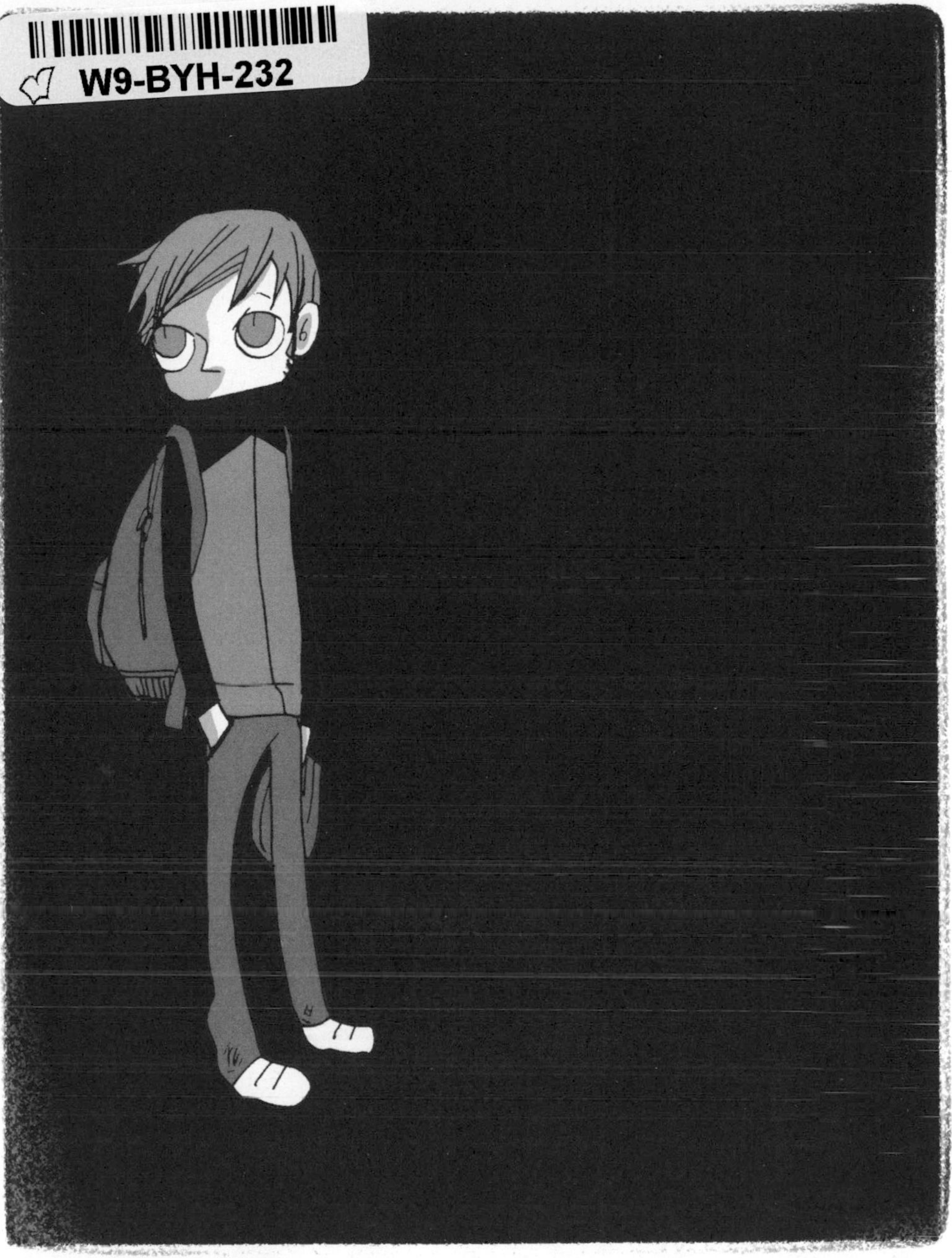

not simple

NATSUME ONO

contents

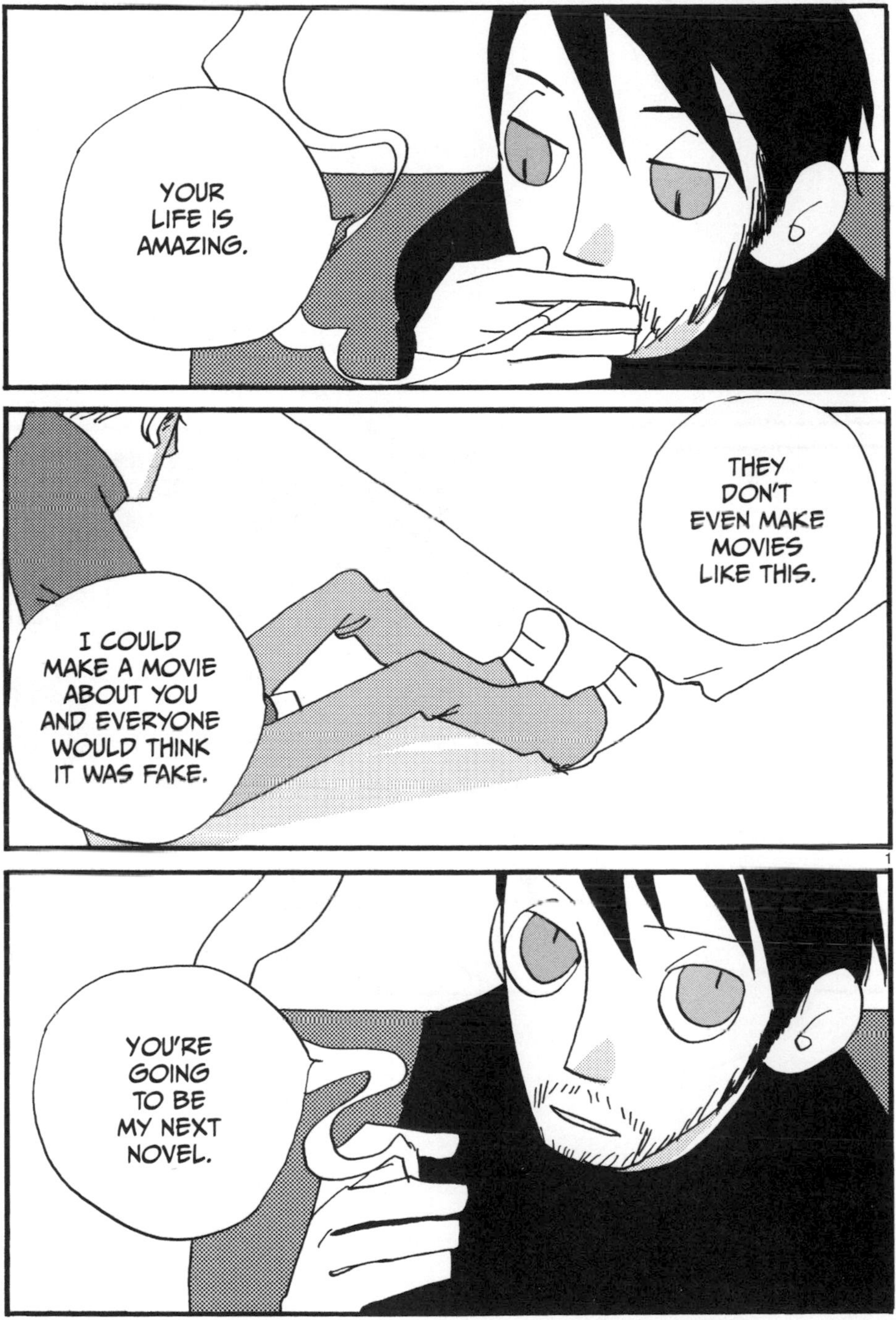
YOUR LIFE IS AMAZING.
THEY DON'T EVEN MAKE MOVIES LIKE THIS.
I COULD MAKE A MOVIE ABOUT YOU AND EVERYONE WOULD THINK IT WAS FAKE.
YOU'RE GOING TO BE MY NEXT NOVEL.

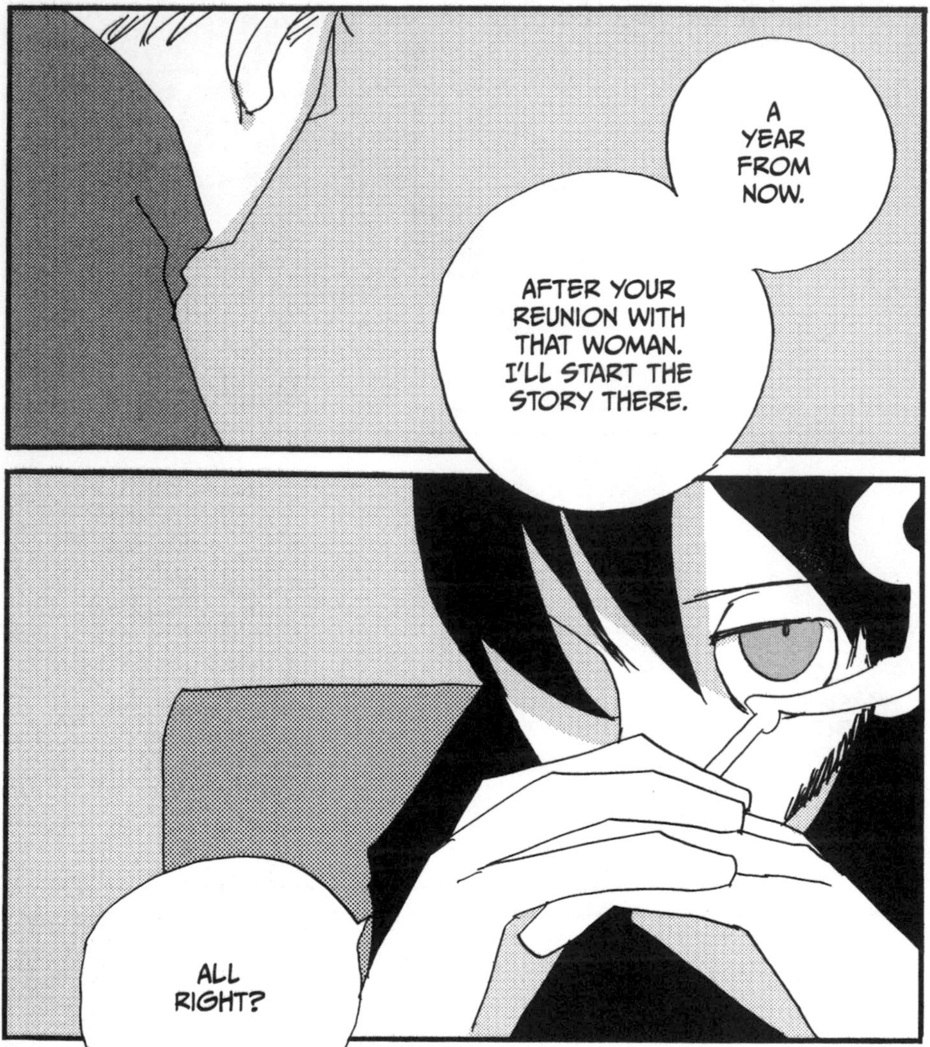
A YEAR FROM NOW.
AFTER YOUR REUNION WITH THAT WOMAN. I'LL START THE STORY THERE.
ALL RIGHT?

prologue not simple

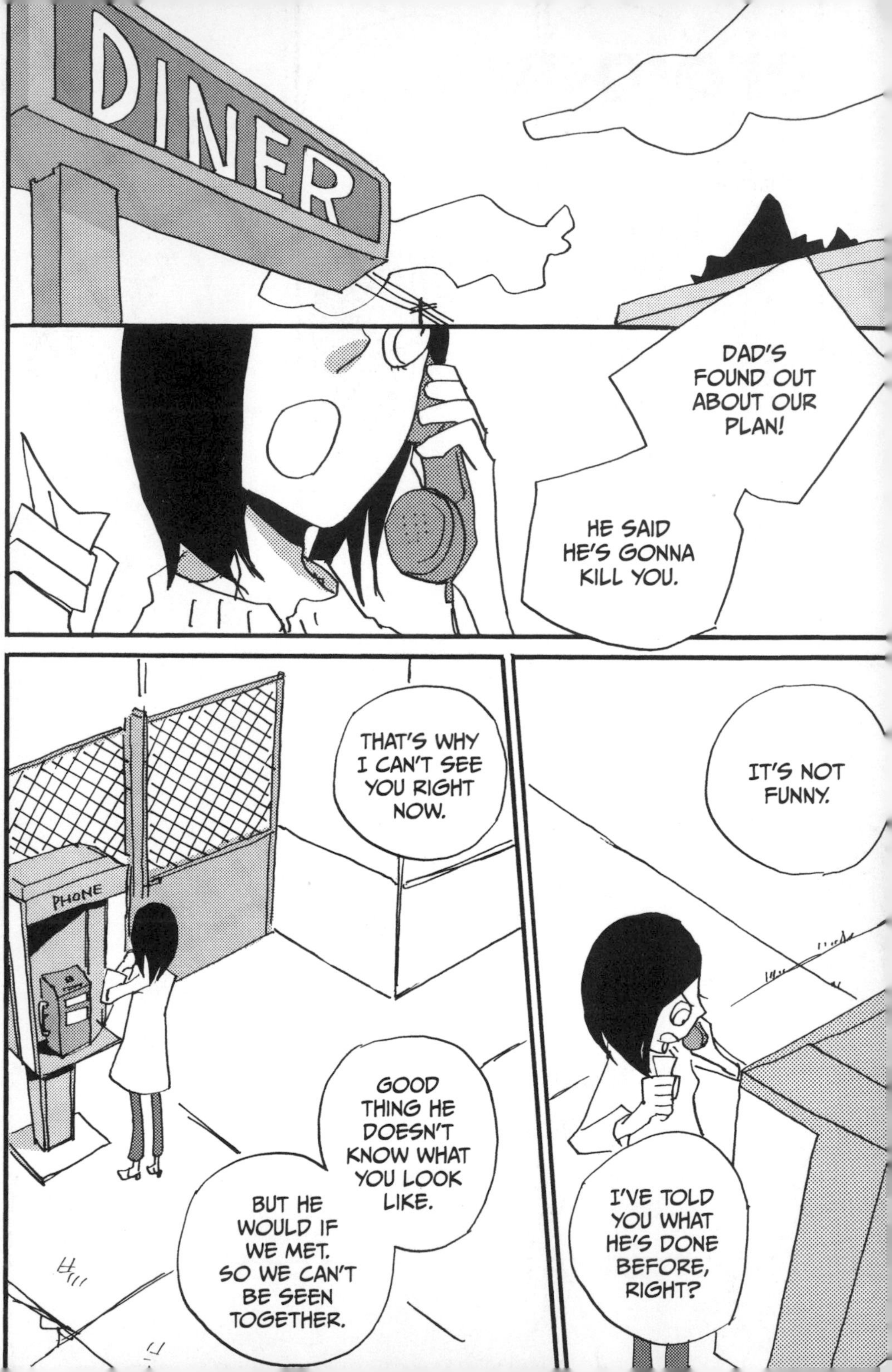
DINER
DAD'S FOUND OUT ABOUT OUR PLAN!
HE SAID HE'S GONNA KILL YOU.
IT'S NOT FUNNY.
I'VE TOLD YOU WHAT HE'S DONE BEFORE, RIGHT?
THAT'S WHY I CAN'T SEE YOU RIGHT NOW.
PHONE
GOOD THING HE DOESN'T KNOW WHAT YOU LOOK LIKE.
BUT HE WOULD IF WE MET. SO WE CAN'T BE SEEN TOGETHER.

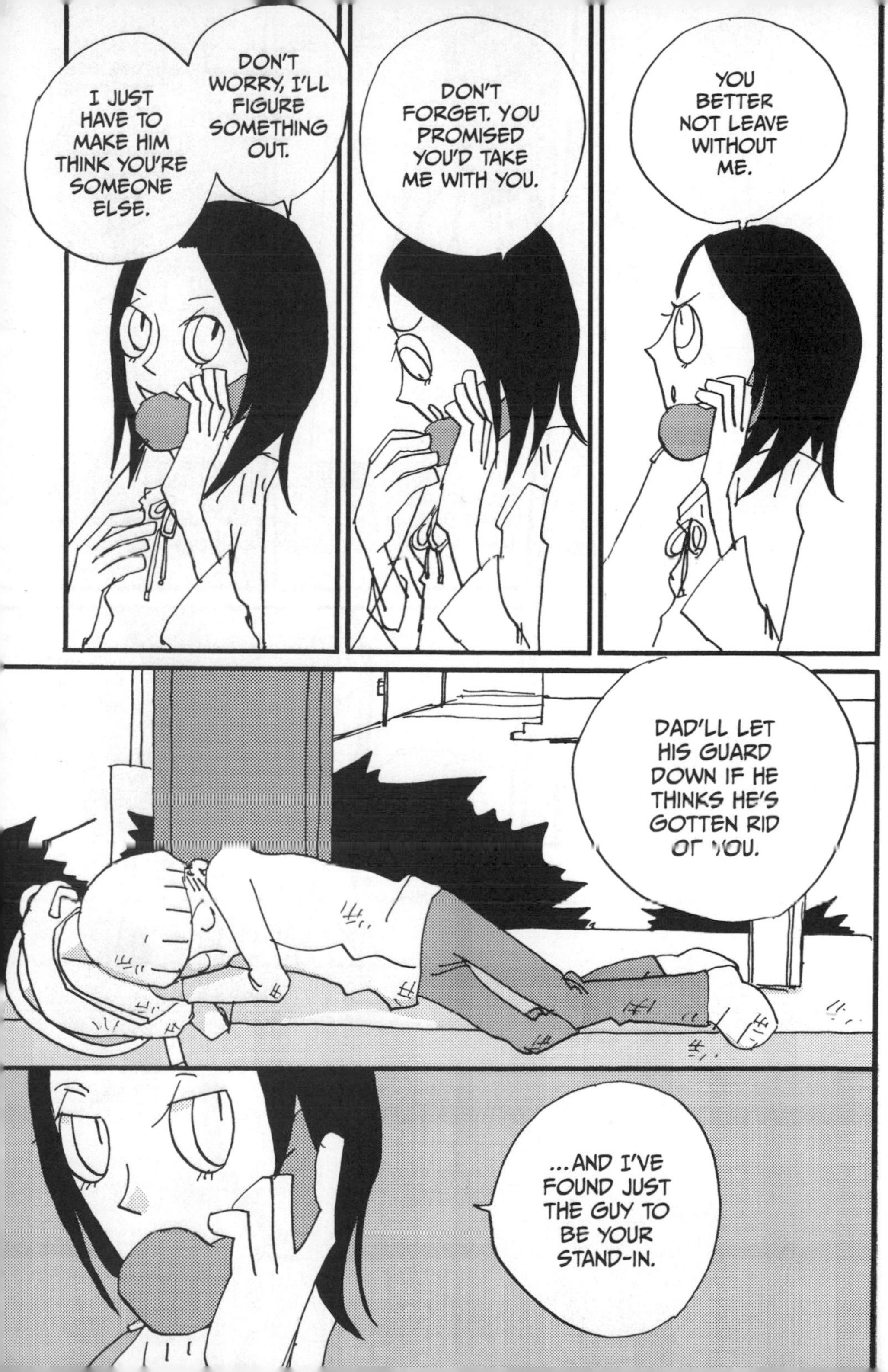
YOU BETTER NOT LEAVE WITHOUT ME.
DON'T FORGET. YOU PROMISED YOU'D TAKE ME WITH YOU.
DON'T WORRY, I'LL FIGURE SOMETHING OUT.
I JUST HAVE TO MAKE HIM THINK YOU'RE SOMEONE ELSE.
DAD'LL LET HIS GUARD DOWN IF HE THINKS HE'S GOTTEN RID OF YOU.
...AND I'VE FOUND JUST THE GUY TO BE YOUR STAND-IN.

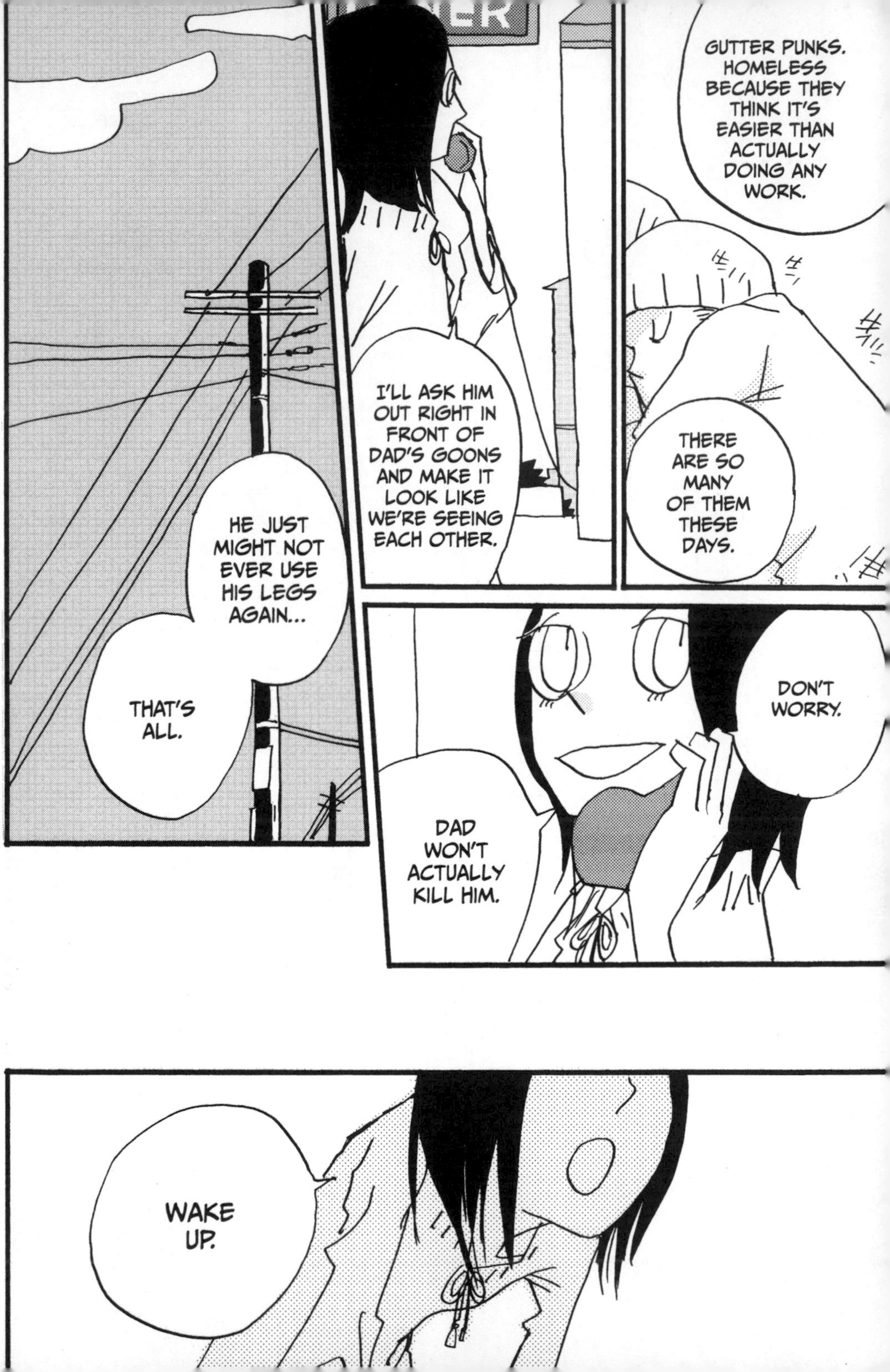
GUTTER PUNKS. HOMELESS BECAUSE THEY THINK IT'S EASIER THAN ACTUALLY DOING ANY WORK.
THERE ARE SO MANY OF THEM THESE DAYS.
I'LL ASK HIM OUT RIGHT IN FRONT OF DAD'S GOONS AND MAKE IT LOOK LIKE WE'RE SEEING EACH OTHER.
DON'T WORRY.
DAD WON'T ACTUALLY KILL HIM.
HE JUST MIGHT NOT EVER USE HIS LEGS AGAIN...
THAT'S ALL.
WAKE UP.

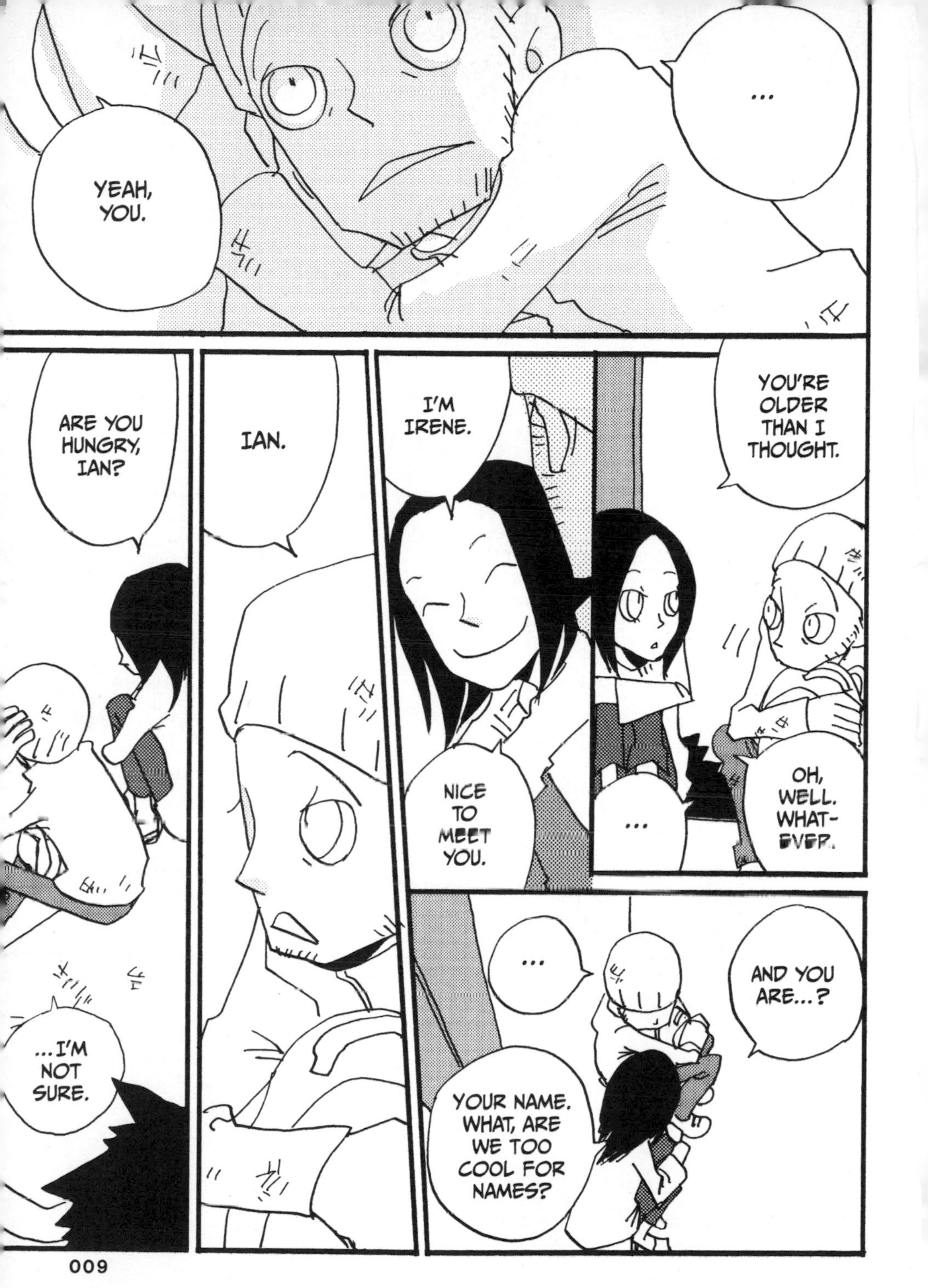
...
YEAH, YOU.
YOU'RE OLDER THAN I THOUGHT.
...
OH, WELL. WHAT-EVER.
I'M IRENE.
NICE TO MEET YOU.
AND YOU ARE...?
...
YOUR NAME. WHAT, ARE WE TOO COOL FOR NAMES?
IAN.
ARE YOU HUNGRY, IAN?
...I'M NOT SURE.

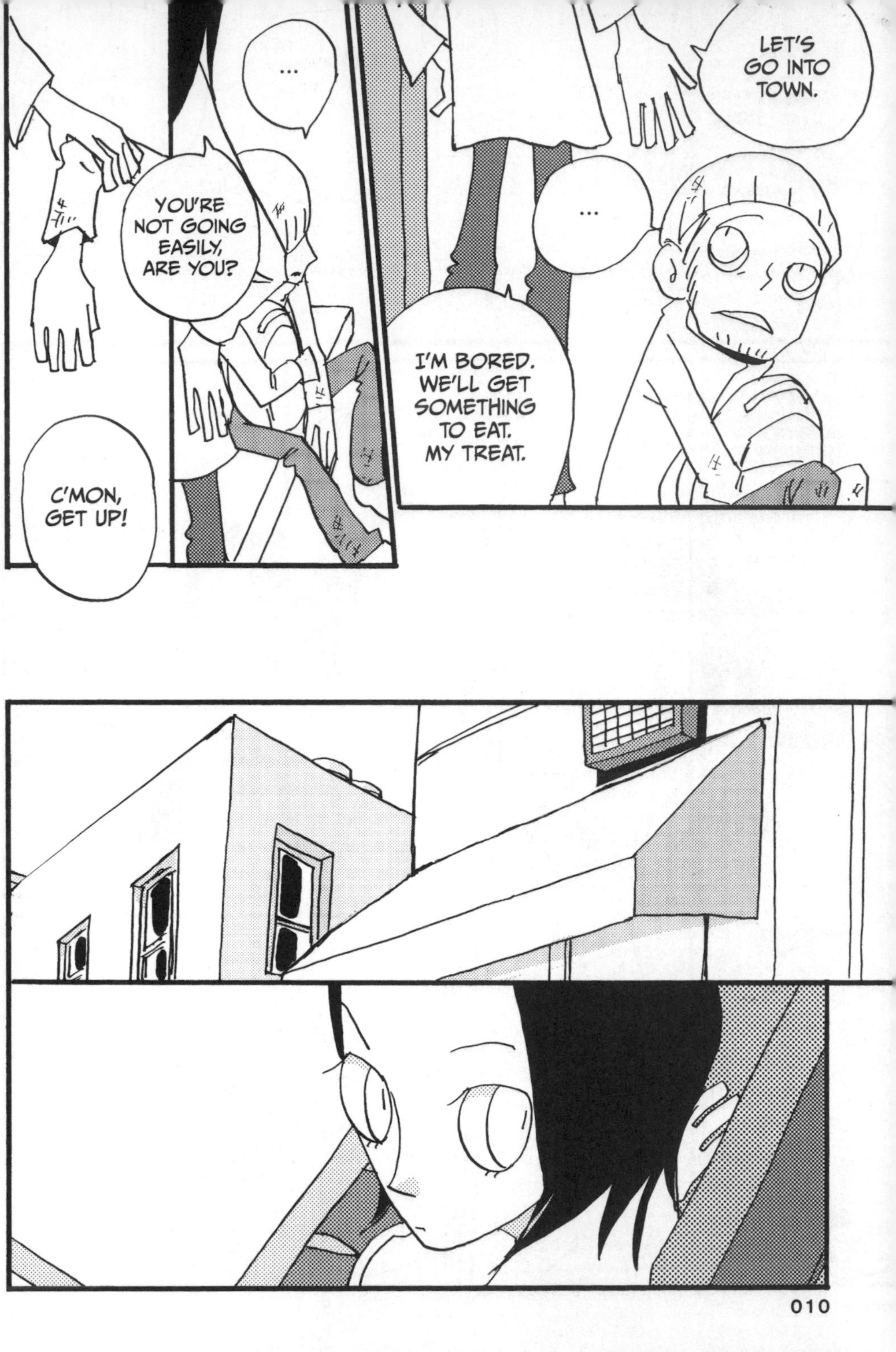
LET'S GO INTO TOWN.
...
I'M BORED. WE'LL GET SOMETHING TO EAT. MY TREAT.
...
YOU'RE NOT GOING EASILY, ARE YOU?
C'MON, GET UP!

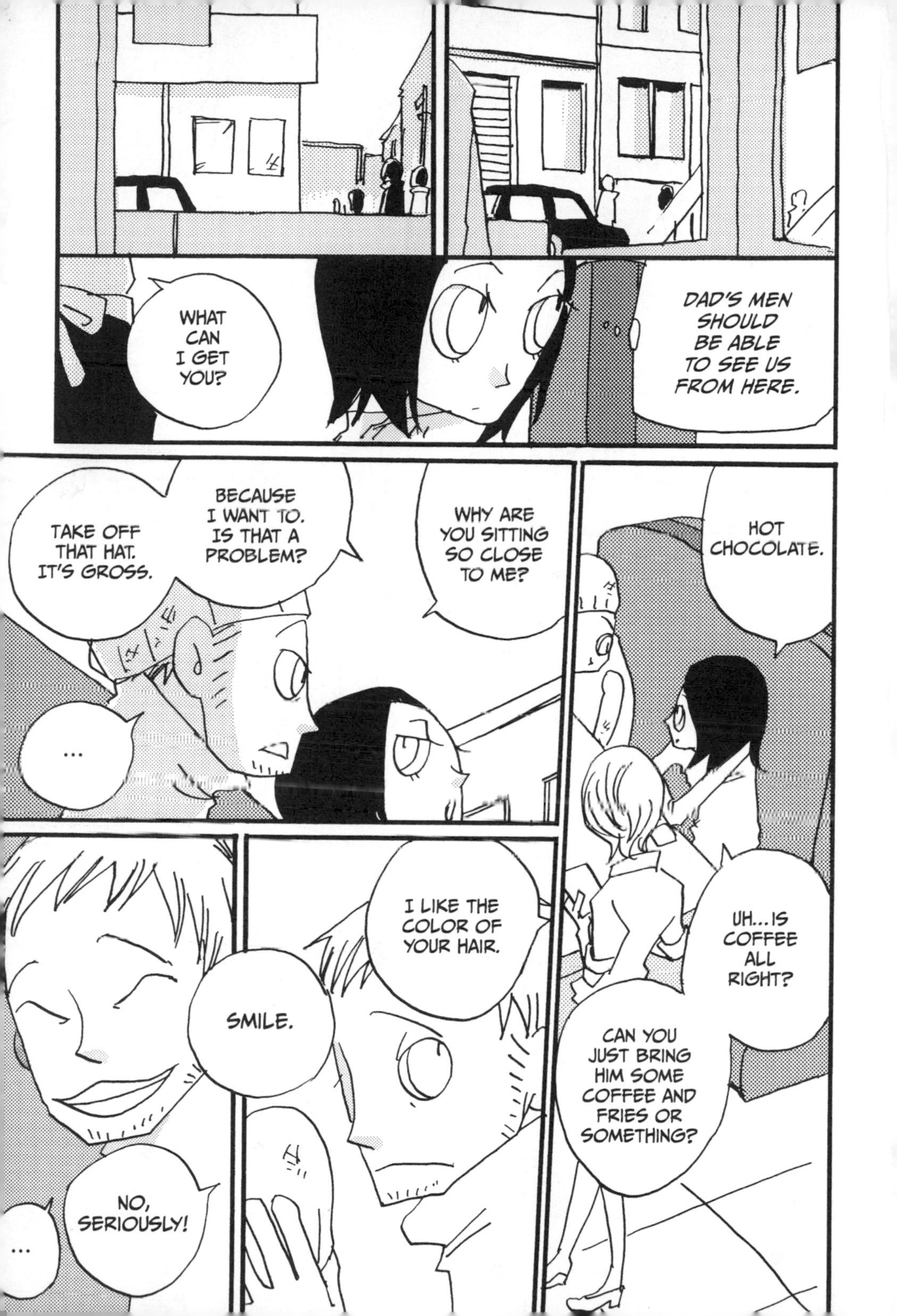
DAD'S MEN SHOULD BE ABLE TO SEE US FROM HERE.
WHAT CAN I GET YOU?
HOT CHOCOLATE.
UH...IS COFFEE ALL RIGHT?
CAN YOU JUST BRING HIM SOME COFFEE AND FRIES OR SOMETHING?
WHY ARE YOU SITTING SO CLOSE TO ME?
BECAUSE I WANT TO. IS THAT A PROBLEM?
TAKE OFF THAT HAT. IT'S GROSS.
...
I LIKE THE COLOR OF YOUR HAIR.
SMILE.
NO, SERIOUSLY!
...

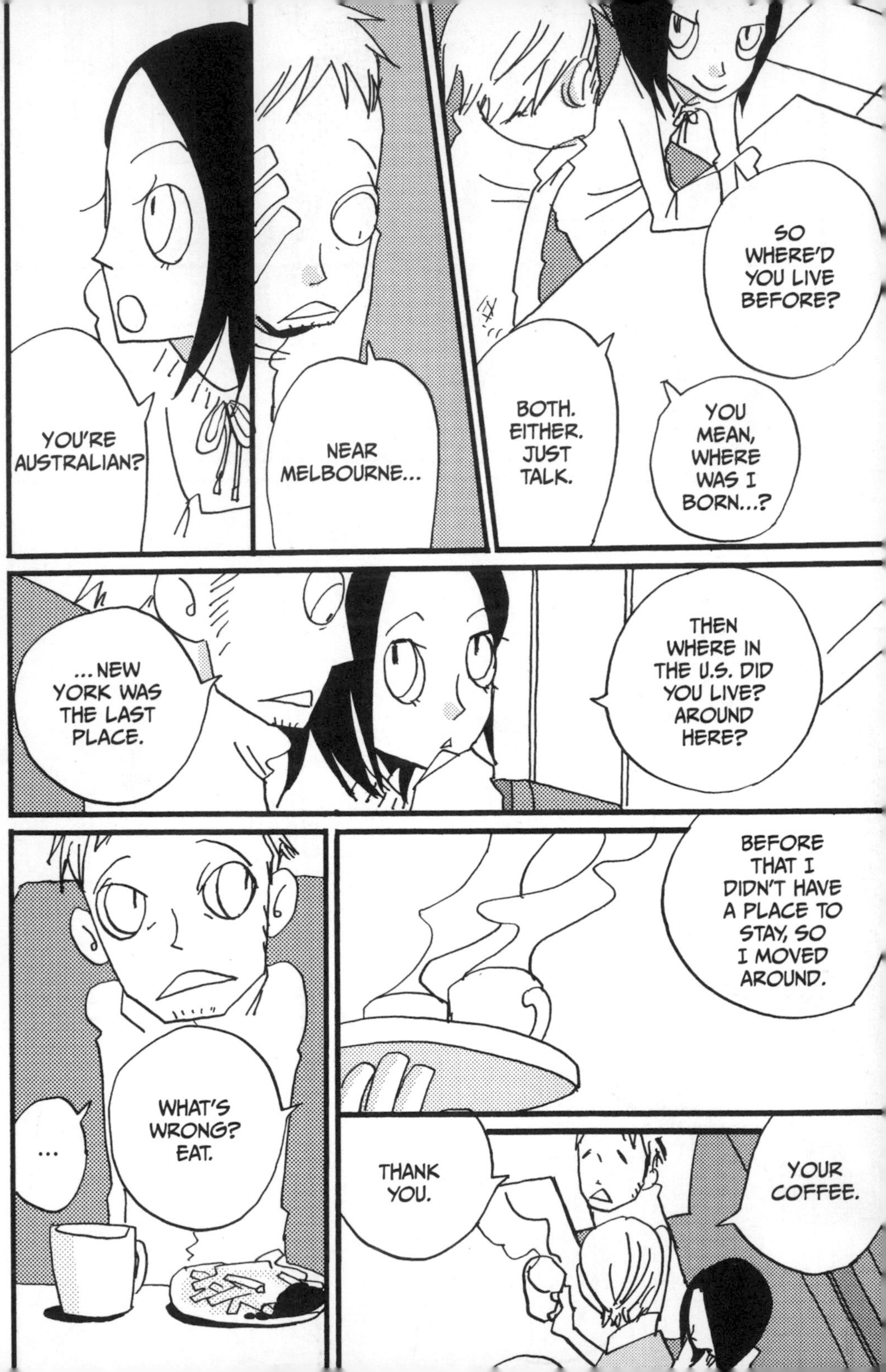
SO WHERE'D YOU LIVE BEFORE?
YOU MEAN, WHERE WAS I BORN...?
BOTH. EITHER. JUST TALK.
NEAR MELBOURNE...
YOU'RE AUSTRALIAN?
THEN WHERE IN THE U.S. DID YOU LIVE? AROUND HERE?
...NEW YORK WAS THE LAST PLACE.
BEFORE THAT I DIDN'T HAVE A PLACE TO STAY, SO I MOVED AROUND.
YOUR COFFEE.
THANK YOU.
WHAT'S WRONG? EAT.
...

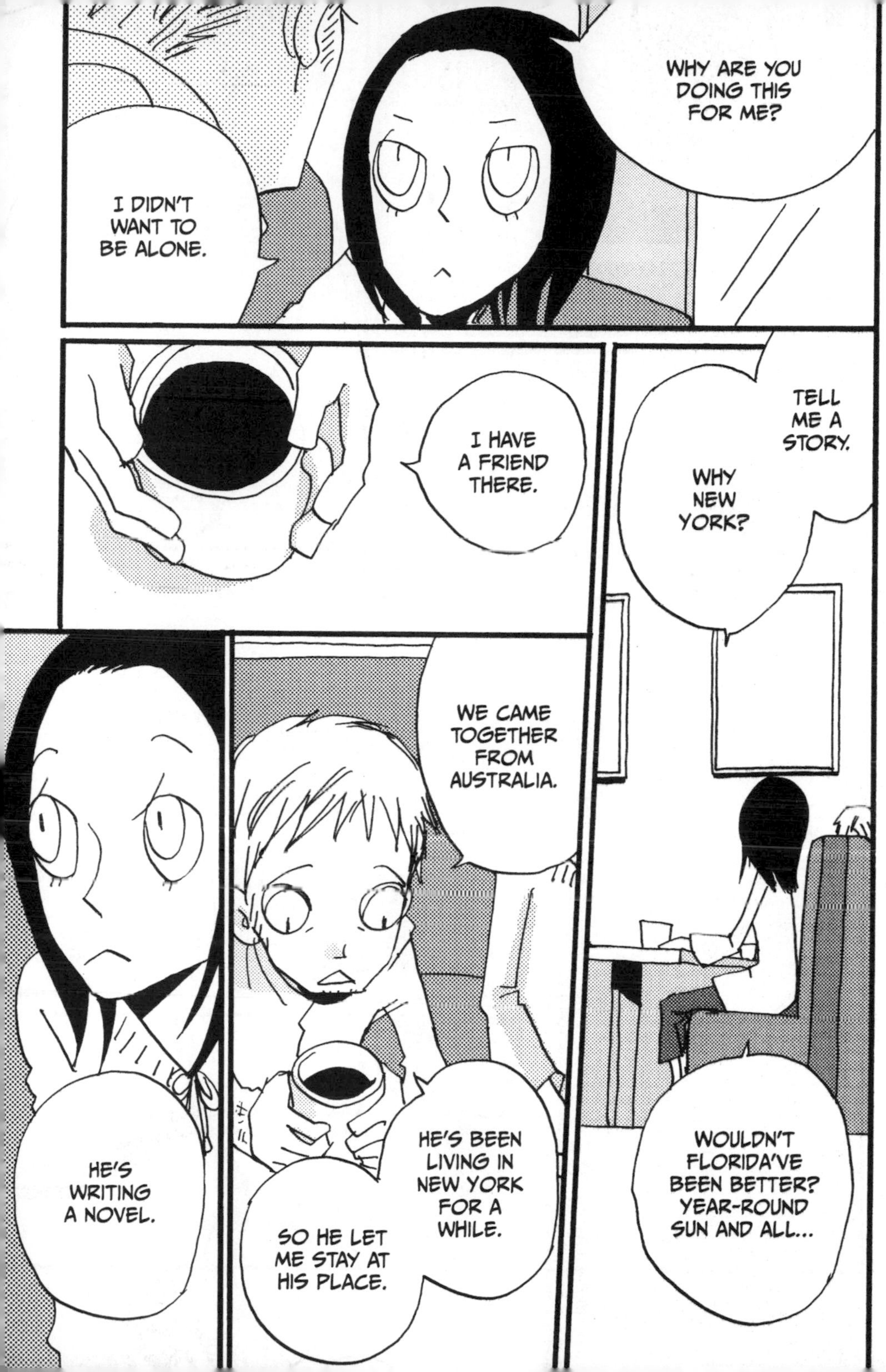
WHY ARE YOU DOING THIS FOR ME?
I DIDN'T WANT TO BE ALONE.
TELL ME A STORY.
WHY NEW YORK?
WOULDN'T FLORIDA'VE BEEN BETTER? YEAR-ROUND SUN AND ALL...
I HAVE A FRIEND THERE.
WE CAME TOGETHER FROM AUSTRALIA.
HE'S BEEN LIVING IN NEW YORK FOR A WHILE.
SO HE LET ME STAY AT HIS PLACE.
HE'S WRITING A NOVEL.

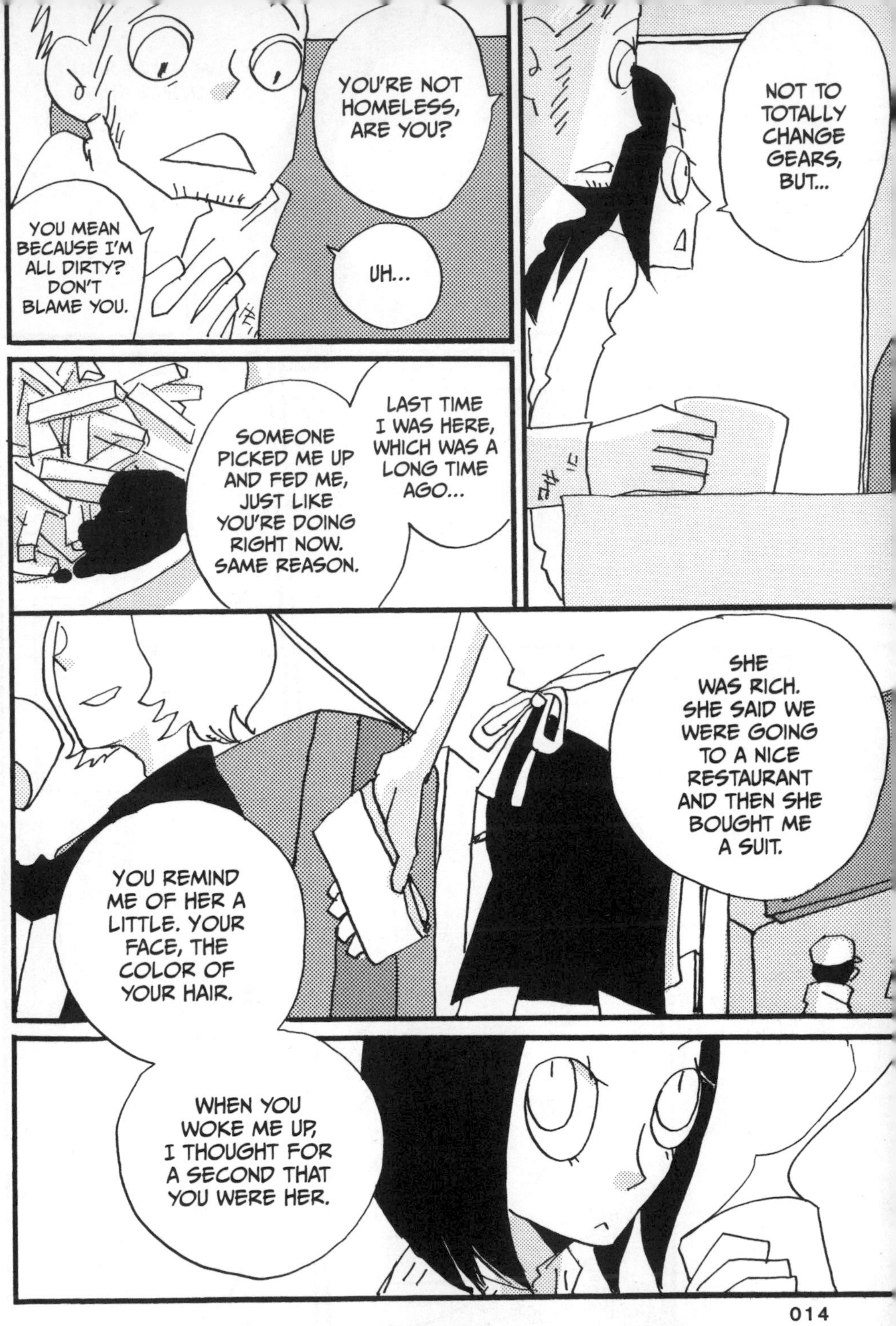
NOT TO TOTALLY CHANGE GEARS, BUT...
YOU'RE NOT HOMELESS, ARE YOU?
UH...
YOU MEAN BECAUSE I'M ALL DIRTY? DON'T BLAME YOU.
LAST TIME I WAS HERE, WHICH WAS A LONG TIME AGO...
SOMEONE PICKED ME UP AND FED ME, JUST LIKE YOU'RE DOING RIGHT NOW. SAME REASON.
SHE WAS RICH. SHE SAID WE WERE GOING TO A NICE RESTAURANT AND THEN SHE BOUGHT ME A SUIT.
YOU REMIND ME OF HER A LITTLE. YOUR FACE, THE COLOR OF YOUR HAIR.
WHEN YOU WOKE ME UP, I THOUGHT FOR A SECOND THAT YOU WERE HER.

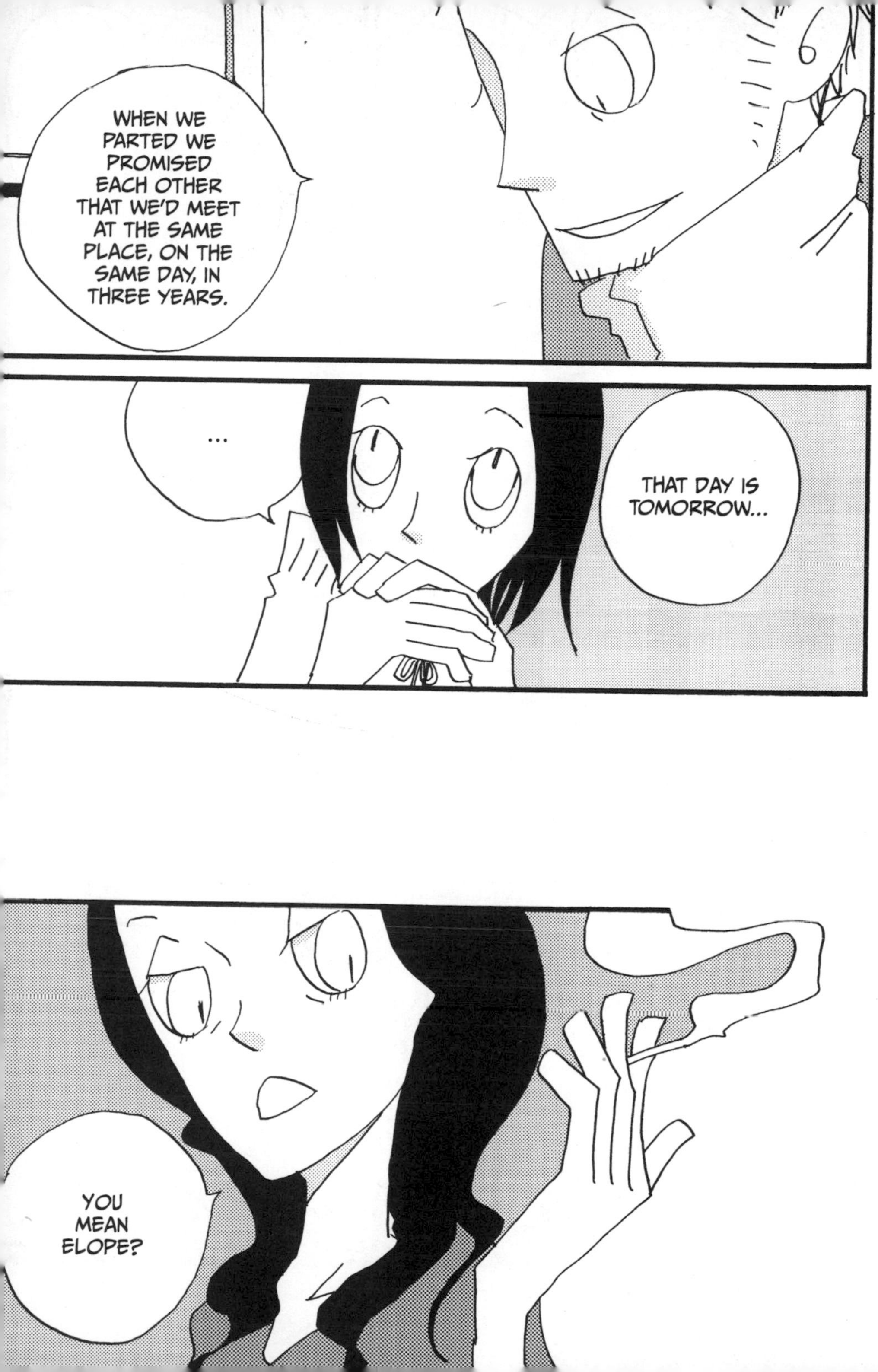
WHEN WE PARTED WE PROMISED EACH OTHER THAT WE'D MEET AT THE SAME PLACE, ON THE SAME DAY, IN THREE YEARS.
THAT DAY IS TOMORROW...
...
YOU MEAN ELOPE?

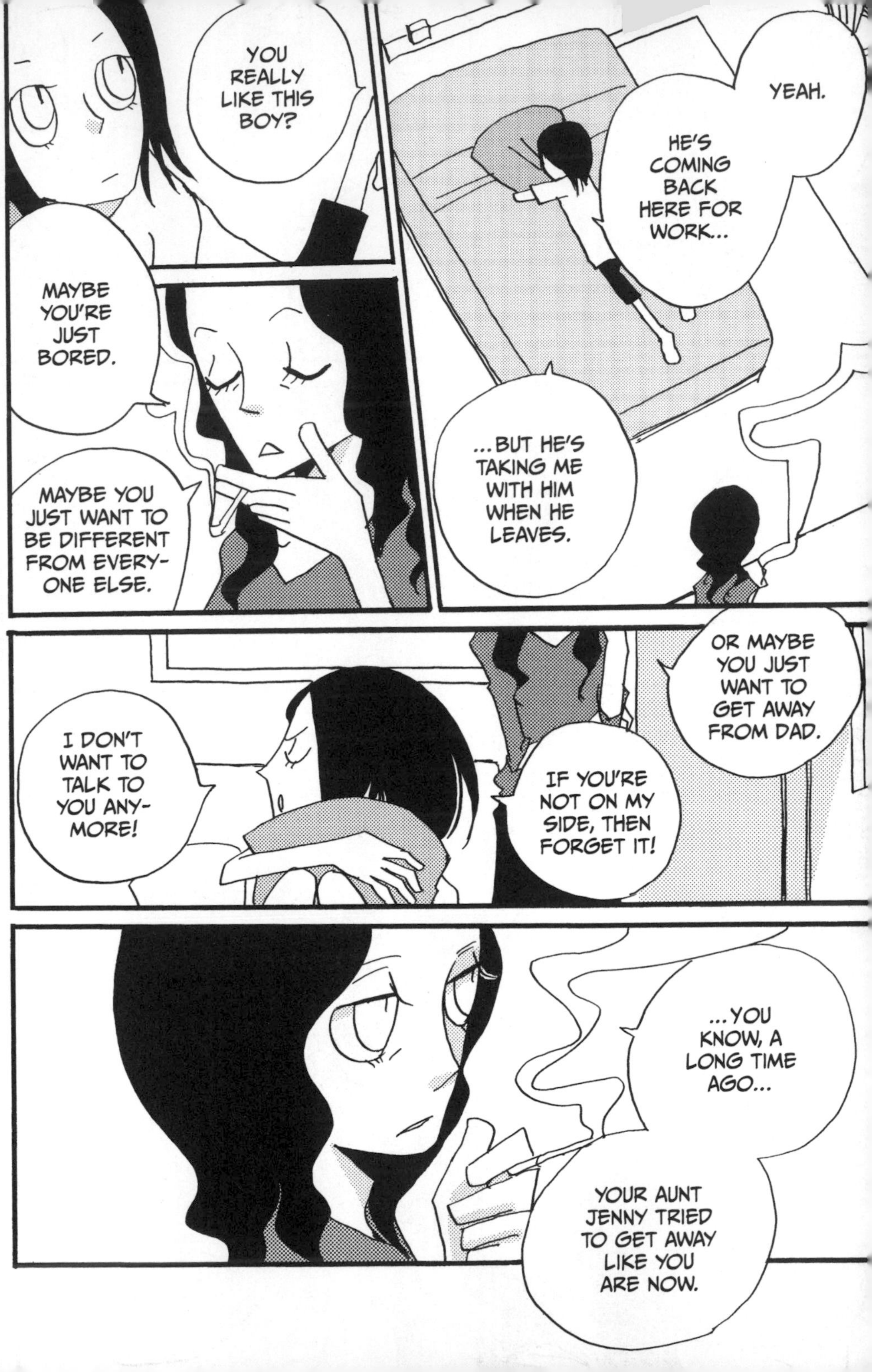
YEAH.
HE'S COMING BACK HERE FOR WORK...
...BUT HE'S TAKING ME WITH HIM WHEN HE LEAVES.
YOU REALLY LIKE THIS BOY?
MAYBE YOU'RE JUST BORED.
MAYBE YOU JUST WANT TO BE DIFFERENT FROM EVERY-ONE ELSE.
OR MAYBE YOU JUST WANT TO GET AWAY FROM DAD.
IF YOU'RE NOT ON MY SIDE, THEN FORGET IT!
I DON'T WANT TO TALK TO YOU ANY-MORE!
...YOU KNOW, A LONG TIME AGO...
YOUR AUNT JENNY TRIED TO GET AWAY LIKE YOU ARE NOW.

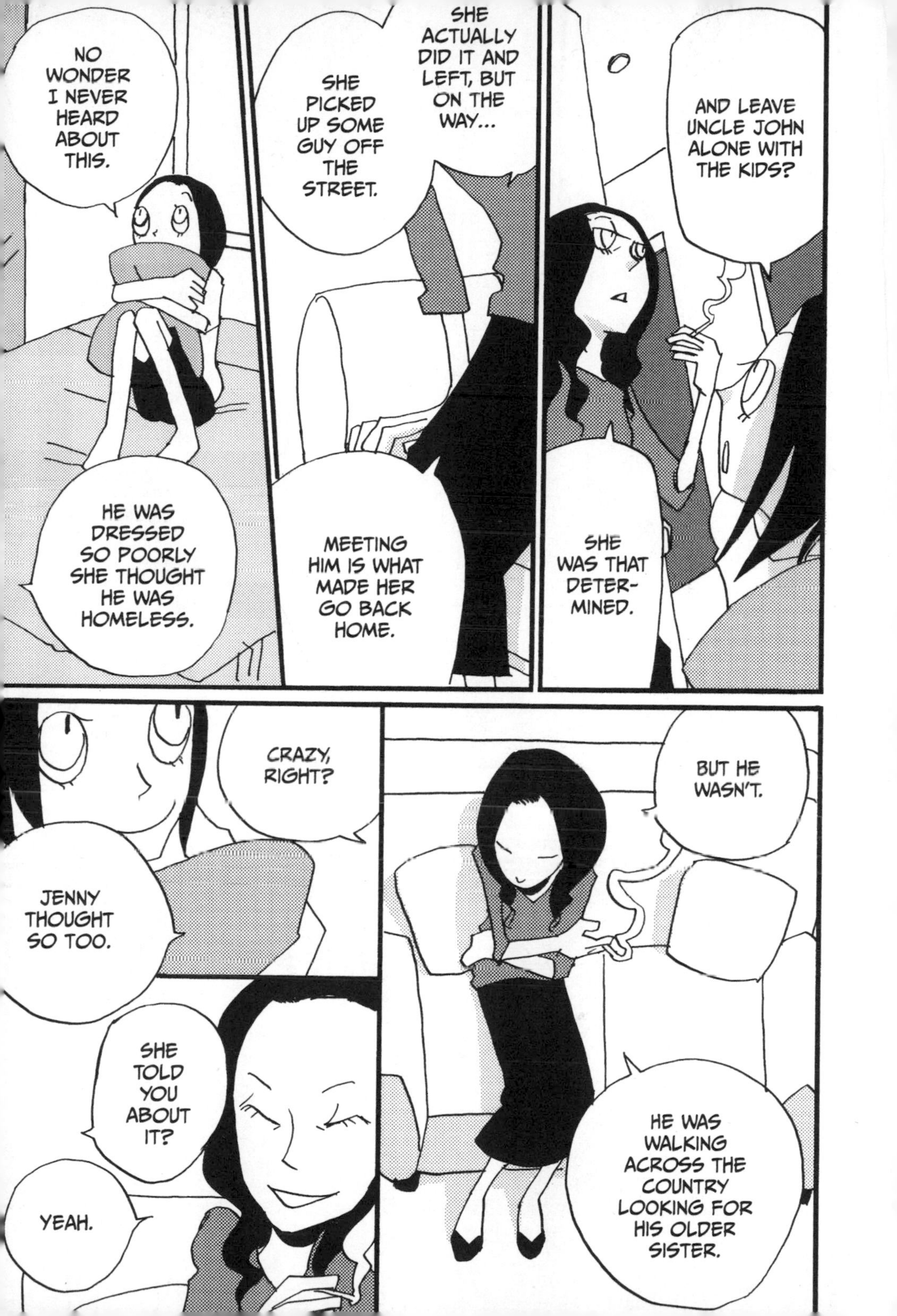
AND LEAVE UNCLE JOHN ALONE WITH THE KIDS?
SHE WAS THAT DETER-MINED.
SHE ACTUALLY DID IT AND LEFT, BUT ON THE WAY...
SHE PICKED UP SOME GUY OFF THE STREET.
MEETING HIM IS WHAT MADE HER GO BACK HOME.
NO WONDER I NEVER HEARD ABOUT THIS.
HE WAS DRESSED SO POORLY SHE THOUGHT HE WAS HOMELESS.
BUT HE WASN'T.
HE WAS WALKING ACROSS THE COUNTRY LOOKING FOR HIS OLDER SISTER.
CRAZY, RIGHT?
JENNY THOUGHT SO TOO.
SHE TOLD YOU ABOUT IT?
YEAH.

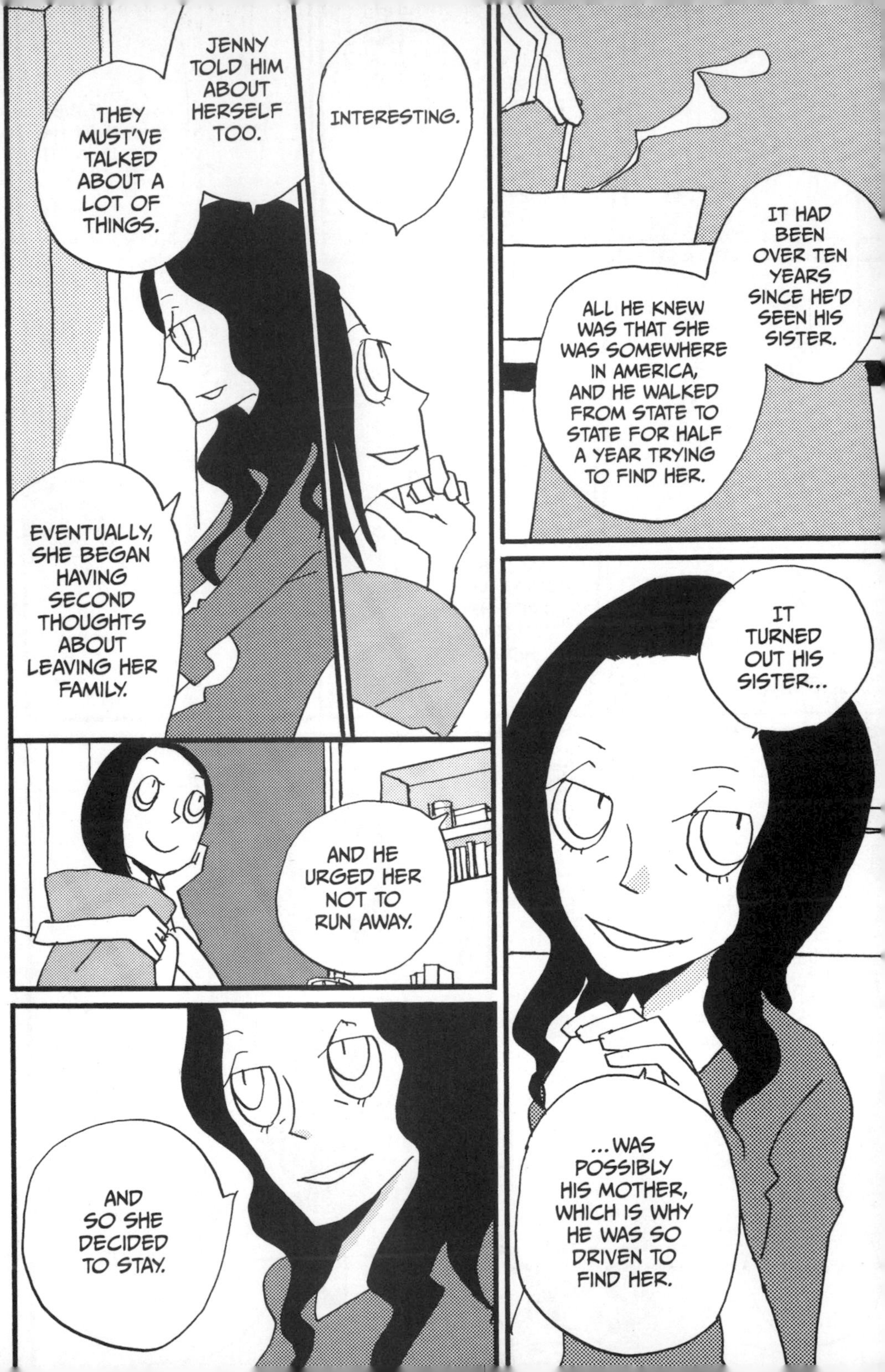
IT HAD BEEN OVER TEN YEARS SINCE HE'D SEEN HIS SISTER.
ALL HE KNEW WAS THAT SHE WAS SOMEWHERE IN AMERICA, AND HE WALKED FROM STATE TO STATE FOR HALF A YEAR TRYING TO FIND HER.
THEY MUST'VE TALKED ABOUT A LOT OF THINGS.
JENNY TOLD HIM ABOUT HERSELF TOO.
INTERESTING.
EVENTUALLY, SHE BEGAN HAVING SECOND THOUGHTS ABOUT LEAVING HER FAMILY.
IT TURNED OUT HIS SISTER...
...WAS POSSIBLY HIS MOTHER, WHICH IS WHY HE WAS SO DRIVEN TO FIND HER.
AND HE URGED HER NOT TO RUN AWAY.
AND SO SHE DECIDED TO STAY.

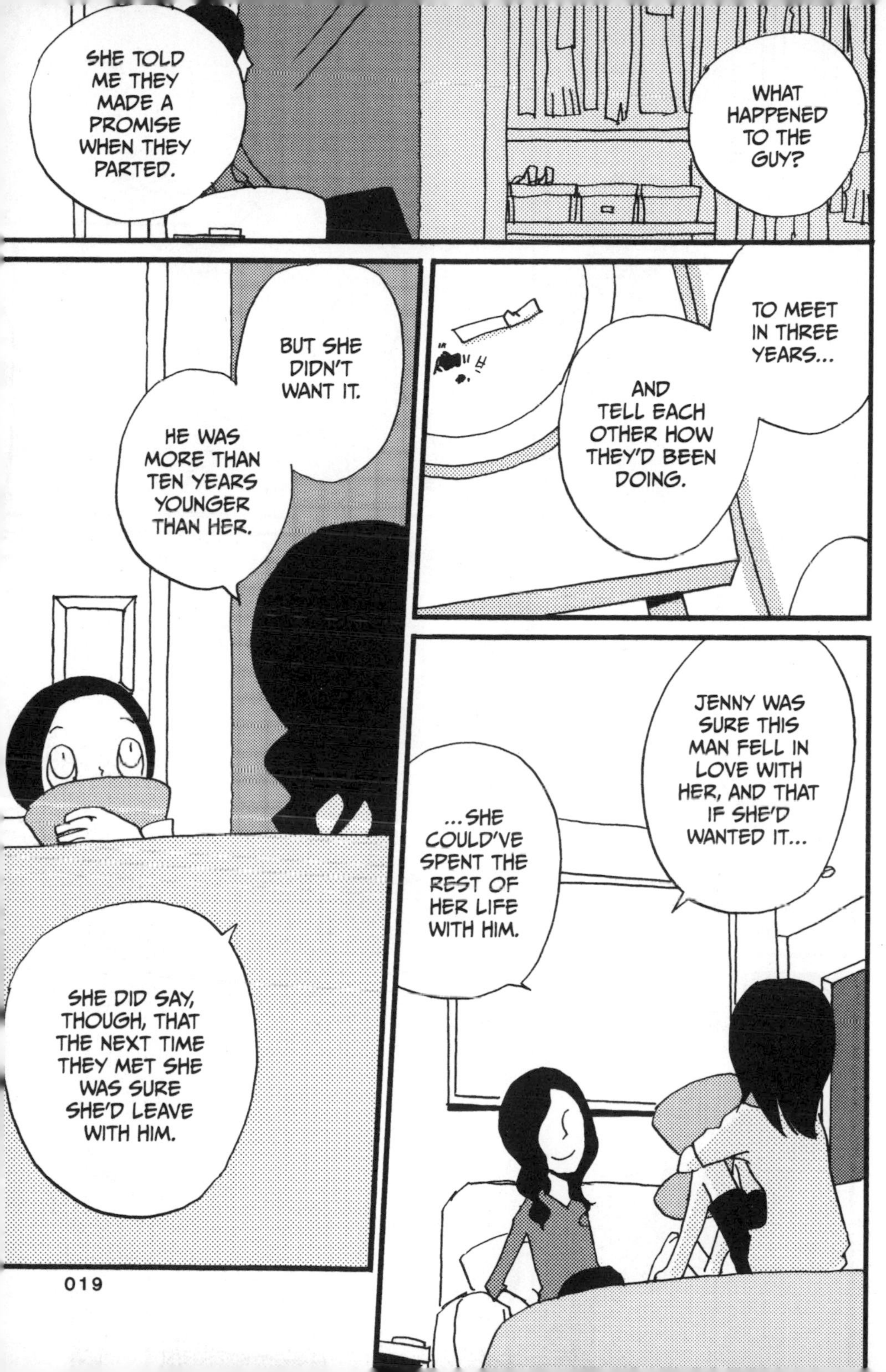
WHAT HAPPENED TO THE GUY?
SHE TOLD ME THEY MADE A PROMISE WHEN THEY PARTED.
TO MEET IN THREE YEARS...
AND TELL EACH OTHER HOW THEY'D BEEN DOING.
JENNY WAS SURE THIS MAN FELL IN LOVE WITH HER, AND THAT IF SHE'D WANTED IT...
...SHE COULD'VE SPENT THE REST OF HER LIFE WITH HIM.
BUT SHE DIDN'T WANT IT.
HE WAS MORE THAN TEN YEARS YOUNGER THAN HER.
SHE DID SAY, THOUGH, THAT THE NEXT TIME THEY MET SHE WAS SURE SHE'D LEAVE WITH HIM.

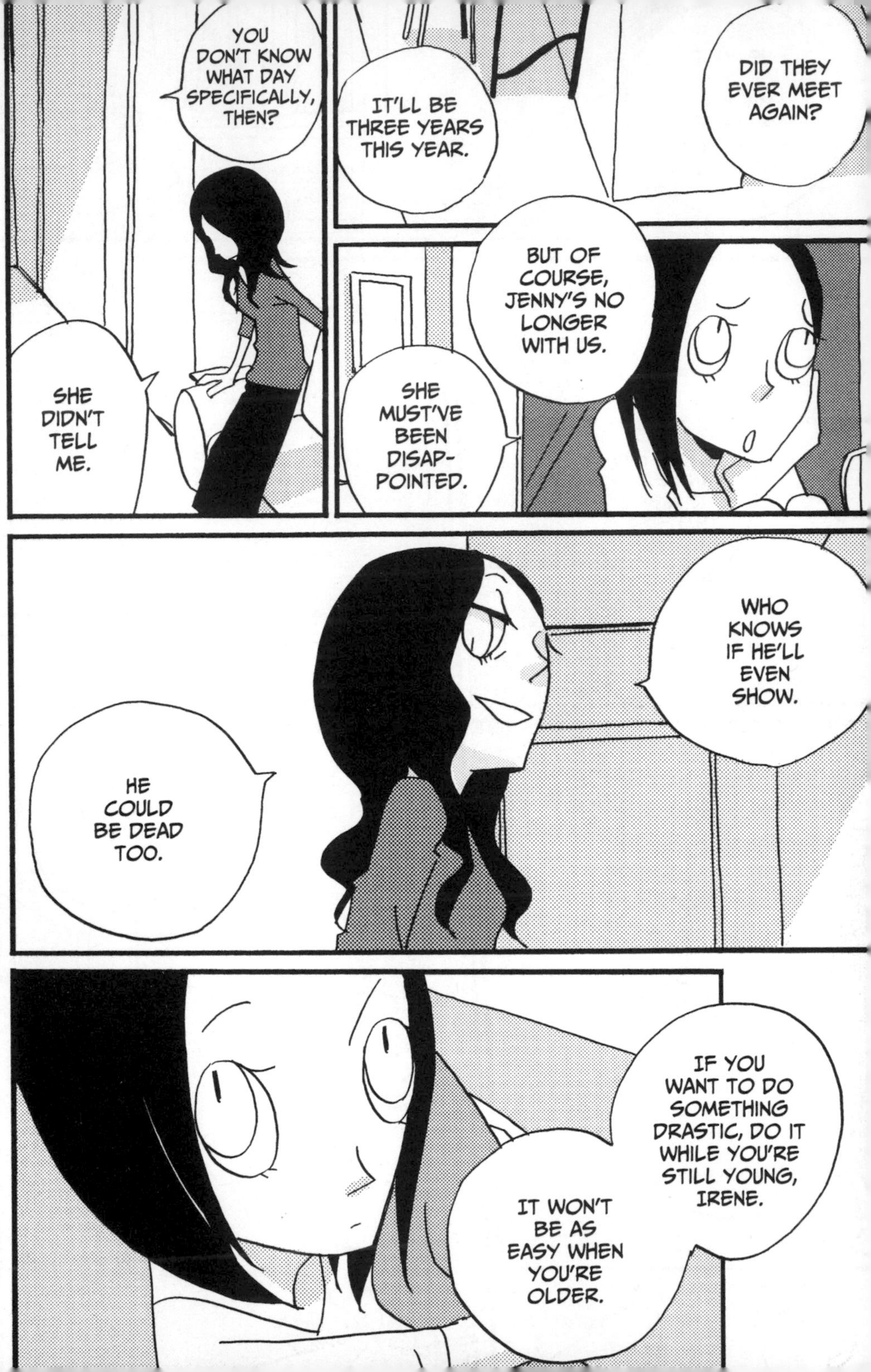
DID THEY EVER MEET AGAIN?
IT'LL BE THREE YEARS THIS YEAR.
BUT OF COURSE, JENNY'S NO LONGER WITH US.
SHE MUST'VE BEEN DISAP-POINTED.
YOU DON'T KNOW WHAT DAY SPECIFICALLY, THEN?
SHE DIDN'T TELL ME.
WHO KNOWS IF HE'LL EVEN SHOW.
HE COULD BE DEAD TOO.
IF YOU WANT TO DO SOMETHING DRASTIC, DO IT WHILE YOU'RE STILL YOUNG, IRENE.
IT WON'T BE AS EASY WHEN YOU'RE OLDER.

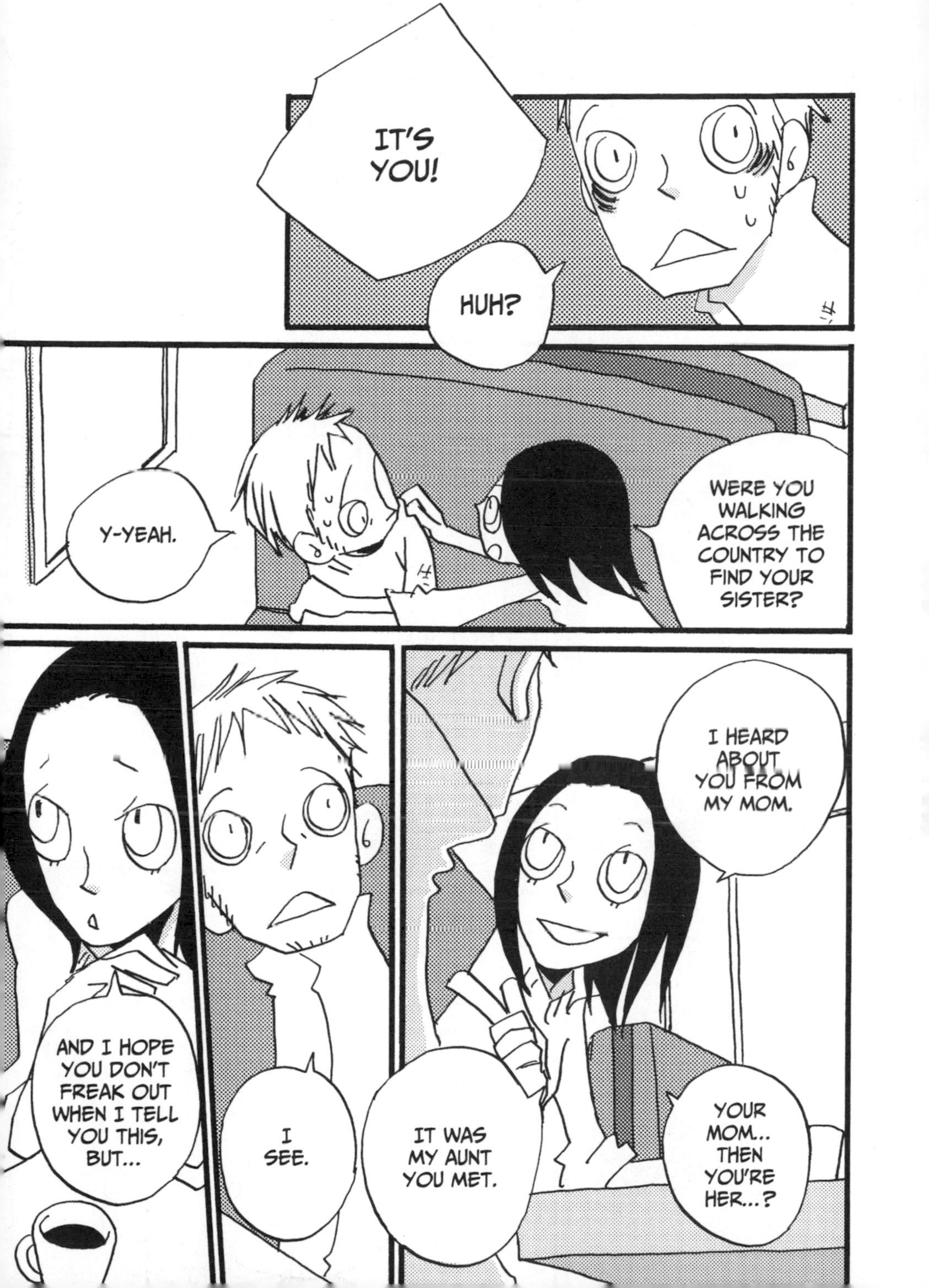
IT'S YOU!
HUH?
WERE YOU WALKING ACROSS THE COUNTRY TO FIND YOUR SISTER?
Y-YEAH.
I HEARD ABOUT YOU FROM MY MOM.
YOUR MOM.. THEN YOU'RE HER...?
IT WAS MY AUNT YOU MET.
I SEE.
AND I HOPE YOU DON'T FREAK OUT WHEN I TELL YOU THIS, BUT...

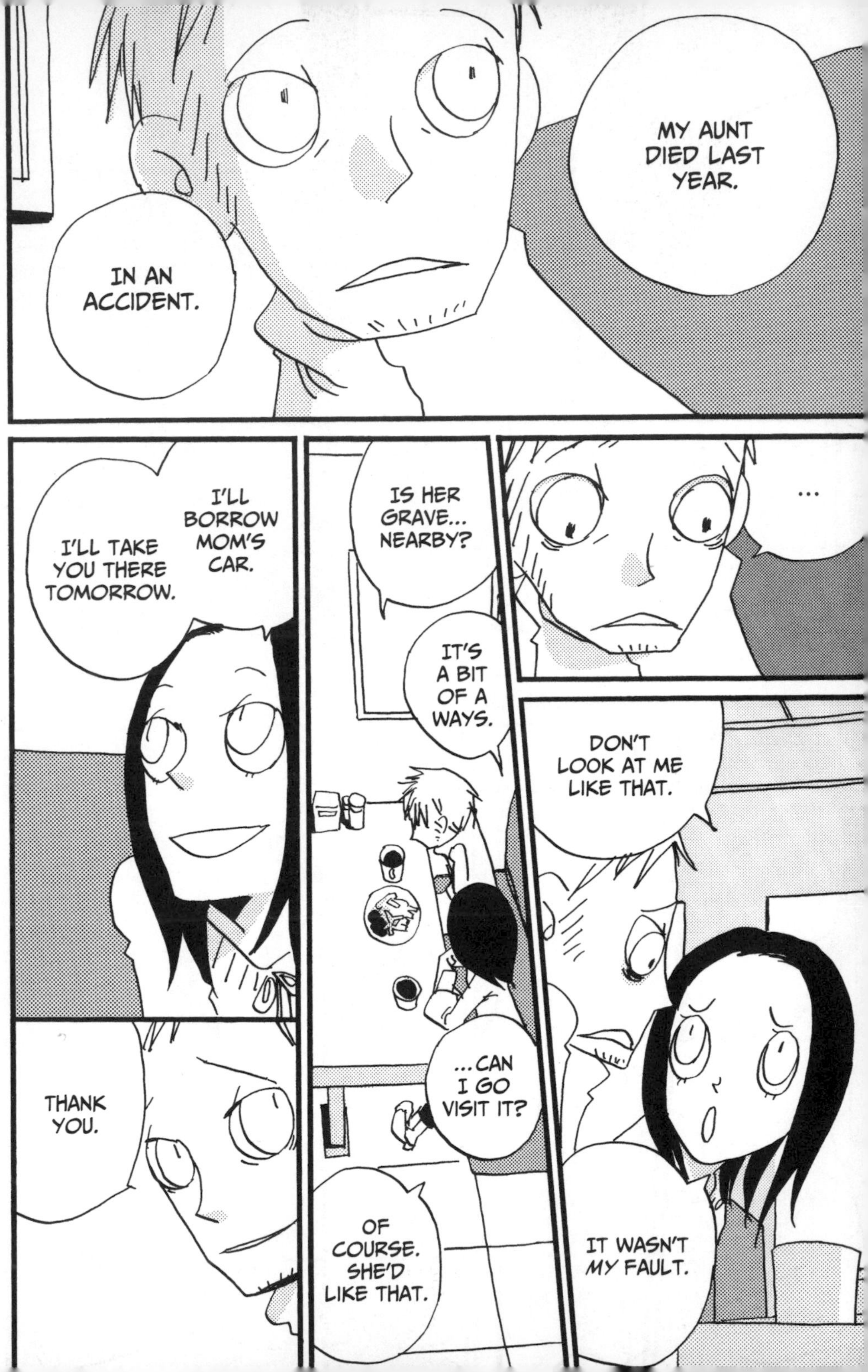
MY AUNT DIED LAST YEAR.
IN AN ACCIDENT.
...
DON'T LOOK AT ME LIKE THAT.
IT WASN'T MY FAULT.
IS HER GRAVE... NEARBY?
IT'S A BIT OF A WAYS.
...CAN I GO VISIT IT?
OF COURSE. SHE'D LIKE THAT.
I'LL BORROW MOM'S CAR.
I'LL TAKE YOU THERE TOMORROW.
THANK YOU.

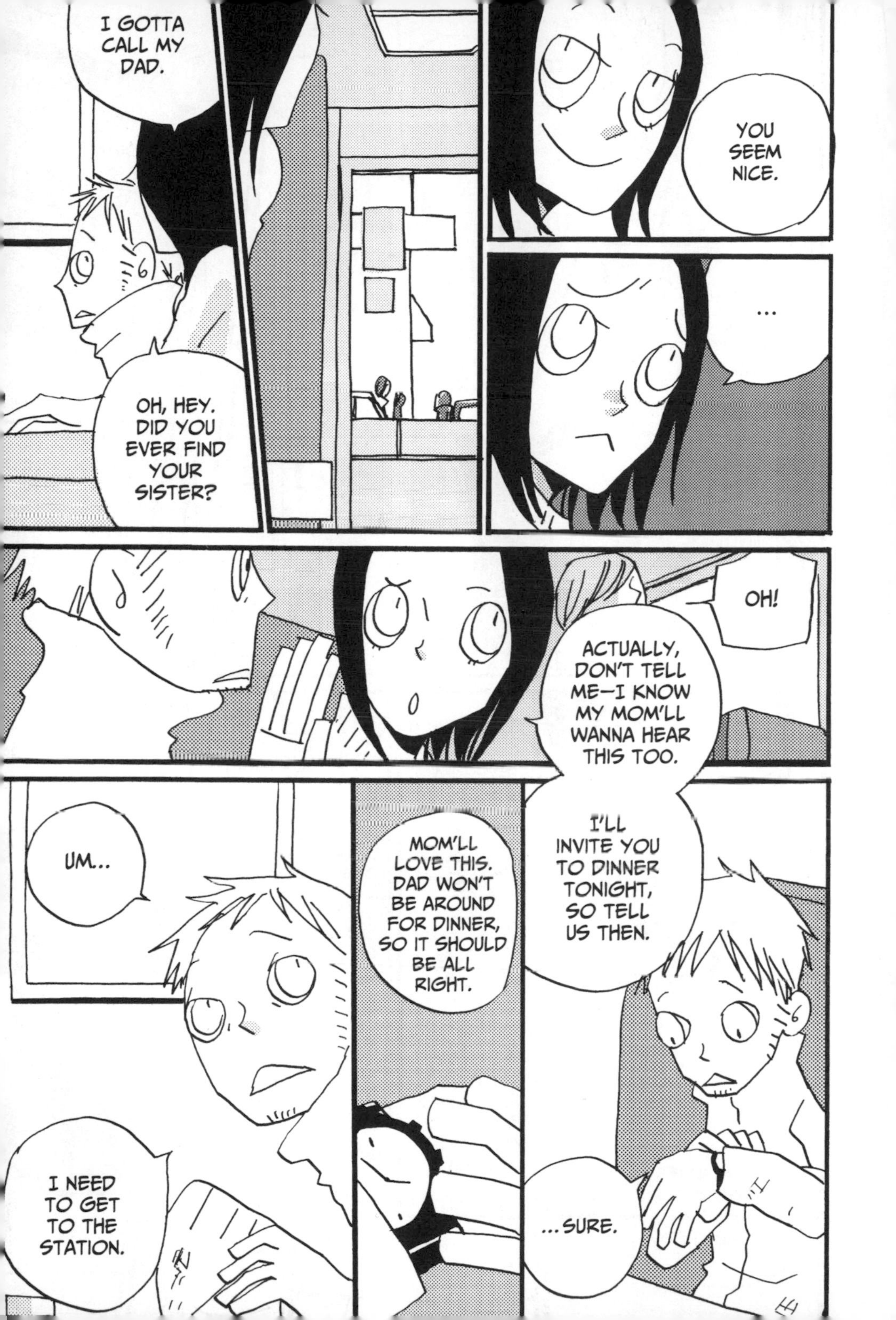
YOU SEEM NICE.
...
I GOTTA CALL MY DAD.
OH, HEY. DID YOU EVER FIND YOUR SISTER?
OH!
ACTUALLY, DON'T TELL ME—I KNOW MY MOM'LL WANNA HEAR THIS TOO.
I'LL INVITE YOU TO DINNER TONIGHT, SO TELL US THEN.
...SURE.
MOM'LL LOVE THIS. DAD WON'T BE AROUND FOR DINNER, SO IT SHOULD BE ALL RIGHT.
UM...
I NEED TO GET TO THE STATION.

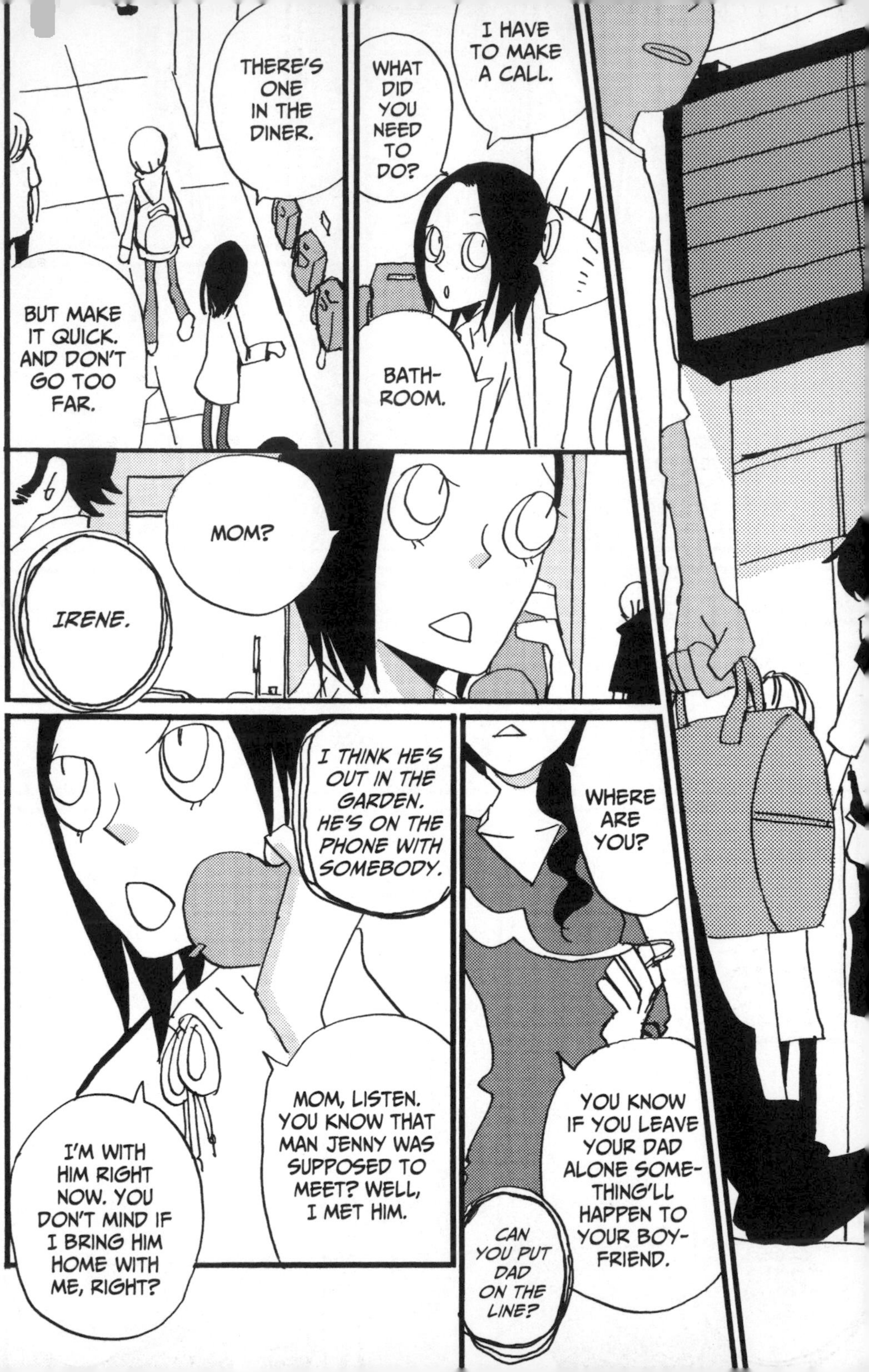
I HAVE TO MAKE A CALL.
WHAT DID YOU NEED TO DO?
BATHROOM.
THERE'S ONE IN THE DINER.
BUT MAKE IT QUICK. AND DON'T GO TOO FAR.
MOM?
IRENE.
WHERE ARE YOU?
YOU KNOW IF YOU LEAVE YOUR DAD ALONE SOME-THING'LL HAPPEN TO YOUR BOY-FRIEND.
CAN YOU PUT DAD ON THE LINE?
I THINK HE'S OUT IN THE GARDEN. HE'S ON THE PHONE WITH SOMEBODY.
MOM, LISTEN. YOU KNOW THAT MAN JENNY WAS SUPPOSED TO MEET? WELL, I MET HIM.
I'M WITH HIM RIGHT NOW. YOU DON'T MIND IF I BRING HIM HOME WITH ME, RIGHT?

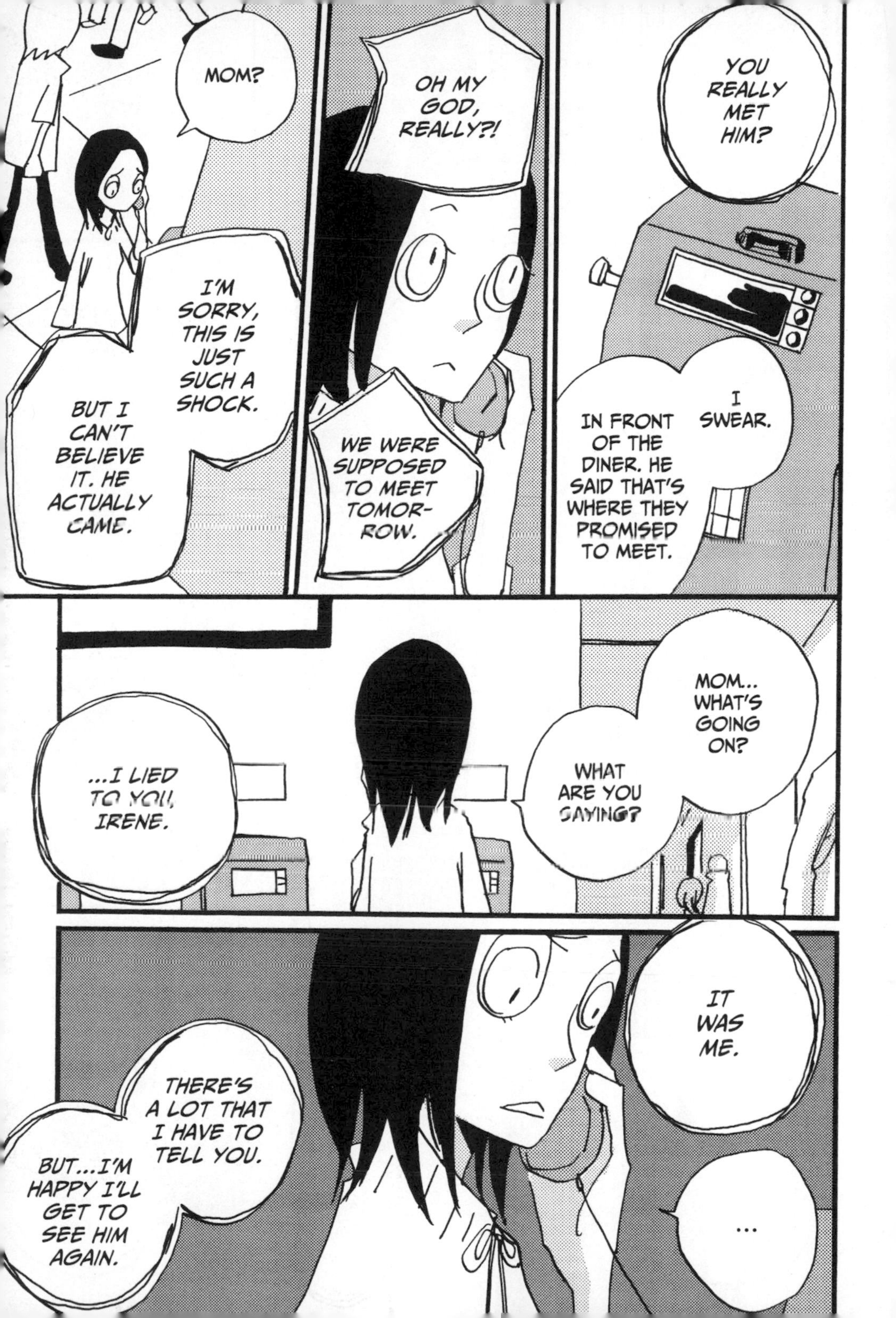
YOU REALLY MET HIM?
I SWEAR.
IN FRONT OF THE DINER. HE SAID THAT'S WHERE THEY PROMISED TO MEET.
OH MY GOD, REALLY?!
WE WERE SUPPOSED TO MEET TOMOR-ROW.
MOM?
I'M SORRY, THIS IS JUST SUCH A SHOCK.
BUT I CAN'T BELIEVE IT. HE ACTUALLY CAME.
MOM... WHAT'S GOING ON?
WHAT ARE YOU SAYING?
...I LIED TO YOU, IRENE.
IT WAS ME.
...
THERE'S A LOT THAT I HAVE TO TELL YOU.
BUT...I'M HAPPY I'LL GET TO SEE HIM AGAIN.

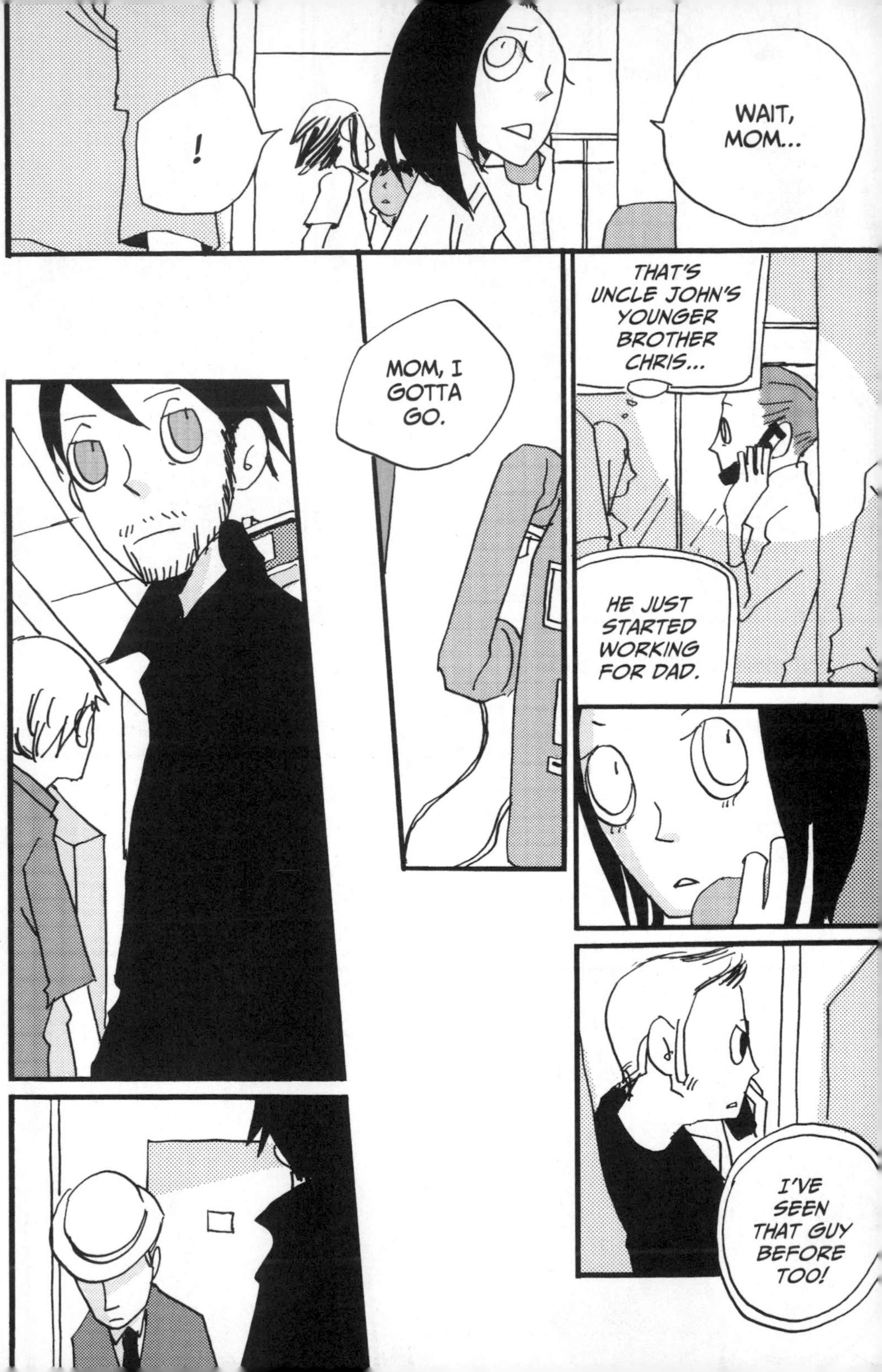
WAIT, MOM...
!
THAT'S UNCLE JOHN'S YOUNGER BROTHER CHRIS...
HE JUST STARTED WORKING FOR DAD.
I'VE SEEN THAT GUY BEFORE TOO!
MOM, I GOTTA GO.

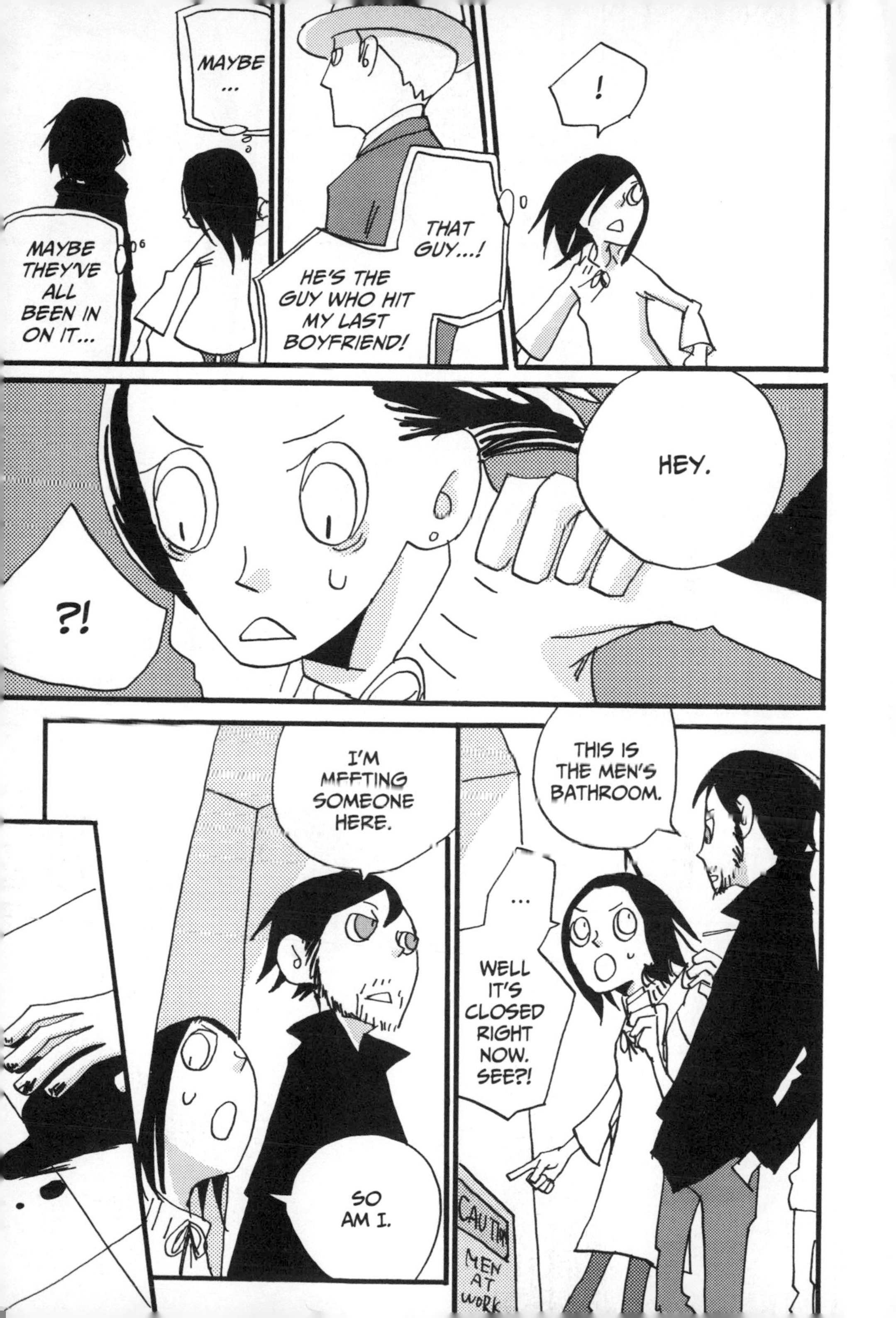
!
THAT GUY...!
HE'S THE GUY WHO HIT MY LAST BOYFRIEND!
MAYBE ...
MAYBE THEY'VE ALL BEEN IN ON IT...
HEY.
?!
THIS IS THE MEN'S BATHROOM.
...
WELL IT'S CLOSED RIGHT NOW. SEE?!
CAUTI
MEN AT WORK
I'M MEETING SOMEONE HERE.
SO AM I.

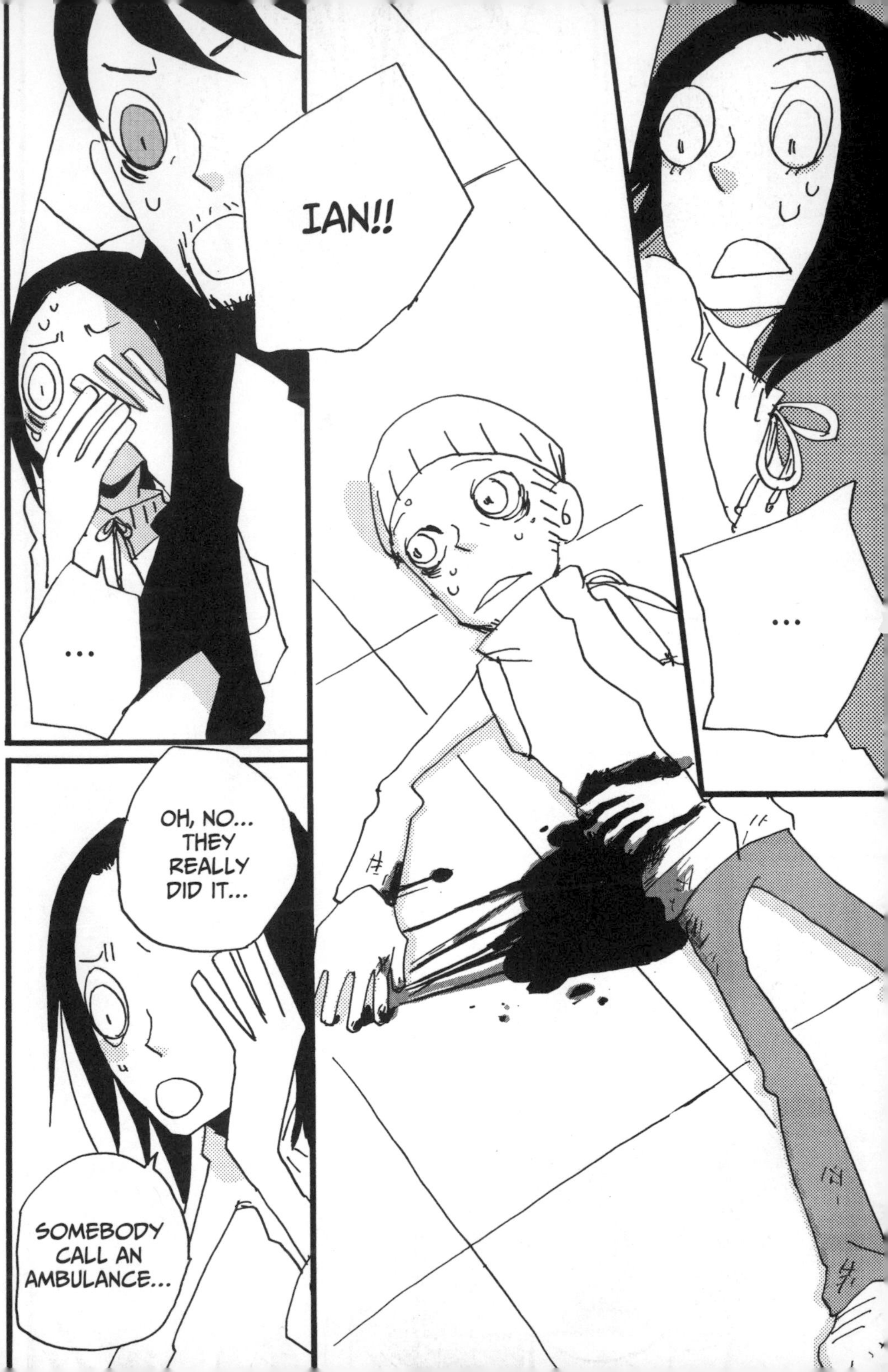
...
IAN!!
...
OH, NO... THEY REALLY DID IT...
SOMEBODY CALL AN AMBULANCE...

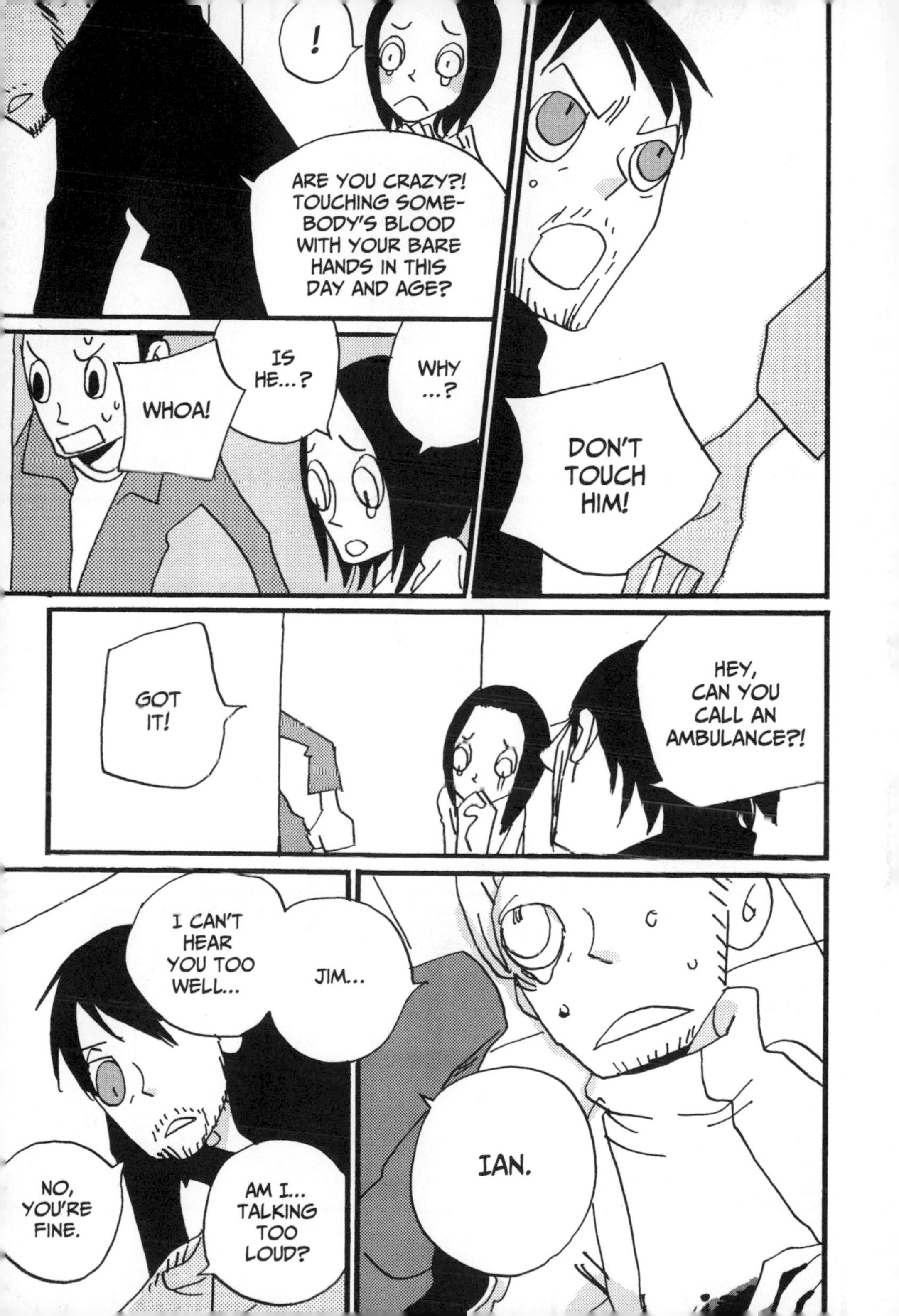
DON'T TOUCH HIM!
!
ARE YOU CRAZY?! TOUCHING SOME-BODY'S BLOOD WITH YOUR BARE HANDS IN THIS DAY AND AGE?
WHY ...?
IS HE...?
WHOA!
HEY, CAN YOU CALL AN AMBULANCE?!
GOT IT!
IAN.
JIM...
I CAN'T HEAR YOU TOO WELL...
AM I... TALKING TOO LOUD?
NO, YOU'RE FINE.

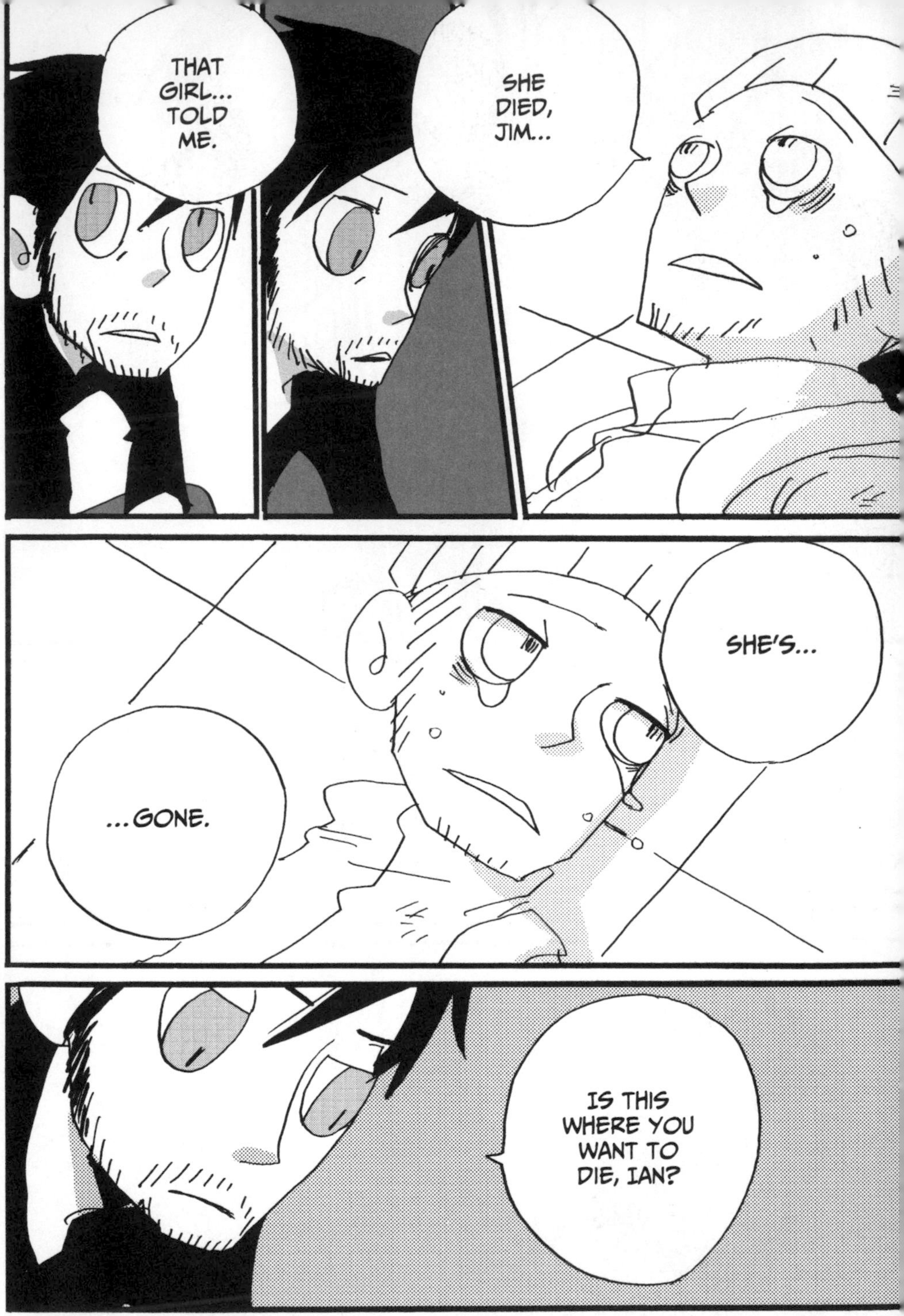
SHE DIED, JIM...
THAT GIRL... TOLD ME.
SHE'S...
...GONE.
IS THIS WHERE YOU WANT TO DIE, IAN?

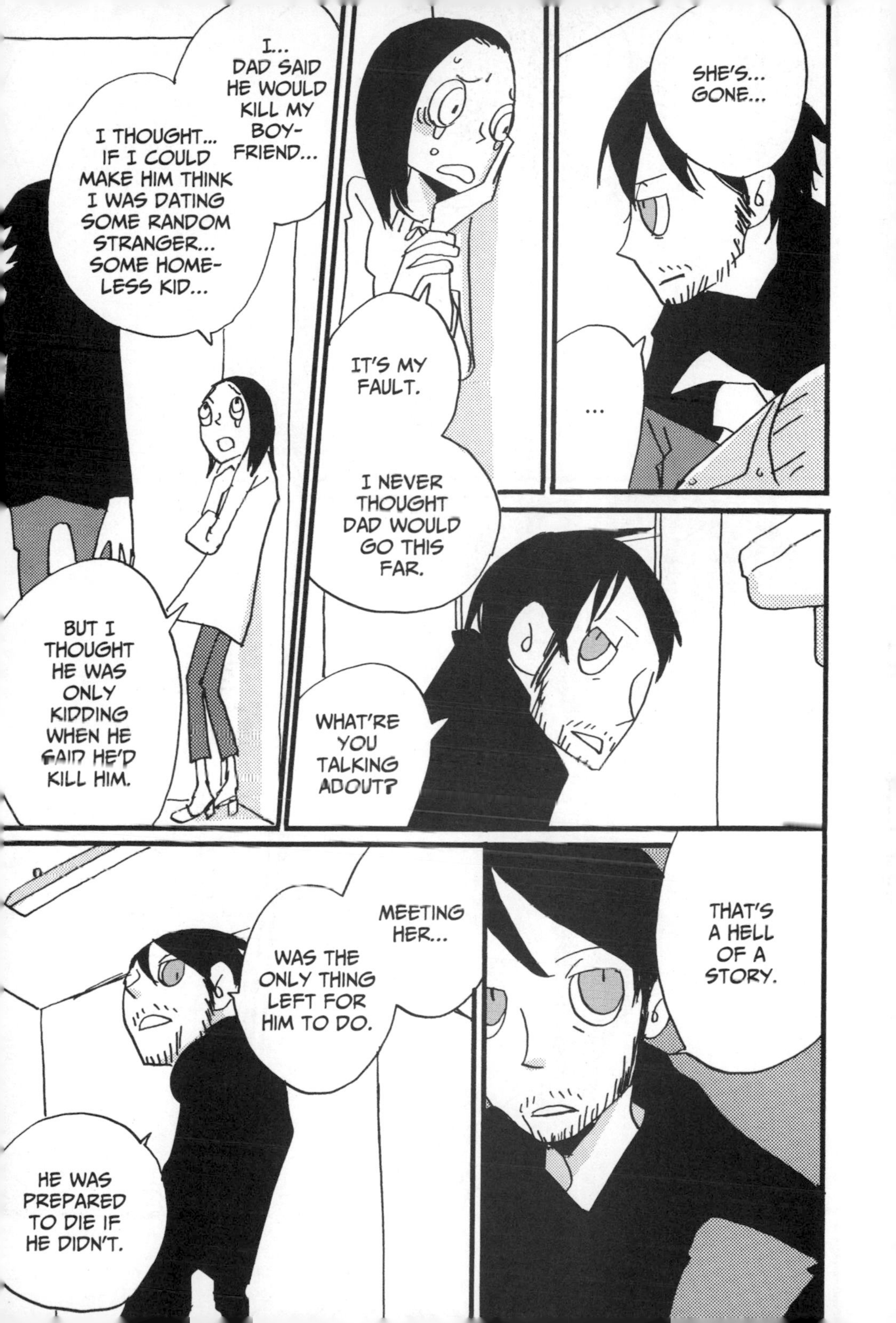
SHE'S... GONE...
...
I... DAD SAID HE WOULD KILL MY BOY-FRIEND...
IT'S MY FAULT.
I NEVER THOUGHT DAD WOULD GO THIS FAR.
WHAT'RE YOU TALKING ABOUT?
I THOUGHT... IF I COULD MAKE HIM THINK I WAS DATING SOME RANDOM STRANGER... SOME HOME-LESS KID...
BUT I THOUGHT HE WAS ONLY KIDDING WHEN HE SAID HE'D KILL HIM.
THAT'S A HELL OF A STORY.
MEETING HER...
WAS THE ONLY THING LEFT FOR HIM TO DO.
HE WAS PREPARED TO DIE IF HE DIDN'T.

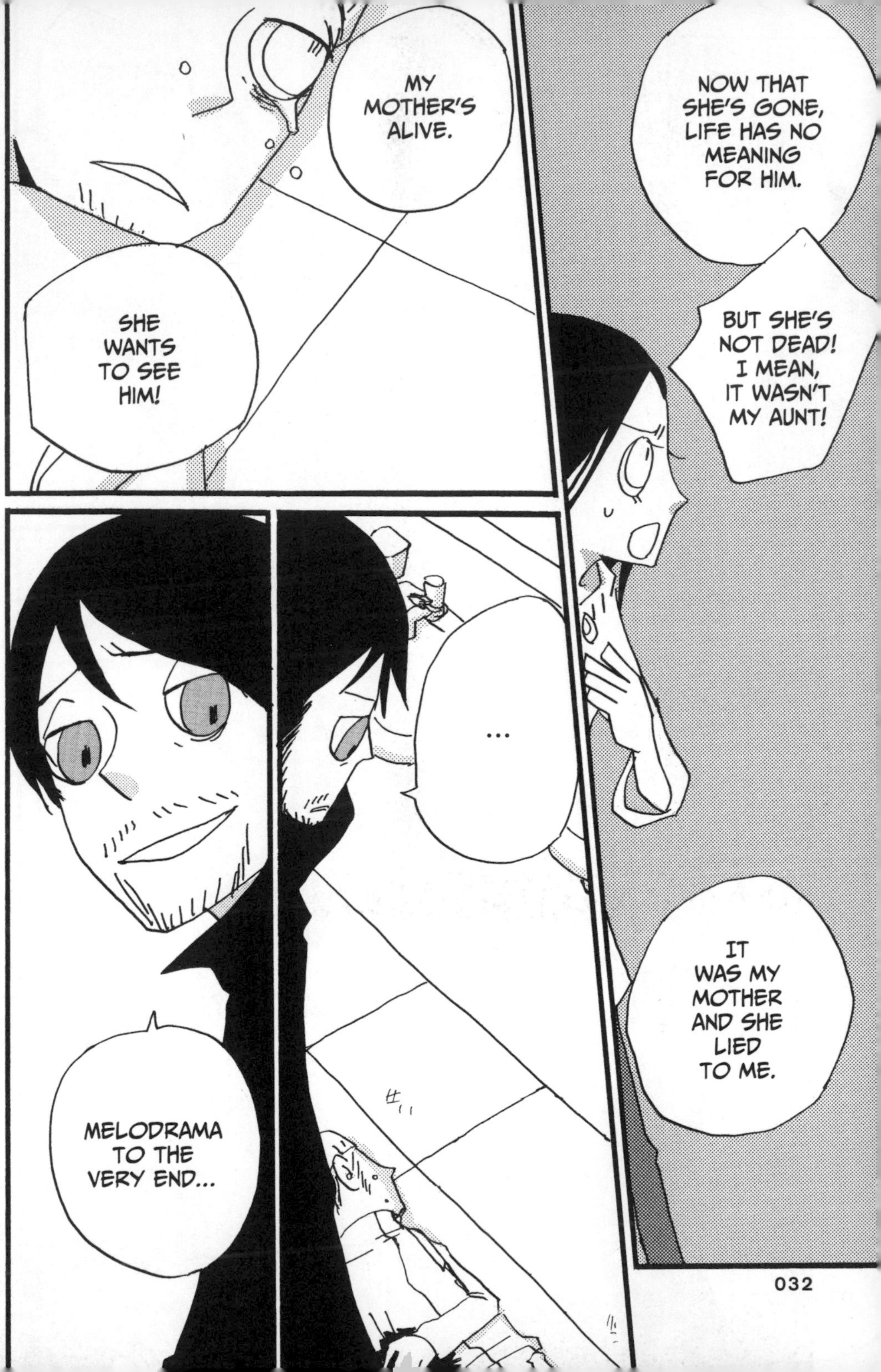
NOW THAT SHE'S GONE, LIFE HAS NO MEANING FOR HIM.
BUT SHE'S NOT DEAD! I MEAN, IT WASN'T MY AUNT!
IT WAS MY MOTHER AND SHE LIED TO ME.
MY MOTHER'S ALIVE.
SHE WANTS TO SEE HIM!
...
MELODRAMA TO THE VERY END...

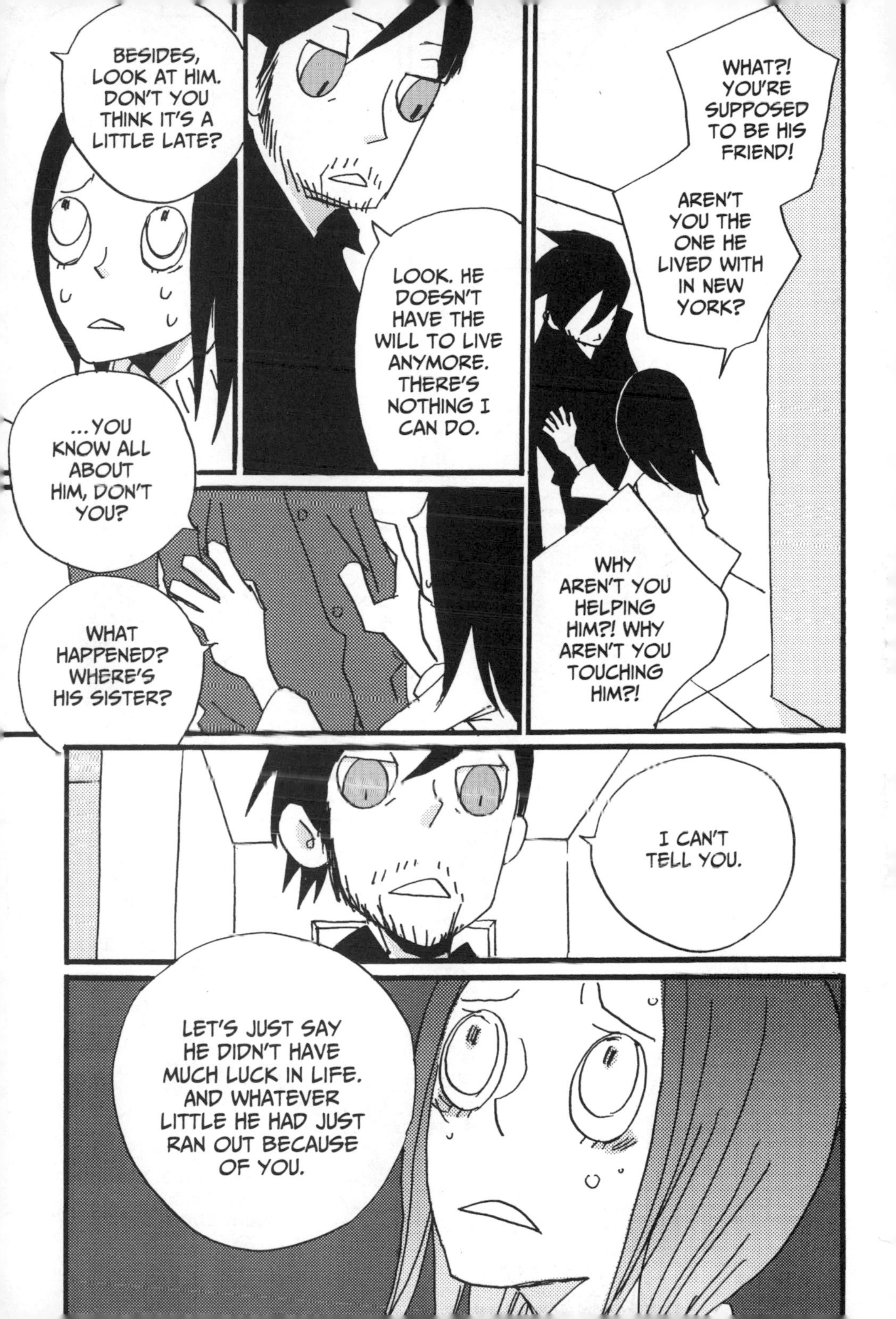
WHAT?! YOU'RE SUPPOSED TO BE HIS FRIEND!
AREN'T YOU THE ONE HE LIVED WITH IN NEW YORK?
WHY AREN'T YOU HELPING HIM?! WHY AREN'T YOU TOUCHING HIM?!
LOOK. HE DOESN'T HAVE THE WILL TO LIVE ANYMORE. THERE'S NOTHING I CAN DO.
BESIDES, LOOK AT HIM. DON'T YOU THINK IT'S A LITTLE LATE?
...YOU KNOW ALL ABOUT HIM, DON'T YOU?
WHAT HAPPENED? WHERE'S HIS SISTER?
I CAN'T TELL YOU.
LET'S JUST SAY HE DIDN'T HAVE MUCH LUCK IN LIFE. AND WHATEVER LITTLE HE HAD JUST RAN OUT BECAUSE OF YOU.

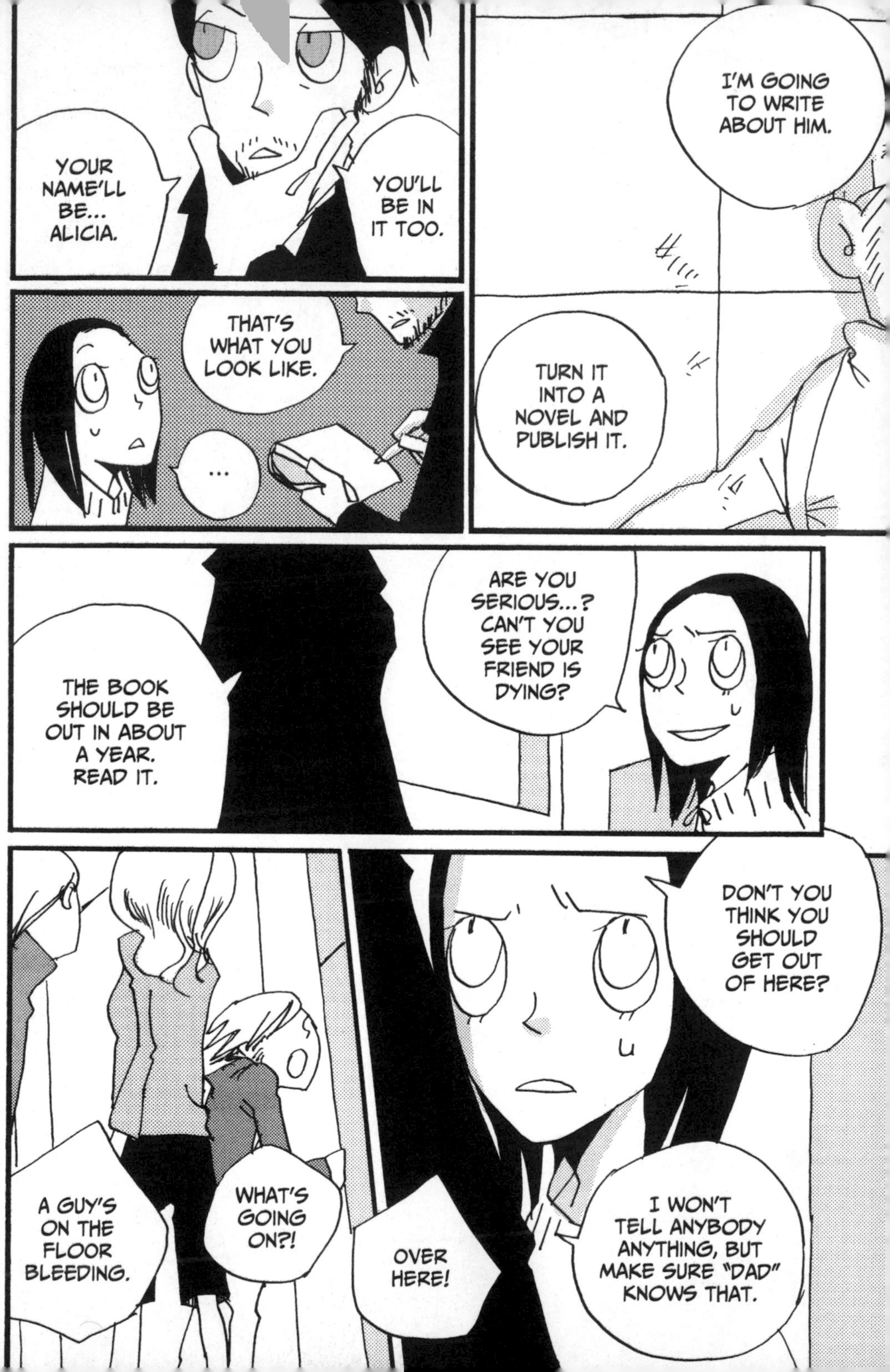
I'M GOING TO WRITE ABOUT HIM.
TURN IT INTO A NOVEL AND PUBLISH IT.
YOU'LL BE IN IT TOO.
YOUR NAME'LL BE... ALICIA.
THAT'S WHAT YOU LOOK LIKE.
...
ARE YOU SERIOUS...? CAN'T YOU SEE YOUR FRIEND IS DYING?
THE BOOK SHOULD BE OUT IN ABOUT A YEAR. READ IT.
DON'T YOU THINK YOU SHOULD GET OUT OF HERE?
I WON'T TELL ANYBODY ANYTHING, BUT MAKE SURE "DAD" KNOWS THAT.
OVER HERE!
WHAT'S GOING ON?!
A GUY'S ON THE FLOOR BLEEDING.

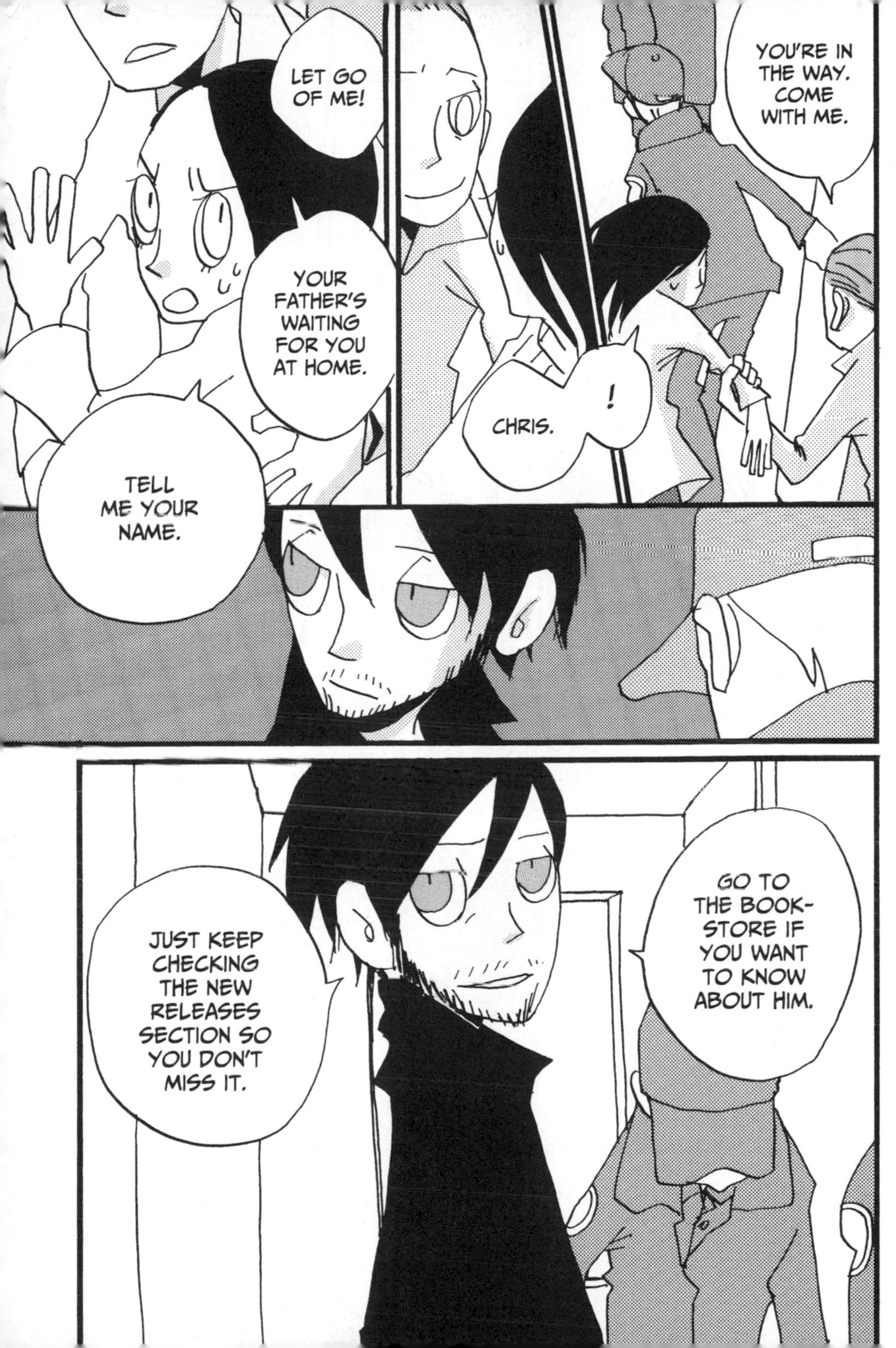
YOU'RE IN THE WAY. COME WITH ME.
!
CHRIS.
LET GO OF ME!
YOUR FATHER'S WAITING FOR YOU AT HOME.
TELL ME YOUR NAME.
GO TO THE BOOK-STORE IF YOU WANT TO KNOW ABOUT HIM.
JUST KEEP CHECKING THE NEW RELEASES SECTION SO YOU DON'T MISS IT.

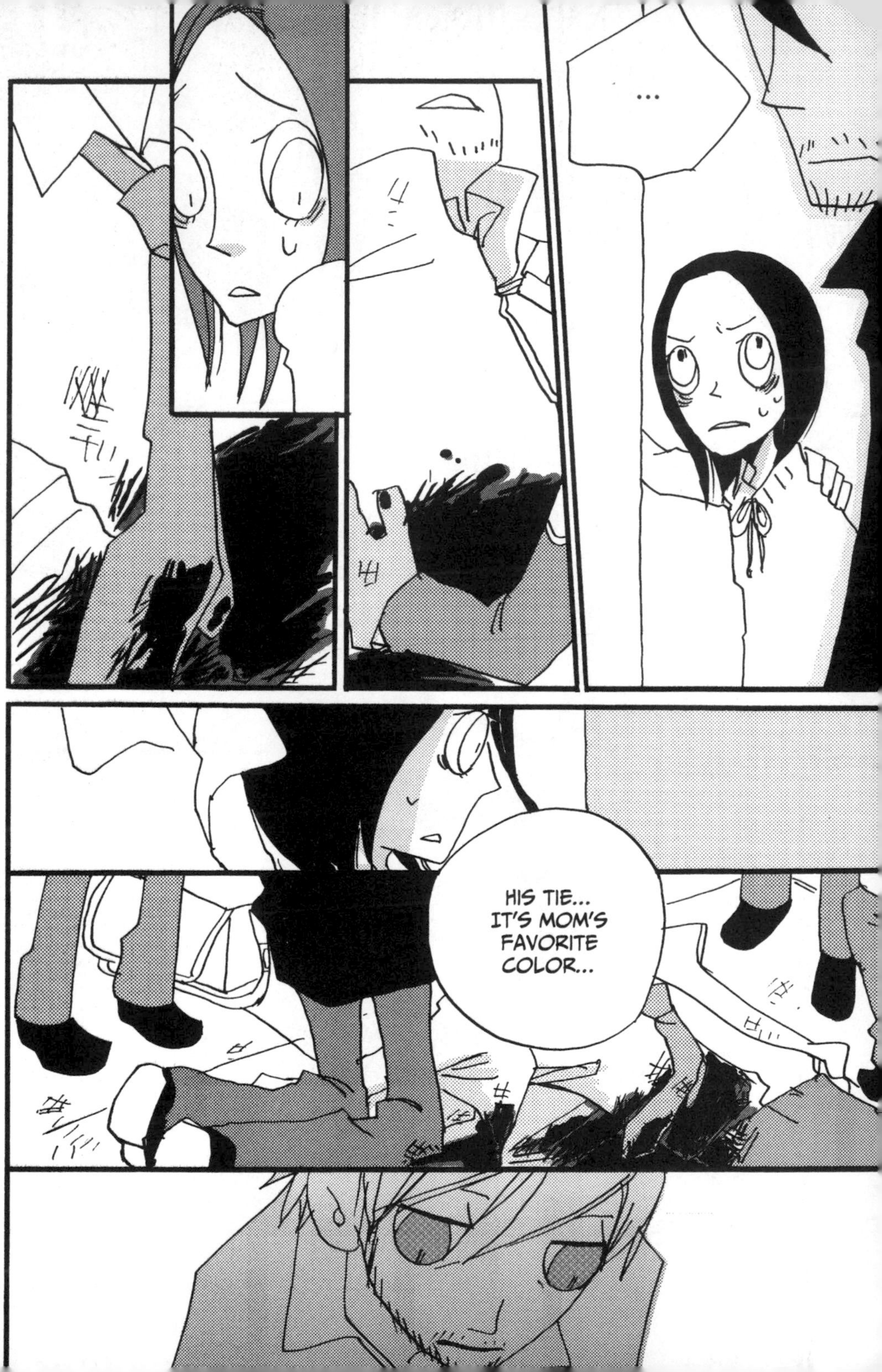
...
HIS TIE... IT'S MOM'S FAVORITE COLOR...

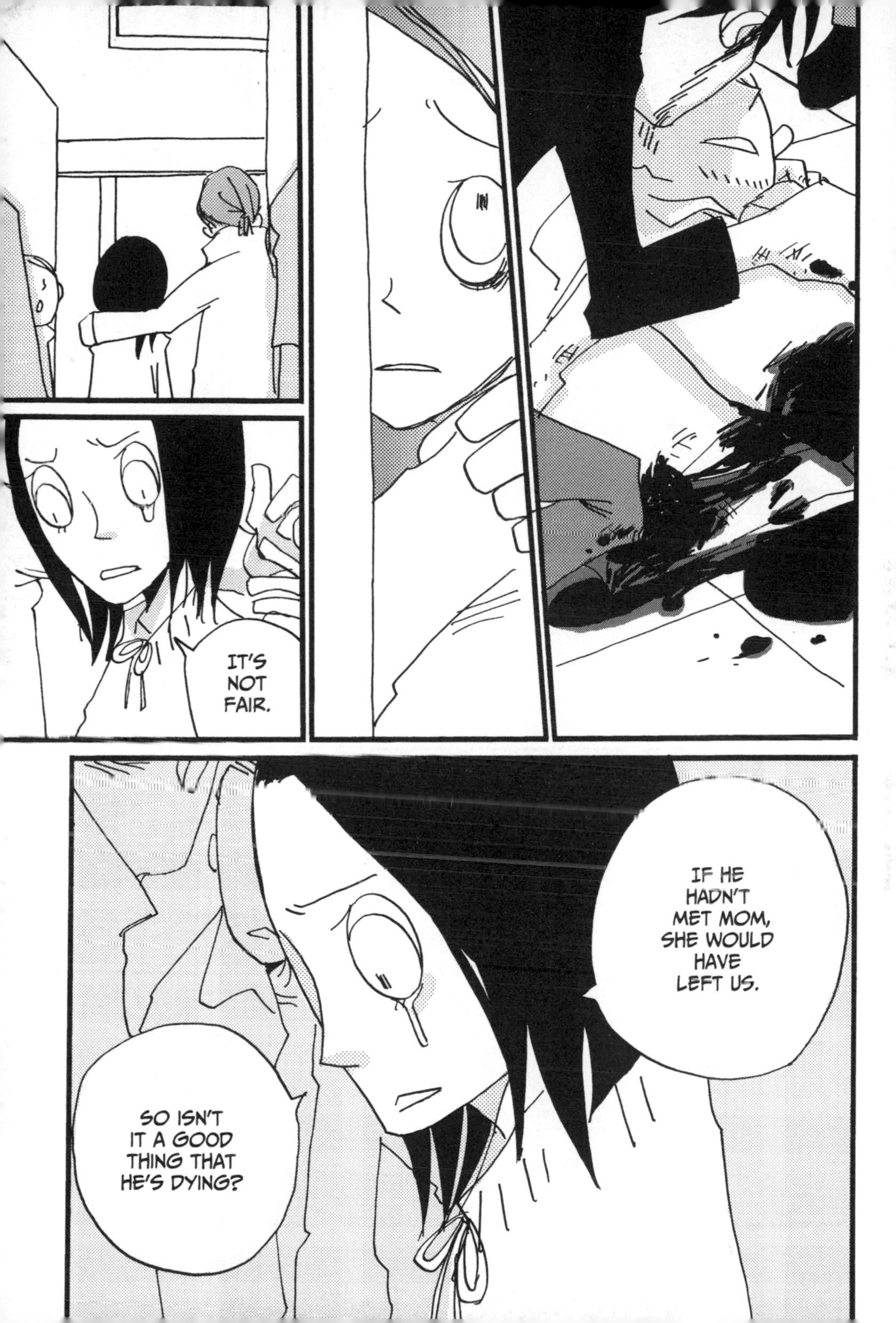
IT'S NOT FAIR.
IF HE HADN'T MET MOM, SHE WOULD HAVE LEFT US.
SO ISN'T IT A GOOD THING THAT HE'S DYING?

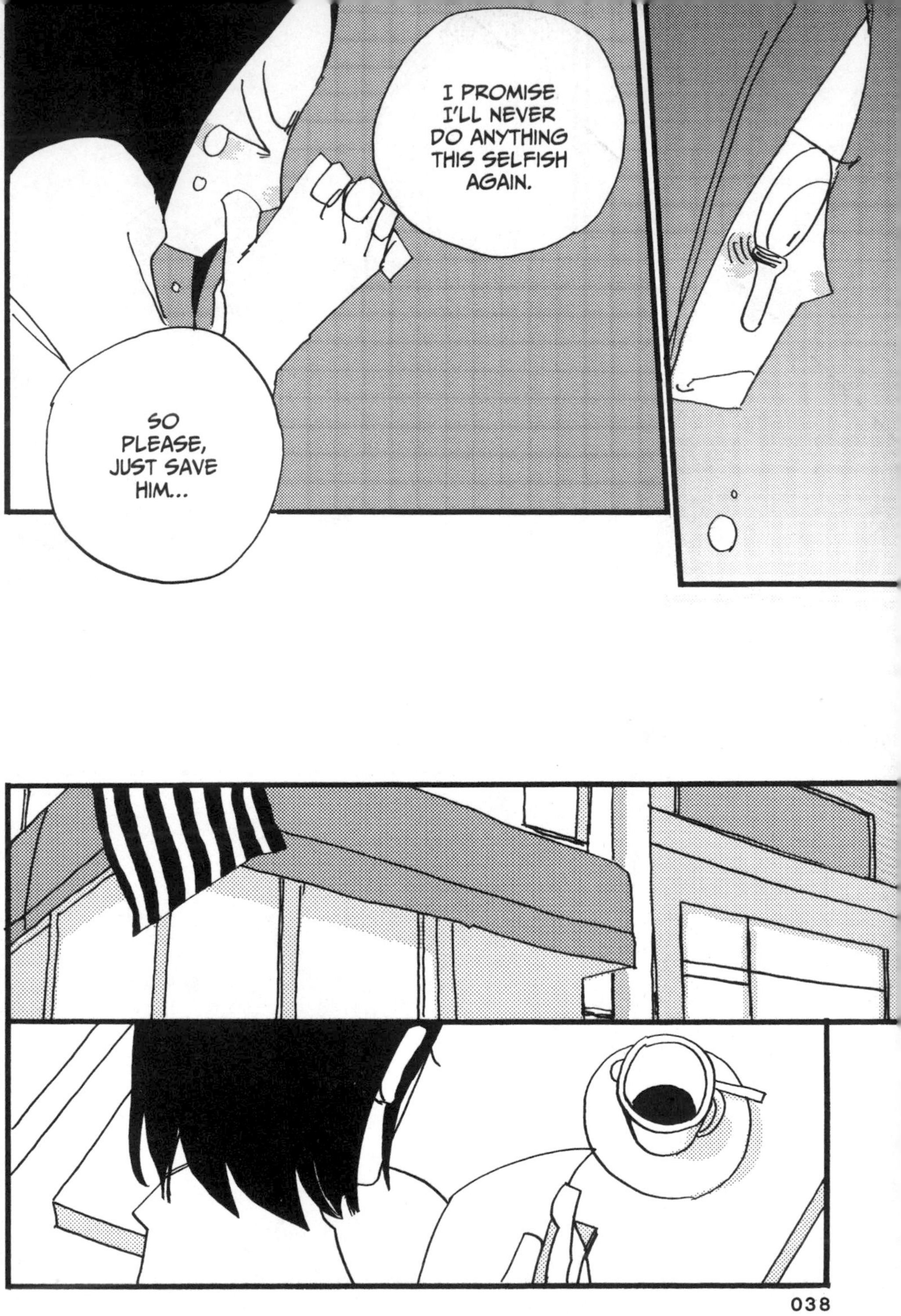
I PROMISE I'LL NEVER DO ANYTHING THIS SELFISH AGAIN.
SO PLEASE, JUST SAVE HIM...

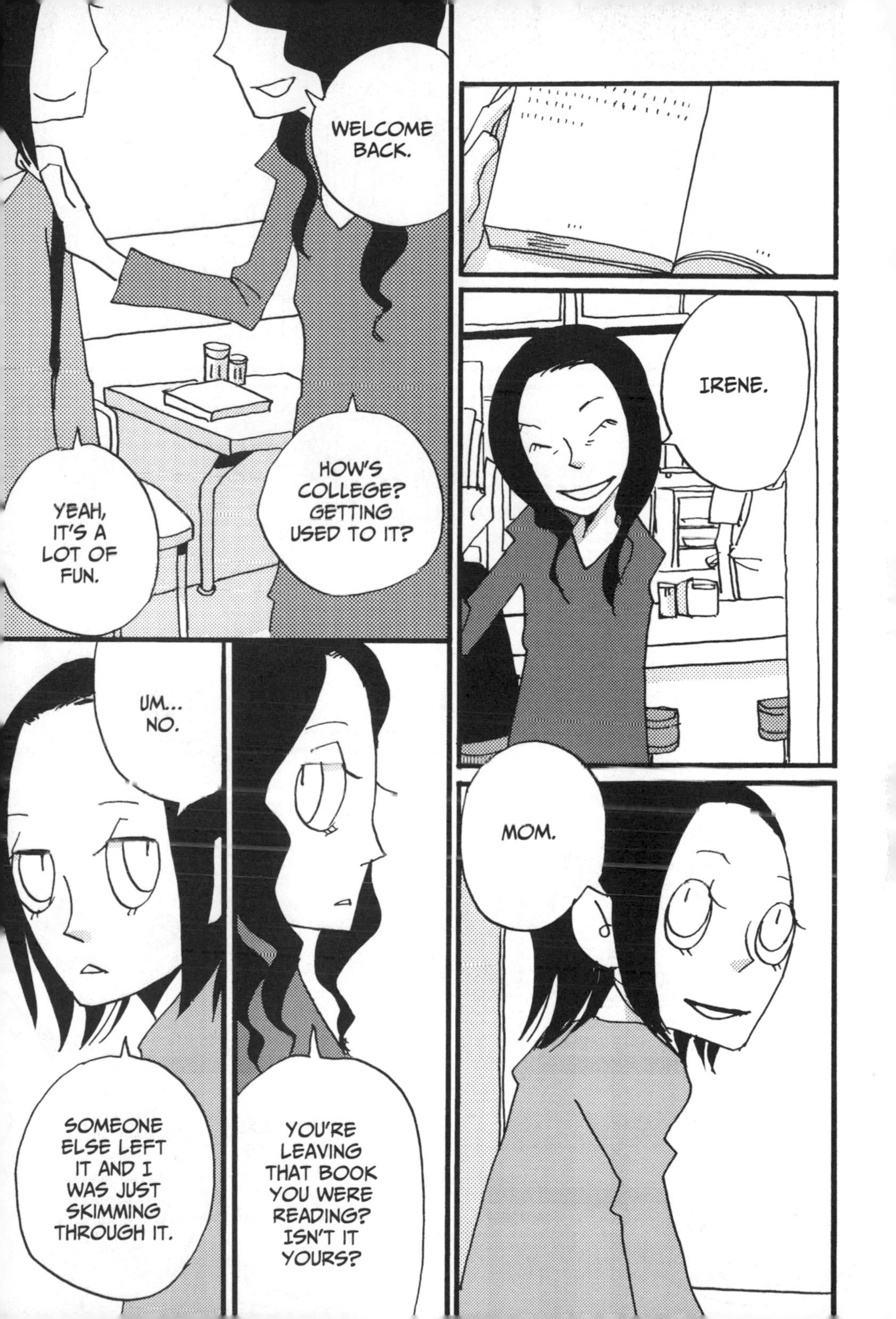
IRENE.
MOM.
WELCOME BACK.
HOW'S COLLEGE? GETTING USED TO IT?
YEAH, IT'S A LOT OF FUN.
YOU'RE LEAVING THAT BOOK YOU WERE READING? ISN'T IT YOURS?
UM... NO.
SOMEONE ELSE LEFT IT AND I WAS JUST SKIMMING THROUGH IT.

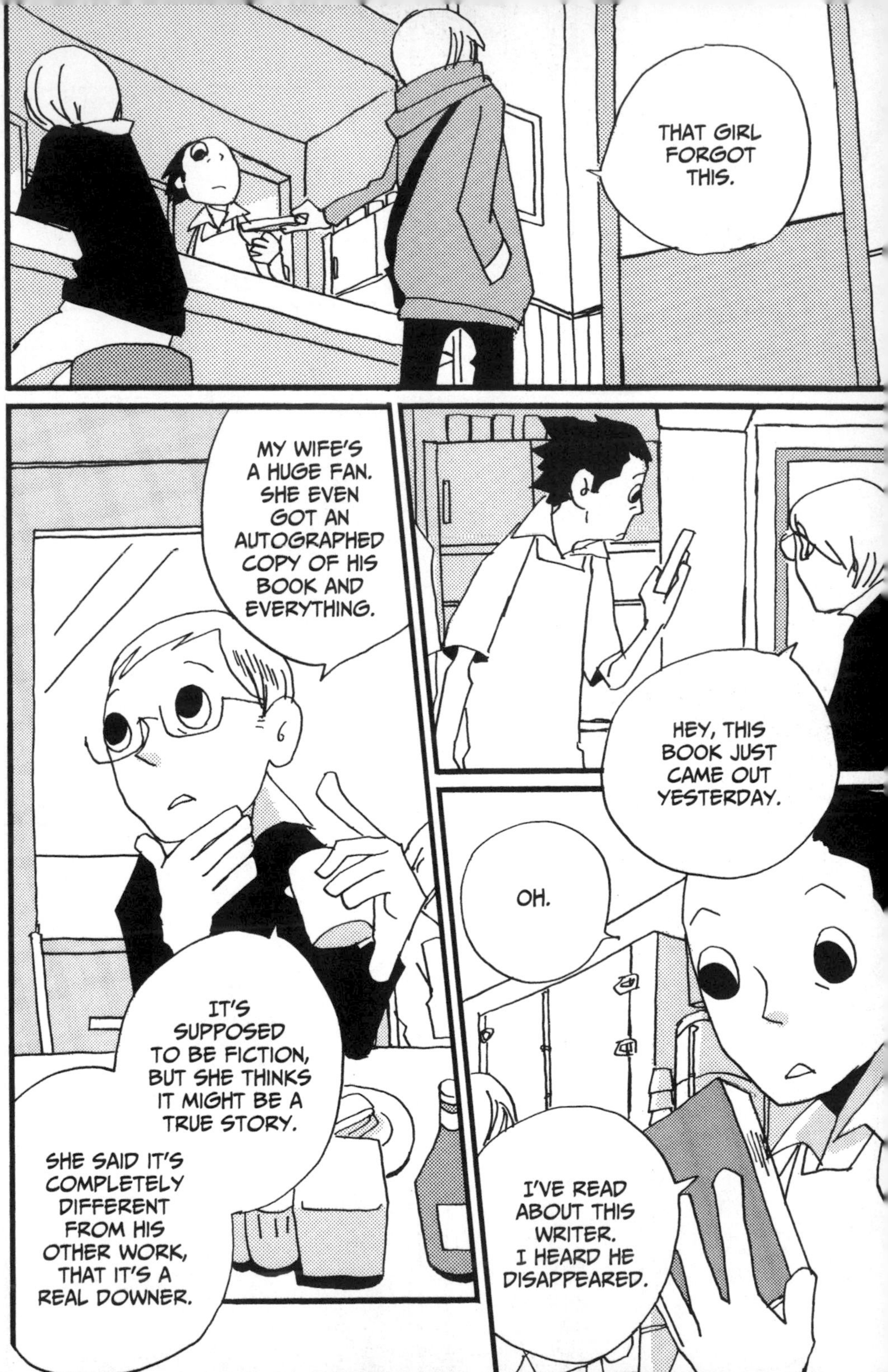
THAT GIRL FORGOT THIS.
HEY, THIS BOOK JUST CAME OUT YESTERDAY.
OH.
I'VE READ ABOUT THIS WRITER. I HEARD HE DISAPPEARED.
MY WIFE'S A HUGE FAN. SHE EVEN GOT AN AUTOGRAPHED COPY OF HIS BOOK AND EVERYTHING.
IT'S SUPPOSED TO BE FICTION, BUT SHE THINKS IT MIGHT BE A TRUE STORY.
SHE SAID IT'S COMPLETELY DIFFERENT FROM HIS OTHER WORK, THAT IT'S A REAL DOWNER.

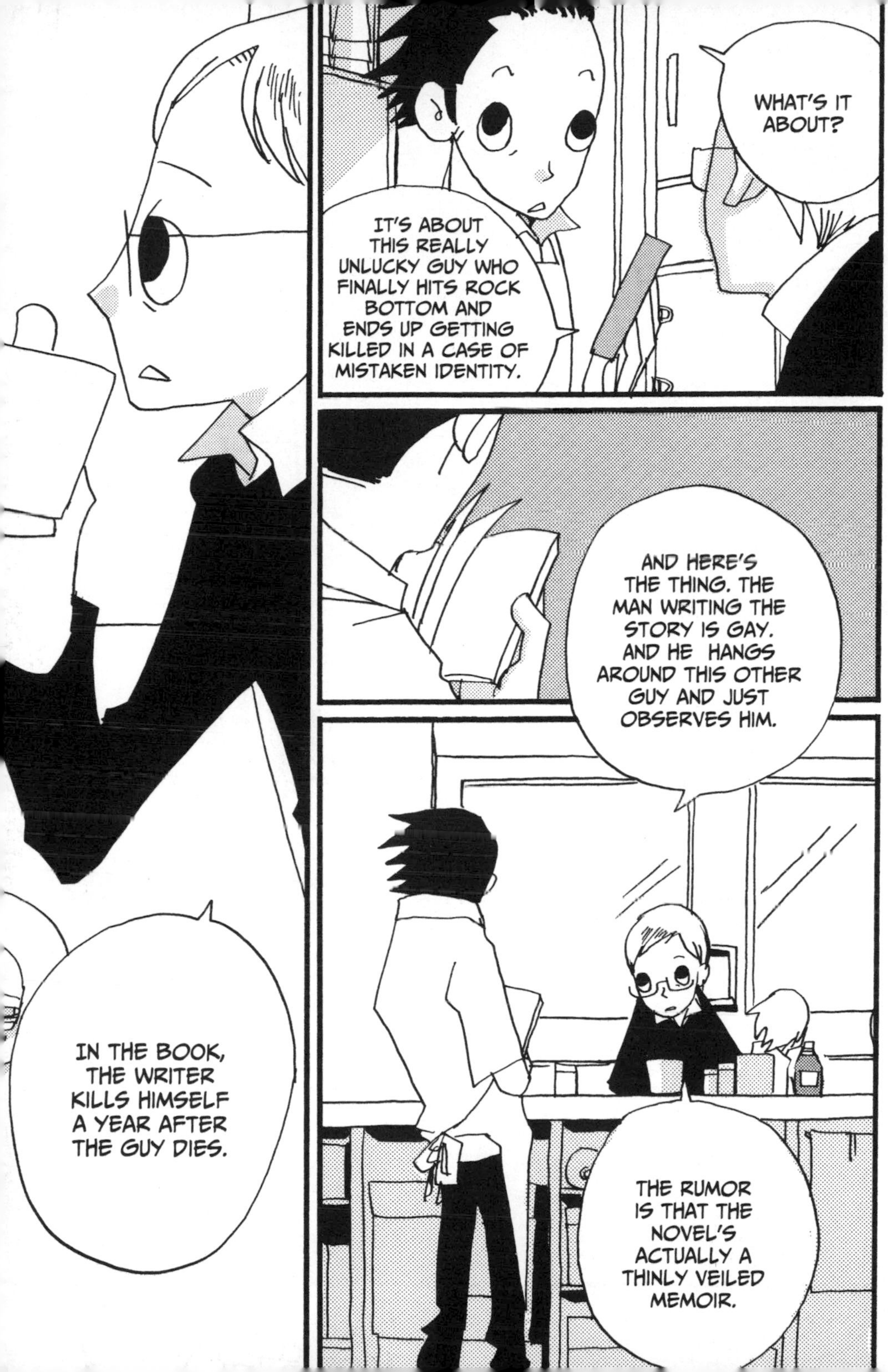
WHAT'S IT ABOUT?
IT'S ABOUT THIS REALLY UNLUCKY GUY WHO FINALLY HITS ROCK BOTTOM AND ENDS UP GETTING KILLED IN A CASE OF MISTAKEN IDENTITY.
AND HERE'S THE THING. THE MAN WRITING THE STORY IS GAY. AND HE HANGS AROUND THIS OTHER GUY AND JUST OBSERVES HIM.
THE RUMOR IS THAT THE NOVEL'S ACTUALLY A THINLY VEILED MEMOIR.
IN THE BOOK, THE WRITER KILLS HIMSELF A YEAR AFTER THE GUY DIES.

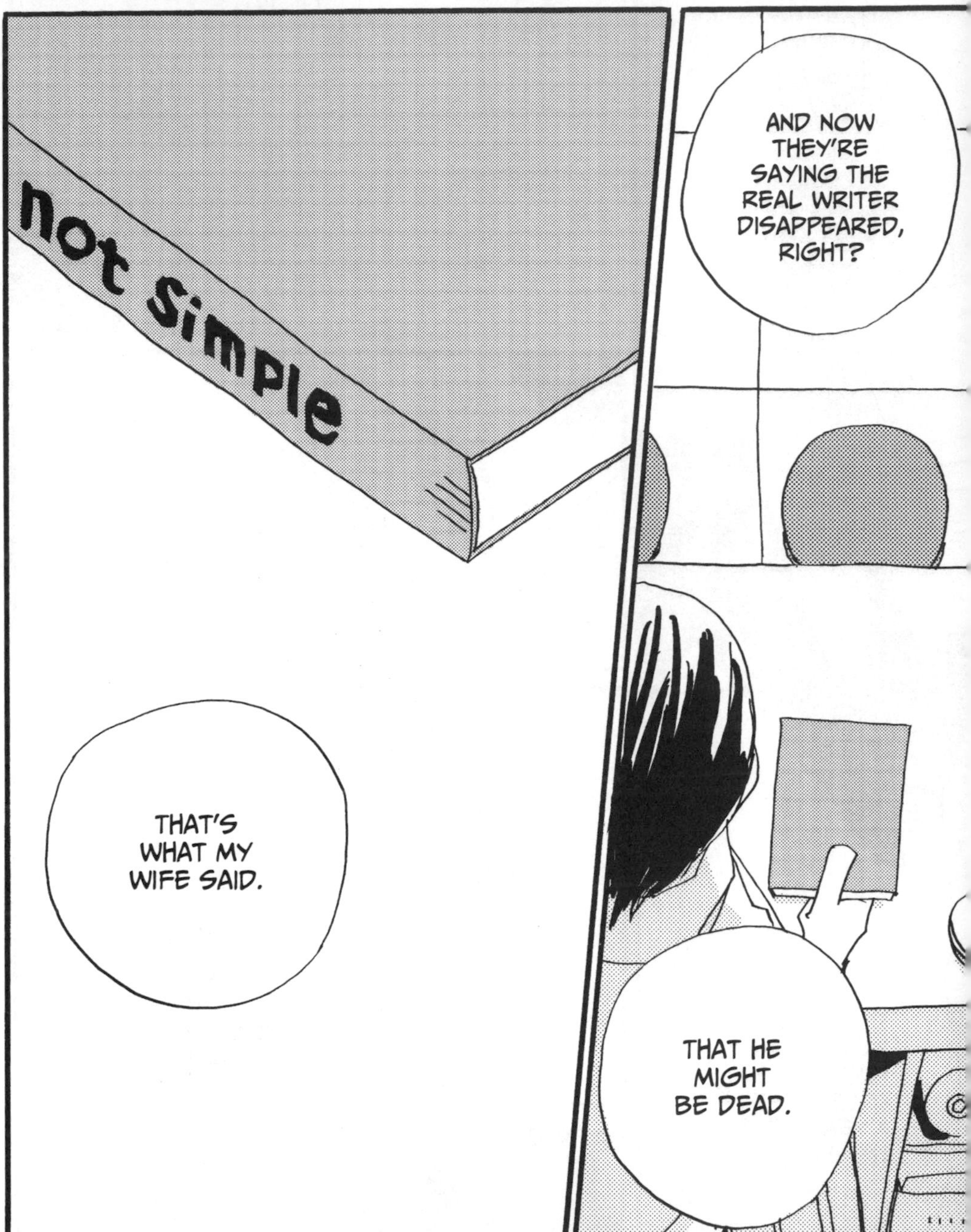
AND NOW THEY'RE SAYING THE REAL WRITER DISAPPEARED, RIGHT?
THAT HE MIGHT BE DEAD.
not simple
THAT'S WHAT MY WIFE SAID.

#01 not simple

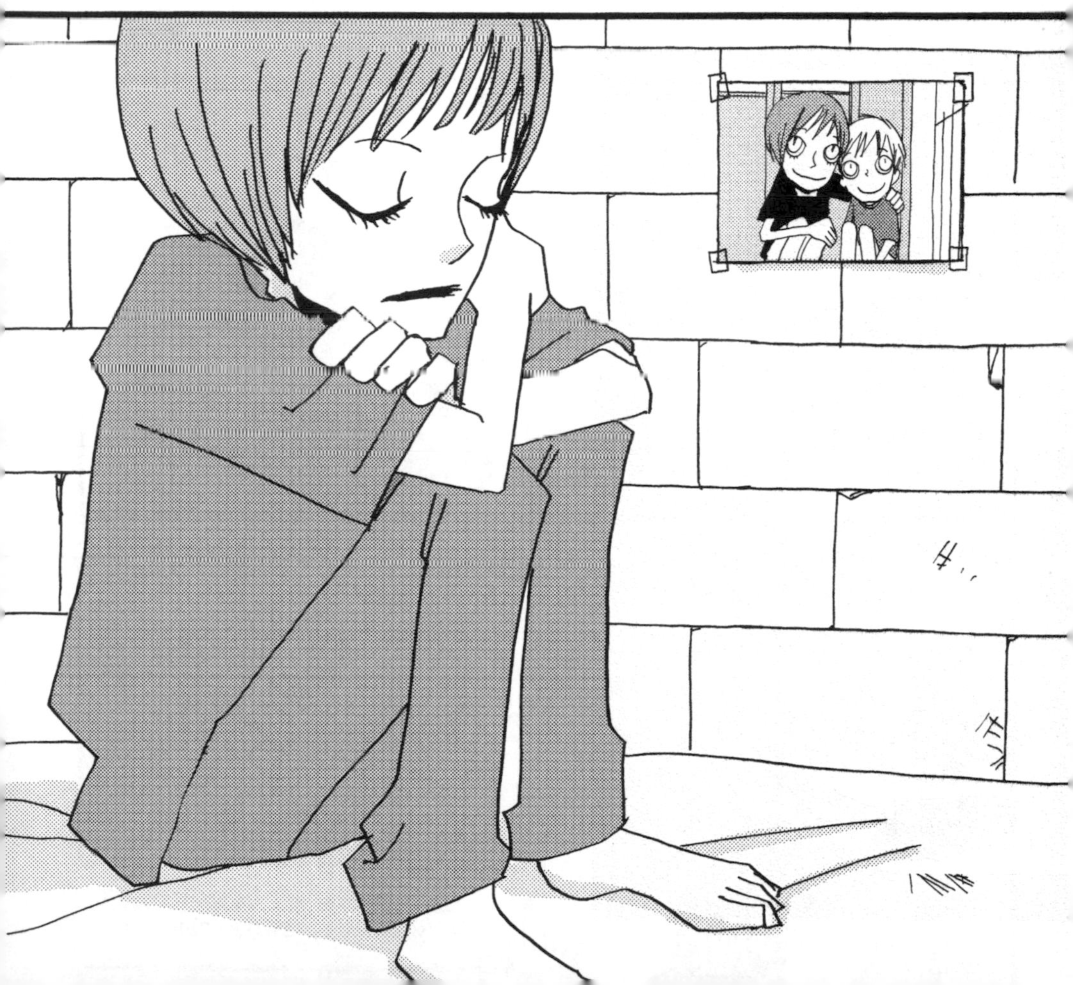

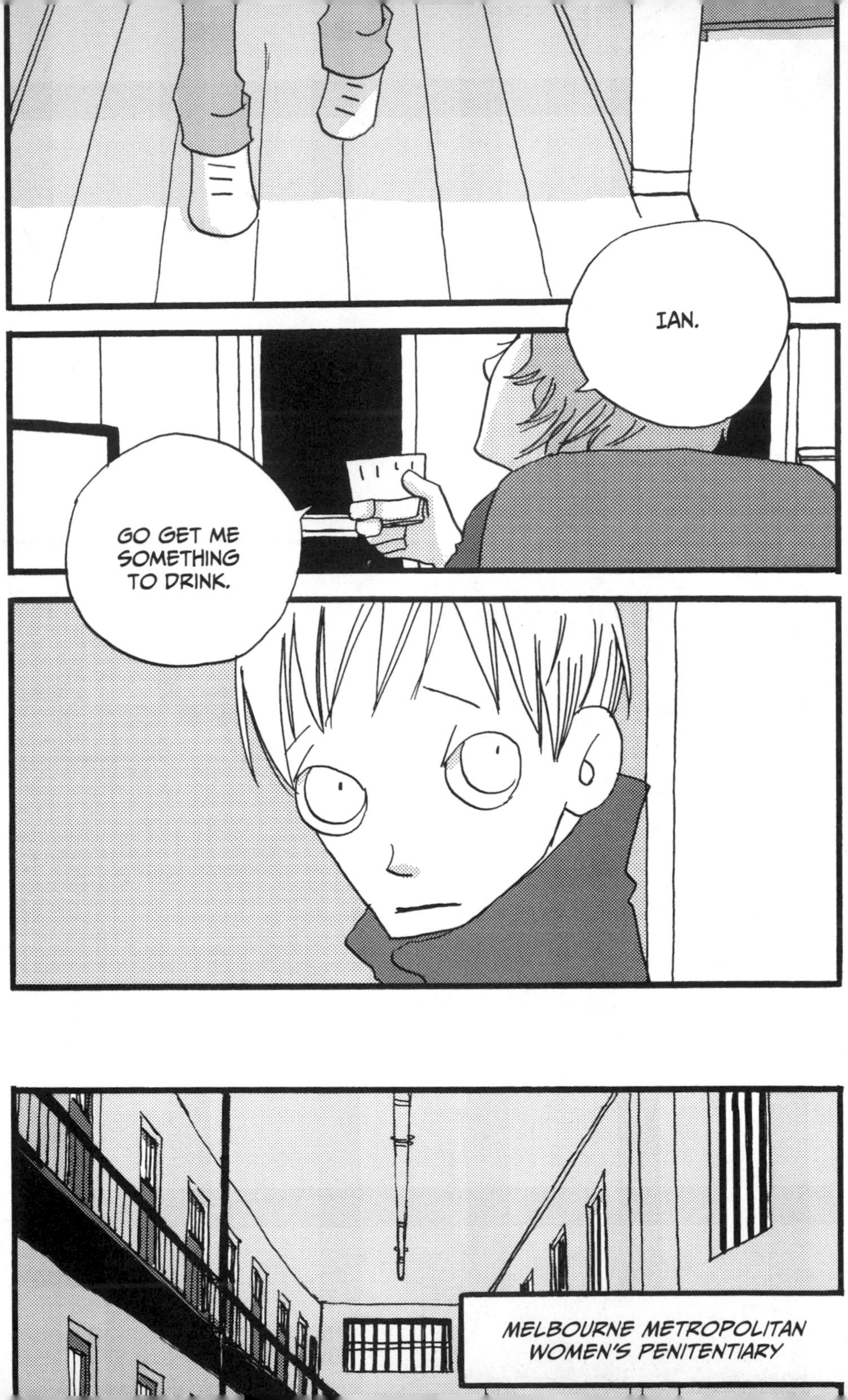
IAN.
GO GET ME SOMETHING TO DRINK.
MELBOURNE METROPOLITAN WOMEN'S PENITENTIARY

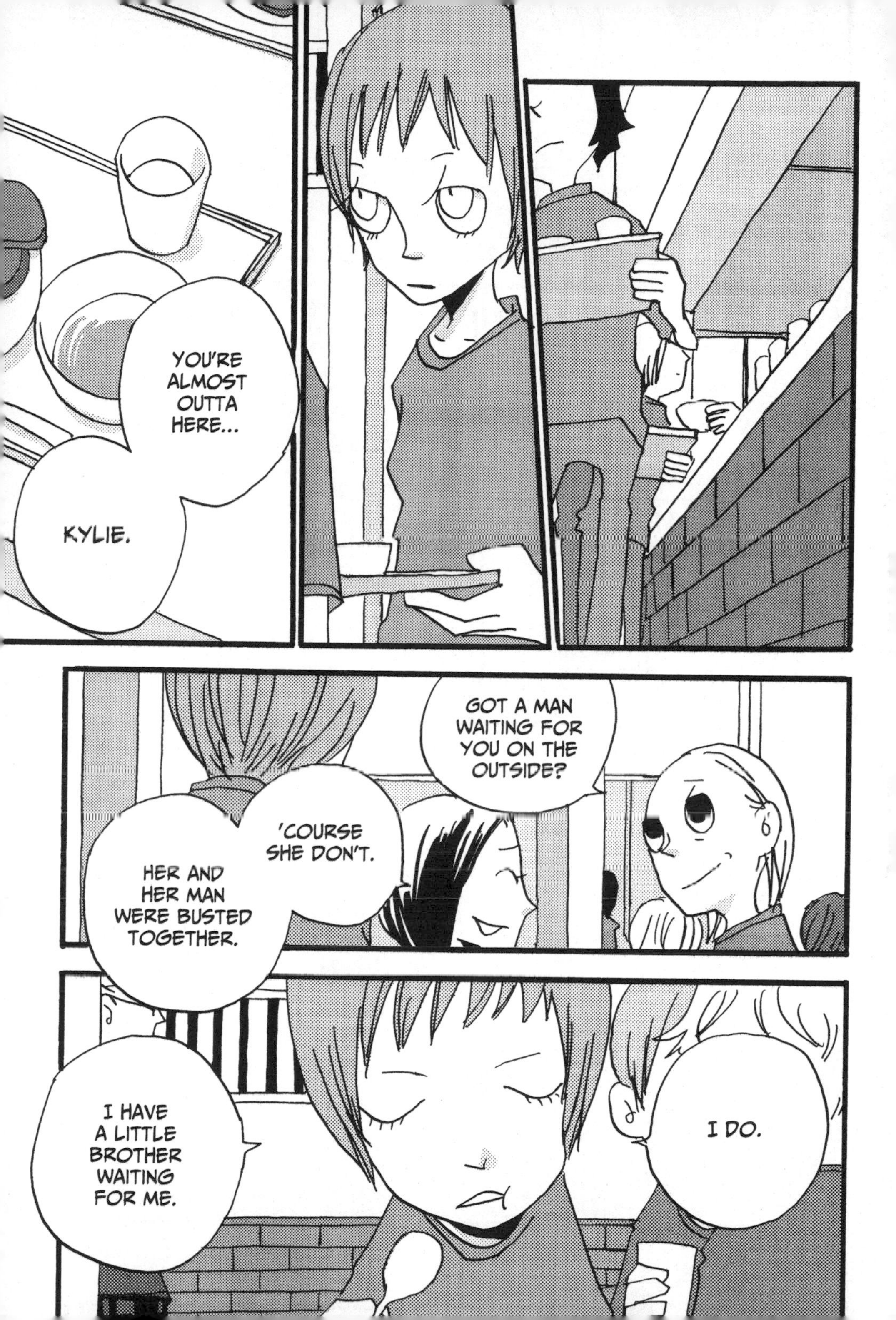
YOU'RE ALMOST OUTTA HERE...
KYLIE.
GOT A MAN WAITING FOR YOU ON THE OUTSIDE?
'COURSE SHE DON'T.
HER AND HER MAN WERE BUSTED TOGETHER.
I DO.
I HAVE A LITTLE BROTHER WAITING FOR ME.

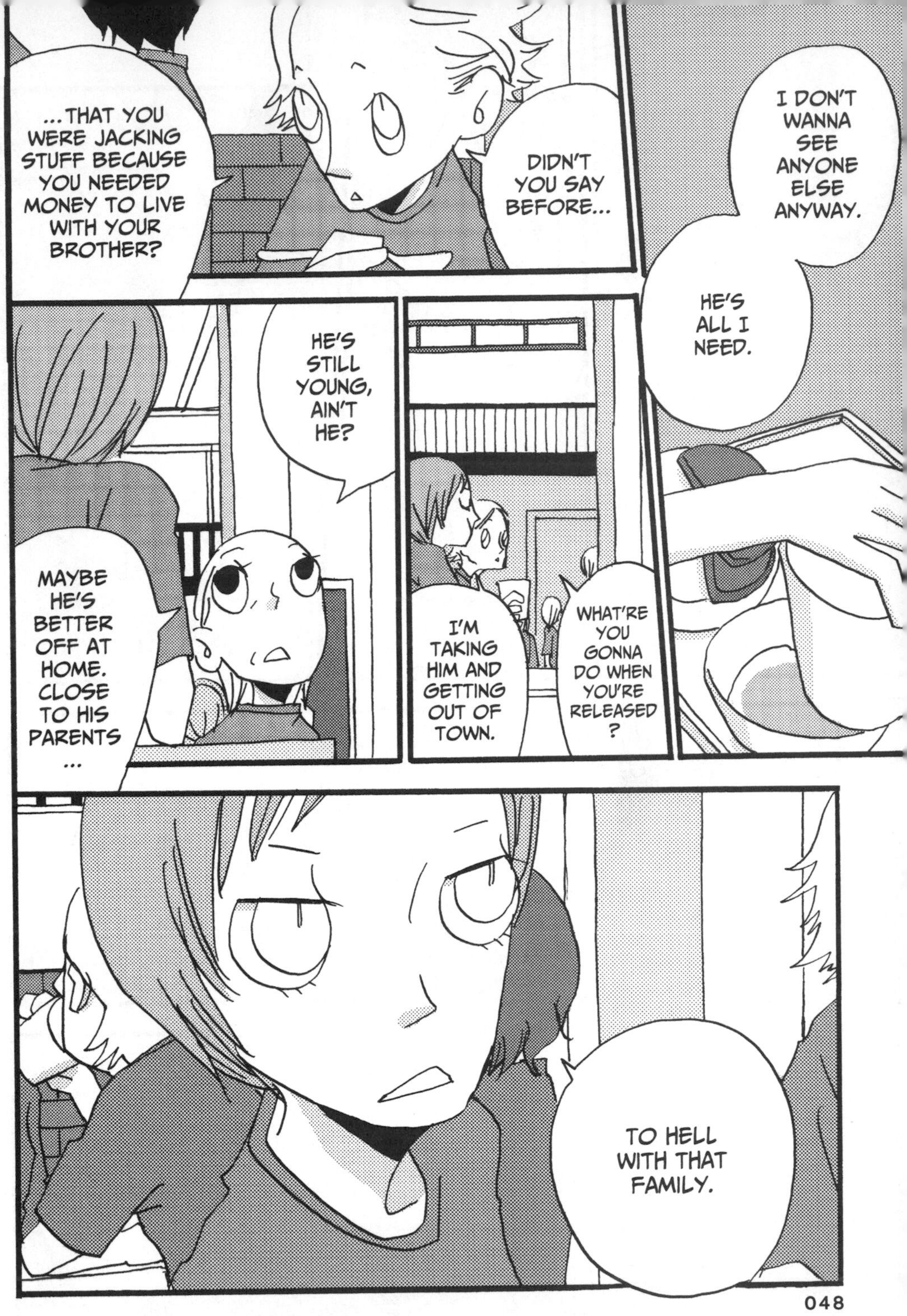
I DON'T WANNA SEE ANYONE ELSE ANYWAY.
HE'S ALL I NEED.
DIDN'T YOU SAY BEFORE...
...THAT YOU WERE JACKING STUFF BECAUSE YOU NEEDED MONEY TO LIVE WITH YOUR BROTHER?
WHAT'RE YOU GONNA DO WHEN YOU'RE RELEASED?
I'M TAKING HIM AND GETTING OUT OF TOWN.
HE'S STILL YOUNG, AIN'T HE?
MAYBE HE'S BETTER OFF AT HOME. CLOSE TO HIS PARENTS...
TO HELL WITH THAT FAMILY.

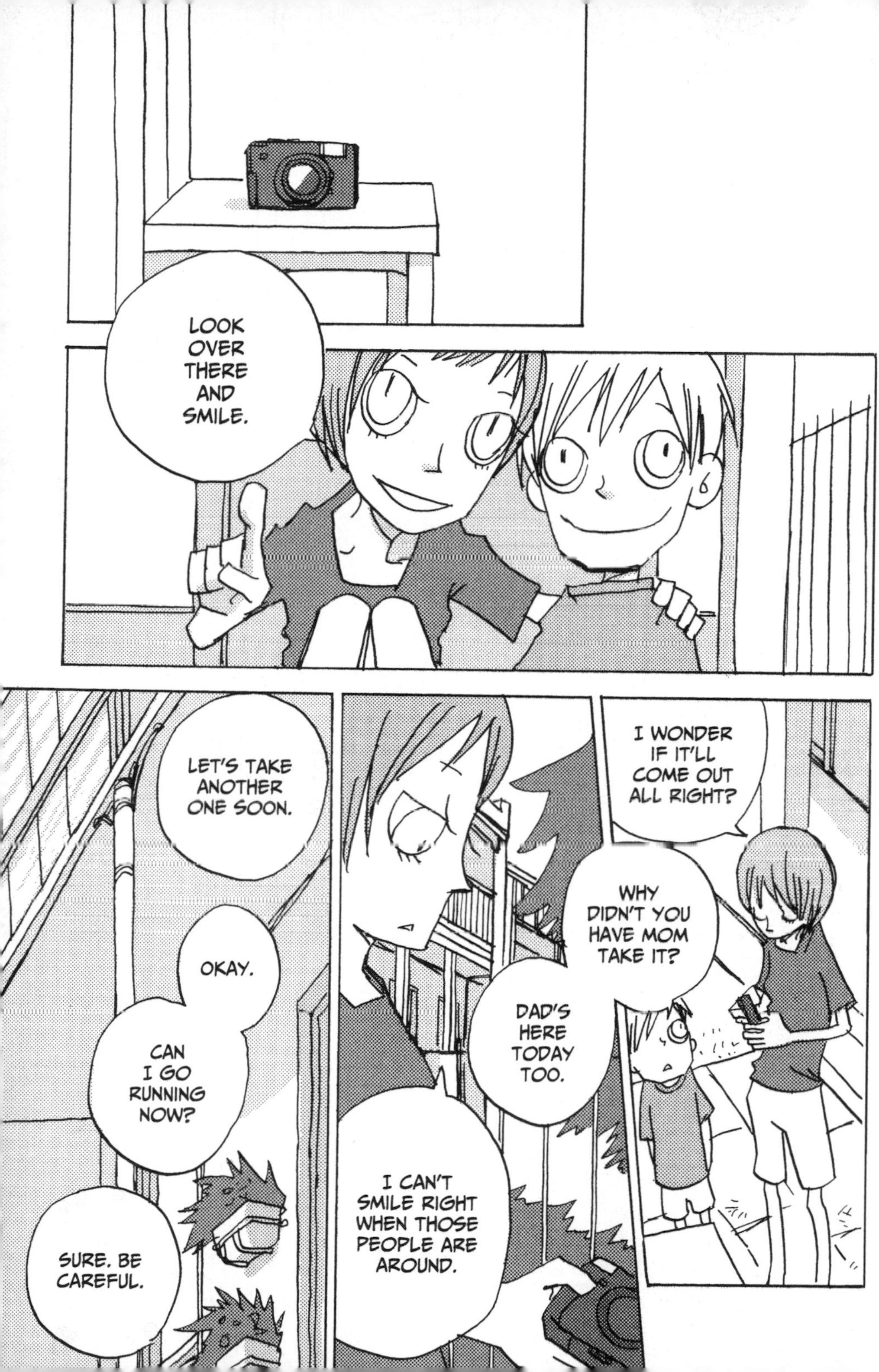
LOOK OVER THERE AND SMILE.
I WONDER IF IT'LL COME OUT ALL RIGHT?
WHY DIDN'T YOU HAVE MOM TAKE IT?
DAD'S HERE TODAY TOO.
I CAN'T SMILE RIGHT WHEN THOSE PEOPLE ARE AROUND.
LET'S TAKE ANOTHER ONE SOON.
OKAY.
CAN I GO RUNNING NOW?
SURE. BE CAREFUL.

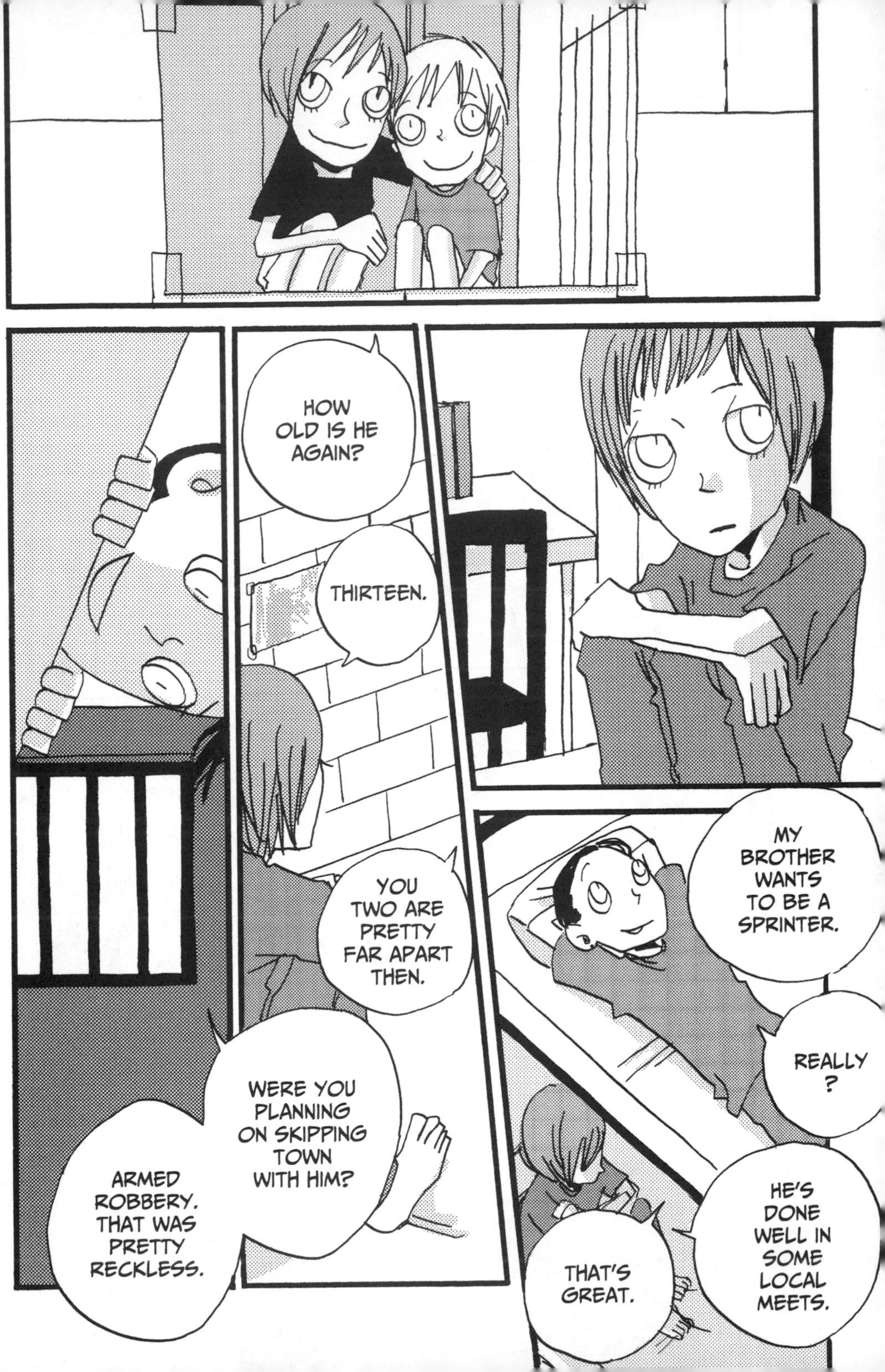
MY BROTHER WANTS TO BE A SPRINTER.
REALLY?
HE'S DONE WELL IN SOME LOCAL MEETS.
THAT'S GREAT.
HOW OLD IS HE AGAIN?
THIRTEEN.
YOU TWO ARE PRETTY FAR APART THEN.
WERE YOU PLANNING ON SKIPPING TOWN WITH HIM?
ARMED ROBBERY. THAT WAS PRETTY RECKLESS.

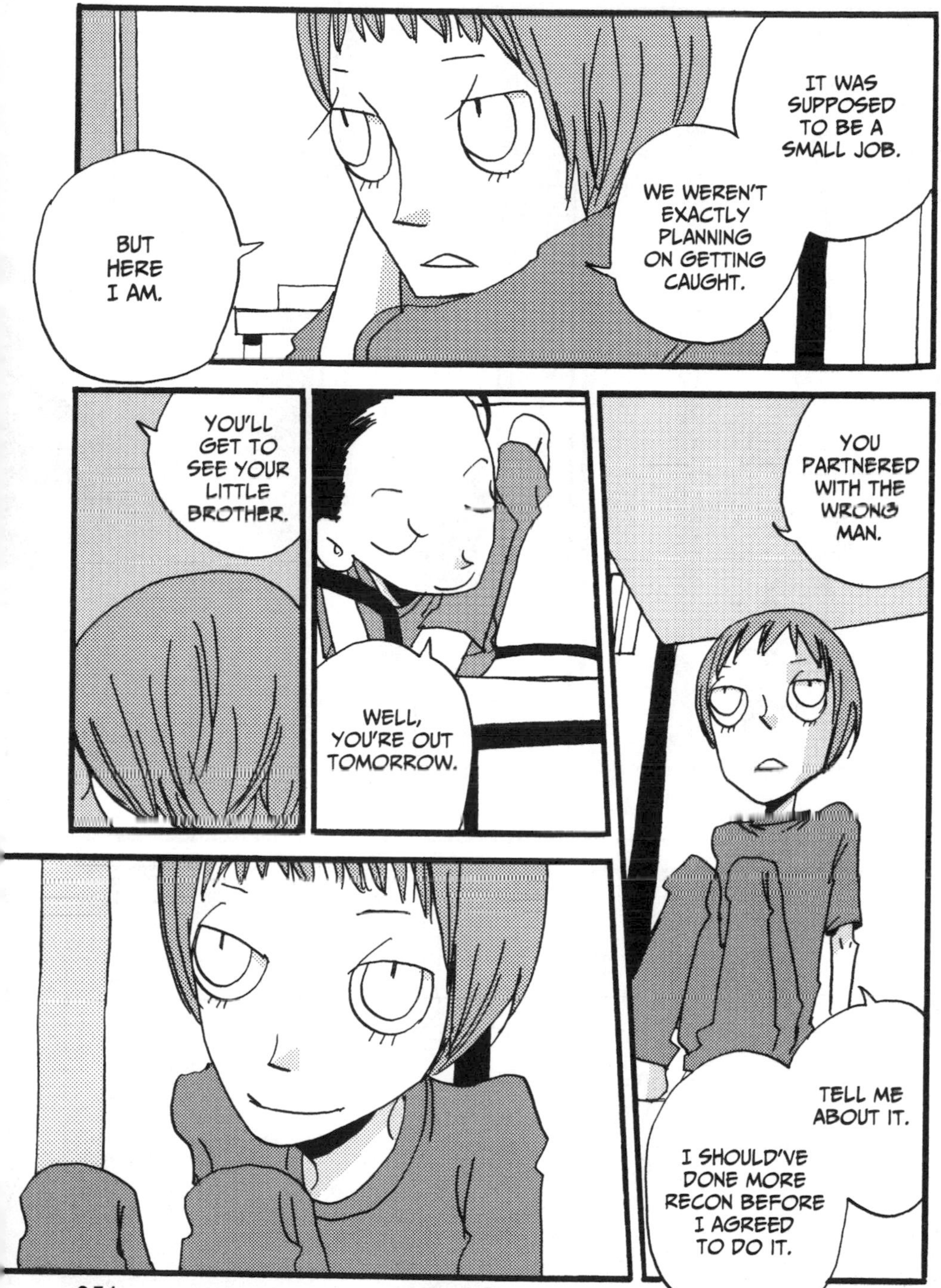
IT WAS SUPPOSED TO BE A SMALL JOB.
WE WEREN'T EXACTLY PLANNING ON GETTING CAUGHT.
BUT HERE I AM.
YOU PARTNERED WITH THE WRONG MAN.
TELL ME ABOUT IT.
I SHOULD'VE DONE MORE RECON BEFORE I AGREED TO DO IT.
WELL, YOU'RE OUT TOMORROW.
YOU'LL GET TO SEE YOUR LITTLE BROTHER.

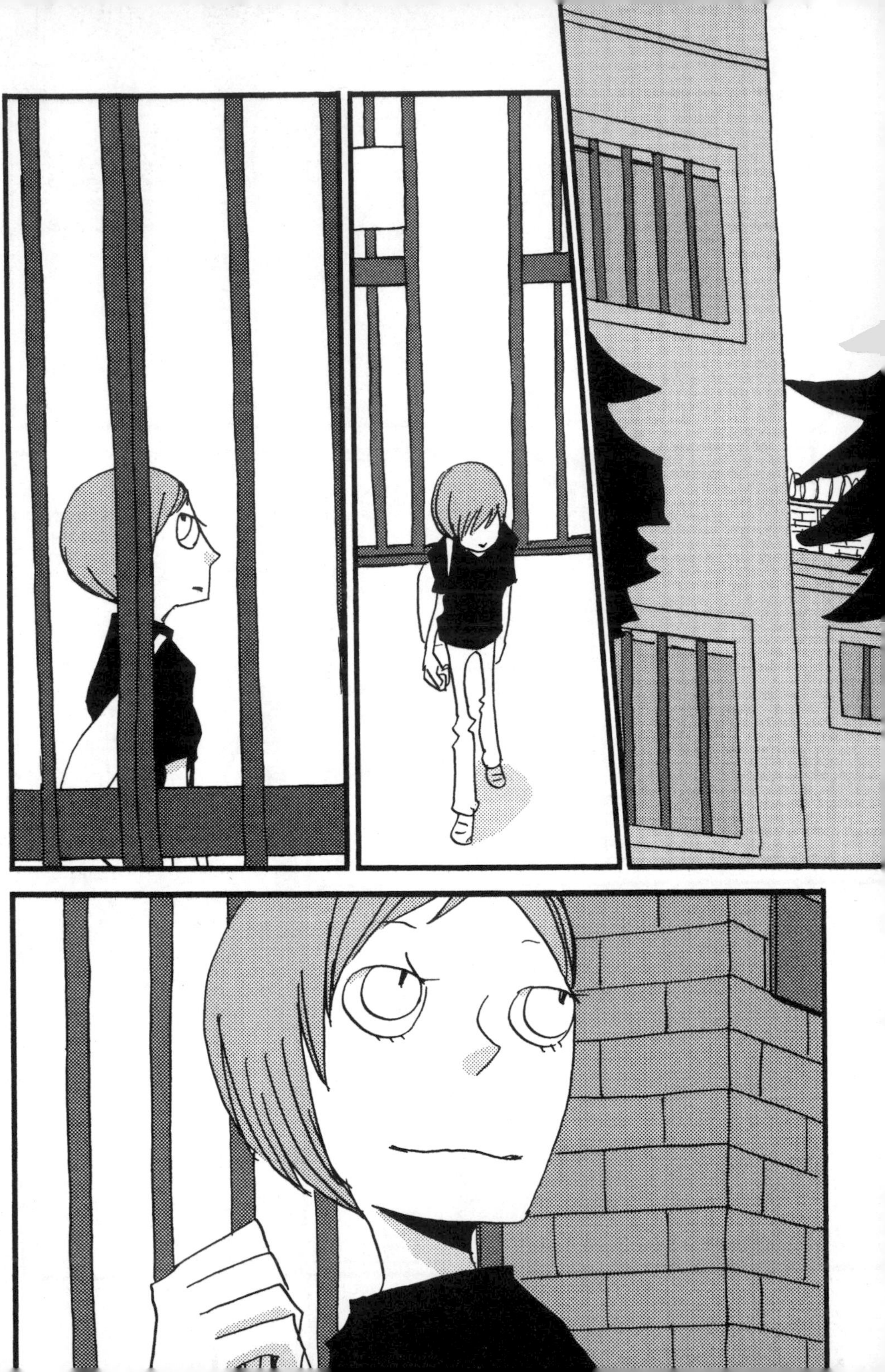

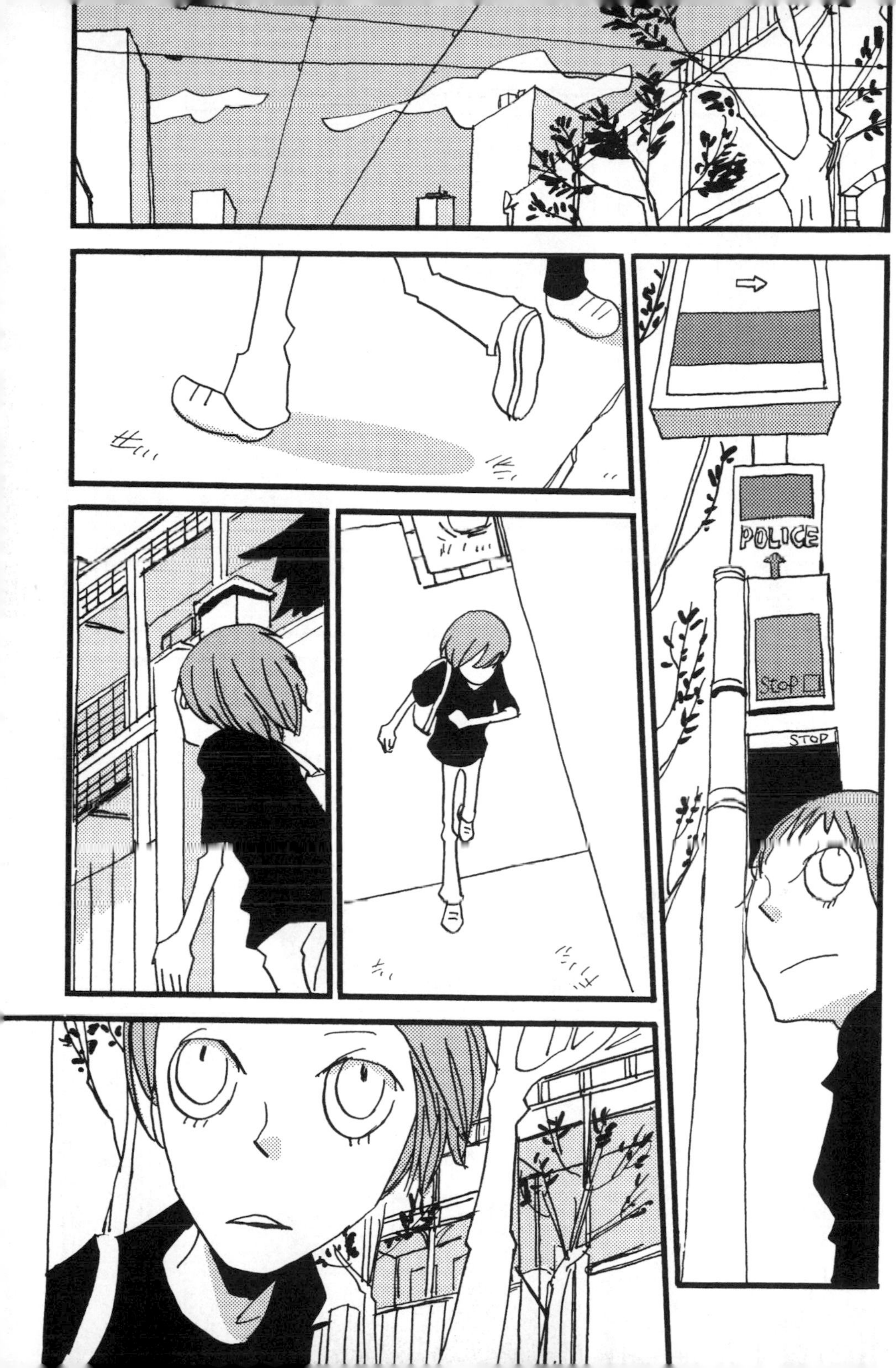
POLICE
STOP
STOP

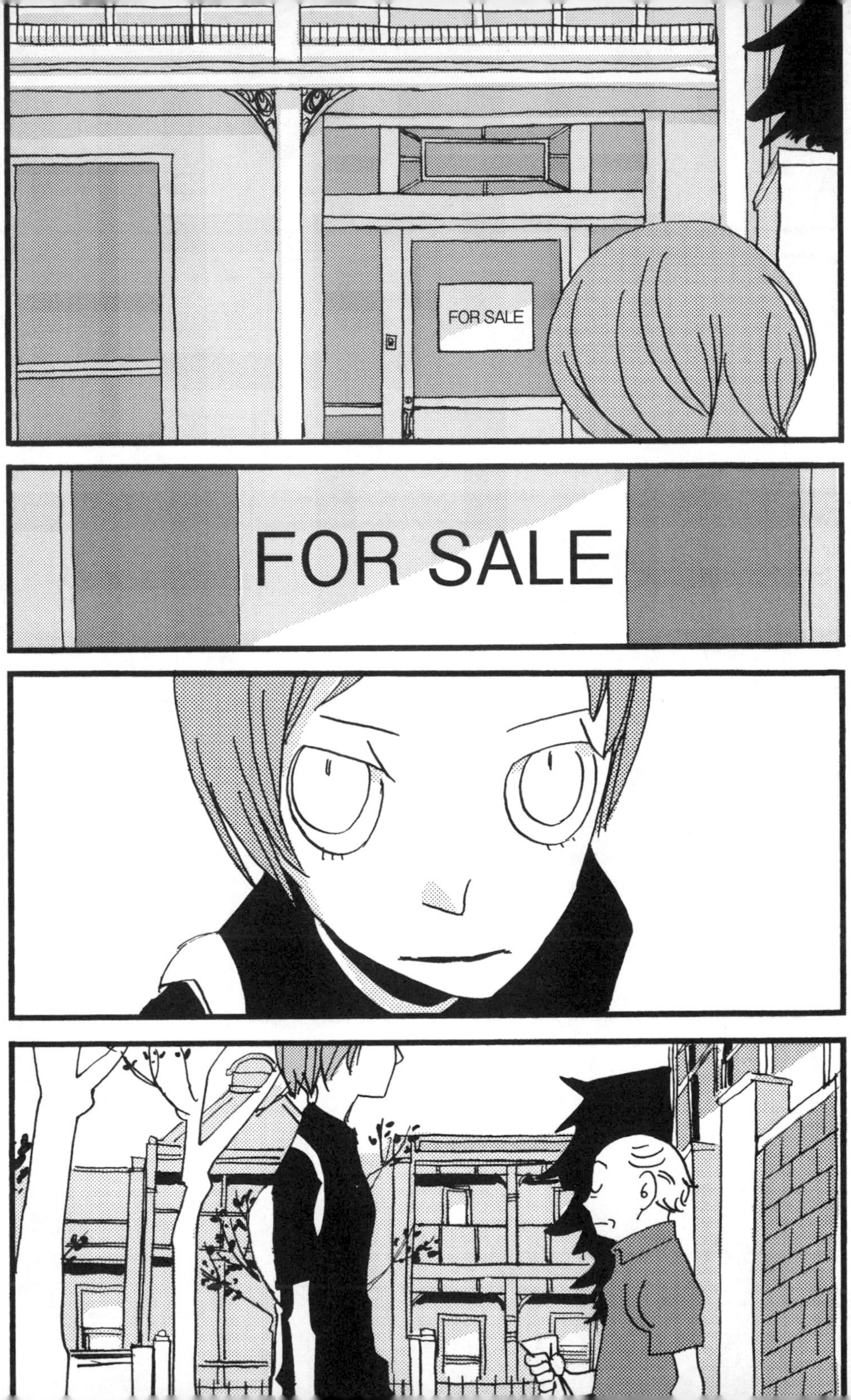
FOR SALE
FOR SALE

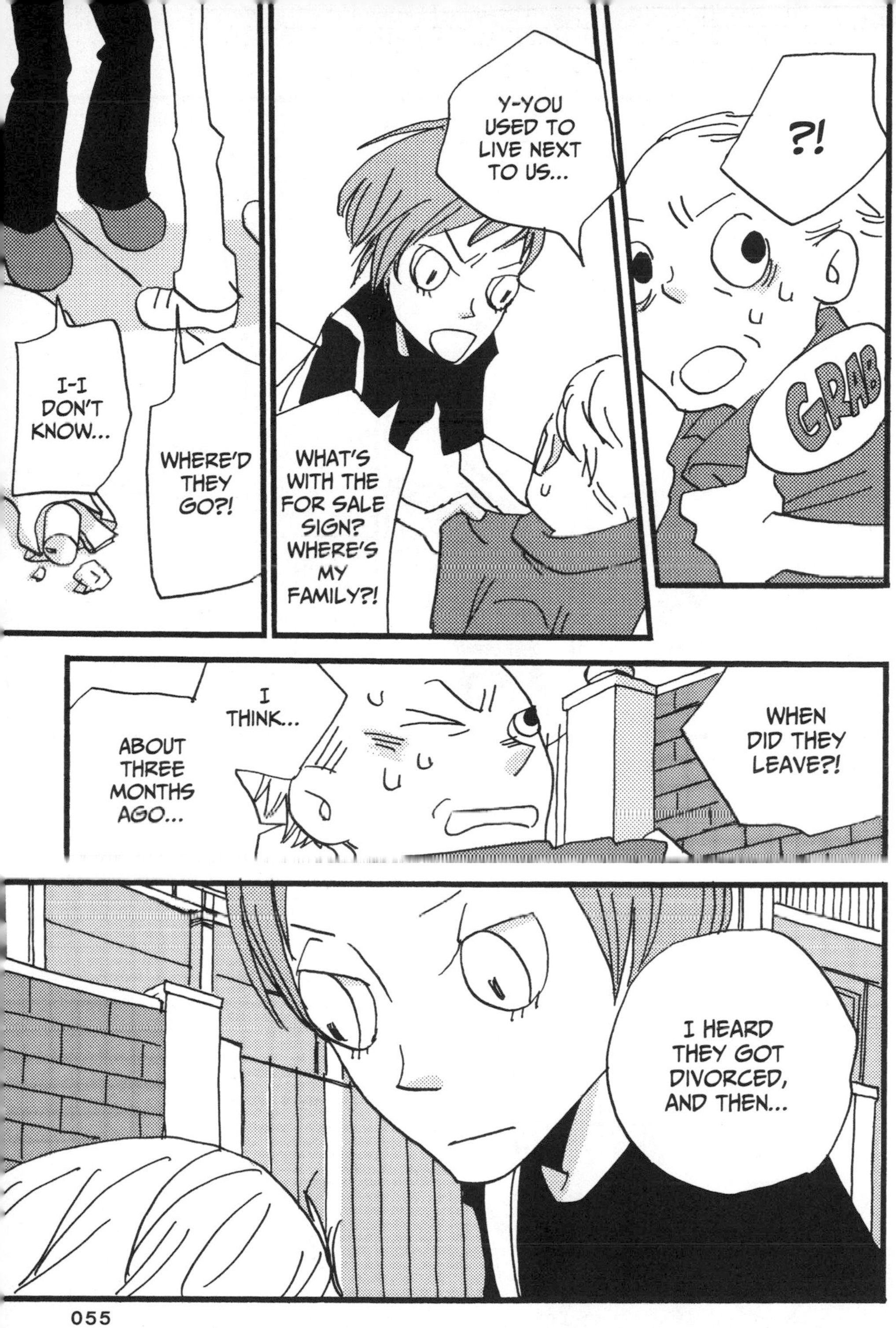
?!
GRAB
Y-YOU USED TO LIVE NEXT TO US...
WHAT'S WITH THE FOR SALE SIGN? WHERE'S MY FAMILY?!
WHERE'D THEY GO?!
I-I DON'T KNOW...
WHEN DID THEY LEAVE?!
I THINK...
ABOUT THREE MONTHS AGO...
I HEARD THEY GOT DIVORCED, AND THEN...

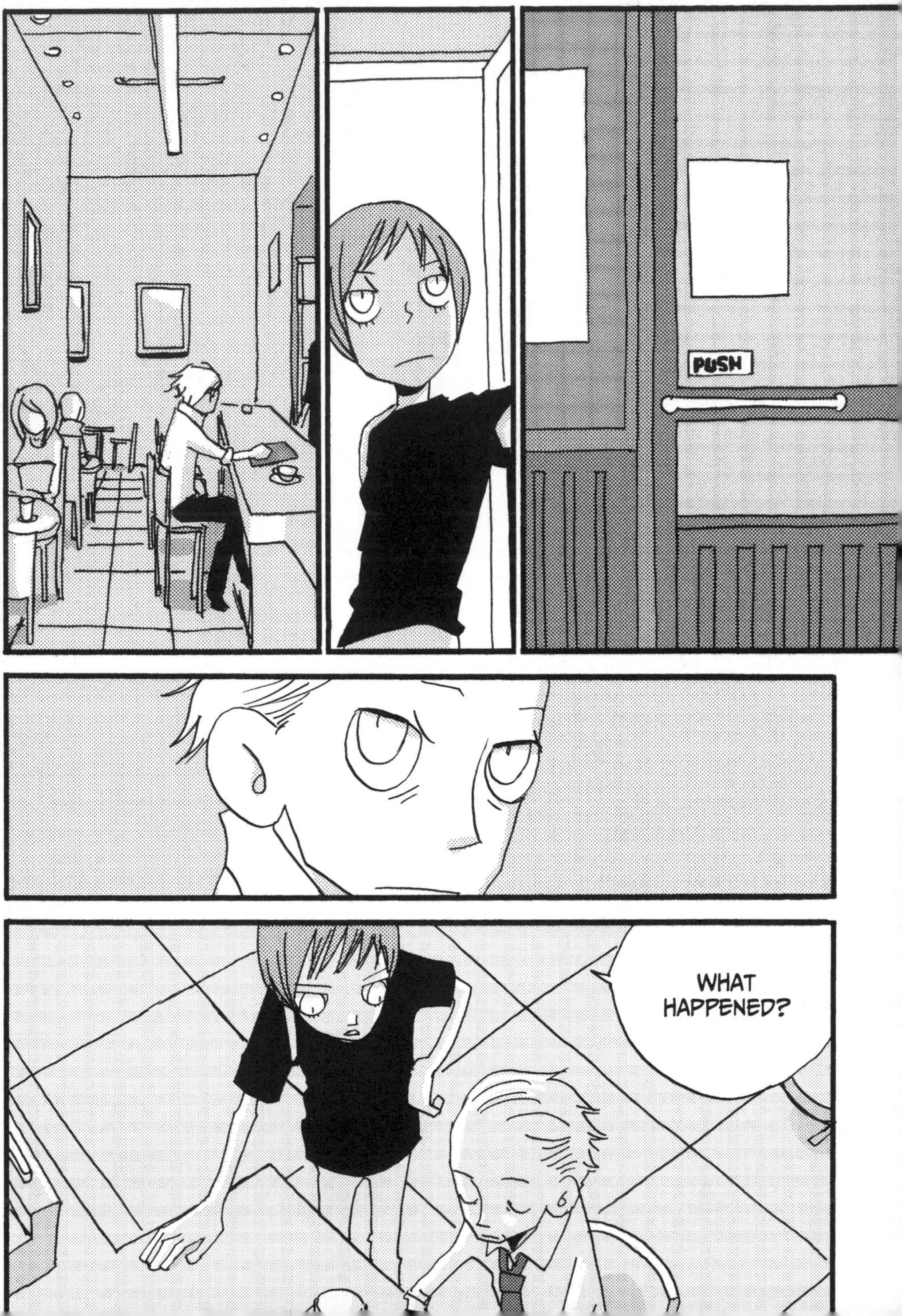
PUSH
WHAT HAPPENED?

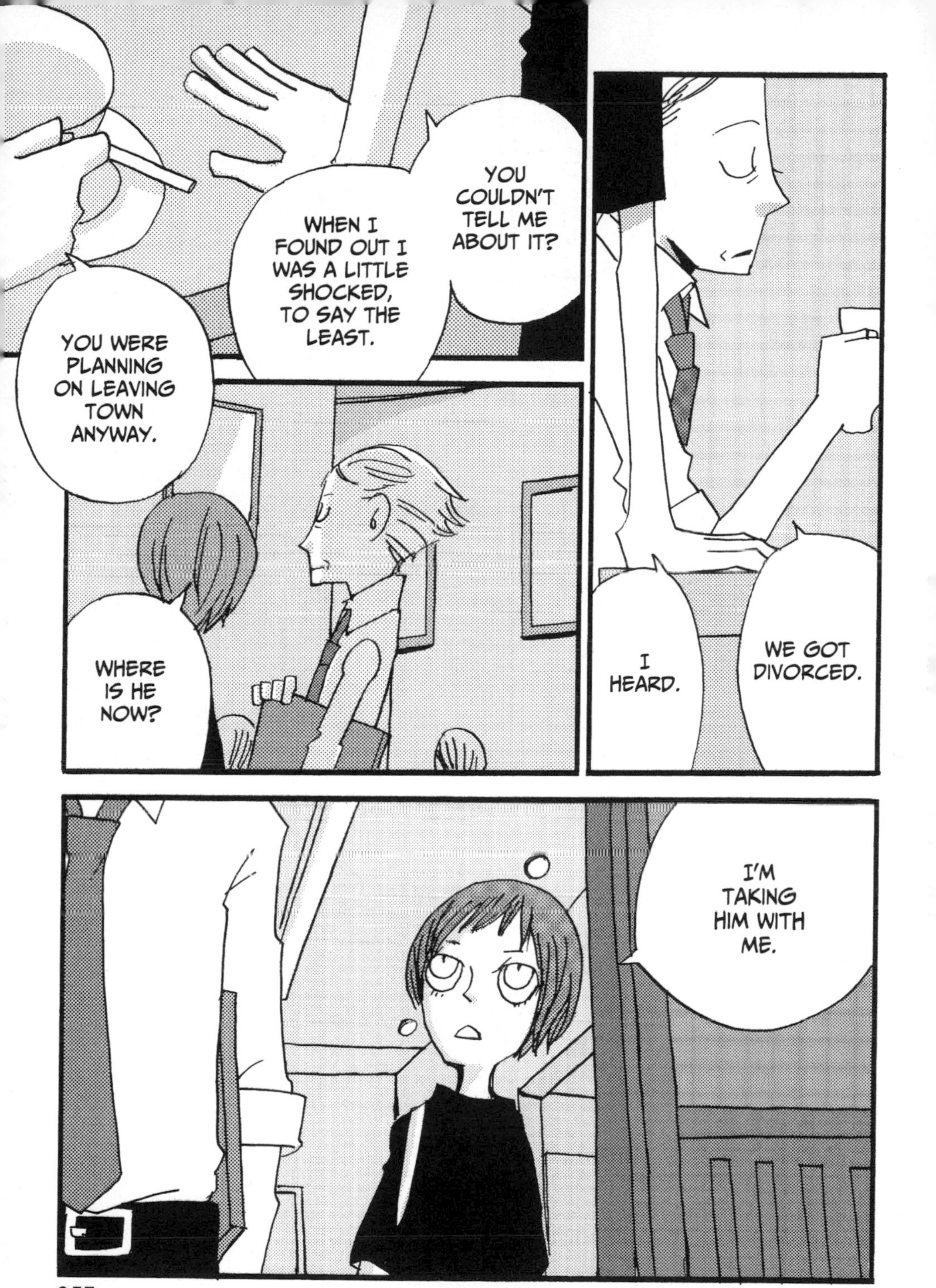
WE GOT DIVORCED.
I HEARD.
YOU COULDN'T TELL ME ABOUT IT?
WHEN I FOUND OUT I WAS A LITTLE SHOCKED, TO SAY THE LEAST.
YOU WERE PLANNING ON LEAVING TOWN ANYWAY.
WHERE IS HE NOW?
I'M TAKING HIM WITH ME.

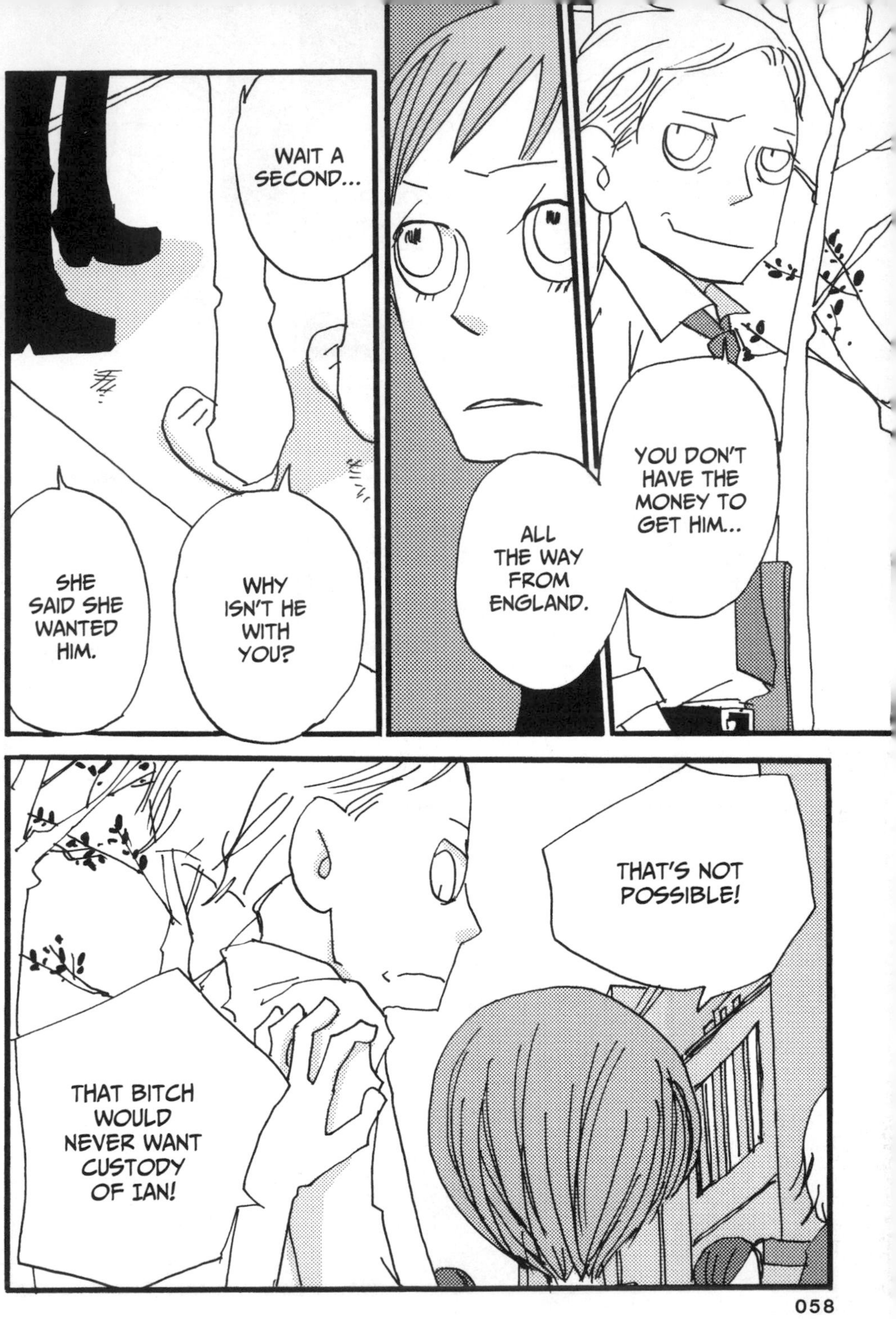
YOU DON'T HAVE THE MONEY TO GET HIM...
ALL THE WAY FROM ENGLAND.
WAIT A SECOND...
WHY ISN'T HE WITH YOU?
SHE SAID SHE WANTED HIM.
THAT'S NOT POSSIBLE!
THAT BITCH WOULD NEVER WANT CUSTODY OF IAN!

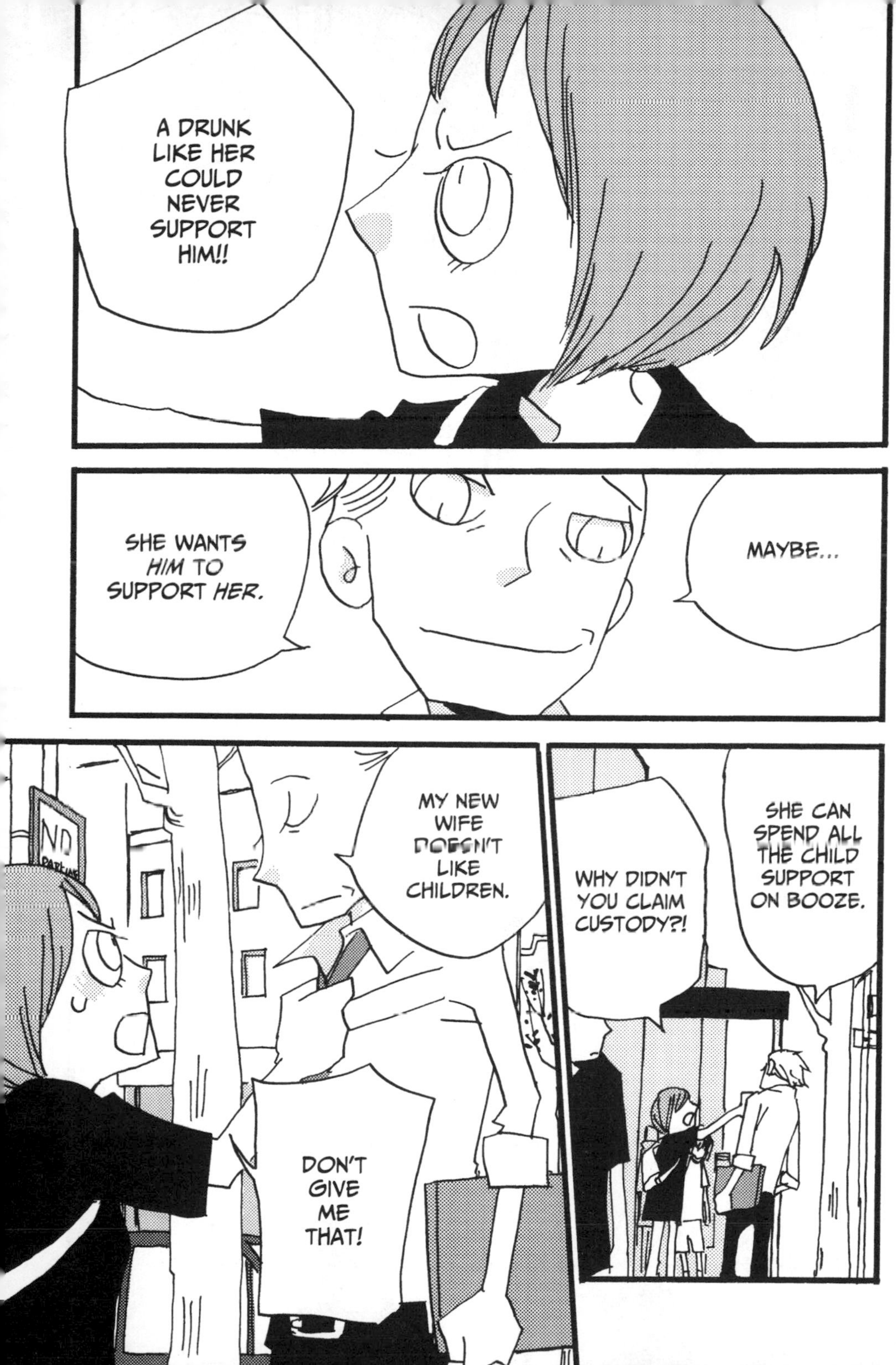
A DRUNK LIKE HER COULD NEVER SUPPORT HIM!!
MAYBE...
SHE WANTS *HIM* TO SUPPORT *HER.*
SHE CAN SPEND ALL THE CHILD SUPPORT ON BOOZE.
WHY DIDN'T YOU CLAIM CUSTODY?!
MY NEW WIFE DOESN'T LIKE CHILDREN.
DON'T GIVE ME THAT!

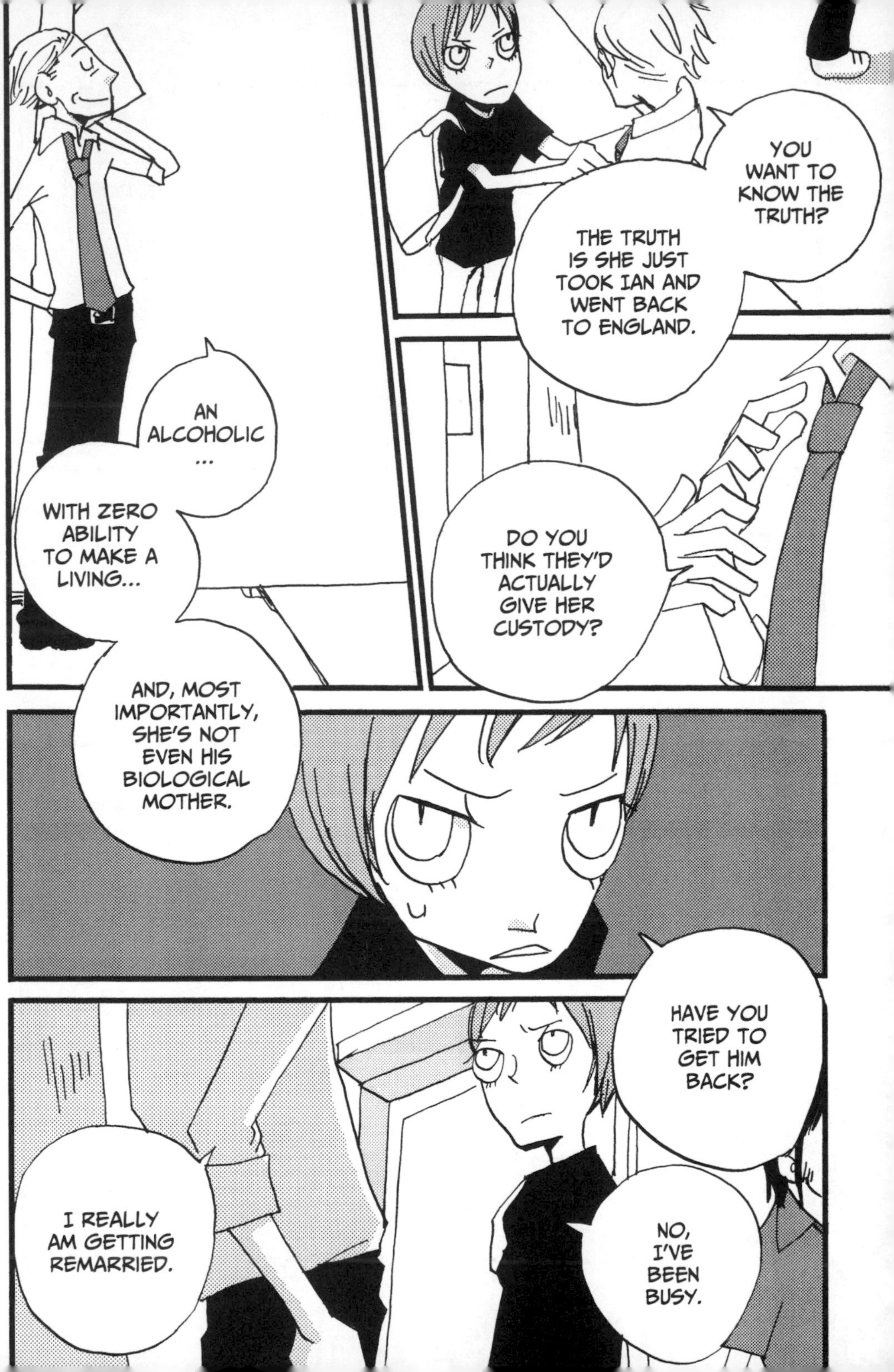
YOU WANT TO KNOW THE TRUTH?
THE TRUTH IS SHE JUST TOOK IAN AND WENT BACK TO ENGLAND.
DO YOU THINK THEY'D ACTUALLY GIVE HER CUSTODY?
AN ALCOHOLIC ...
WITH ZERO ABILITY TO MAKE A LIVING...
AND, MOST IMPORTANTLY, SHE'S NOT EVEN HIS BIOLOGICAL MOTHER.
HAVE YOU TRIED TO GET HIM BACK?
NO, I'VE BEEN BUSY.
I REALLY AM GETTING REMARRIED.

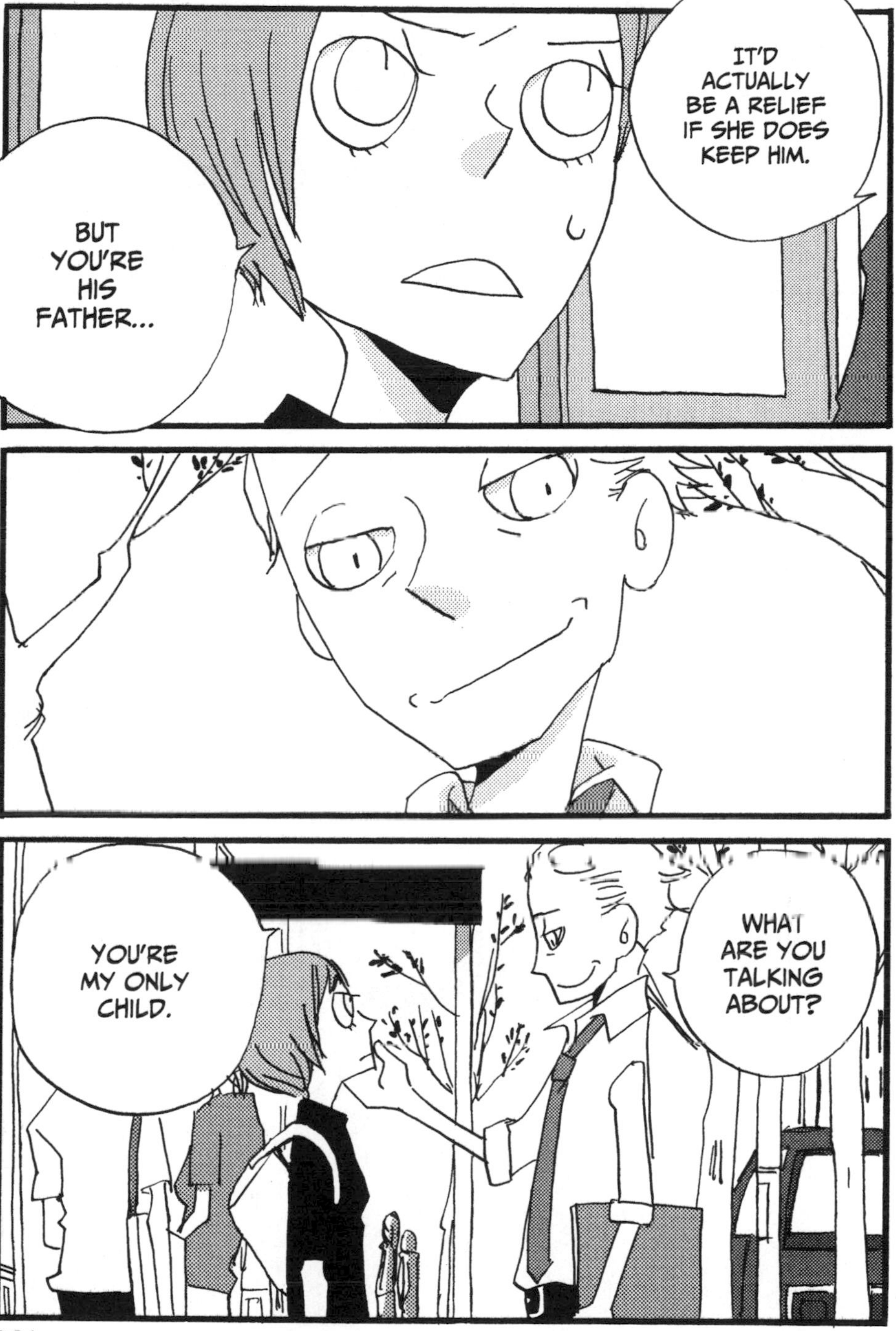
IT'D ACTUALLY BE A RELIEF IF SHE DOES KEEP HIM.
BUT YOU'RE HIS FATHER...
WHAT ARE YOU TALKING ABOUT?
YOU'RE MY ONLY CHILD.

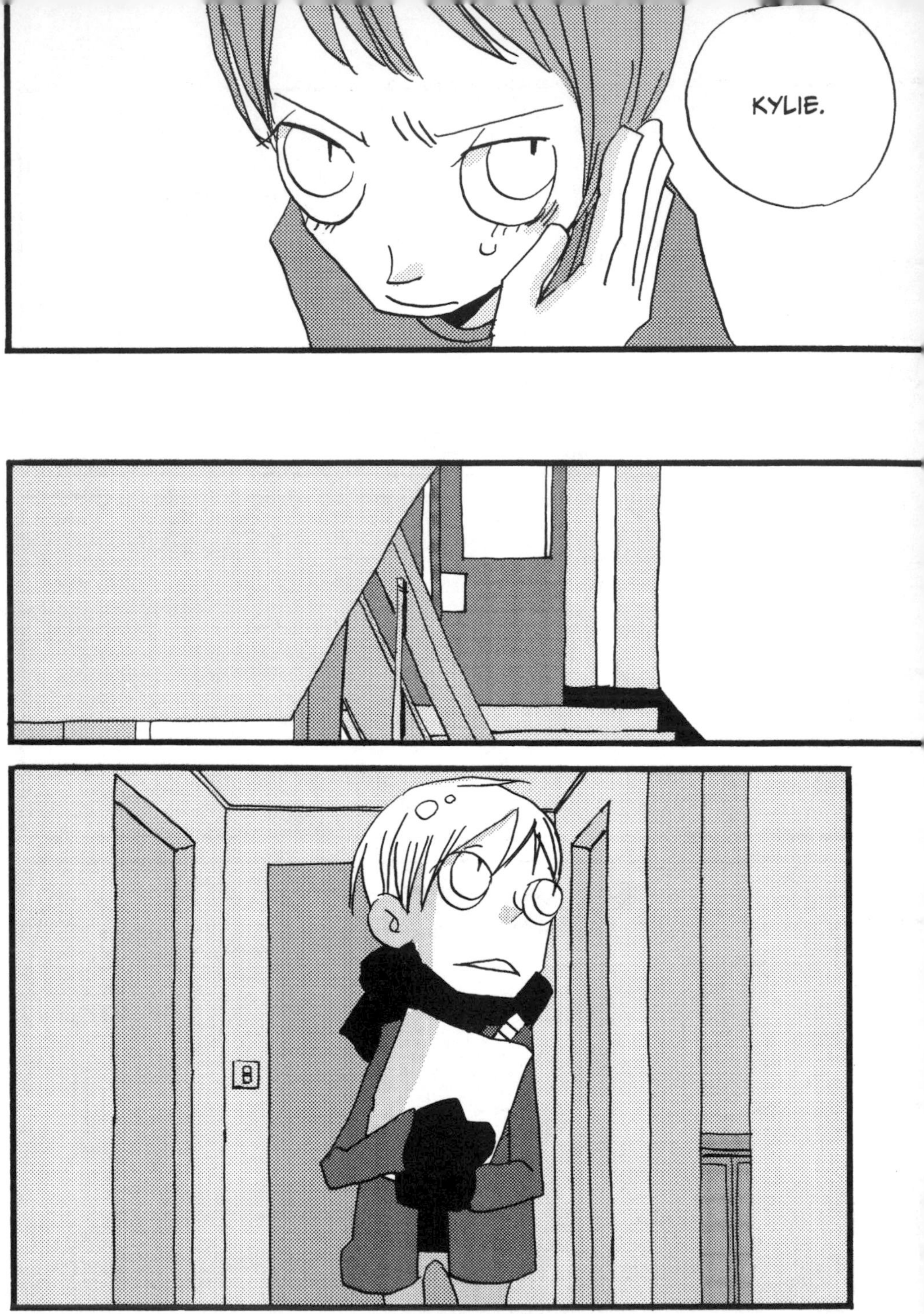
KYLIE.

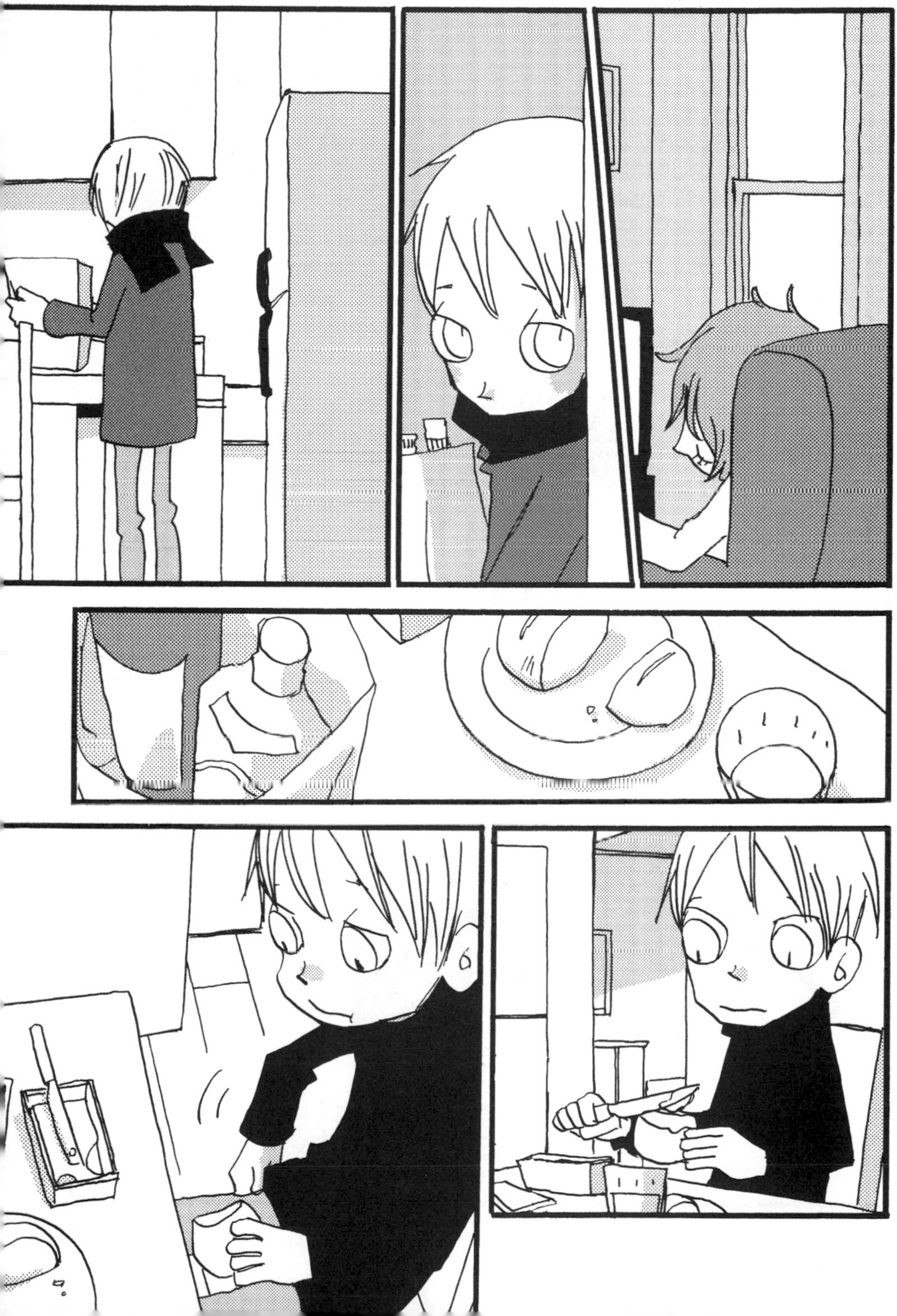

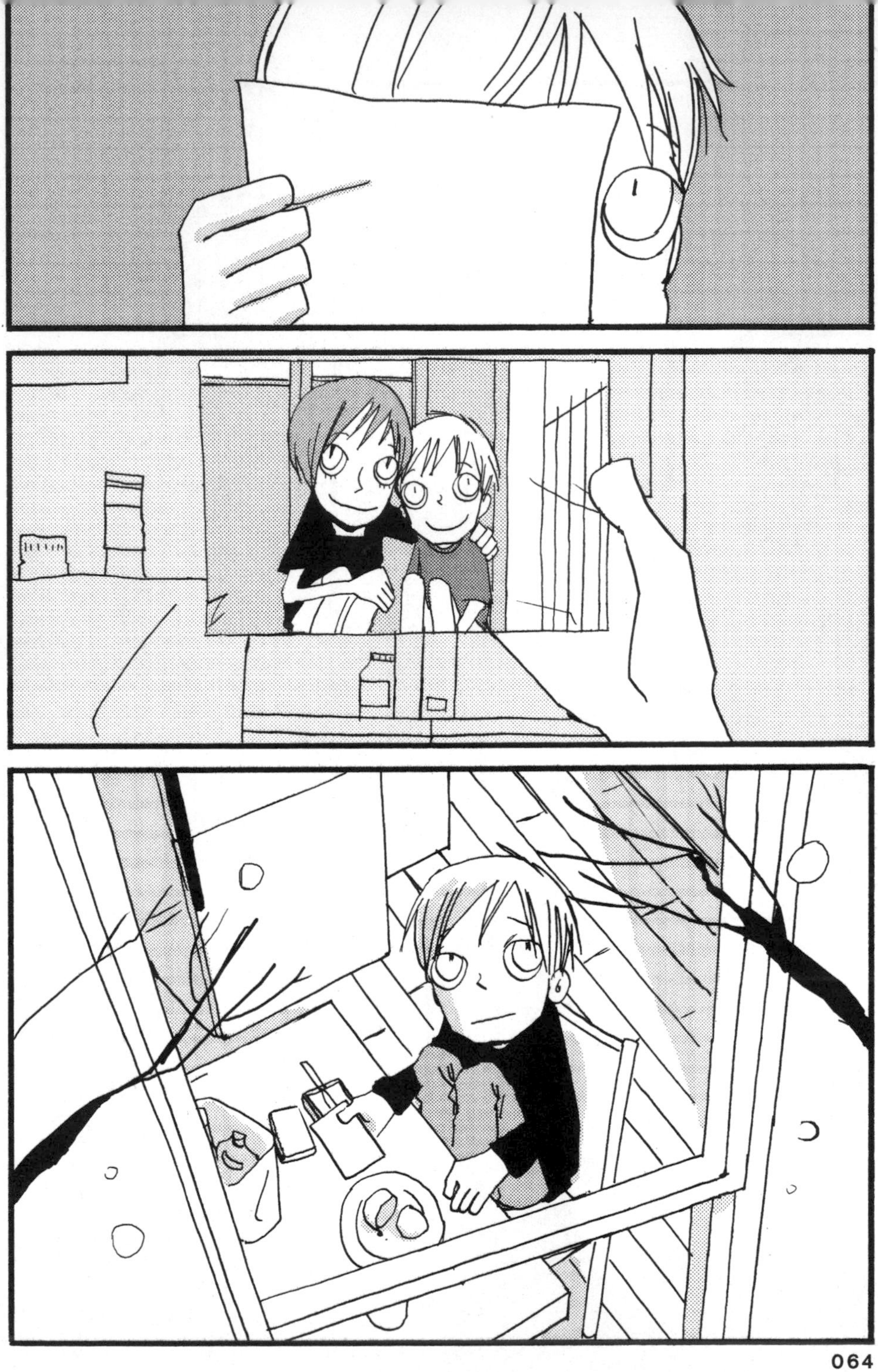

#02 not simple

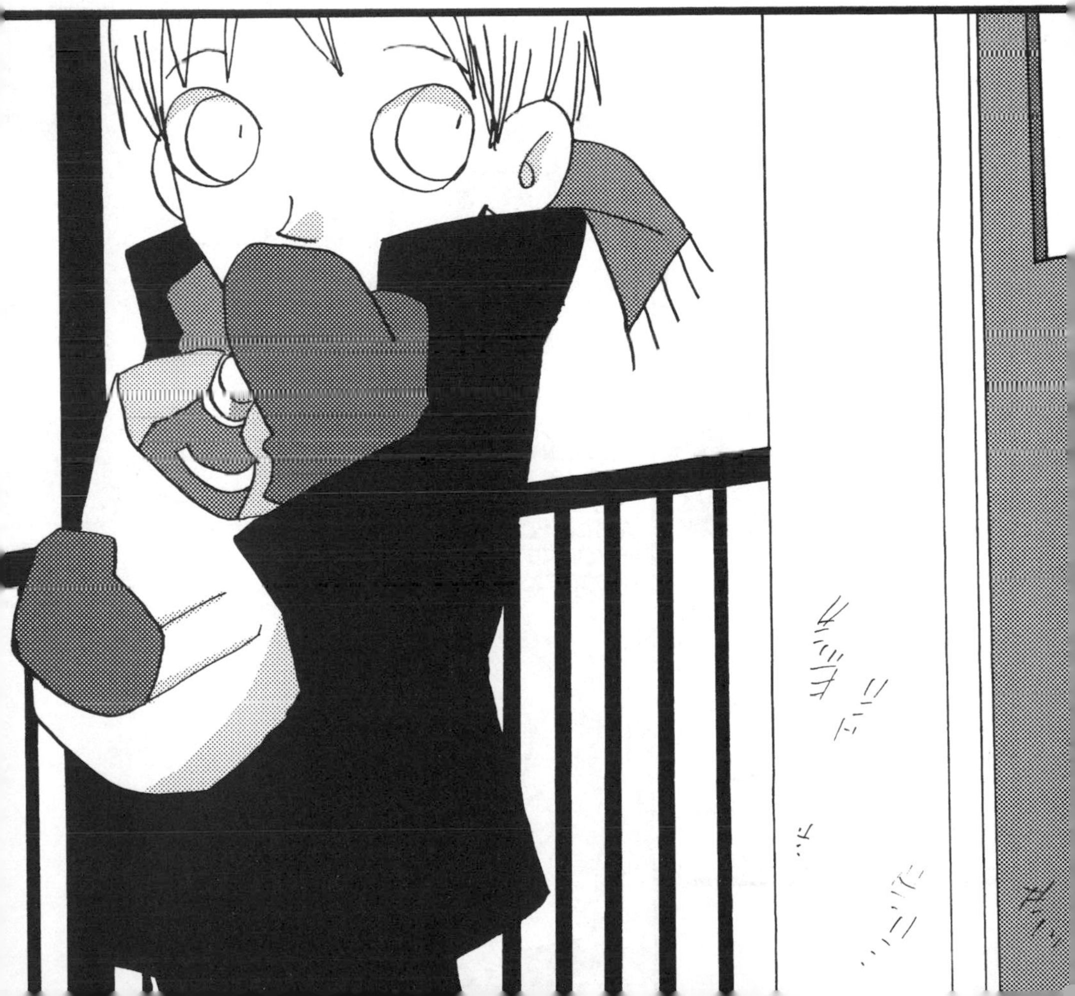

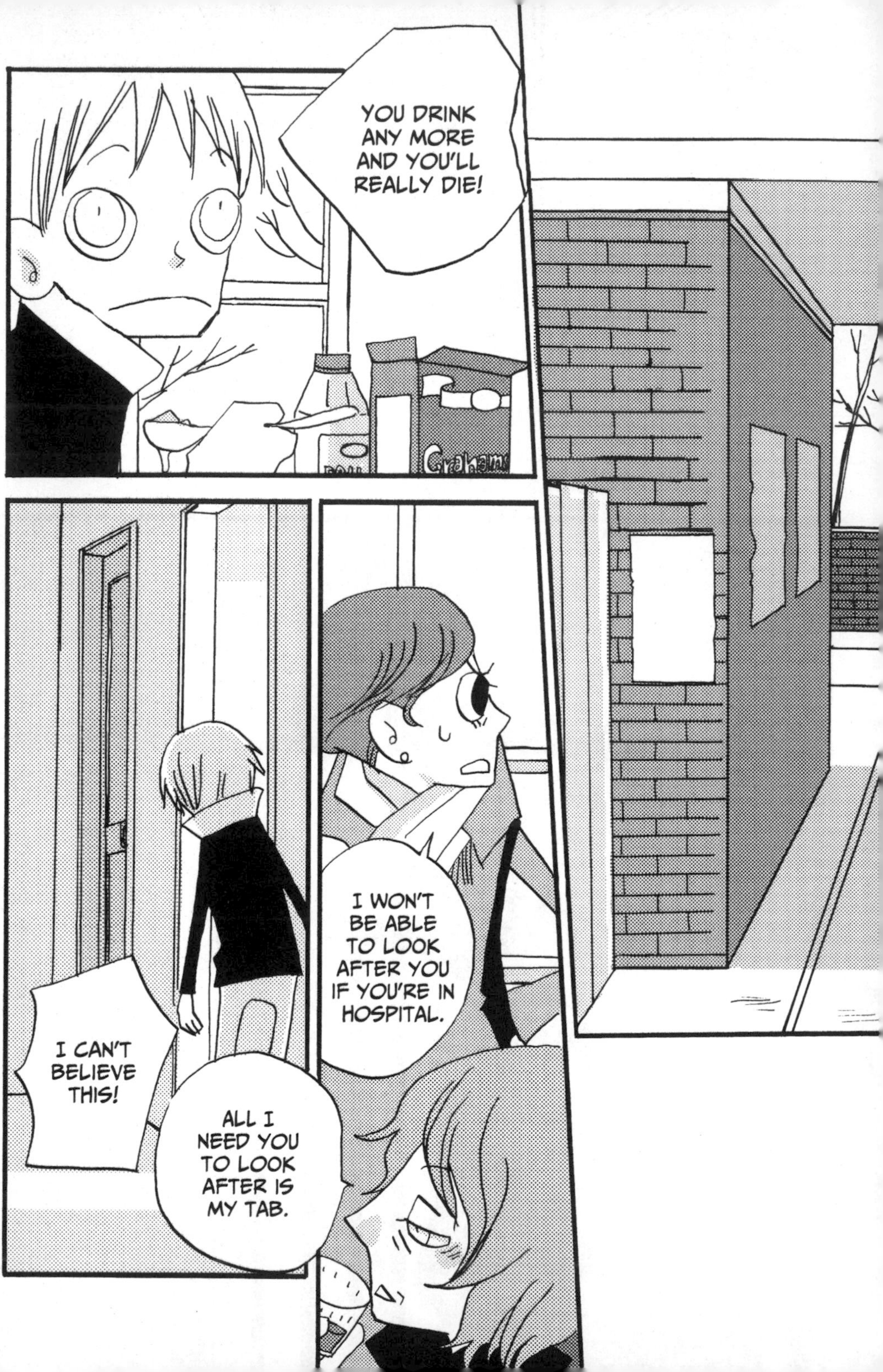

YOU DRINK ANY MORE AND YOU'LL REALLY DIE!
I WON'T BE ABLE TO LOOK AFTER YOU IF YOU'RE IN HOSPITAL.
ALL I NEED YOU TO LOOK AFTER IS MY TAB.
I CAN'T BELIEVE THIS!

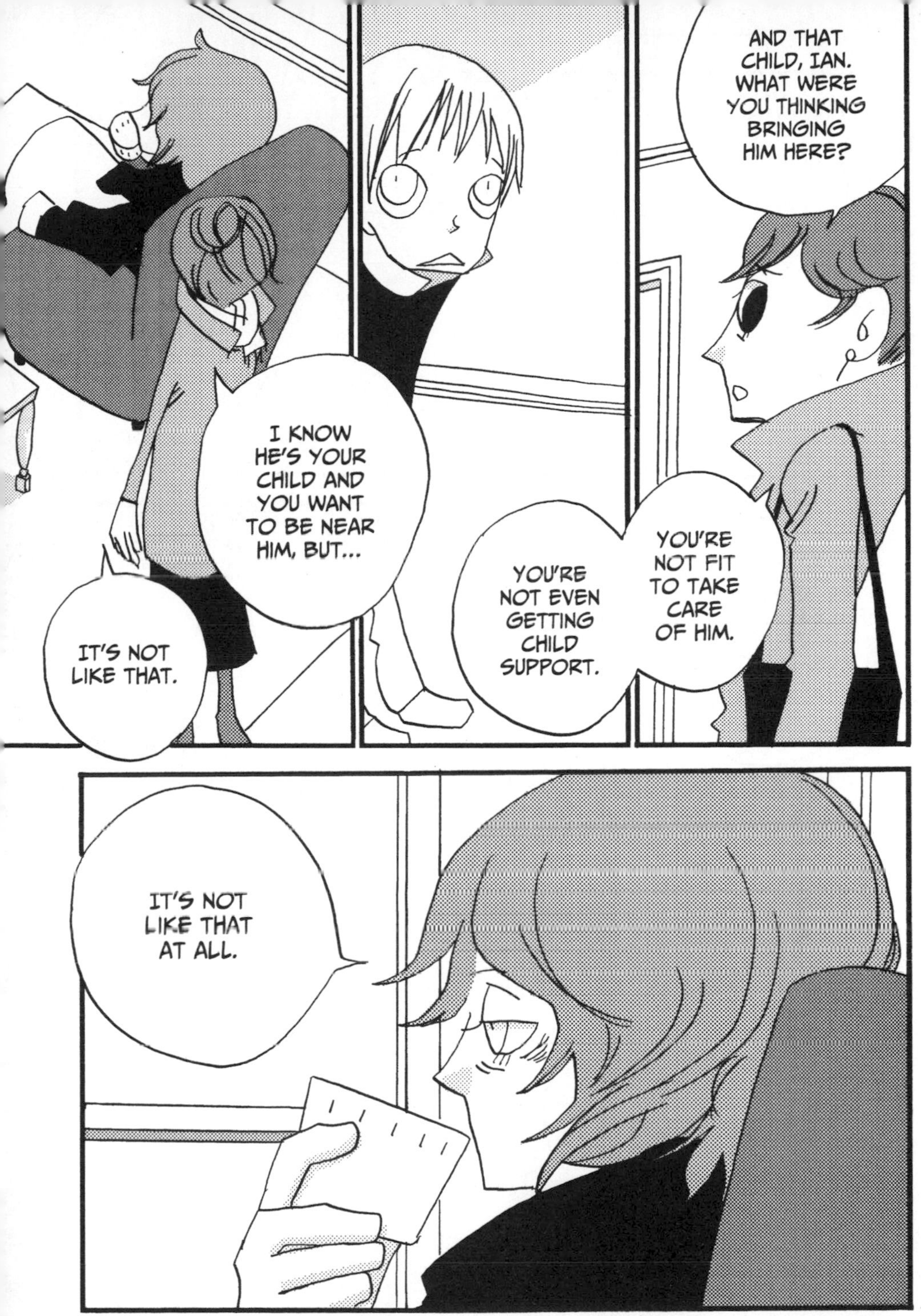
AND THAT CHILD, IAN. WHAT WERE YOU THINKING BRINGING HIM HERE?
YOU'RE NOT FIT TO TAKE CARE OF HIM.
YOU'RE NOT EVEN GETTING CHILD SUPPORT.
I KNOW HE'S YOUR CHILD AND YOU WANT TO BE NEAR HIM, BUT...
IT'S NOT LIKE THAT.
IT'S NOT LIKE THAT AT ALL.

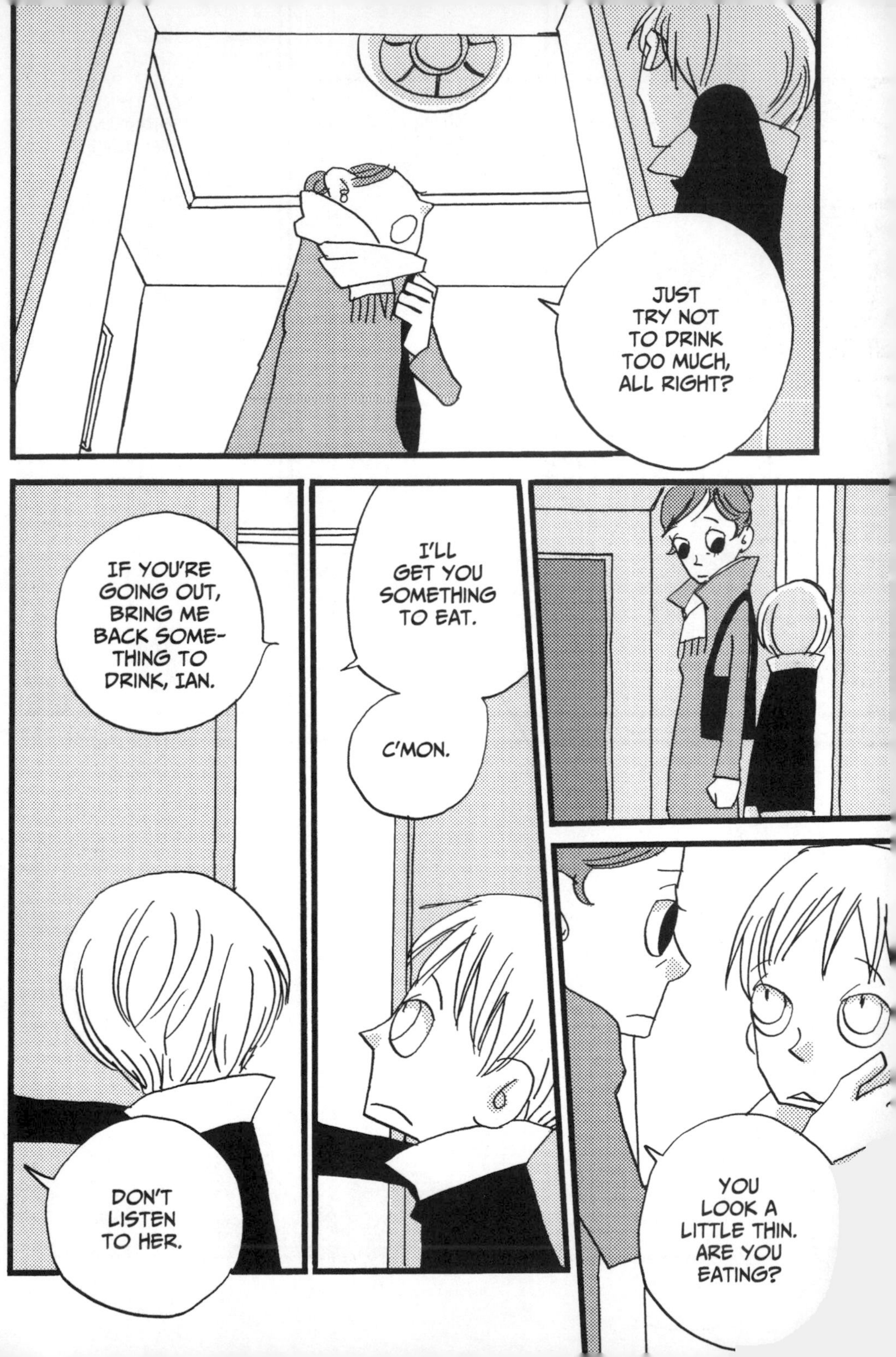
JUST TRY NOT TO DRINK TOO MUCH, ALL RIGHT?
YOU LOOK A LITTLE THIN. ARE YOU EATING?
I'LL GET YOU SOMETHING TO EAT.
C'MON.
IF YOU'RE GOING OUT, BRING ME BACK SOMETHING TO DRINK, IAN.
DON'T LISTEN TO HER.

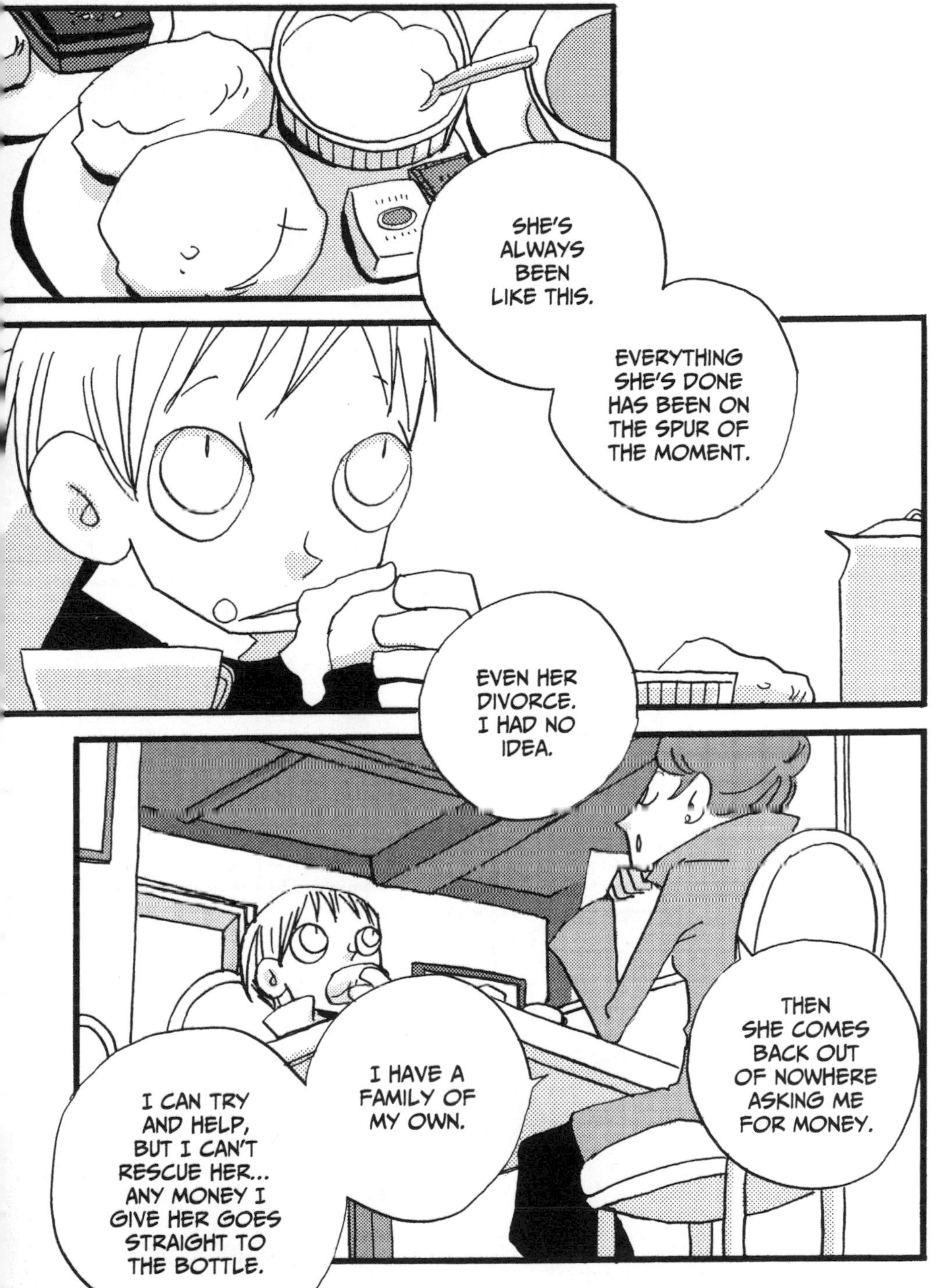
SHE'S ALWAYS BEEN LIKE THIS.
EVERYTHING SHE'S DONE HAS BEEN ON THE SPUR OF THE MOMENT.
EVEN HER DIVORCE. I HAD NO IDEA.
THEN SHE COMES BACK OUT OF NOWHERE ASKING ME FOR MONEY.
I HAVE A FAMILY OF MY OWN.
I CAN TRY AND HELP, BUT I CAN'T RESCUE HER... ANY MONEY I GIVE HER GOES STRAIGHT TO THE BOTTLE.

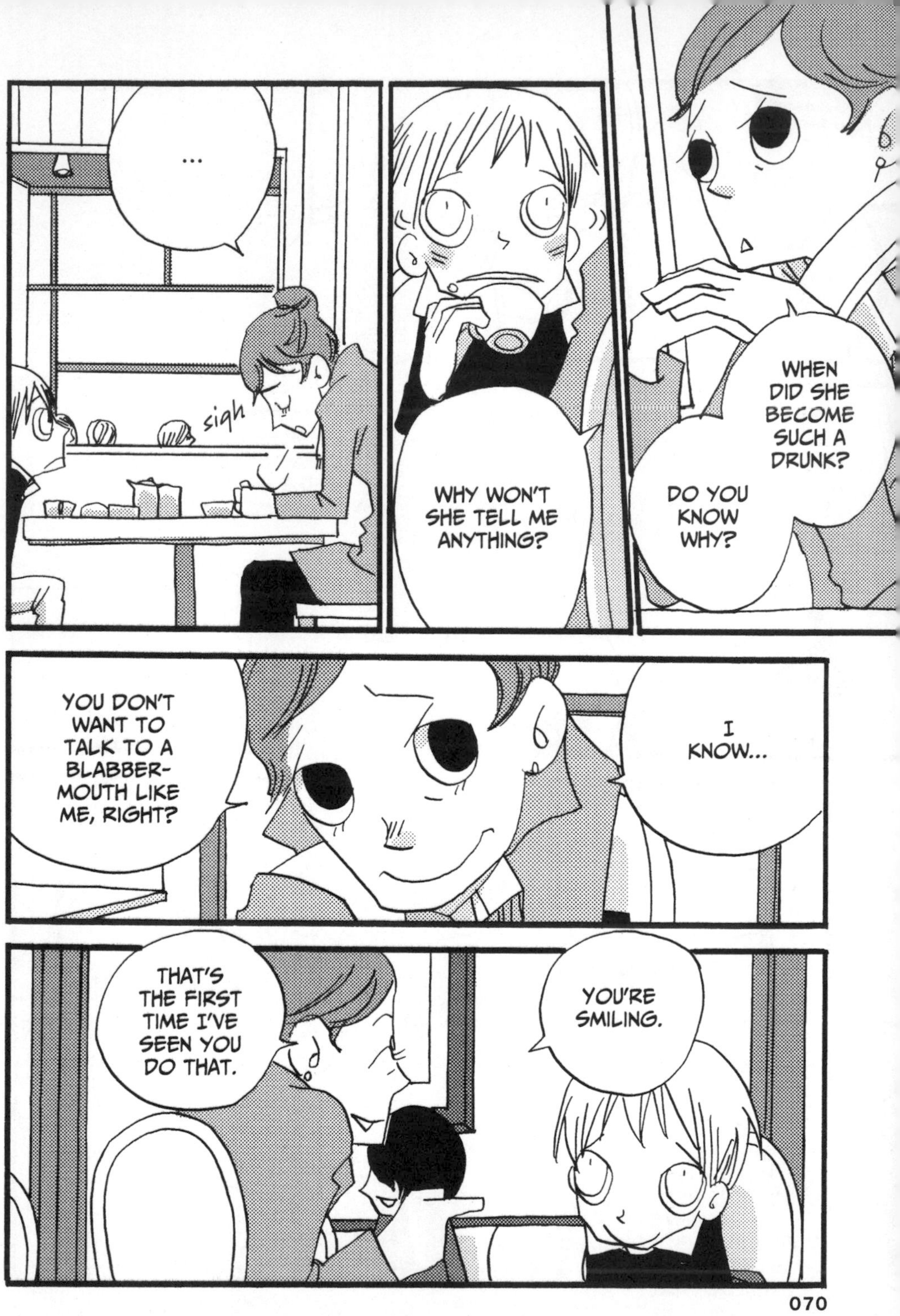
WHEN DID SHE BECOME SUCH A DRUNK?
DO YOU KNOW WHY?
WHY WON'T SHE TELL ME ANYTHING?
...
sigh
I KNOW...
YOU DON'T WANT TO TALK TO A BLABBER-MOUTH LIKE ME, RIGHT?
YOU'RE SMILING.
THAT'S THE FIRST TIME I'VE SEEN YOU DO THAT.

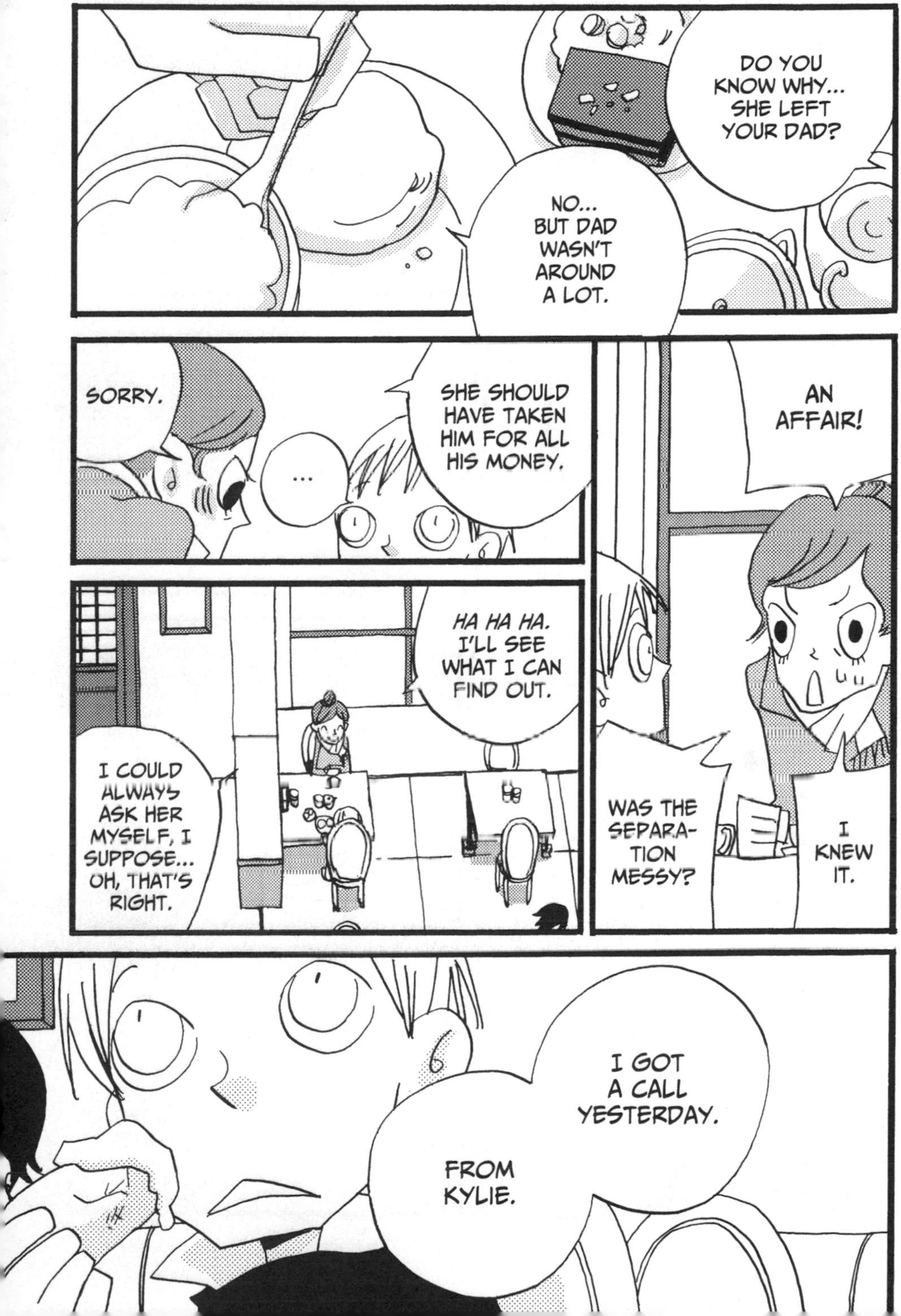
DO YOU KNOW WHY... SHE LEFT YOUR DAD?
NO... BUT DAD WASN'T AROUND A LOT.
AN AFFAIR!
I KNEW IT.
WAS THE SEPARATION MESSY?
SHE SHOULD HAVE TAKEN HIM FOR ALL HIS MONEY.
...
SORRY.
HA HA HA. I'LL SEE WHAT I CAN FIND OUT.
I COULD ALWAYS ASK HER MYSELF, I SUPPOSE... OH, THAT'S RIGHT.
I GOT A CALL YESTERDAY.
FROM KYLIE.

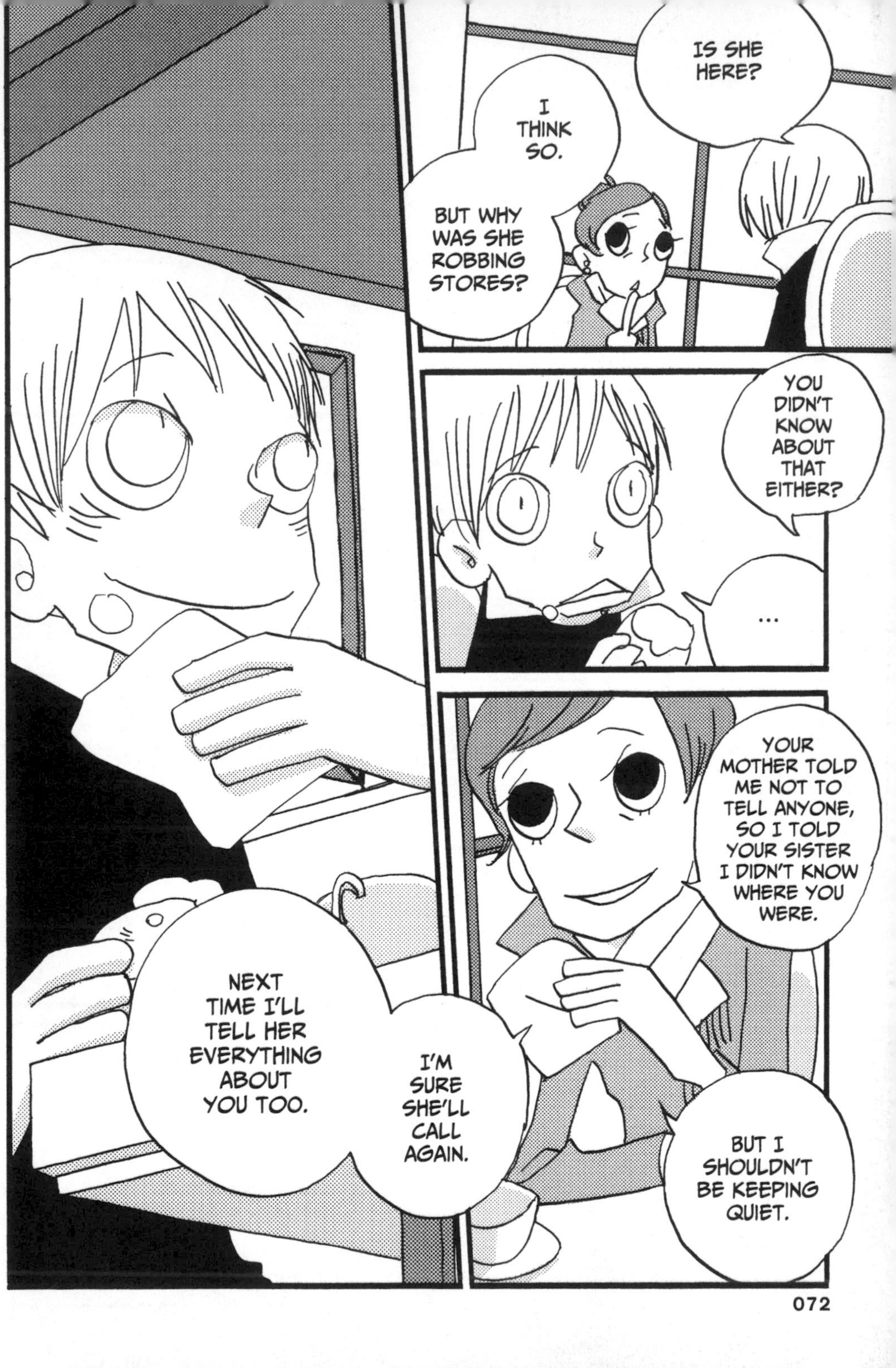
IS SHE HERE?
I THINK SO.
BUT WHY WAS SHE ROBBING STORES?
YOU DIDN'T KNOW ABOUT THAT EITHER?
...
YOUR MOTHER TOLD ME NOT TO TELL ANYONE, SO I TOLD YOUR SISTER I DIDN'T KNOW WHERE YOU WERE.
BUT I SHOULDN'T BE KEEPING QUIET.
I'M SURE SHE'LL CALL AGAIN.
NEXT TIME I'LL TELL HER EVERYTHING ABOUT YOU TOO.

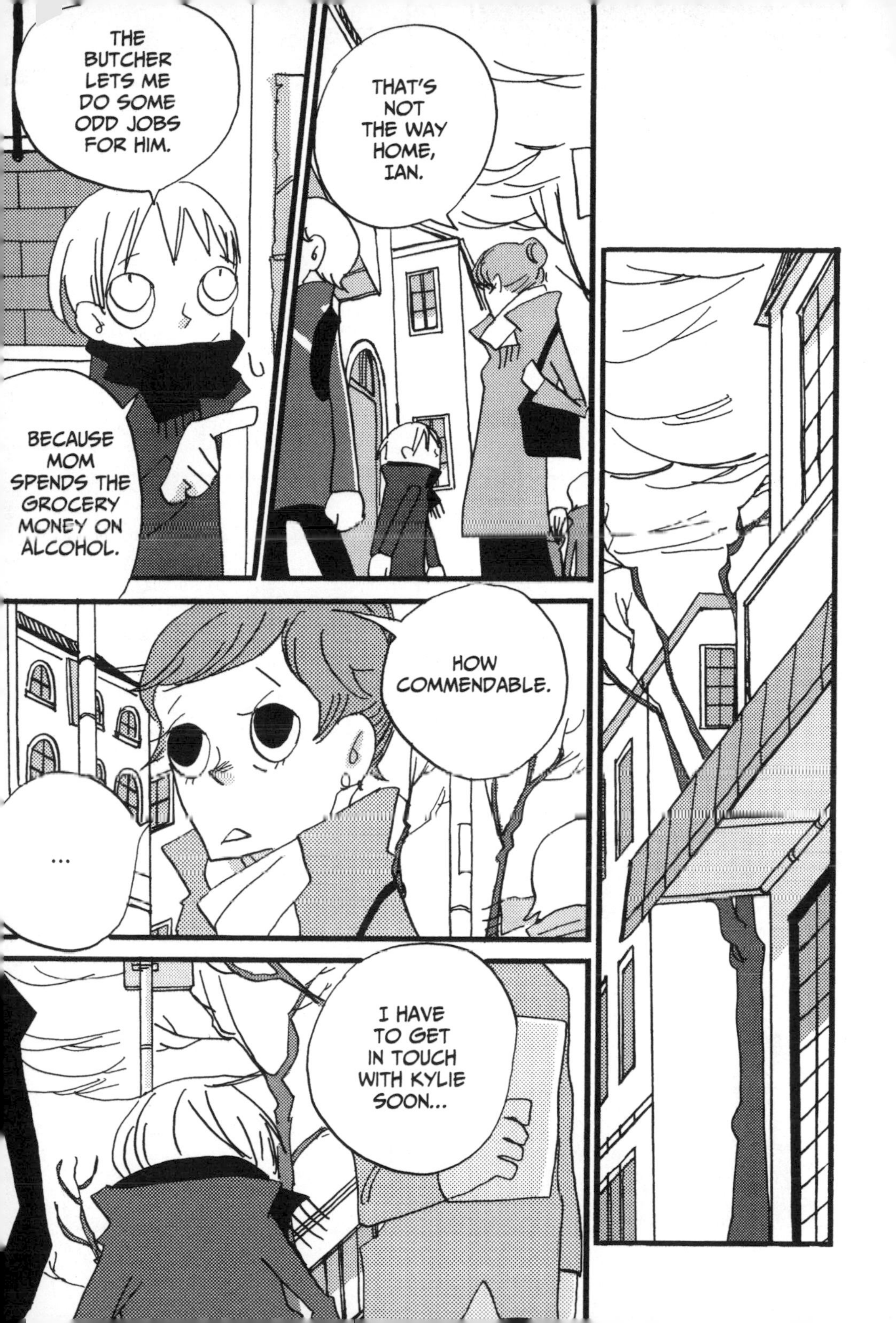
THAT'S NOT THE WAY HOME, IAN.
THE BUTCHER LETS ME DO SOME ODD JOBS FOR HIM.
BECAUSE MOM SPENDS THE GROCERY MONEY ON ALCOHOL.
HOW COMMENDABLE.
...
I HAVE TO GET IN TOUCH WITH KYLIE SOON...

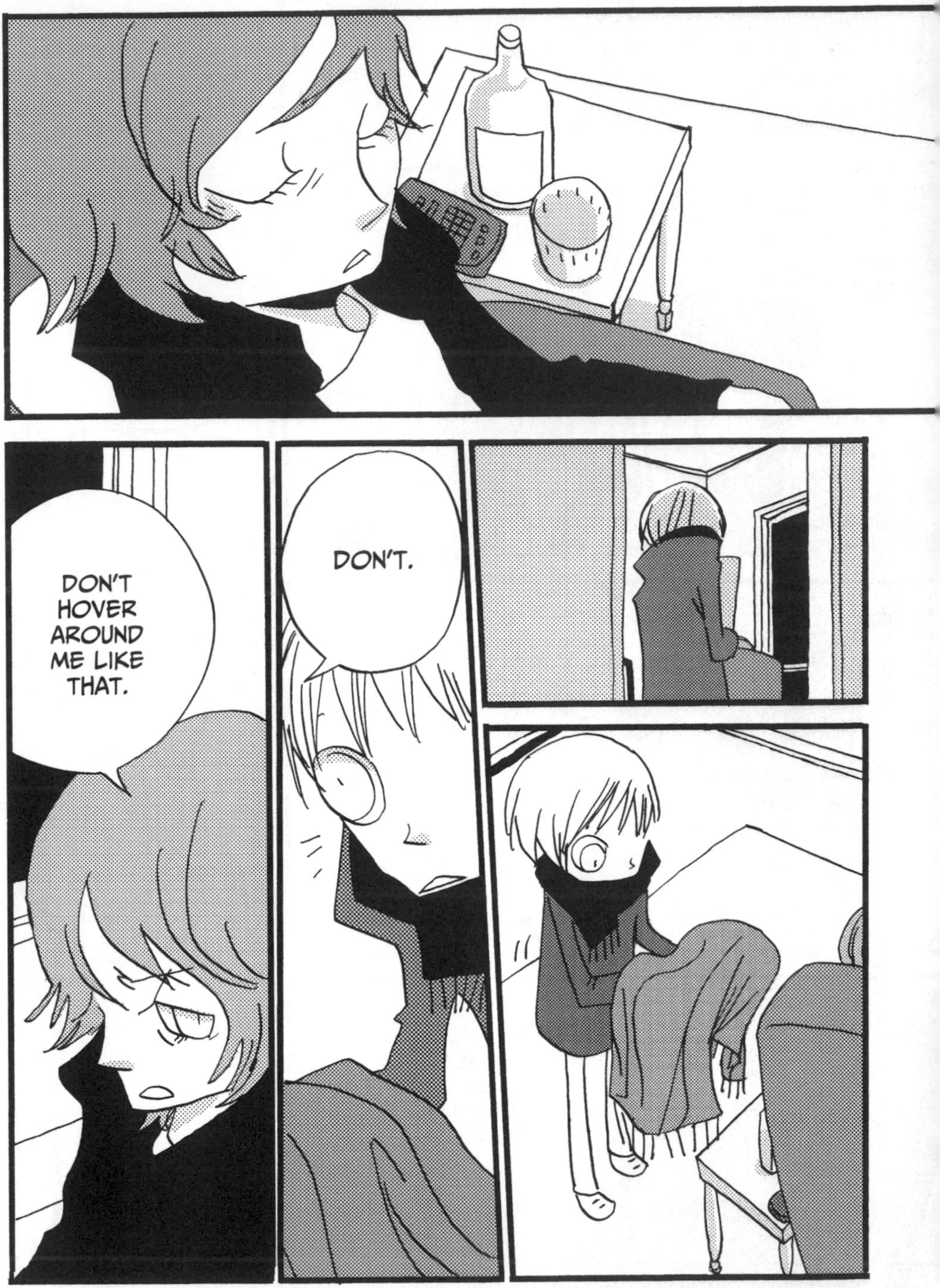
DON'T.
DON'T HOVER AROUND ME LIKE THAT.

WHAT ABOUT MY DRINK? DID YOU GET IT?

YEAH...

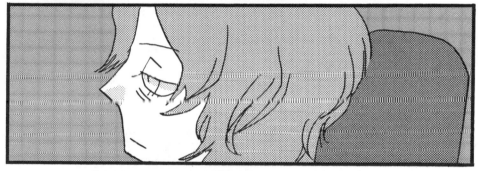

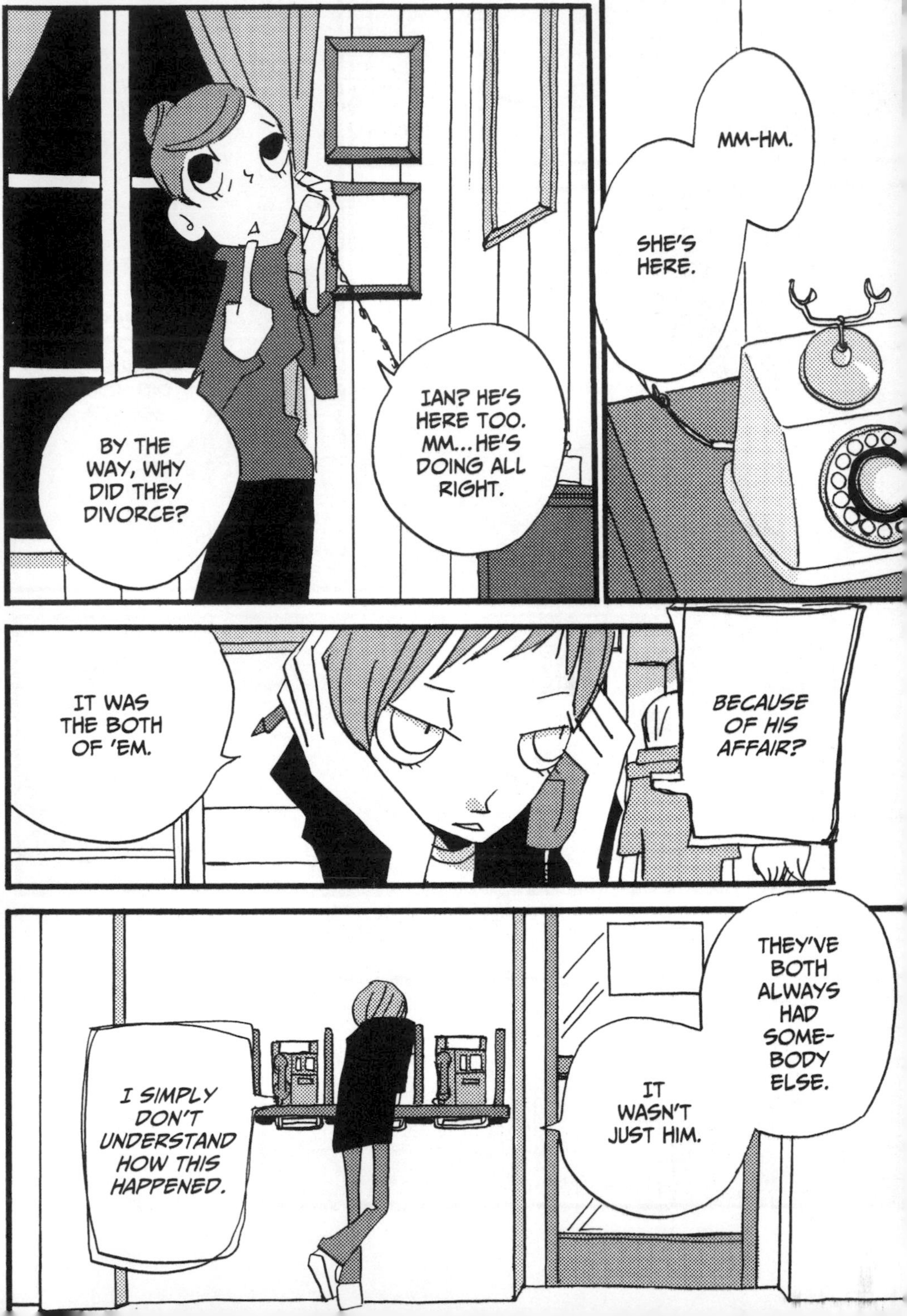
MM-HM.
SHE'S HERE.
IAN? HE'S HERE TOO. MM...HE'S DOING ALL RIGHT.
BY THE WAY, WHY DID THEY DIVORCE?
BECAUSE OF HIS AFFAIR?
IT WAS THE BOTH OF 'EM.
THEY'VE BOTH ALWAYS HAD SOME-BODY ELSE.
IT WASN'T JUST HIM.
I SIMPLY DON'T UNDERSTAND HOW THIS HAPPENED.

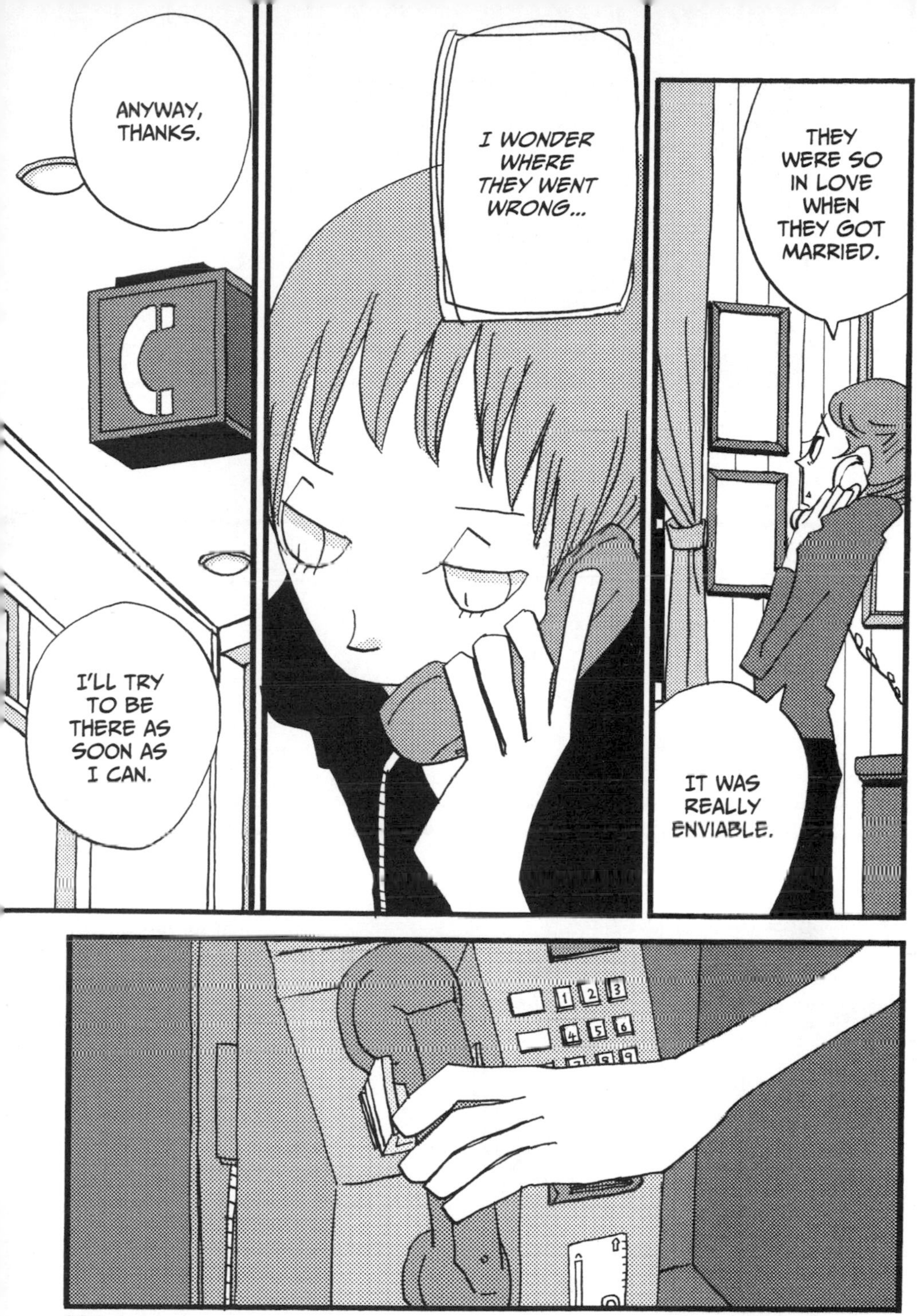
THEY WERE SO IN LOVE WHEN THEY GOT MARRIED.
IT WAS REALLY ENVIABLE.
I WONDER WHERE THEY WENT WRONG...
ANYWAY, THANKS.
I'LL TRY TO BE THERE AS SOON AS I CAN.

...

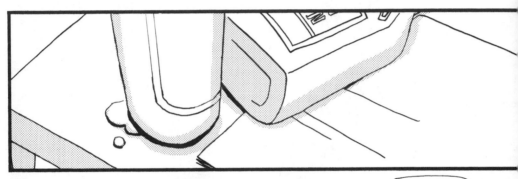

GO GET ME MORE.

I'M ALMOST OUT, IAN.

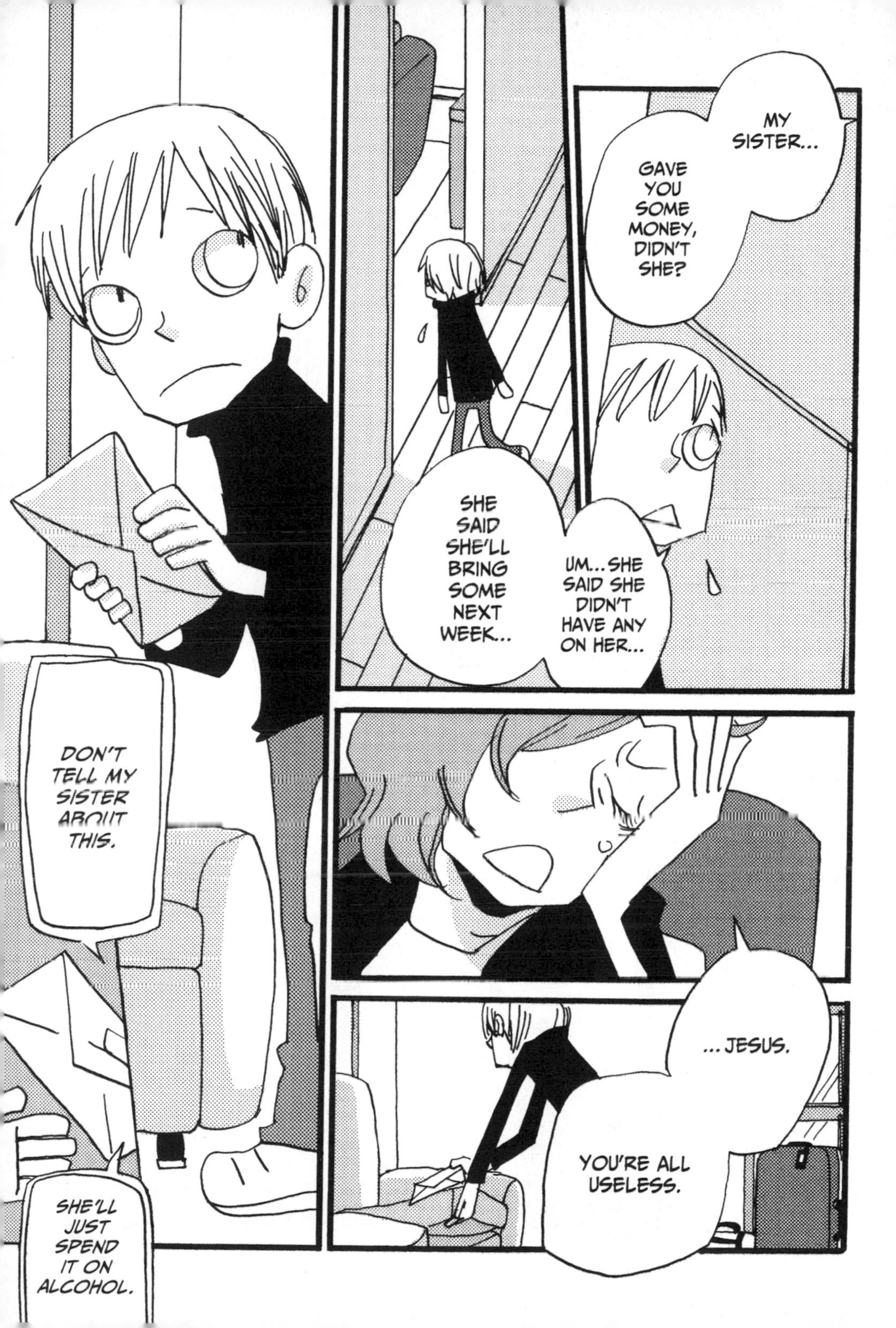
MY SISTER...
GAVE YOU SOME MONEY, DIDN'T SHE?
UM... SHE SAID SHE DIDN'T HAVE ANY ON HER...
SHE SAID SHE'LL BRING SOME NEXT WEEK...
...JESUS.
YOU'RE ALL USELESS.
DON'T TELL MY SISTER ABOUT THIS.
SHE'LL JUST SPEND IT ON ALCOHOL.

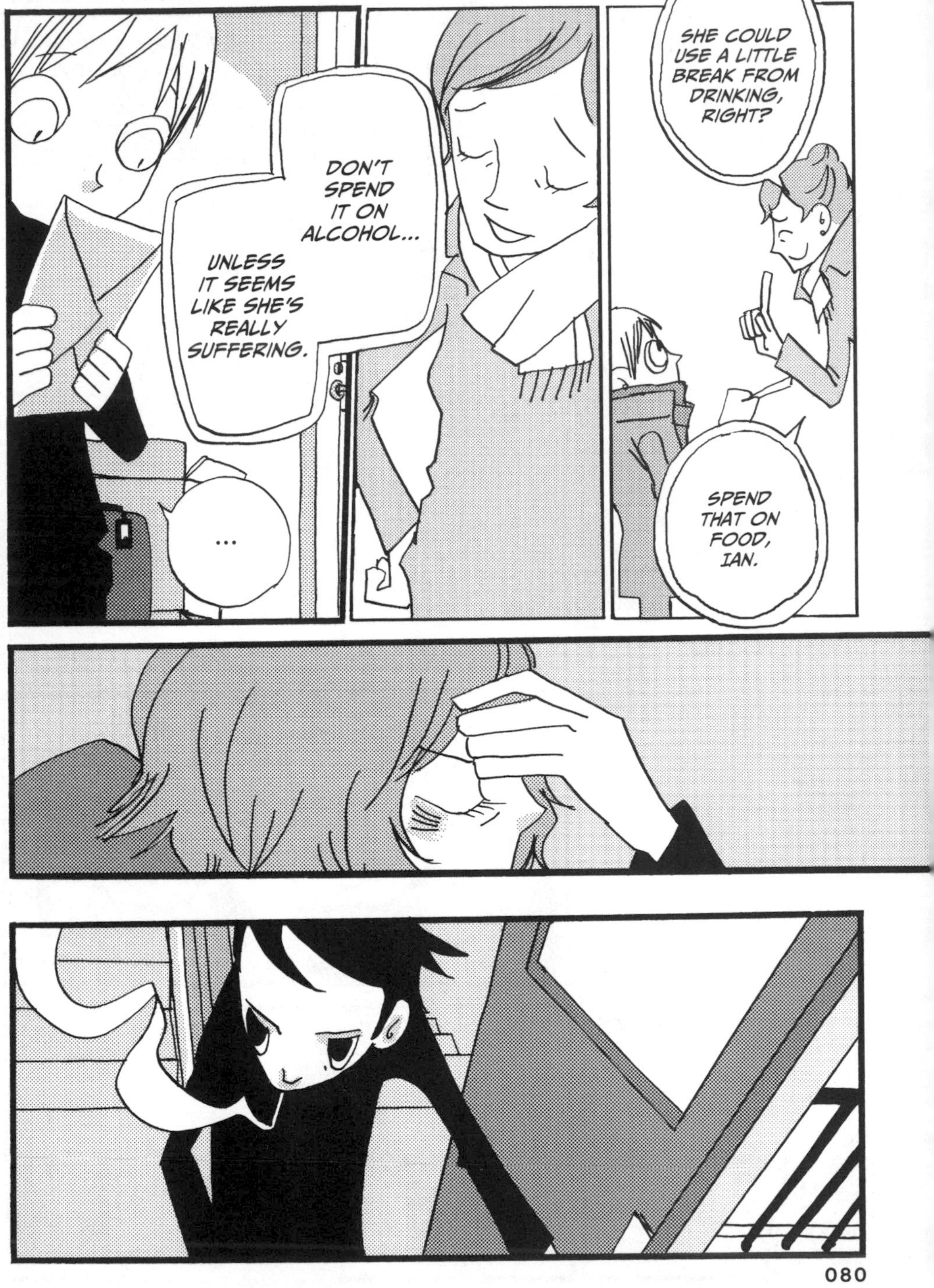
SHE COULD USE A LITTLE BREAK FROM DRINKING, RIGHT?
SPEND THAT ON FOOD, IAN.
DON'T SPEND IT ON ALCOHOL...
UNLESS IT SEEMS LIKE SHE'S REALLY SUFFERING.
...

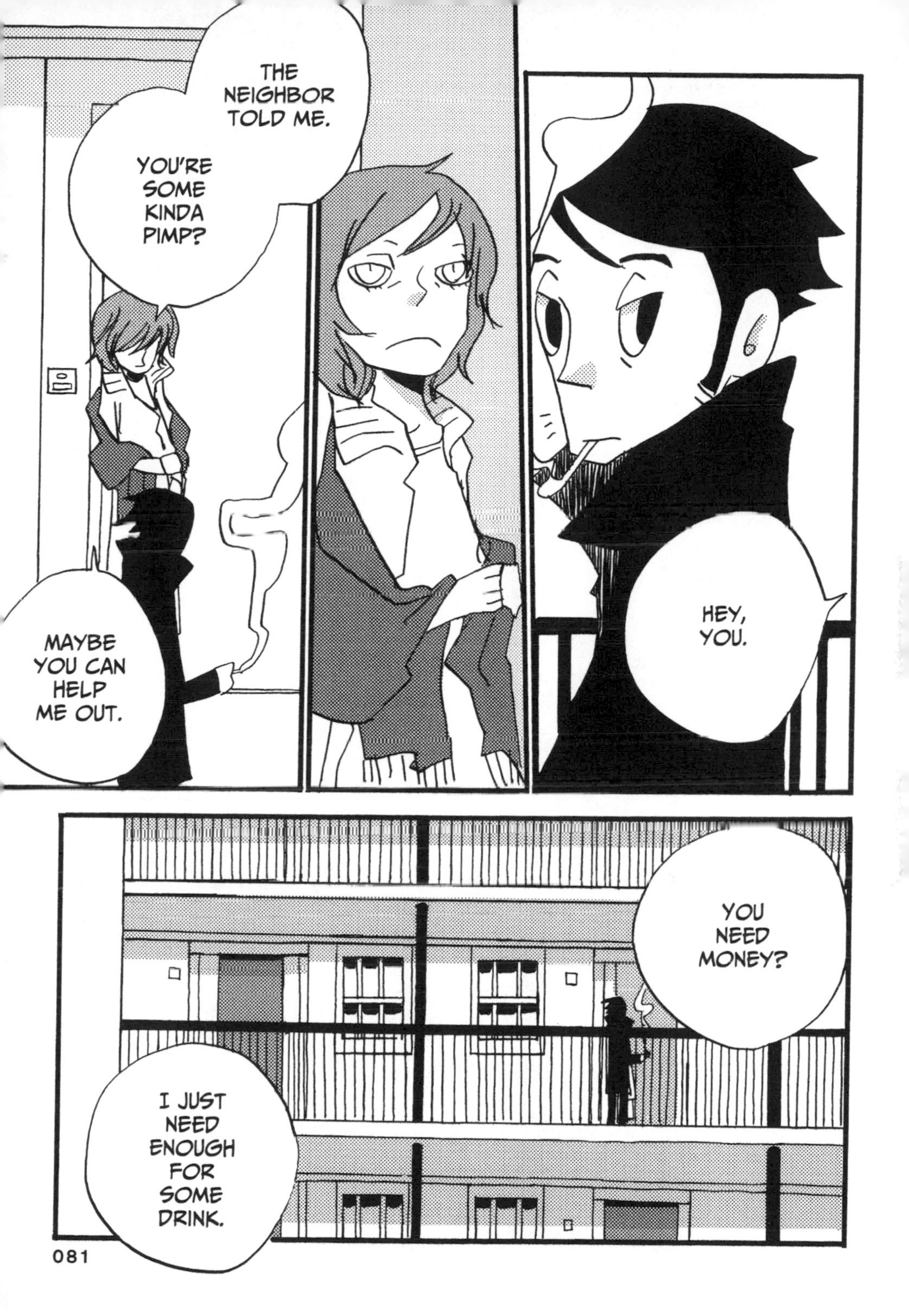
HEY, YOU.
THE NEIGHBOR TOLD ME.
YOU'RE SOME KINDA PIMP?
MAYBE YOU CAN HELP ME OUT.
YOU NEED MONEY?
I JUST NEED ENOUGH FOR SOME DRINK.

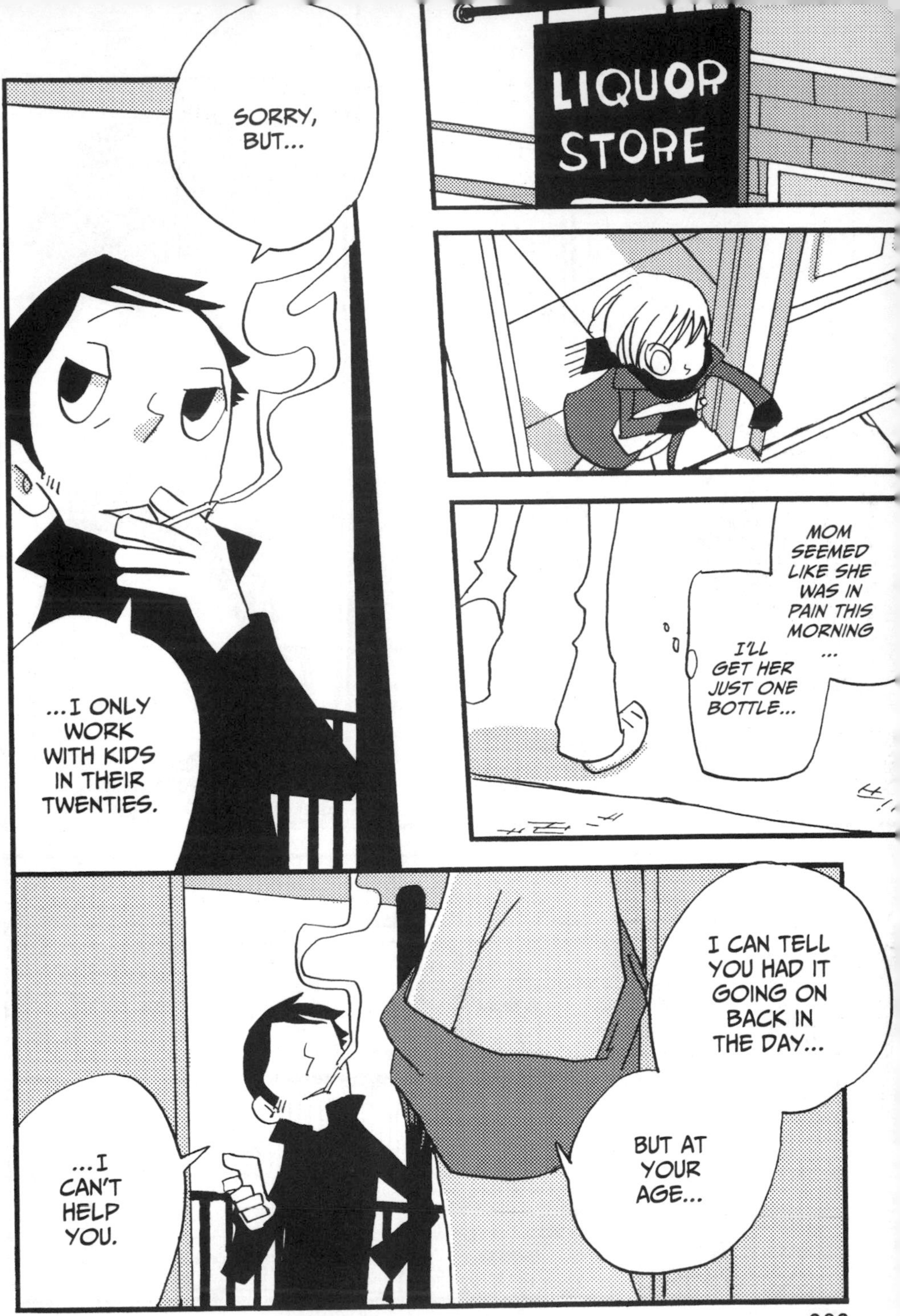
LIQUOR STORE
MOM SEEMED LIKE SHE WAS IN PAIN THIS MORNING...
I'LL GET HER JUST ONE BOTTLE...
SORRY, BUT...
...I ONLY WORK WITH KIDS IN THEIR TWENTIES.
I CAN TELL YOU HAD IT GOING ON BACK IN THE DAY...
BUT AT YOUR AGE...
...I CAN'T HELP YOU.

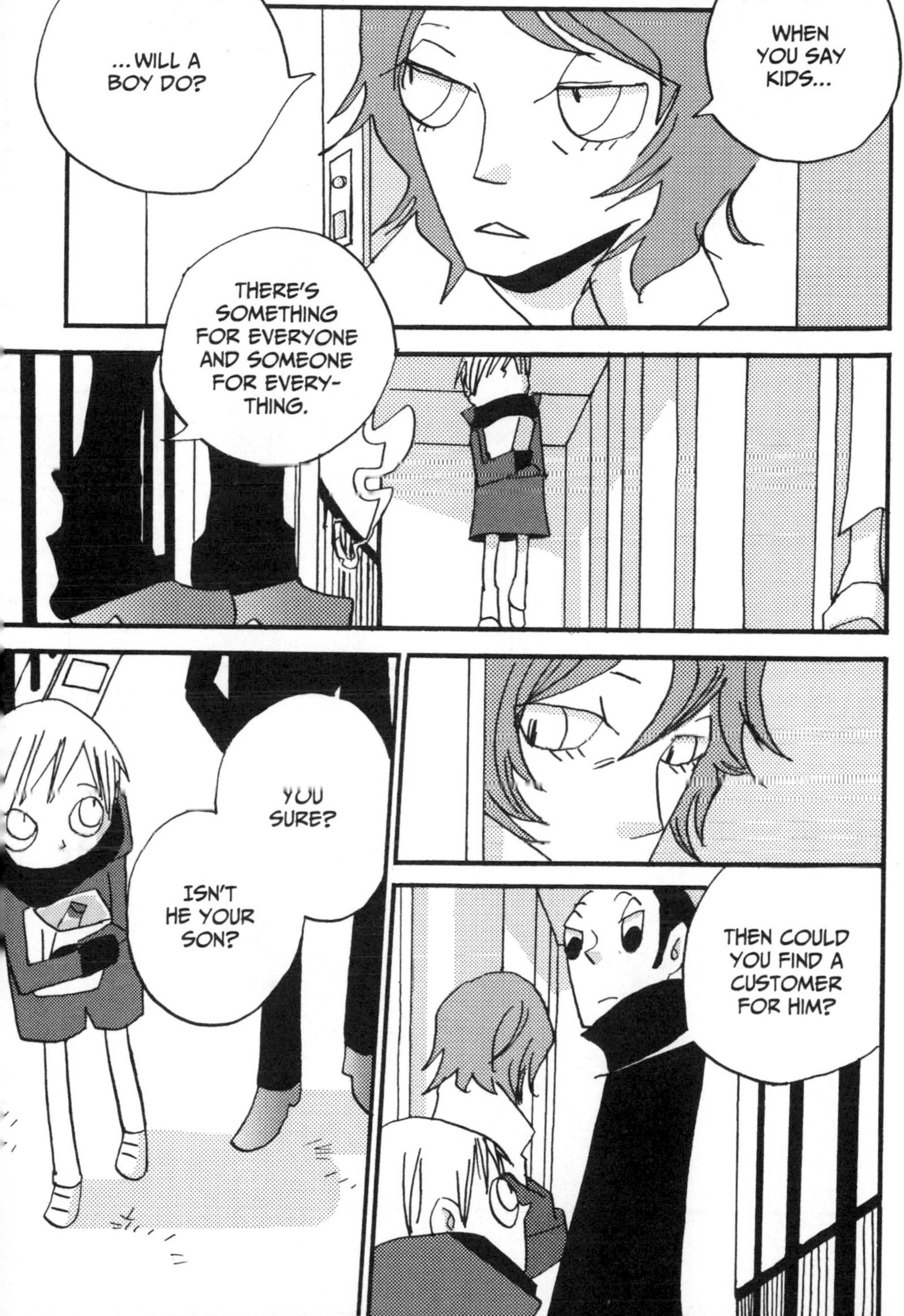
WHEN YOU SAY KIDS...
...WILL A BOY DO?
THERE'S SOMETHING FOR EVERYONE AND SOMEONE FOR EVERY-THING.
THEN COULD YOU FIND A CUSTOMER FOR HIM?
YOU SURE?
ISN'T HE YOUR SON?

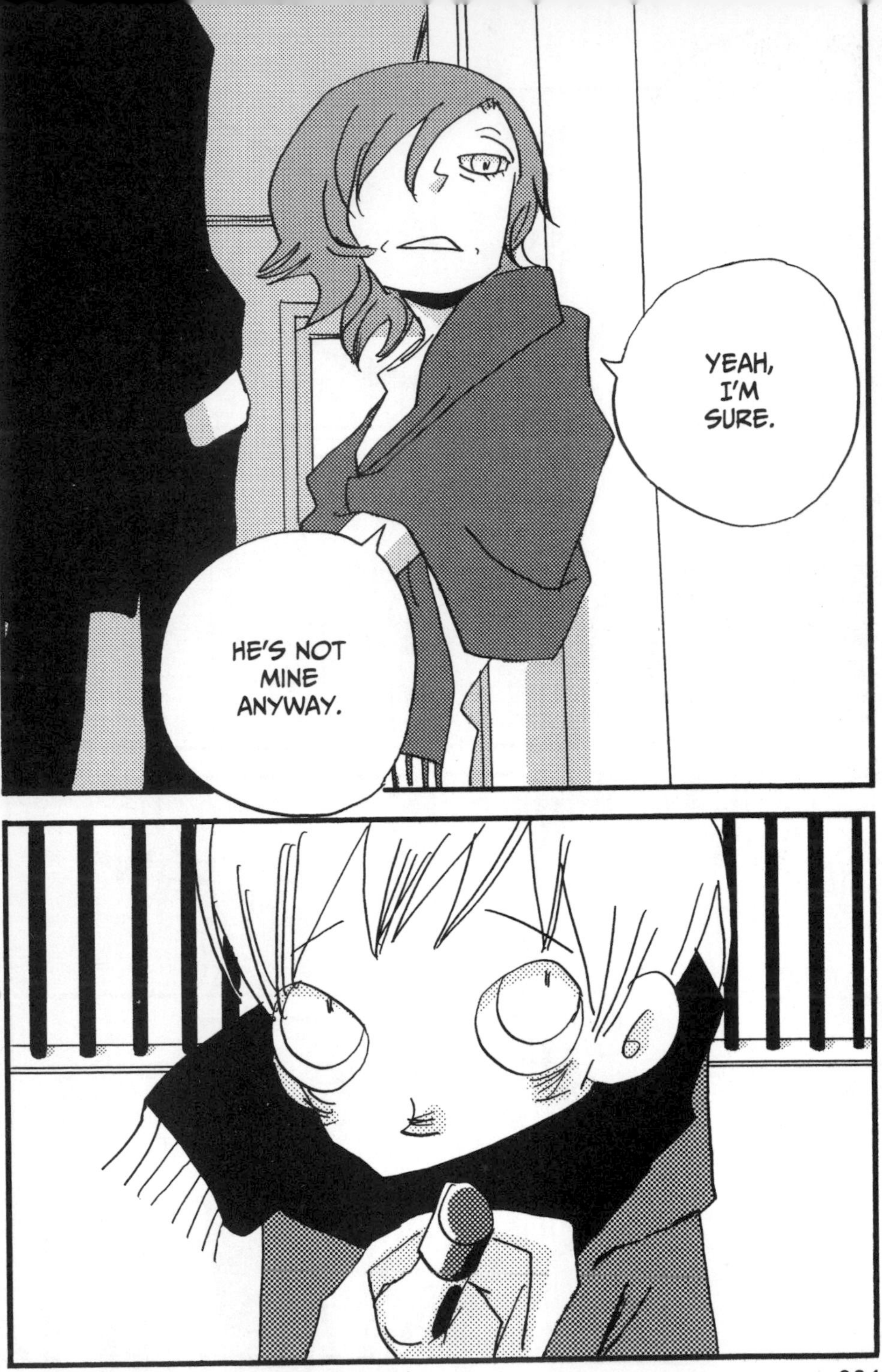
YEAH, I'M SURE.
HE'S NOT MINE ANYWAY.

#03 not simple

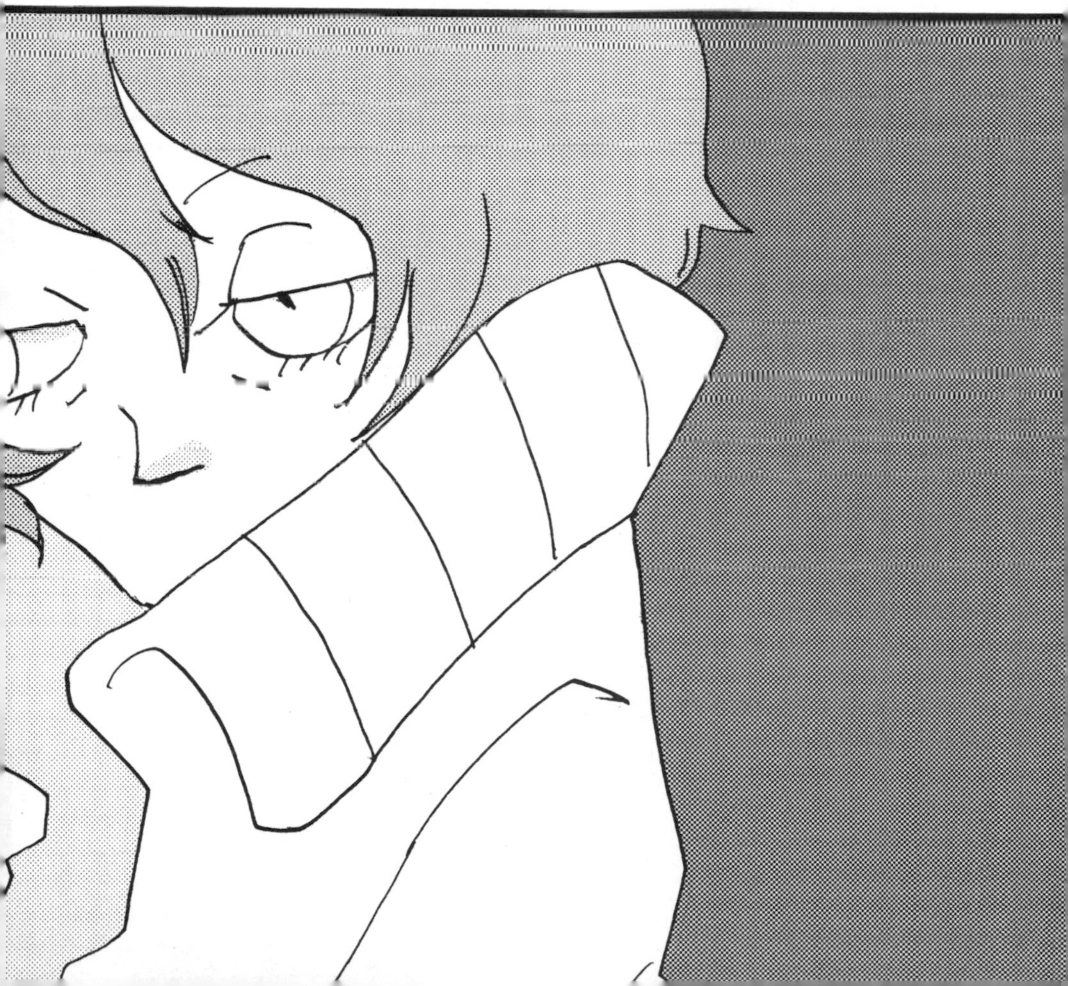

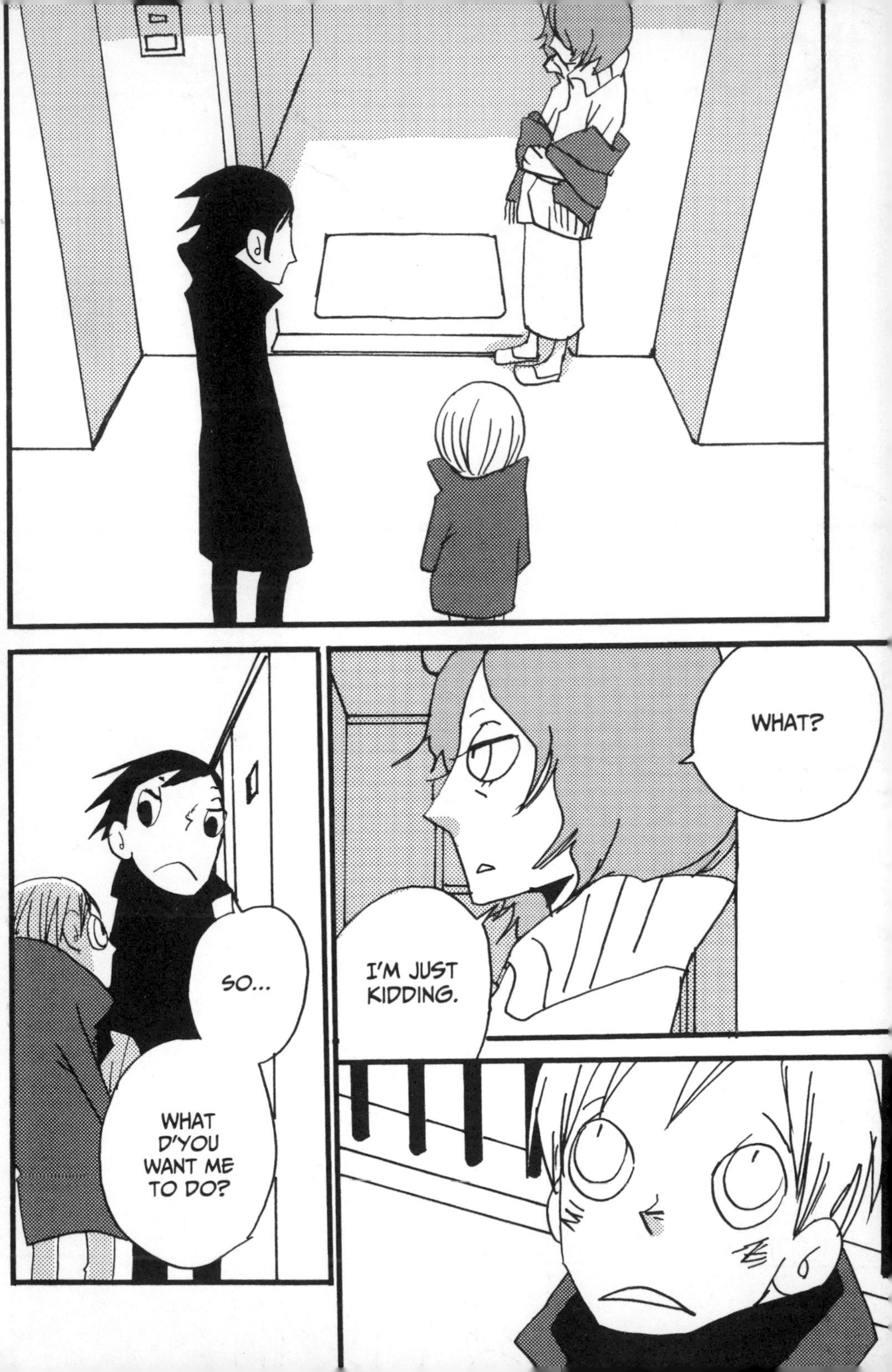
WHAT?
I'M JUST KIDDING.
SO...
WHAT D'YOU WANT ME TO DO?

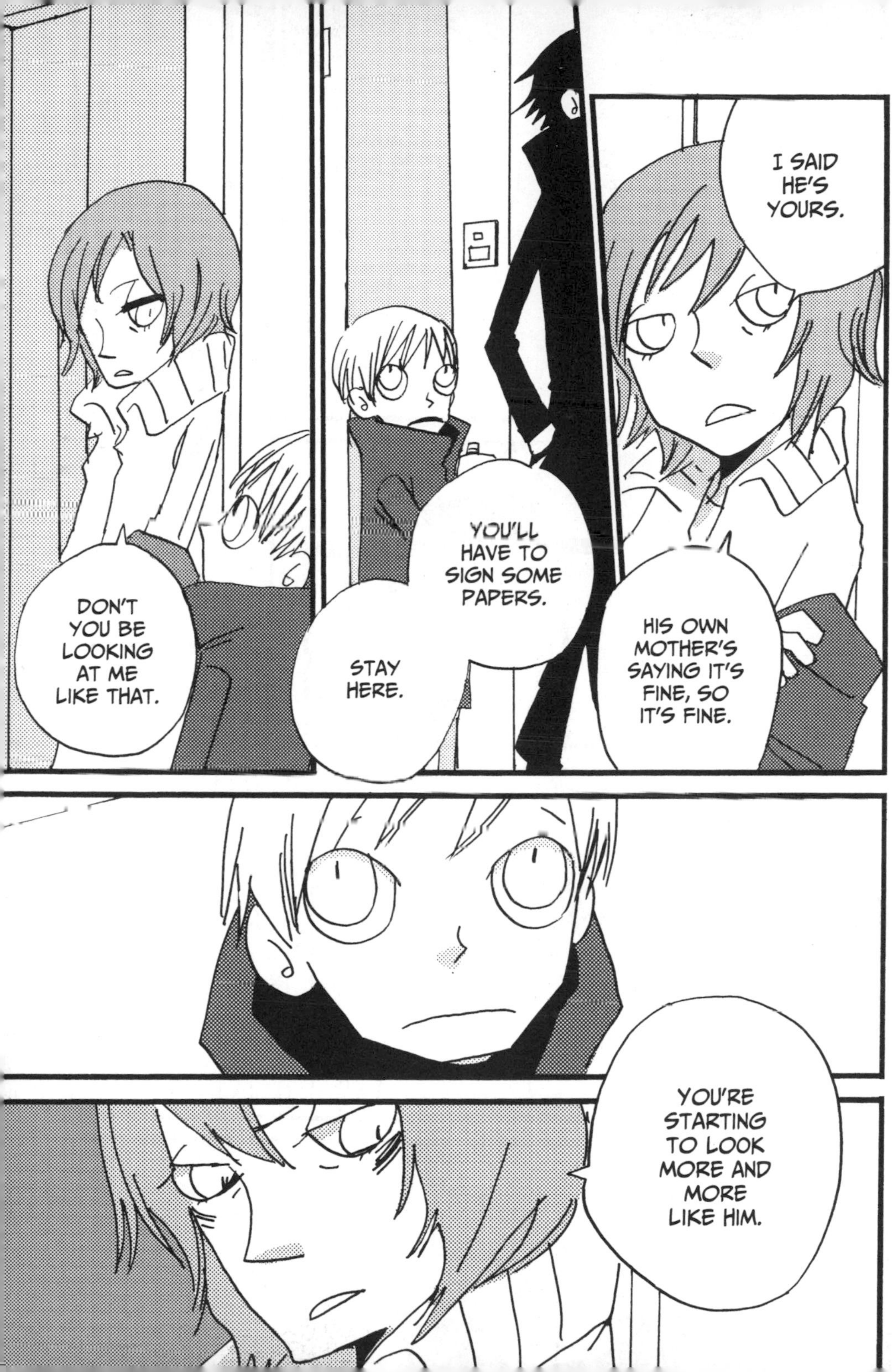
I SAID HE'S YOURS.
HIS OWN MOTHER'S SAYING IT'S FINE, SO IT'S FINE.
YOU'LL HAVE TO SIGN SOME PAPERS.
STAY HERE.
DON'T YOU BE LOOKING AT ME LIKE THAT.
YOU'RE STARTING TO LOOK MORE AND MORE LIKE HIM.

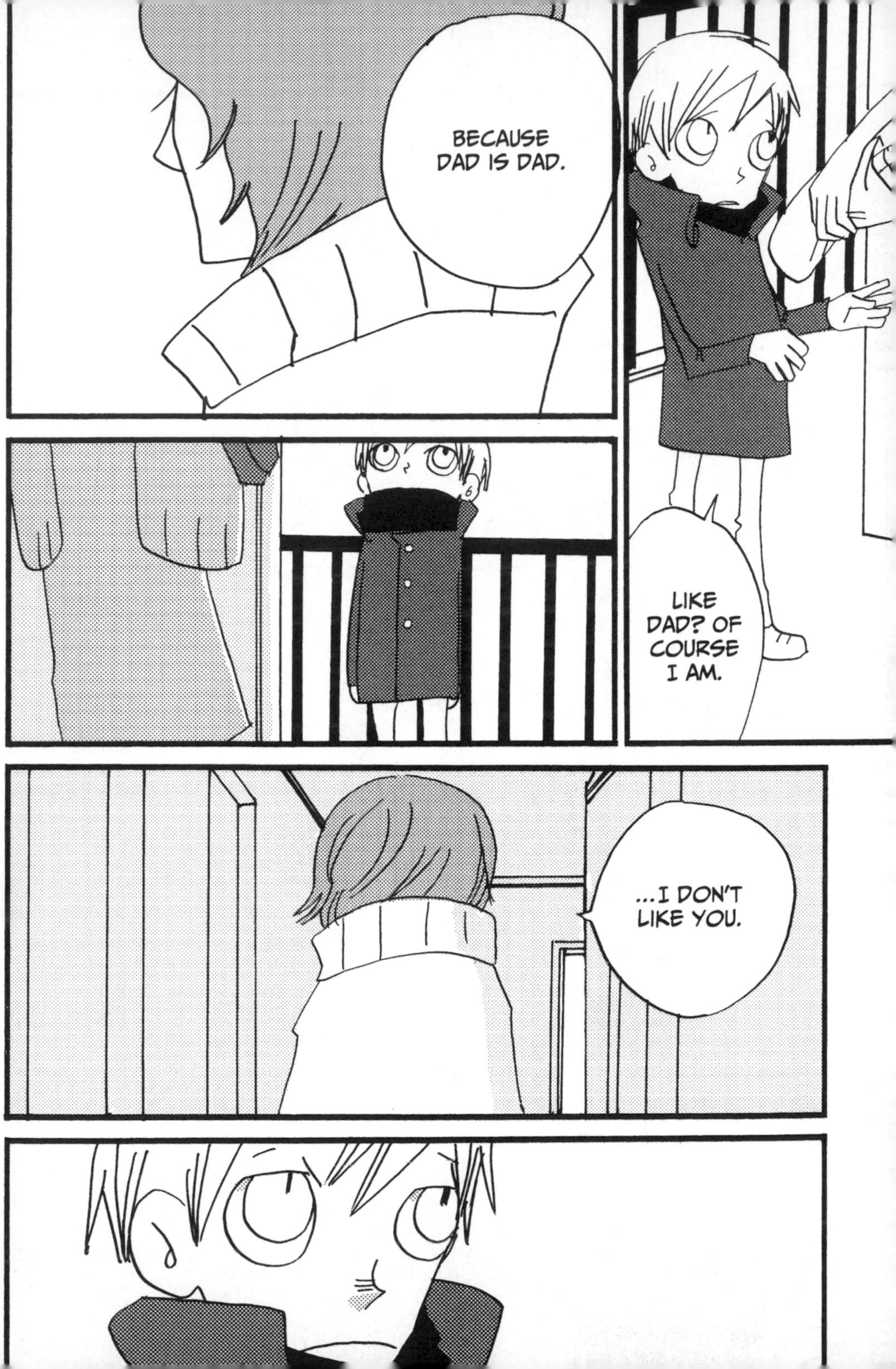
LIKE DAD? OF COURSE I AM.
BECAUSE DAD IS DAD.
...I DON'T LIKE YOU.

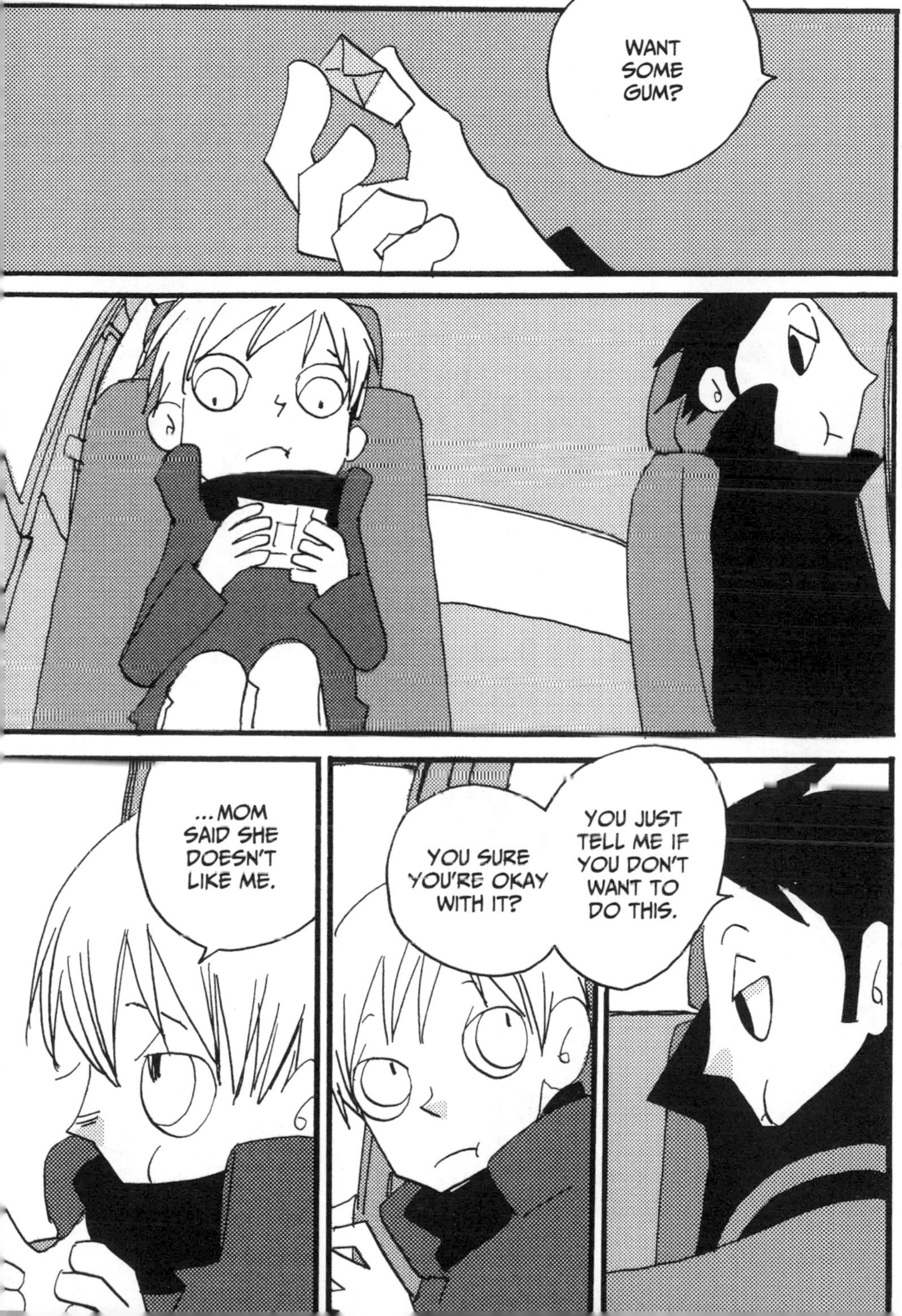
WANT SOME GUM?
YOU JUST TELL ME IF YOU DON'T WANT TO DO THIS.
YOU SURE YOU'RE OKAY WITH IT?
...MOM SAID SHE DOESN'T LIKE ME.

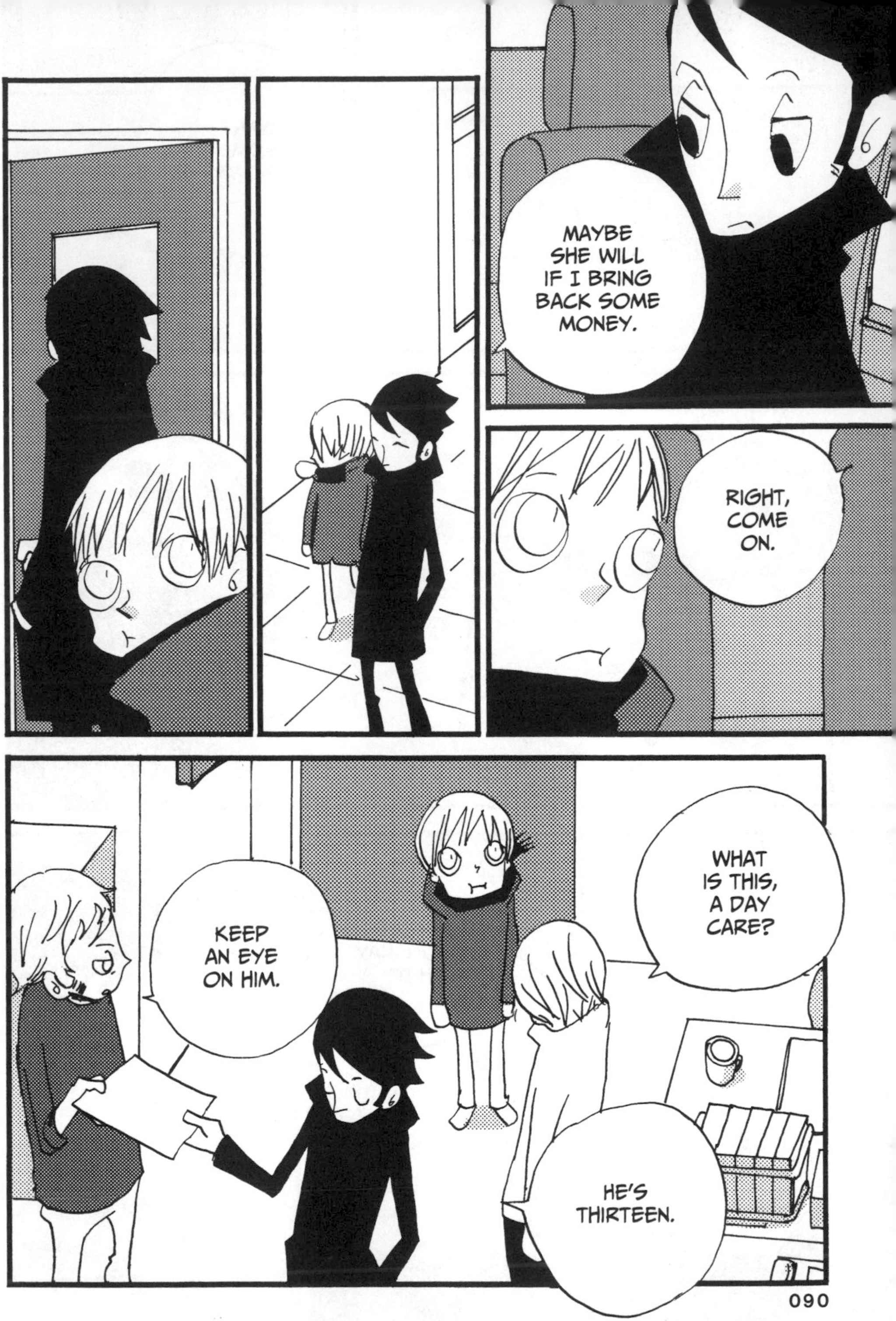
MAYBE SHE WILL IF I BRING BACK SOME MONEY.
RIGHT, COME ON.
WHAT IS THIS, A DAY CARE?
HE'S THIRTEEN.
KEEP AN EYE ON HIM.

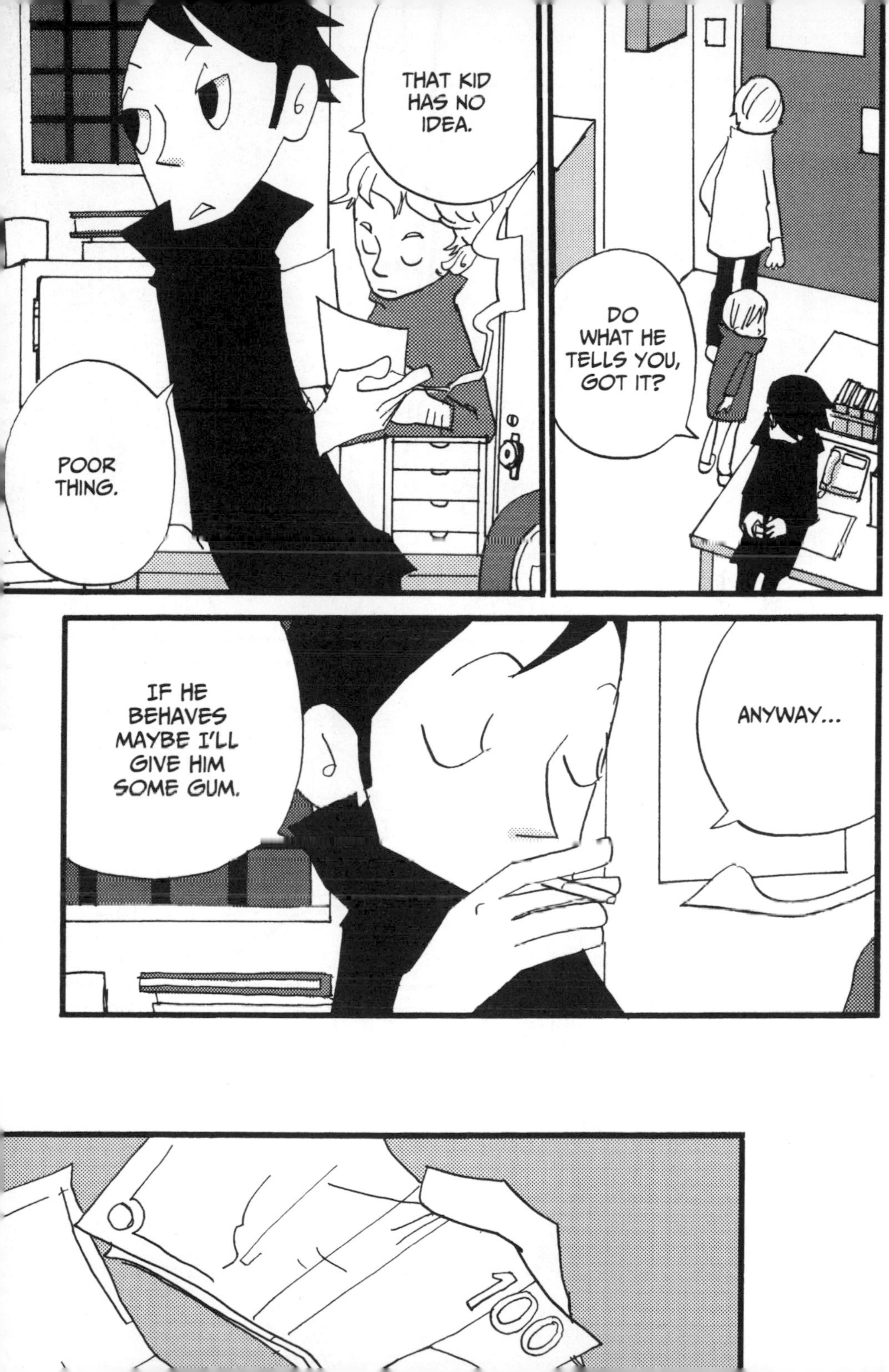
DO WHAT HE TELLS YOU, GOT IT?
THAT KID HAS NO IDEA.
POOR THING.
ANYWAY...
IF HE BEHAVES MAYBE I'LL GIVE HIM SOME GUM.
100

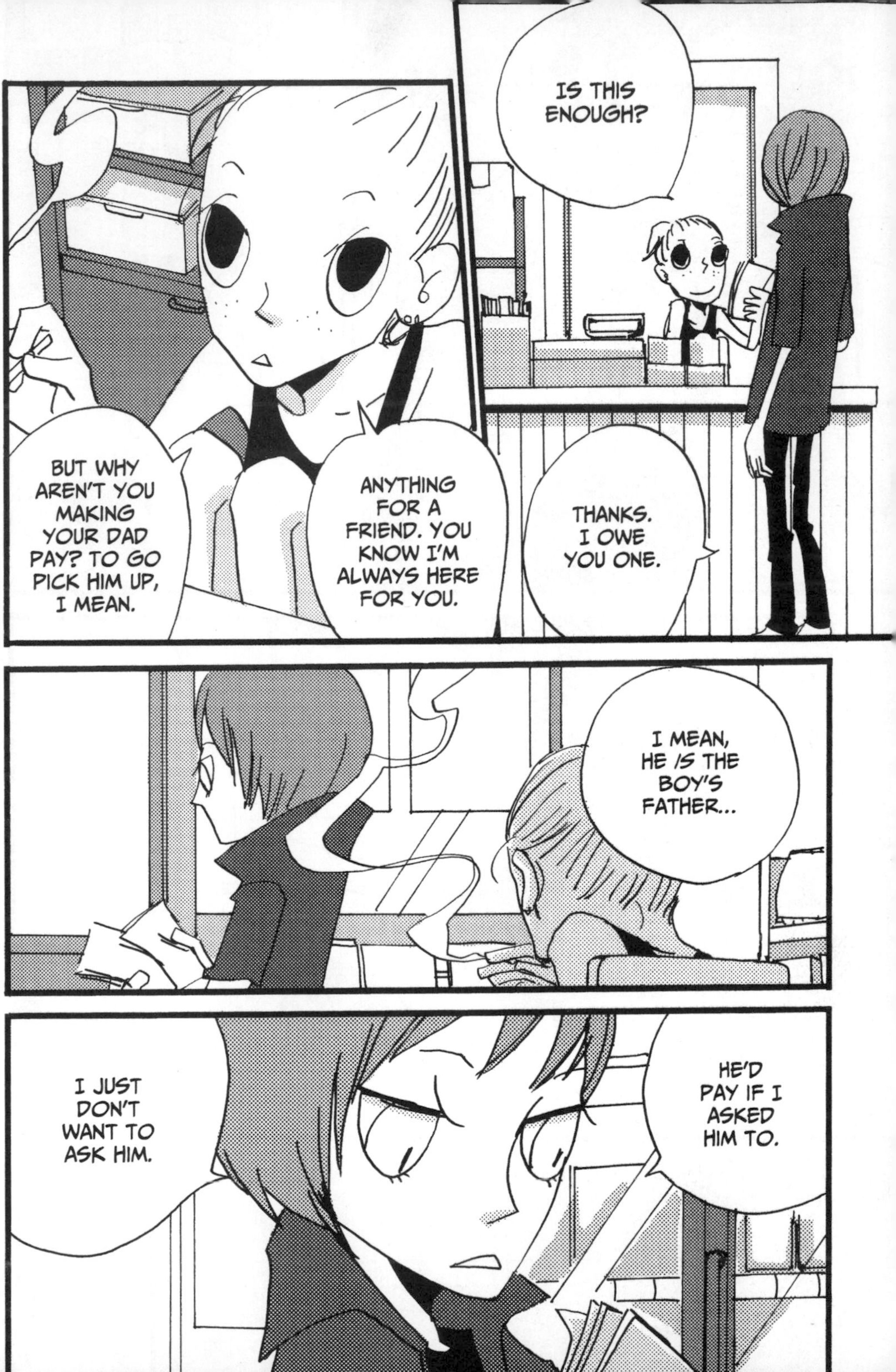
IS THIS ENOUGH?
THANKS. I OWE YOU ONE.
ANYTHING FOR A FRIEND. YOU KNOW I'M ALWAYS HERE FOR YOU.
BUT WHY AREN'T YOU MAKING YOUR DAD PAY? TO GO PICK HIM UP, I MEAN.
I MEAN, HE *IS* THE BOY'S FATHER...
HE'D PAY IF I ASKED HIM TO.
I JUST DON'T WANT TO ASK HIM.

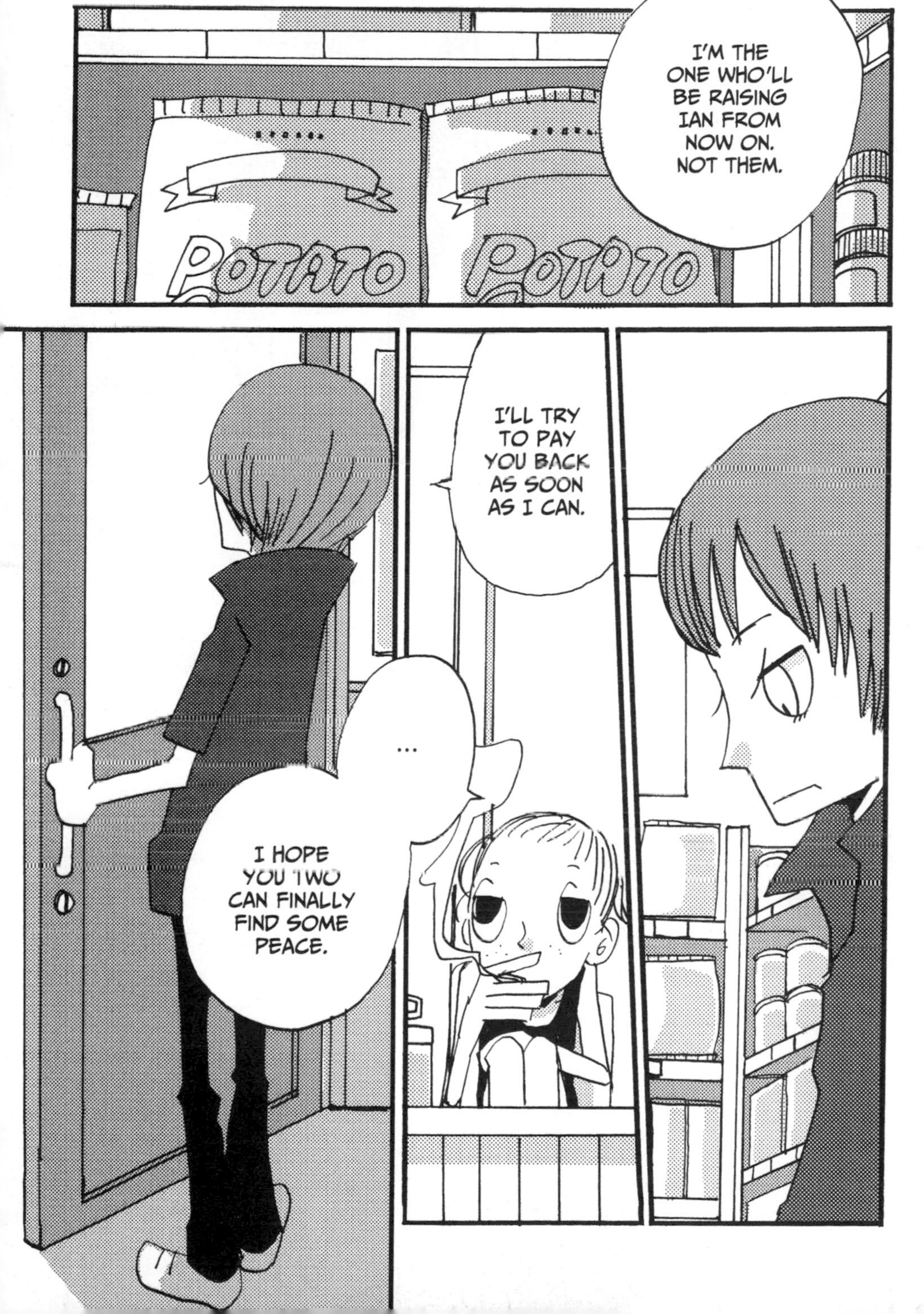
I'M THE ONE WHO'LL BE RAISING IAN FROM NOW ON. NOT THEM.
I'LL TRY TO PAY YOU BACK AS SOON AS I CAN.
...
I HOPE YOU TWO CAN FINALLY FIND SOME PEACE.

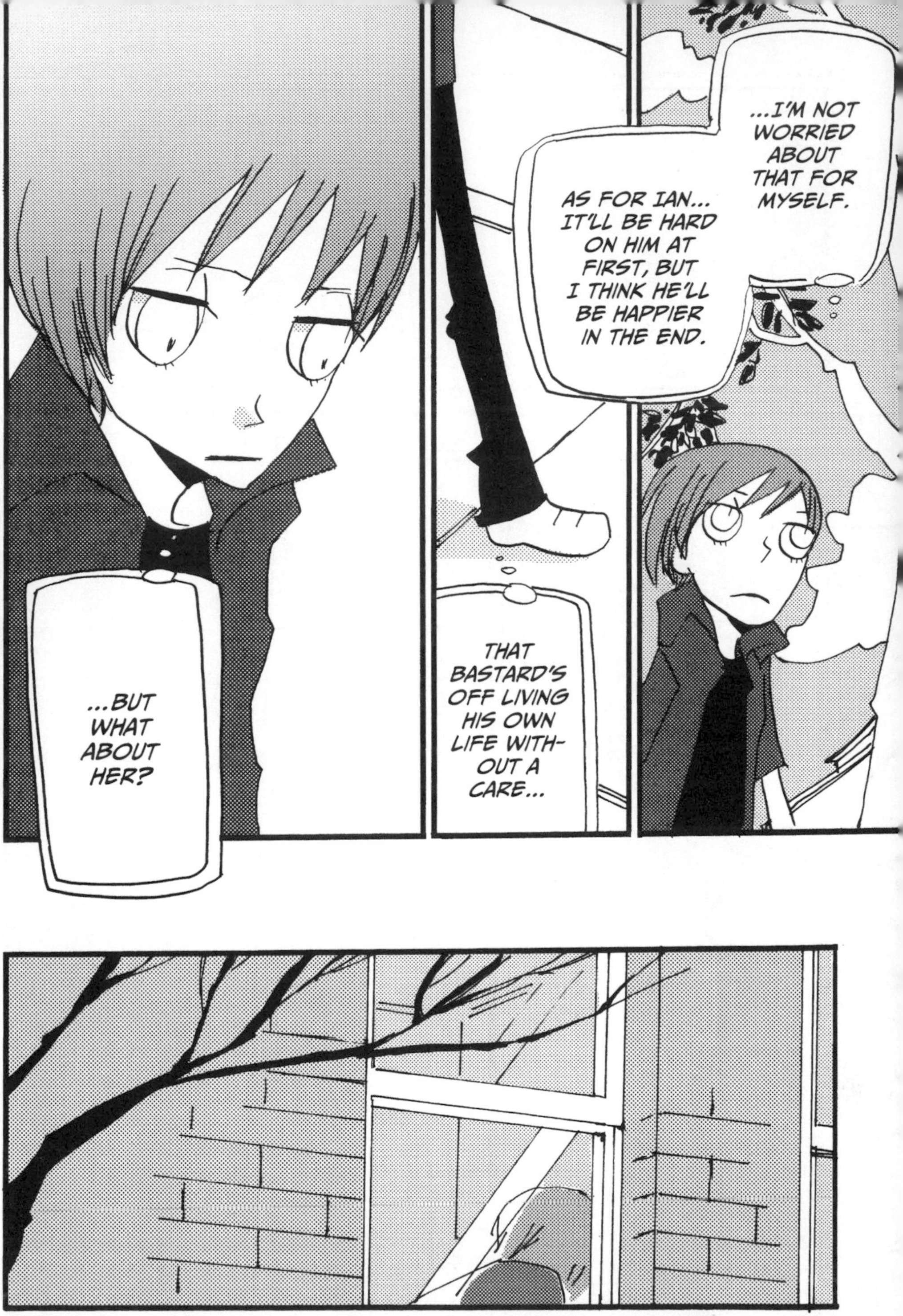
...I'M NOT WORRIED ABOUT THAT FOR MYSELF.
AS FOR IAN... IT'LL BE HARD ON HIM AT FIRST, BUT I THINK HE'LL BE HAPPIER IN THE END.
THAT BASTARD'S OFF LIVING HIS OWN LIFE WITH-OUT A CARE...
...BUT WHAT ABOUT HER?

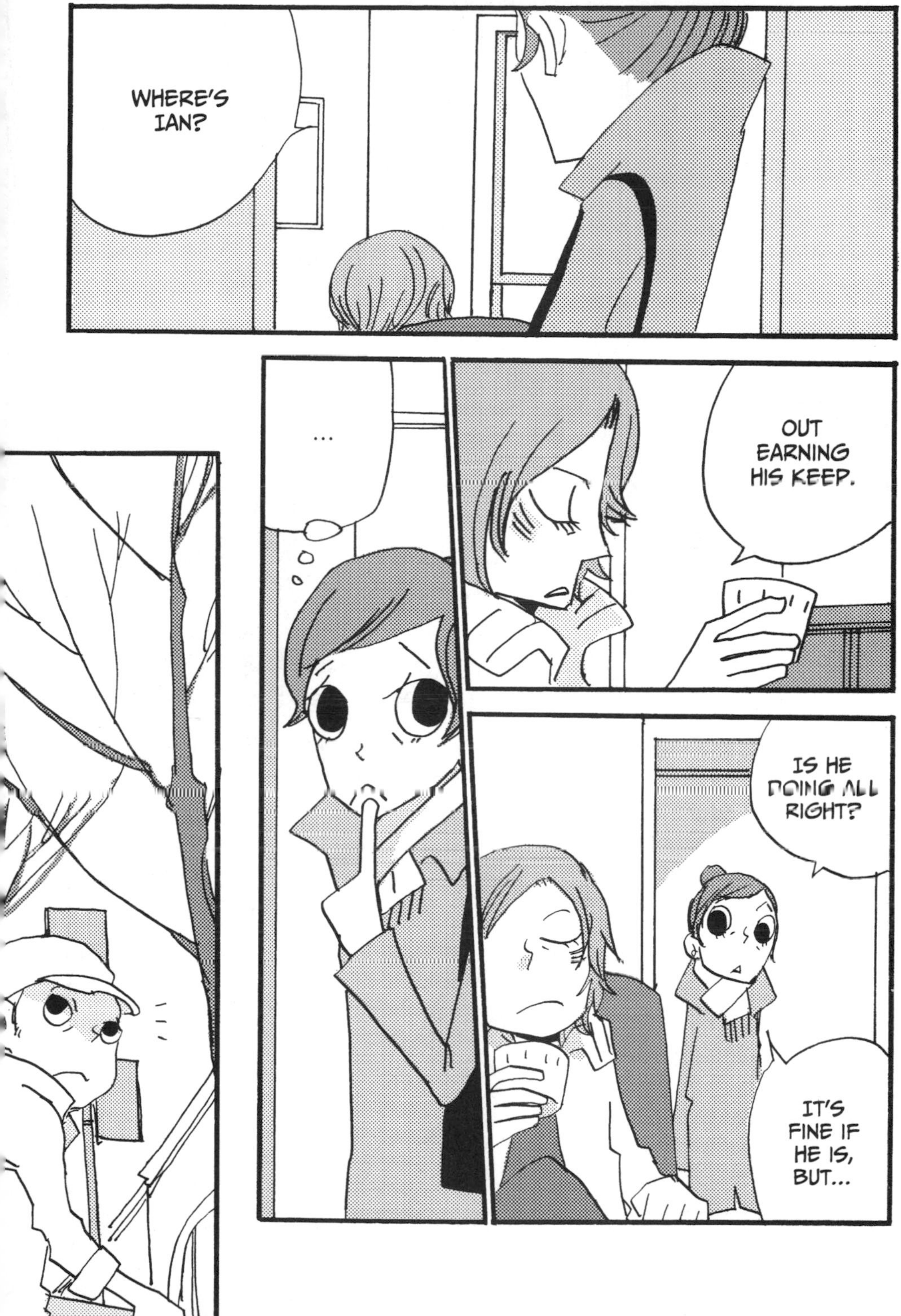
WHERE'S IAN?
OUT EARNING HIS KEEP.
IS HE DOING ALL RIGHT?
IT'S FINE IF HE IS, BUT...
...

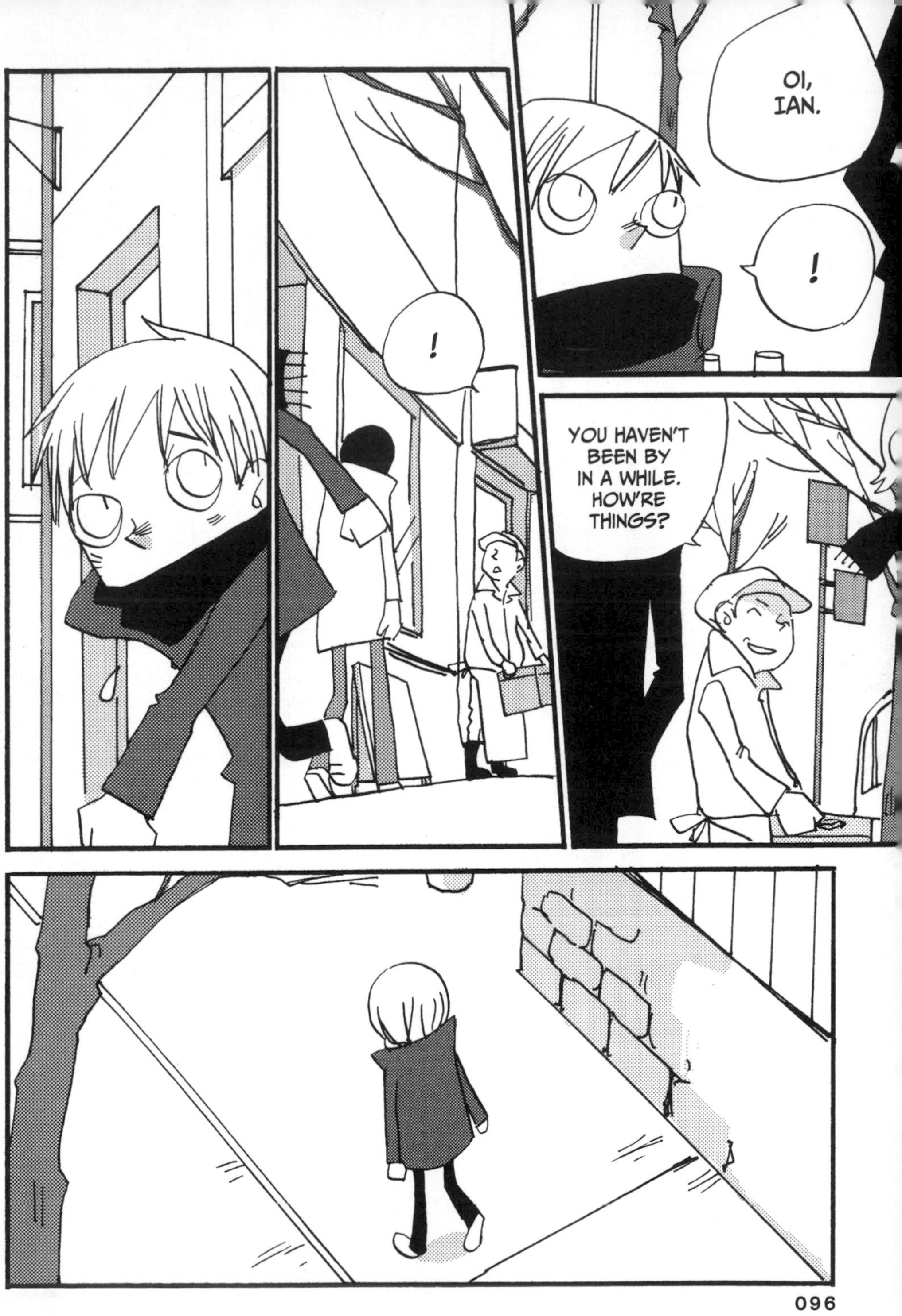
OI, IAN.
!
YOU HAVEN'T BEEN BY IN A WHILE. HOW'RE THINGS?
!

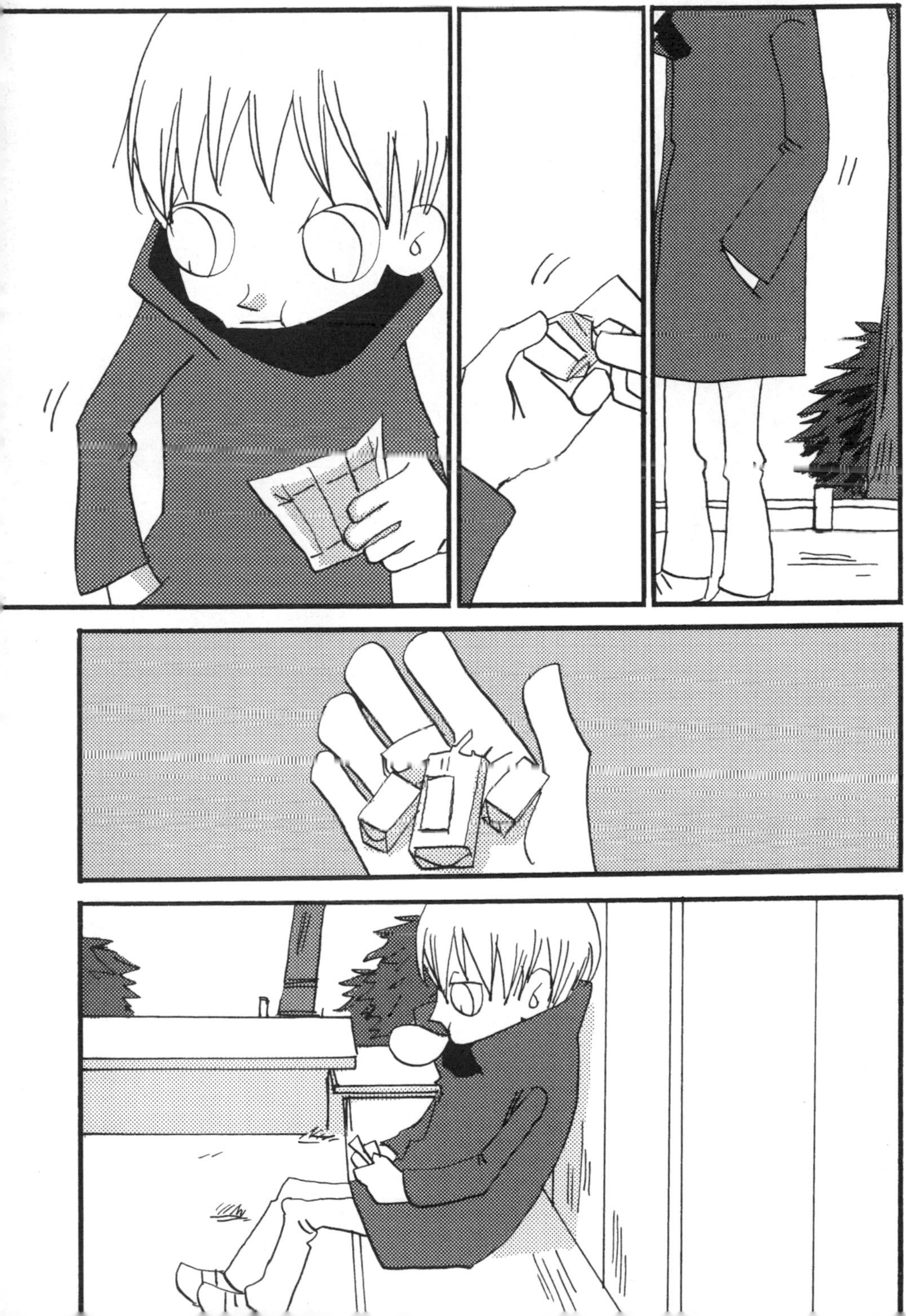

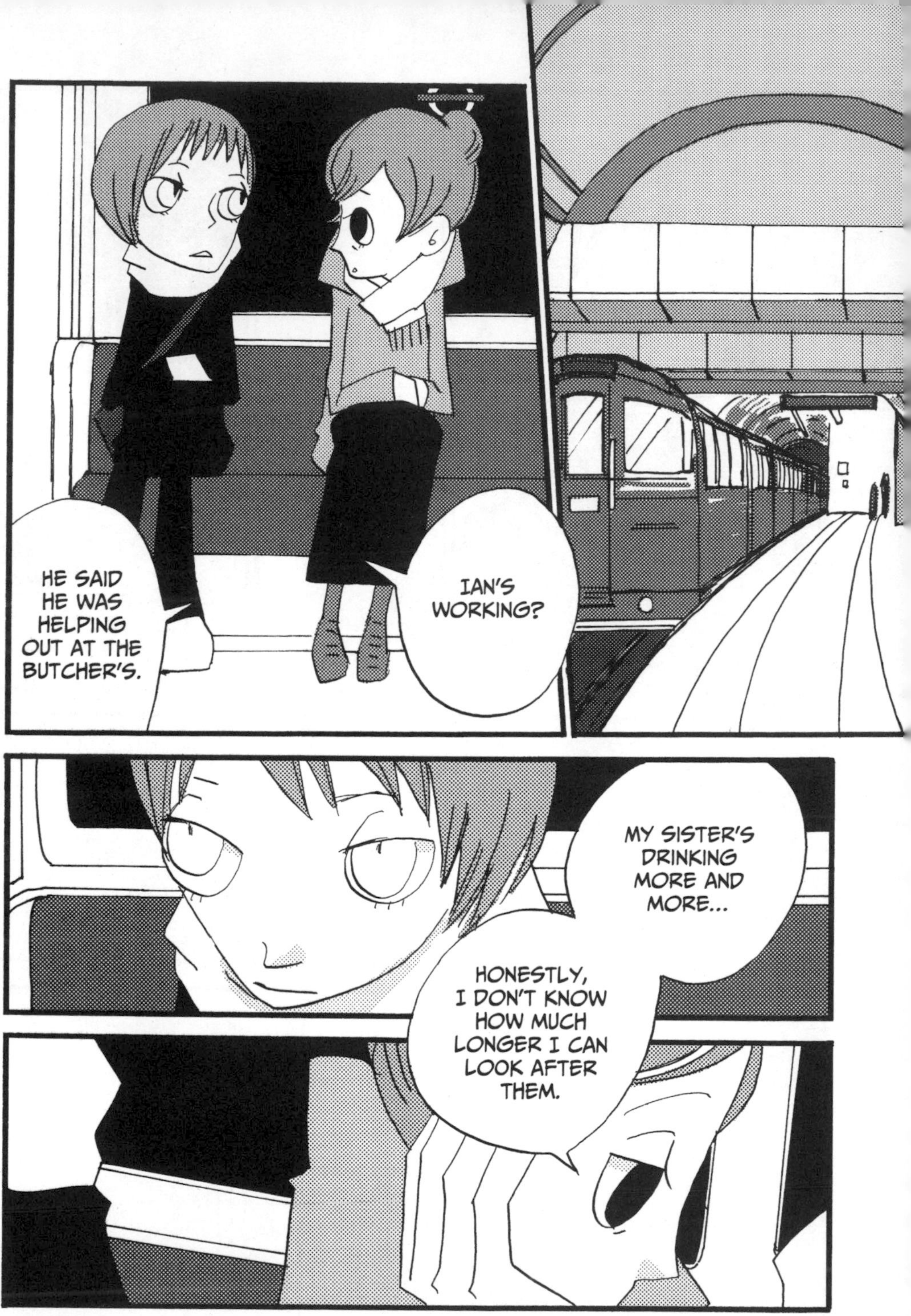
IAN'S WORKING?
HE SAID HE WAS HELPING OUT AT THE BUTCHER'S.
MY SISTER'S DRINKING MORE AND MORE...
HONESTLY, I DON'T KNOW HOW MUCH LONGER I CAN LOOK AFTER THEM.

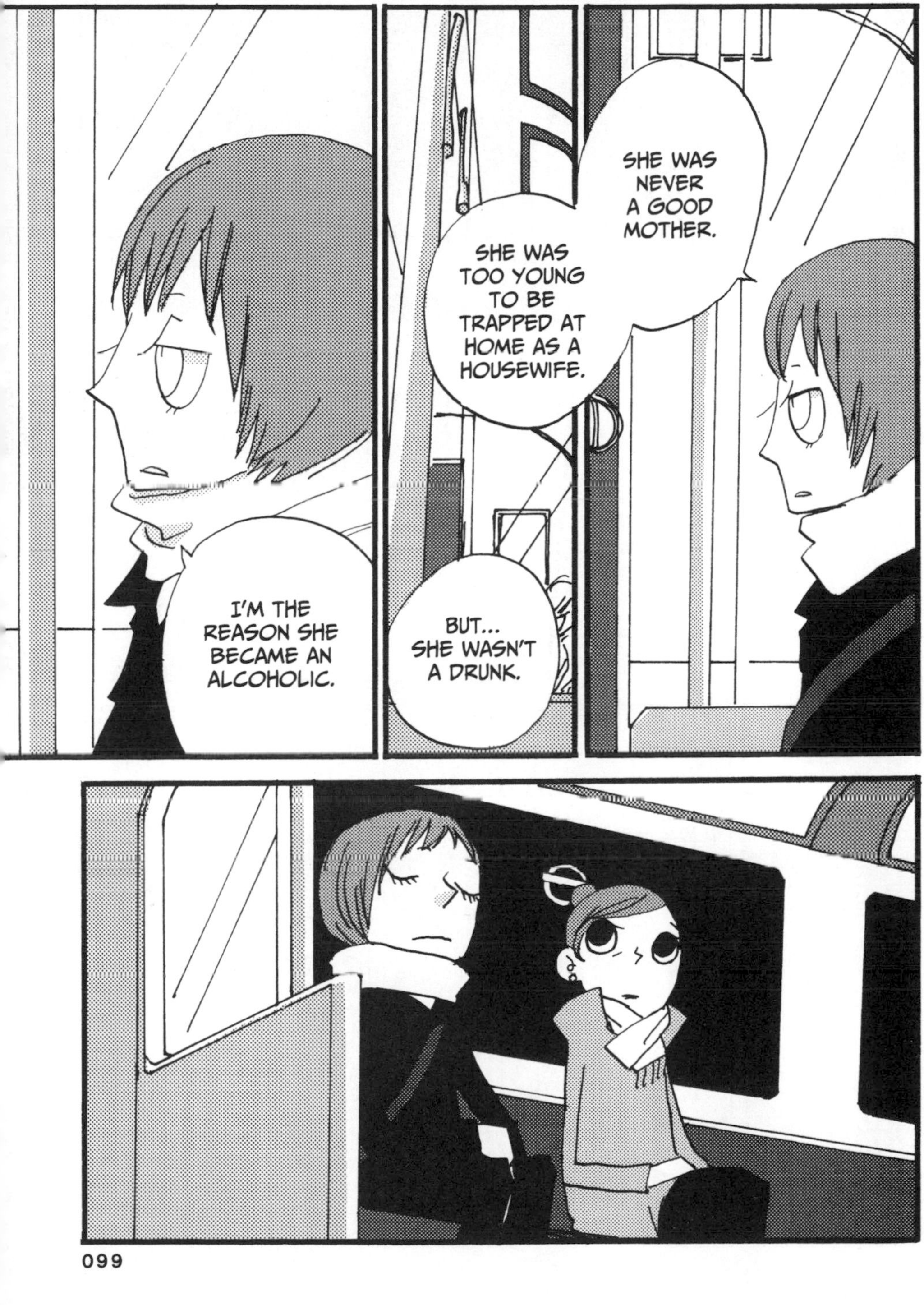
SHE WAS NEVER A GOOD MOTHER.
SHE WAS TOO YOUNG TO BE TRAPPED AT HOME AS A HOUSEWIFE.
BUT... SHE WASN'T A DRUNK.
I'M THE REASON SHE BECAME AN ALCOHOLIC.

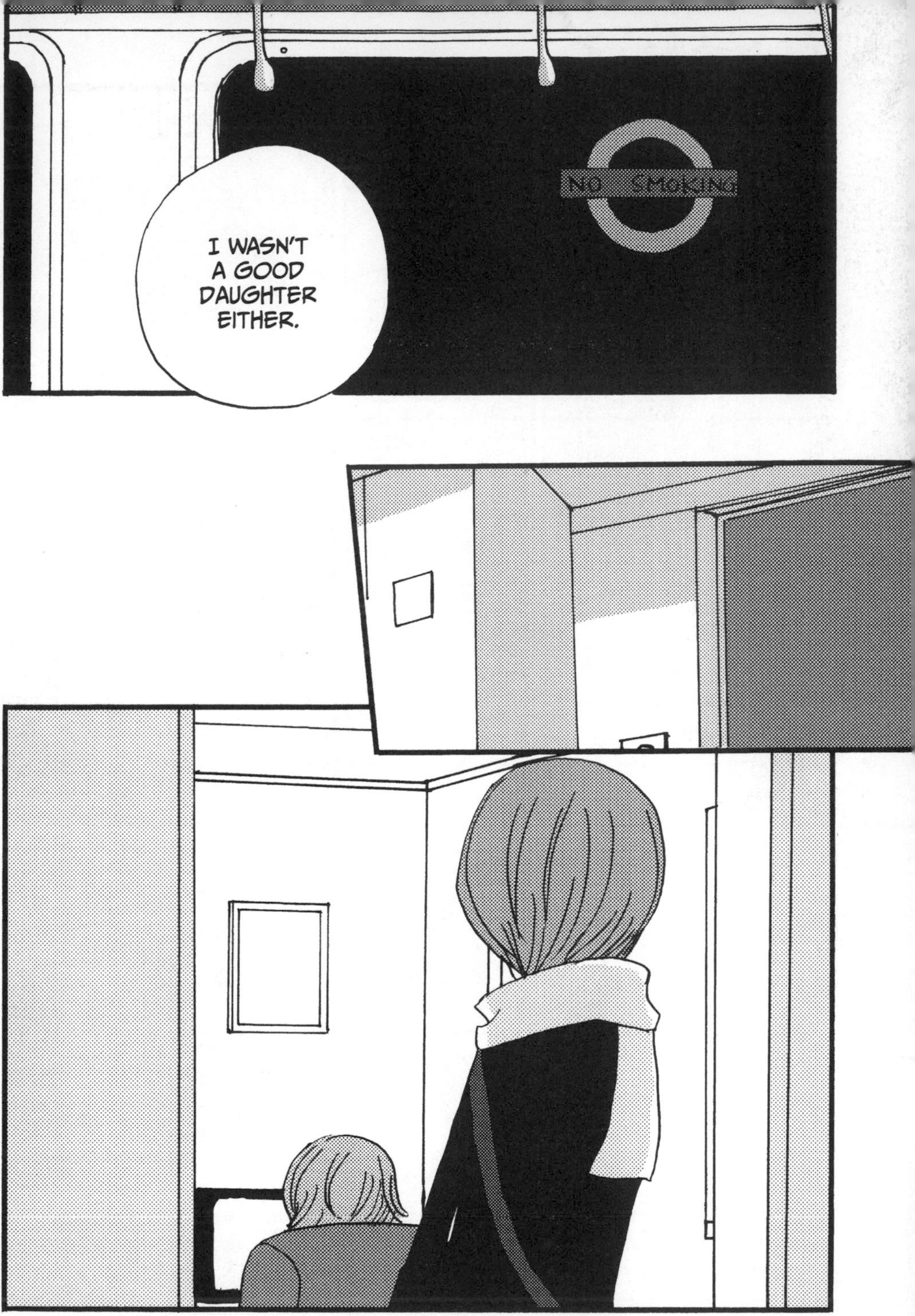
NO SMOKING
I WASN'T A GOOD DAUGHTER EITHER.

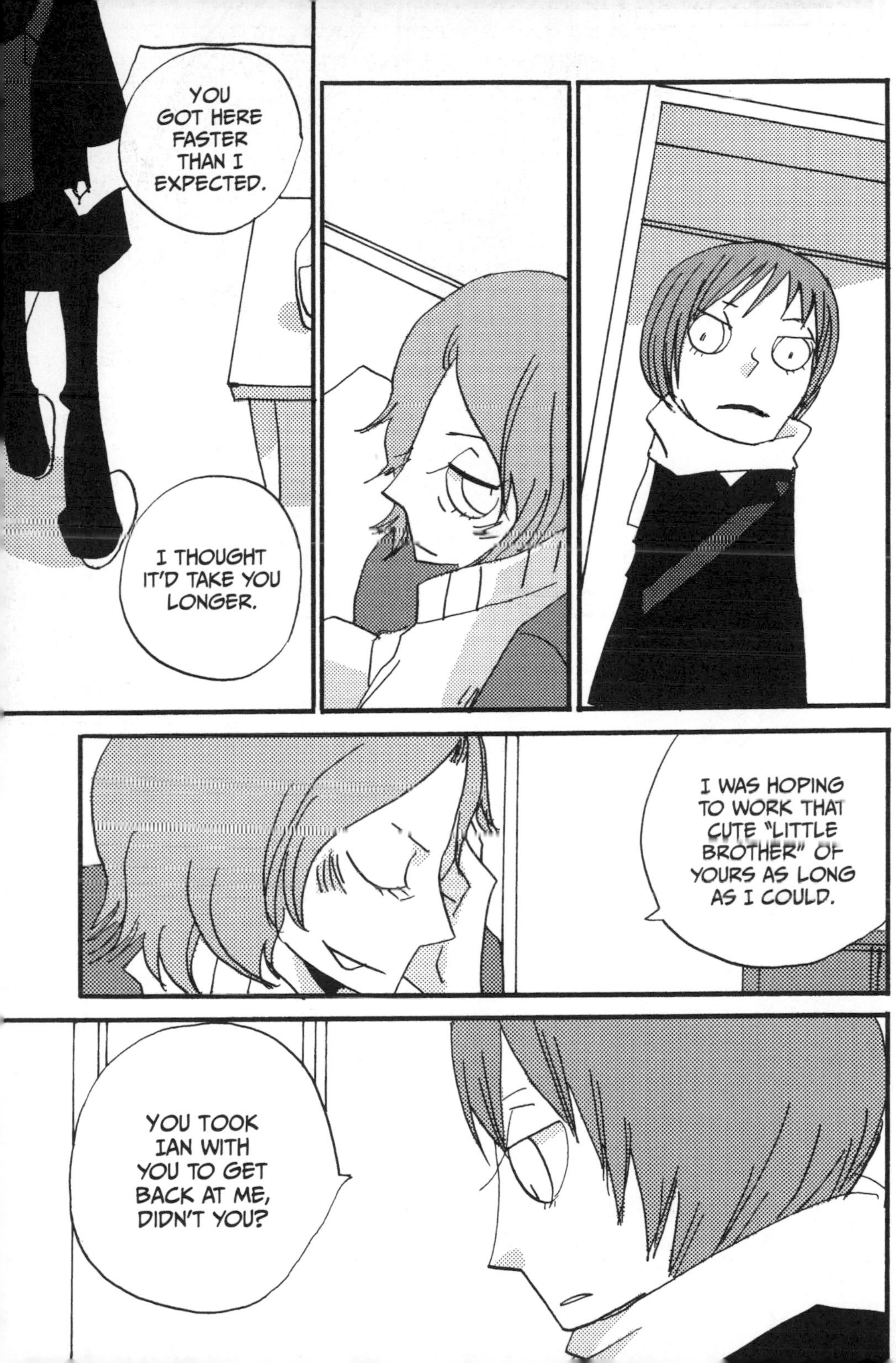
YOU GOT HERE FASTER THAN I EXPECTED.
I THOUGHT IT'D TAKE YOU LONGER.
I WAS HOPING TO WORK THAT CUTE "LITTLE BROTHER" OF YOURS AS LONG AS I COULD.
YOU TOOK IAN WITH YOU TO GET BACK AT ME, DIDN'T YOU?

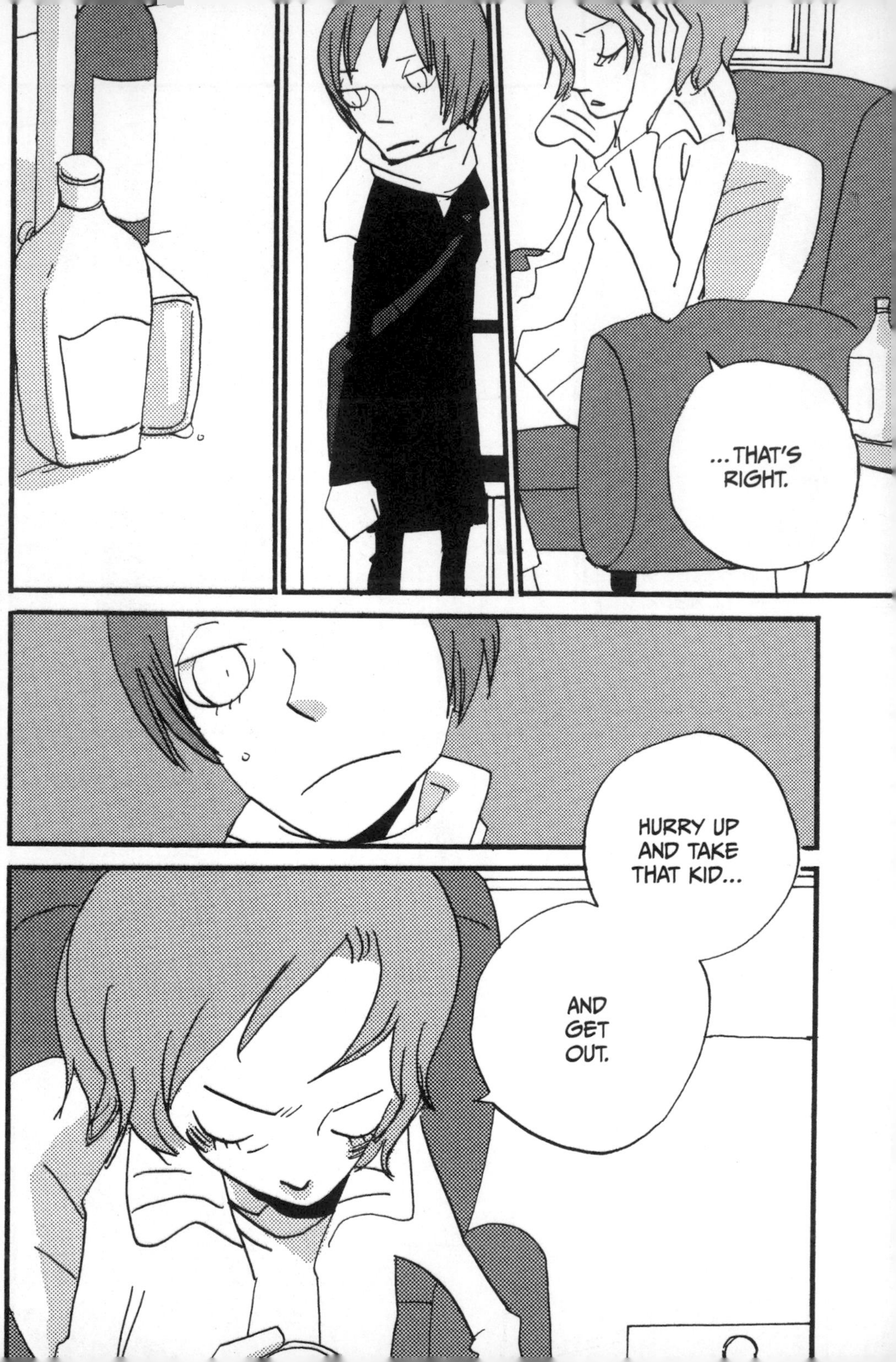
...THAT'S RIGHT.
HURRY UP AND TAKE THAT KID...
AND GET OUT.

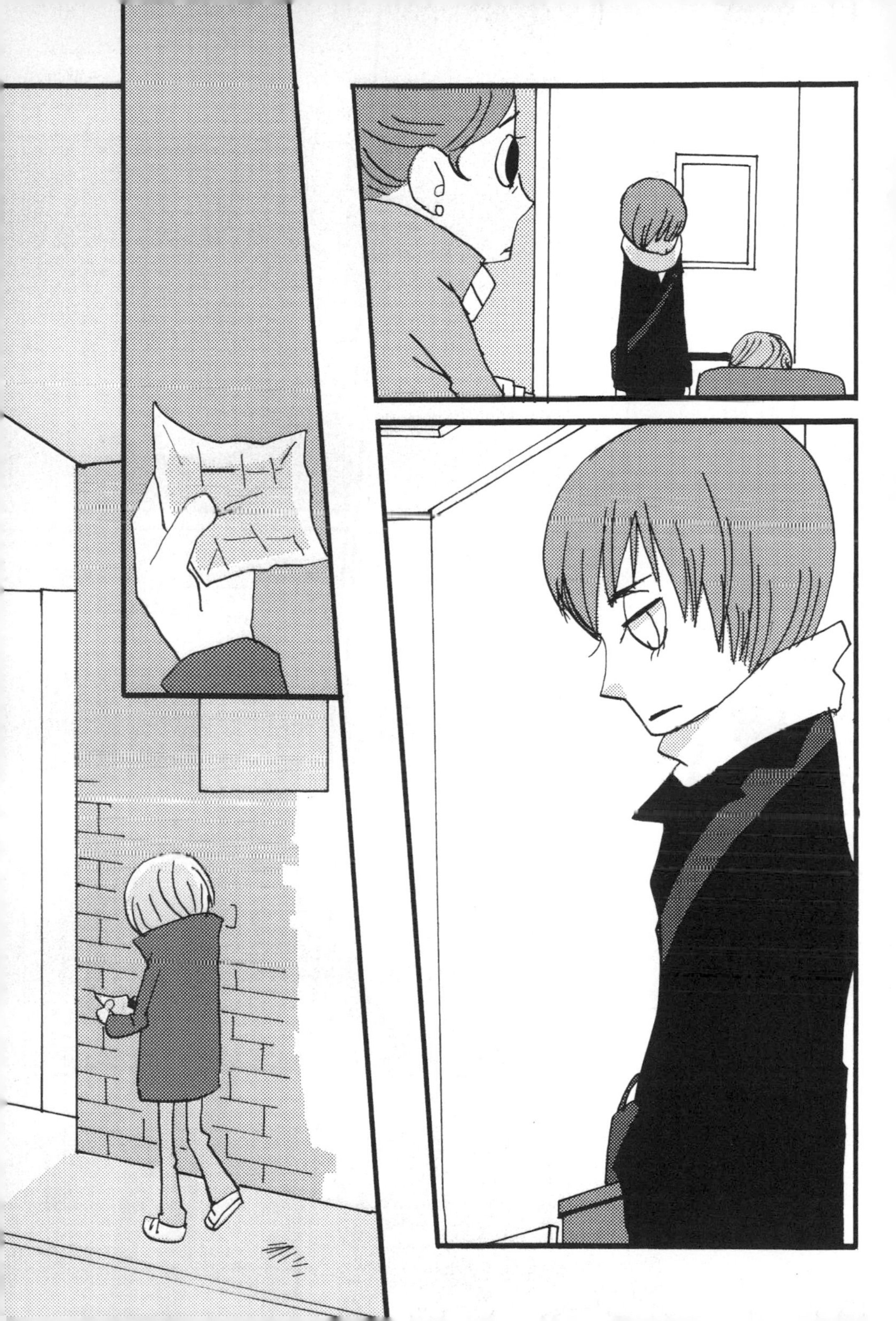

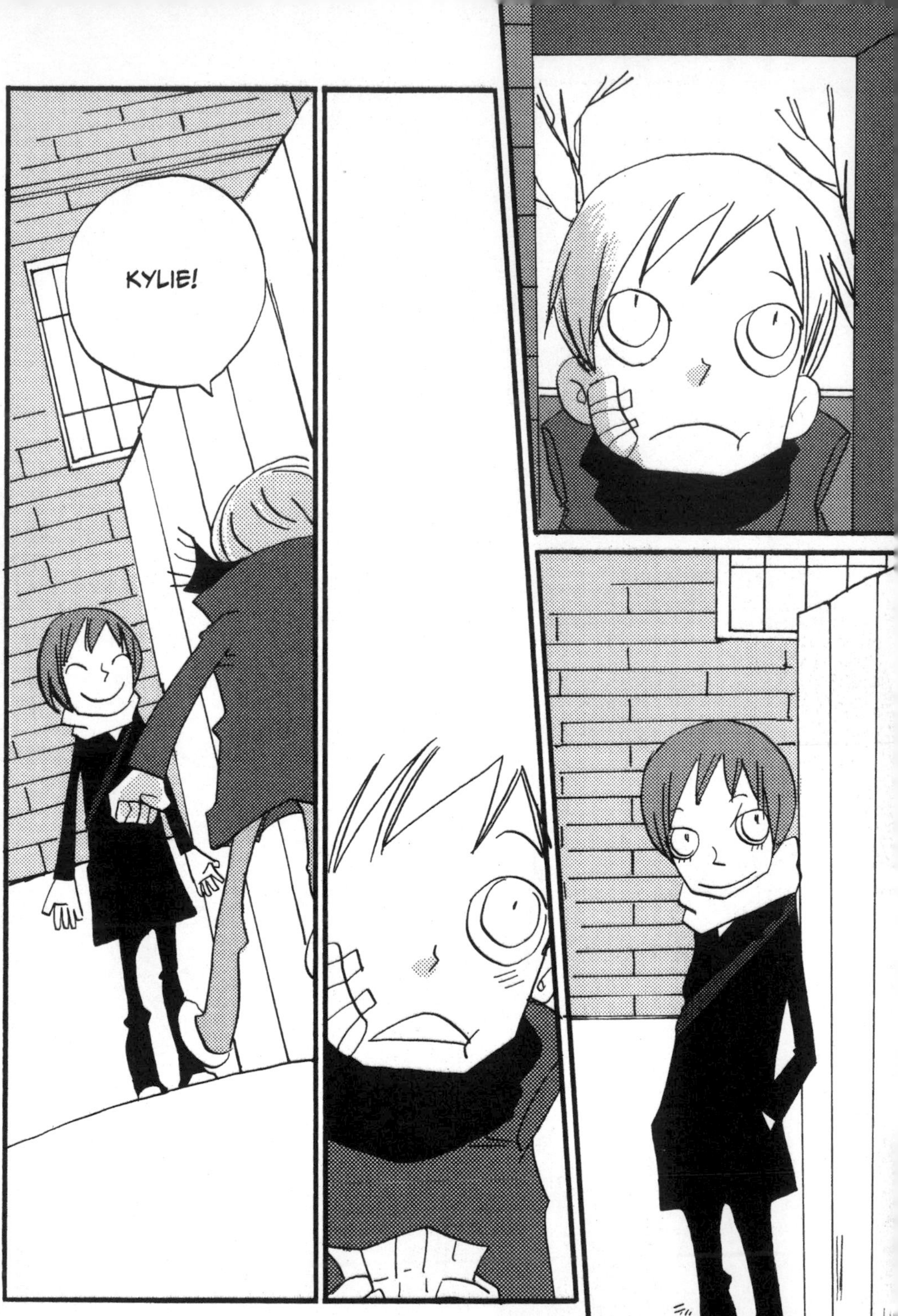
KYLIE!

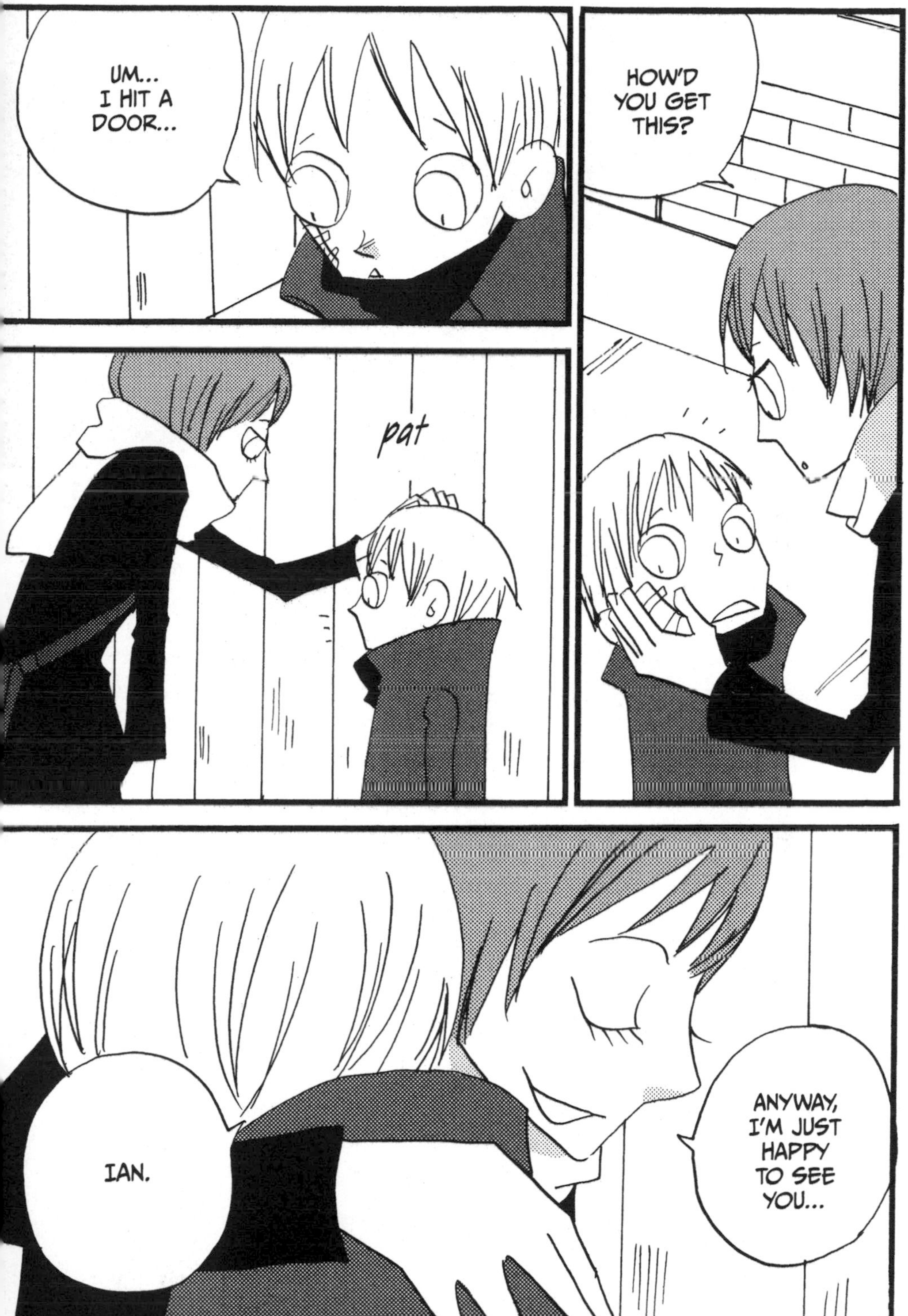
HOW'D YOU GET THIS?
UM... I HIT A DOOR...
pat
ANYWAY, I'M JUST HAPPY TO SEE YOU...
IAN.

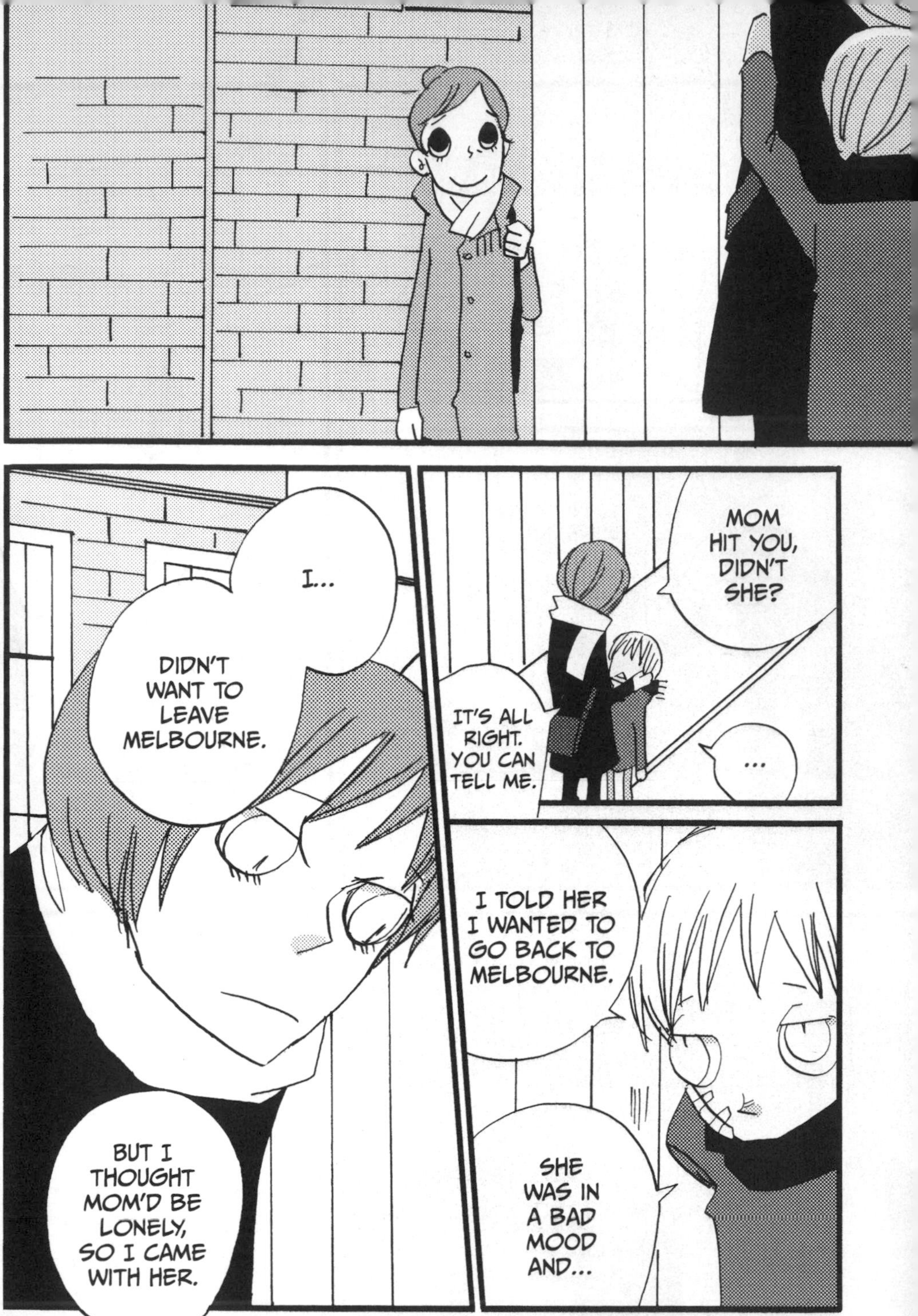
MOM HIT YOU, DIDN'T SHE?
...
IT'S ALL RIGHT. YOU CAN TELL ME.
I TOLD HER I WANTED TO GO BACK TO MELBOURNE.
SHE WAS IN A BAD MOOD AND...
I...
DIDN'T WANT TO LEAVE MELBOURNE.
BUT I THOUGHT MOM'D BE LONELY, SO I CAME WITH HER.

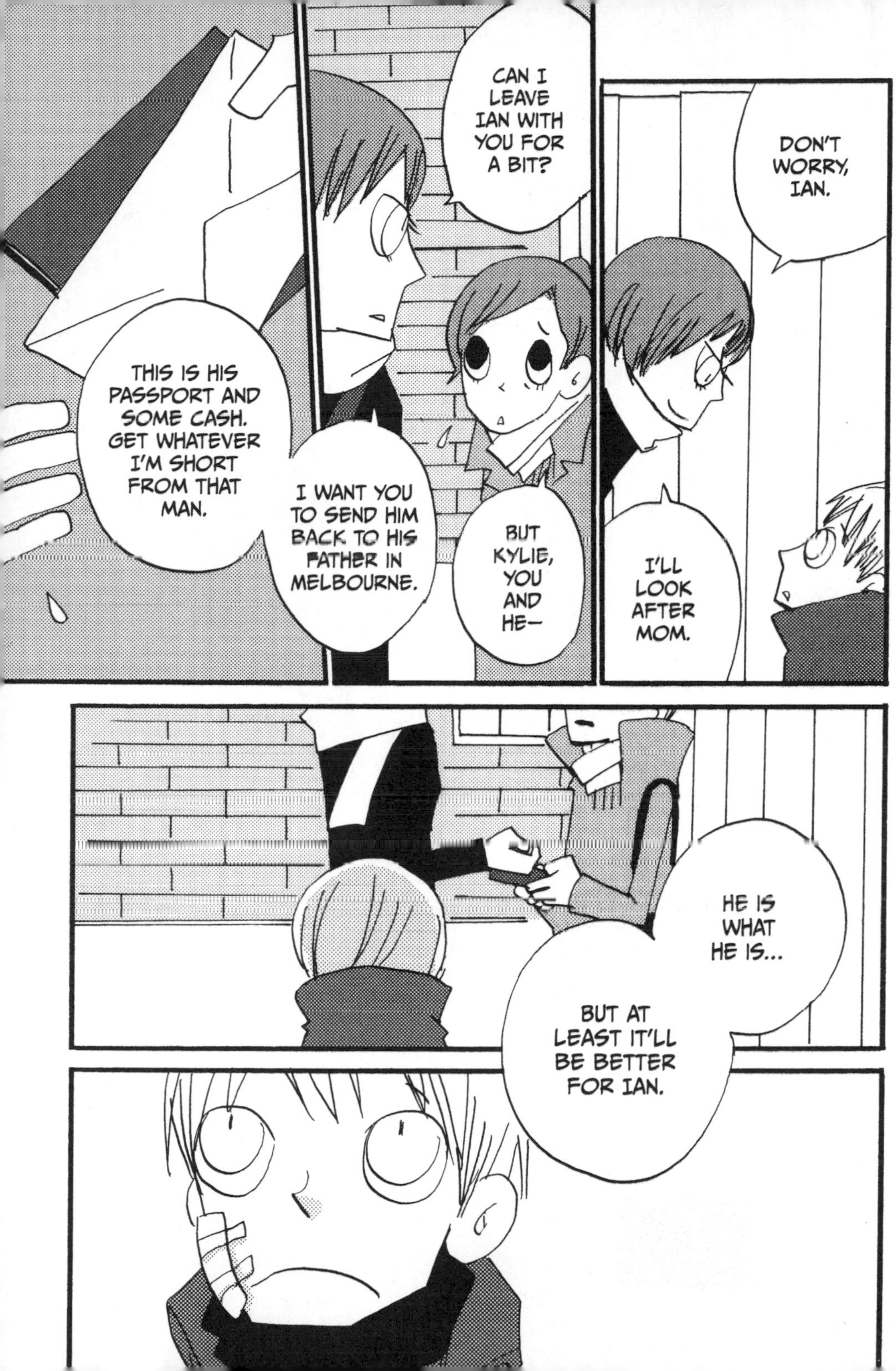
DON'T WORRY, IAN.
I'LL LOOK AFTER MOM.
CAN I LEAVE IAN WITH YOU FOR A BIT?
I WANT YOU TO SEND HIM BACK TO HIS FATHER IN MELBOURNE.
BUT KYLIE, YOU AND HE—
THIS IS HIS PASSPORT AND SOME CASH. GET WHATEVER I'M SHORT FROM THAT MAN.
HE IS WHAT HE IS...
BUT AT LEAST IT'LL BE BETTER FOR IAN.

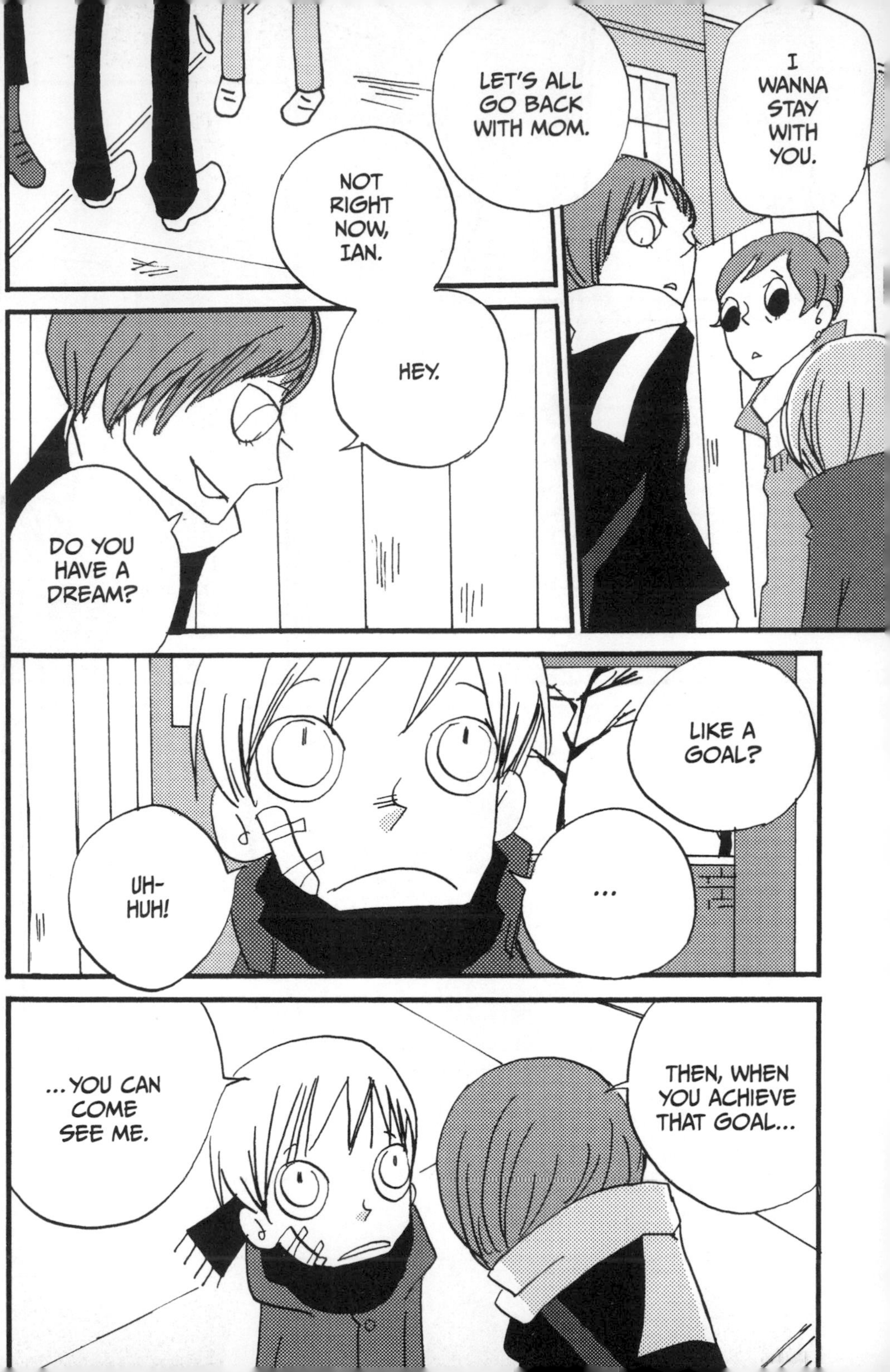
I WANNA STAY WITH YOU.
LET'S ALL GO BACK WITH MOM.
NOT RIGHT NOW, IAN.
HEY.
DO YOU HAVE A DREAM?
LIKE A GOAL?
...
UH-HUH!
THEN, WHEN YOU ACHIEVE THAT GOAL...
...YOU CAN COME SEE ME.

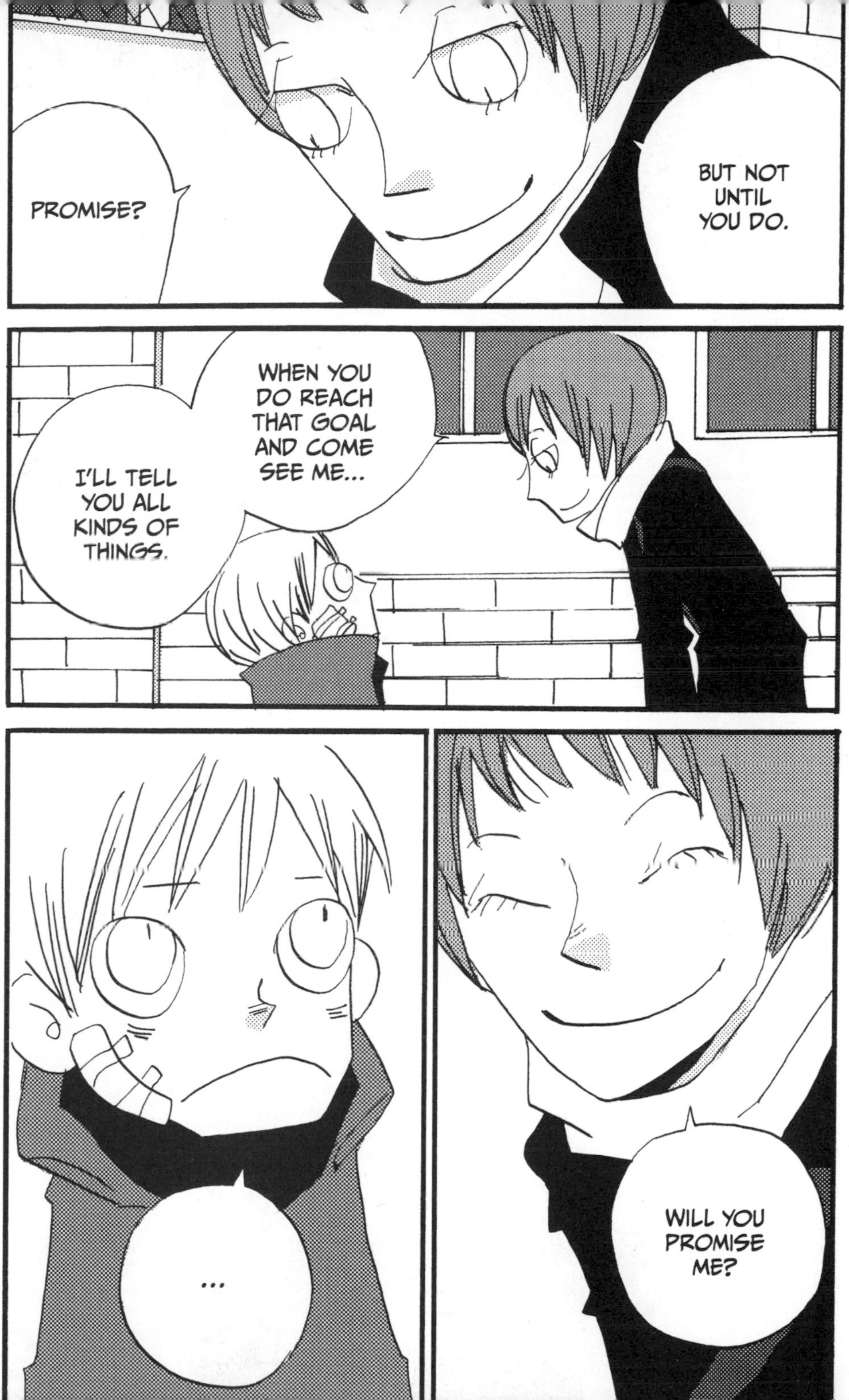
BUT NOT UNTIL YOU DO.
PROMISE?
WHEN YOU DO REACH THAT GOAL AND COME SEE ME...
I'LL TELL YOU ALL KINDS OF THINGS.
WILL YOU PROMISE ME?
...

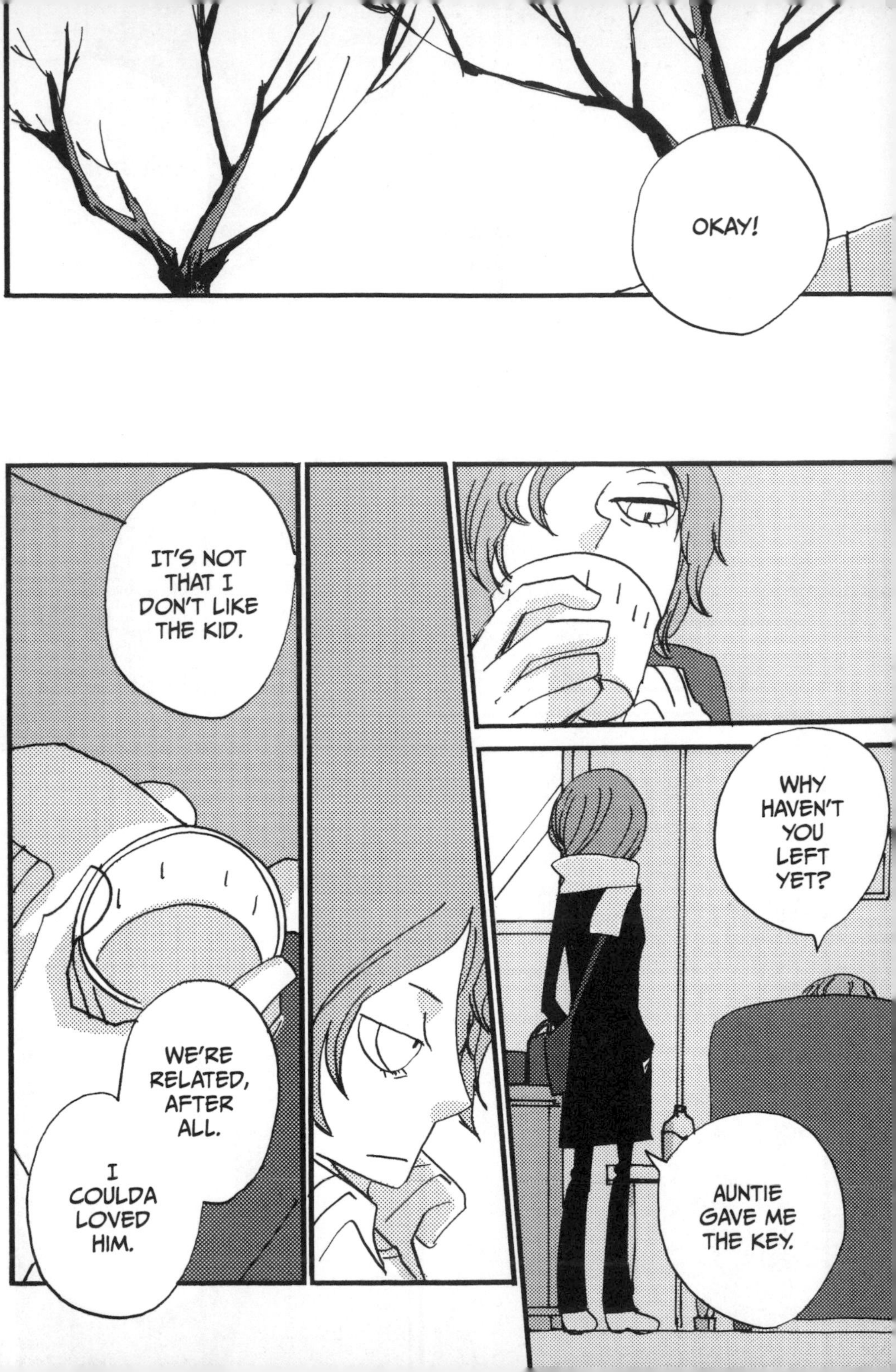
OKAY!
WHY HAVEN'T YOU LEFT YET?
AUNTIE GAVE ME THE KEY.
IT'S NOT THAT I DON'T LIKE THE KID.
WE'RE RELATED, AFTER ALL.
I COULDA LOVED HIM.

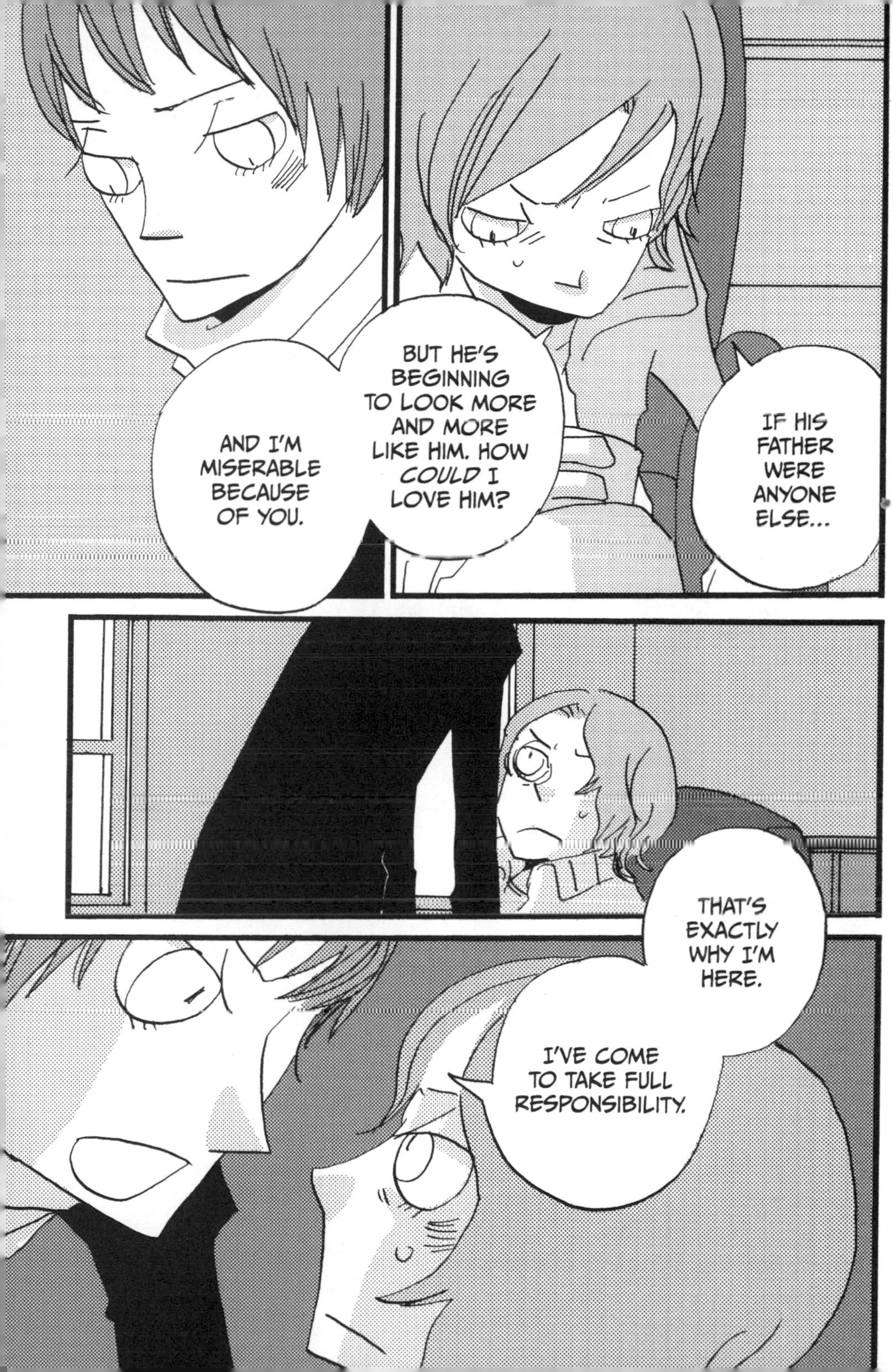
IF HIS FATHER WERE ANYONE ELSE...
BUT HE'S BEGINNING TO LOOK MORE AND MORE LIKE HIM. HOW *COULD* I LOVE HIM?
AND I'M MISERABLE BECAUSE OF YOU.
THAT'S EXACTLY WHY I'M HERE.
I'VE COME TO TAKE FULL RESPONSIBILITY.

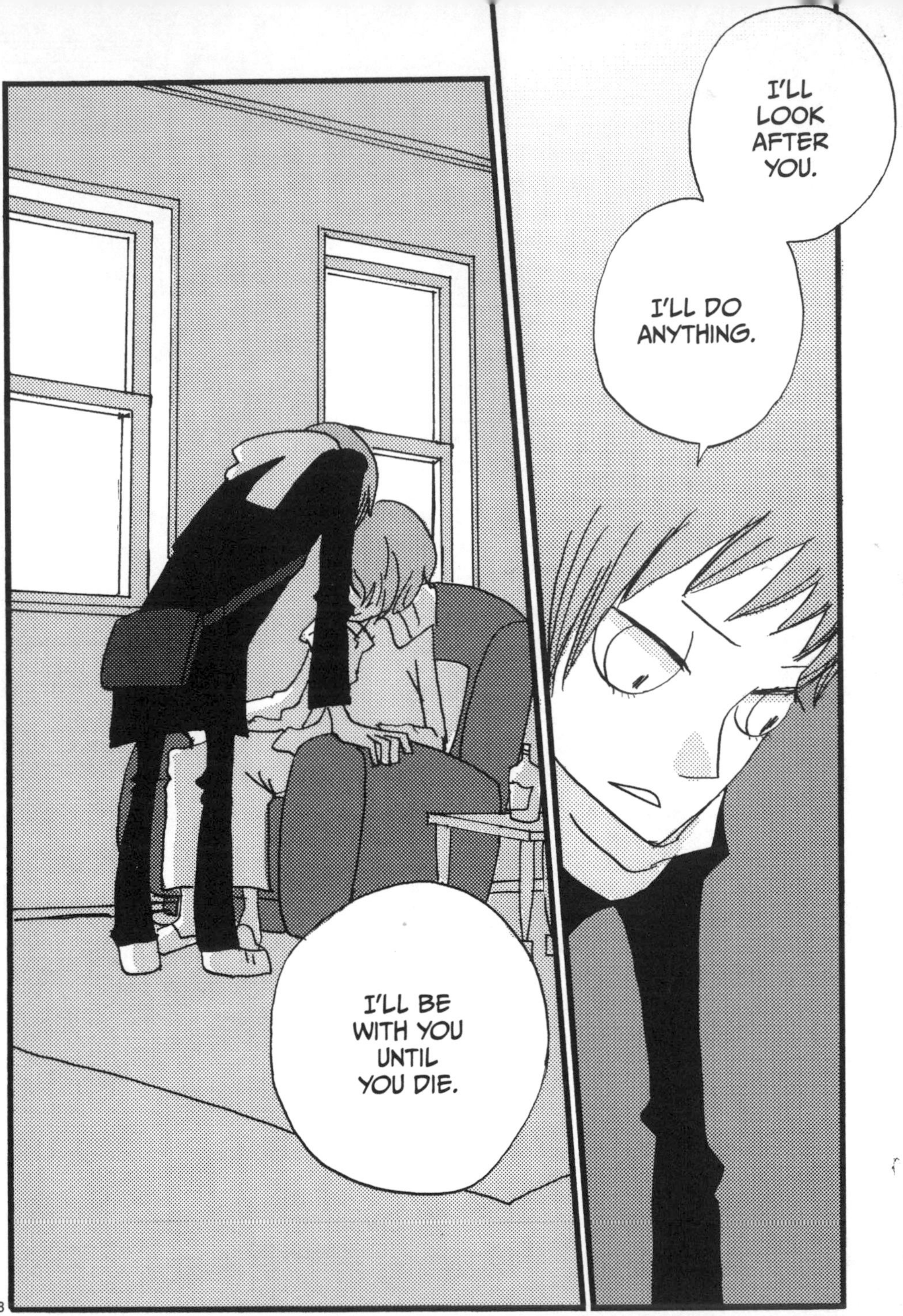
I'LL LOOK AFTER YOU.
I'LL DO ANYTHING.
I'LL BE WITH YOU UNTIL YOU DIE.

#04 not simple

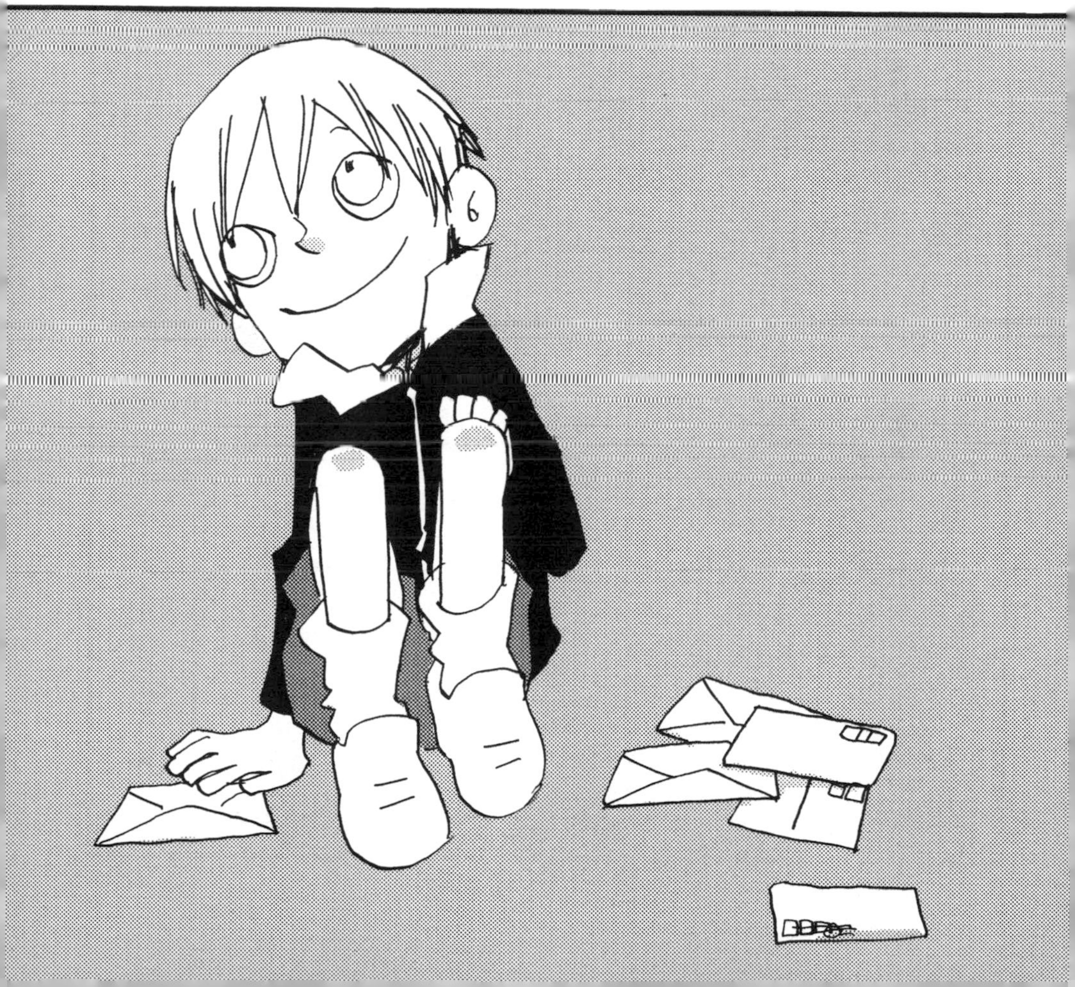

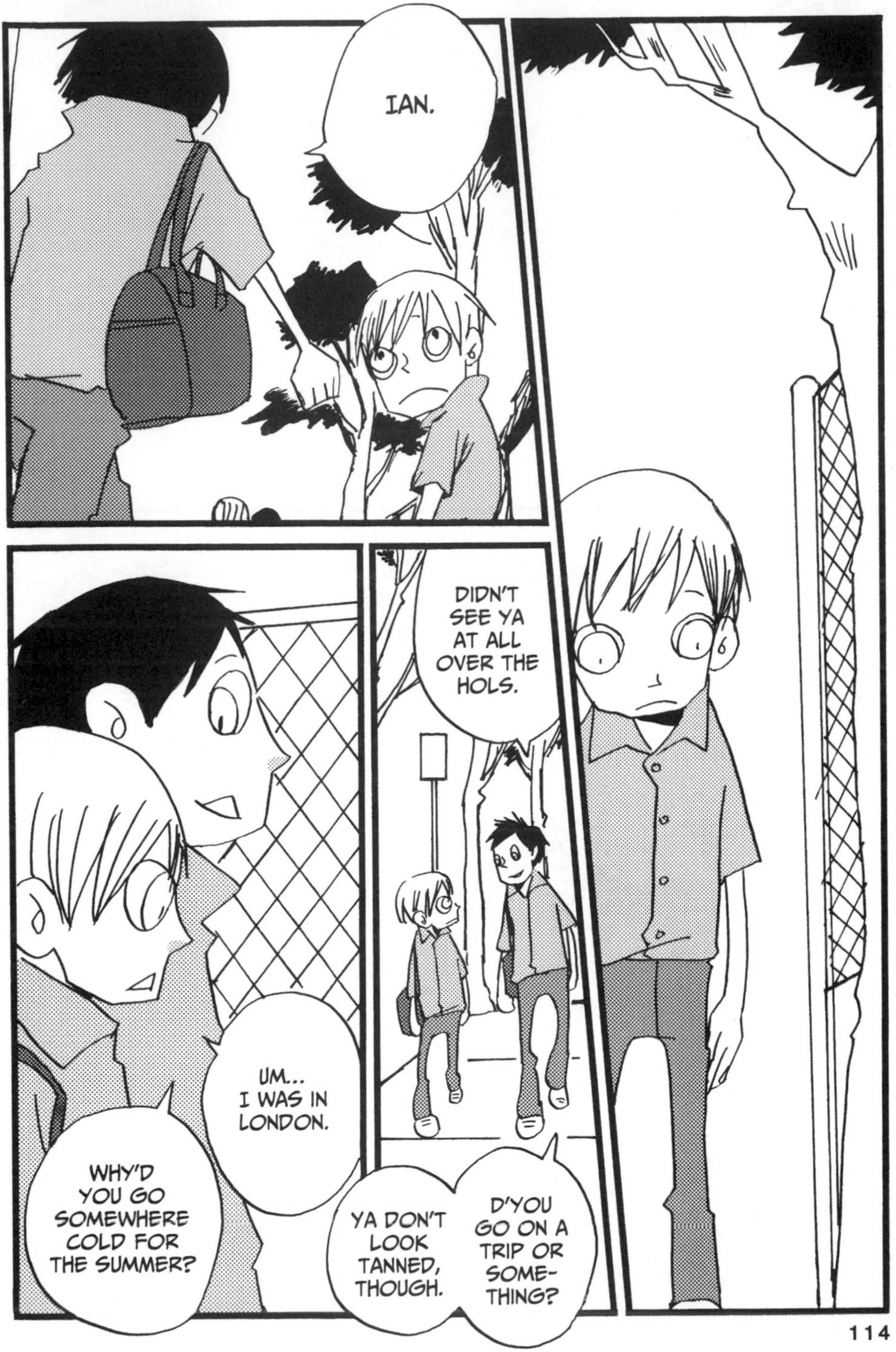
IAN.
DIDN'T SEE YA AT ALL OVER THE HOLS.
D'YOU GO ON A TRIP OR SOME-THING?
YA DON'T LOOK TANNED, THOUGH.
UM... I WAS IN LONDON.
WHY'D YOU GO SOMEWHERE COLD FOR THE SUMMER?

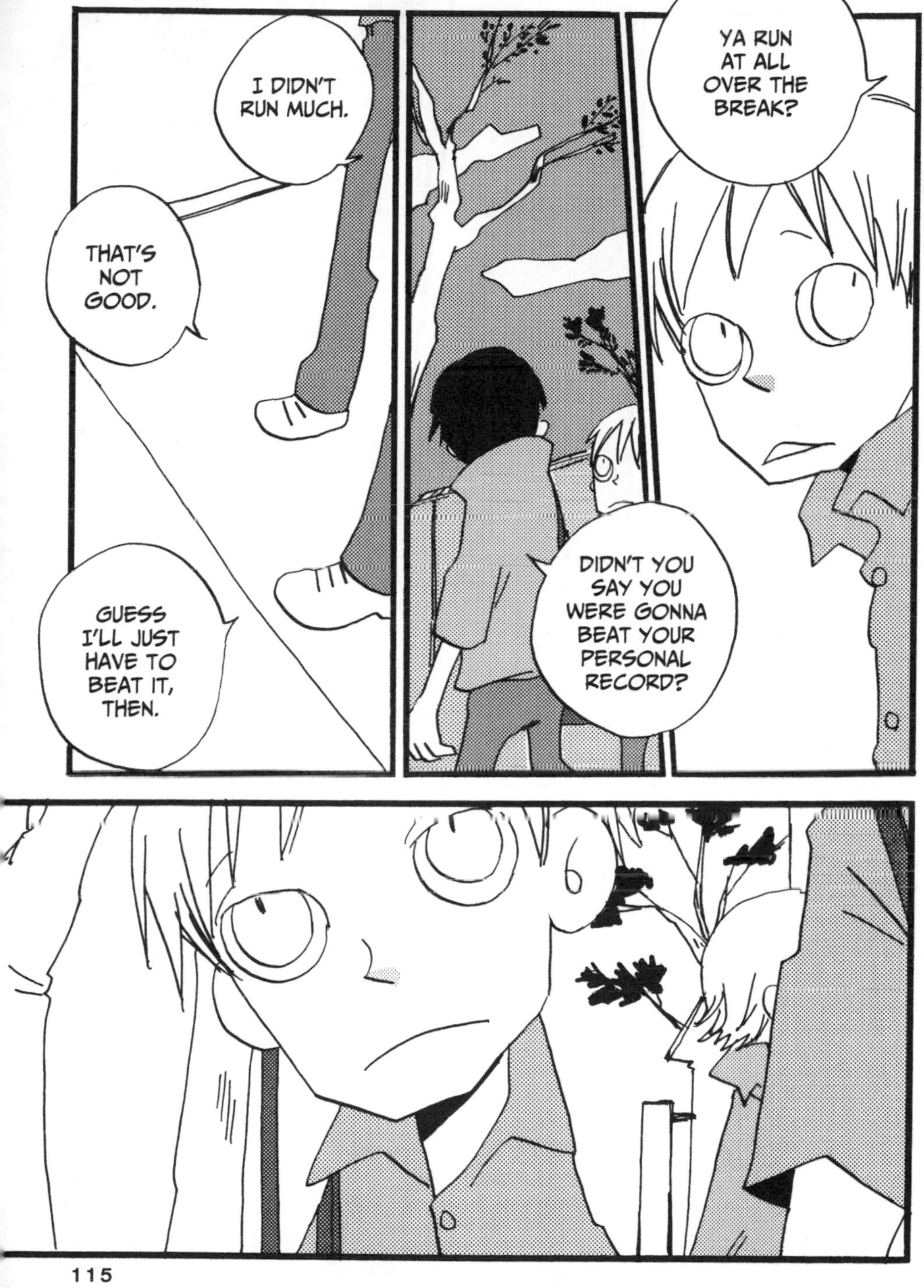
YA RUN AT ALL OVER THE BREAK?
DIDN'T YOU SAY YOU WERE GONNA BEAT YOUR PERSONAL RECORD?
I DIDN'T RUN MUCH.
THAT'S NOT GOOD.
GUESS I'LL JUST HAVE TO BEAT IT, THEN.

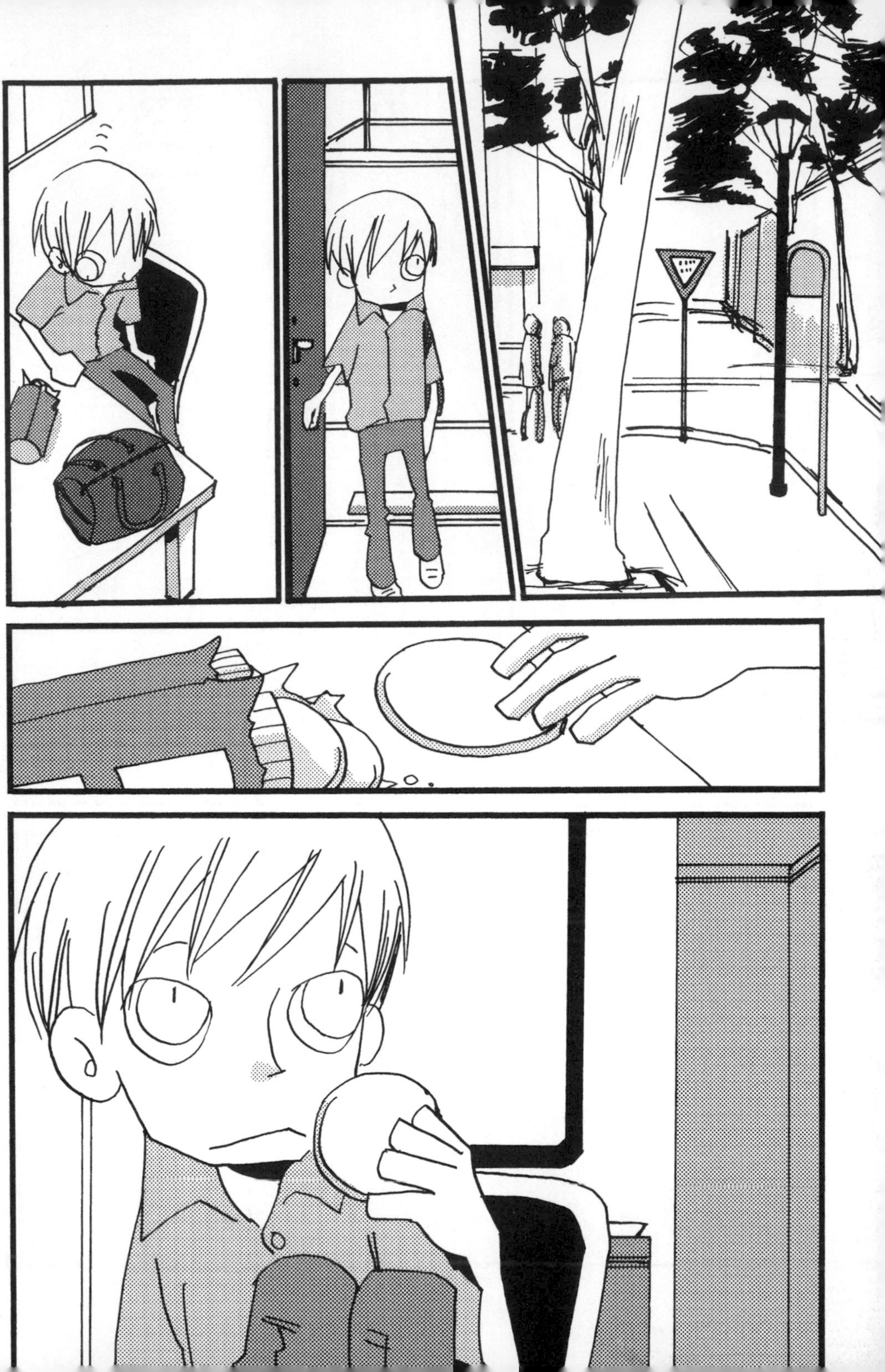

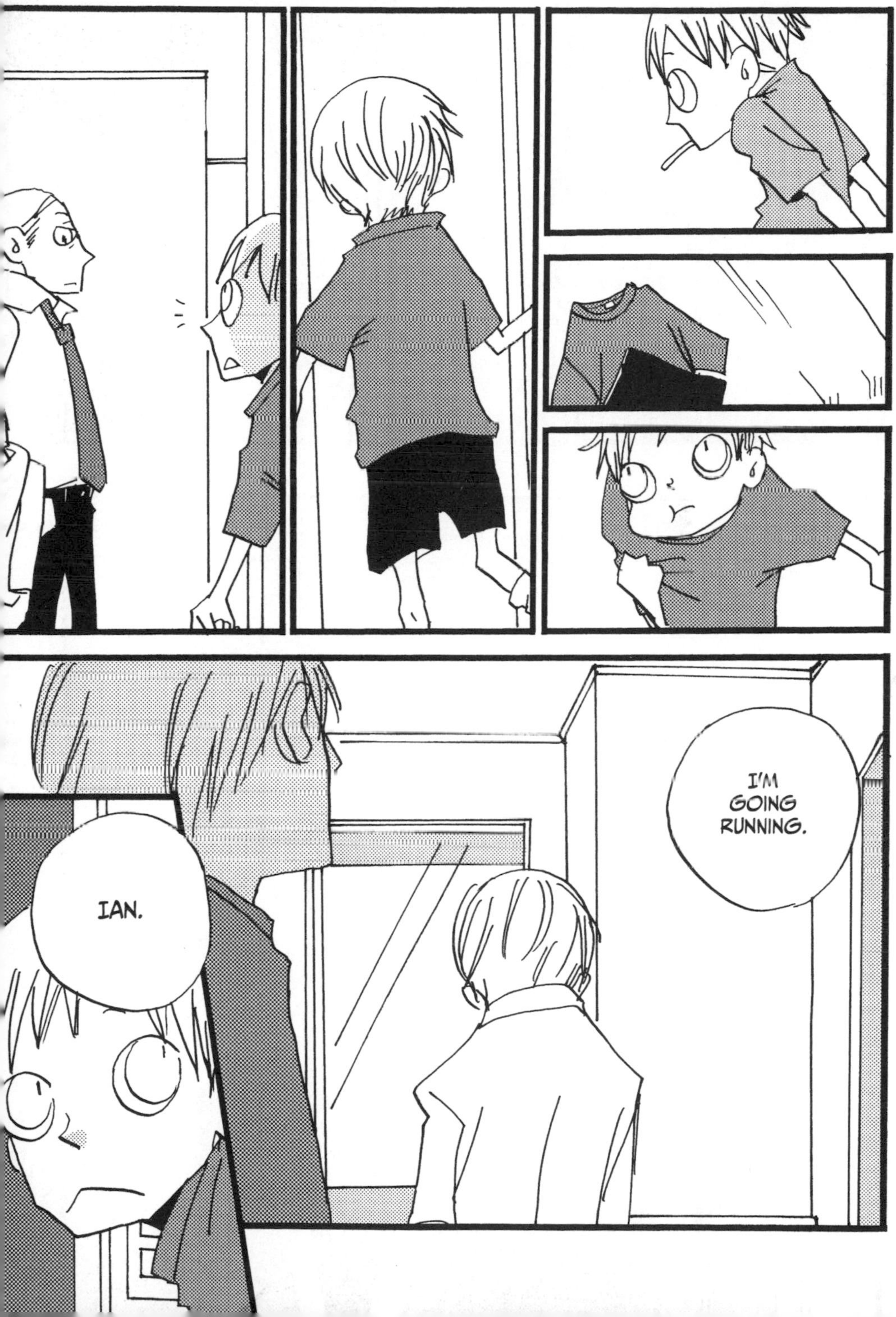
I'M GOING RUNNING.
IAN.

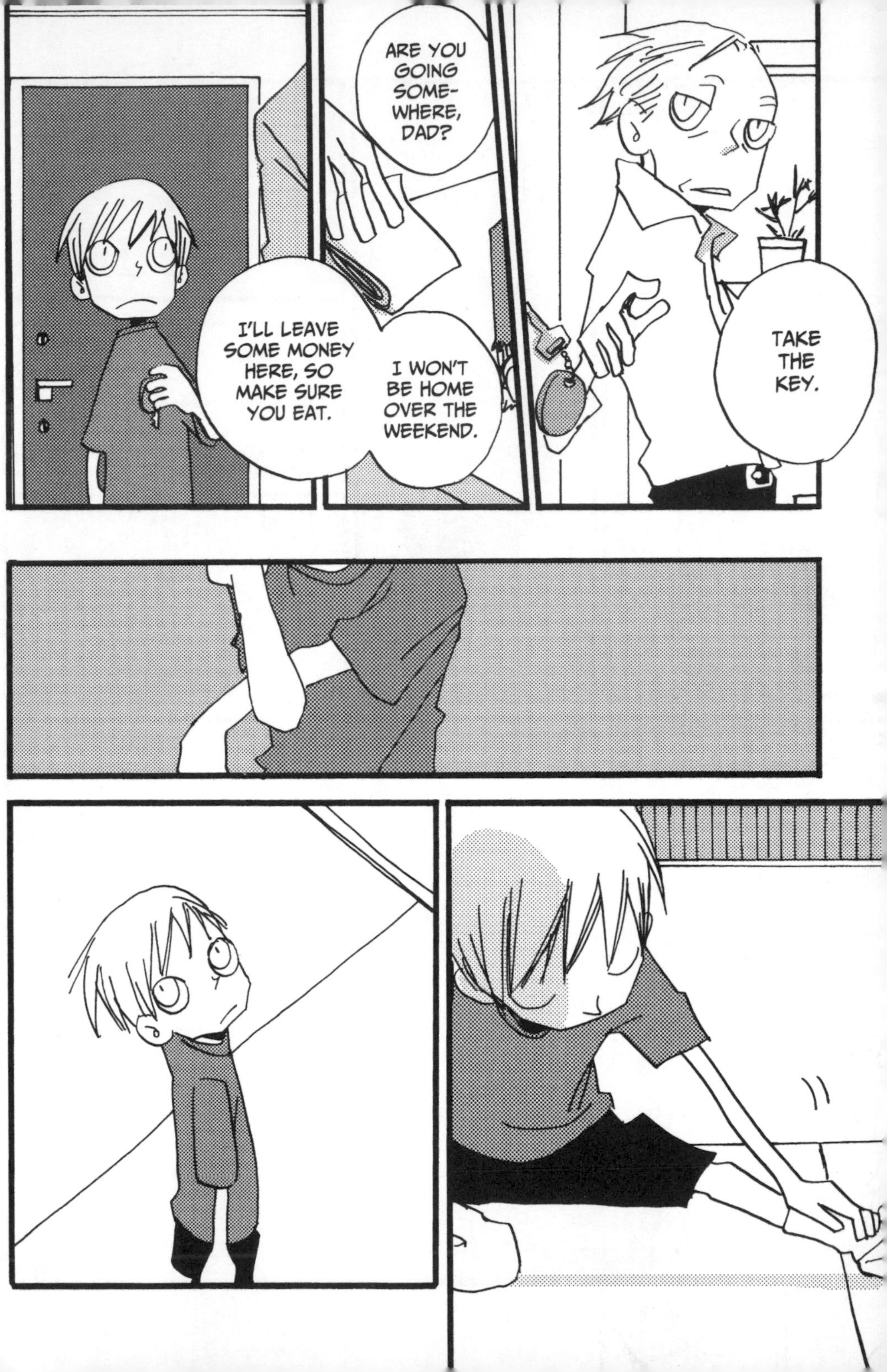
TAKE THE KEY.
ARE YOU GOING SOME-WHERE, DAD?
I WON'T BE HOME OVER THE WEEKEND.
I'LL LEAVE SOME MONEY HERE, SO MAKE SURE YOU EAT.

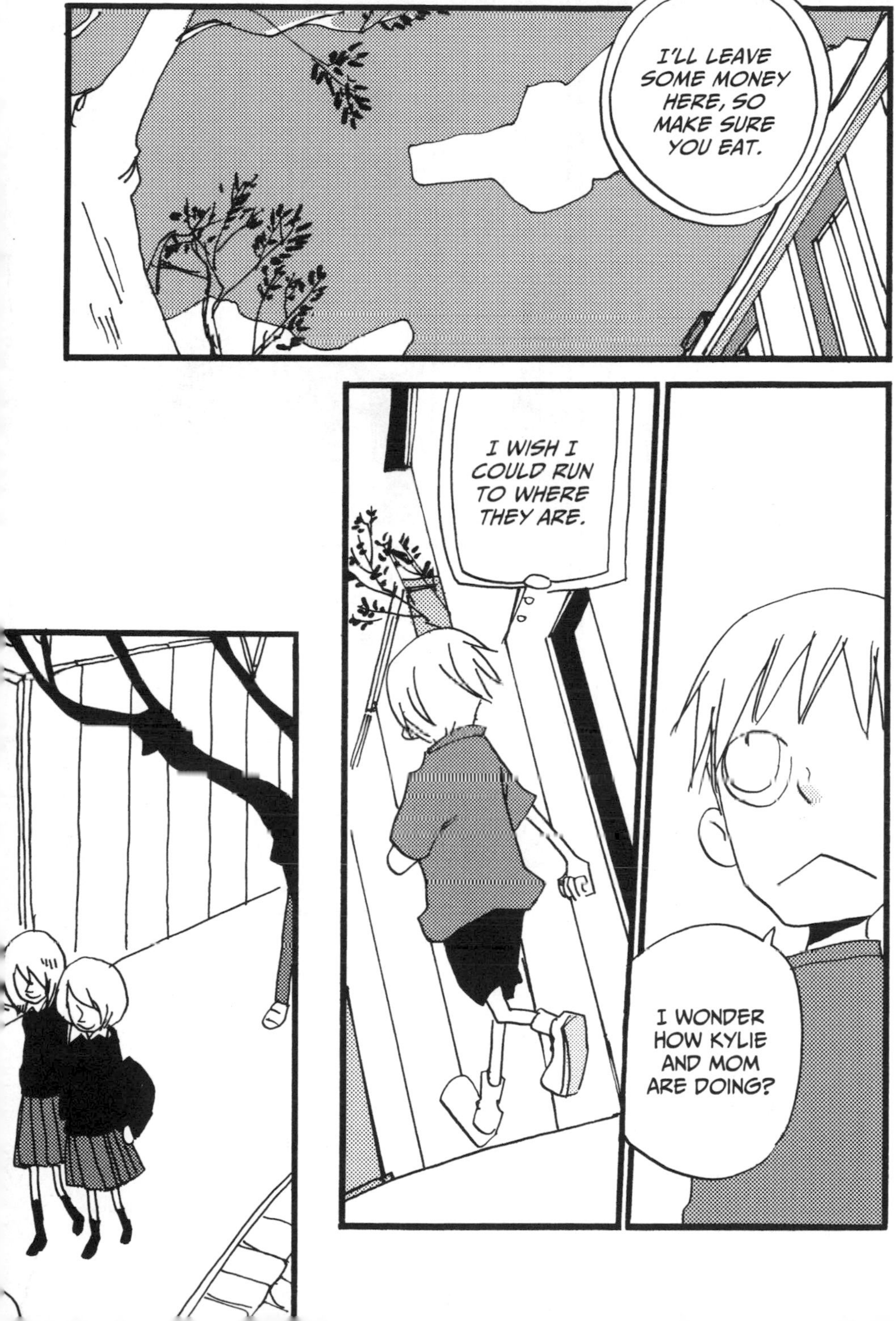
I'LL LEAVE SOME MONEY HERE, SO MAKE SURE YOU EAT.
I WONDER HOW KYLIE AND MOM ARE DOING?
I WISH I COULD RUN TO WHERE THEY ARE.

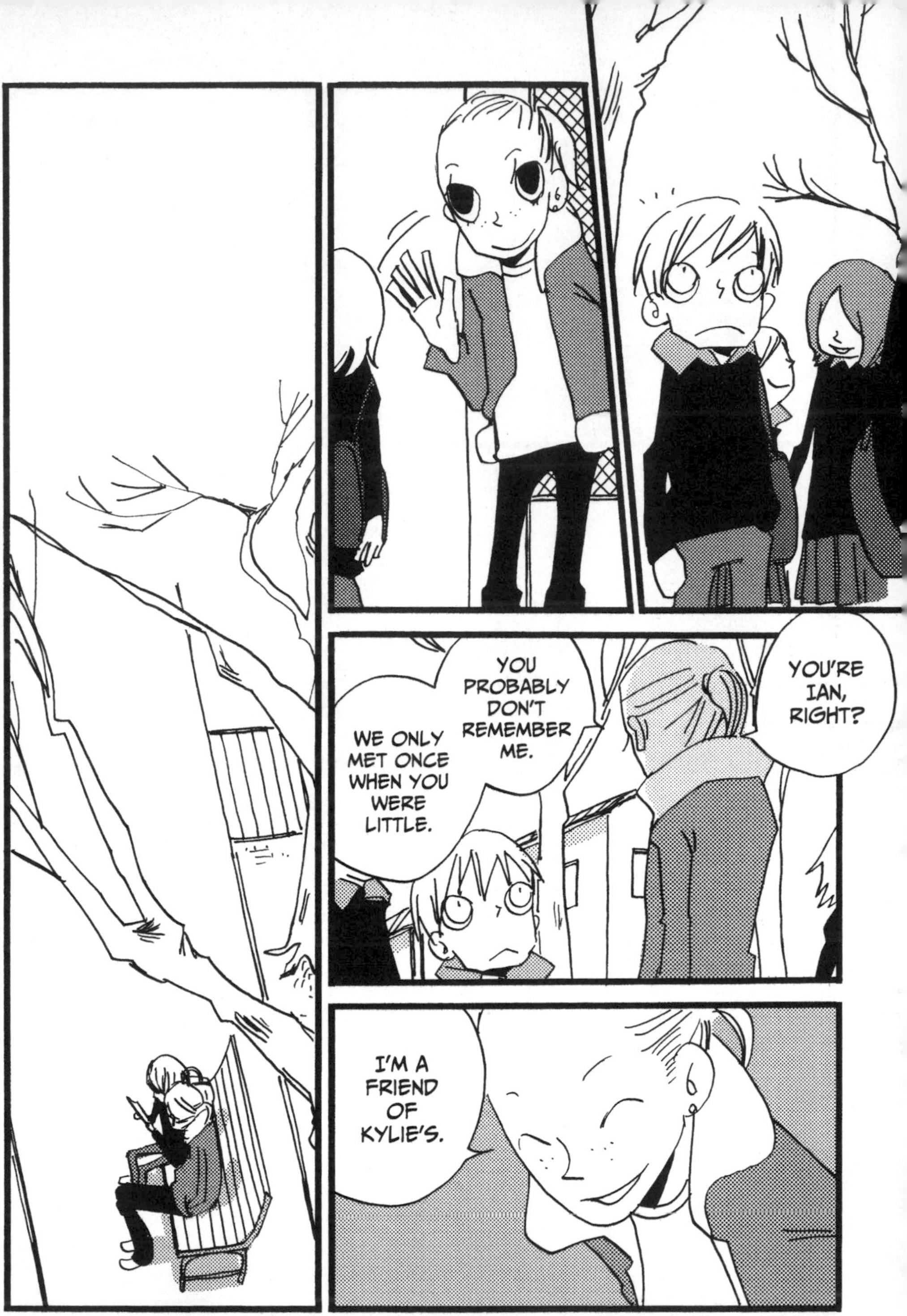
YOU'RE IAN, RIGHT?
YOU PROBABLY DON'T REMEMBER ME.
WE ONLY MET ONCE WHEN YOU WERE LITTLE.
I'M A FRIEND OF KYLIE'S.

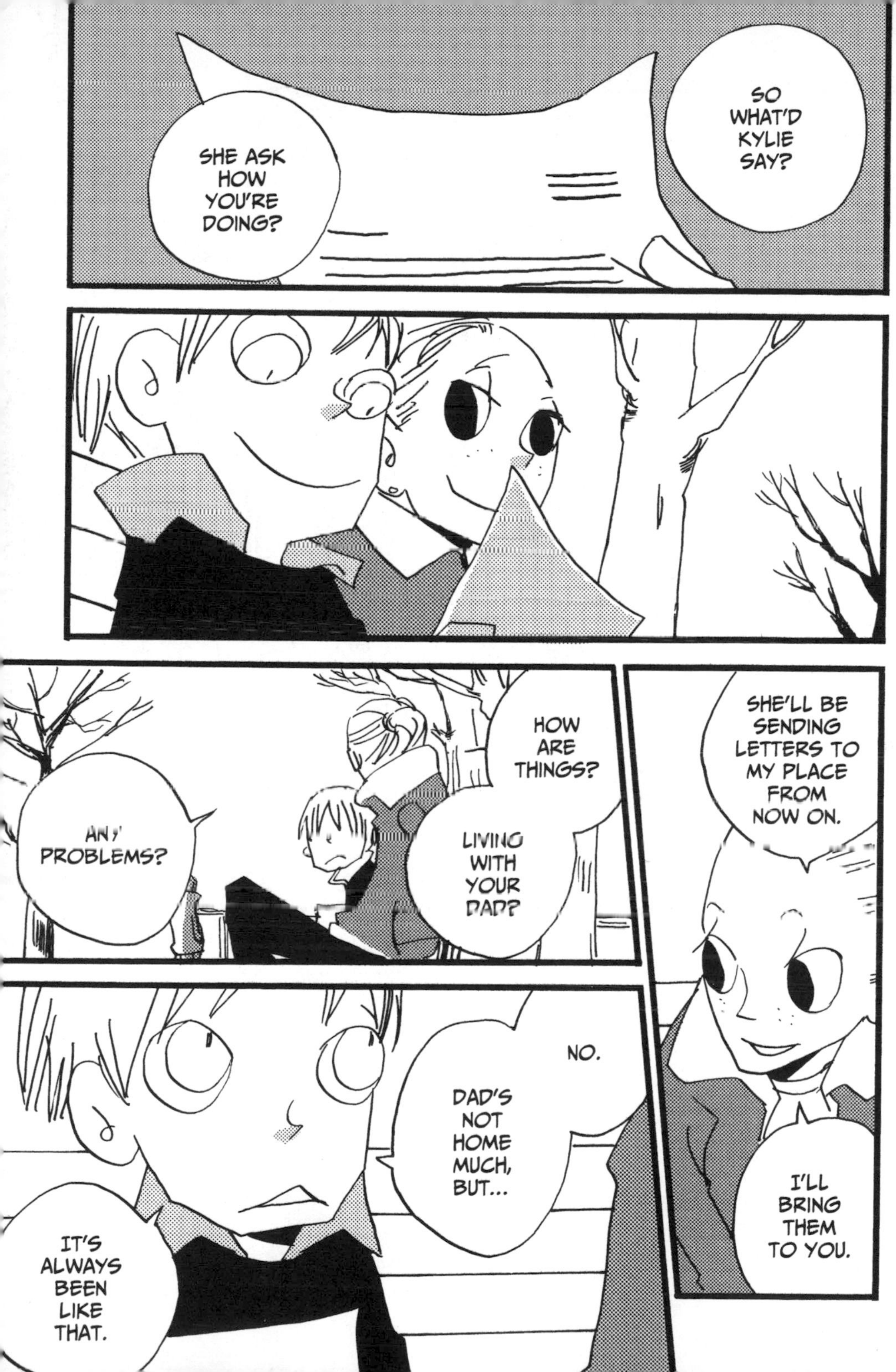
SO WHAT'D KYLIE SAY?
SHE ASK HOW YOU'RE DOING?
SHE'LL BE SENDING LETTERS TO MY PLACE FROM NOW ON.
I'LL BRING THEM TO YOU.
HOW ARE THINGS?
LIVING WITH YOUR DAD?
ANY PROBLEMS?
NO.
DAD'S NOT HOME MUCH, BUT...
IT'S ALWAYS BEEN LIKE THAT.

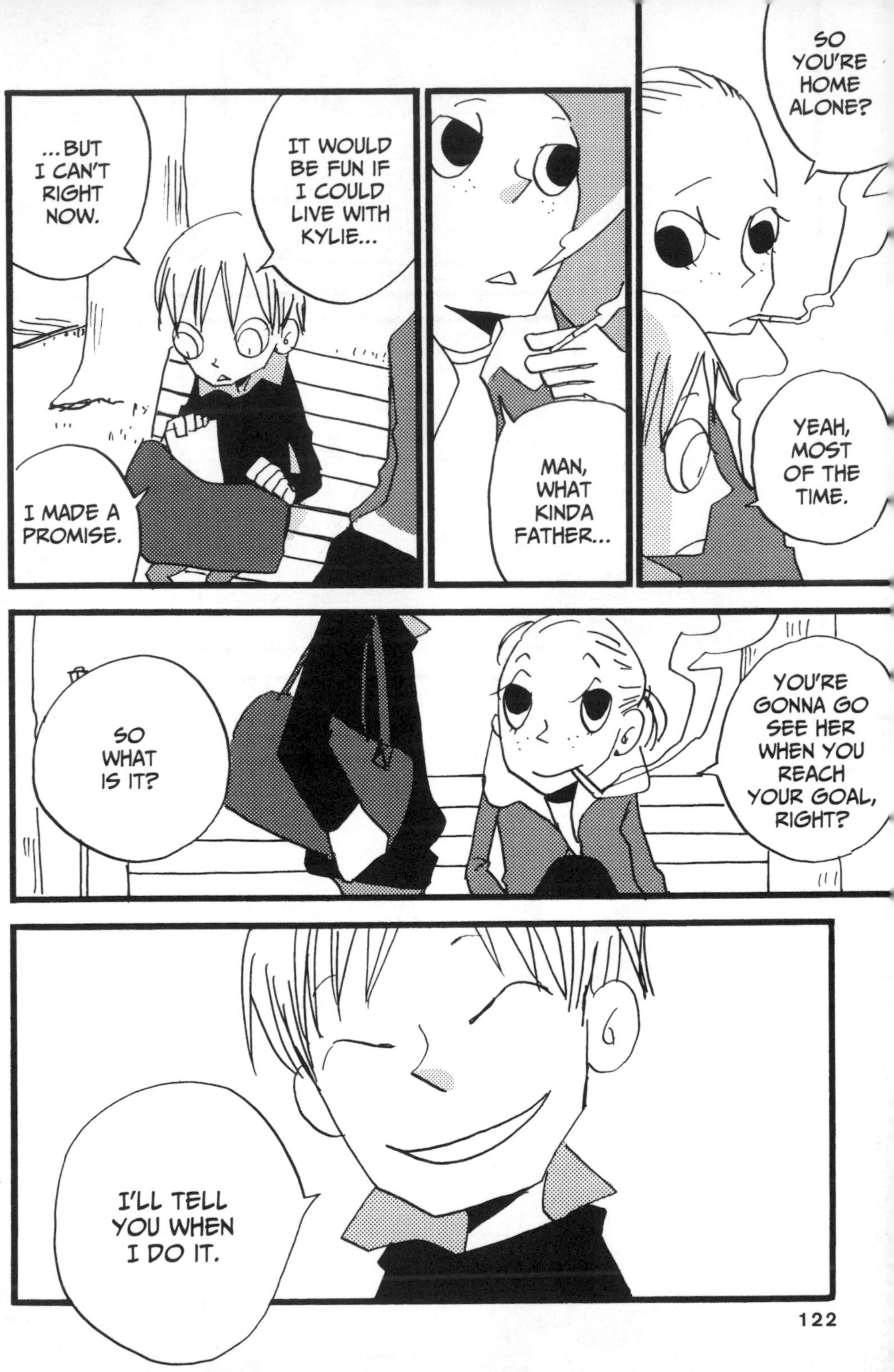
SO YOU'RE HOME ALONE?
YEAH, MOST OF THE TIME.
MAN, WHAT KINDA FATHER...
IT WOULD BE FUN IF I COULD LIVE WITH KYLIE...
...BUT I CAN'T RIGHT NOW.
I MADE A PROMISE.
YOU'RE GONNA GO SEE HER WHEN YOU REACH YOUR GOAL, RIGHT?
SO WHAT IS IT?
I'LL TELL YOU WHEN I DO IT.

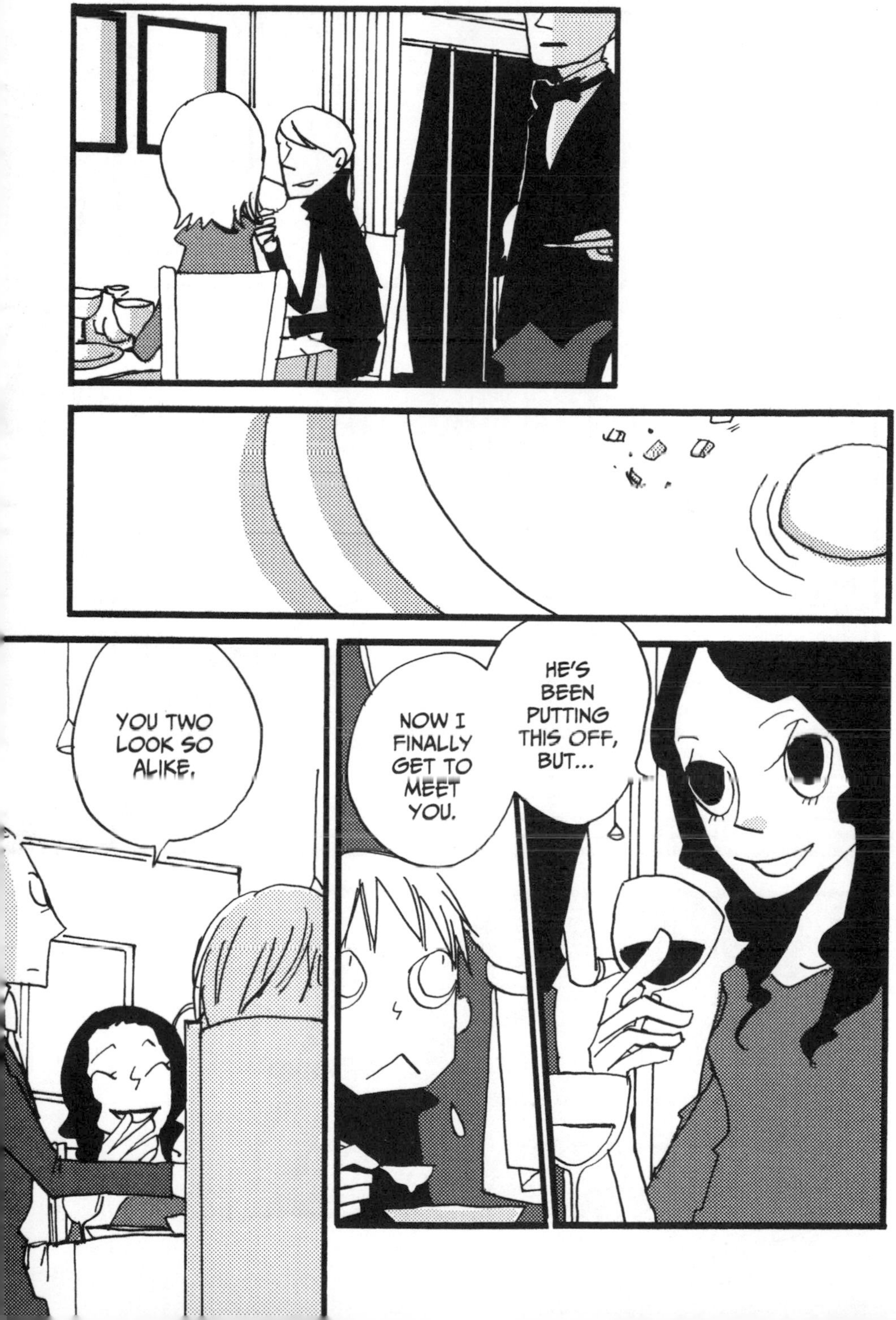
HE'S BEEN PUTTING THIS OFF, BUT...
NOW I FINALLY GET TO MEET YOU.
YOU TWO LOOK SO ALIKE.

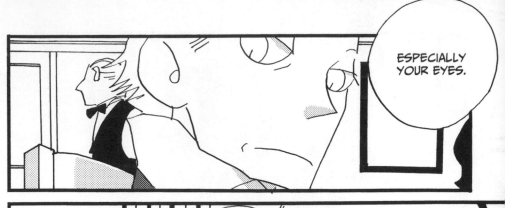

ESPECIALLY YOUR EYES.

WELL, I AM HIS FATHER.

THAT'S TRUE.

IAN.

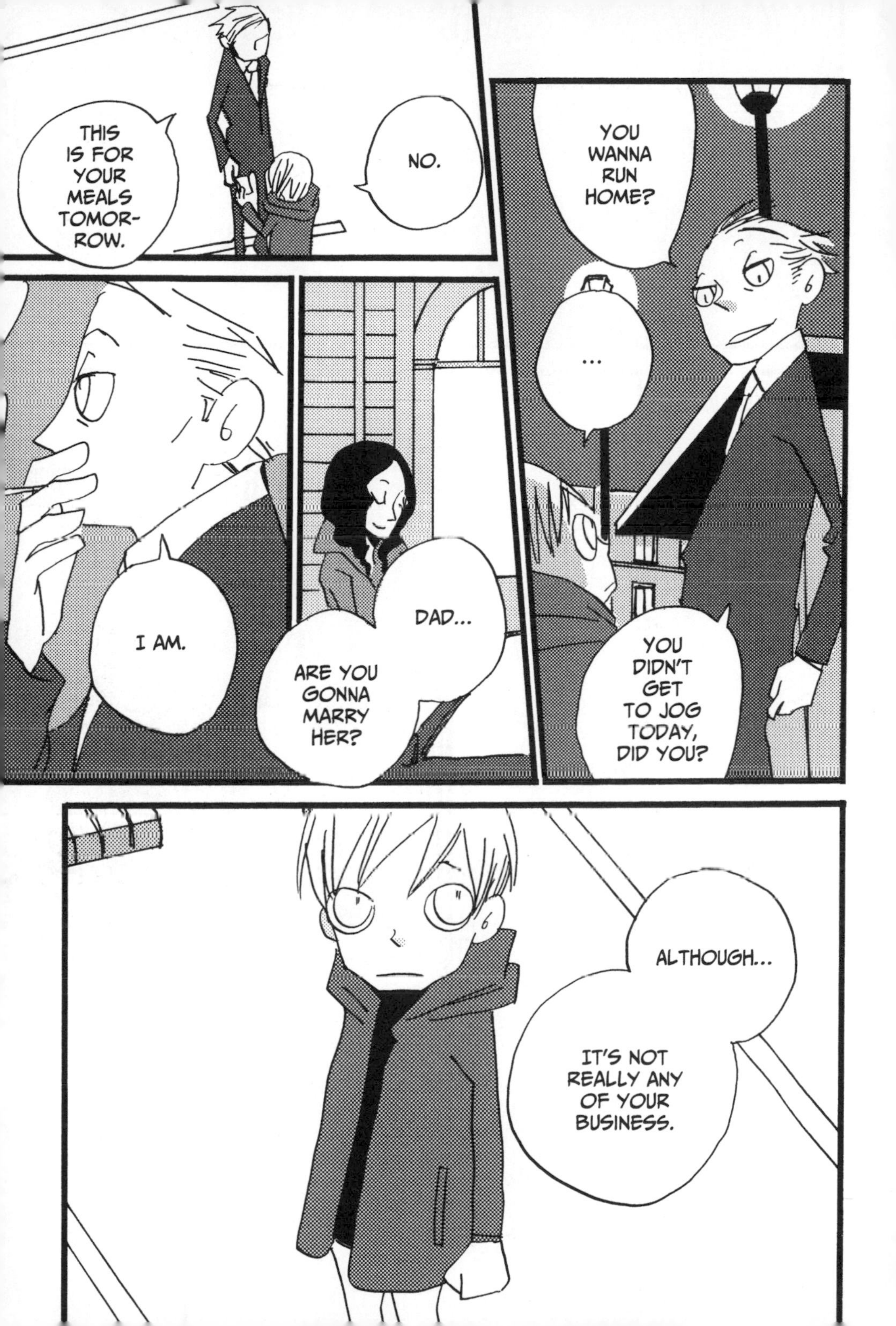
YOU WANNA RUN HOME?
...
YOU DIDN'T GET TO JOG TODAY, DID YOU?
NO.
THIS IS FOR YOUR MEALS TOMOR-ROW.
DAD...
ARE YOU GONNA MARRY HER?
I AM.
ALTHOUGH...
IT'S NOT REALLY ANY OF YOUR BUSINESS.

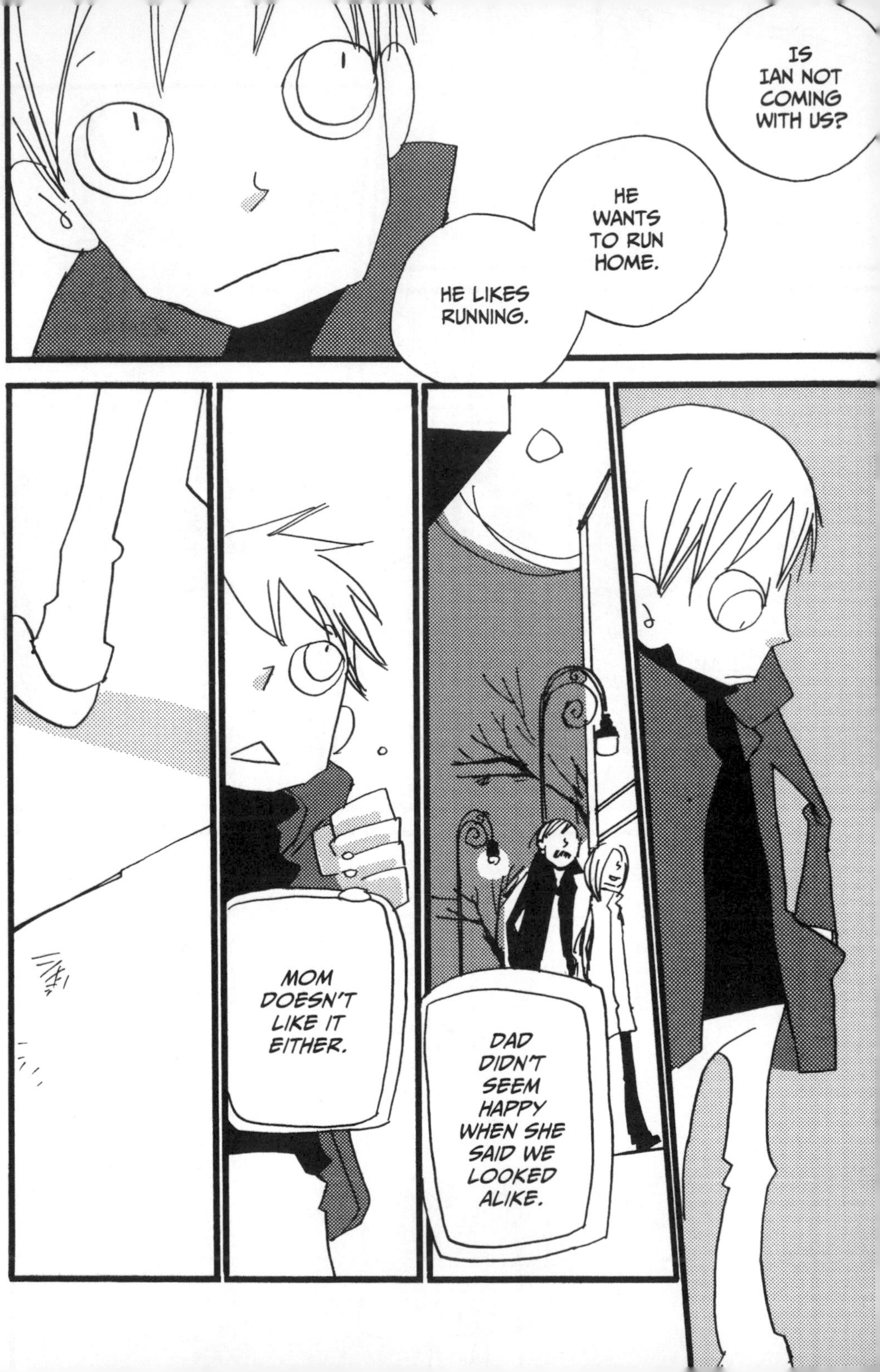
IS IAN NOT COMING WITH US?
HE WANTS TO RUN HOME.
HE LIKES RUNNING.
DAD DIDN'T SEEM HAPPY WHEN SHE SAID WE LOOKED ALIKE.
MOM DOESN'T LIKE IT EITHER.

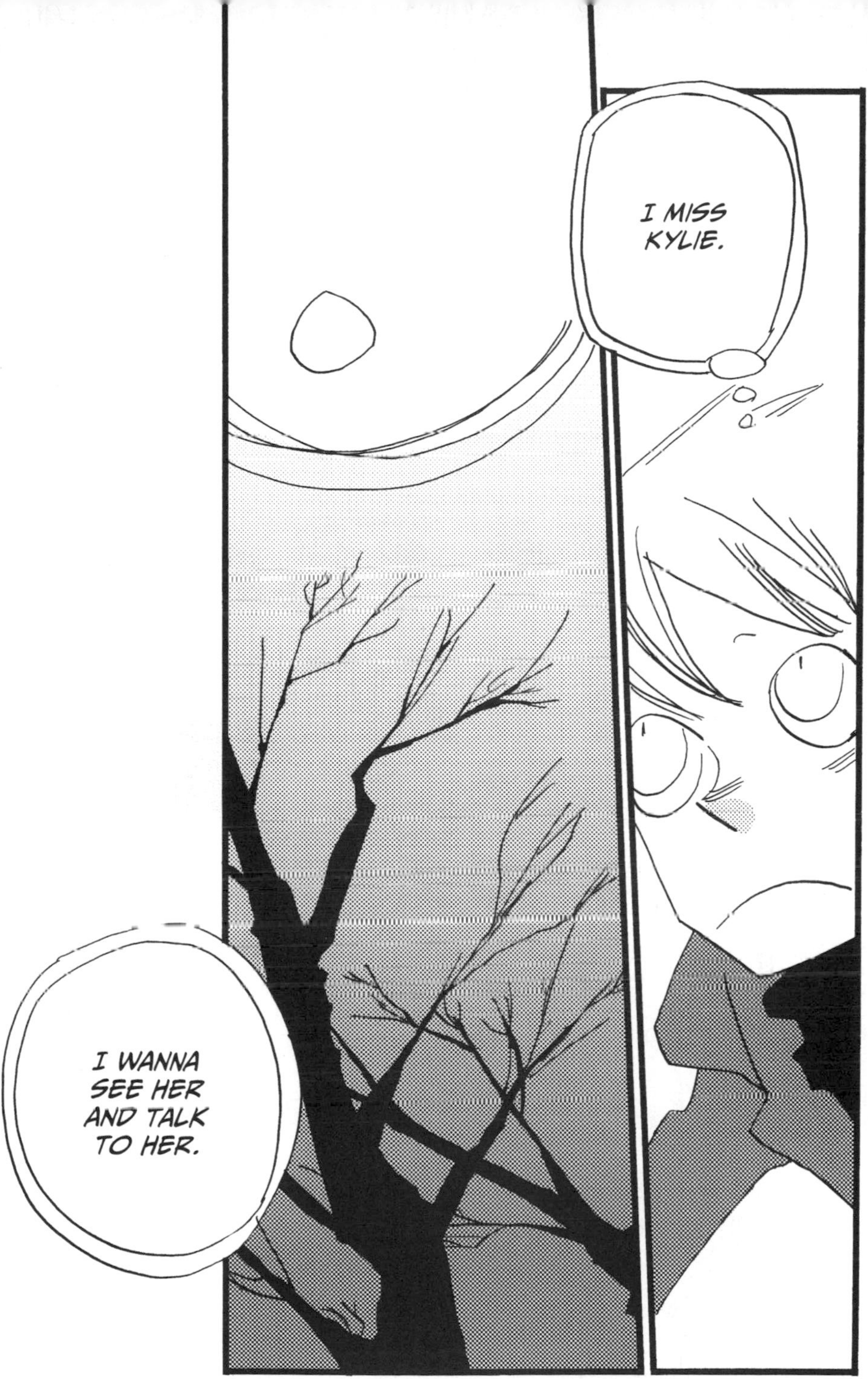
I MISS KYLIE.
I WANNA SEE HER AND TALK TO HER.

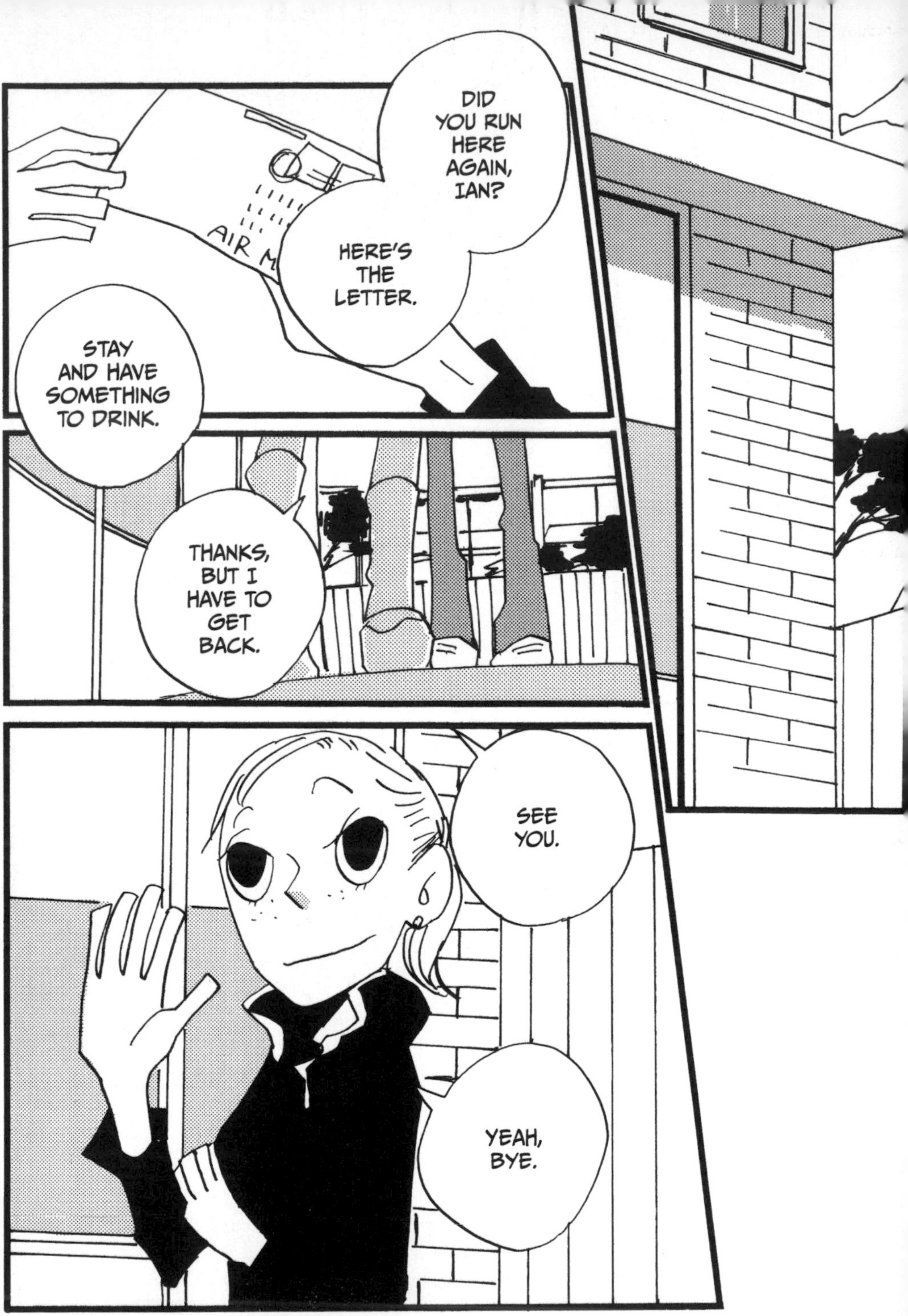
DID YOU RUN HERE AGAIN, IAN?
HERE'S THE LETTER.
AIR M
STAY AND HAVE SOMETHING TO DRINK.
THANKS, BUT I HAVE TO GET BACK.
SEE YOU.
YEAH, BYE.

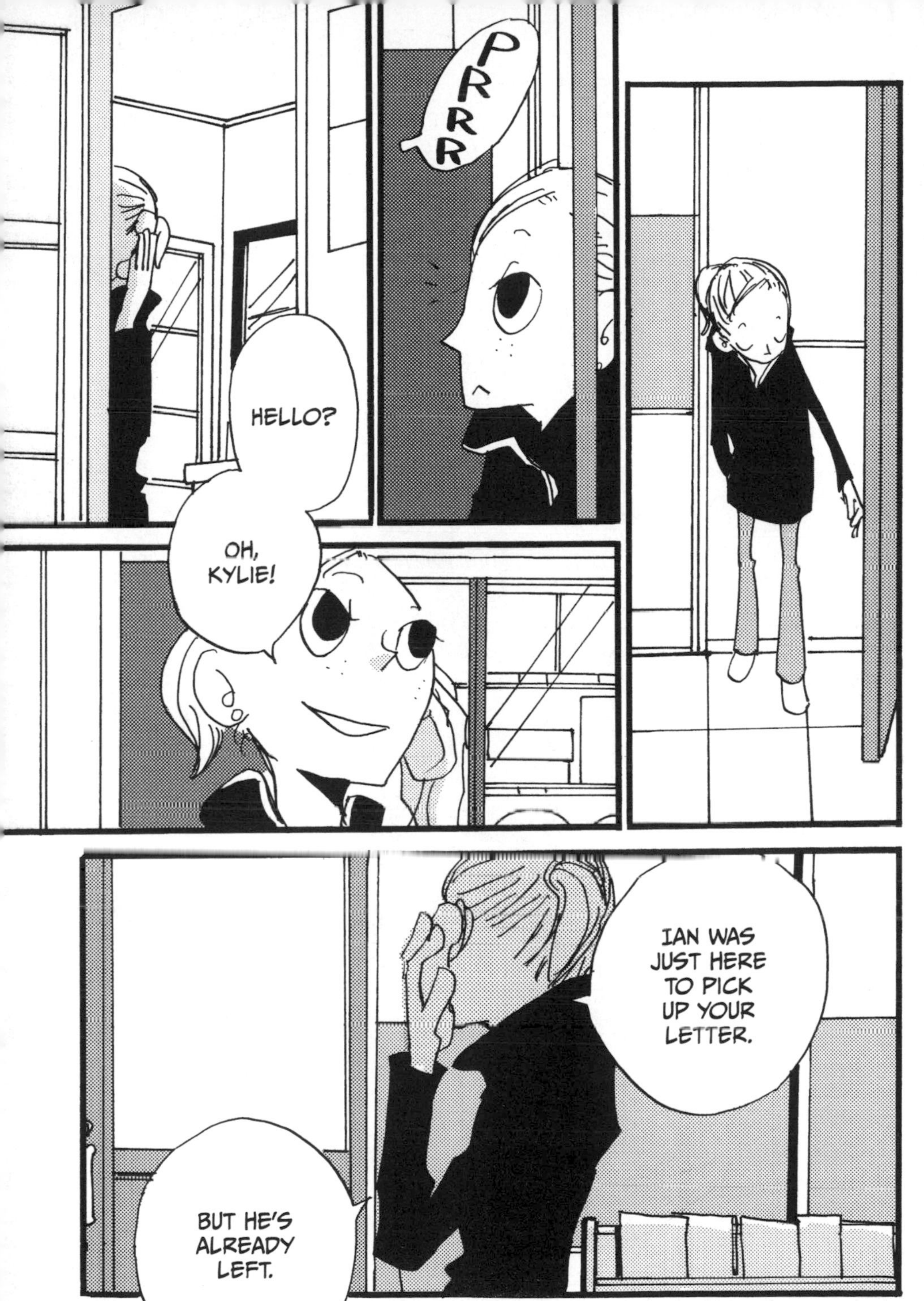
PRRR
HELLO?
OH, KYLIE!
IAN WAS JUST HERE TO PICK UP YOUR LETTER.
BUT HE'S ALREADY LEFT.

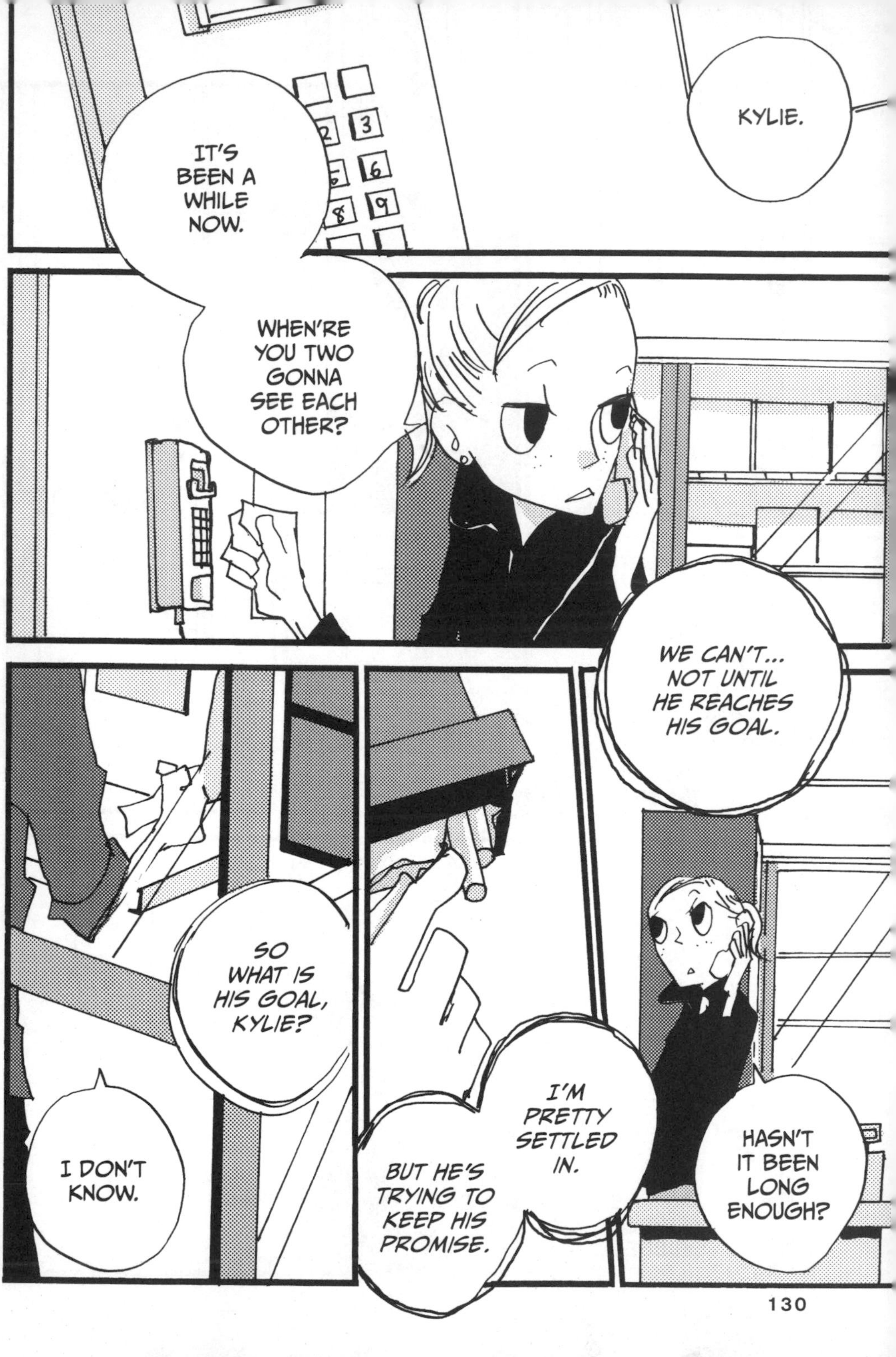
KYLIE.
IT'S BEEN A WHILE NOW.
WHEN'RE YOU TWO GONNA SEE EACH OTHER?
WE CAN'T... NOT UNTIL HE REACHES HIS GOAL.
HASN'T IT BEEN LONG ENOUGH?
I'M PRETTY SETTLED IN.
BUT HE'S TRYING TO KEEP HIS PROMISE.
SO WHAT IS HIS GOAL, KYLIE?
I DON'T KNOW.

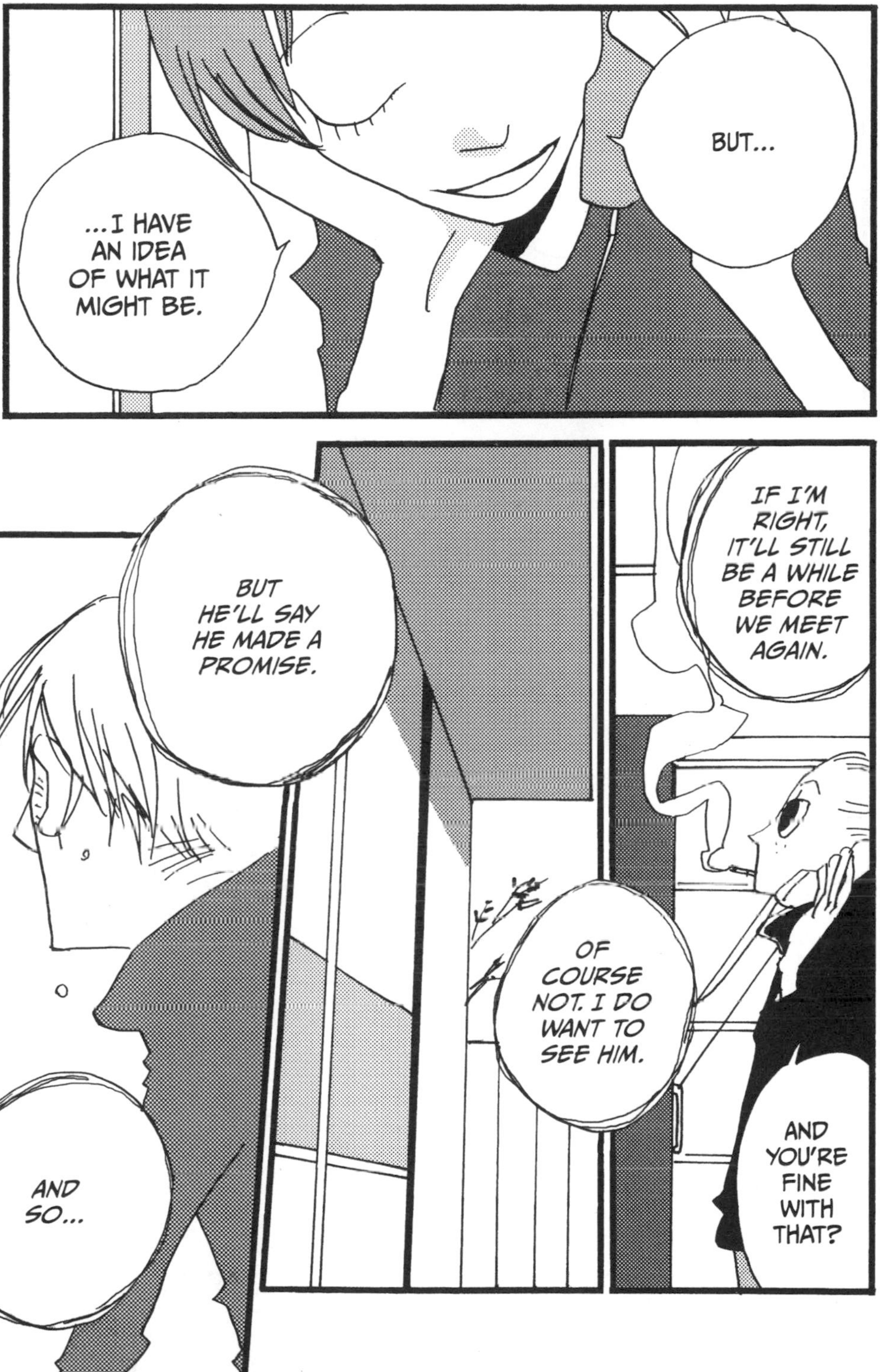
BUT...
...I HAVE AN IDEA OF WHAT IT MIGHT BE.
IF I'M RIGHT, IT'LL STILL BE A WHILE BEFORE WE MEET AGAIN.
AND YOU'RE FINE WITH THAT?
OF COURSE NOT. I DO WANT TO SEE HIM.
BUT HE'LL SAY HE MADE A PROMISE.
AND SO...

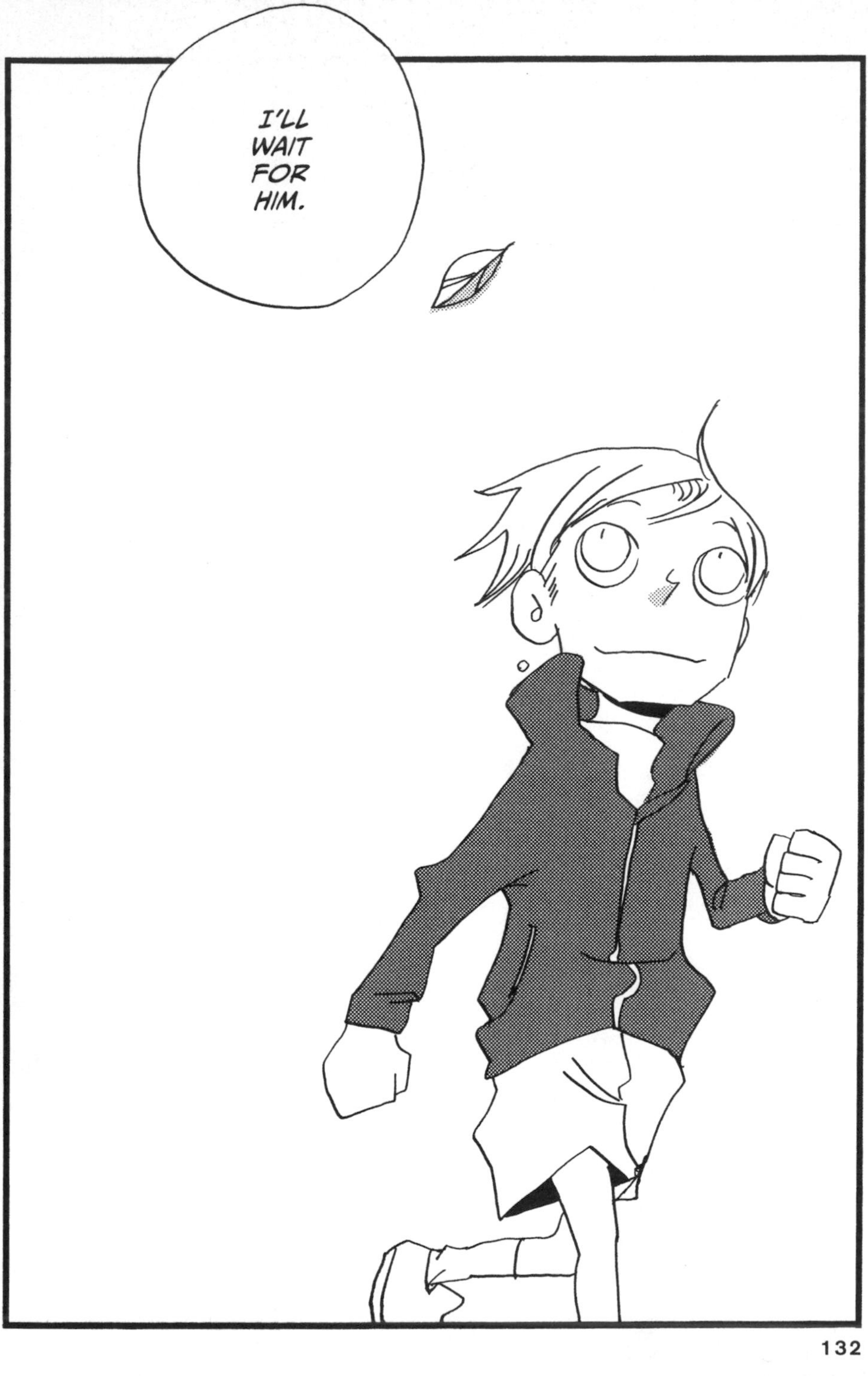
I'LL WAIT FOR HIM.

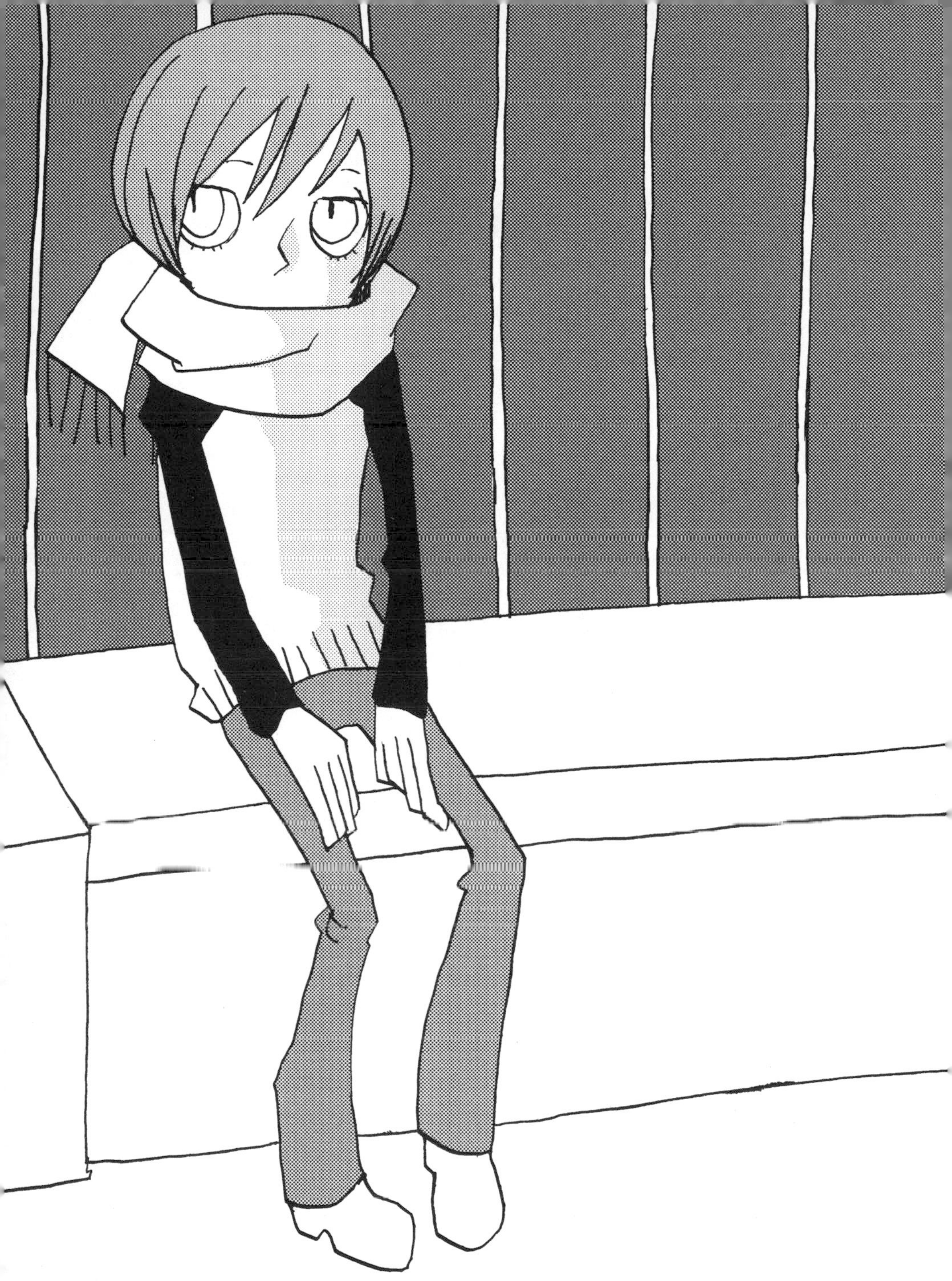

#05 not simple

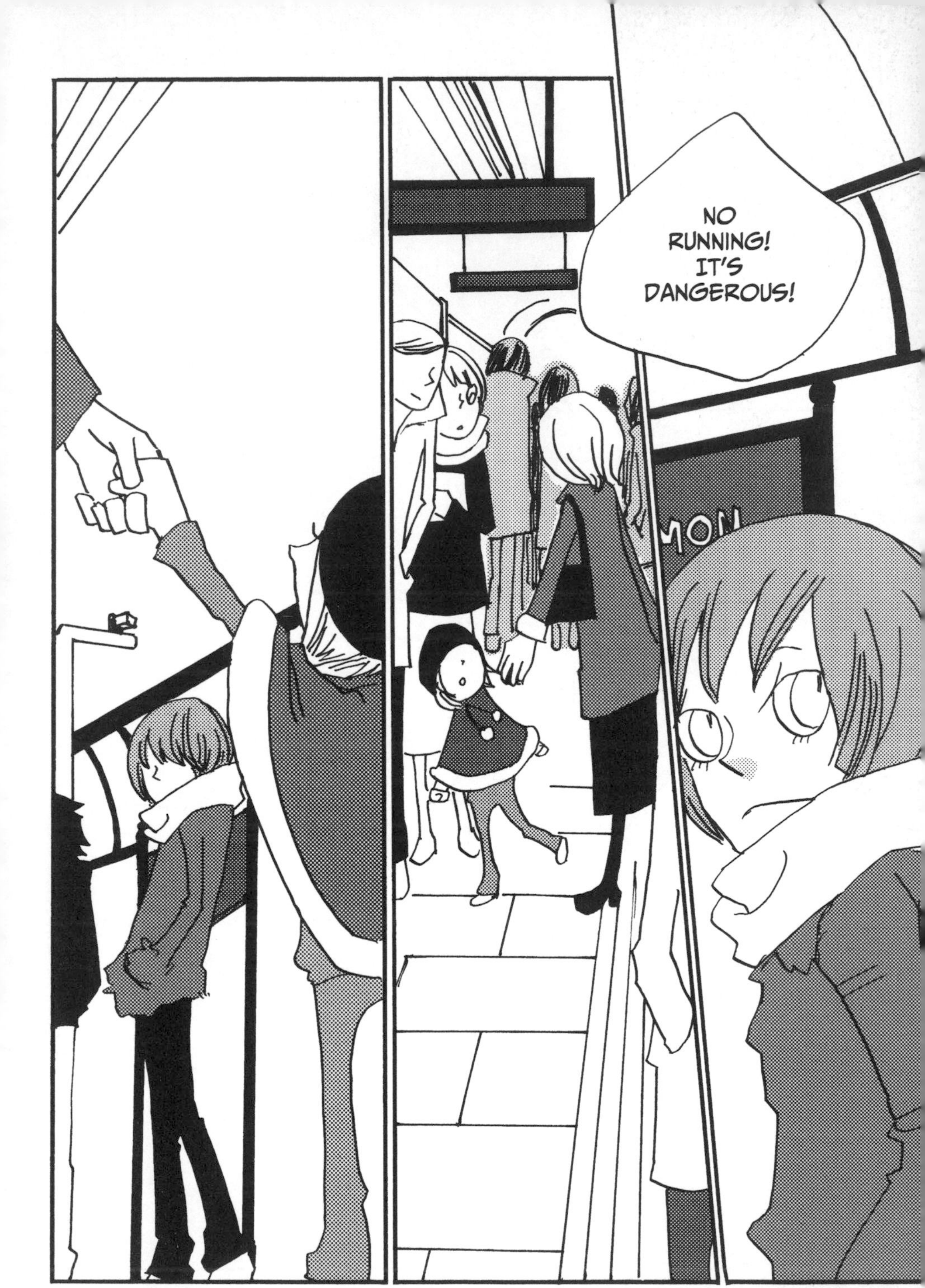
NO RUNNING! IT'S DANGEROUS!
MON

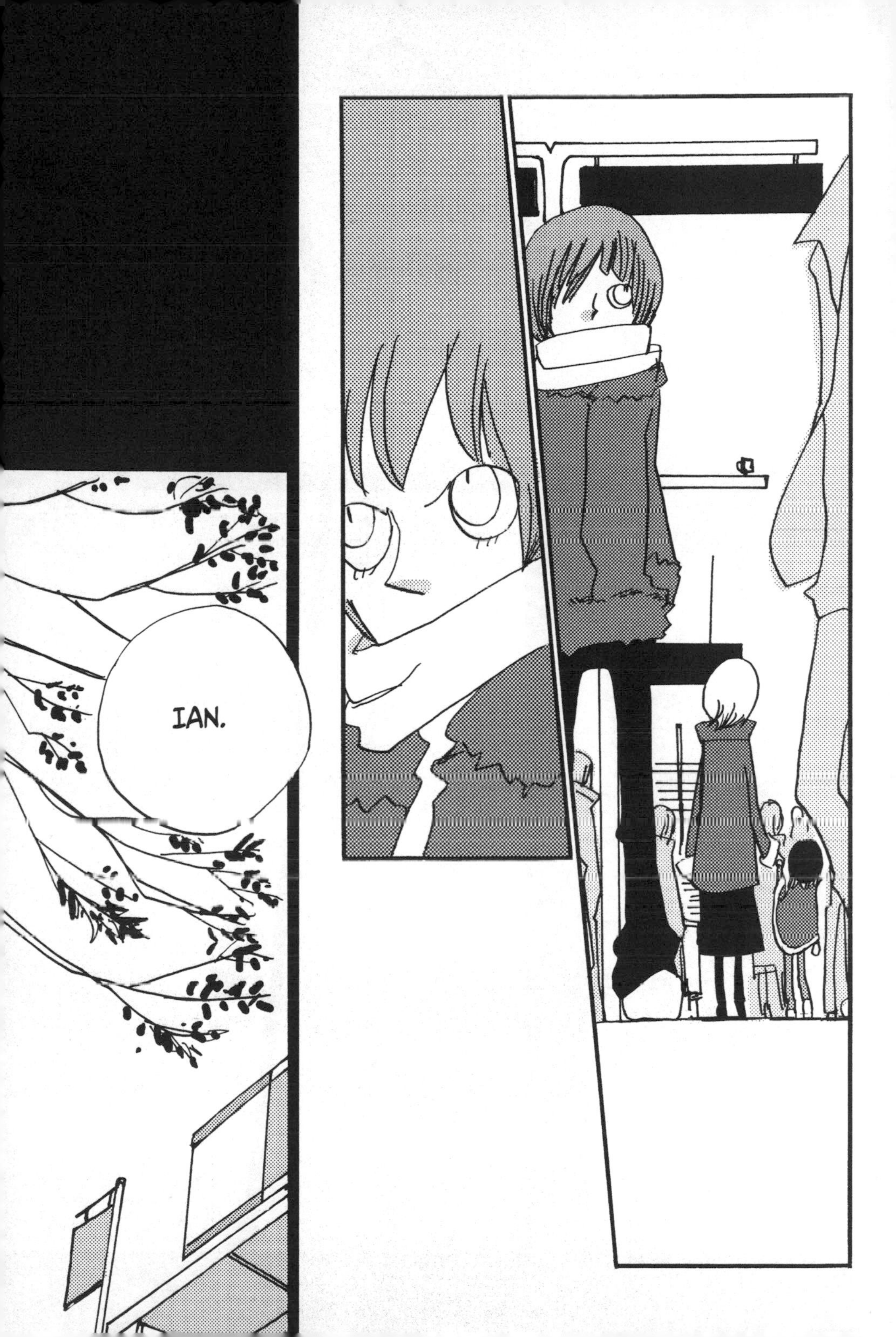
IAN.

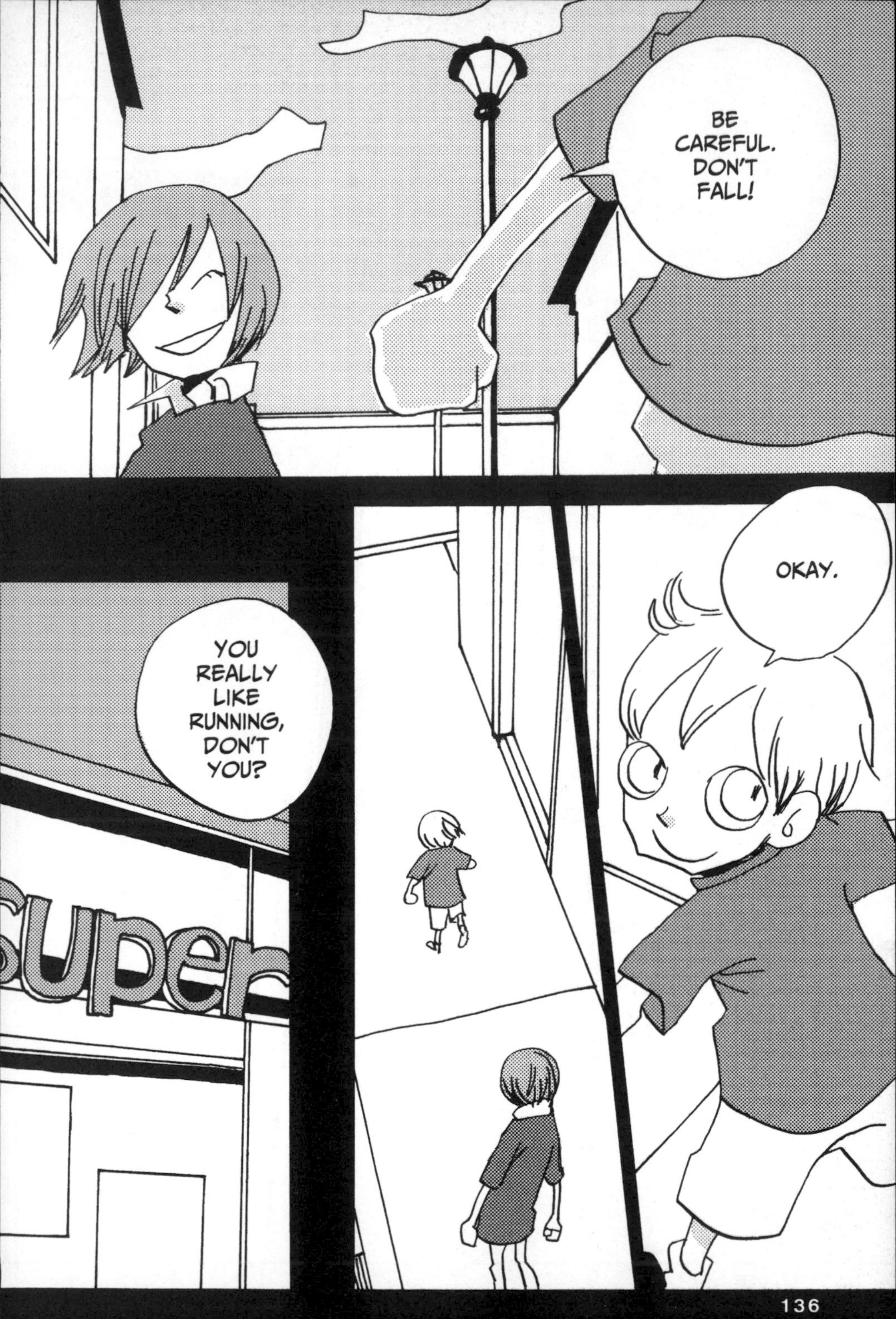
BE CAREFUL. DON'T FALL!
OKAY.
YOU REALLY LIKE RUNNING, DON'T YOU?
Super

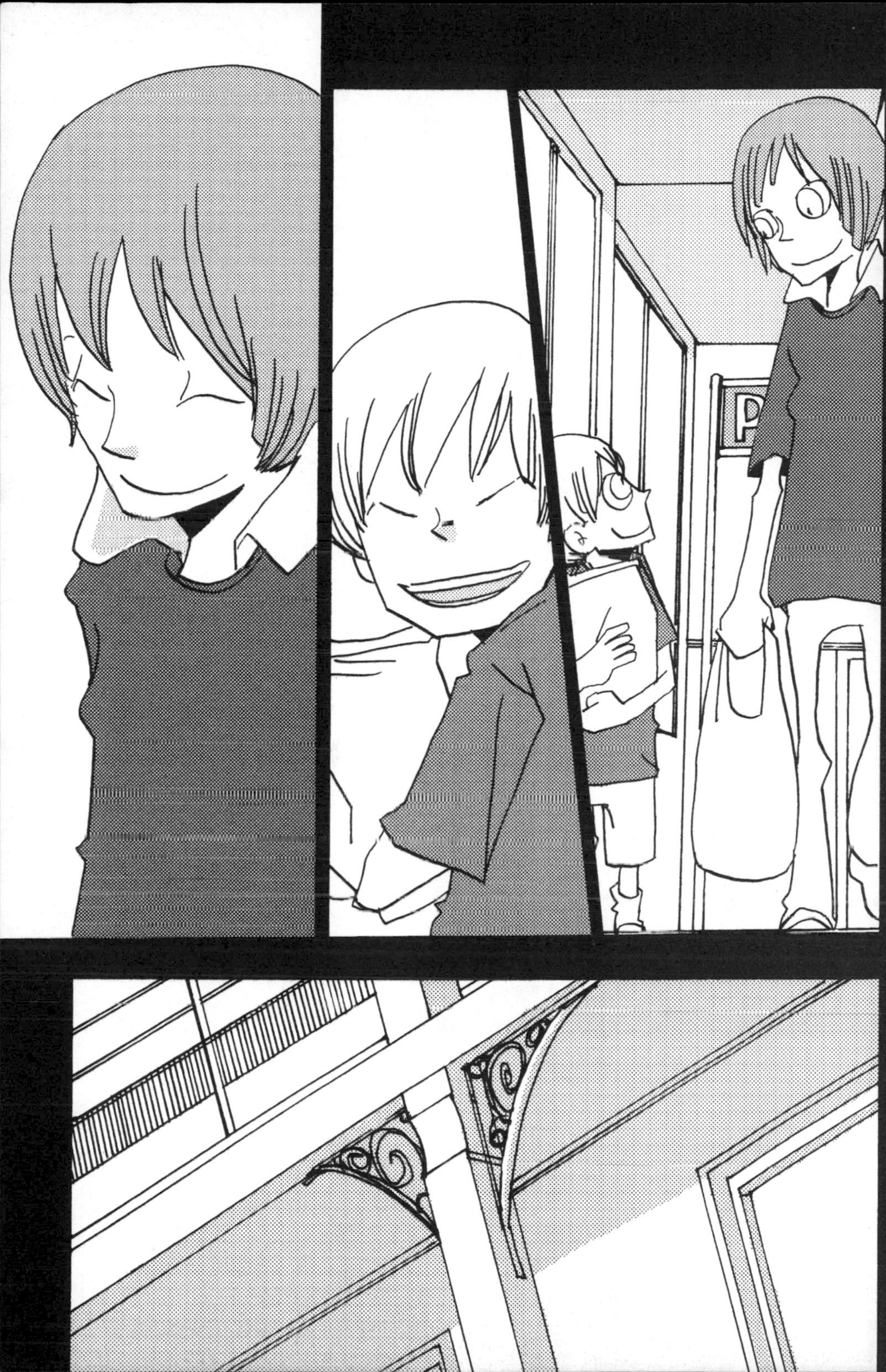

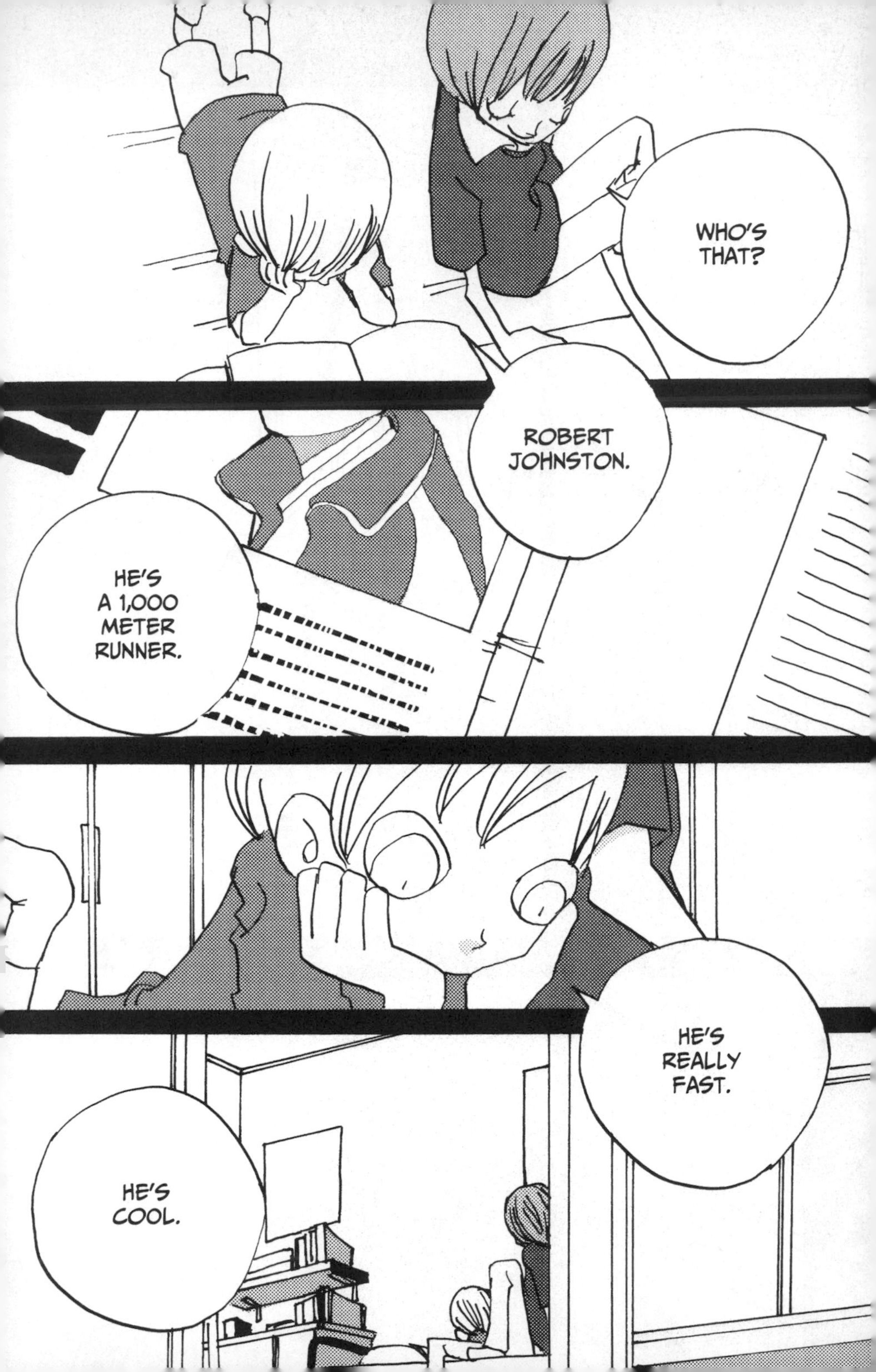
WHO'S THAT?
ROBERT JOHNSTON.
HE'S A 1,000 METER RUNNER.
HE'S REALLY FAST.
HE'S COOL.

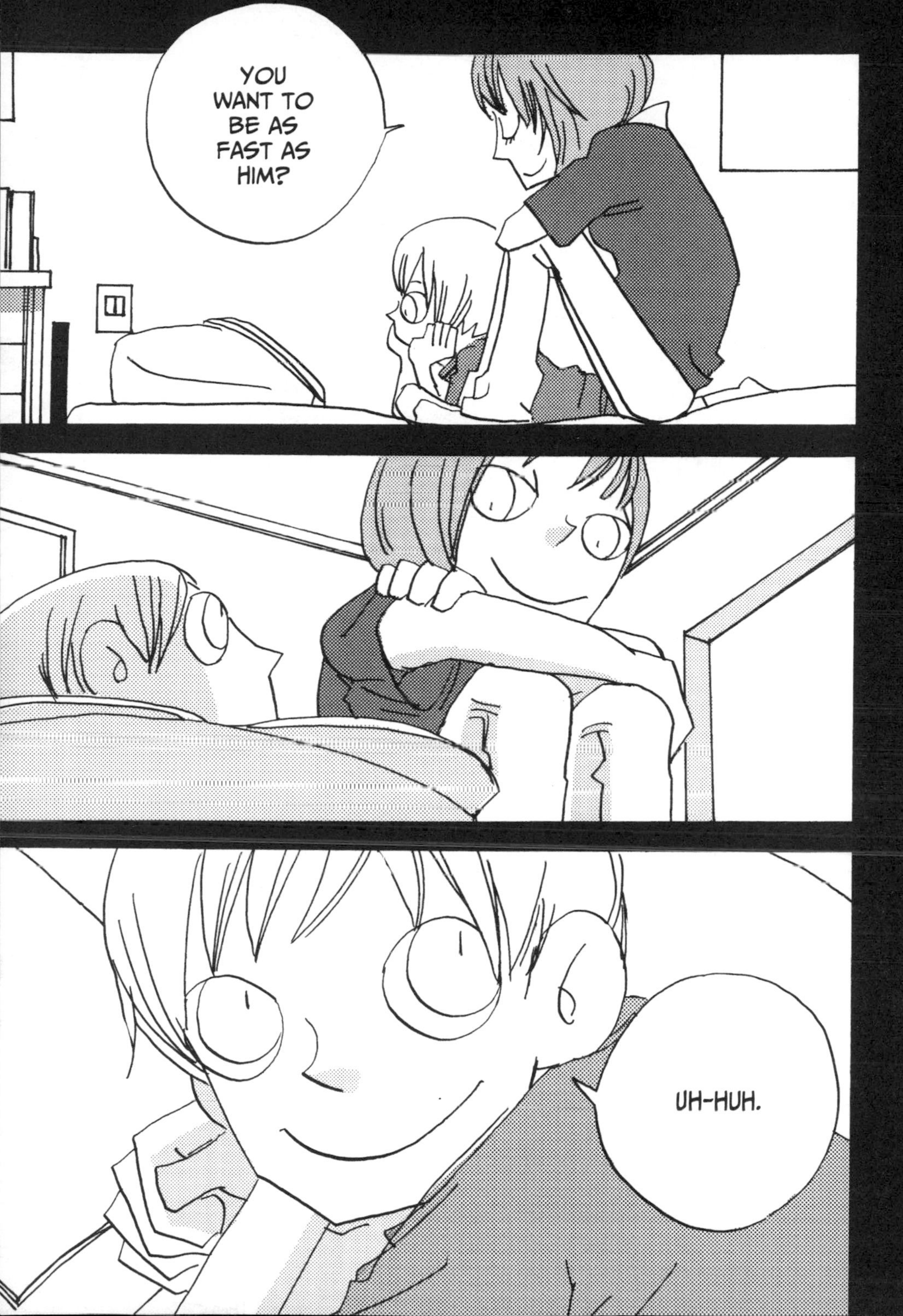
YOU WANT TO BE AS FAST AS HIM?
UH-HUH.

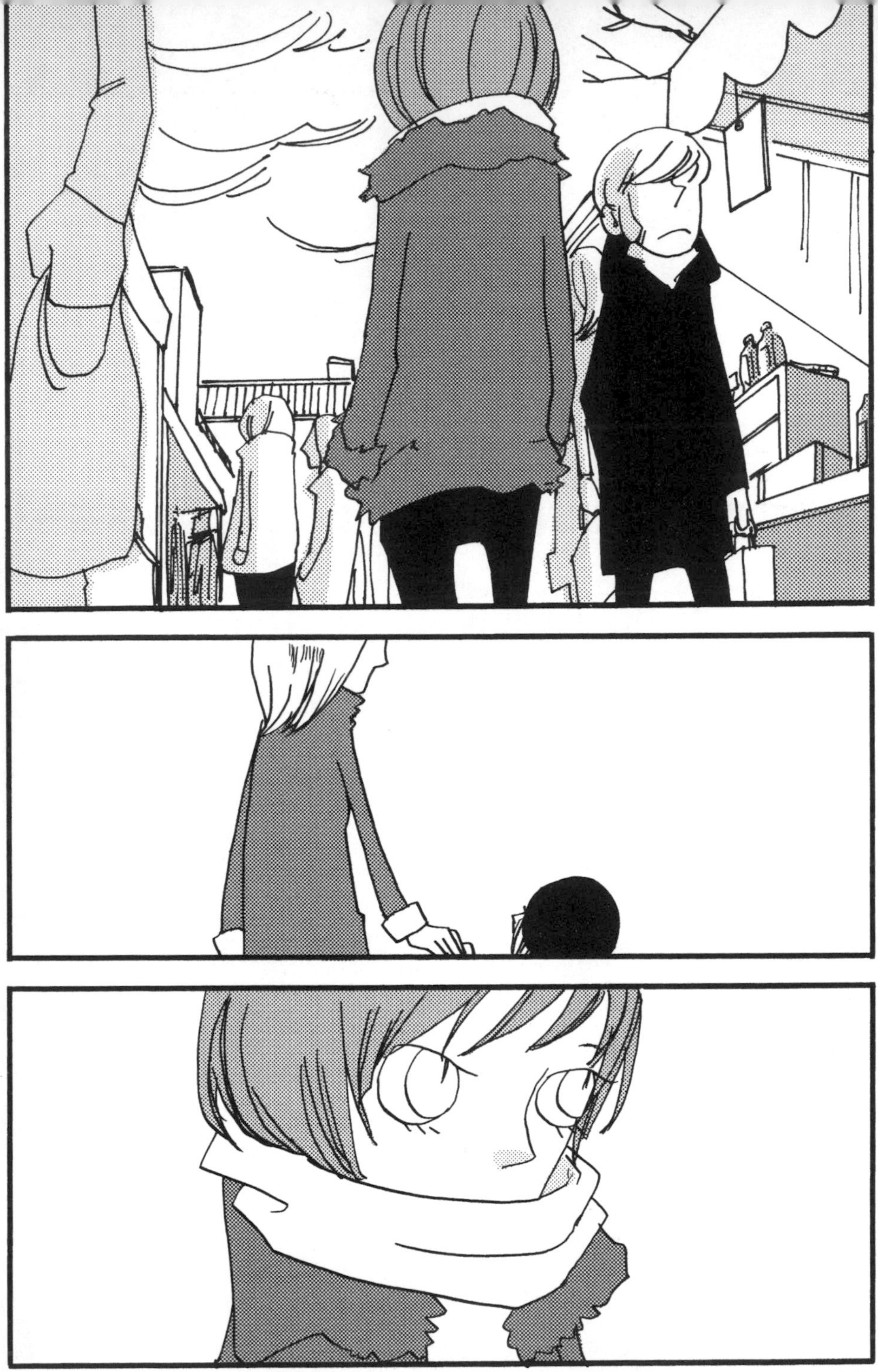

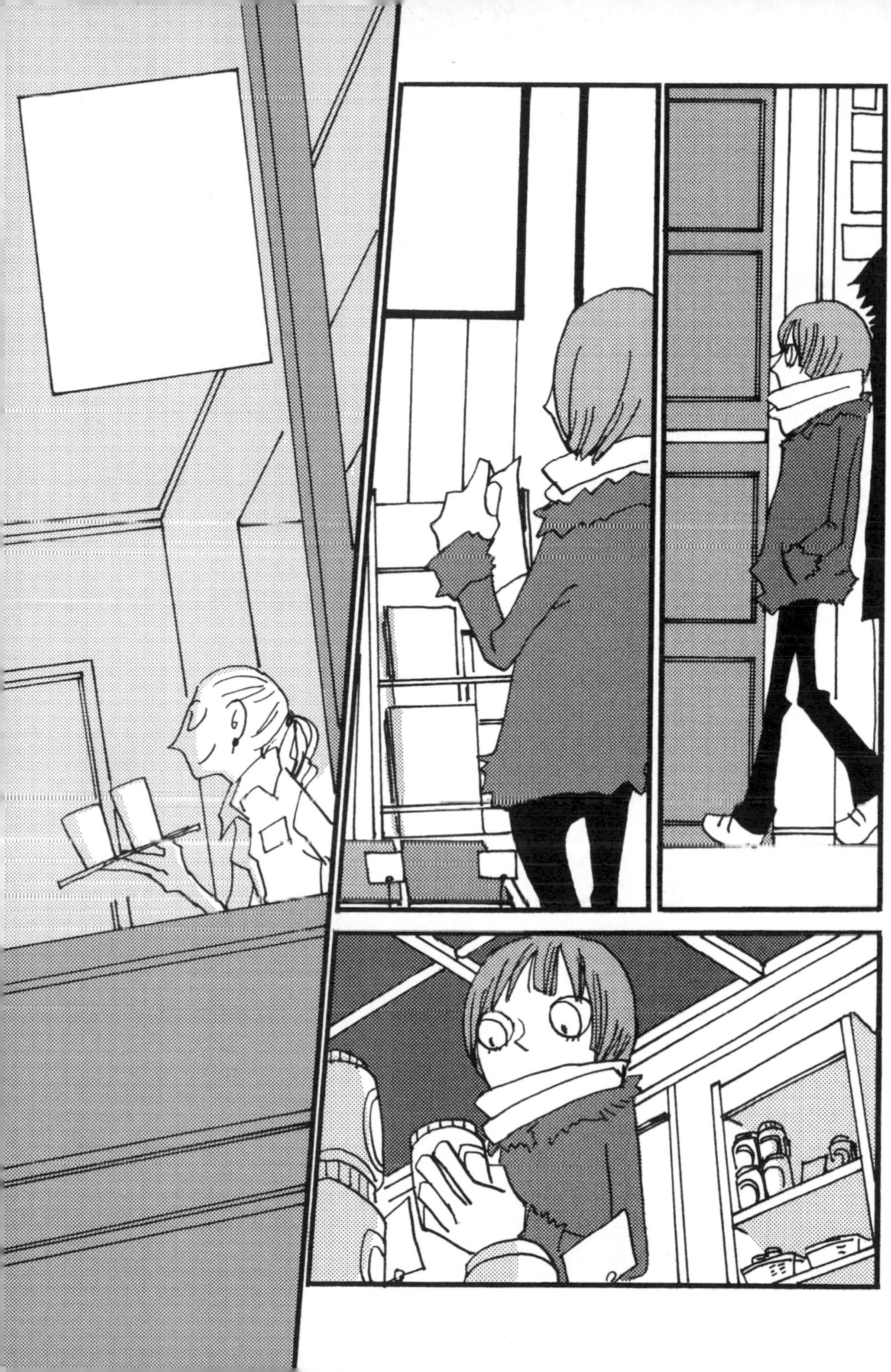

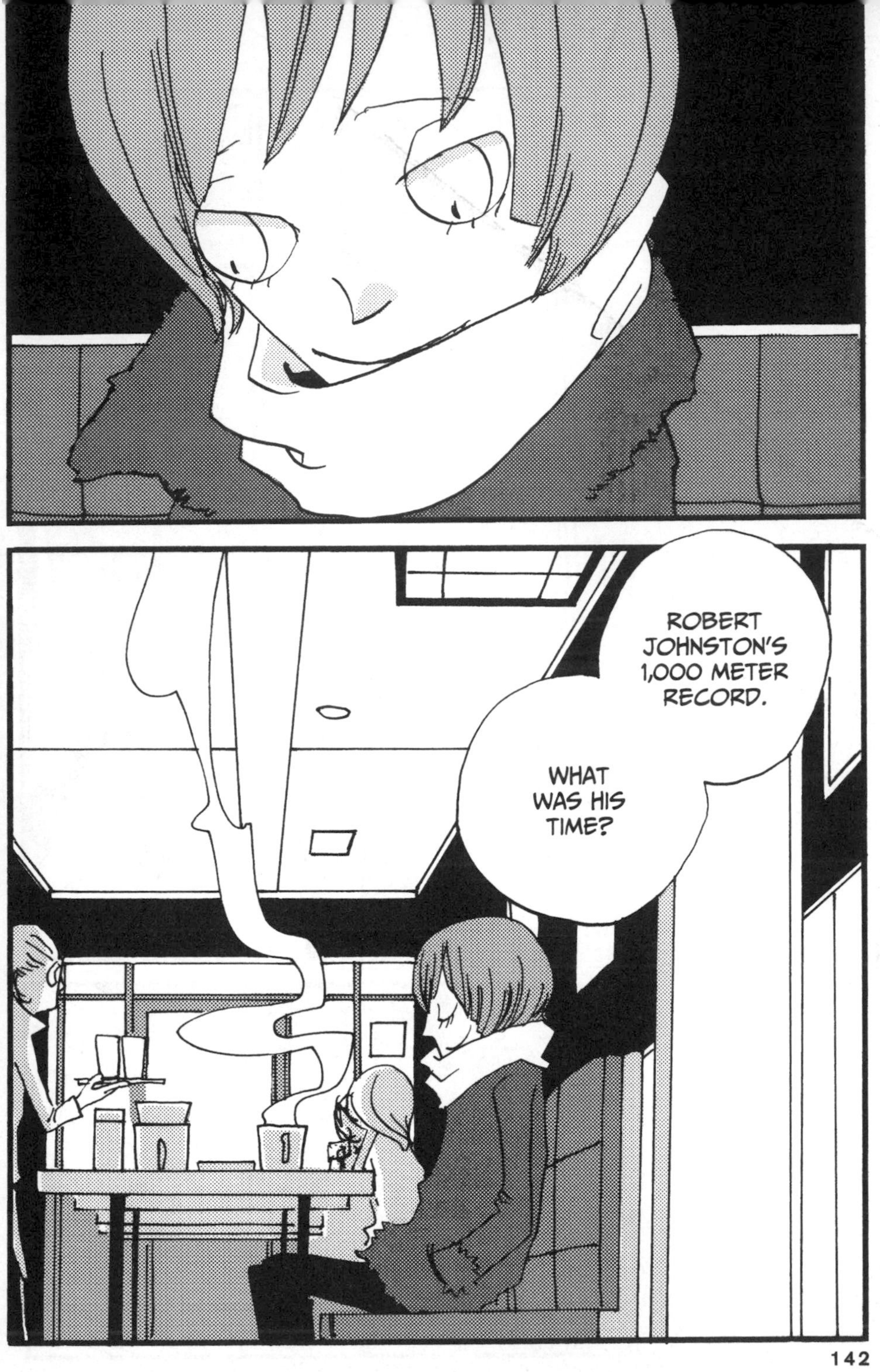
ROBERT JOHNSTON'S 1,000 METER RECORD.
WHAT WAS HIS TIME?

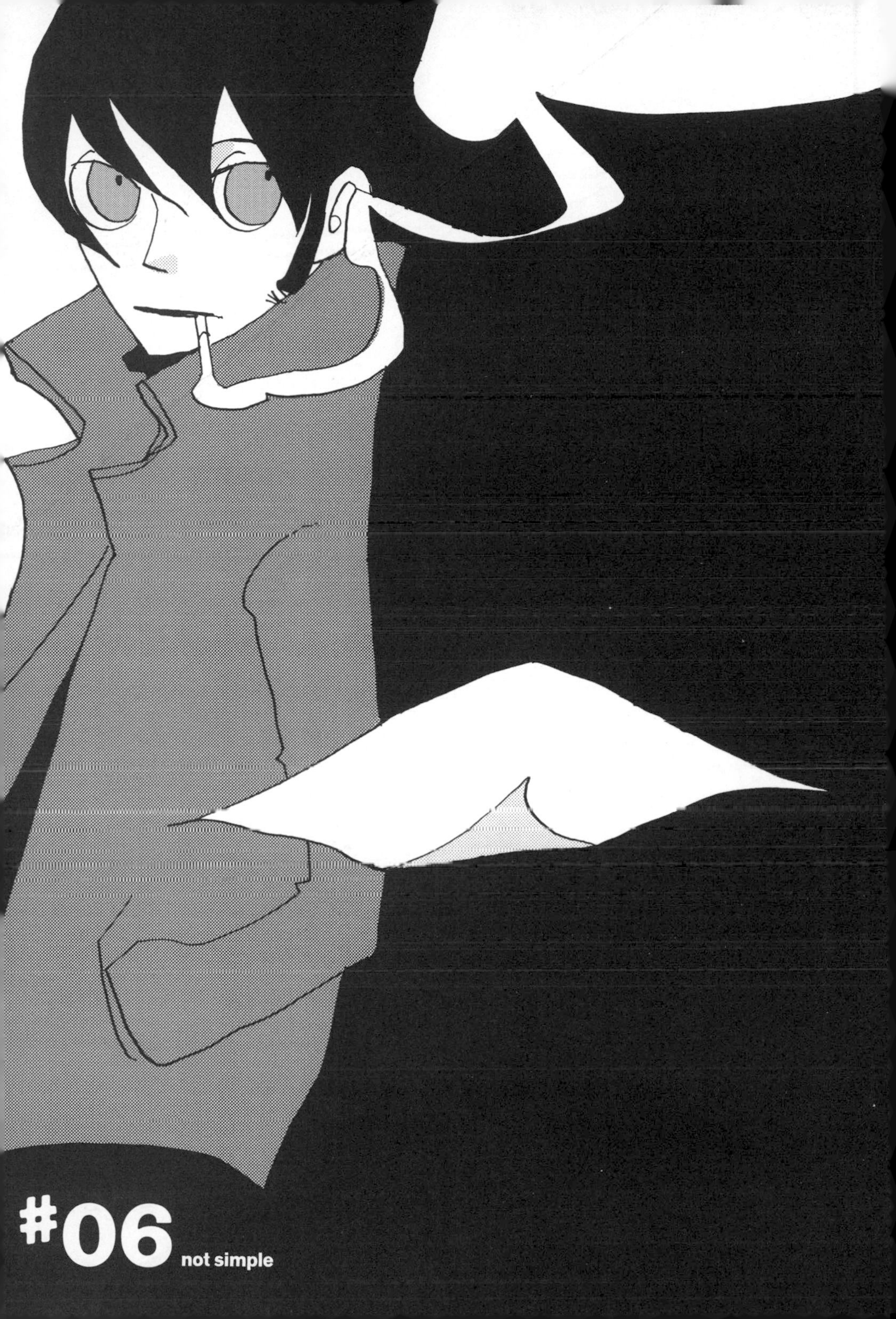
#06
not simple

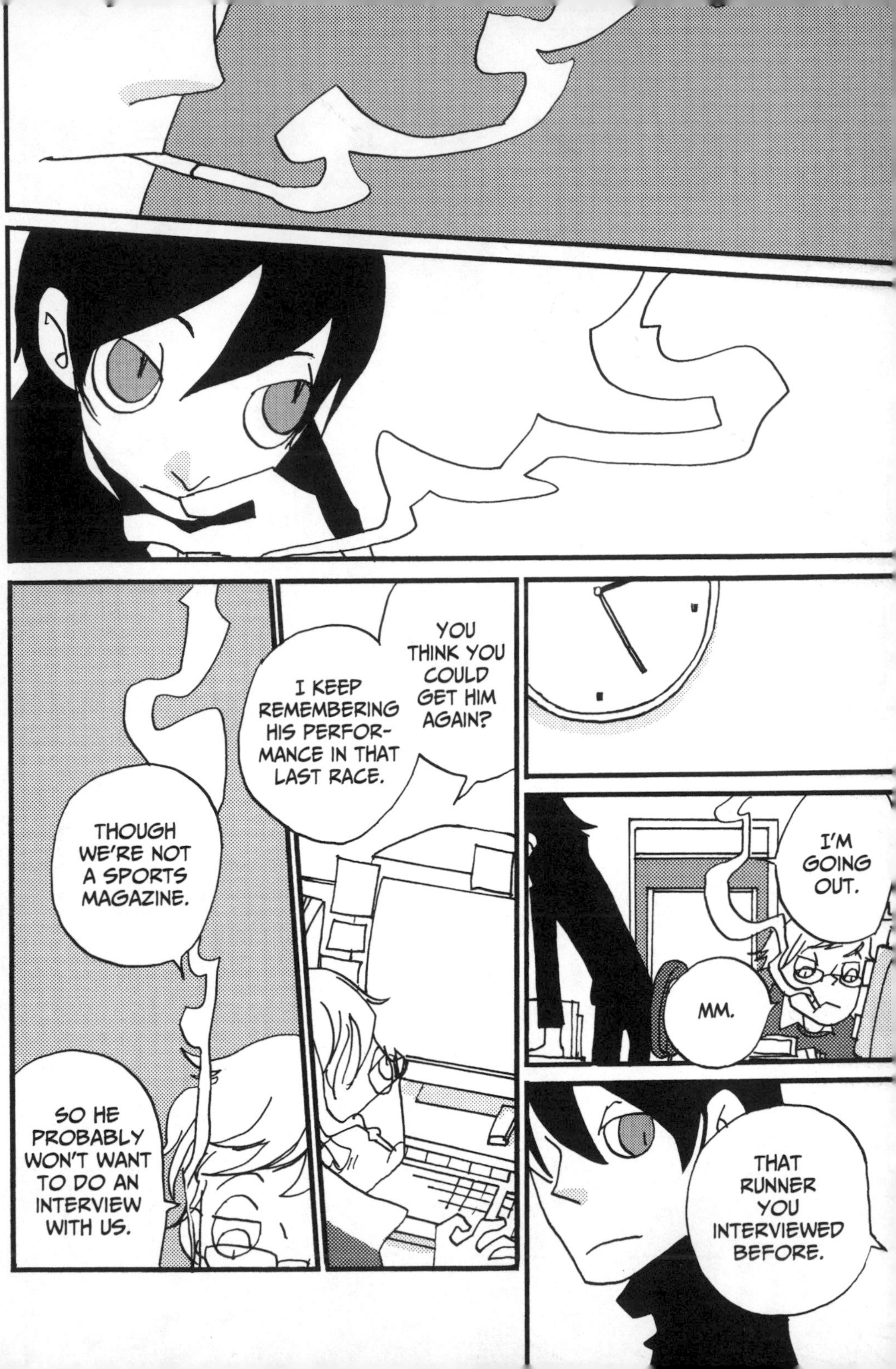
I'M GOING OUT.
MM.
THAT RUNNER YOU INTERVIEWED BEFORE.
YOU THINK YOU COULD GET HIM AGAIN?
I KEEP REMEMBERING HIS PERFOR-MANCE IN THAT LAST RACE.
THOUGH WE'RE NOT A SPORTS MAGAZINE.
SO HE PROBABLY WON'T WANT TO DO AN INTERVIEW WITH US.

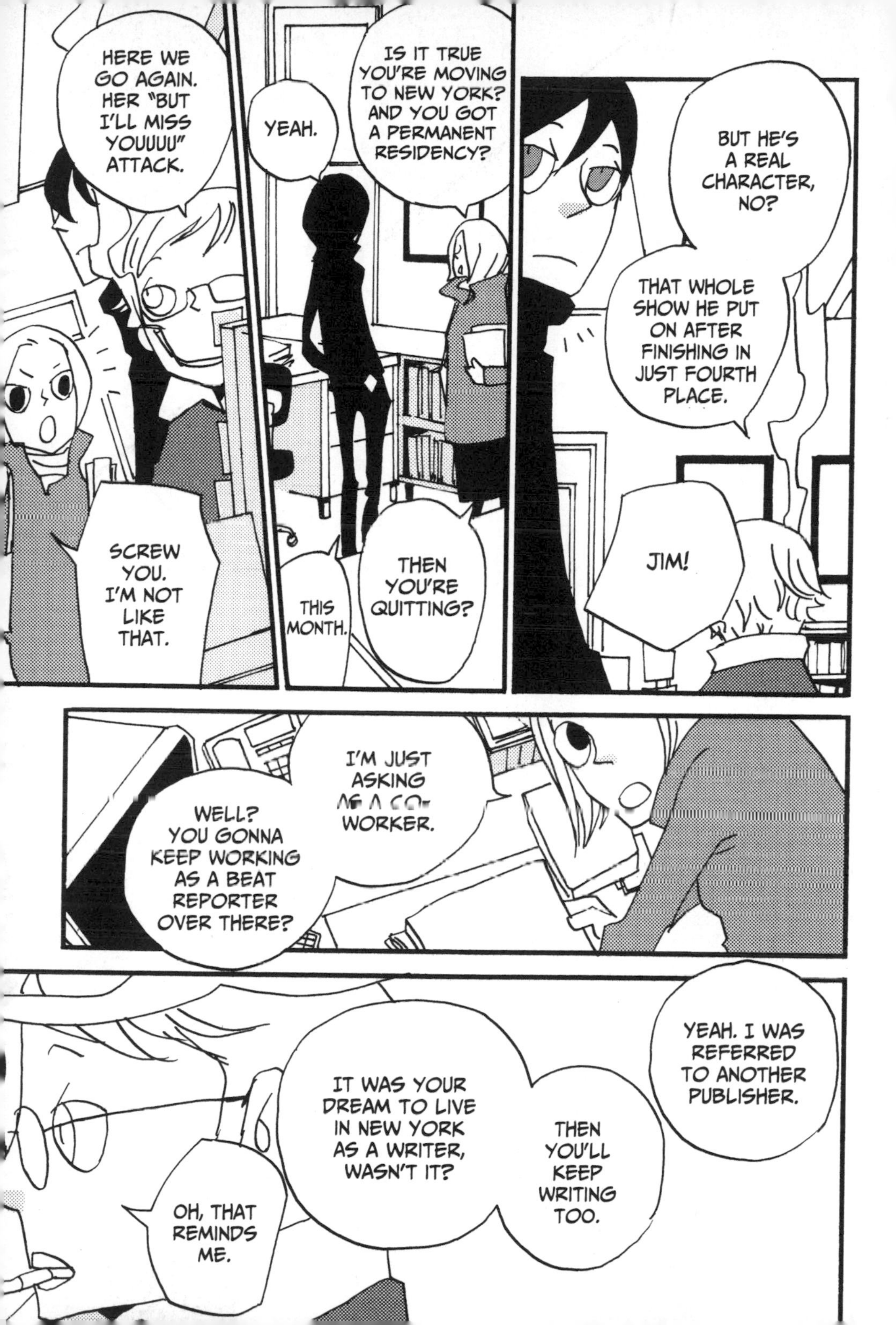
BUT HE'S A REAL CHARACTER, NO?
THAT WHOLE SHOW HE PUT ON AFTER FINISHING IN JUST FOURTH PLACE.
JIM!
IS IT TRUE YOU'RE MOVING TO NEW YORK? AND YOU GOT A PERMANENT RESIDENCY?
YEAH.
THEN YOU'RE QUITTING?
THIS MONTH.
HERE WE GO AGAIN. HER "BUT I'LL MISS YOUUUU" ATTACK.
SCREW YOU. I'M NOT LIKE THAT.
I'M JUST ASKING AS A CO-WORKER.
WELL? YOU GONNA KEEP WORKING AS A BEAT REPORTER OVER THERE?
YEAH. I WAS REFERRED TO ANOTHER PUBLISHER.
THEN YOU'LL KEEP WRITING TOO.
IT WAS YOUR DREAM TO LIVE IN NEW YORK AS A WRITER, WASN'T IT?
OH, THAT REMINDS ME.

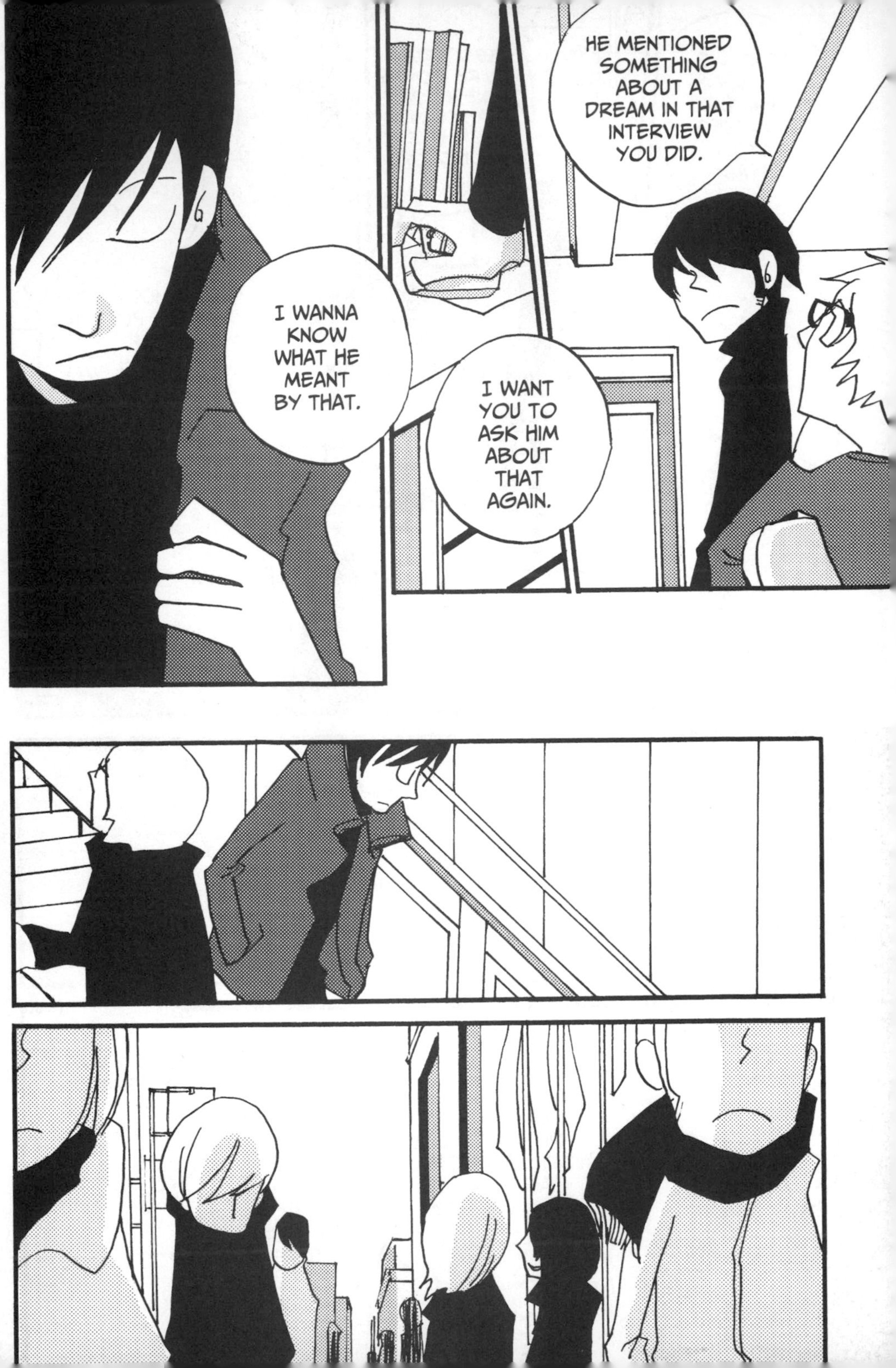
HE MENTIONED SOMETHING ABOUT A DREAM IN THAT INTERVIEW YOU DID.
I WANNA KNOW WHAT HE MEANT BY THAT.
I WANT YOU TO ASK HIM ABOUT THAT AGAIN.

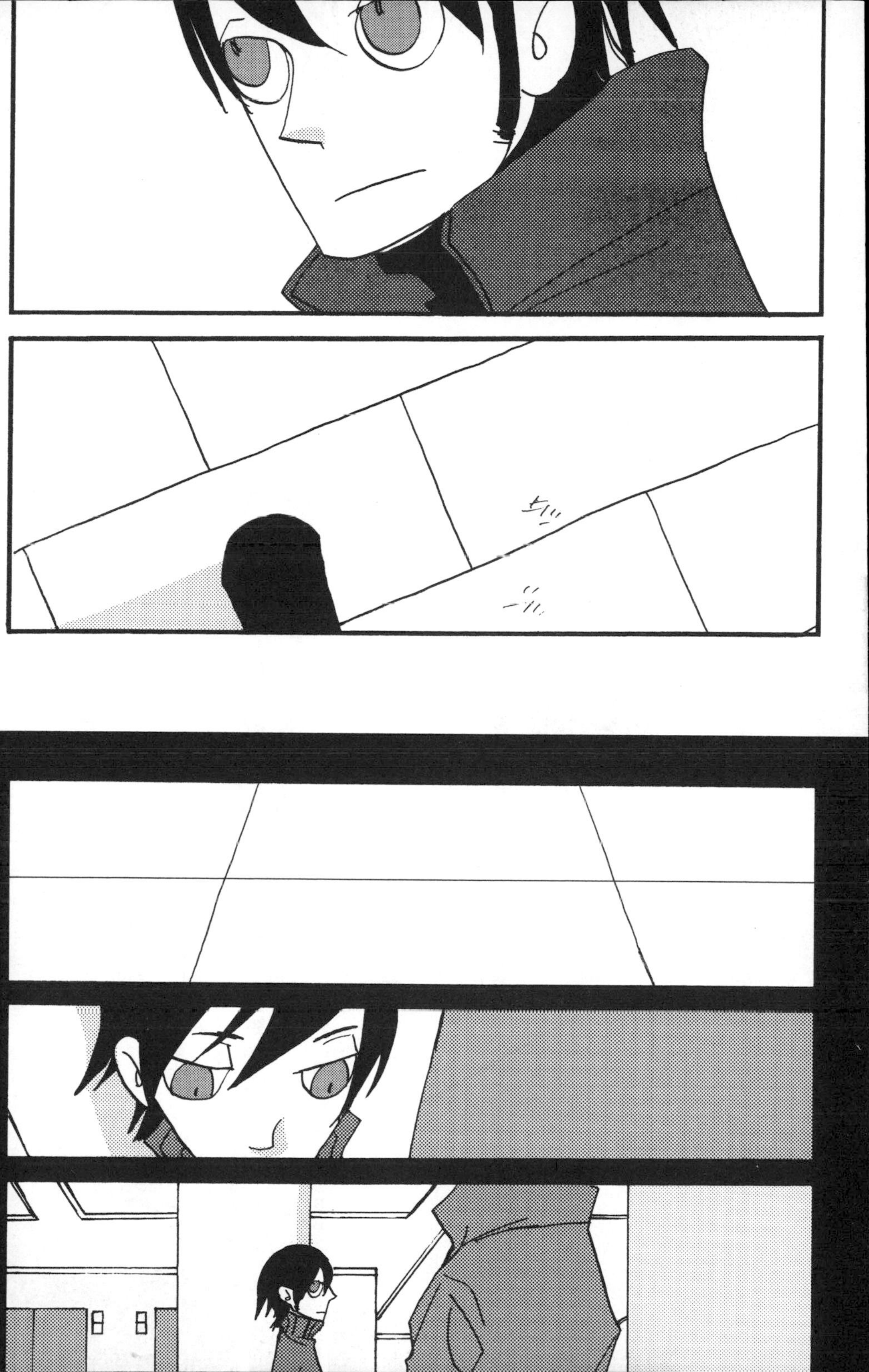

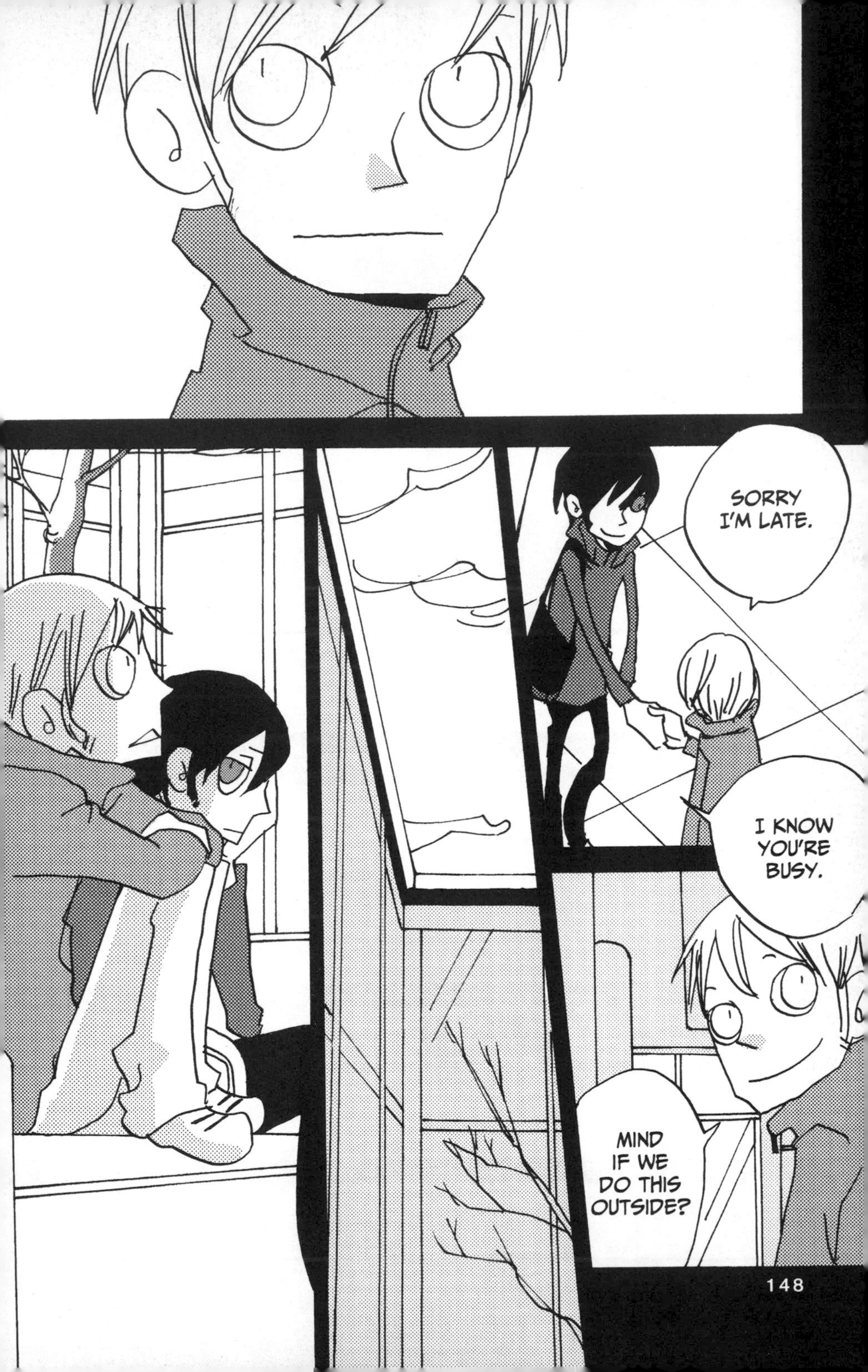
SORRY I'M LATE.
I KNOW YOU'RE BUSY.
MIND IF WE DO THIS OUTSIDE?

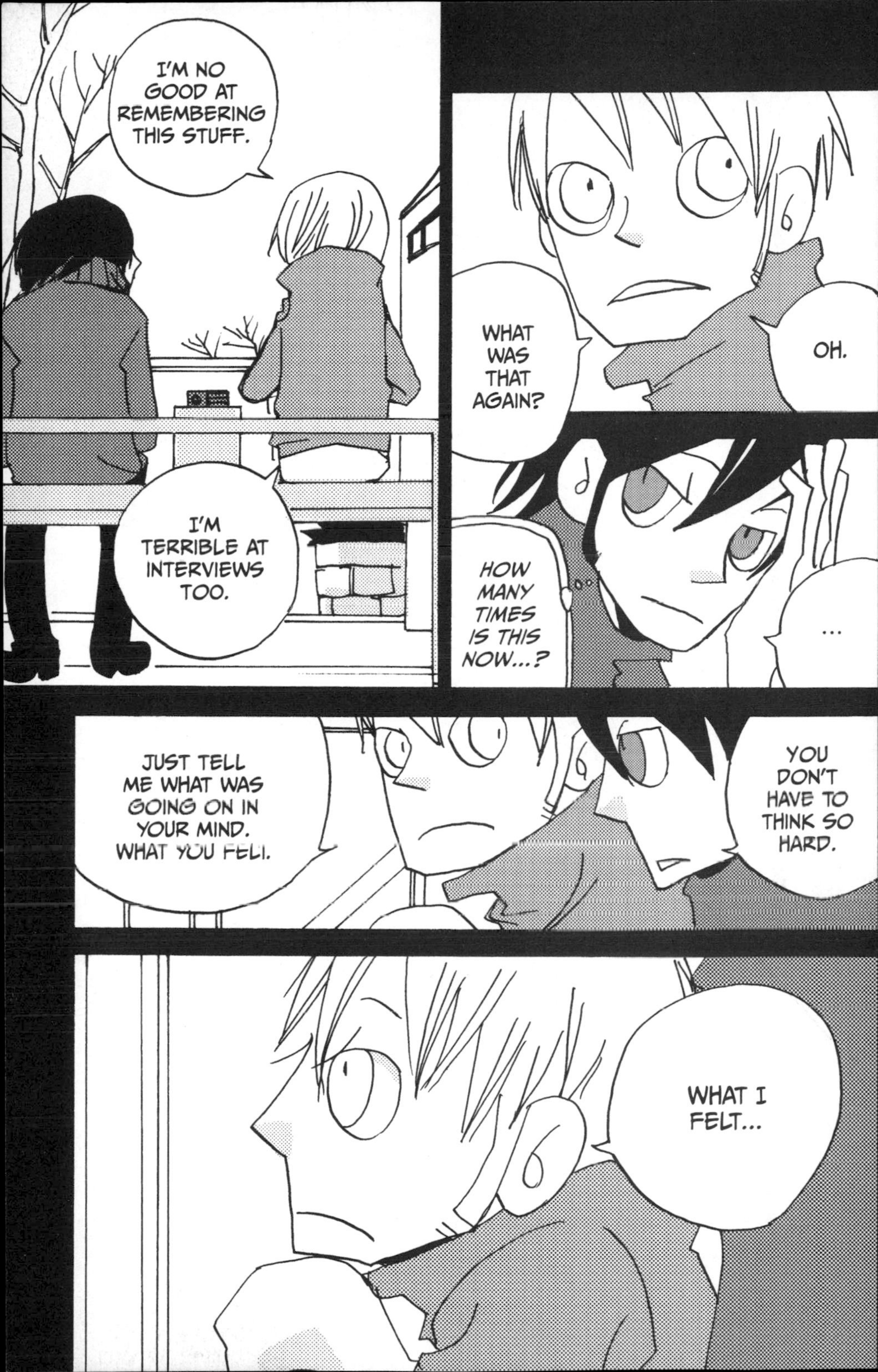
OH.
WHAT WAS THAT AGAIN?
...
HOW MANY TIMES IS THIS NOW...?
I'M NO GOOD AT REMEMBERING THIS STUFF.
I'M TERRIBLE AT INTERVIEWS TOO.
YOU DON'T HAVE TO THINK SO HARD.
JUST TELL ME WHAT WAS GOING ON IN YOUR MIND. WHAT YOU FELT.
WHAT I FELT...

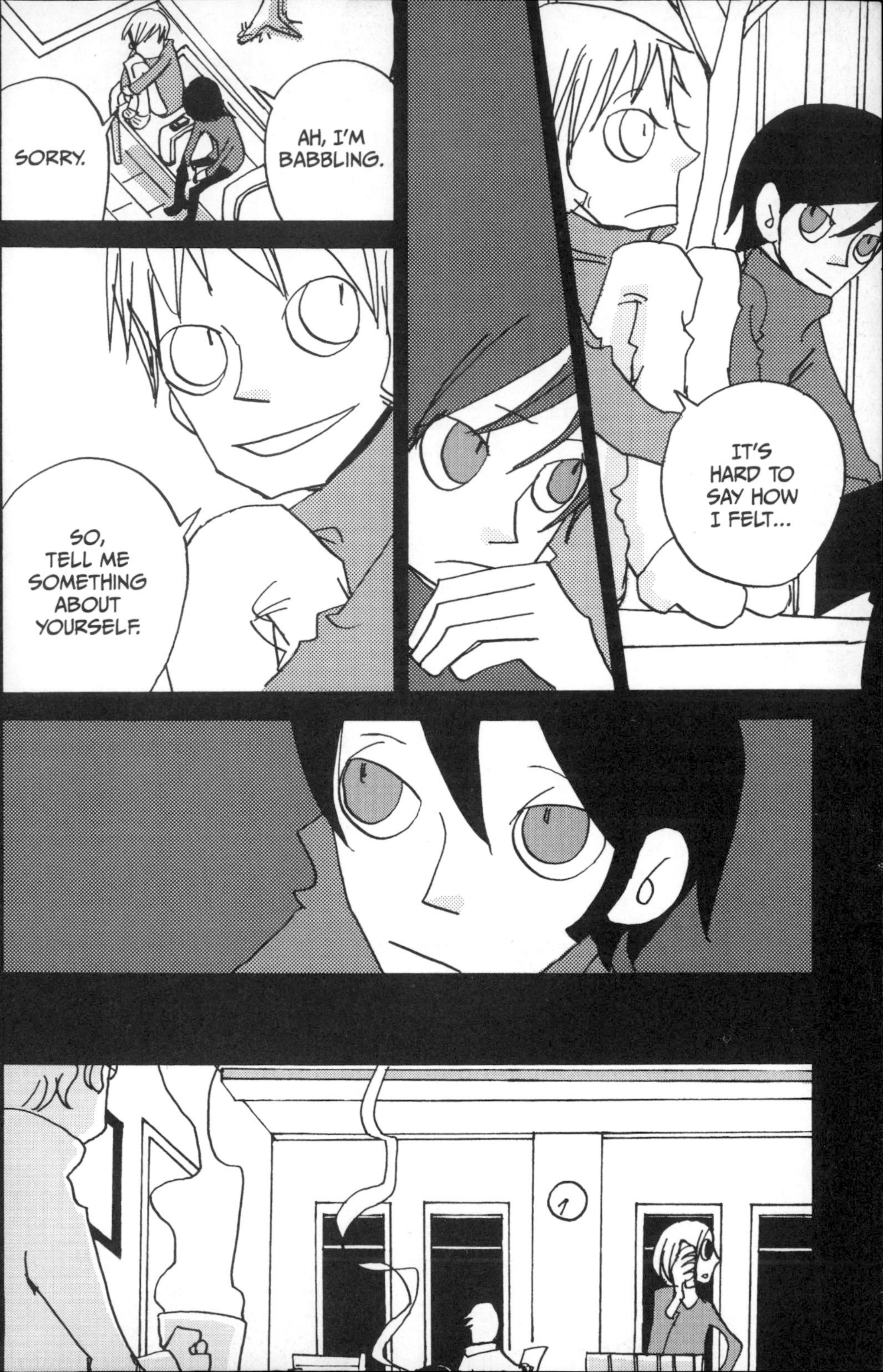
IT'S HARD TO SAY HOW I FELT...
AH, I'M BABBLING.
SORRY.
SO, TELL ME SOMETHING ABOUT YOURSELF.

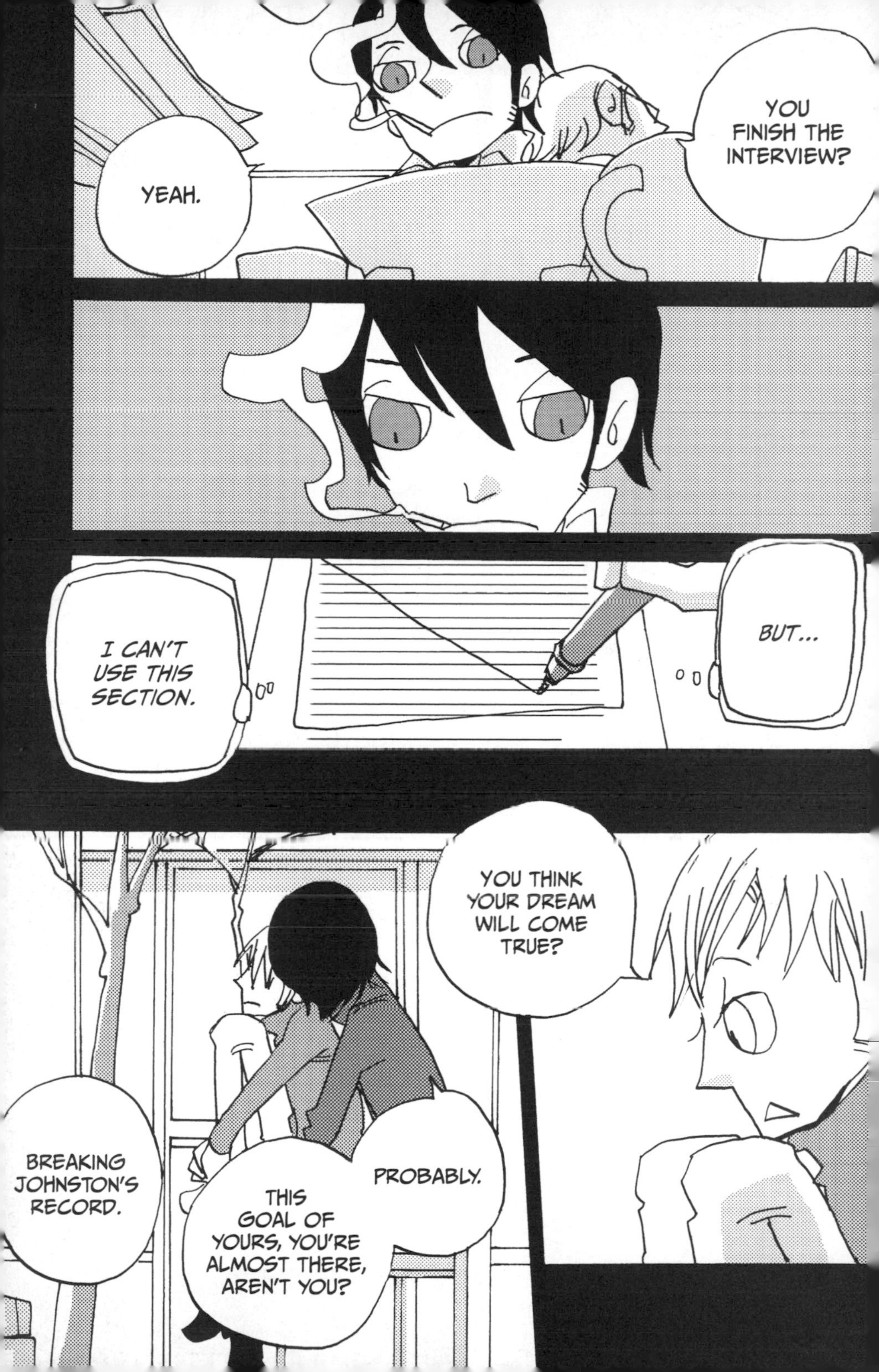
YOU FINISH THE INTERVIEW?
YEAH.
BUT...
I CAN'T USE THIS SECTION.
YOU THINK YOUR DREAM WILL COME TRUE?
PROBABLY.
THIS GOAL OF YOURS, YOU'RE ALMOST THERE, AREN'T YOU?
BREAKING JOHNSTON'S RECORD.

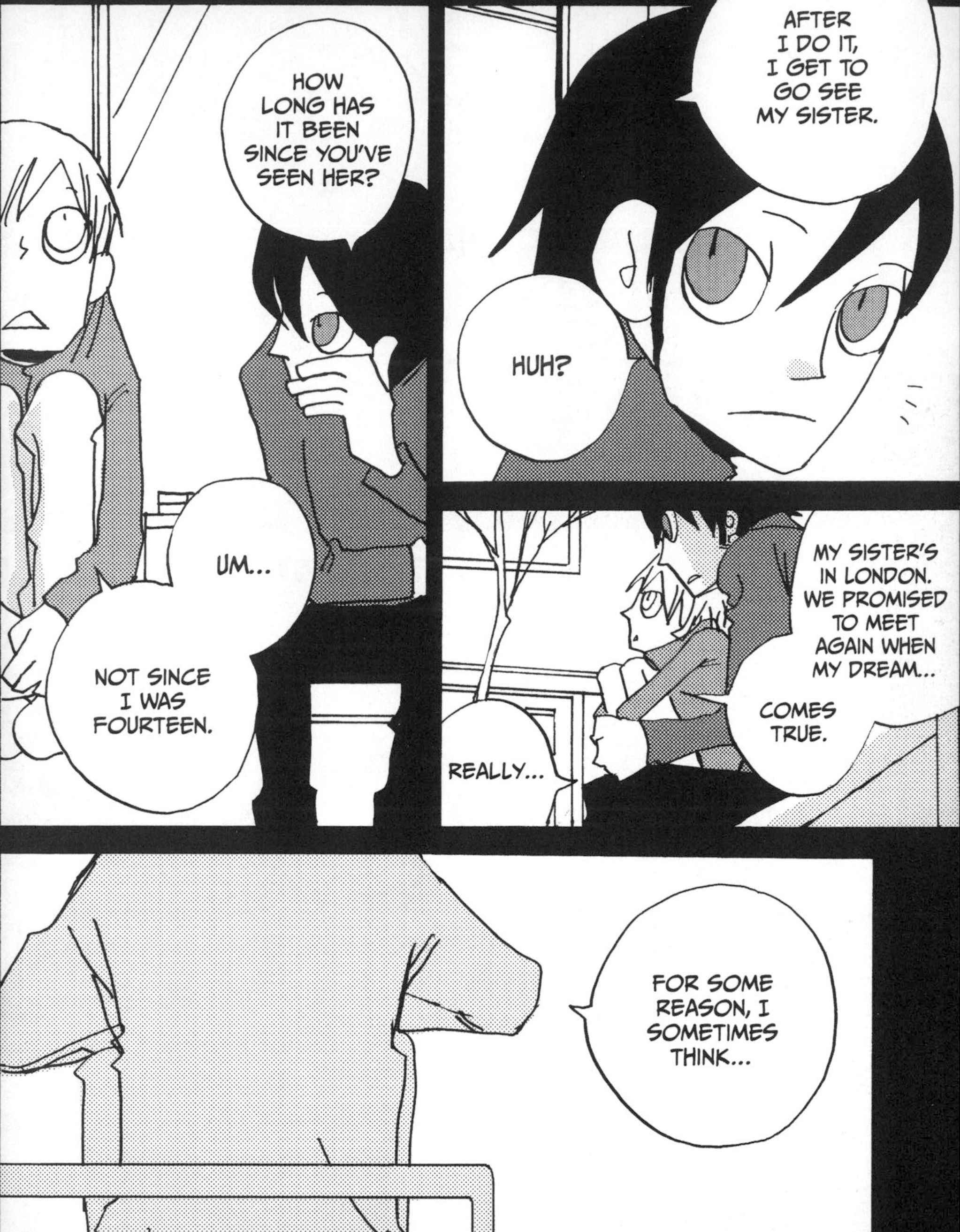
AFTER I DO IT, I GET TO GO SEE MY SISTER.
HUH?
MY SISTER'S IN LONDON. WE PROMISED TO MEET AGAIN WHEN MY DREAM...
COMES TRUE.
REALLY...
HOW LONG HAS IT BEEN SINCE YOU'VE SEEN HER?
UM...
NOT SINCE I WAS FOURTEEN.
FOR SOME REASON, I SOMETIMES THINK...

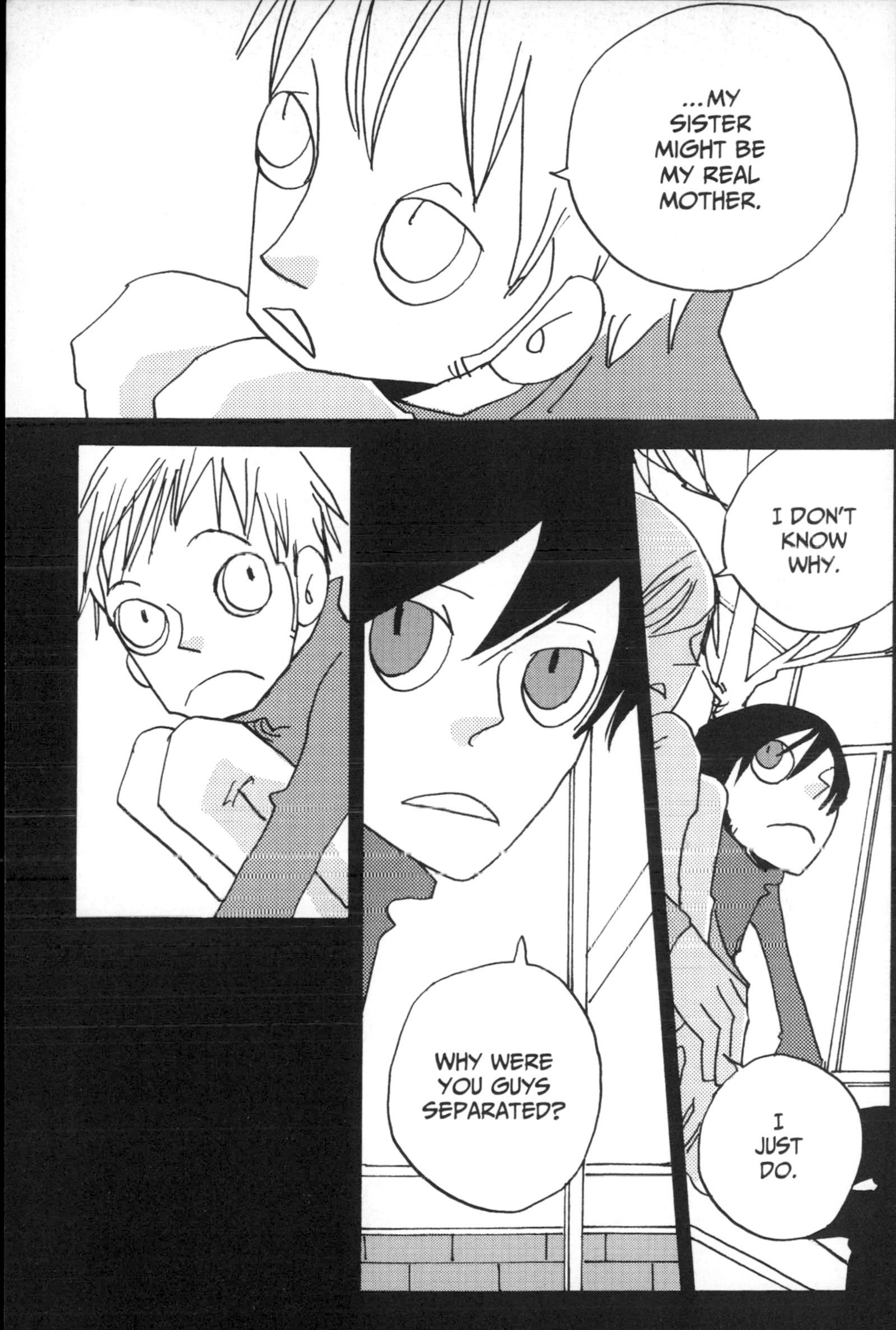
...MY SISTER MIGHT BE MY REAL MOTHER.
I DON'T KNOW WHY.
I JUST DO.
WHY WERE YOU GUYS SEPARATED?

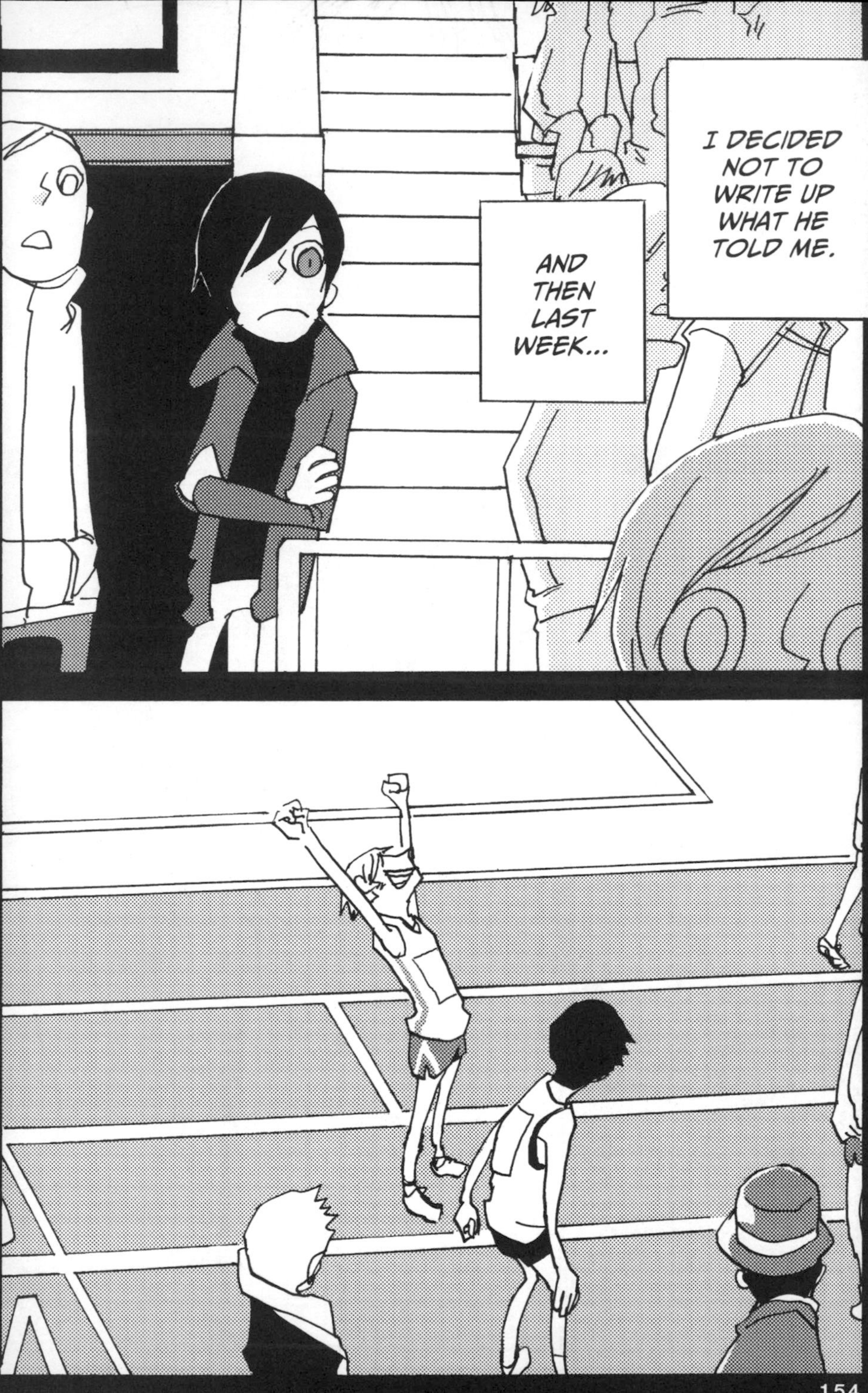
I DECIDED NOT TO WRITE UP WHAT HE TOLD ME.
AND THEN LAST WEEK...

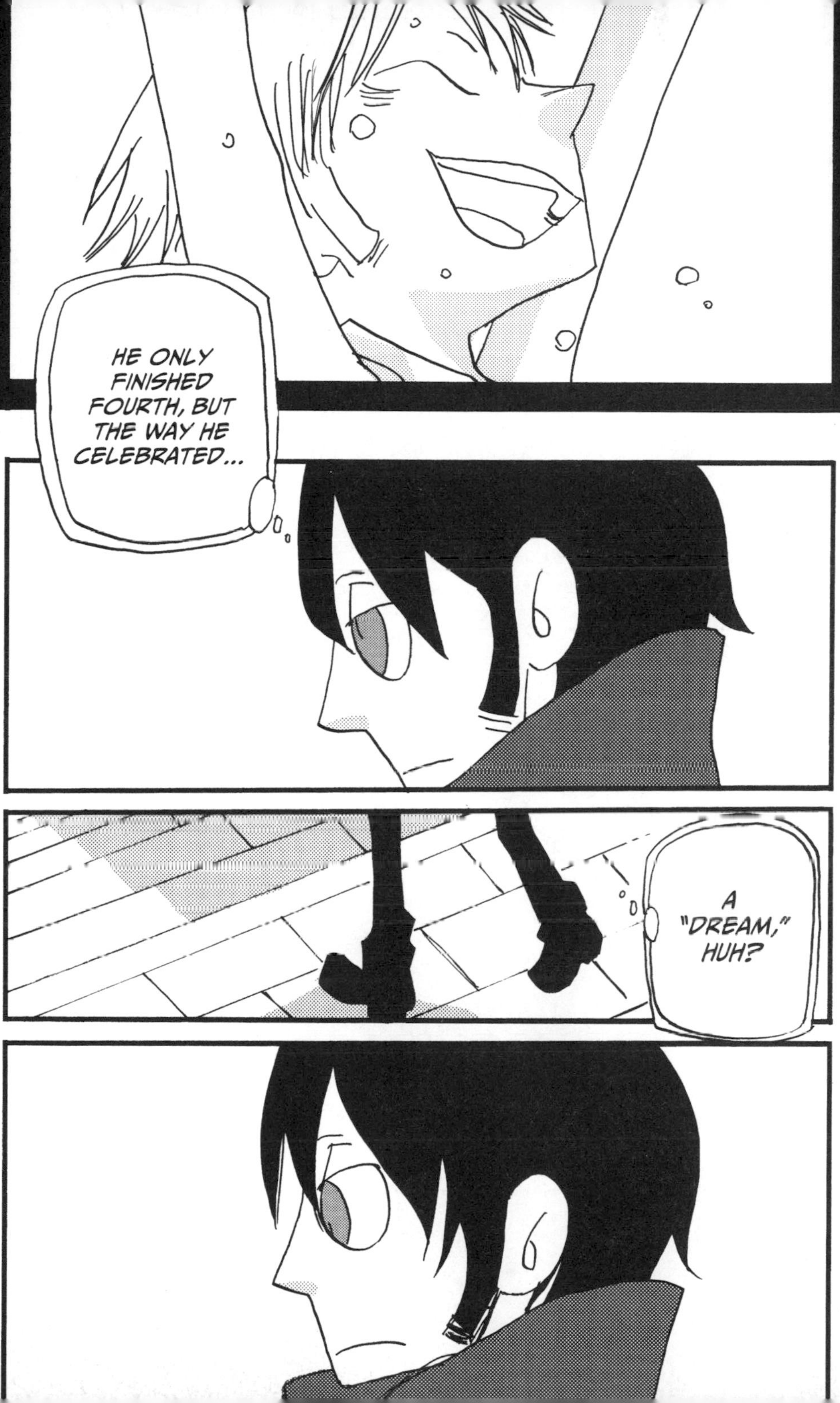
HE ONLY FINISHED FOURTH, BUT THE WAY HE CELEBRATED...
A "DREAM," HUH?

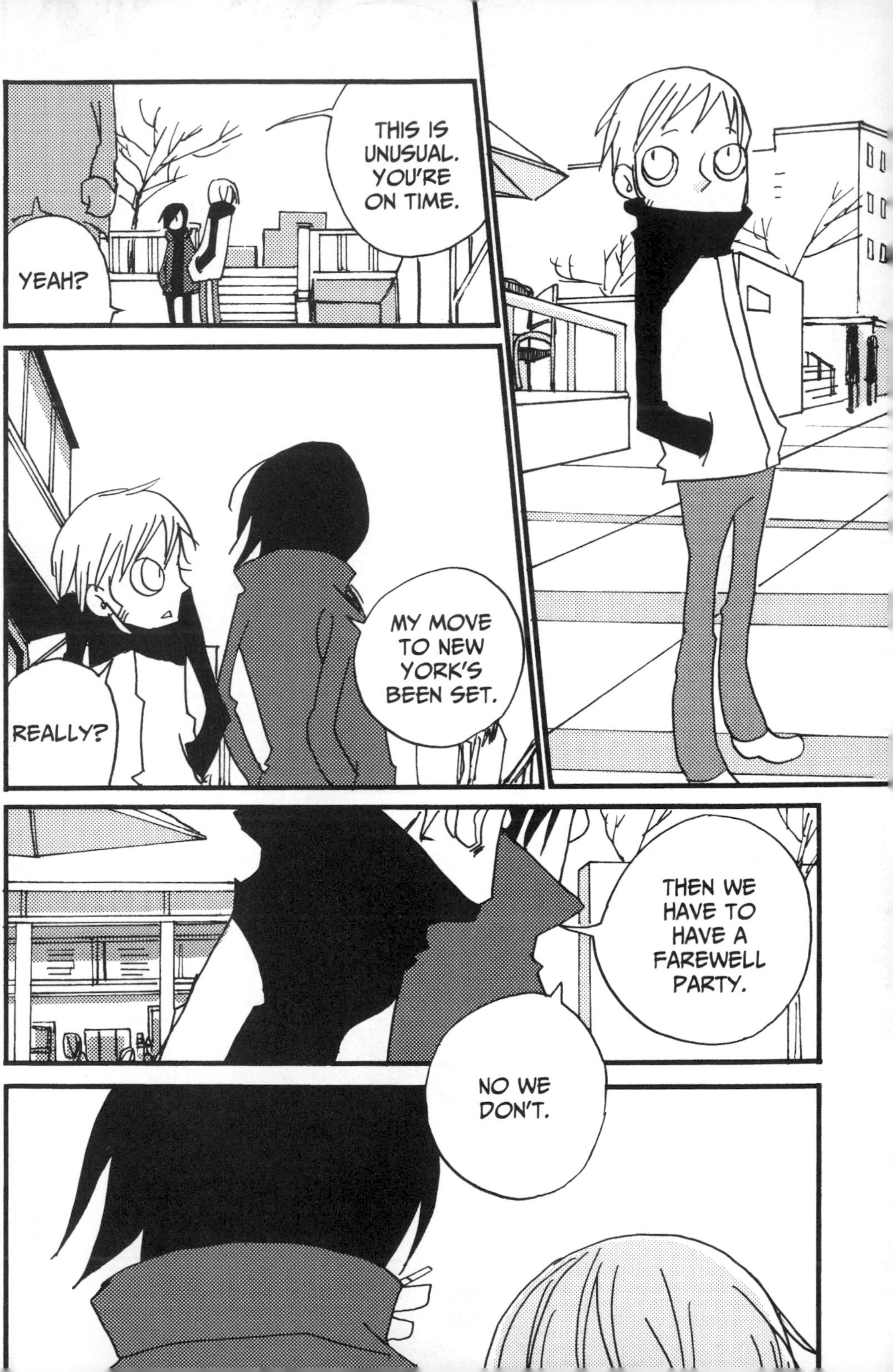
THIS IS UNUSUAL. YOU'RE ON TIME.
YEAH?
MY MOVE TO NEW YORK'S BEEN SET.
REALLY?
THEN WE HAVE TO HAVE A FAREWELL PARTY.
NO WE DON'T.

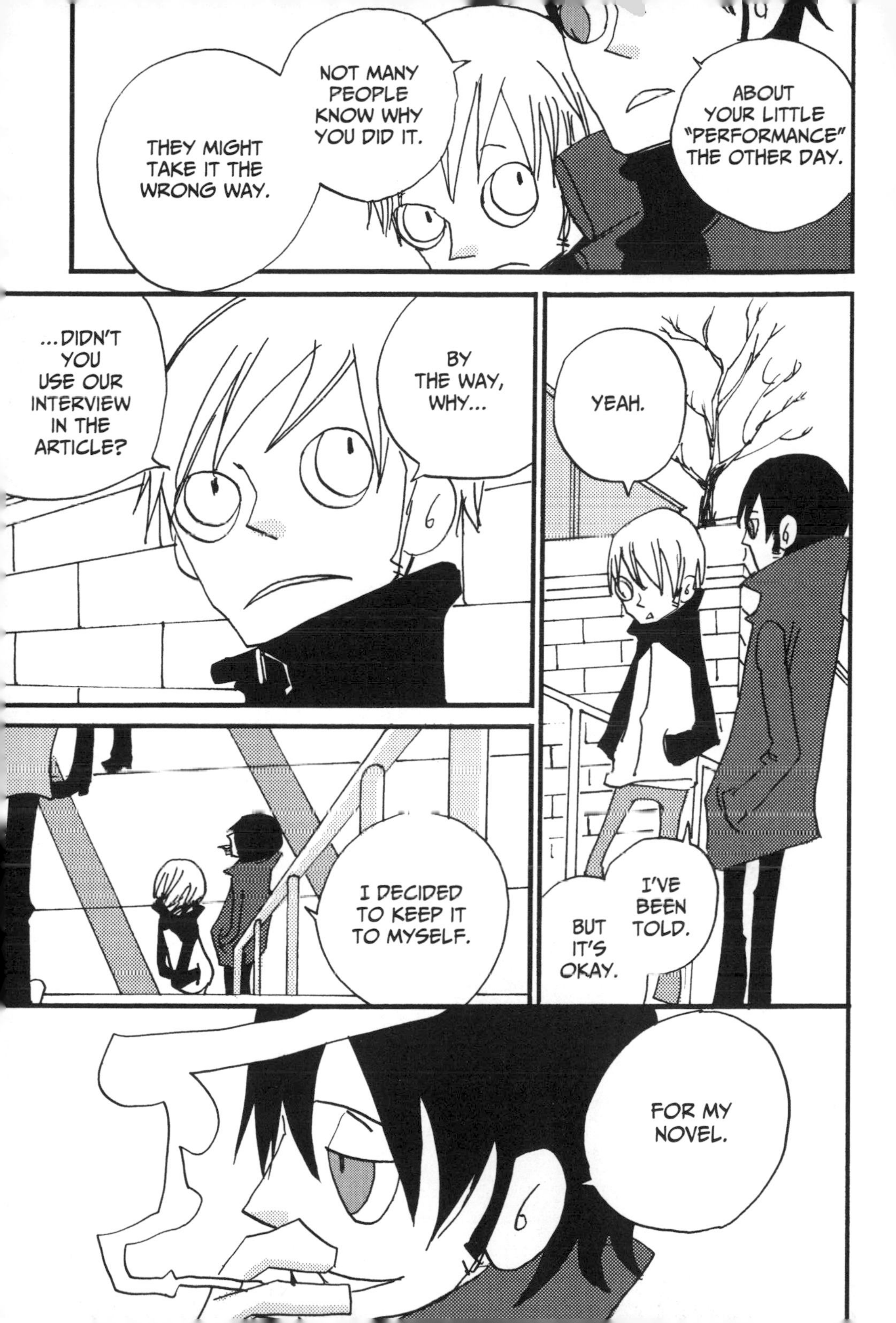

ABOUT YOUR LITTLE "PERFORMANCE" THE OTHER DAY.
NOT MANY PEOPLE KNOW WHY YOU DID IT.
THEY MIGHT TAKE IT THE WRONG WAY.
YEAH.
I'VE BEEN TOLD.
BUT IT'S OKAY.
BY THE WAY, WHY...
...DIDN'T YOU USE OUR INTERVIEW IN THE ARTICLE?
I DECIDED TO KEEP IT TO MYSELF.
FOR MY NOVEL.

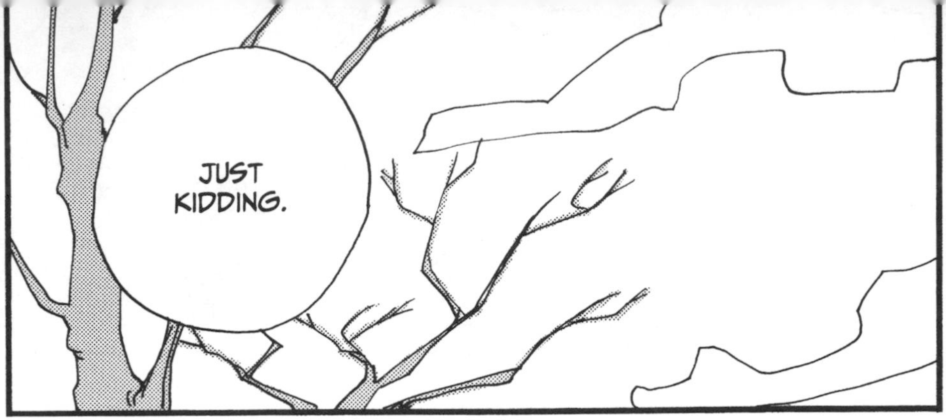
JUST KIDDING.

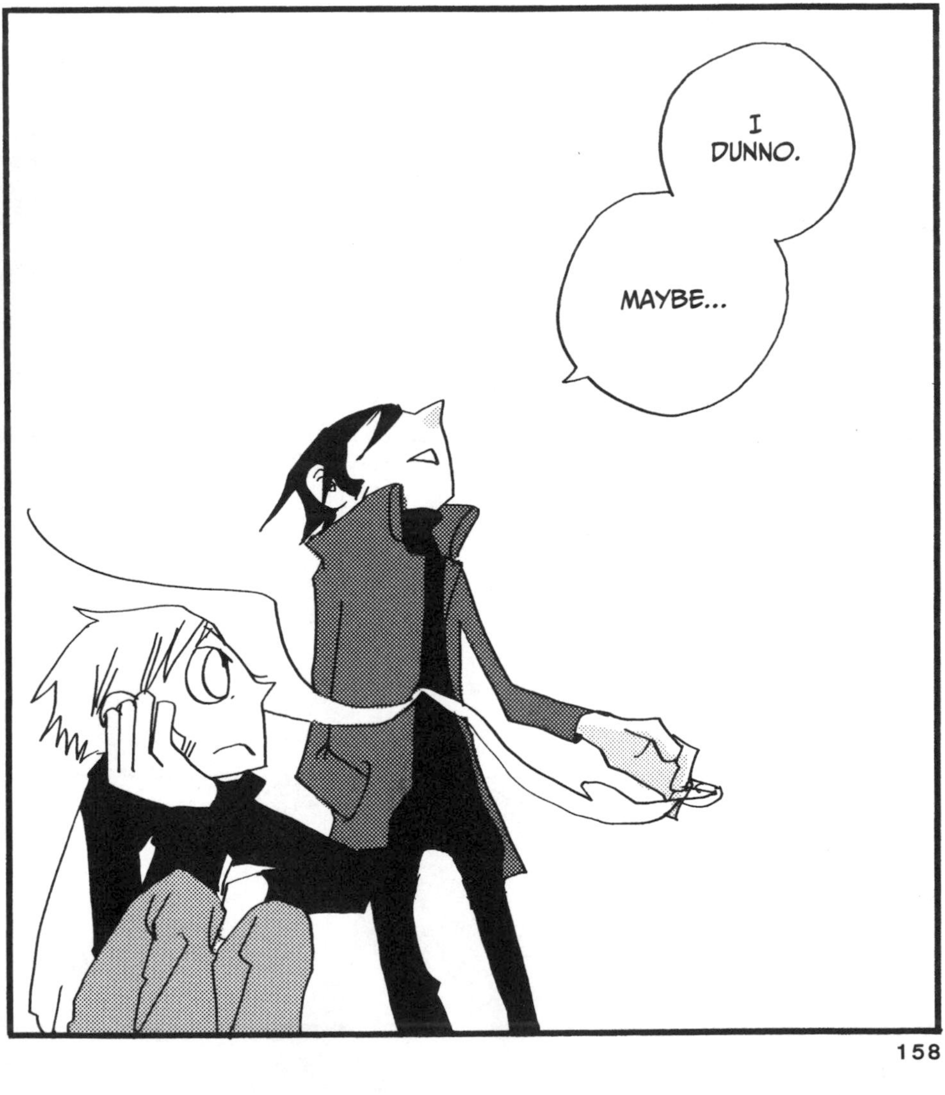
I DUNNO.
MAYBE...

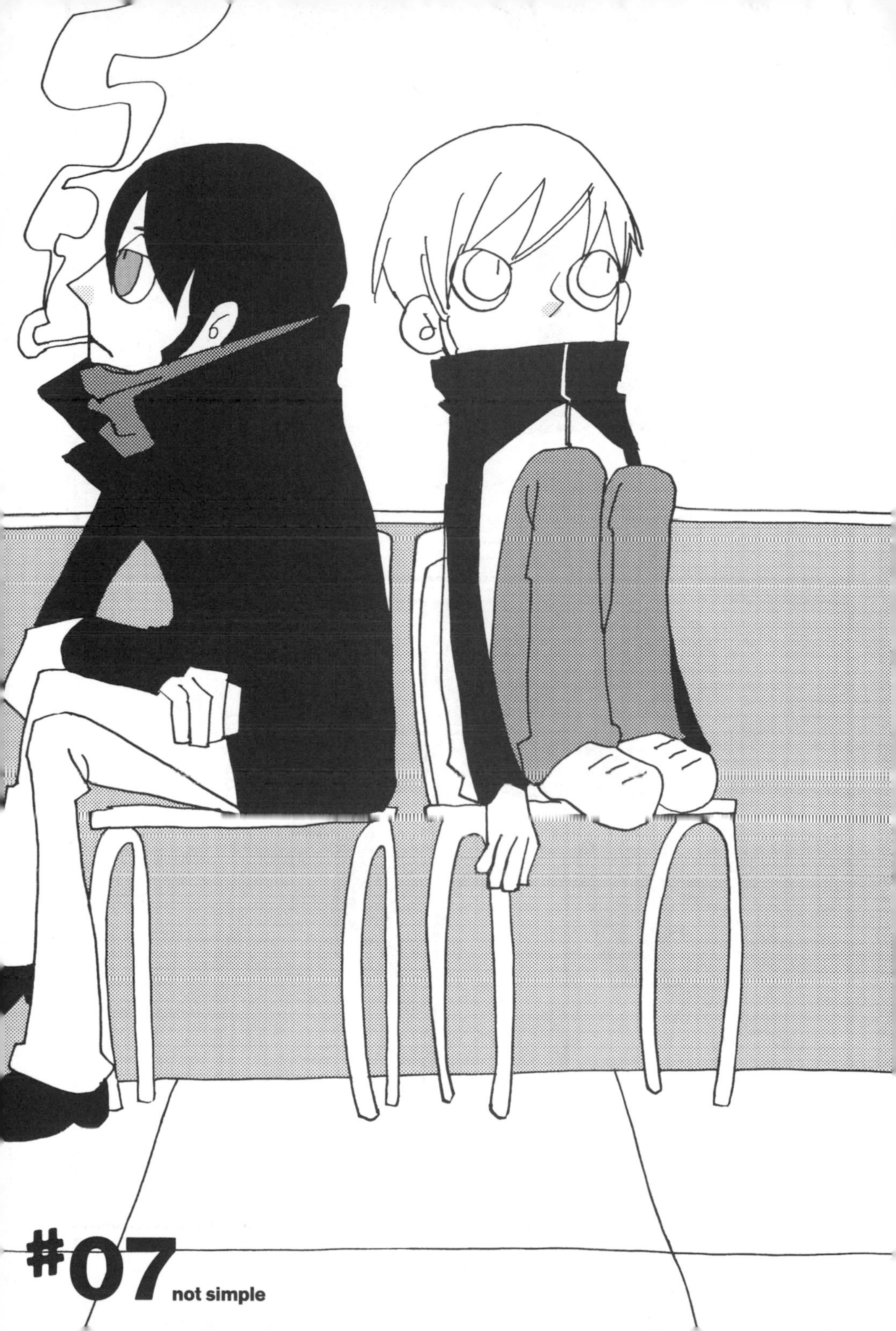

#07 not simple

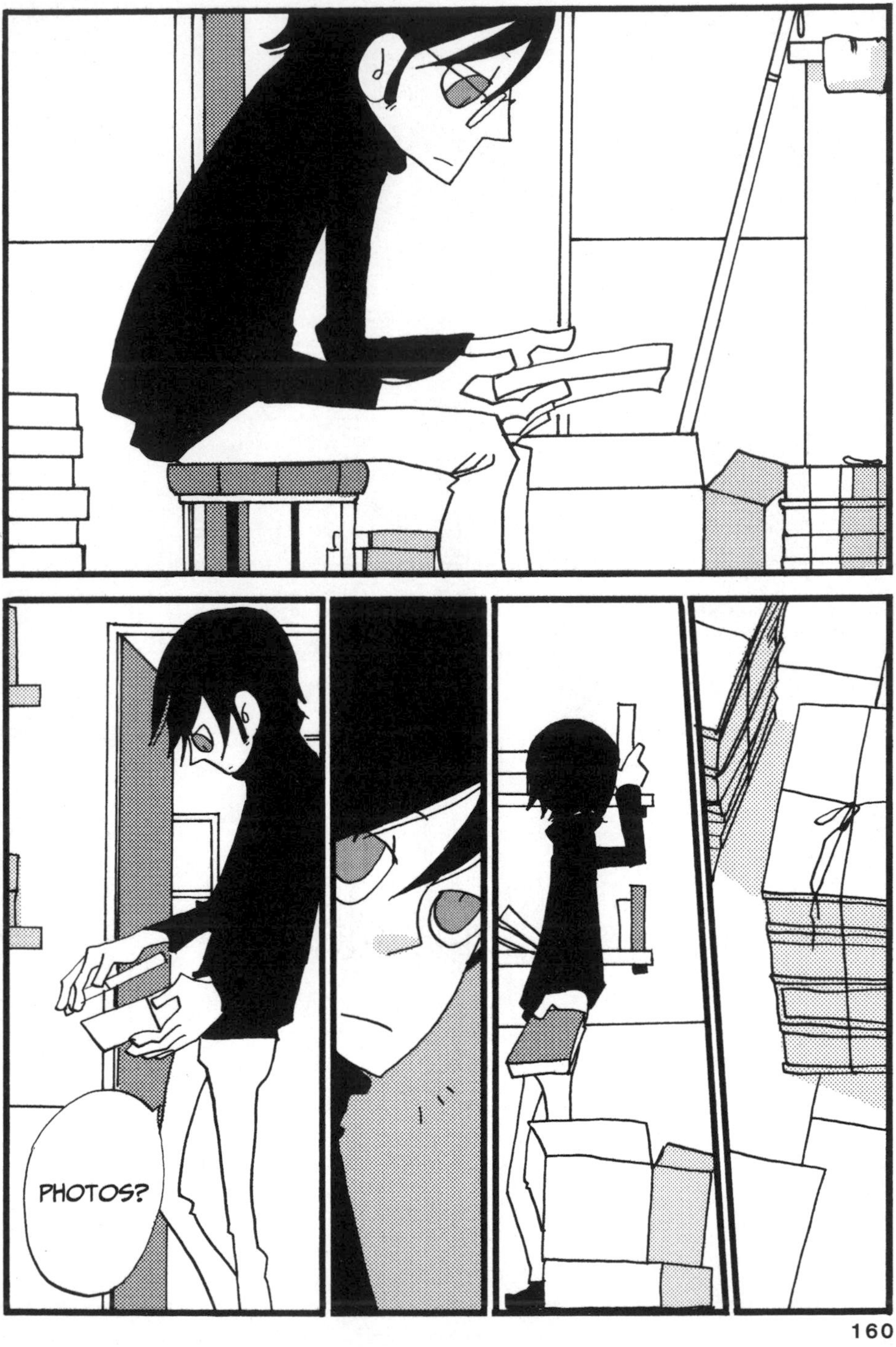
PHOTOS?

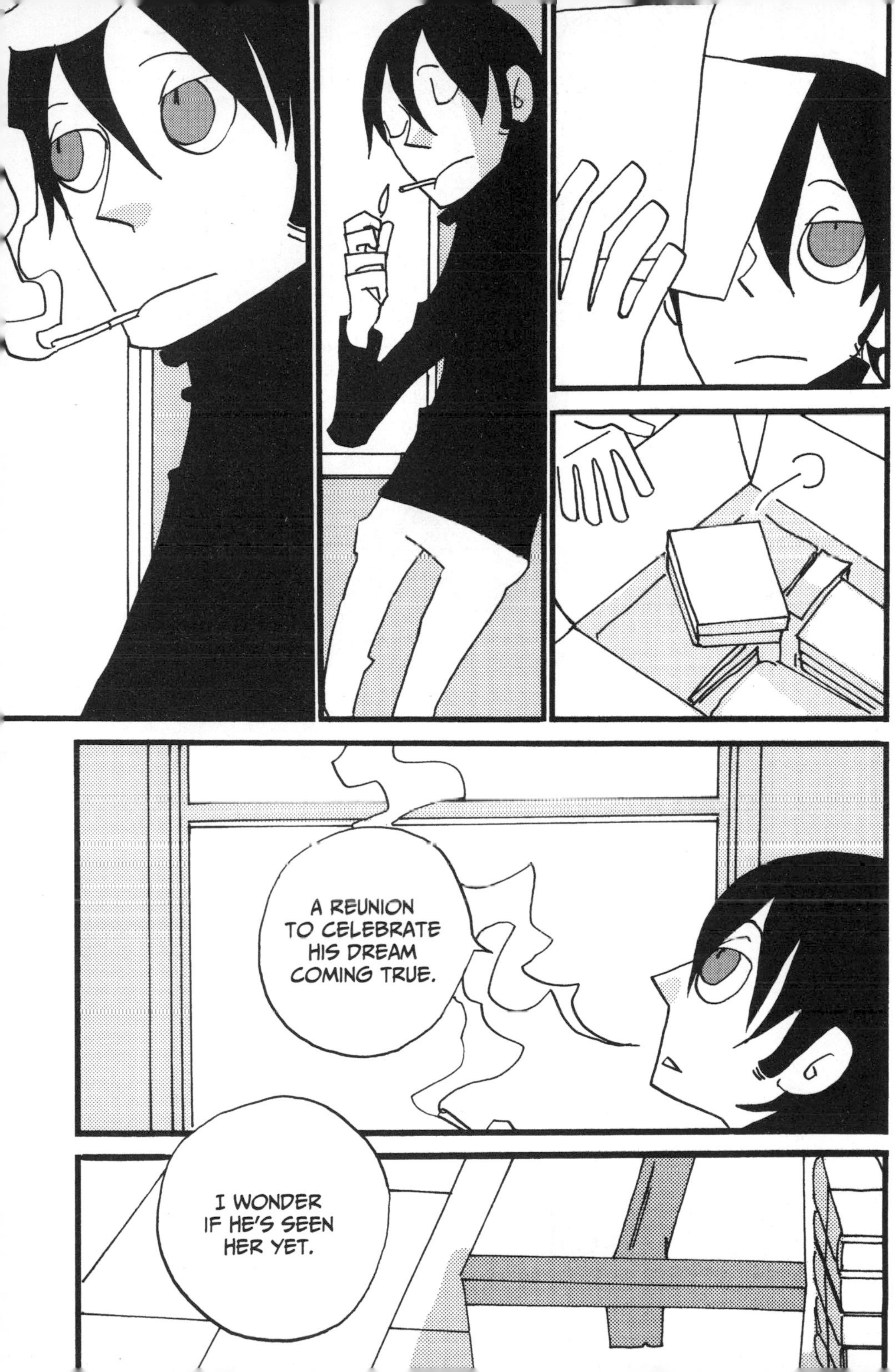
A REUNION TO CELEBRATE HIS DREAM COMING TRUE.
I WONDER IF HE'S SEEN HER YET.

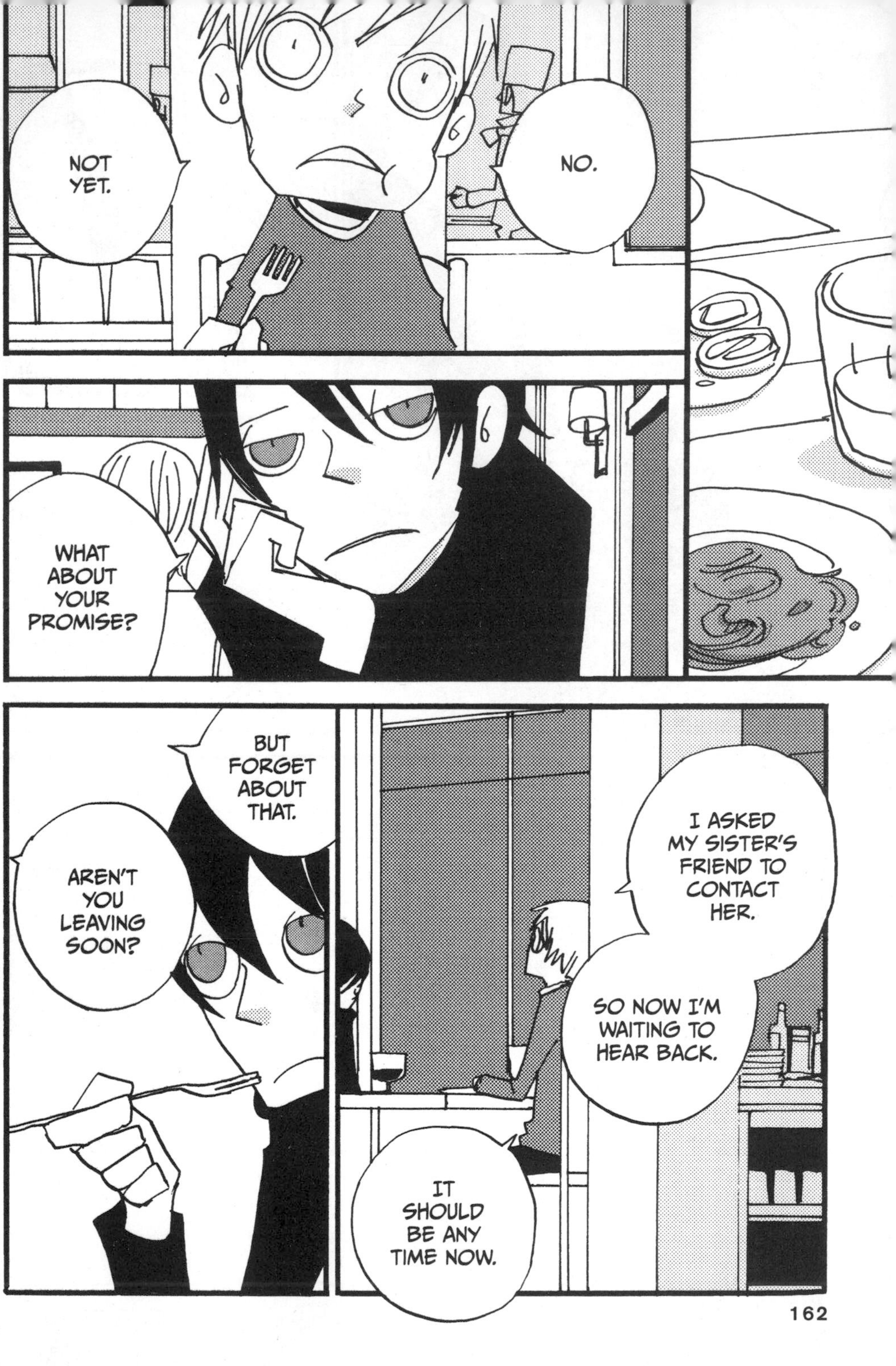
NO.
NOT YET.
WHAT ABOUT YOUR PROMISE?
I ASKED MY SISTER'S FRIEND TO CONTACT HER.
SO NOW I'M WAITING TO HEAR BACK.
IT SHOULD BE ANY TIME NOW.
BUT FORGET ABOUT THAT.
AREN'T YOU LEAVING SOON?

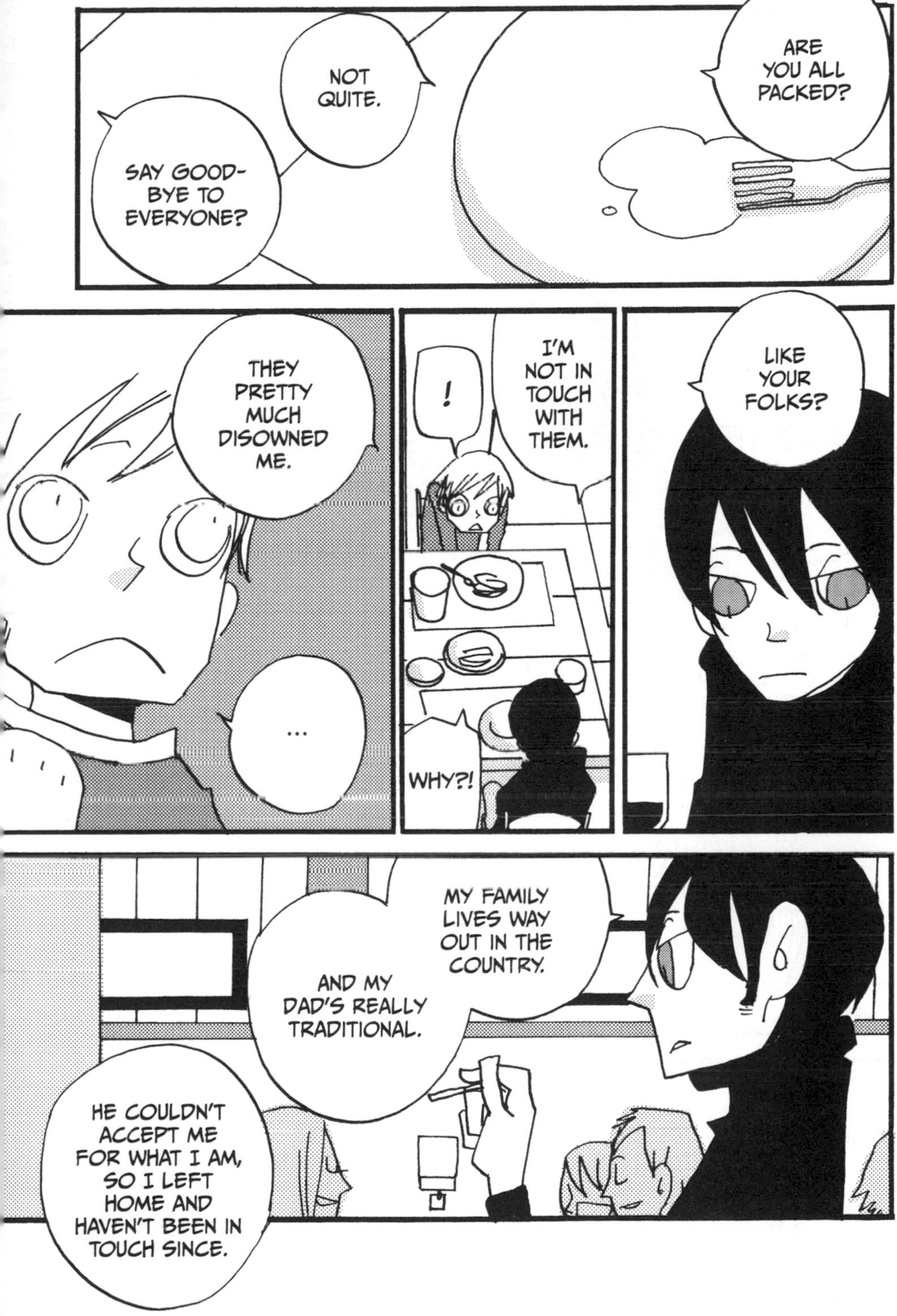
ARE YOU ALL PACKED?
NOT QUITE.
SAY GOOD-BYE TO EVERYONE?
LIKE YOUR FOLKS?
I'M NOT IN TOUCH WITH THEM.
!
WHY?!
THEY PRETTY MUCH DISOWNED ME.
...
MY FAMILY LIVES WAY OUT IN THE COUNTRY.
AND MY DAD'S REALLY TRADITIONAL.
HE COULDN'T ACCEPT ME FOR WHAT I AM, SO I LEFT HOME AND HAVEN'T BEEN IN TOUCH SINCE.

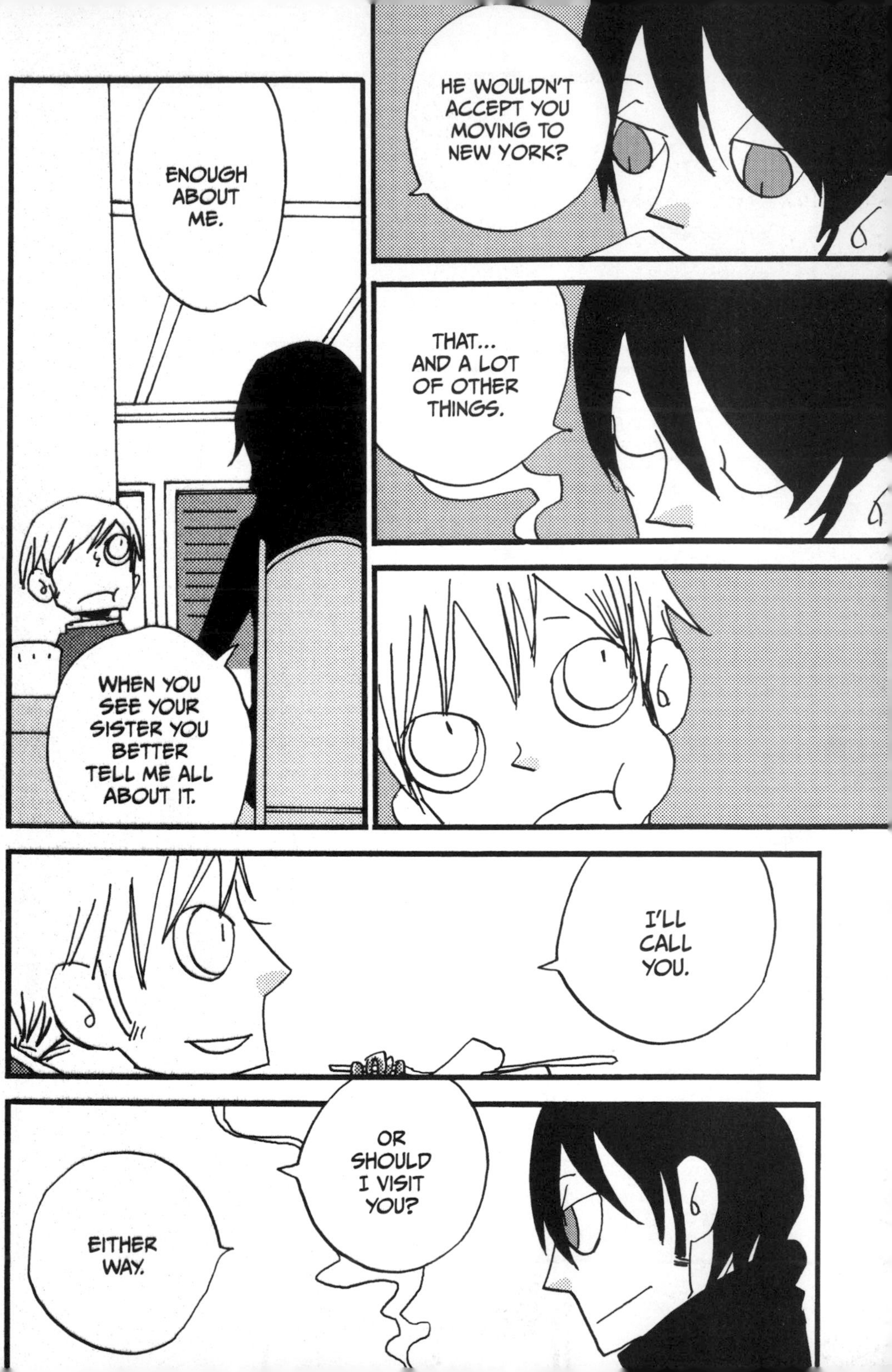
HE WOULDN'T ACCEPT YOU MOVING TO NEW YORK?
THAT... AND A LOT OF OTHER THINGS.
ENOUGH ABOUT ME.
WHEN YOU SEE YOUR SISTER YOU BETTER TELL ME ALL ABOUT IT.
I'LL CALL YOU.
OR SHOULD I VISIT YOU?
EITHER WAY.

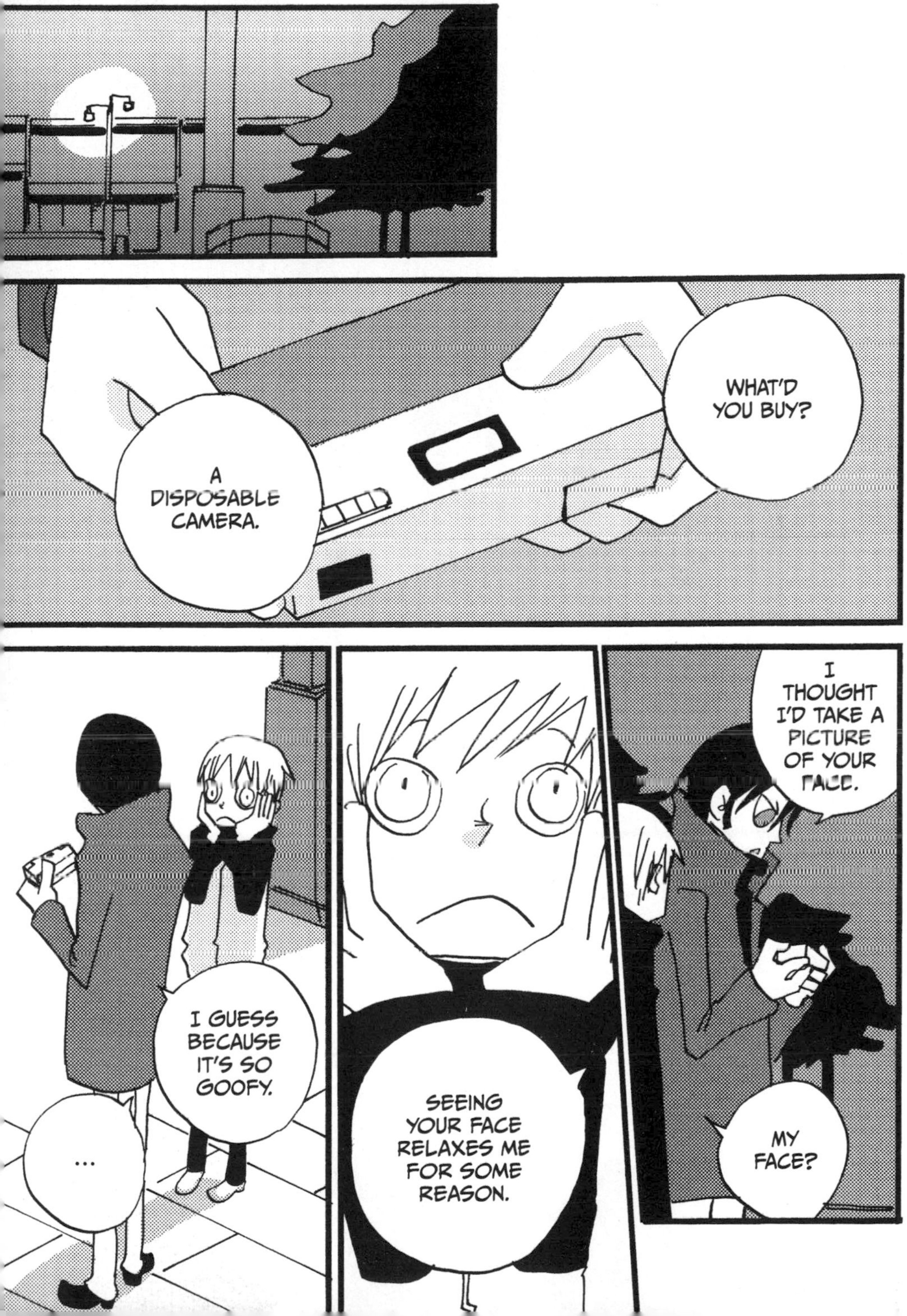
WHAT'D YOU BUY?
A DISPOSABLE CAMERA.
I THOUGHT I'D TAKE A PICTURE OF YOUR FACE.
MY FACE?
SEEING YOUR FACE RELAXES ME FOR SOME REASON.
I GUESS BECAUSE IT'S SO GOOFY.
...

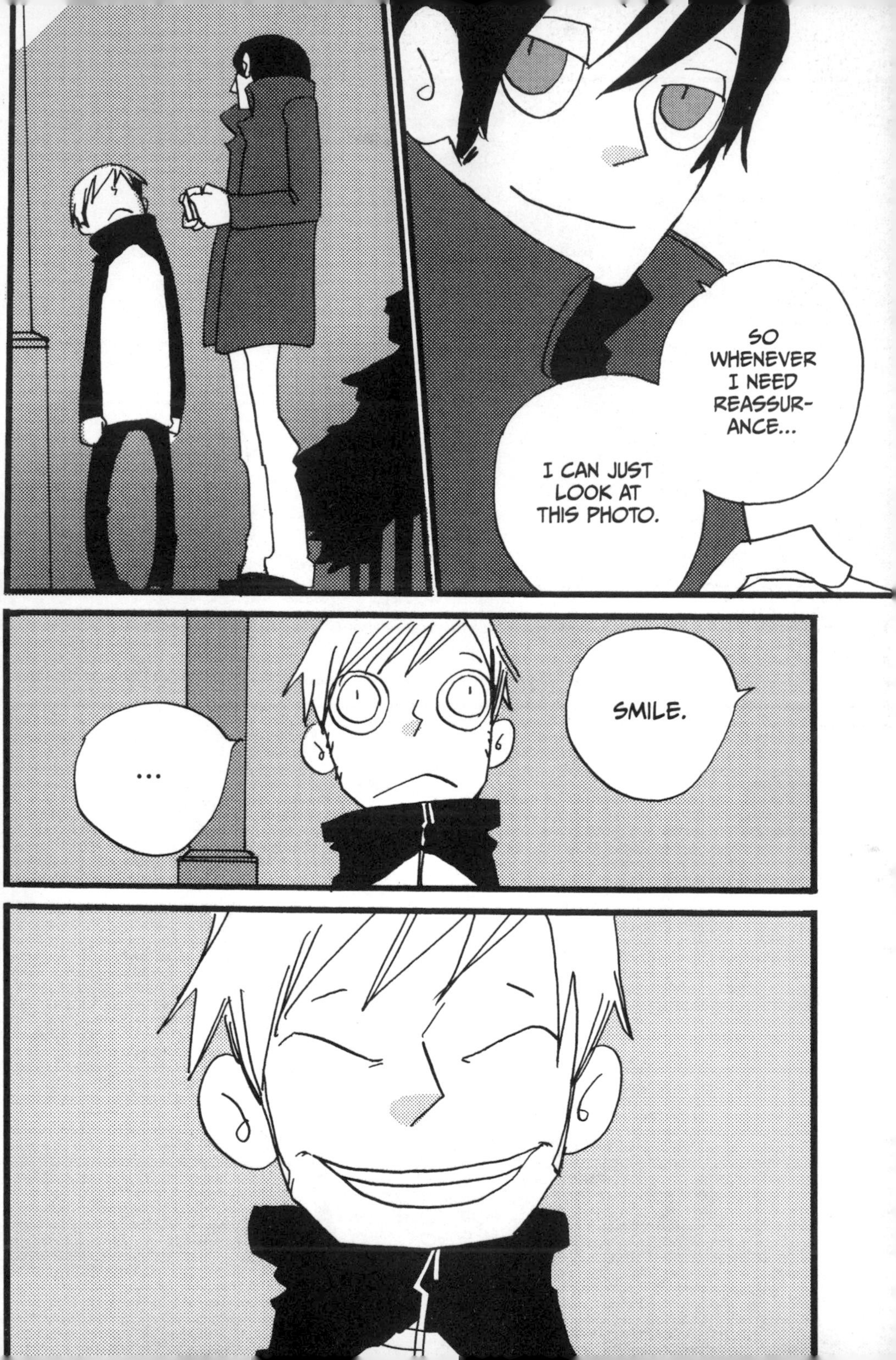
SO WHENEVER I NEED REASSUR-ANCE...
I CAN JUST LOOK AT THIS PHOTO.
SMILE.
...

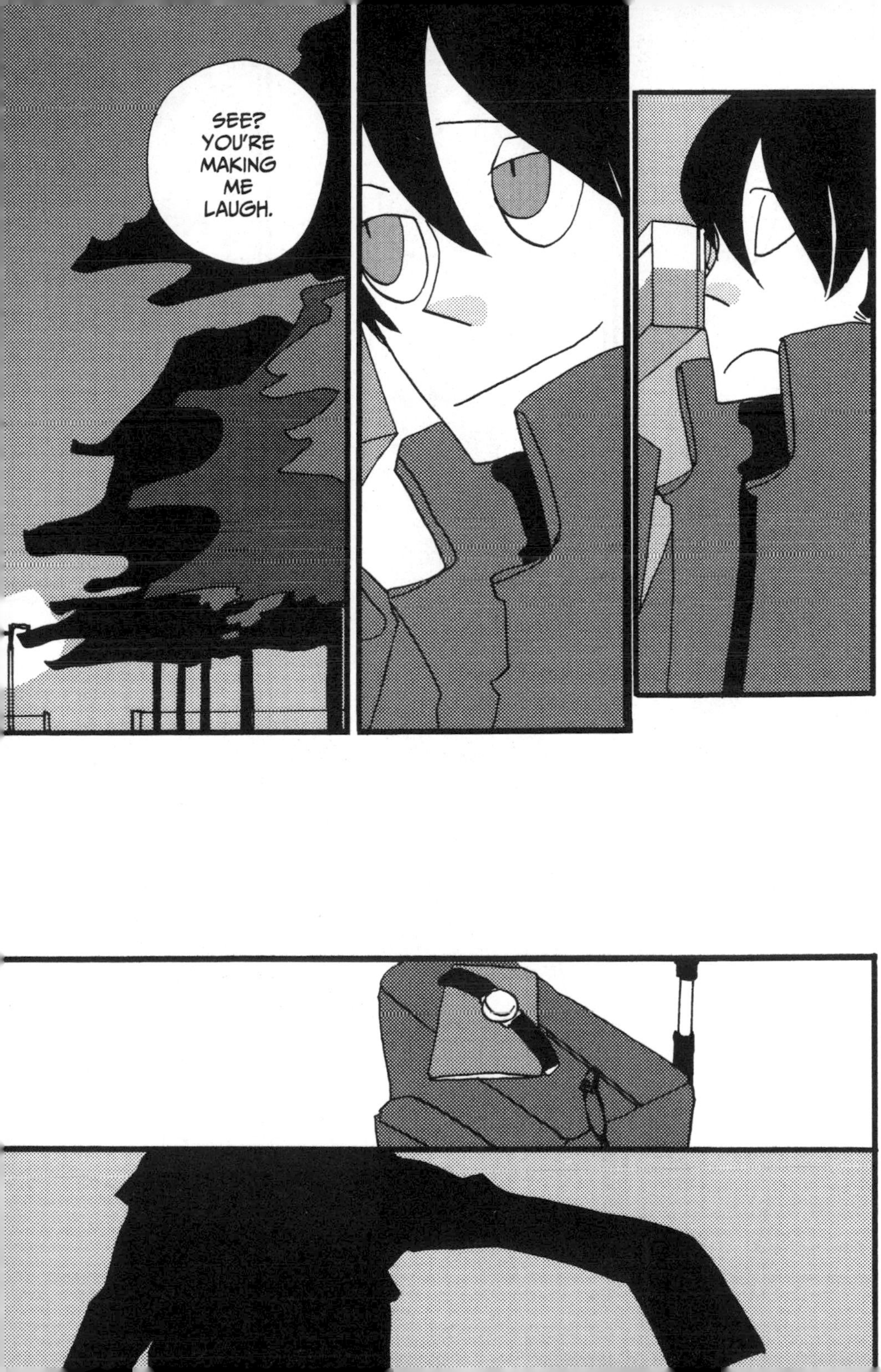
SEE? YOU'RE MAKING ME LAUGH.

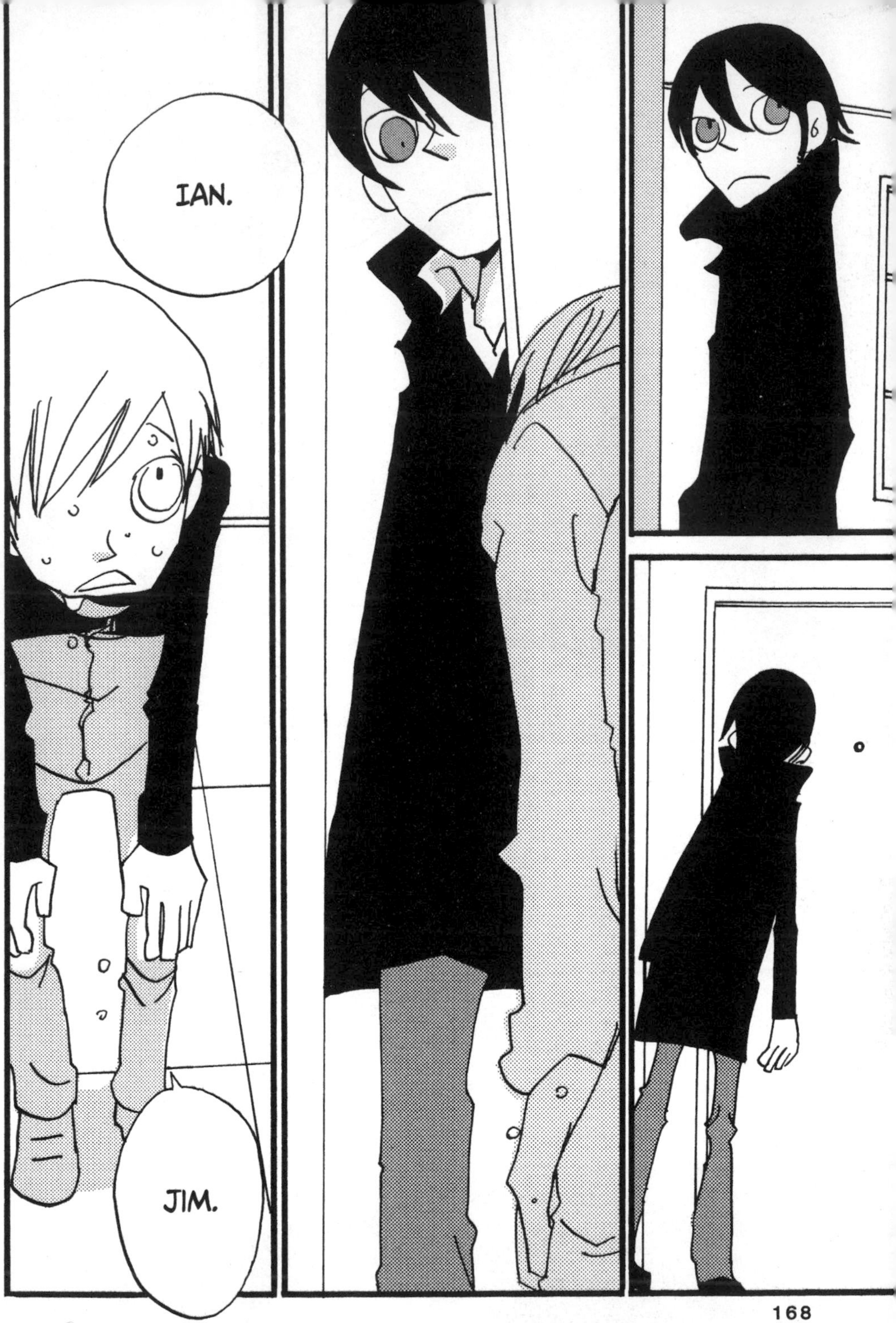
IAN.
JIM.

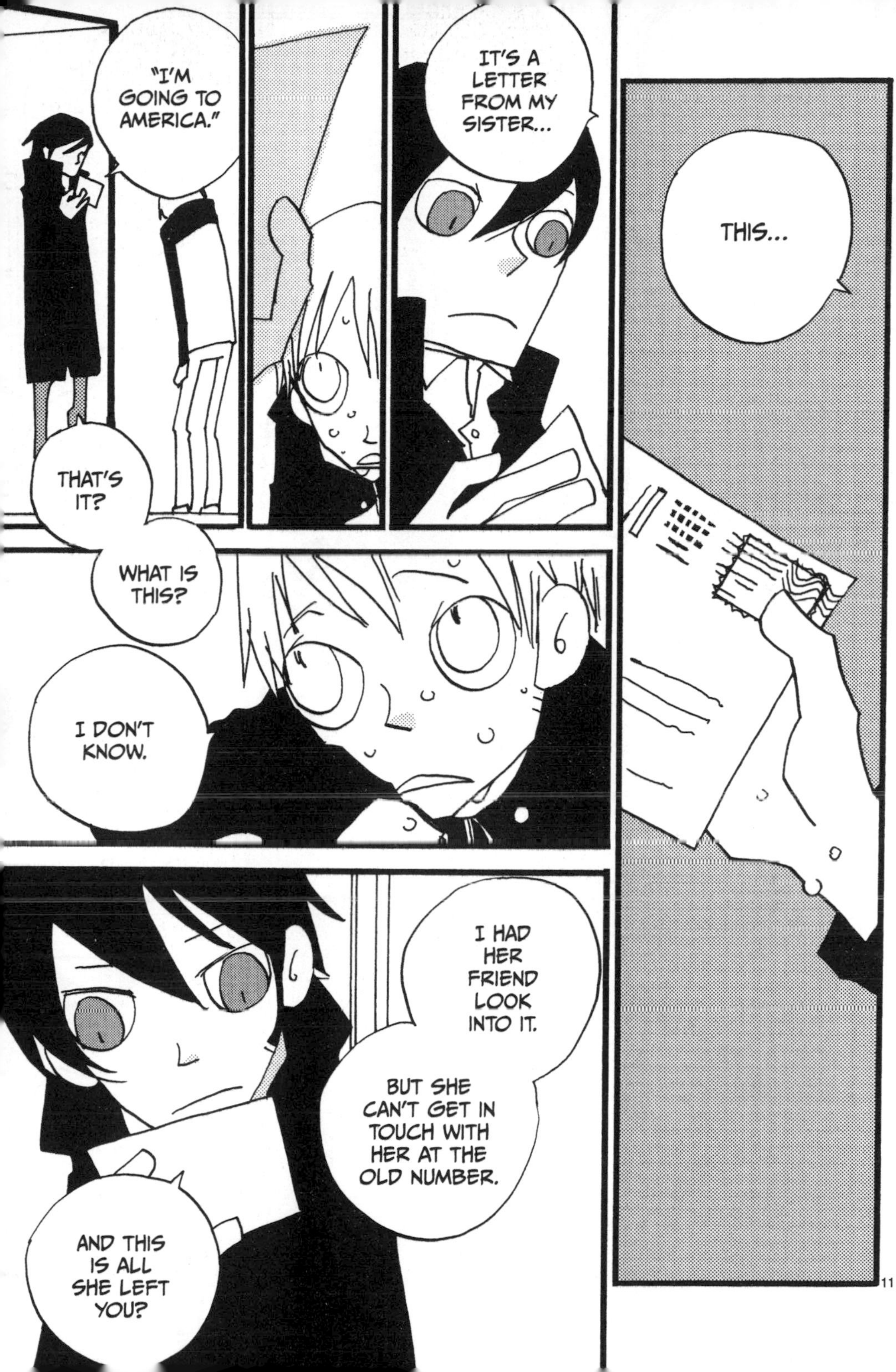
THIS...
IT'S A LETTER FROM MY SISTER...
"I'M GOING TO AMERICA."
THAT'S IT?
WHAT IS THIS?
I DON'T KNOW.
I HAD HER FRIEND LOOK INTO IT.
BUT SHE CAN'T GET IN TOUCH WITH HER AT THE OLD NUMBER.
AND THIS IS ALL SHE LEFT YOU?

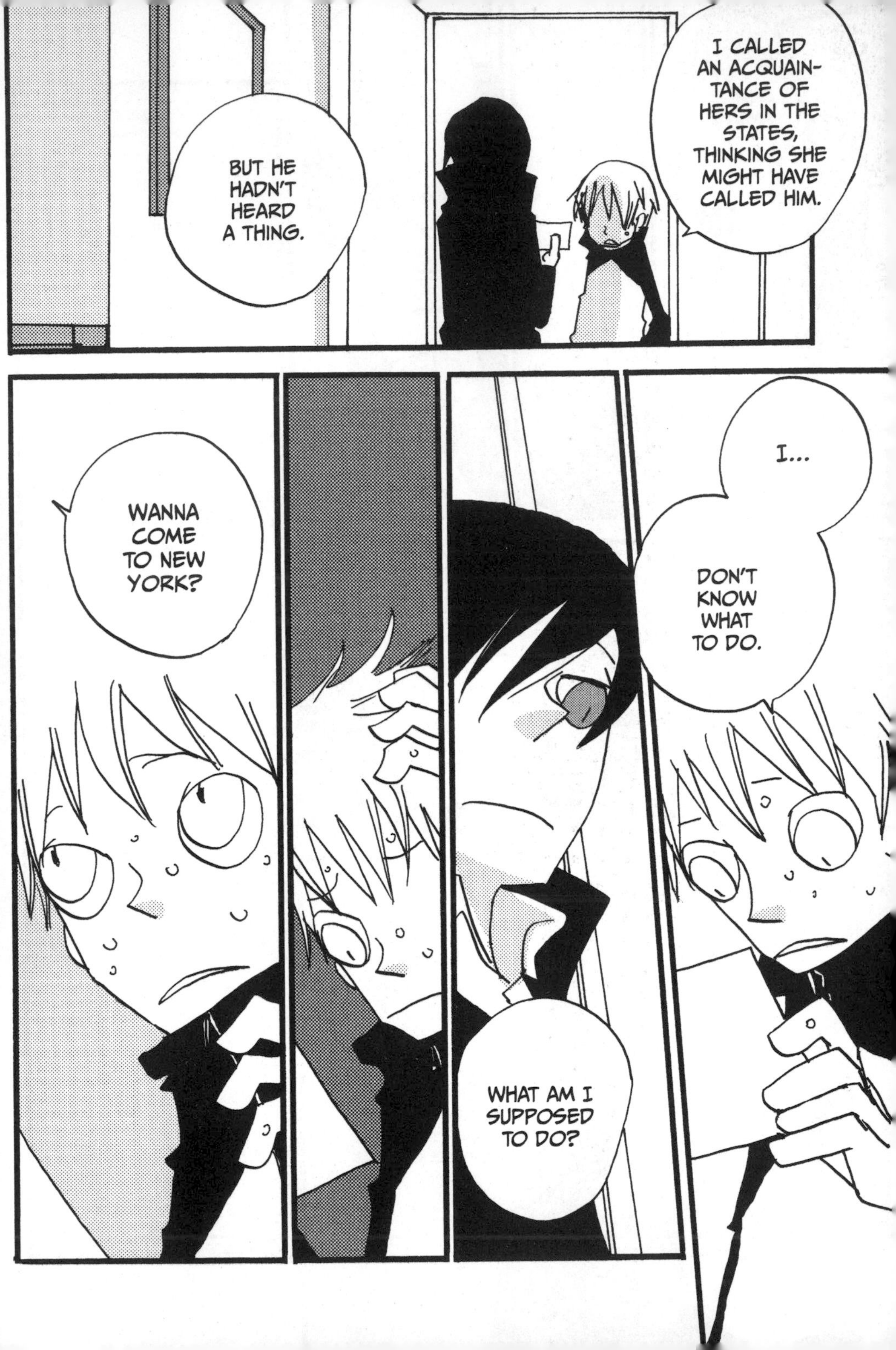
I CALLED AN ACQUAINTANCE OF HERS IN THE STATES, THINKING SHE MIGHT HAVE CALLED HIM.
BUT HE HADN'T HEARD A THING.
I...
DON'T KNOW WHAT TO DO.
WHAT AM I SUPPOSED TO DO?
WANNA COME TO NEW YORK?

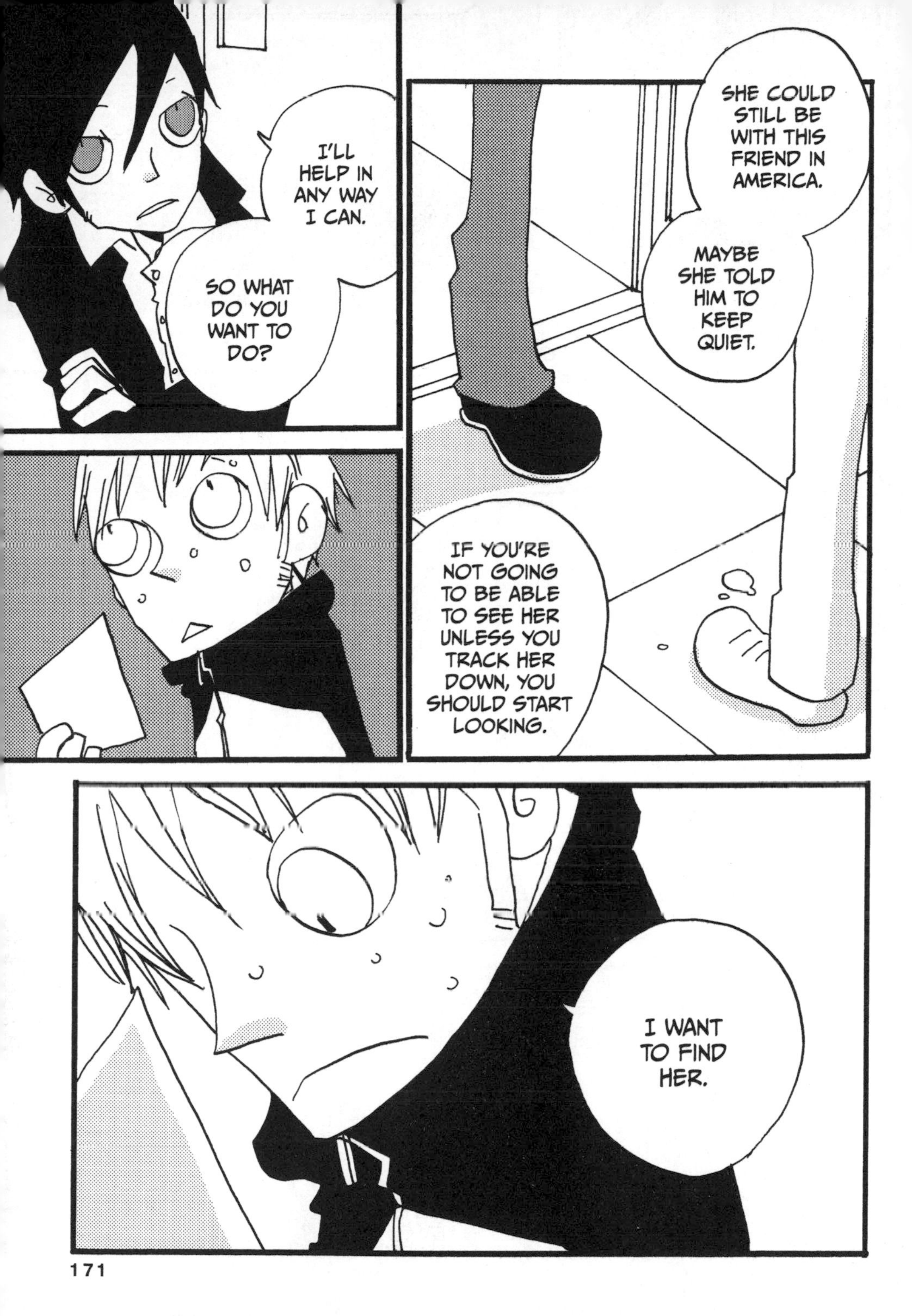
SHE COULD STILL BE WITH THIS FRIEND IN AMERICA.
MAYBE SHE TOLD HIM TO KEEP QUIET.
IF YOU'RE NOT GOING TO BE ABLE TO SEE HER UNLESS YOU TRACK HER DOWN, YOU SHOULD START LOOKING.
I'LL HELP IN ANY WAY I CAN.
SO WHAT DO YOU WANT TO DO?
I WANT TO FIND HER.

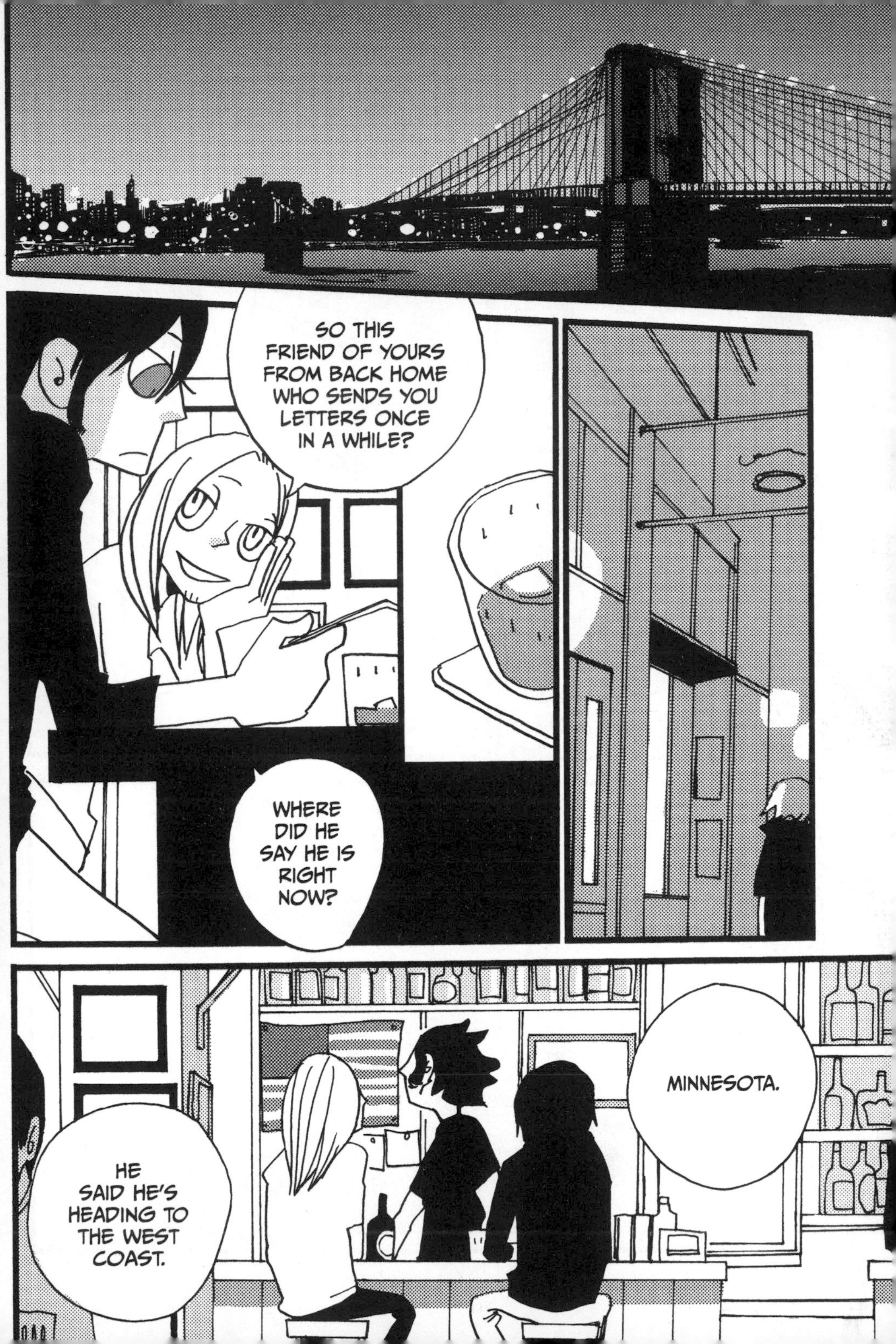
SO THIS FRIEND OF YOURS FROM BACK HOME WHO SENDS YOU LETTERS ONCE IN A WHILE?
WHERE DID HE SAY HE IS RIGHT NOW?
MINNESOTA.
HE SAID HE'S HEADING TO THE WEST COAST.

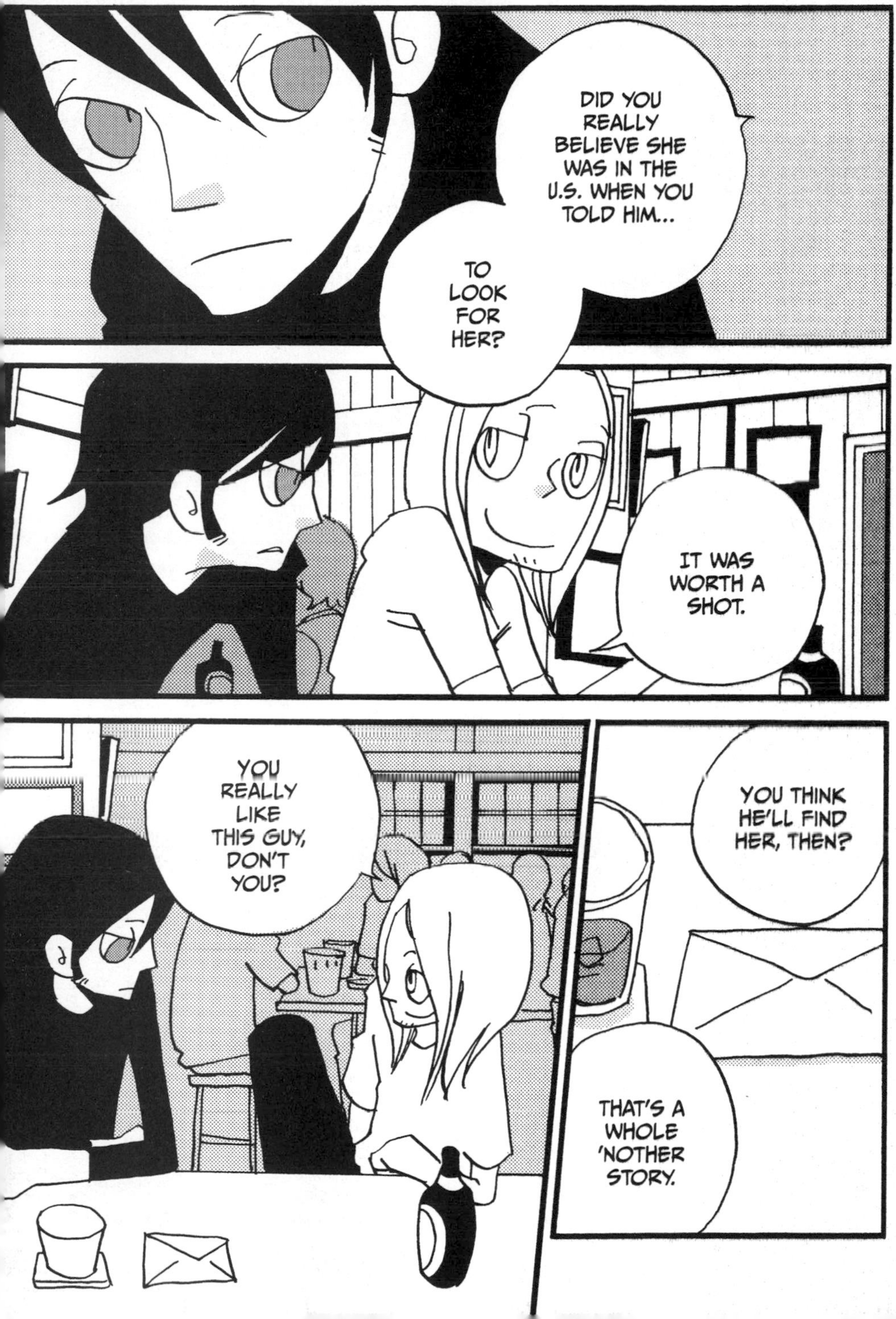
DID YOU REALLY BELIEVE SHE WAS IN THE U.S. WHEN YOU TOLD HIM...
TO LOOK FOR HER?
IT WAS WORTH A SHOT.
YOU THINK HE'LL FIND HER, THEN?
THAT'S A WHOLE 'NOTHER STORY.
YOU REALLY LIKE THIS GUY, DON'T YOU?

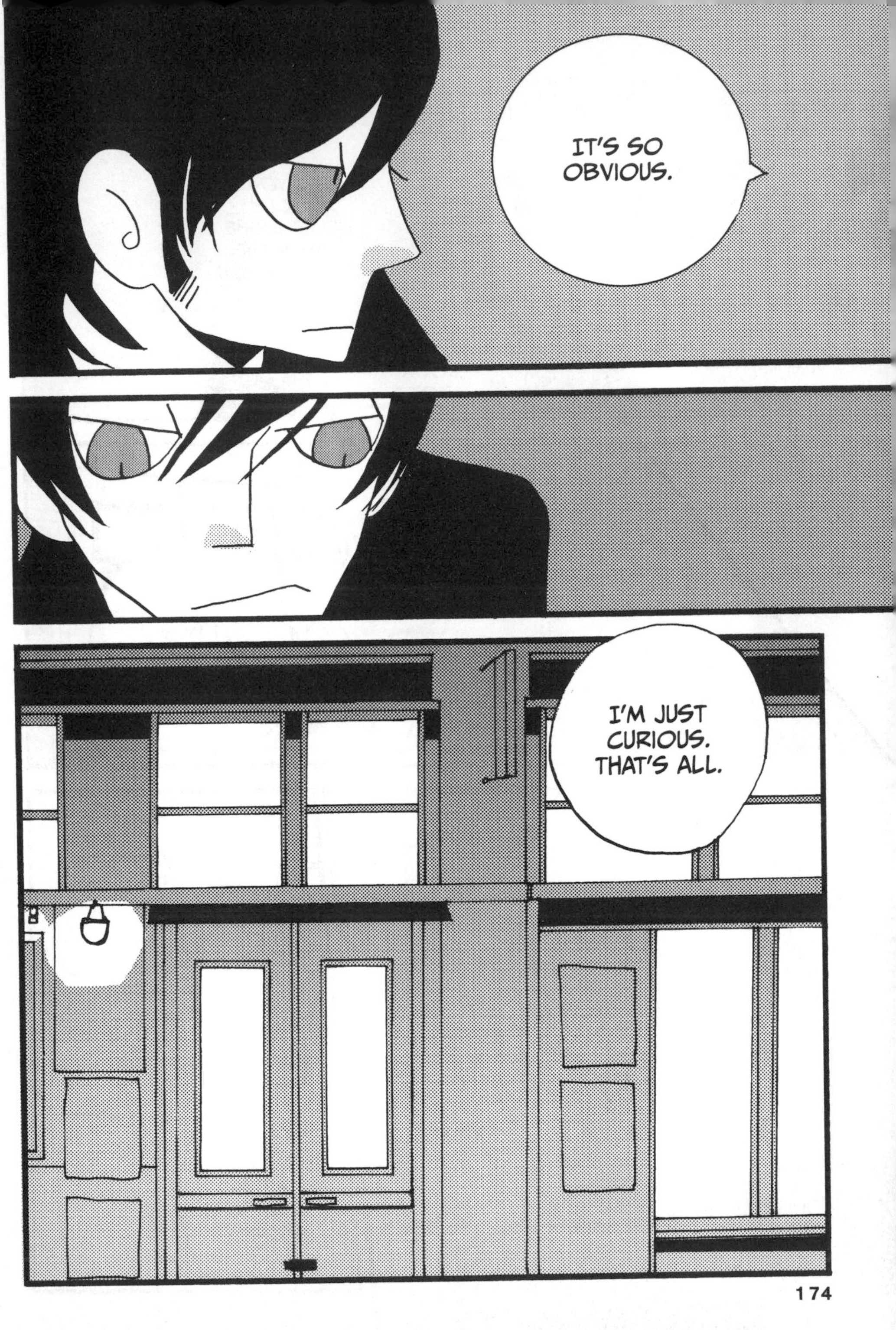
IT'S SO OBVIOUS.
I'M JUST CURIOUS. THAT'S ALL.

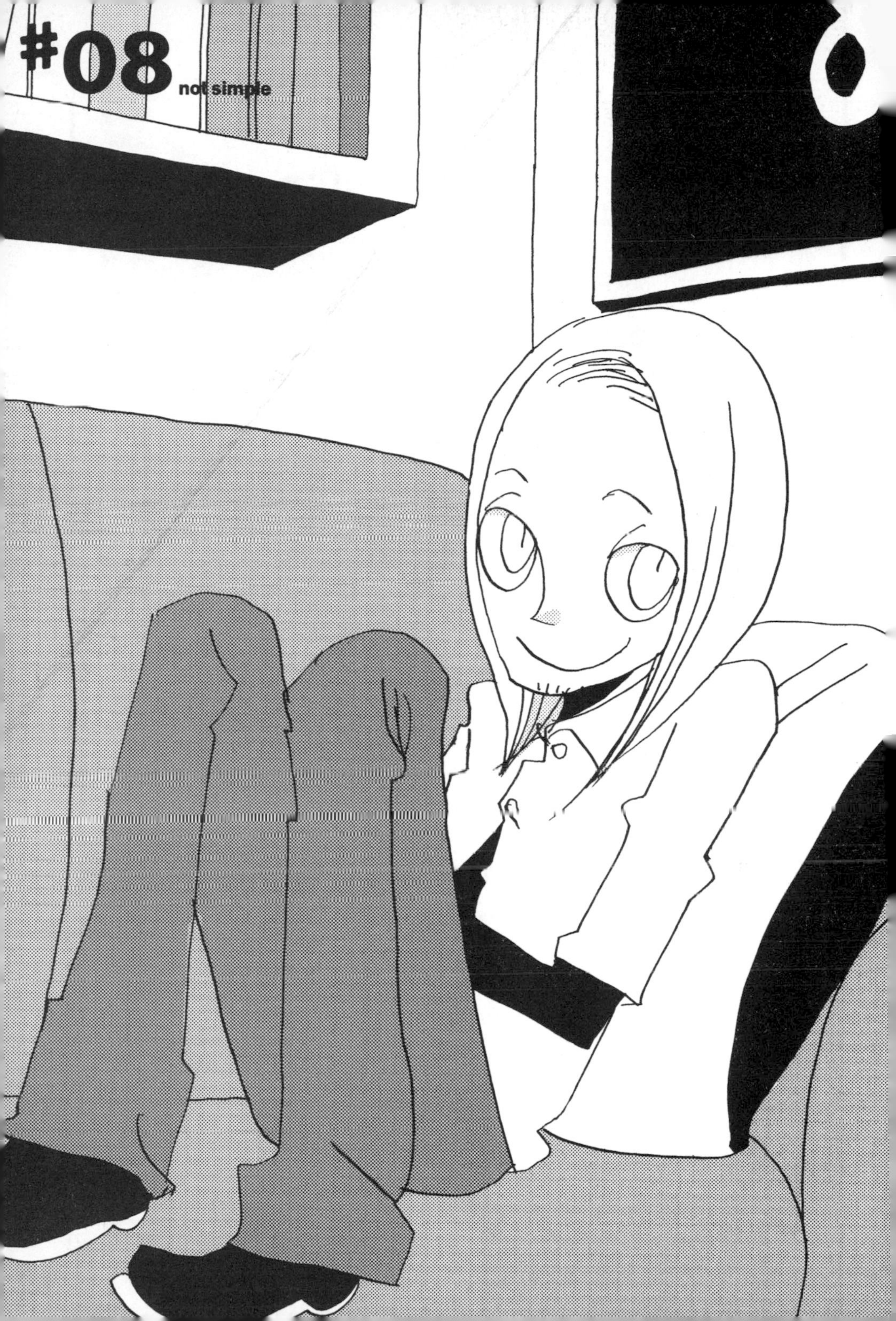
#08
not simple

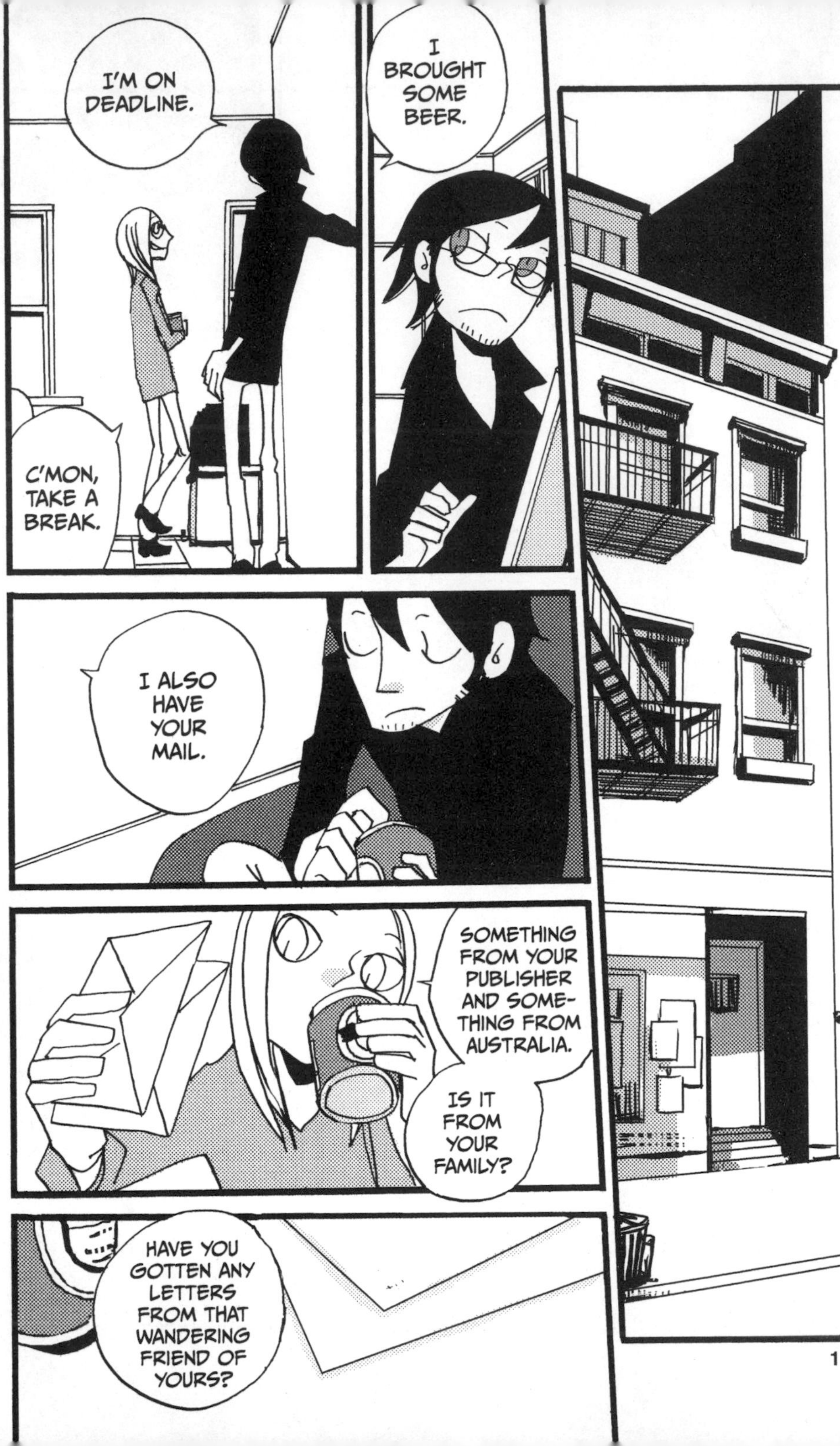
I BROUGHT SOME BEER.
I'M ON DEADLINE.
C'MON, TAKE A BREAK.
I ALSO HAVE YOUR MAIL.
SOMETHING FROM YOUR PUBLISHER AND SOME-THING FROM AUSTRALIA.
IS IT FROM YOUR FAMILY?
HAVE YOU GOTTEN ANY LETTERS FROM THAT WANDERING FRIEND OF YOURS?

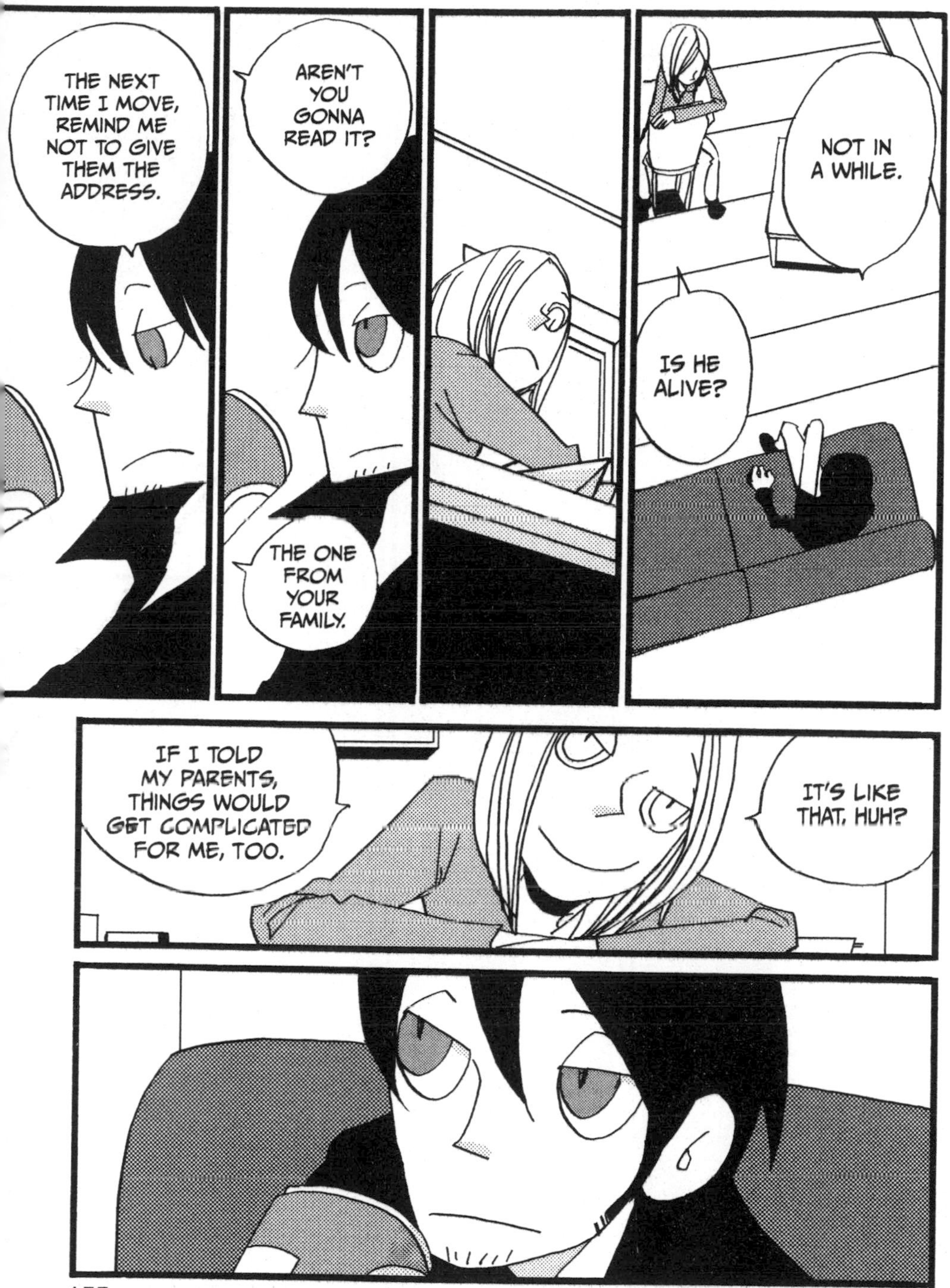
NOT IN A WHILE.
IS HE ALIVE?
AREN'T YOU GONNA READ IT?
THE ONE FROM YOUR FAMILY.
THE NEXT TIME I MOVE, REMIND ME NOT TO GIVE THEM THE ADDRESS.
IT'S LIKE THAT, HUH?
IF I TOLD MY PARENTS, THINGS WOULD GET COMPLICATED FOR ME, TOO.

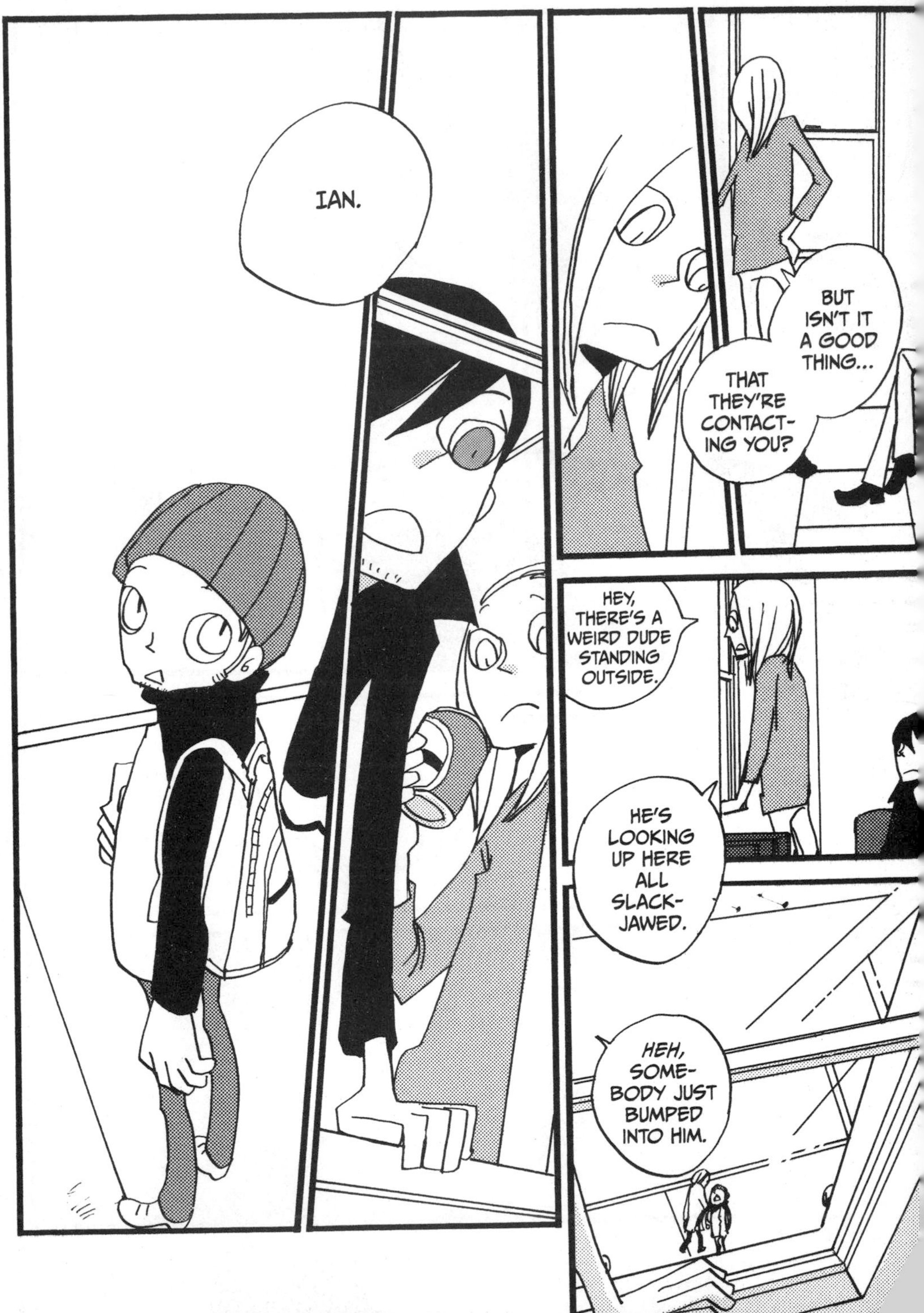
BUT ISN'T IT A GOOD THING...
THAT THEY'RE CONTACTING YOU?
HEY, THERE'S A WEIRD DUDE STANDING OUTSIDE.
HE'S LOOKING UP HERE ALL SLACK-JAWED.
HEH, SOMEBODY JUST BUMPED INTO HIM.
IAN.

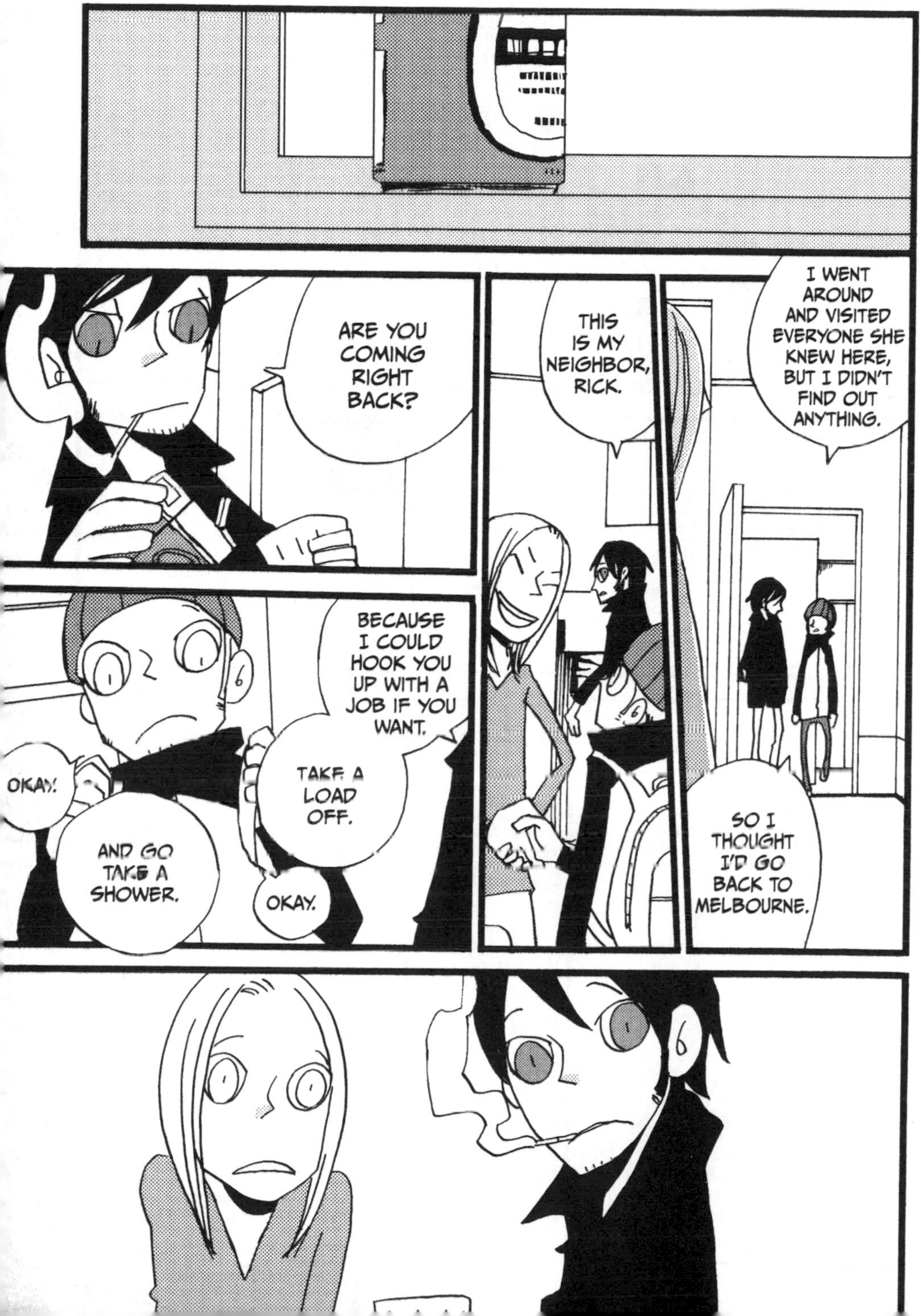
I WENT AROUND AND VISITED EVERYONE SHE KNEW HERE, BUT I DIDN'T FIND OUT ANYTHING.
SO I THOUGHT I'D GO BACK TO MELBOURNE.
THIS IS MY NEIGHBOR, RICK.
ARE YOU COMING RIGHT BACK?
BECAUSE I COULD HOOK YOU UP WITH A JOB IF YOU WANT.
TAKE A LOAD OFF.
OKAY!
AND GO TAKE A SHOWER.
OKAY.

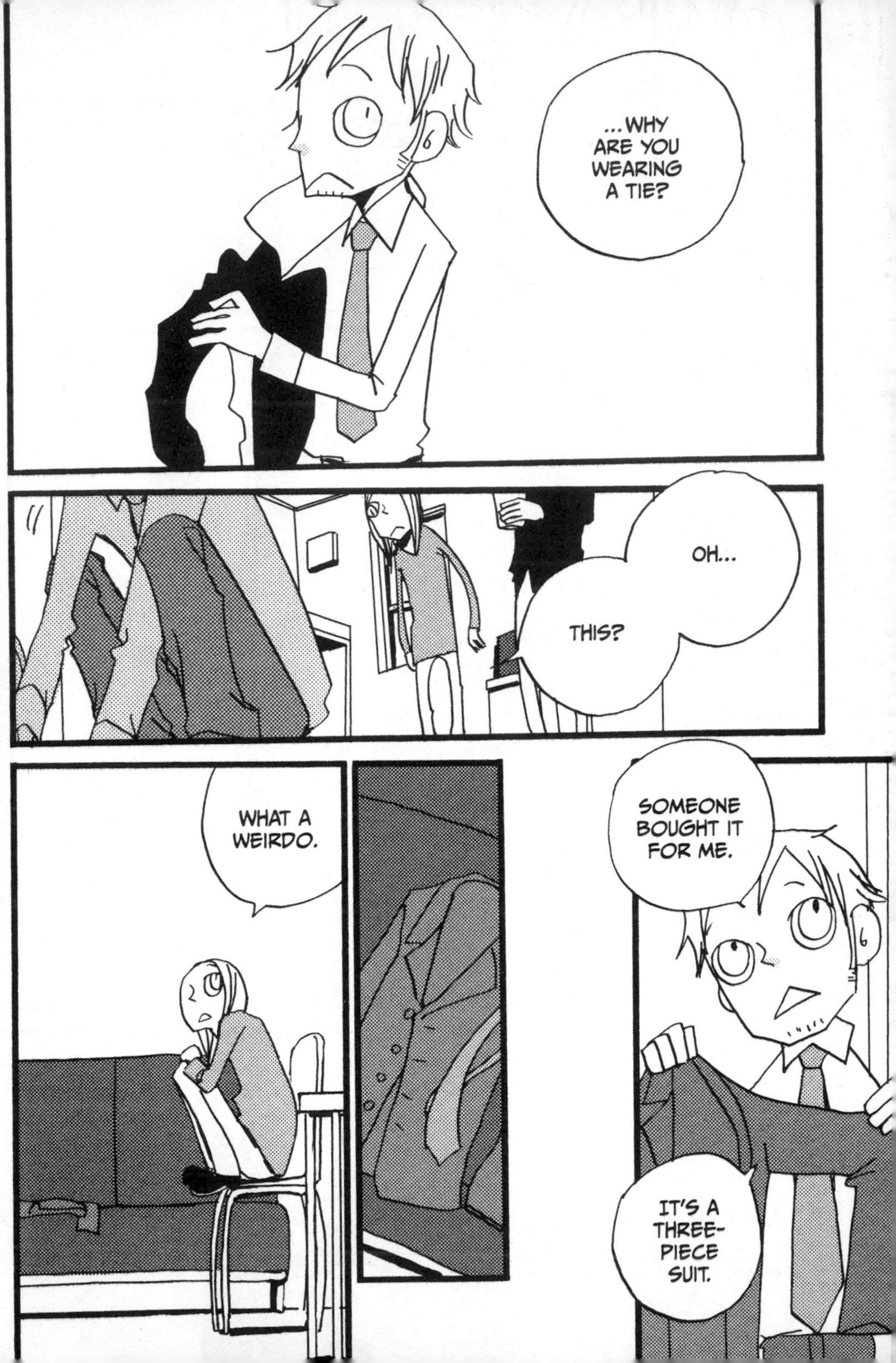
...WHY ARE YOU WEARING A TIE?
OH...
THIS?
SOMEONE BOUGHT IT FOR ME.
IT'S A THREE-PIECE SUIT.
WHAT A WEIRDO.

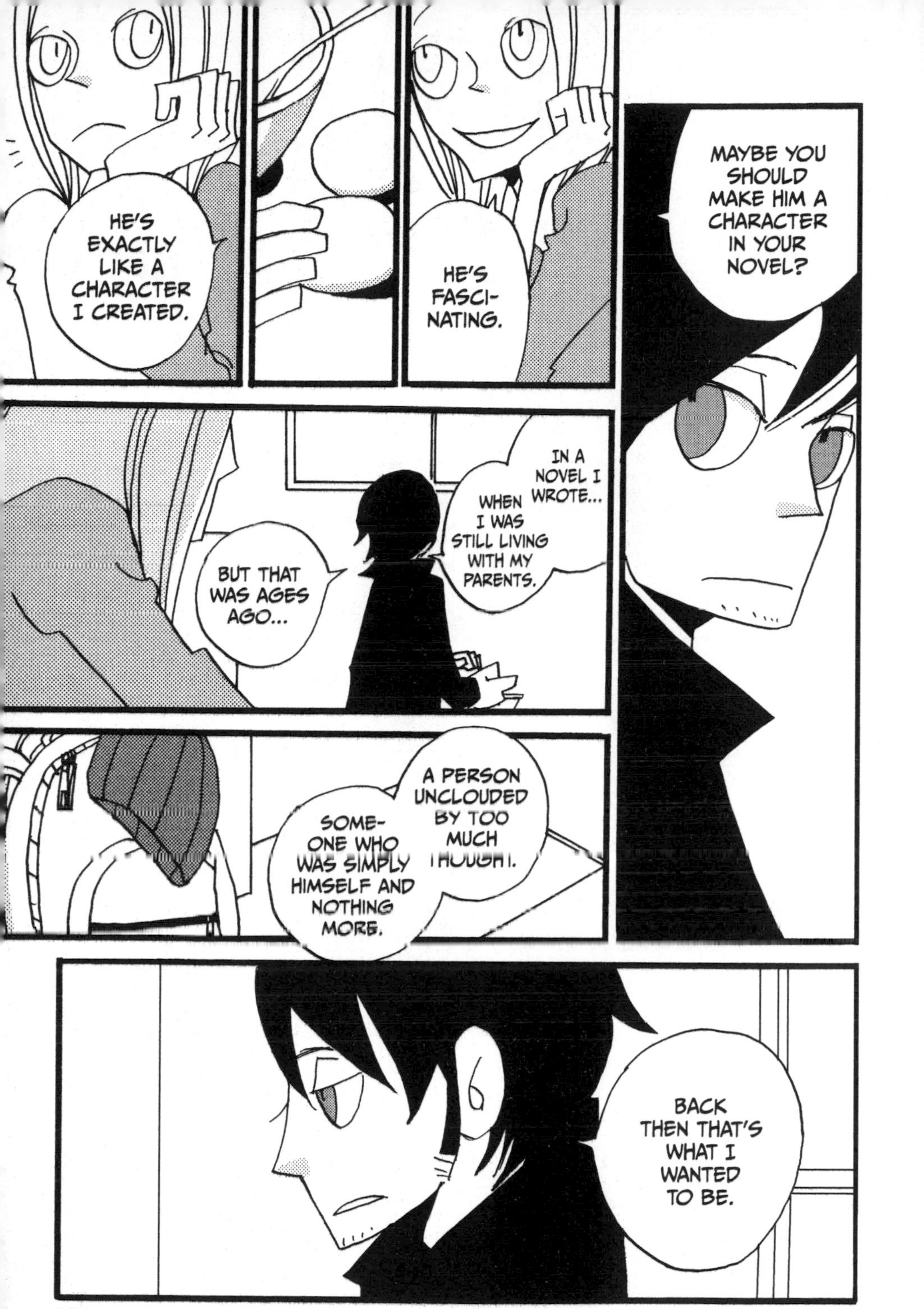
HE'S FASCINATING.
HE'S EXACTLY LIKE A CHARACTER I CREATED.
MAYBE YOU SHOULD MAKE HIM A CHARACTER IN YOUR NOVEL?
IN A NOVEL I WROTE...
WHEN I WAS STILL LIVING WITH MY PARENTS.
BUT THAT WAS AGES AGO...
A PERSON UNCLOUDED BY TOO MUCH THOUGHT.
SOMEONE WHO WAS SIMPLY HIMSELF AND NOTHING MORE.
BACK THEN THAT'S WHAT I WANTED TO BE.

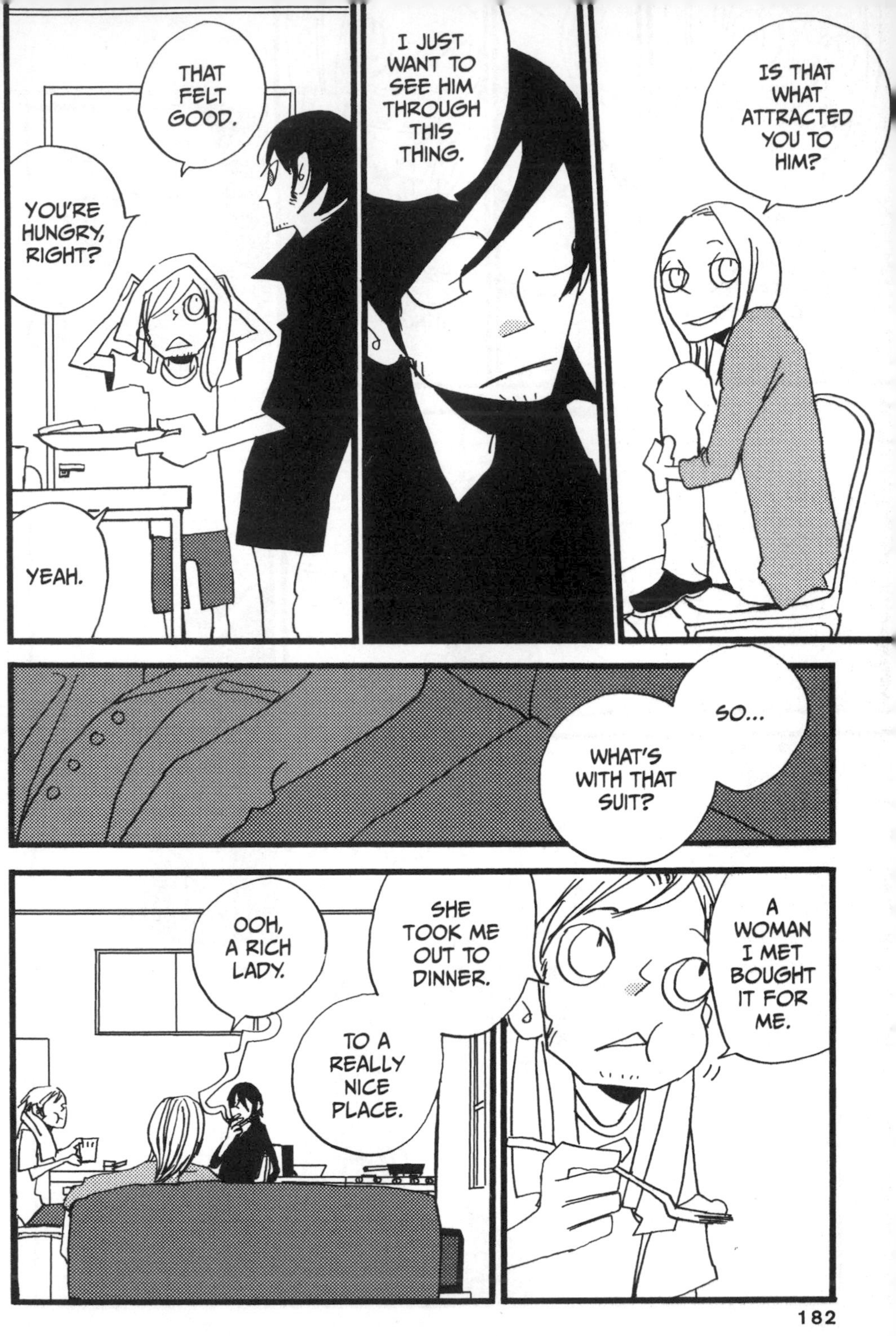
IS THAT WHAT ATTRACTED YOU TO HIM?
I JUST WANT TO SEE HIM THROUGH THIS THING.
THAT FELT GOOD.
YOU'RE HUNGRY, RIGHT?
YEAH.
SO...
WHAT'S WITH THAT SUIT?
A WOMAN I MET BOUGHT IT FOR ME.
SHE TOOK ME OUT TO DINNER.
TO A REALLY NICE PLACE.
OOH, A RICH LADY.

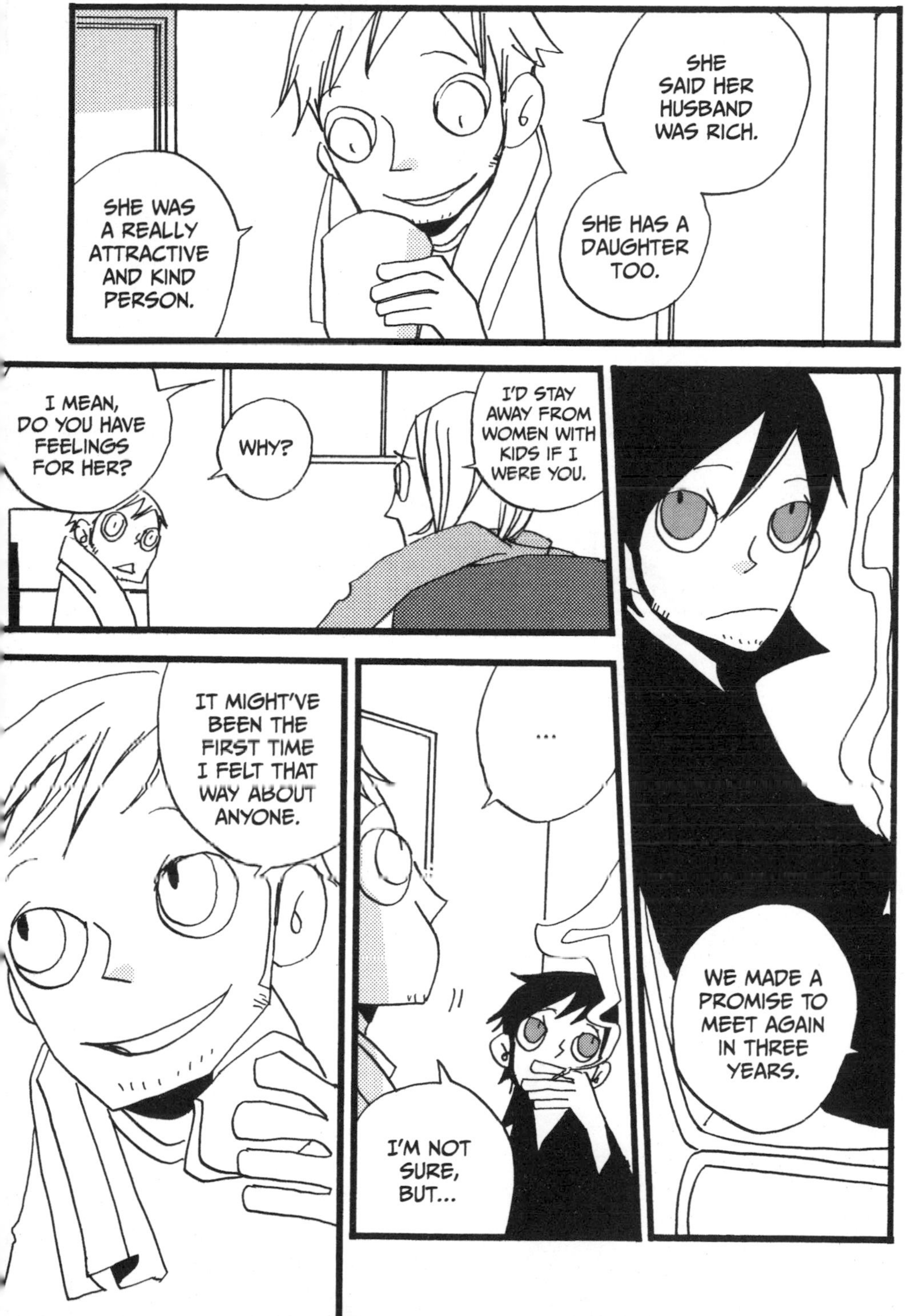
SHE SAID HER HUSBAND WAS RICH.
SHE HAS A DAUGHTER TOO.
SHE WAS A REALLY ATTRACTIVE AND KIND PERSON.
WE MADE A PROMISE TO MEET AGAIN IN THREE YEARS.
I'D STAY AWAY FROM WOMEN WITH KIDS IF I WERE YOU.
WHY?
I MEAN, DO YOU HAVE FEELINGS FOR HER?
...
I'M NOT SURE, BUT...
IT MIGHT'VE BEEN THE FIRST TIME I FELT THAT WAY ABOUT ANYONE.

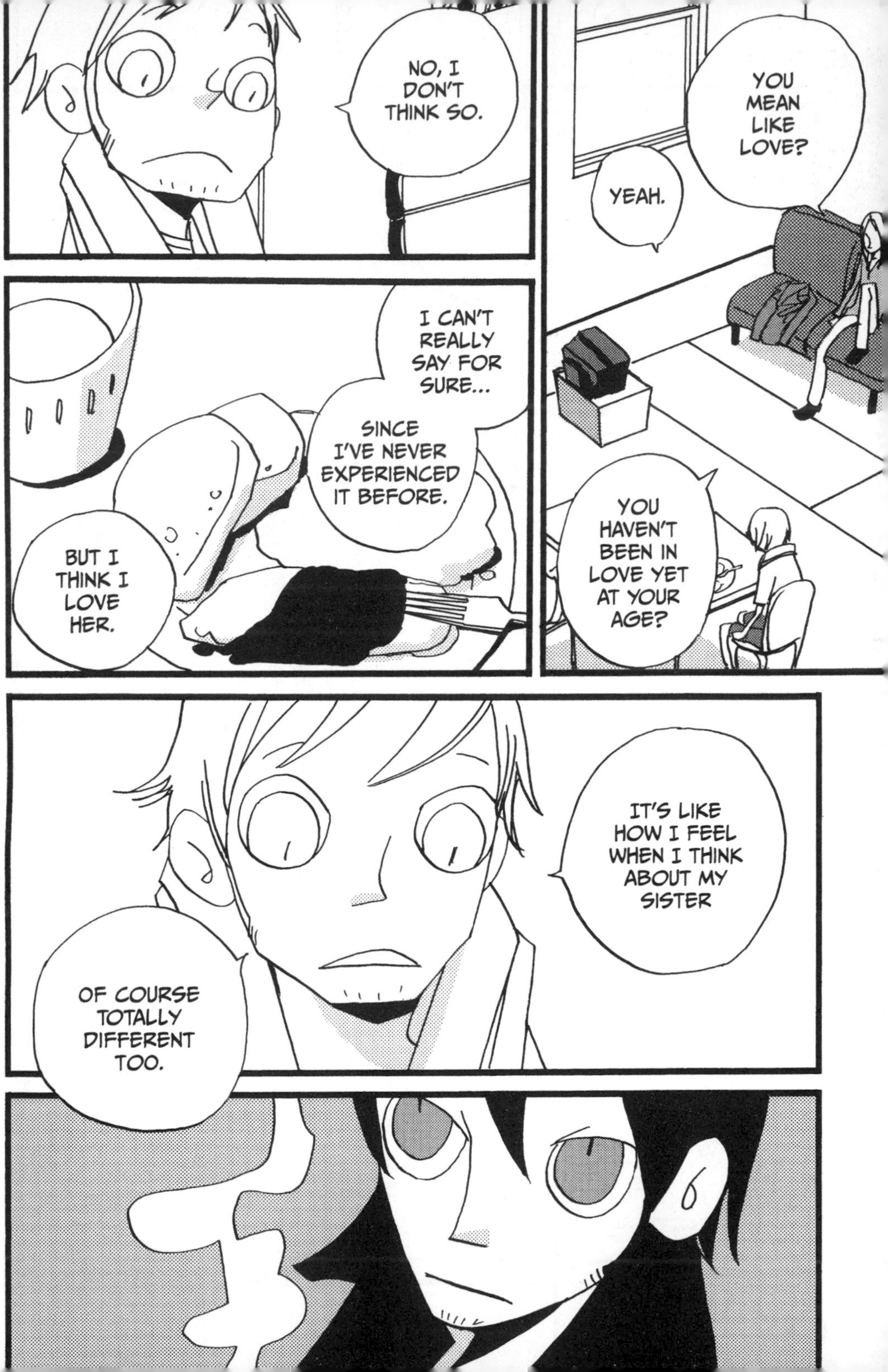
YOU MEAN LIKE LOVE?
YEAH.
YOU HAVEN'T BEEN IN LOVE YET AT YOUR AGE?
NO, I DON'T THINK SO.
I CAN'T REALLY SAY FOR SURE...
SINCE I'VE NEVER EXPERIENCED IT BEFORE.
BUT I THINK I LOVE HER.
IT'S LIKE HOW I FEEL WHEN I THINK ABOUT MY SISTER
OF COURSE TOTALLY DIFFERENT TOO.

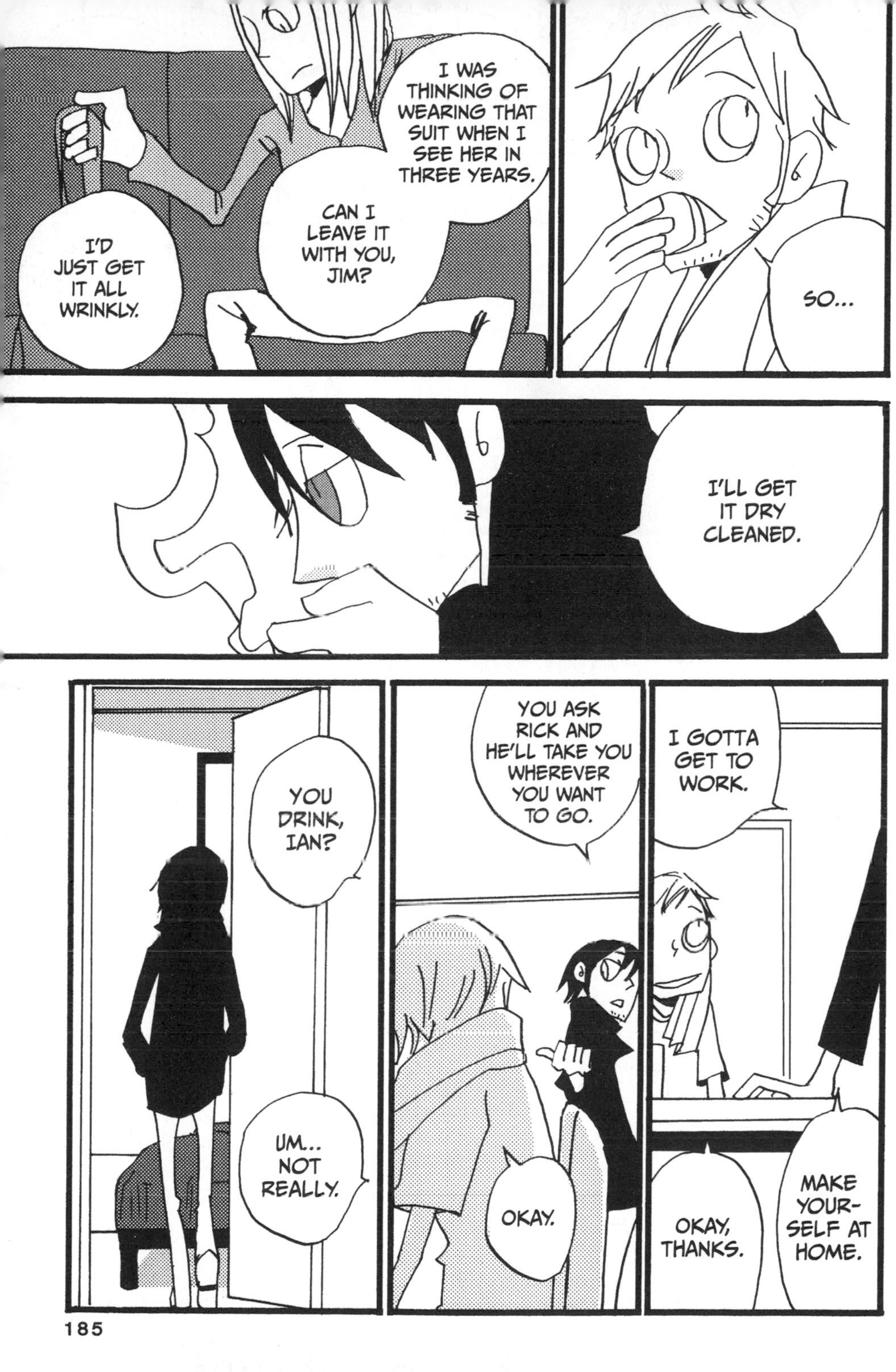
SO...
I WAS THINKING OF WEARING THAT SUIT WHEN I SEE HER IN THREE YEARS.
CAN I LEAVE IT WITH YOU, JIM?
I'D JUST GET IT ALL WRINKLY.
I'LL GET IT DRY CLEANED.
I GOTTA GET TO WORK.
MAKE YOUR-SELF AT HOME.
OKAY, THANKS.
YOU ASK RICK AND HE'LL TAKE YOU WHEREVER YOU WANT TO GO.
OKAY.
YOU DRINK, IAN?
UM... NOT REALLY.

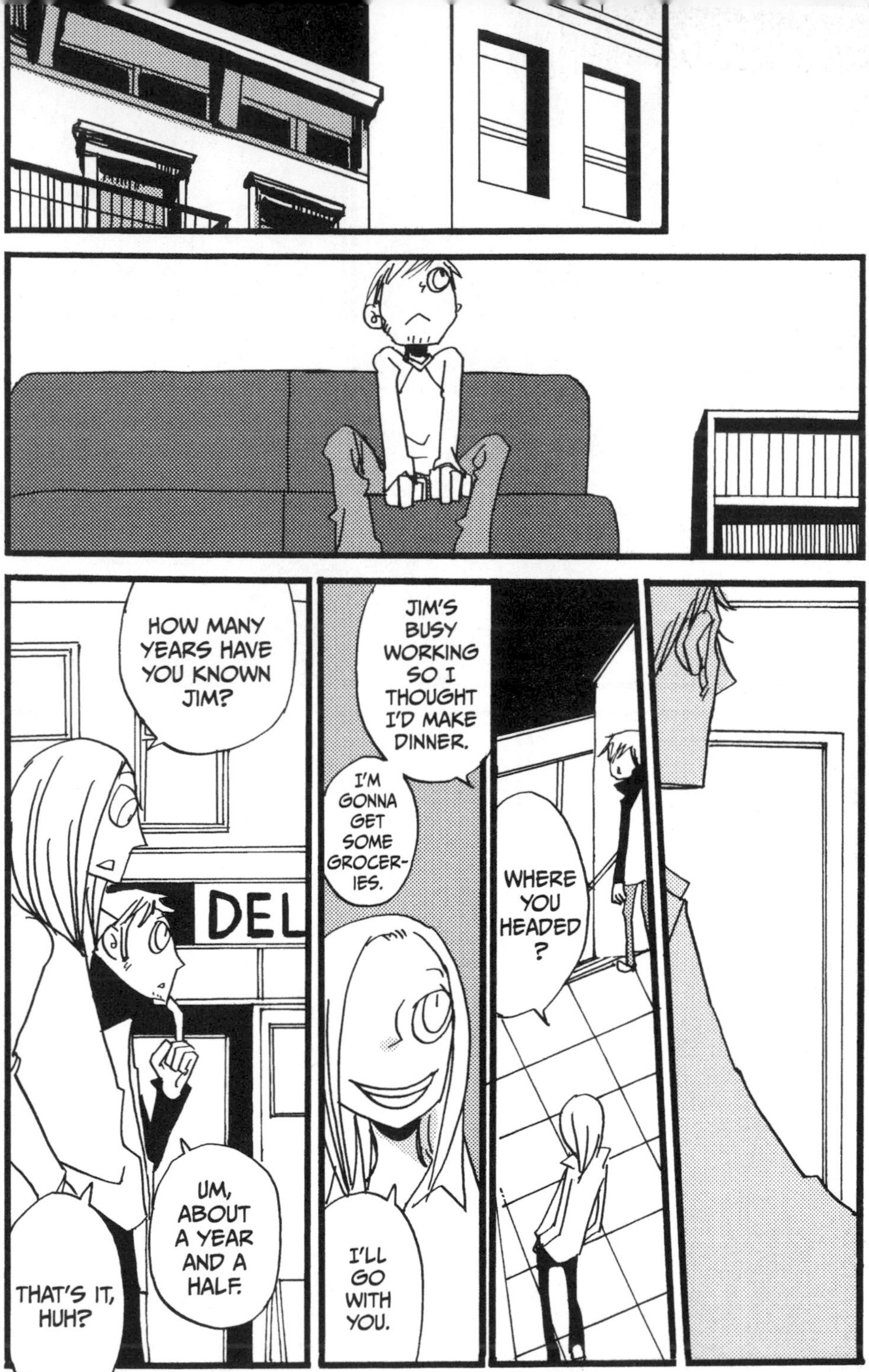
HOW MANY YEARS HAVE YOU KNOWN JIM?
UM, ABOUT A YEAR AND A HALF.
THAT'S IT, HUH?
DELI
JIM'S BUSY WORKING SO I THOUGHT I'D MAKE DINNER.
I'M GONNA GET SOME GROCER-IES.
I'LL GO WITH YOU.
WHERE YOU HEADED?

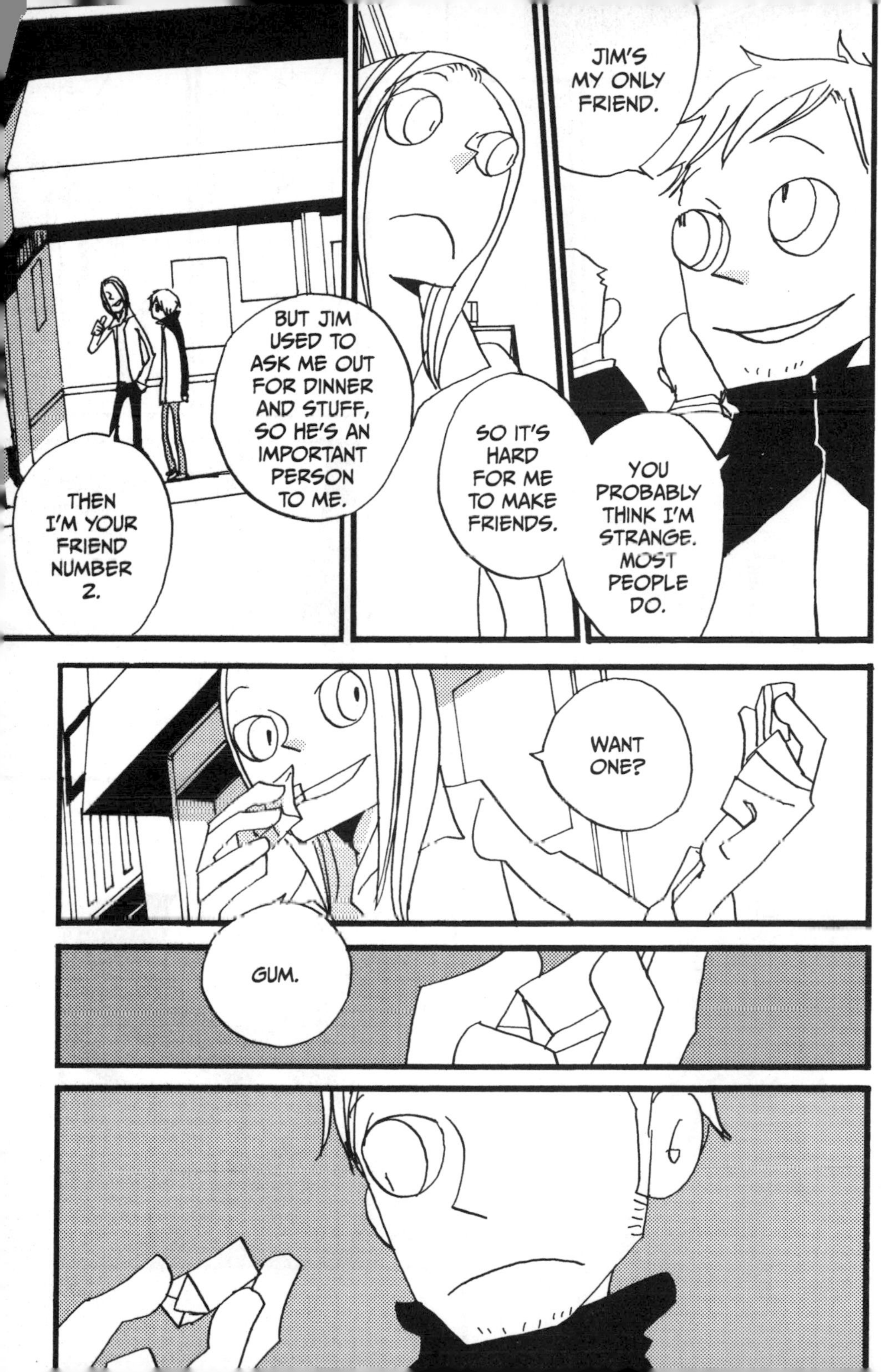
JIM'S MY ONLY FRIEND.
YOU PROBABLY THINK I'M STRANGE. MOST PEOPLE DO.
SO IT'S HARD FOR ME TO MAKE FRIENDS.
BUT JIM USED TO ASK ME OUT FOR DINNER AND STUFF, SO HE'S AN IMPORTANT PERSON TO ME.
THEN I'M YOUR FRIEND NUMBER 2.
WANT ONE?
GUM.

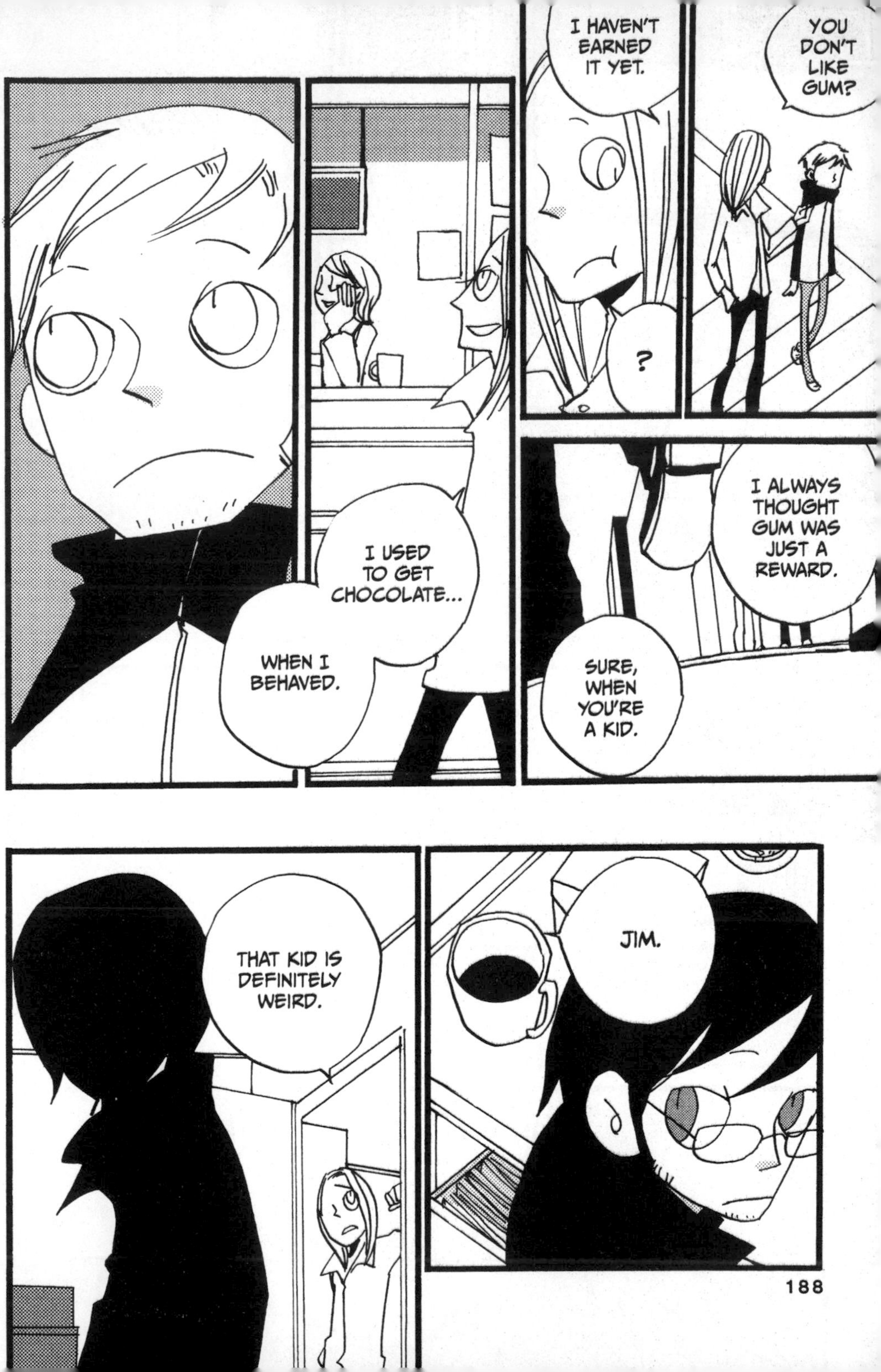
YOU DON'T LIKE GUM?
I HAVEN'T EARNED IT YET.
?
I ALWAYS THOUGHT GUM WAS JUST A REWARD.
SURE, WHEN YOU'RE A KID.
I USED TO GET CHOCOLATE...
WHEN I BEHAVED.
JIM.
THAT KID IS DEFINITELY WEIRD.

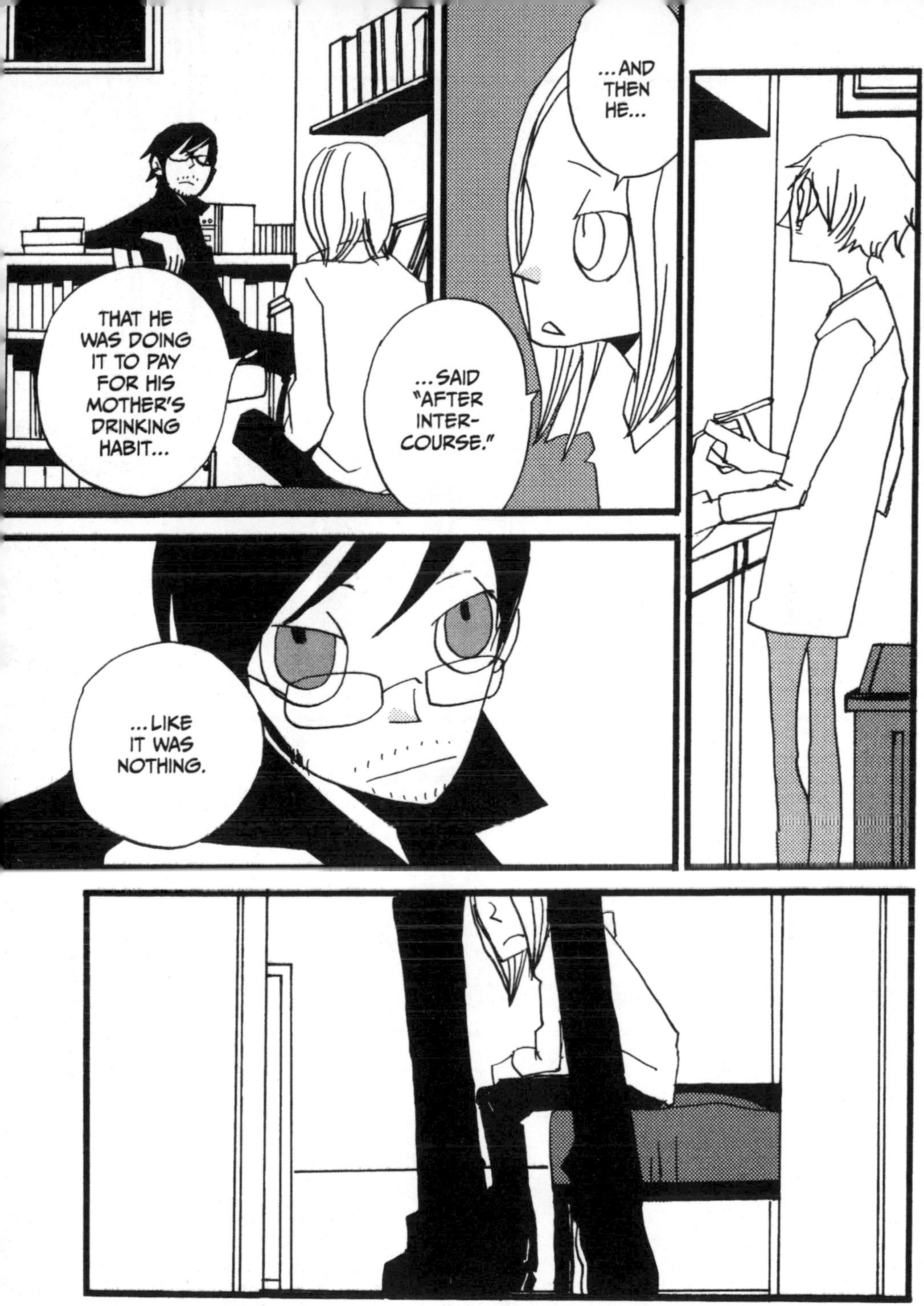
...AND THEN HE...
...SAID "AFTER INTER-COURSE."
THAT HE WAS DOING IT TO PAY FOR HIS MOTHER'S DRINKING HABIT...
...LIKE IT WAS NOTHING.

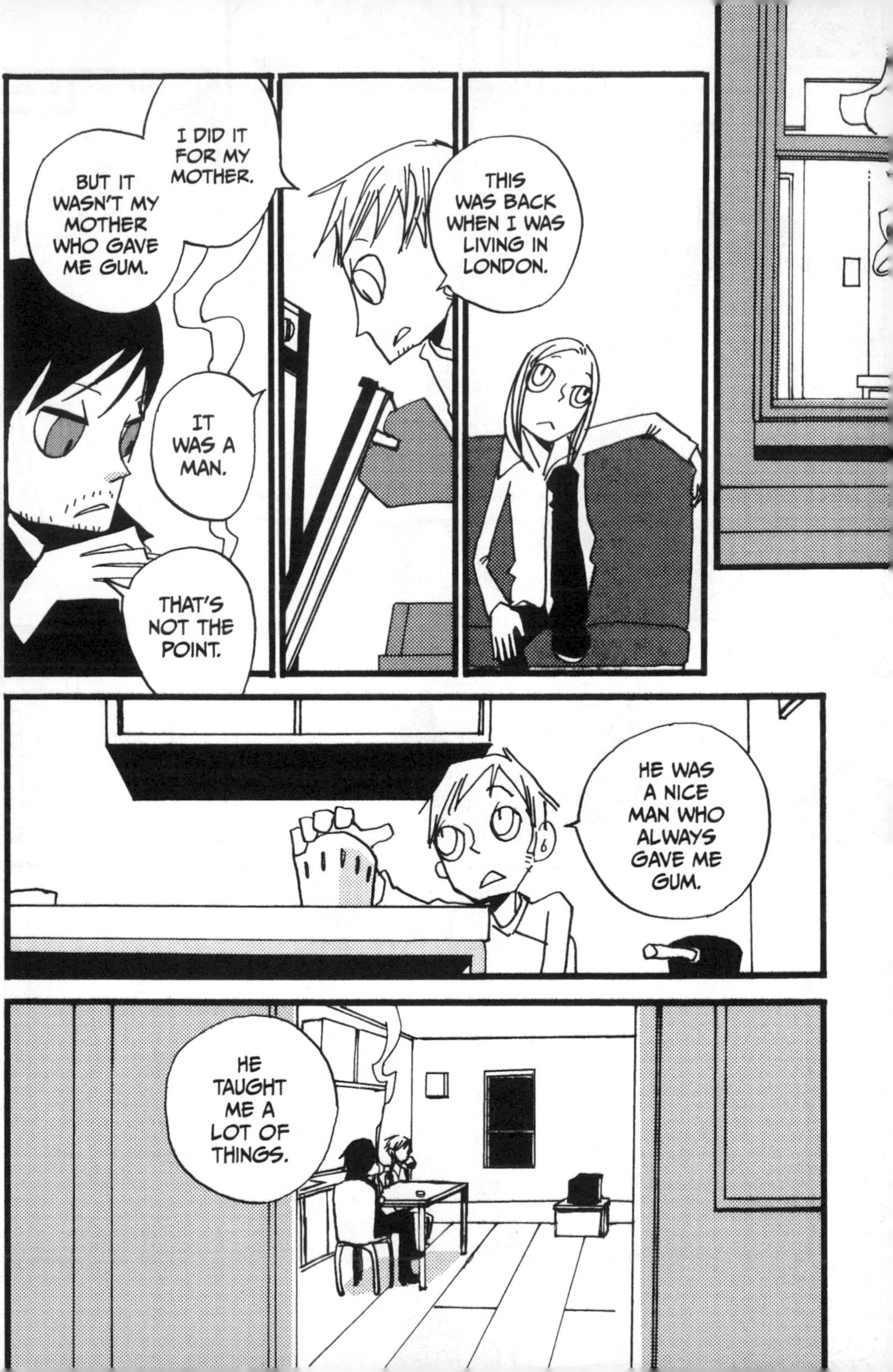
THIS WAS BACK WHEN I WAS LIVING IN LONDON.
I DID IT FOR MY MOTHER.
BUT IT WASN'T MY MOTHER WHO GAVE ME GUM.
IT WAS A MAN.
THAT'S NOT THE POINT.
HE WAS A NICE MAN WHO ALWAYS GAVE ME GUM.
HE TAUGHT ME A LOT OF THINGS.

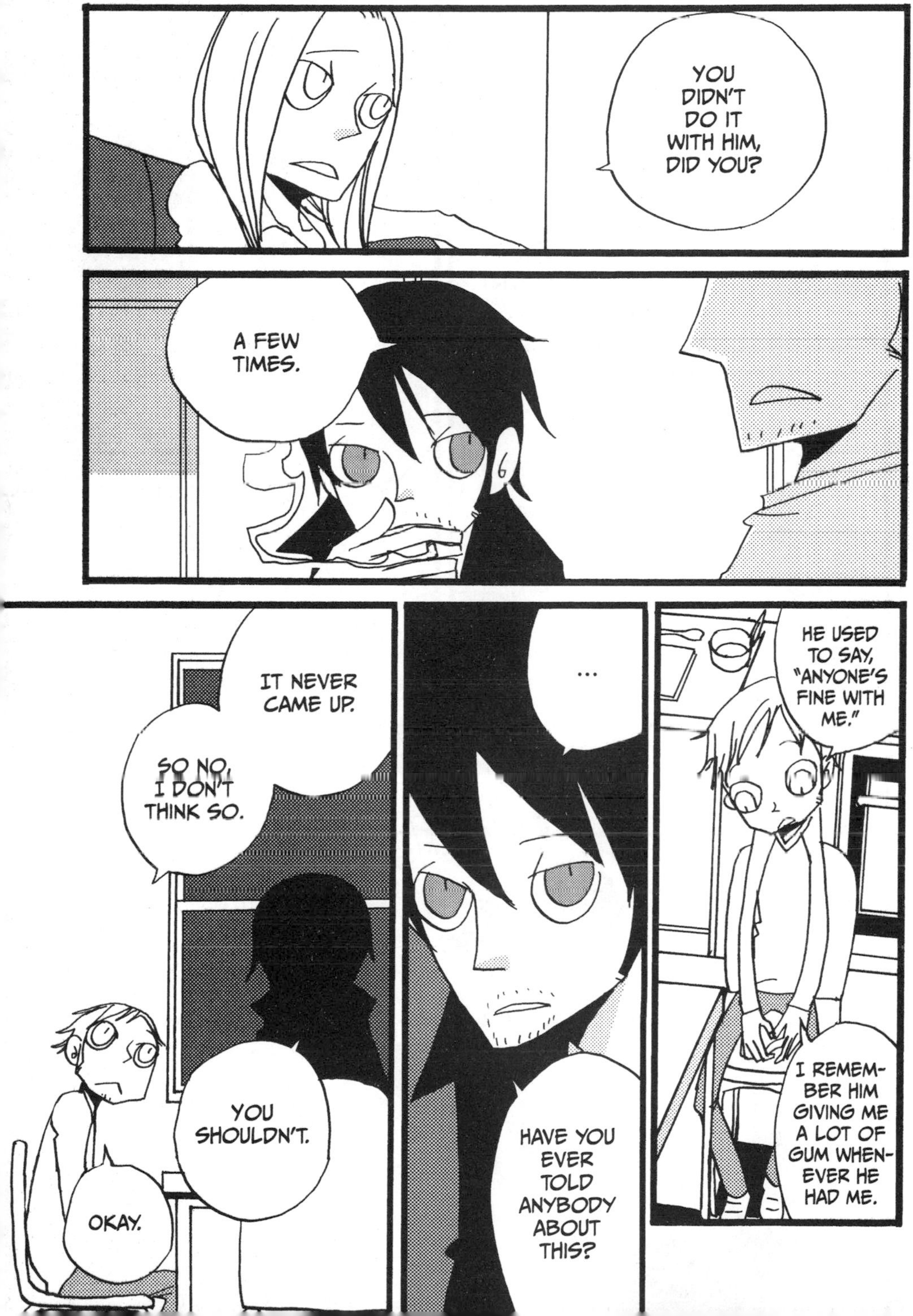
YOU DIDN'T DO IT WITH HIM, DID YOU?
A FEW TIMES.
HE USED TO SAY, "ANYONE'S FINE WITH ME."
I REMEMBER HIM GIVING ME A LOT OF GUM WHENEVER HE HAD ME.
...
HAVE YOU EVER TOLD ANYBODY ABOUT THIS?
IT NEVER CAME UP.
SO NO, I DON'T THINK SO.
YOU SHOULDN'T.
OKAY.

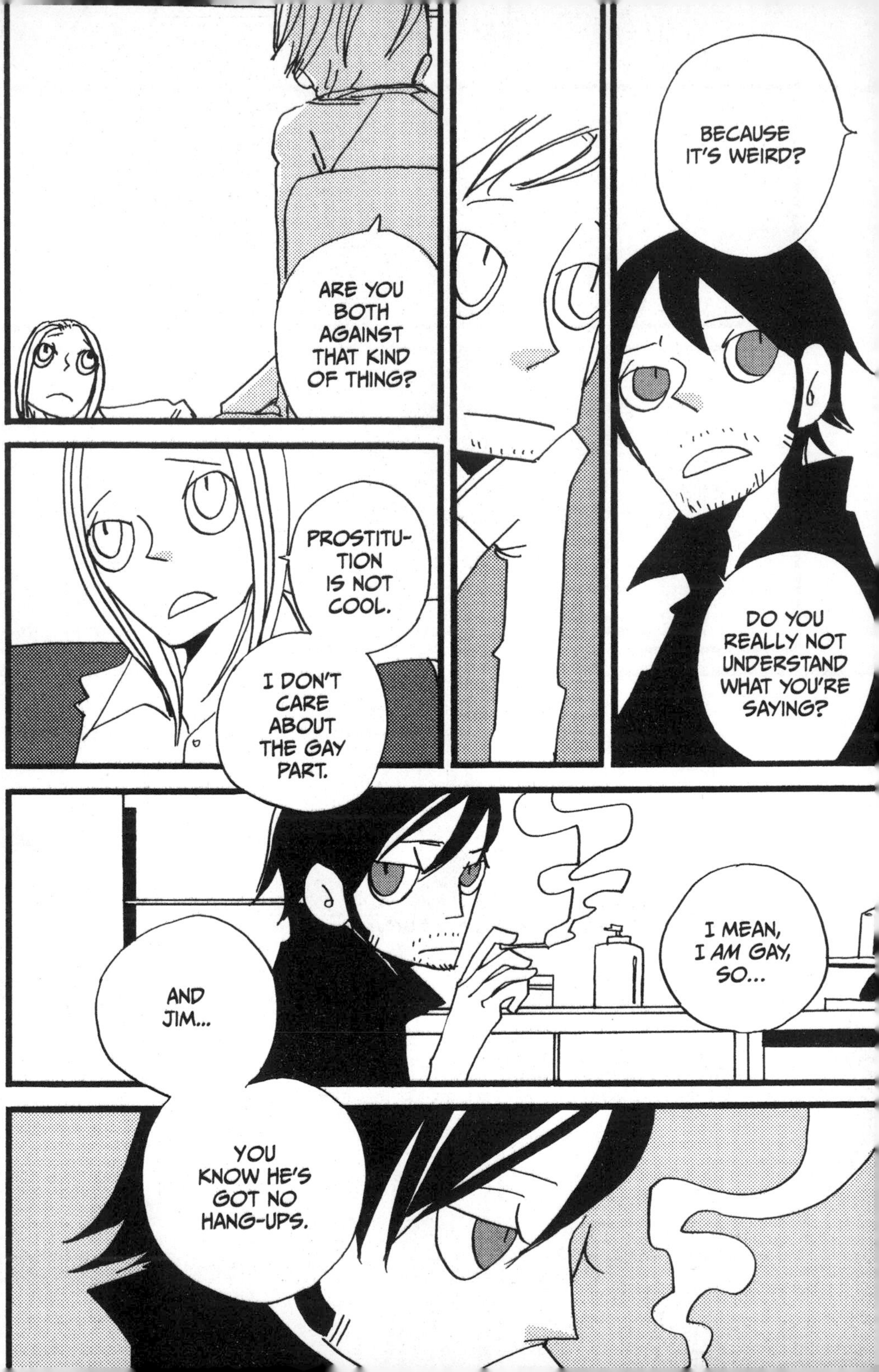
BECAUSE IT'S WEIRD?
DO YOU REALLY NOT UNDERSTAND WHAT YOU'RE SAYING?
ARE YOU BOTH AGAINST THAT KIND OF THING?
PROSTITUTION IS NOT COOL.
I DON'T CARE ABOUT THE GAY PART.
I MEAN, I AM GAY, SO...
AND JIM...
YOU KNOW HE'S GOT NO HANG-UPS.

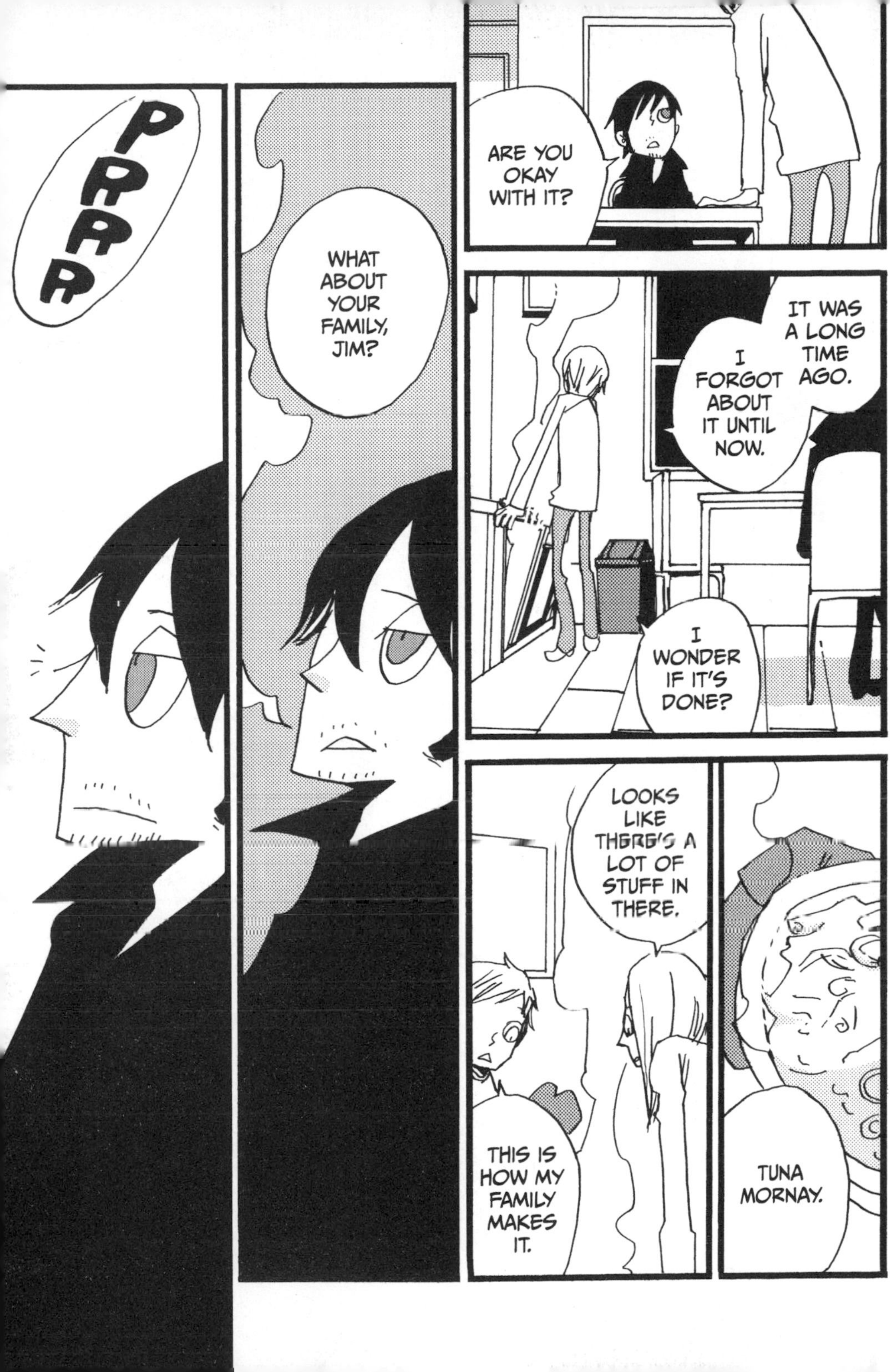
ARE YOU OKAY WITH IT?
IT WAS A LONG TIME AGO.
I FORGOT ABOUT IT UNTIL NOW.
I WONDER IF IT'S DONE?
TUNA MORNAY.
LOOKS LIKE THERE'S A LOT OF STUFF IN THERE.
THIS IS HOW MY FAMILY MAKES IT.
WHAT ABOUT YOUR FAMILY, JIM?
PRRR

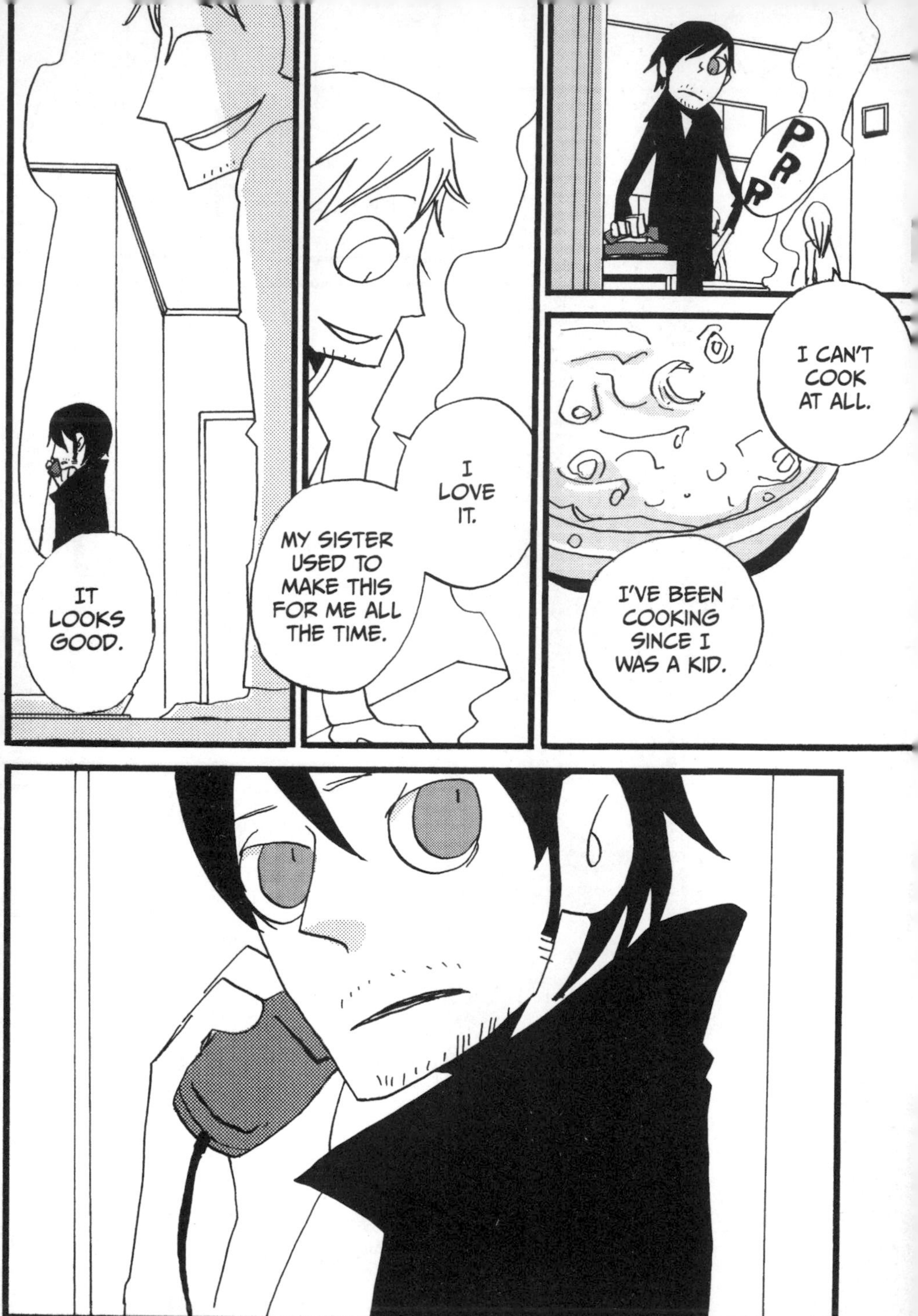
PRR
I CAN'T COOK AT ALL.
I'VE BEEN COOKING SINCE I WAS A KID.
I LOVE IT.
MY SISTER USED TO MAKE THIS FOR ME ALL THE TIME.
IT LOOKS GOOD.

#09 not simple

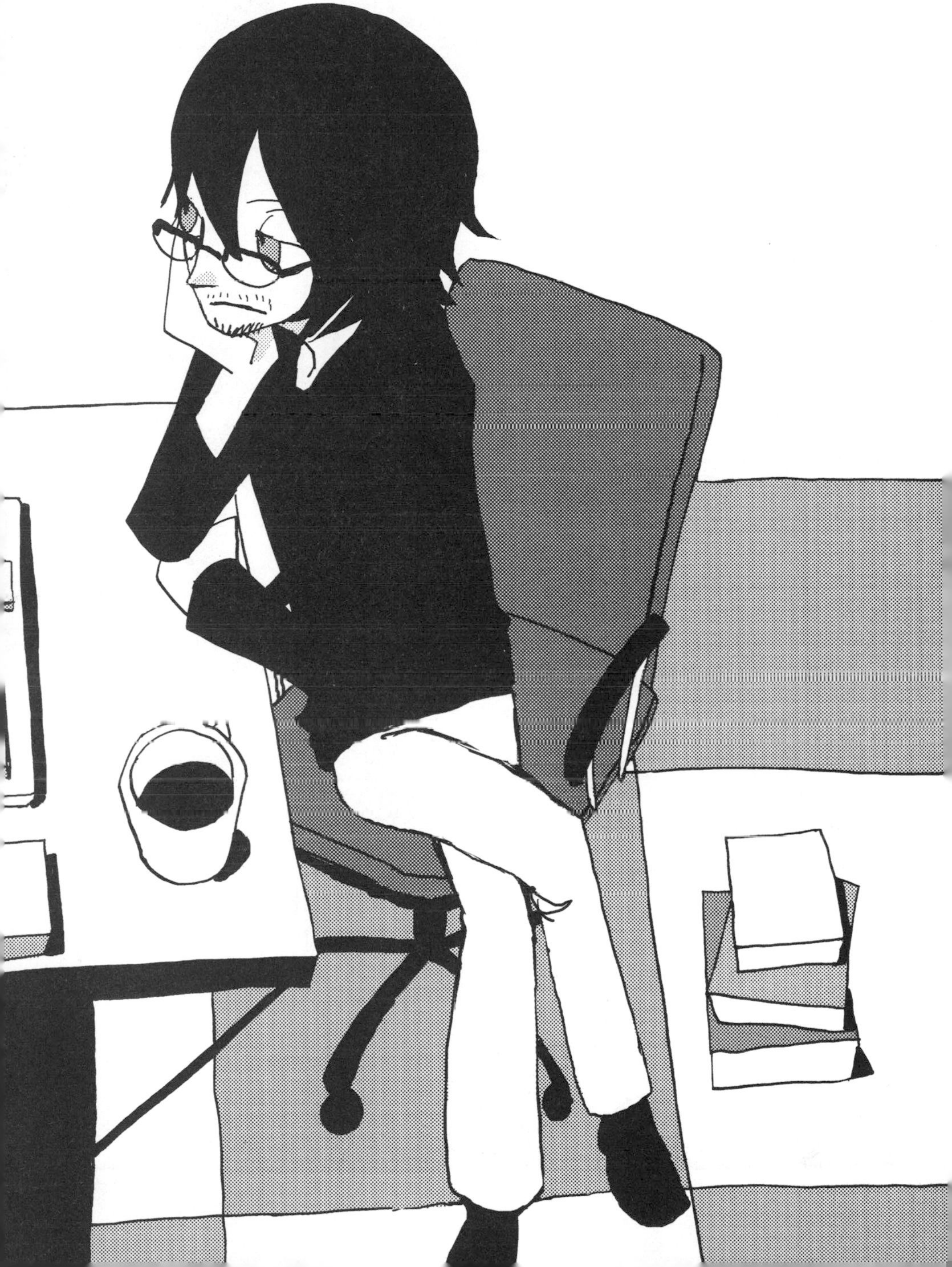

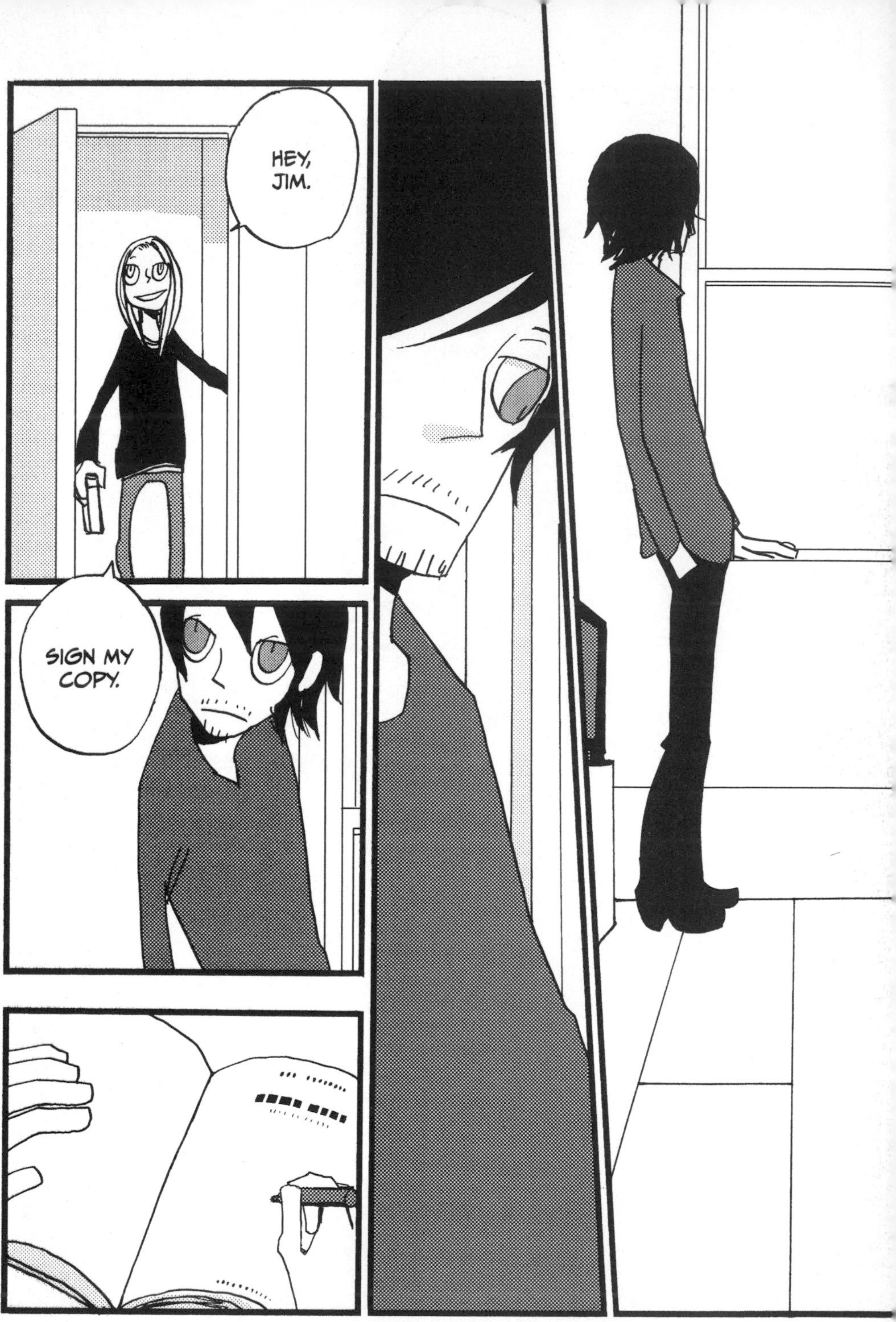
HEY, JIM.
SIGN MY COPY.

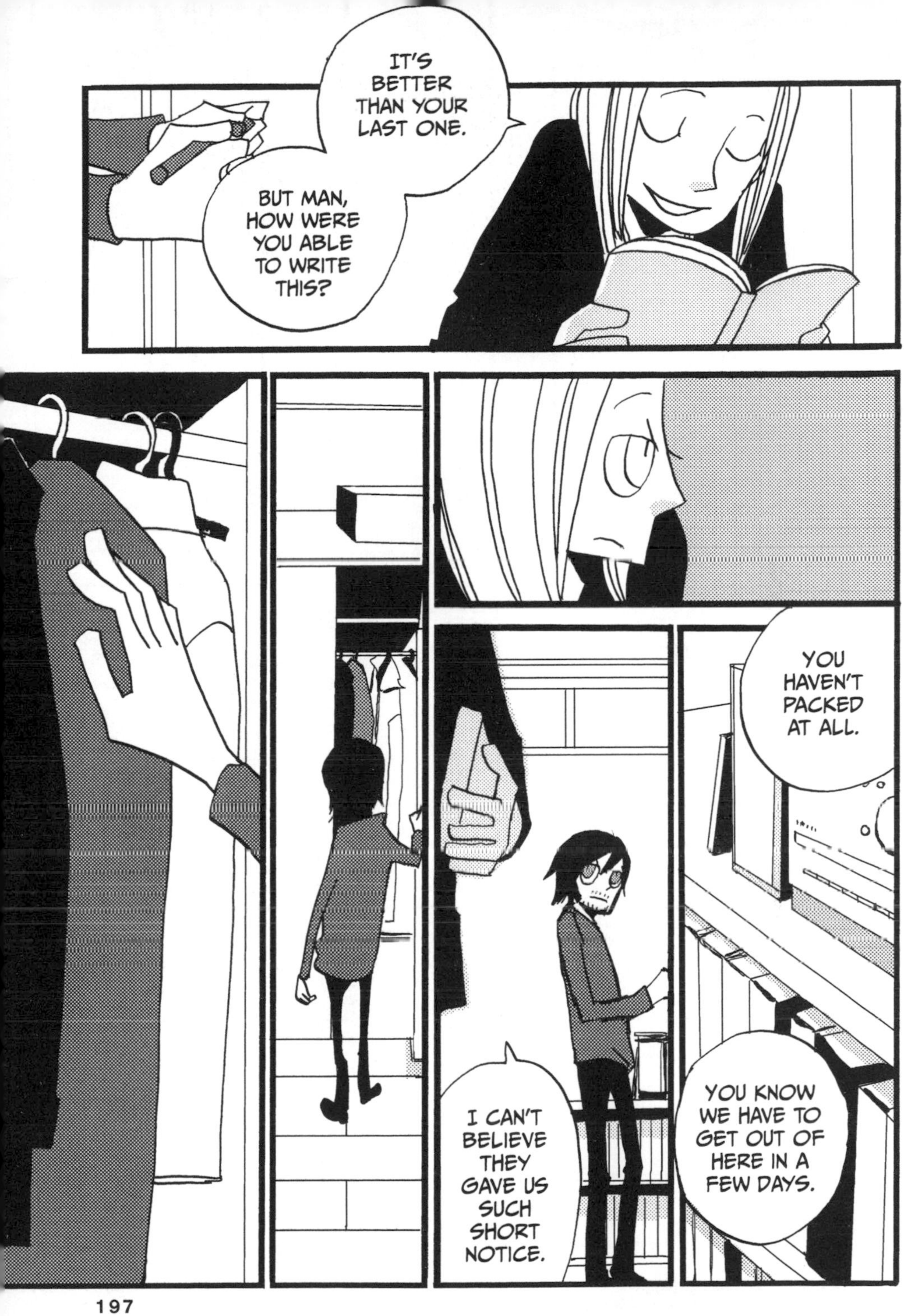
IT'S BETTER THAN YOUR LAST ONE.
BUT MAN, HOW WERE YOU ABLE TO WRITE THIS?
YOU HAVEN'T PACKED AT ALL.
YOU KNOW WE HAVE TO GET OUT OF HERE IN A FEW DAYS.
I CAN'T BELIEVE THEY GAVE US SUCH SHORT NOTICE.

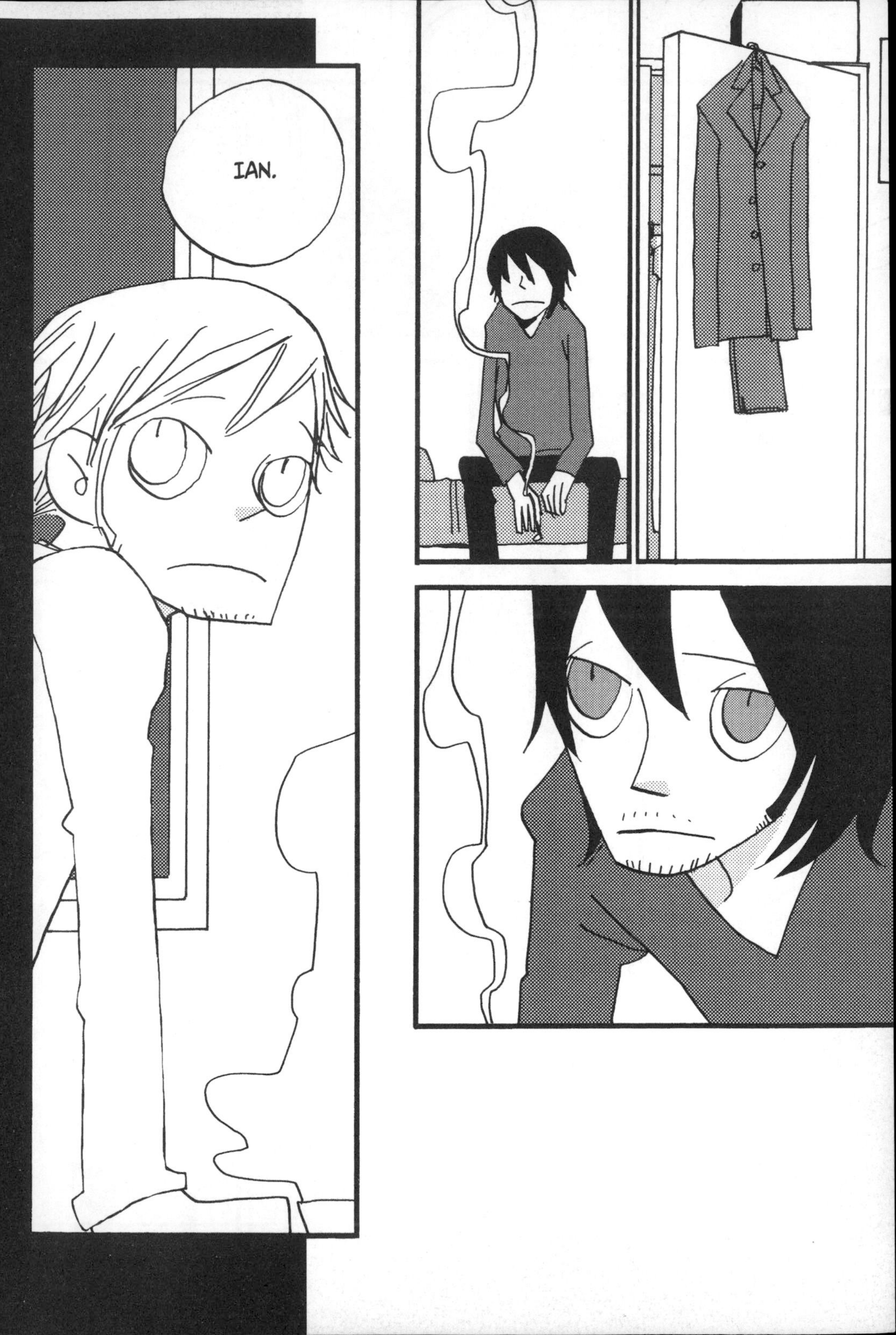
IAN.

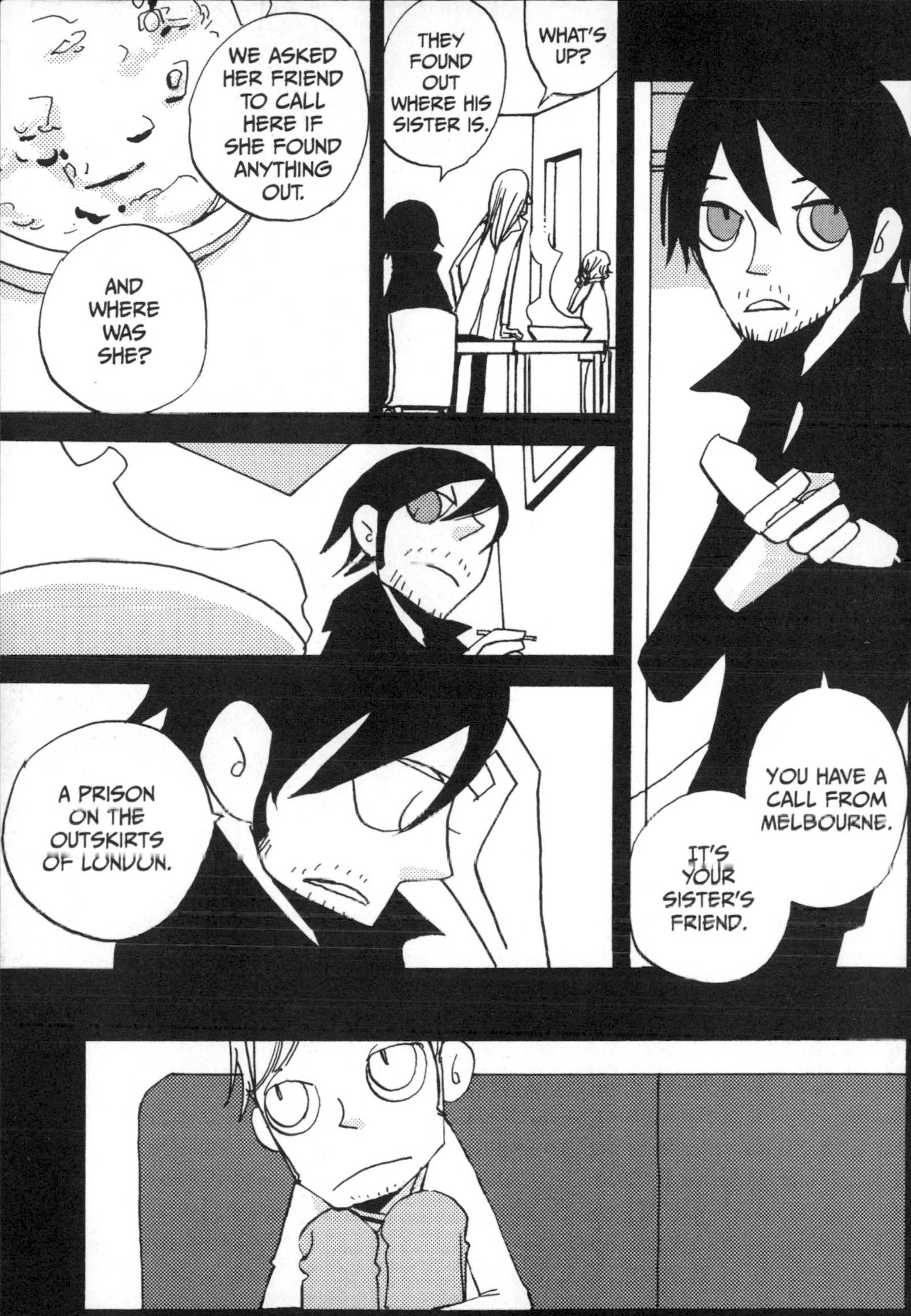
YOU HAVE A CALL FROM MELBOURNE.
IT'S YOUR SISTER'S FRIEND.
WHAT'S UP?
THEY FOUND OUT WHERE HIS SISTER IS.
WE ASKED HER FRIEND TO CALL HERE IF SHE FOUND ANYTHING OUT.
AND WHERE WAS SHE?
A PRISON ON THE OUTSKIRTS OF LONDON.

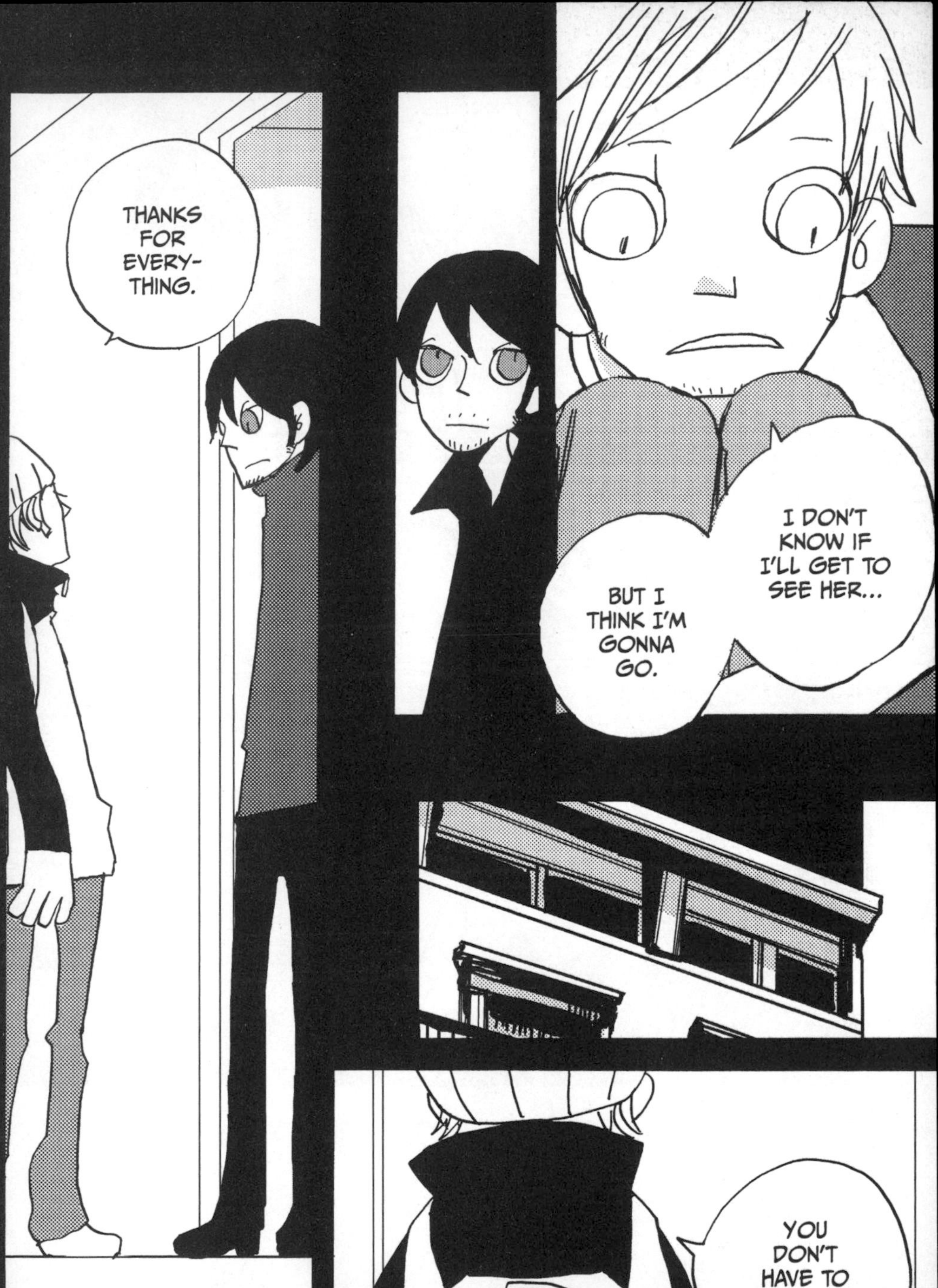
I DON'T KNOW IF I'LL GET TO SEE HER...
BUT I THINK I'M GONNA GO.
THANKS FOR EVERY-THING.
YOU DON'T HAVE TO SEE ME OFF.

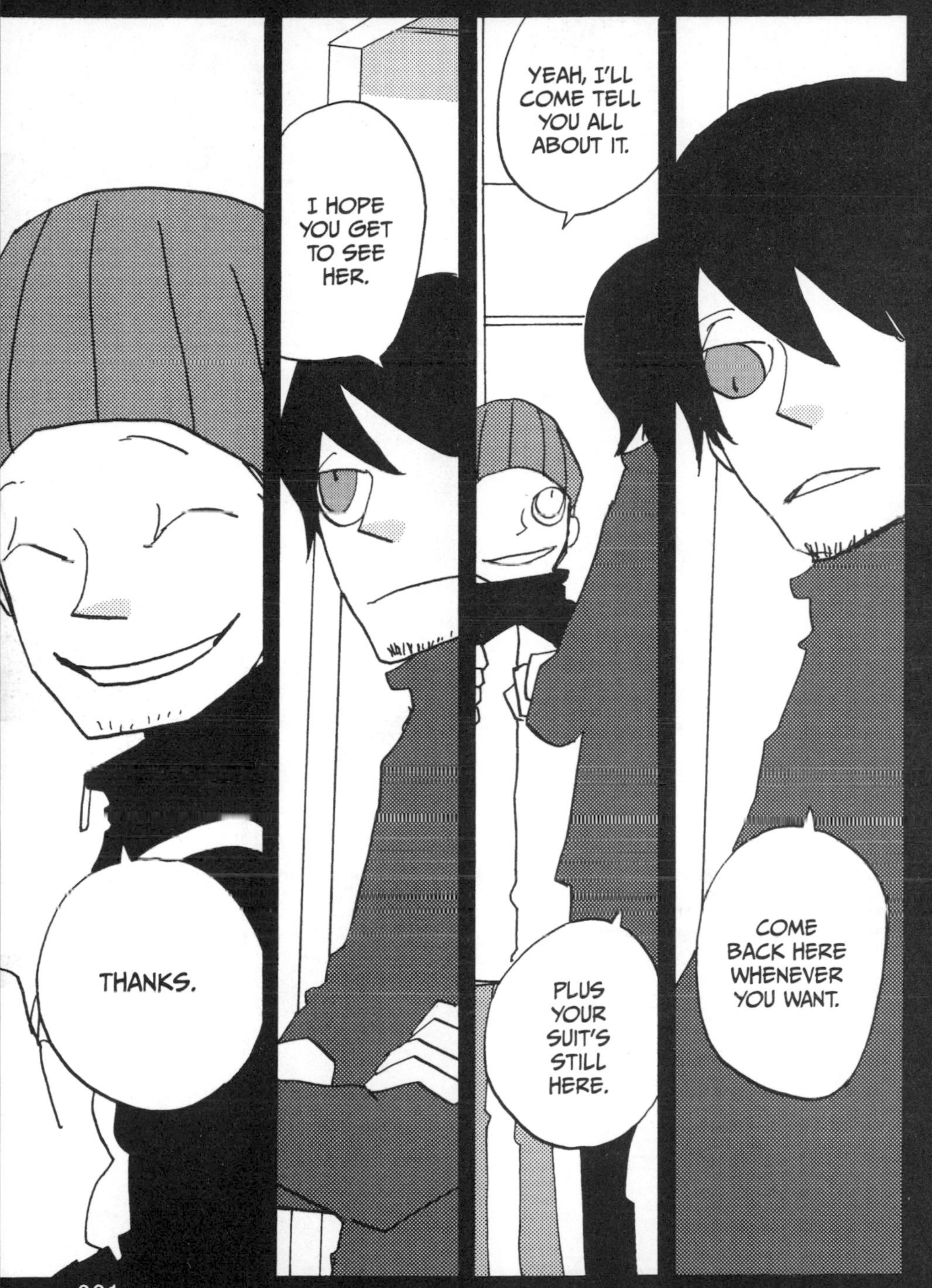
COME BACK HERE WHENEVER YOU WANT.
YEAH, I'LL COME TELL YOU ALL ABOUT IT.
PLUS YOUR SUIT'S STILL HERE.
I HOPE YOU GET TO SEE HER.
THANKS.

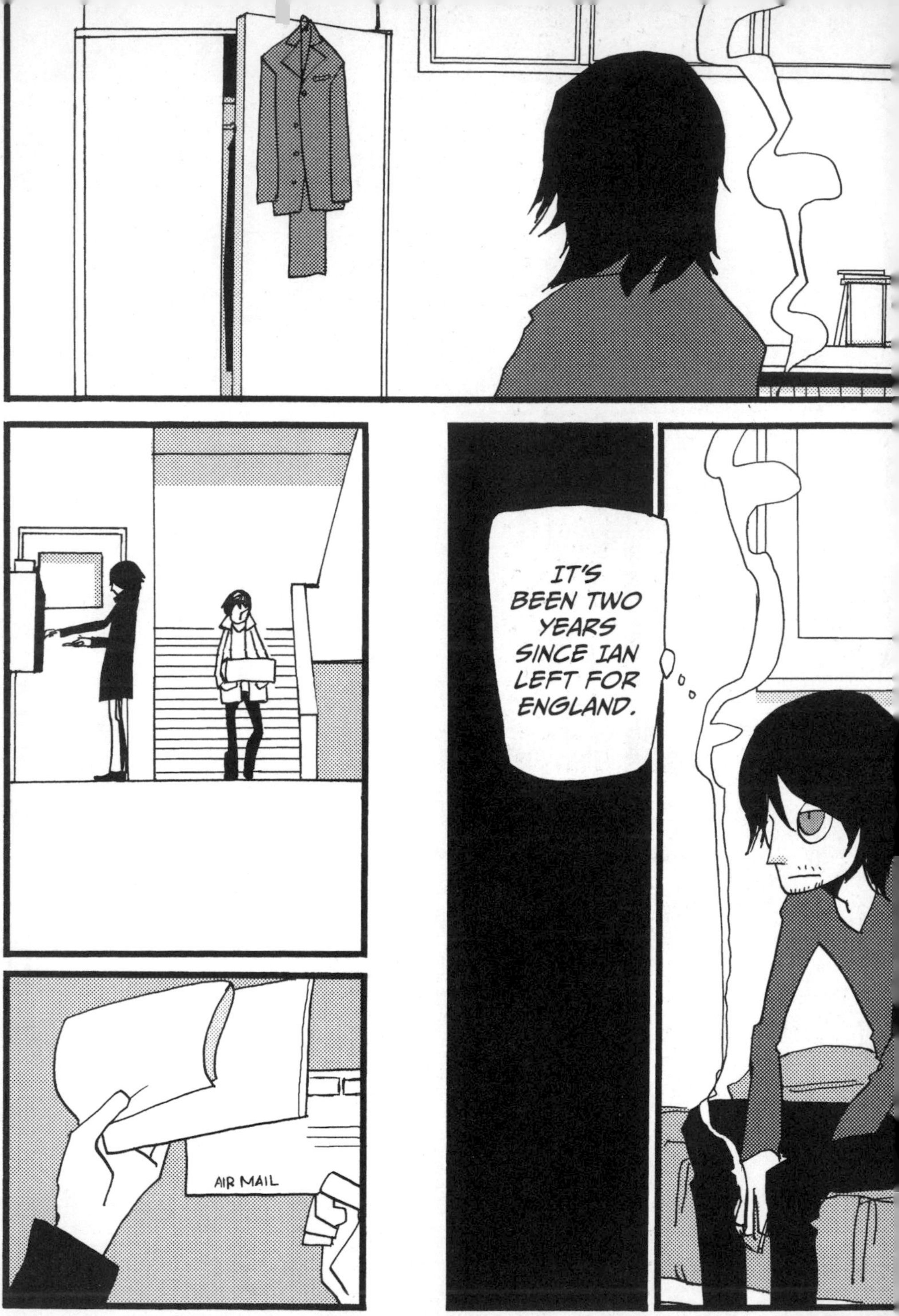
IT'S BEEN TWO YEARS SINCE IAN LEFT FOR ENGLAND.
AIR MAIL

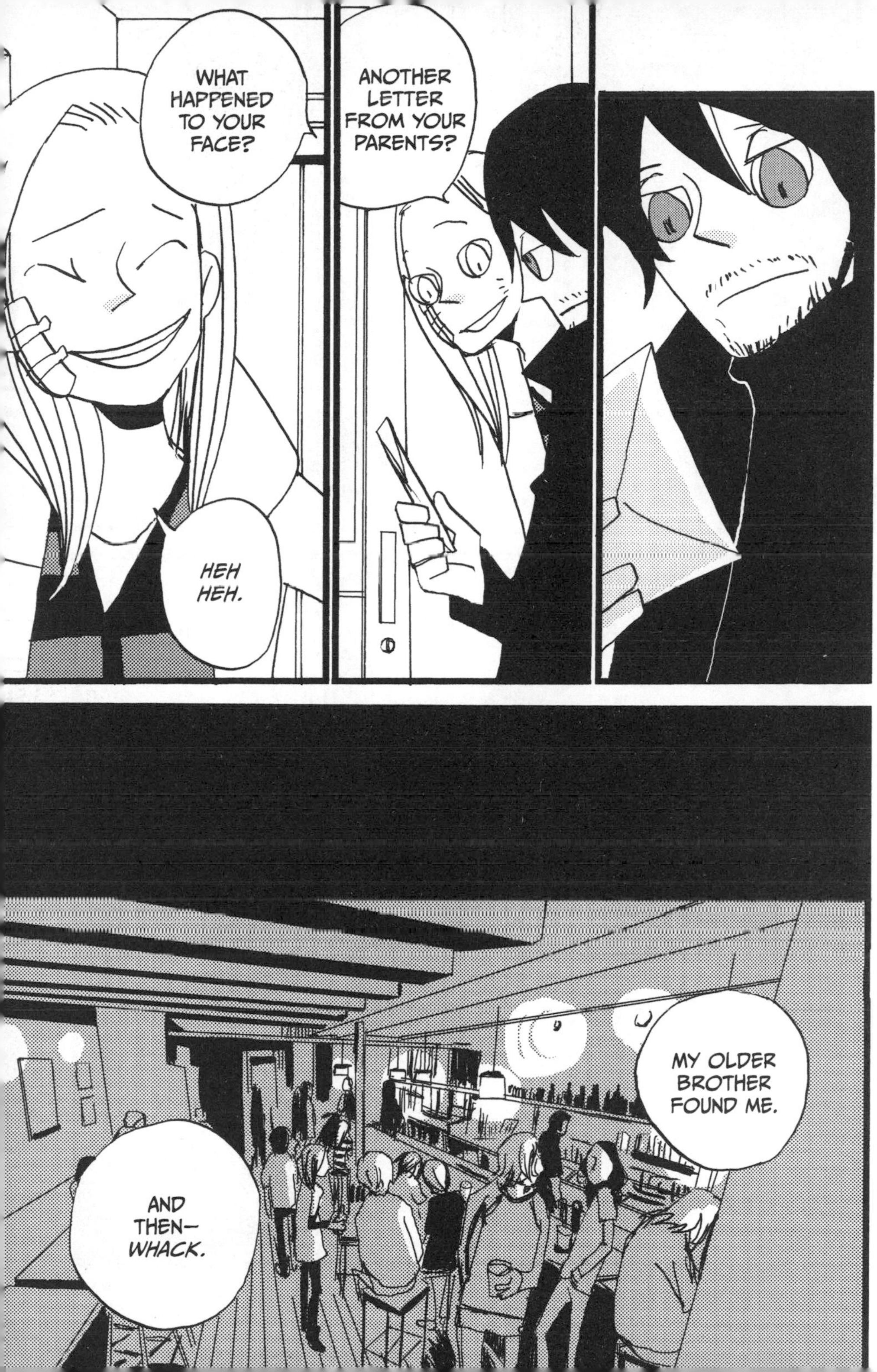
ANOTHER LETTER FROM YOUR PARENTS?
WHAT HAPPENED TO YOUR FACE?
HEH HEH.
MY OLDER BROTHER FOUND ME.
AND THEN— WHACK.

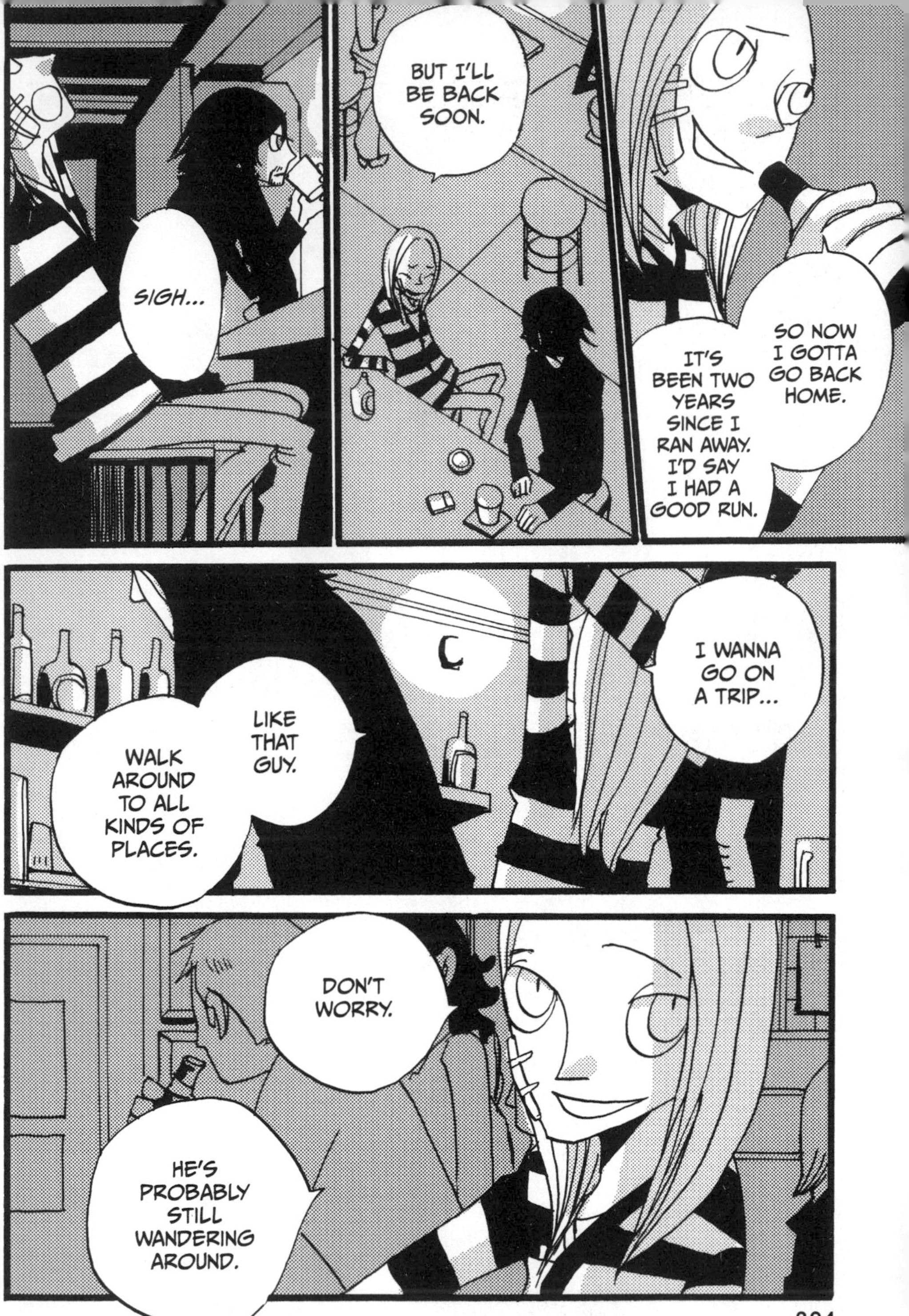
IT'S BEEN TWO YEARS SINCE I RAN AWAY. I'D SAY I HAD A GOOD RUN.
SO NOW I GOTTA GO BACK HOME.
BUT I'LL BE BACK SOON.
SIGH...
I WANNA GO ON A TRIP...
LIKE THAT GUY.
WALK AROUND TO ALL KINDS OF PLACES.
DON'T WORRY.
HE'S PROBABLY STILL WANDERING AROUND.

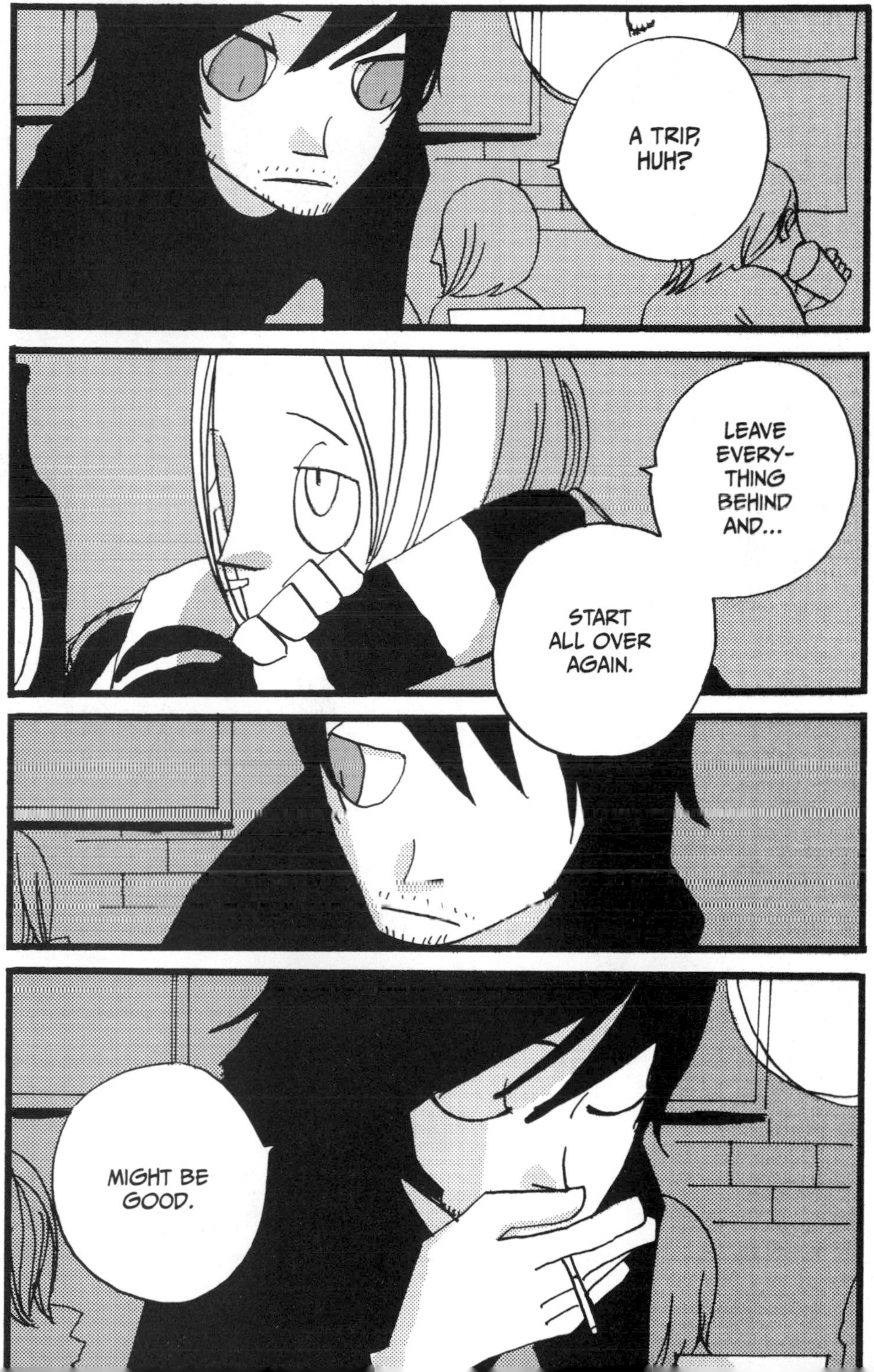
A TRIP, HUH?
LEAVE EVERY-THING BEHIND AND...
START ALL OVER AGAIN.
MIGHT BE GOOD.

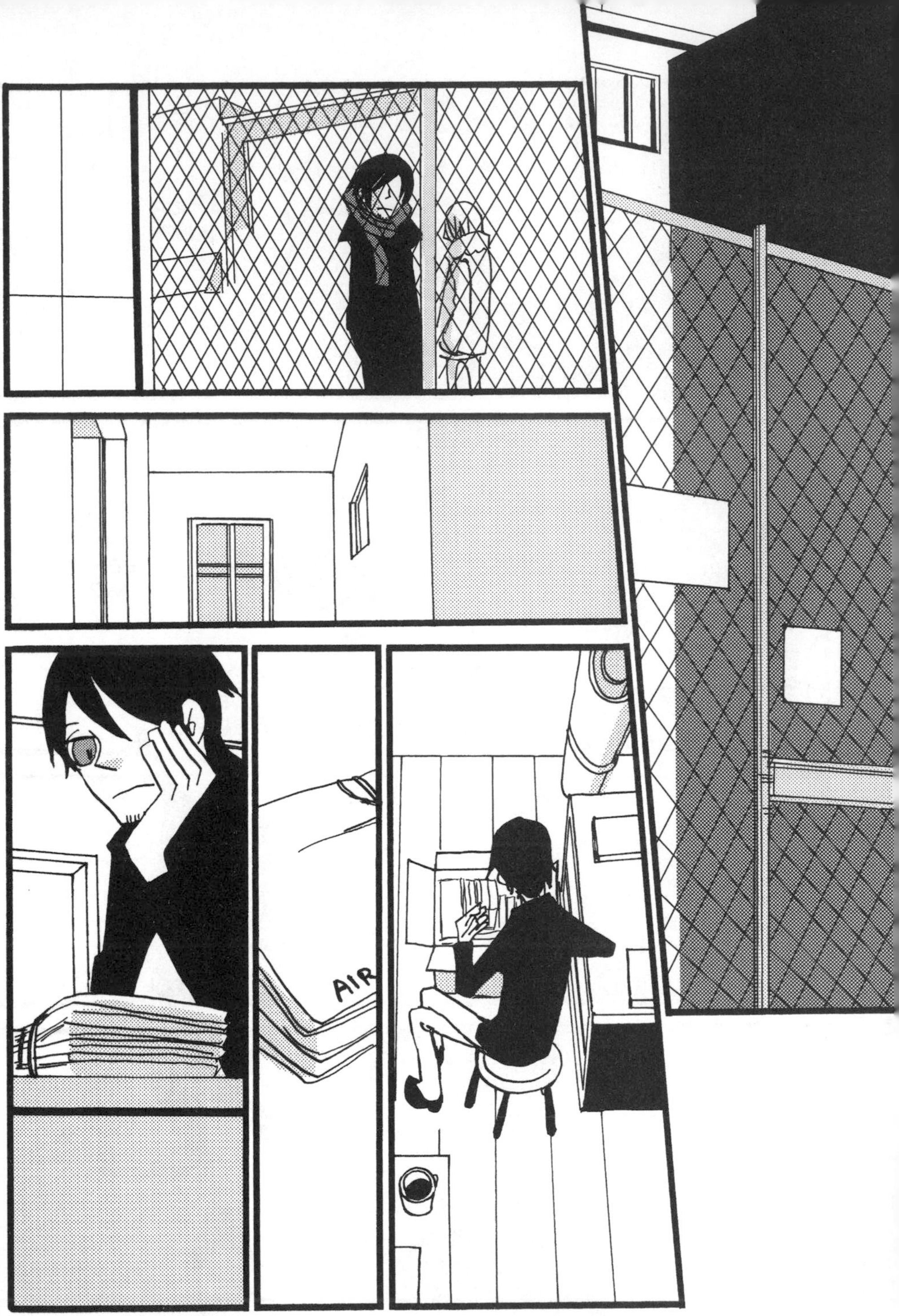
AIR

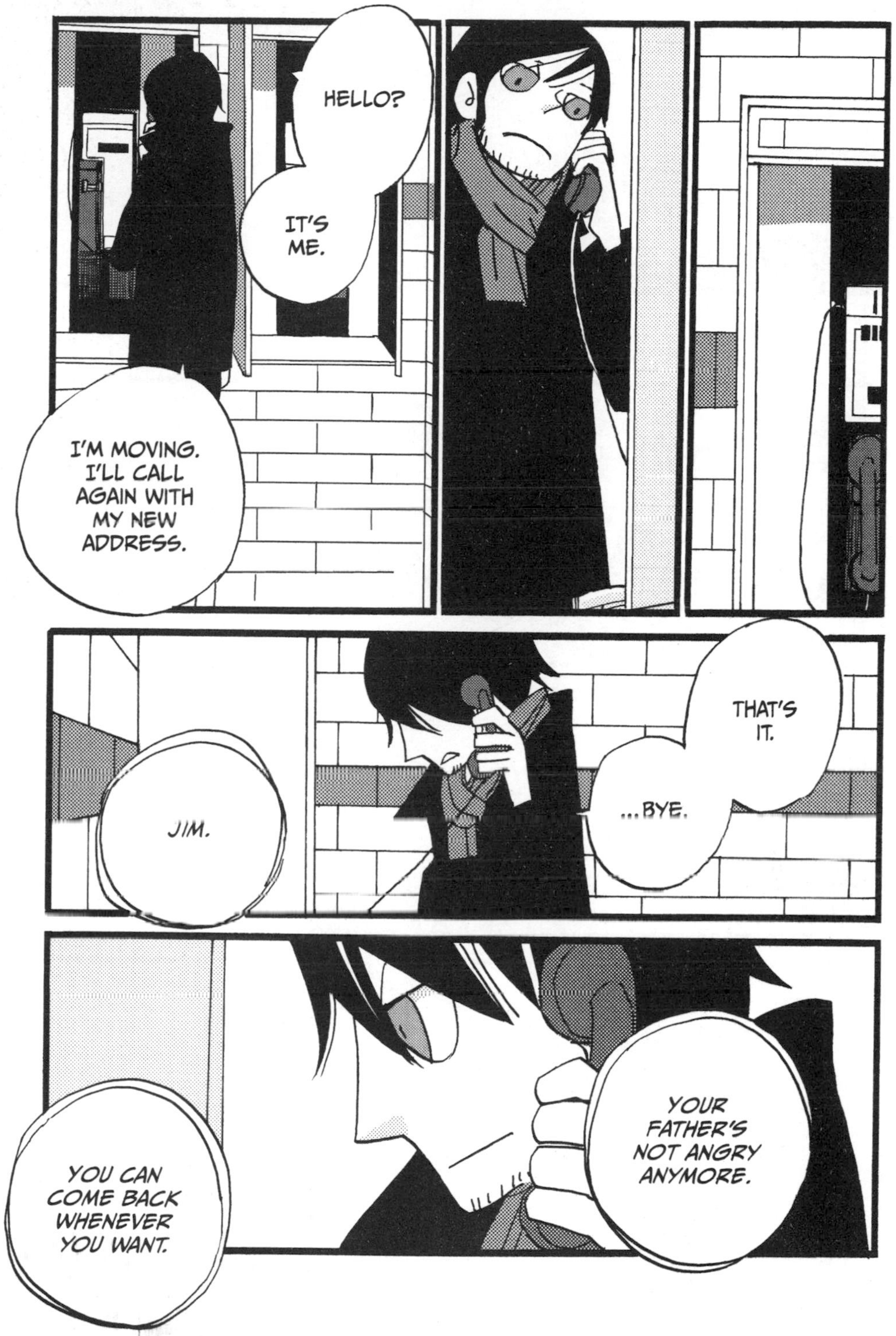
HELLO?
IT'S ME.
I'M MOVING. I'LL CALL AGAIN WITH MY NEW ADDRESS.
THAT'S IT.
...BYE.
JIM.
YOUR FATHER'S NOT ANGRY ANYMORE.
YOU CAN COME BACK WHENEVER YOU WANT.

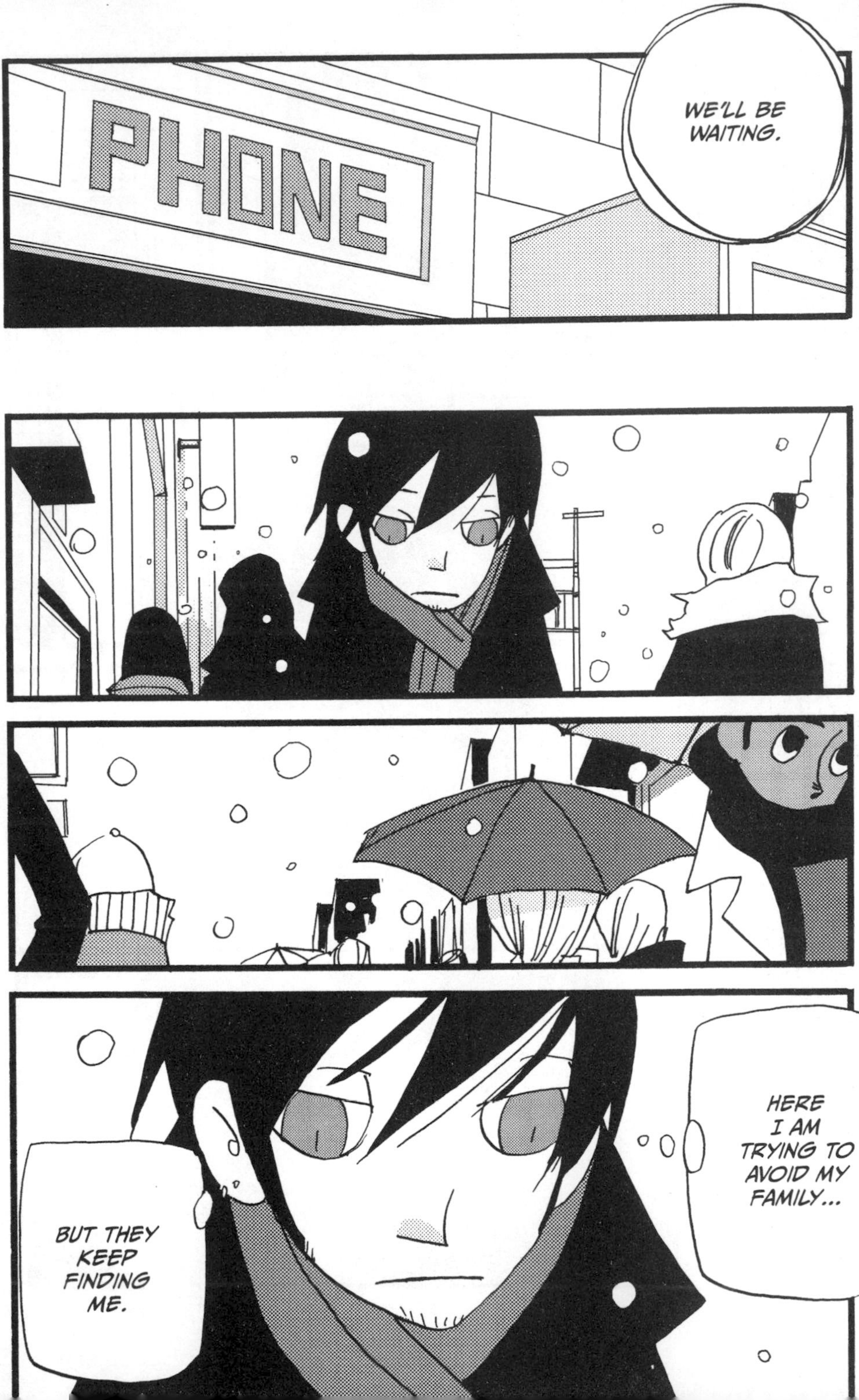
PHONE
WE'LL BE WAITING.
HERE I AM TRYING TO AVOID MY FAMILY...
BUT THEY KEEP FINDING ME.

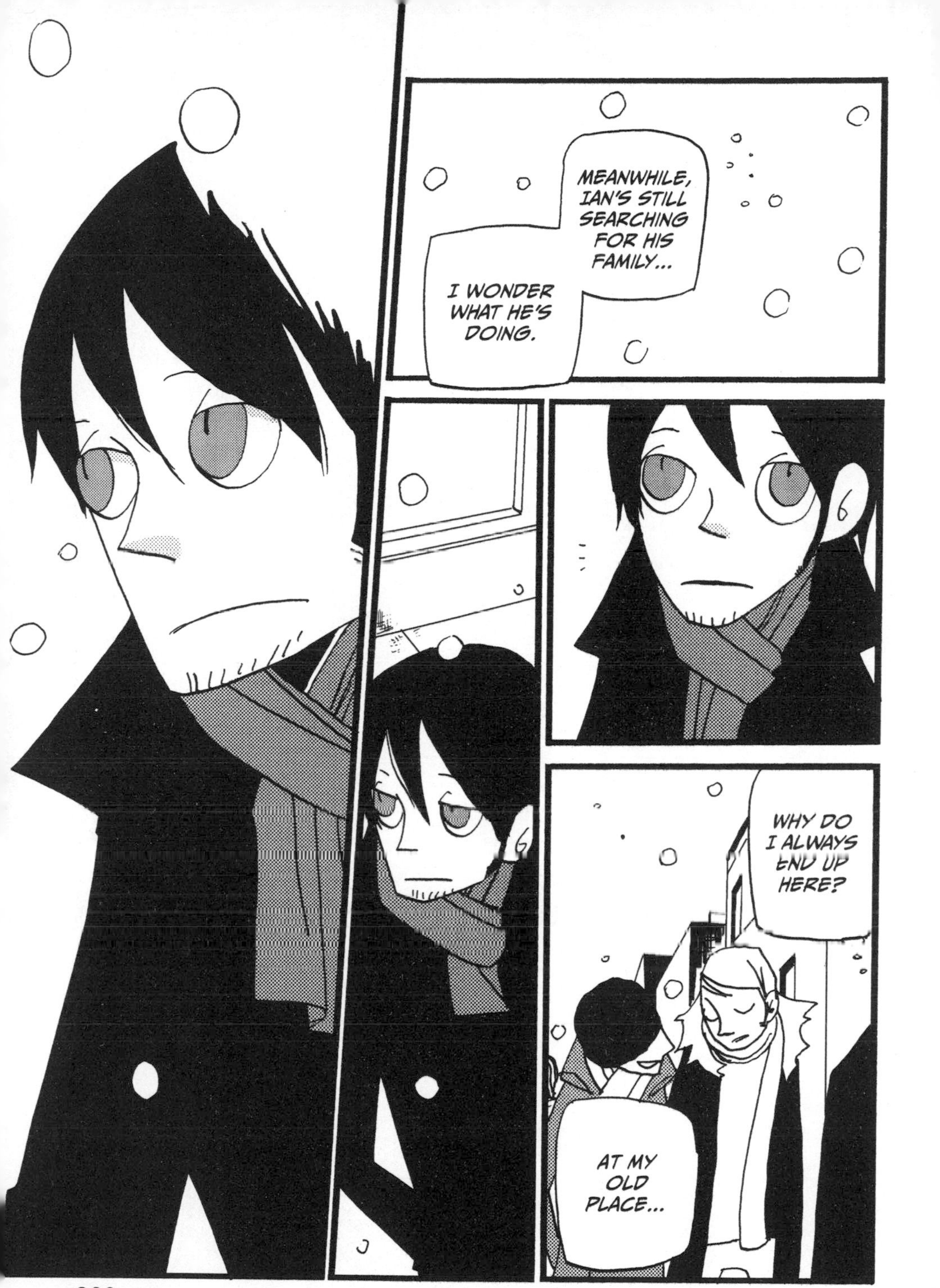
MEANWHILE, IAN'S STILL SEARCHING FOR HIS FAMILY...
I WONDER WHAT HE'S DOING.
WHY DO I ALWAYS END UP HERE?
AT MY OLD PLACE...

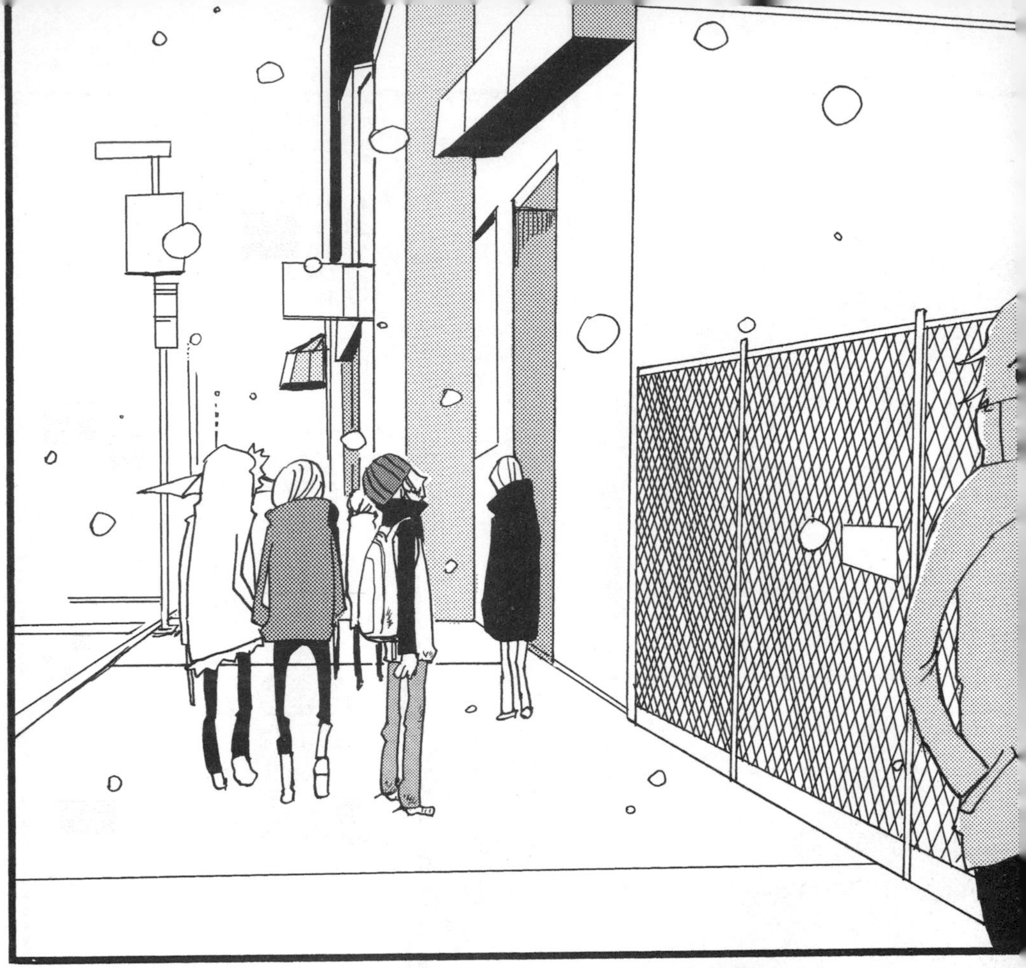
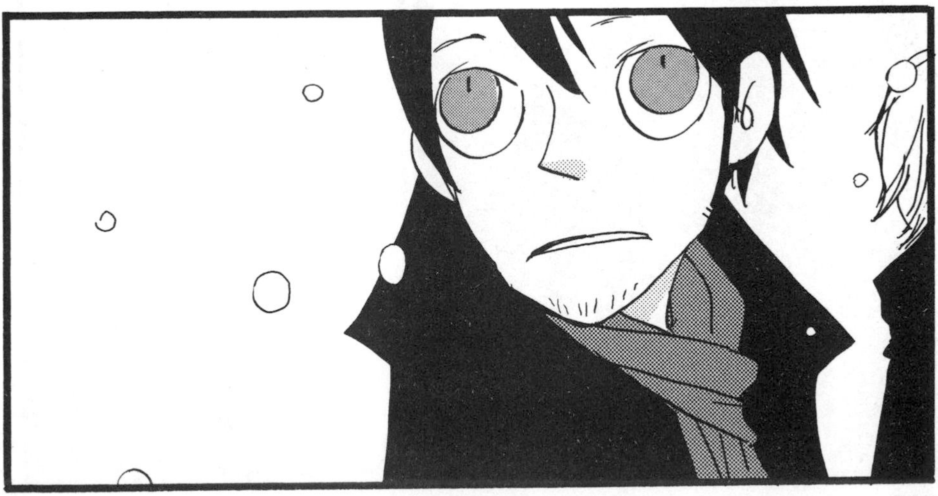

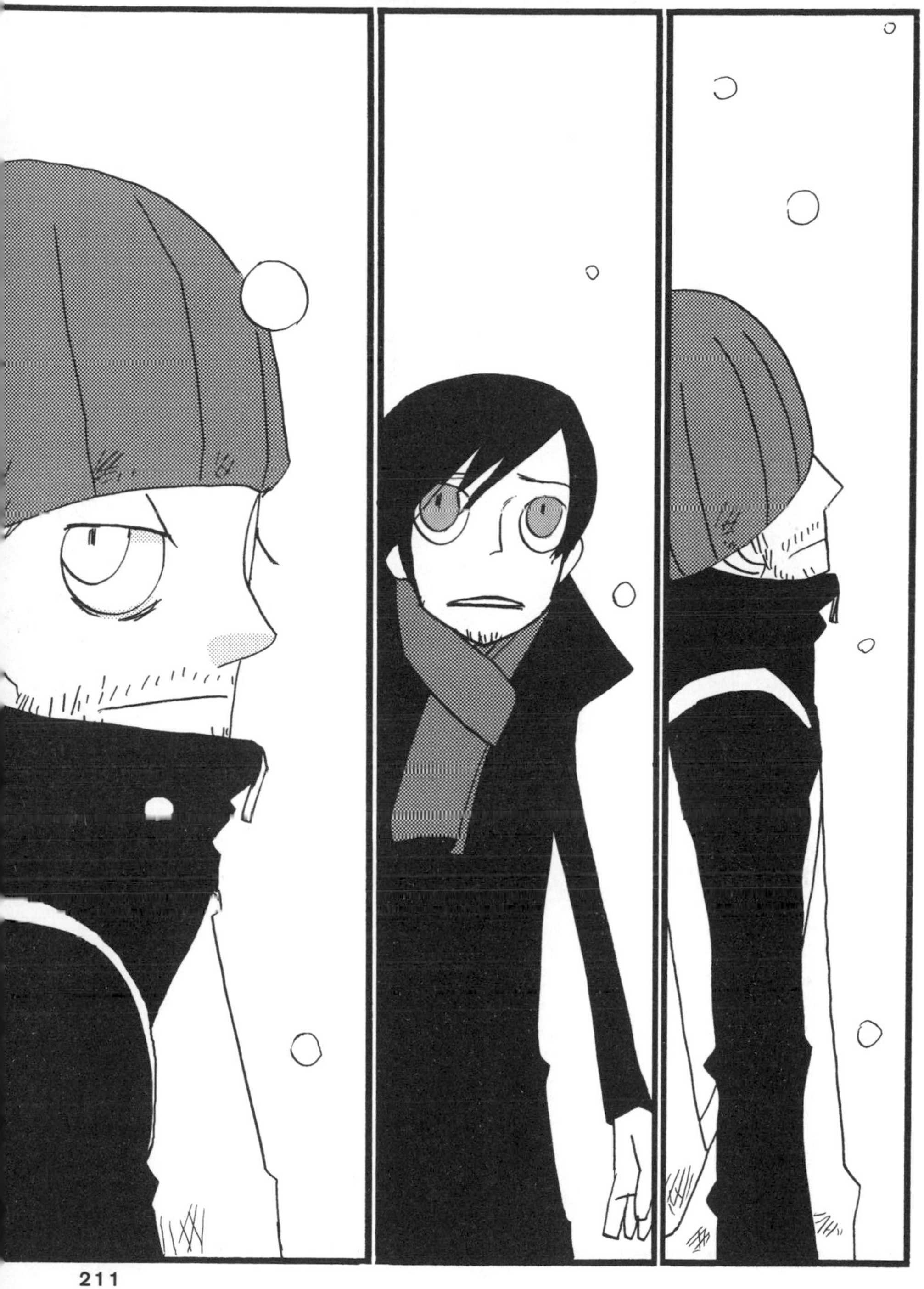

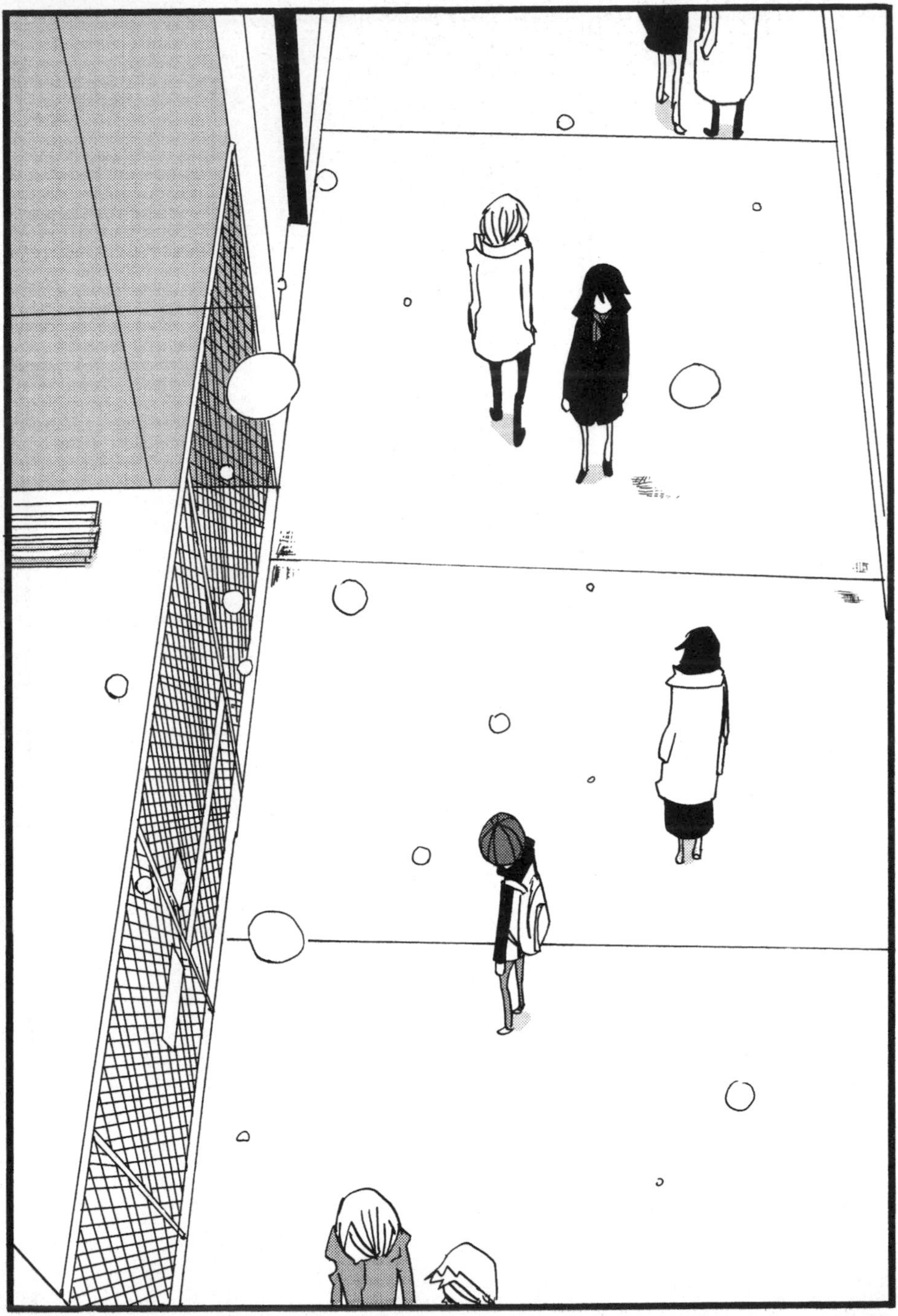

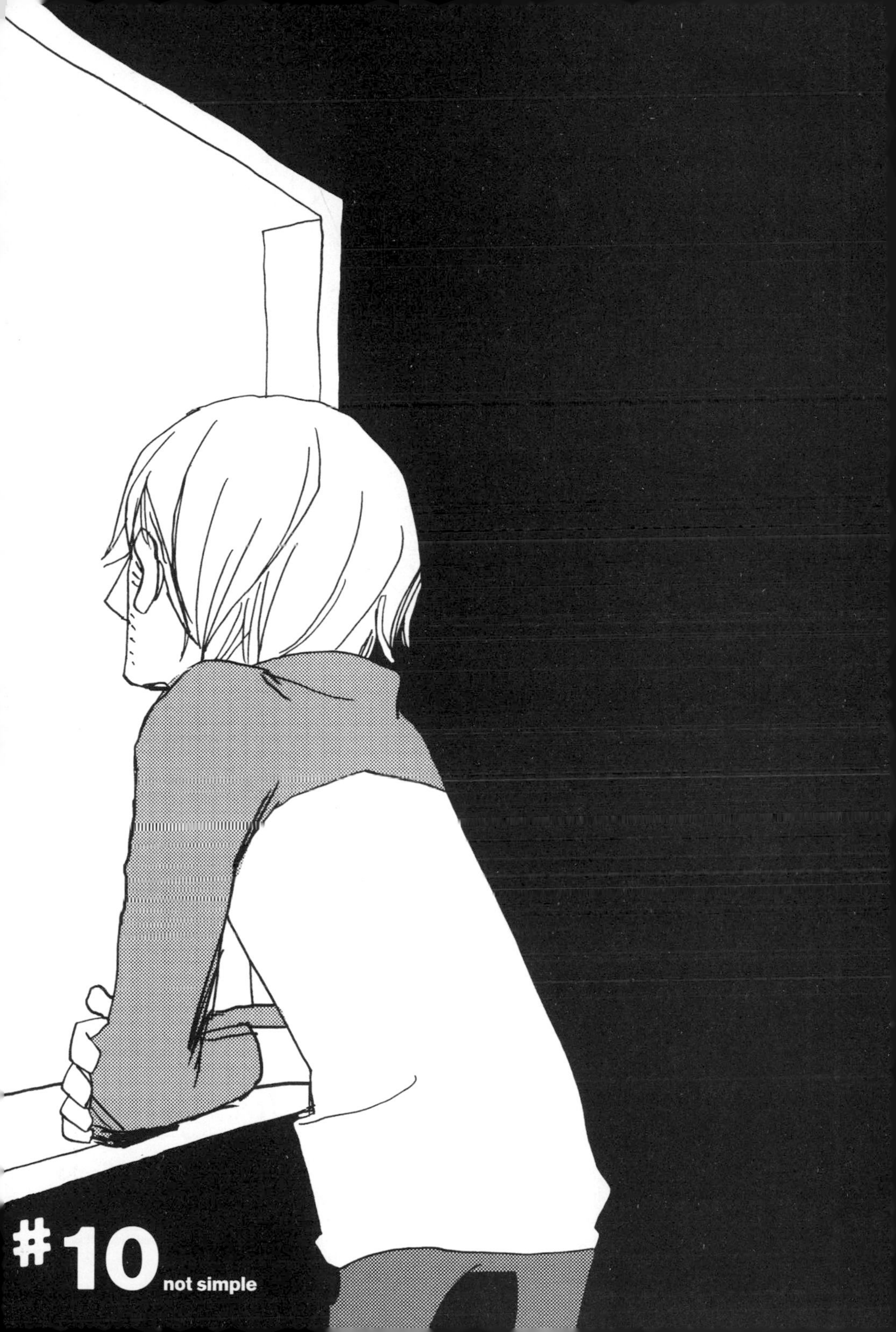

10
not simple

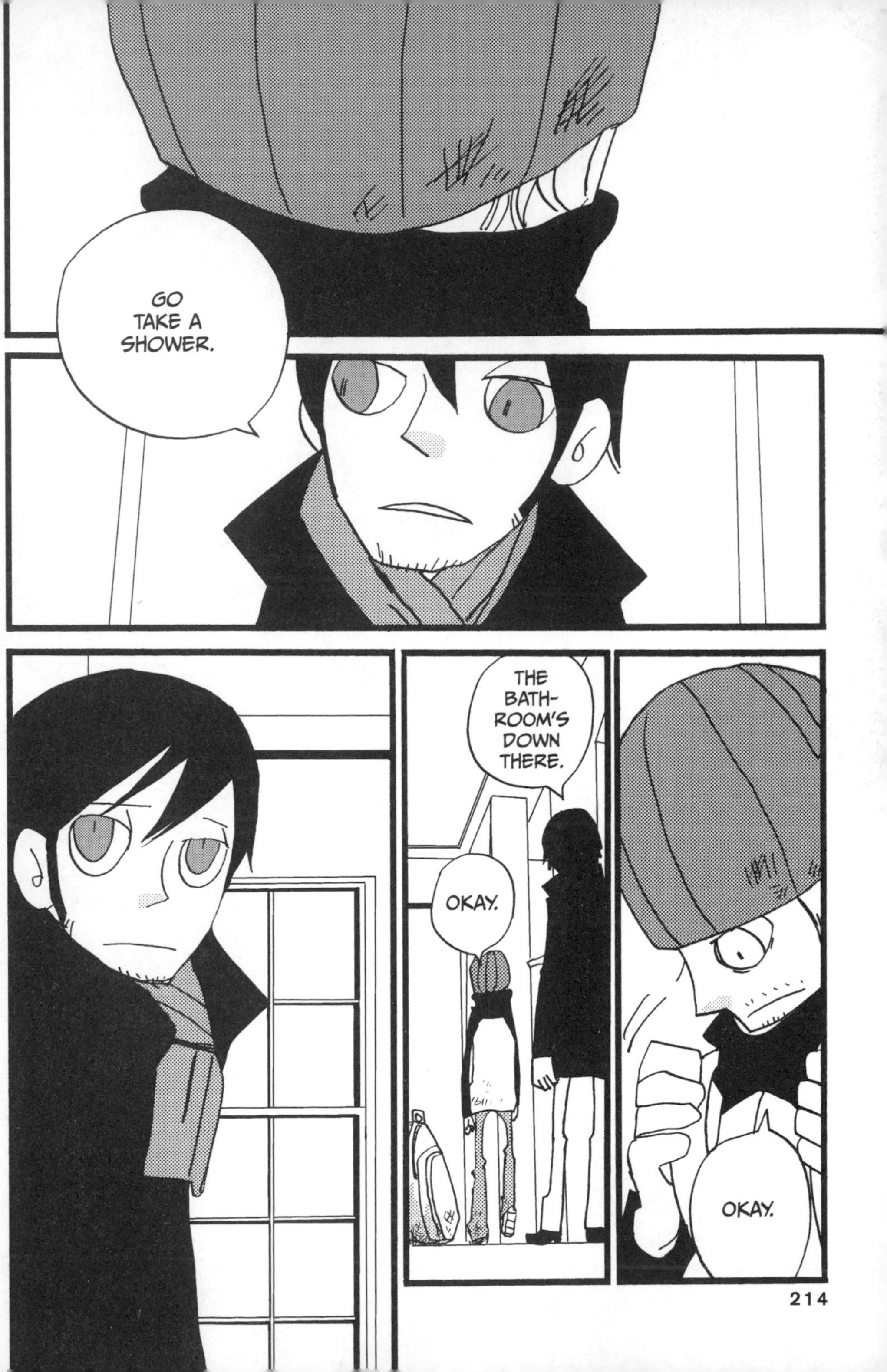
GO TAKE A SHOWER.
OKAY.
THE BATH-ROOM'S DOWN THERE.
OKAY.

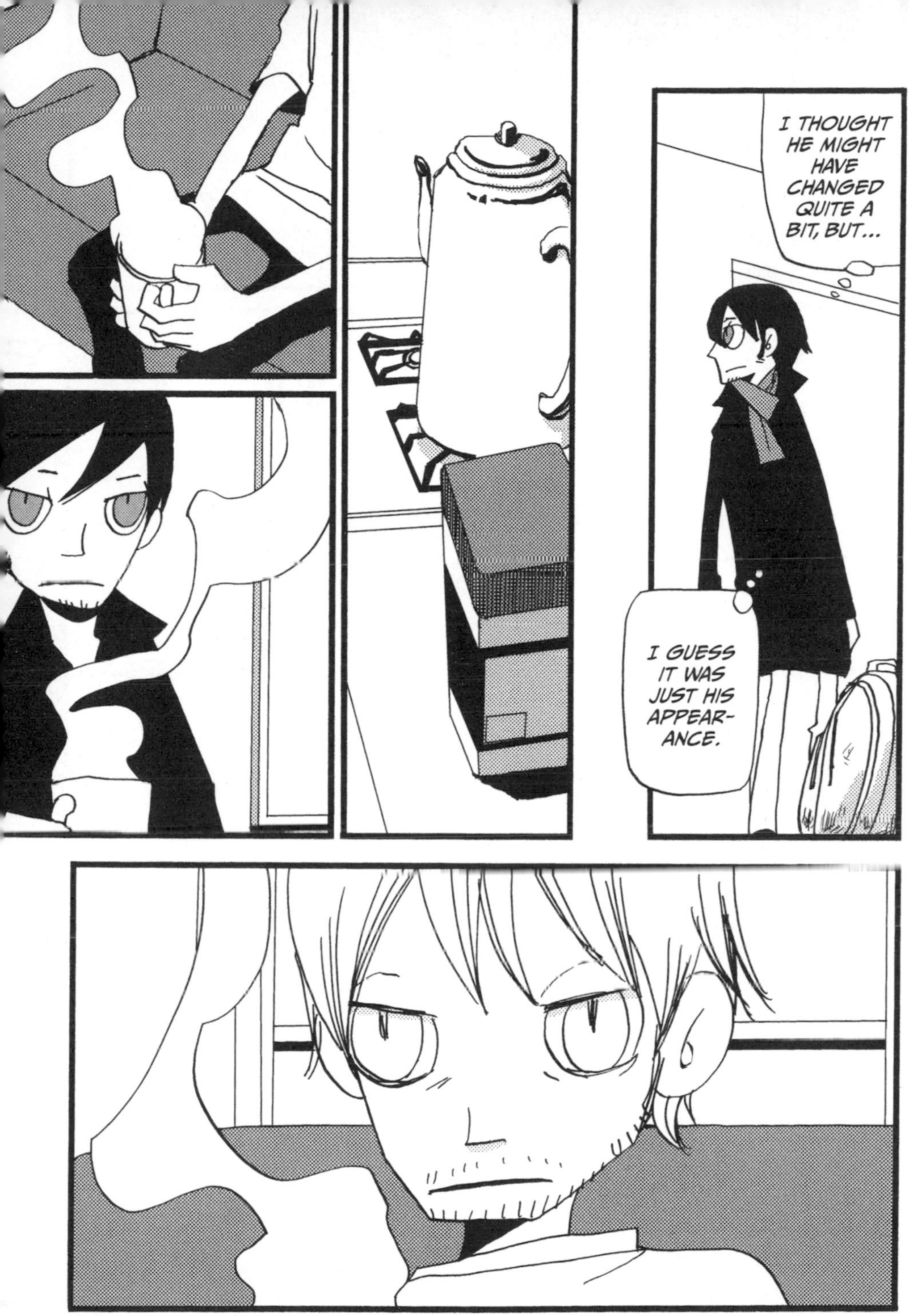
I THOUGHT HE MIGHT HAVE CHANGED QUITE A BIT, BUT...
I GUESS IT WAS JUST HIS APPEARANCE.

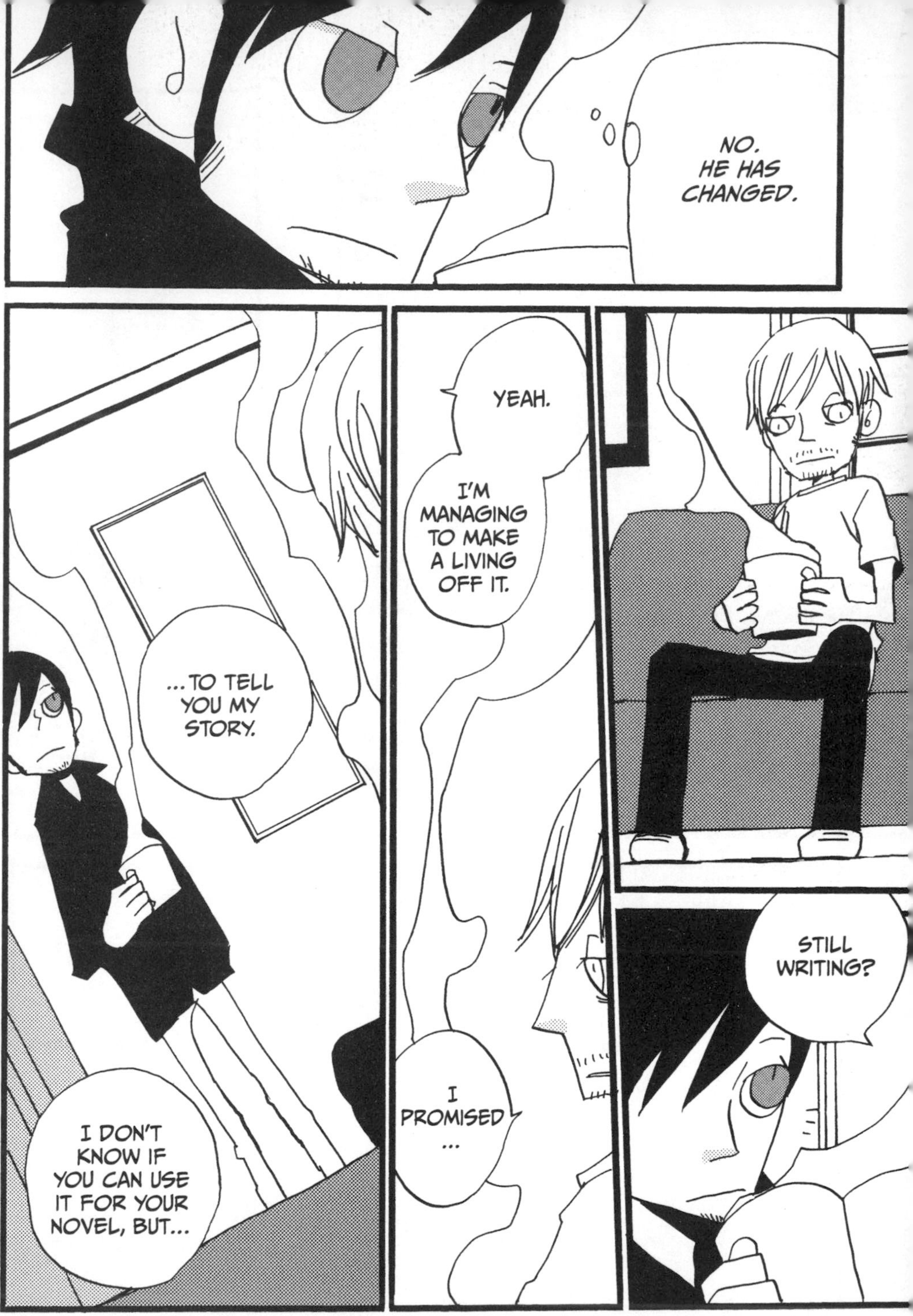
NO. HE HAS CHANGED.
STILL WRITING?
YEAH.
I'M MANAGING TO MAKE A LIVING OFF IT.
I PROMISED...
...TO TELL YOU MY STORY.
I DON'T KNOW IF YOU CAN USE IT FOR YOUR NOVEL, BUT...

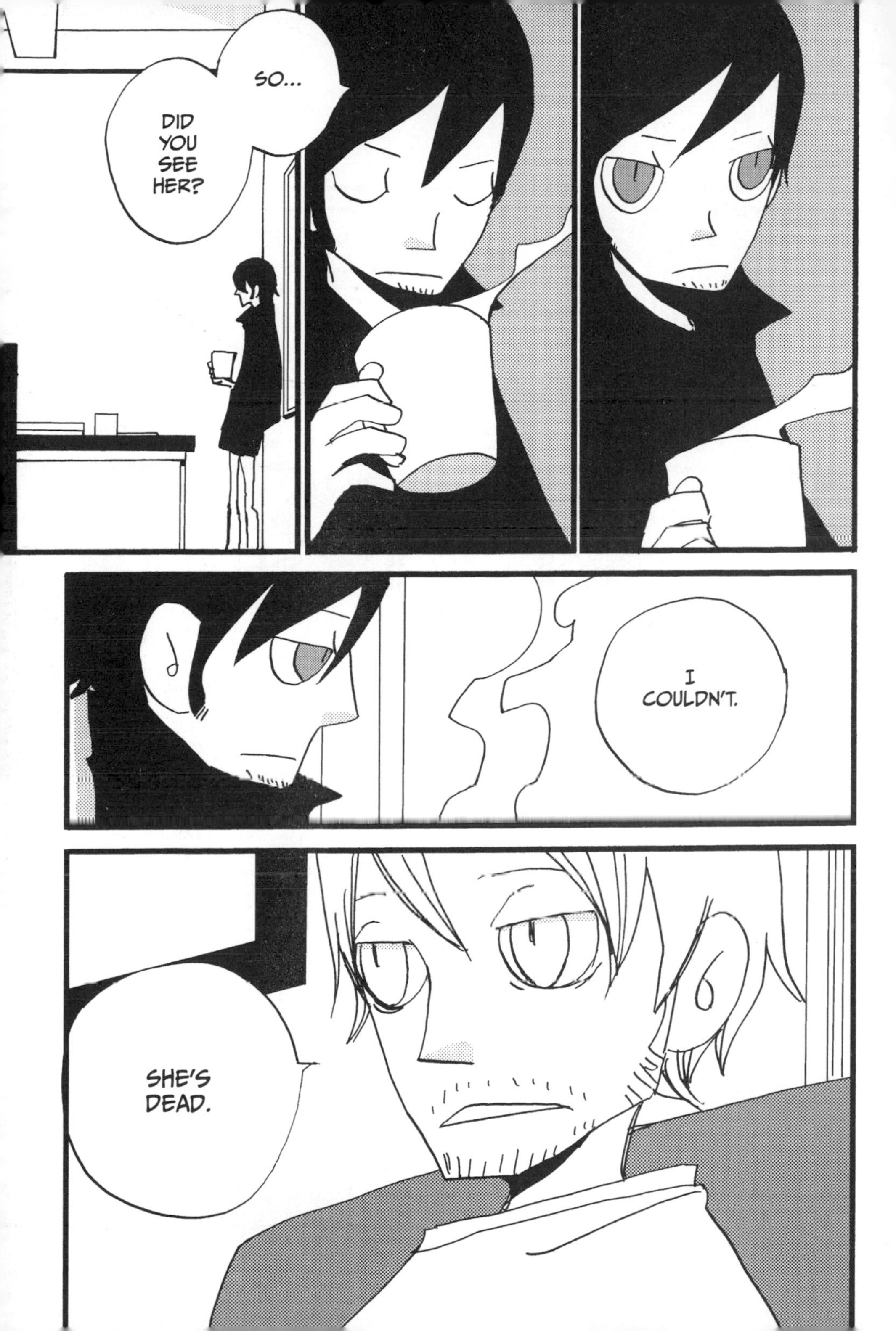
SO...
DID YOU SEE HER?
I COULDN'T.
SHE'S DEAD.

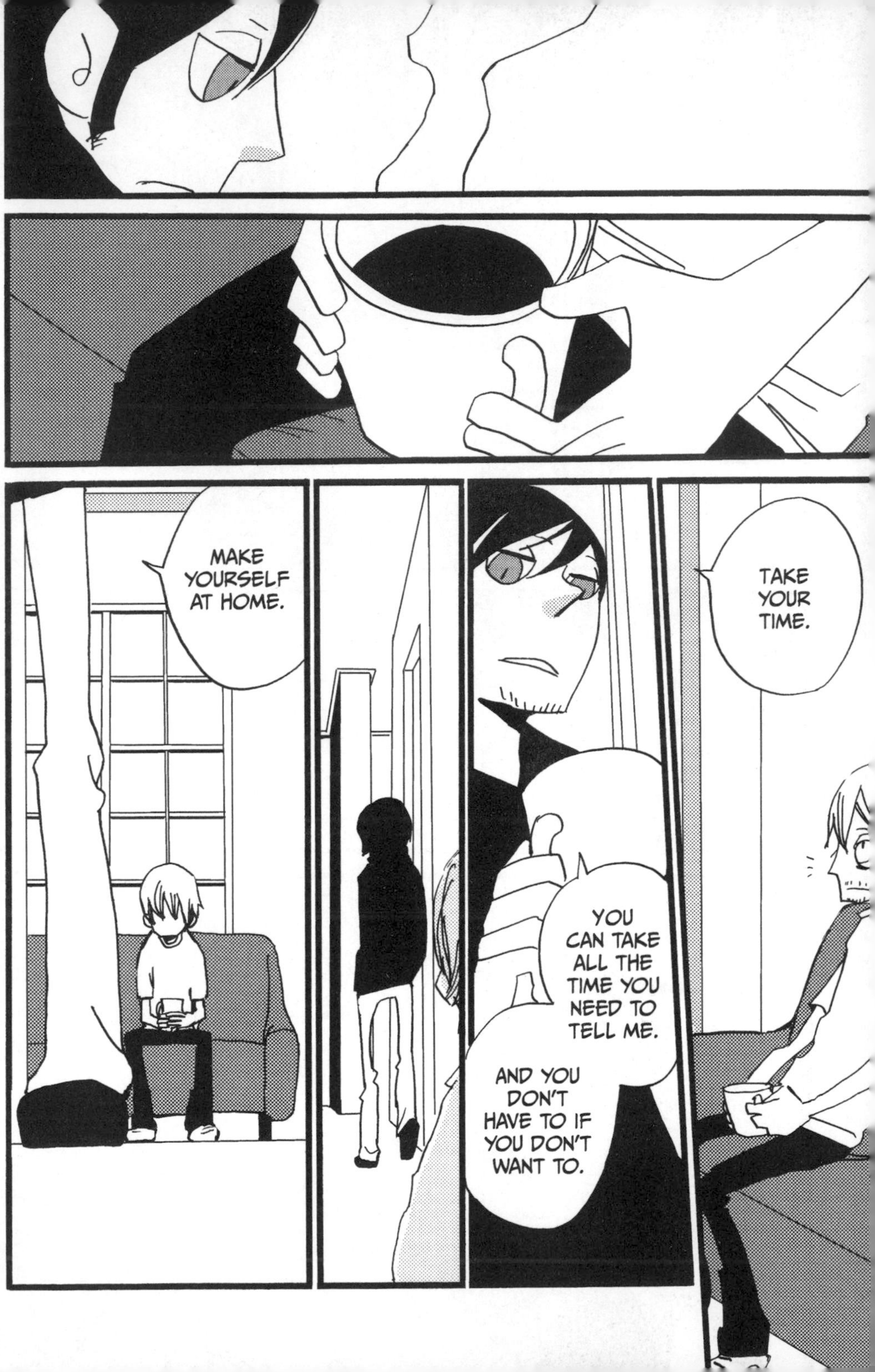
TAKE YOUR TIME.
YOU CAN TAKE ALL THE TIME YOU NEED TO TELL ME.
AND YOU DON'T HAVE TO IF YOU DON'T WANT TO.
MAKE YOURSELF AT HOME.

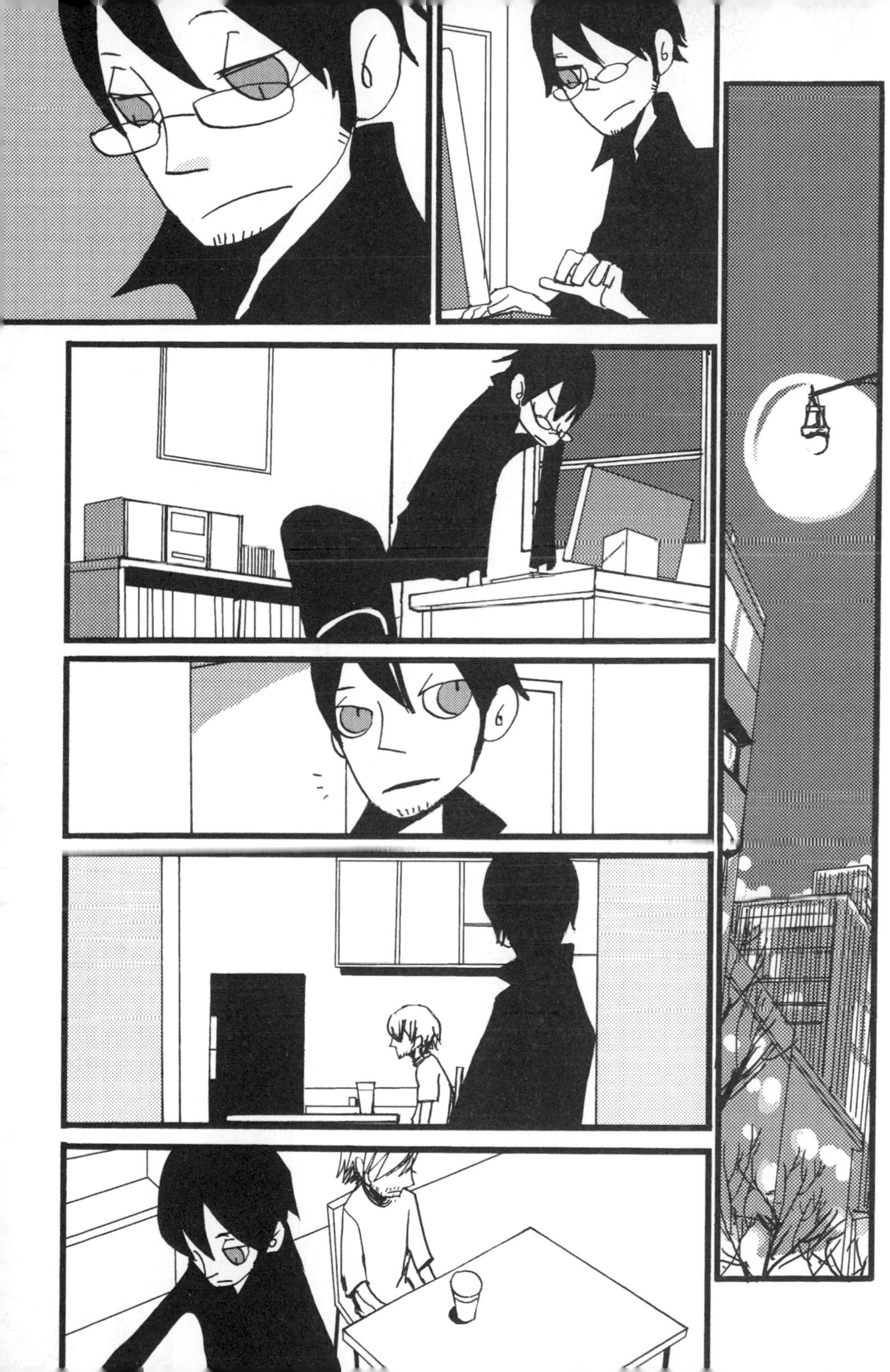

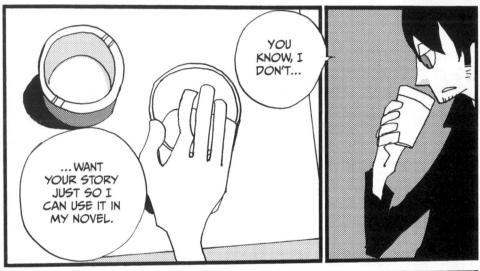

YOU KNOW, I DON'T...

...WANT YOUR STORY JUST SO I CAN USE IT IN MY NOVEL.

I JUST WANT TO KNOW MORE ABOUT YOU.

I CAME HERE BECAUSE I WANTED TO SEE YOU.

...ME TOO.

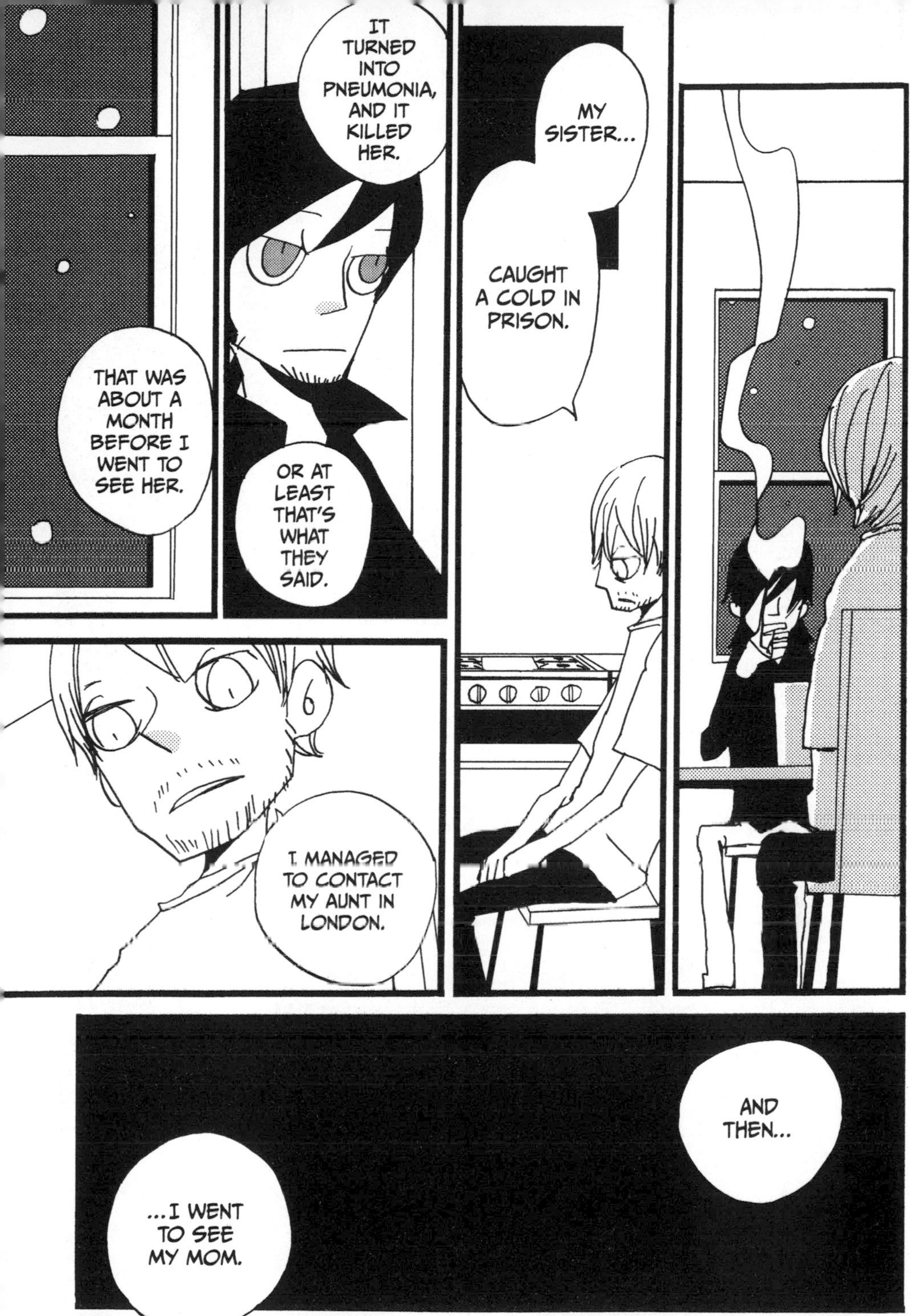
MY SISTER...
CAUGHT A COLD IN PRISON.
IT TURNED INTO PNEUMONIA, AND IT KILLED HER.
OR AT LEAST THAT'S WHAT THEY SAID.
THAT WAS ABOUT A MONTH BEFORE I WENT TO SEE HER.
I MANAGED TO CONTACT MY AUNT IN LONDON.
AND THEN...
...I WENT TO SEE MY MOM.

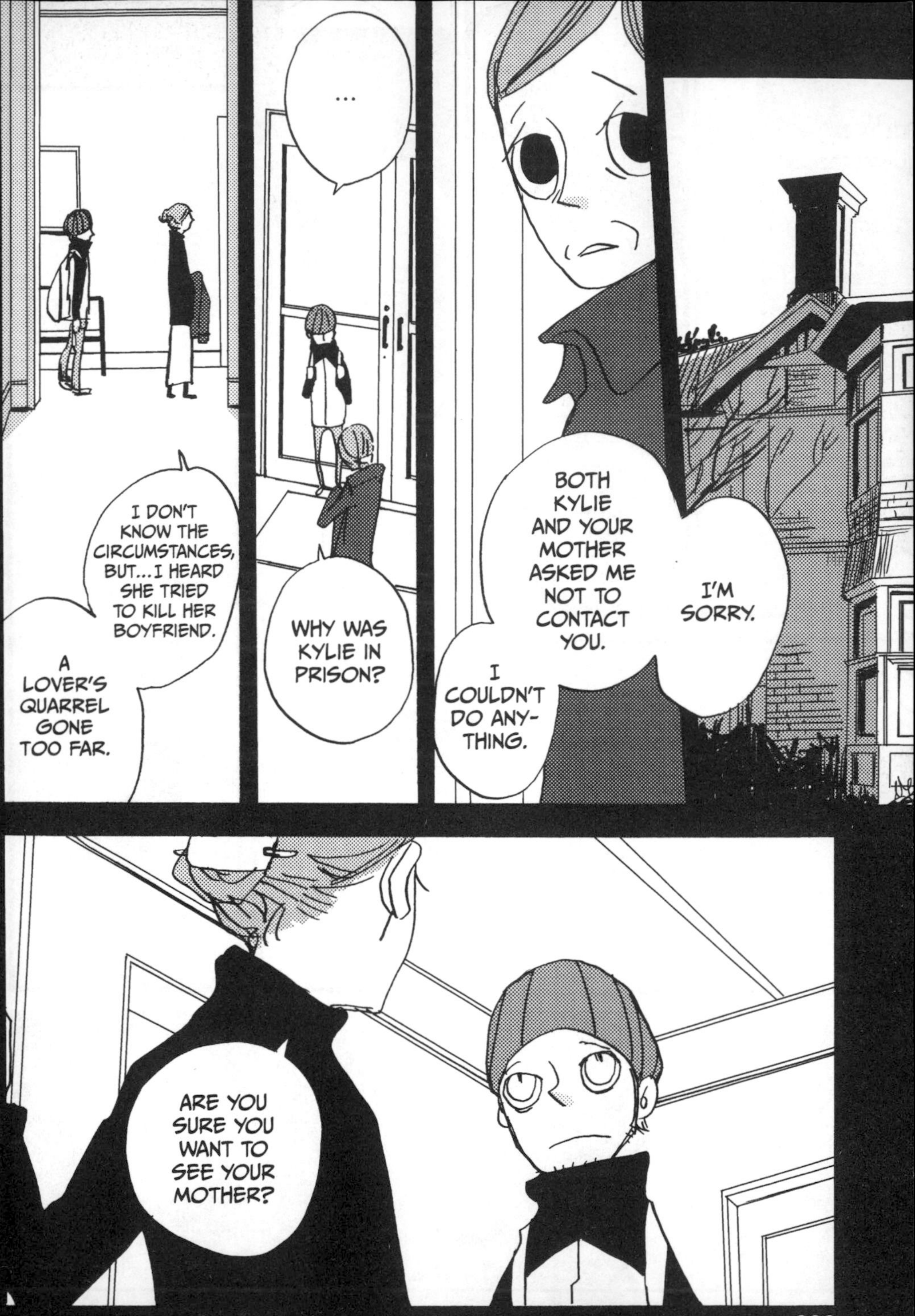
I'M SORRY.
BOTH KYLIE AND YOUR MOTHER ASKED ME NOT TO CONTACT YOU.
I COULDN'T DO ANY-THING.
...
WHY WAS KYLIE IN PRISON?
I DON'T KNOW THE CIRCUMSTANCES, BUT...I HEARD SHE TRIED TO KILL HER BOYFRIEND.
A LOVER'S QUARREL GONE TOO FAR.
ARE YOU SURE YOU WANT TO SEE YOUR MOTHER?

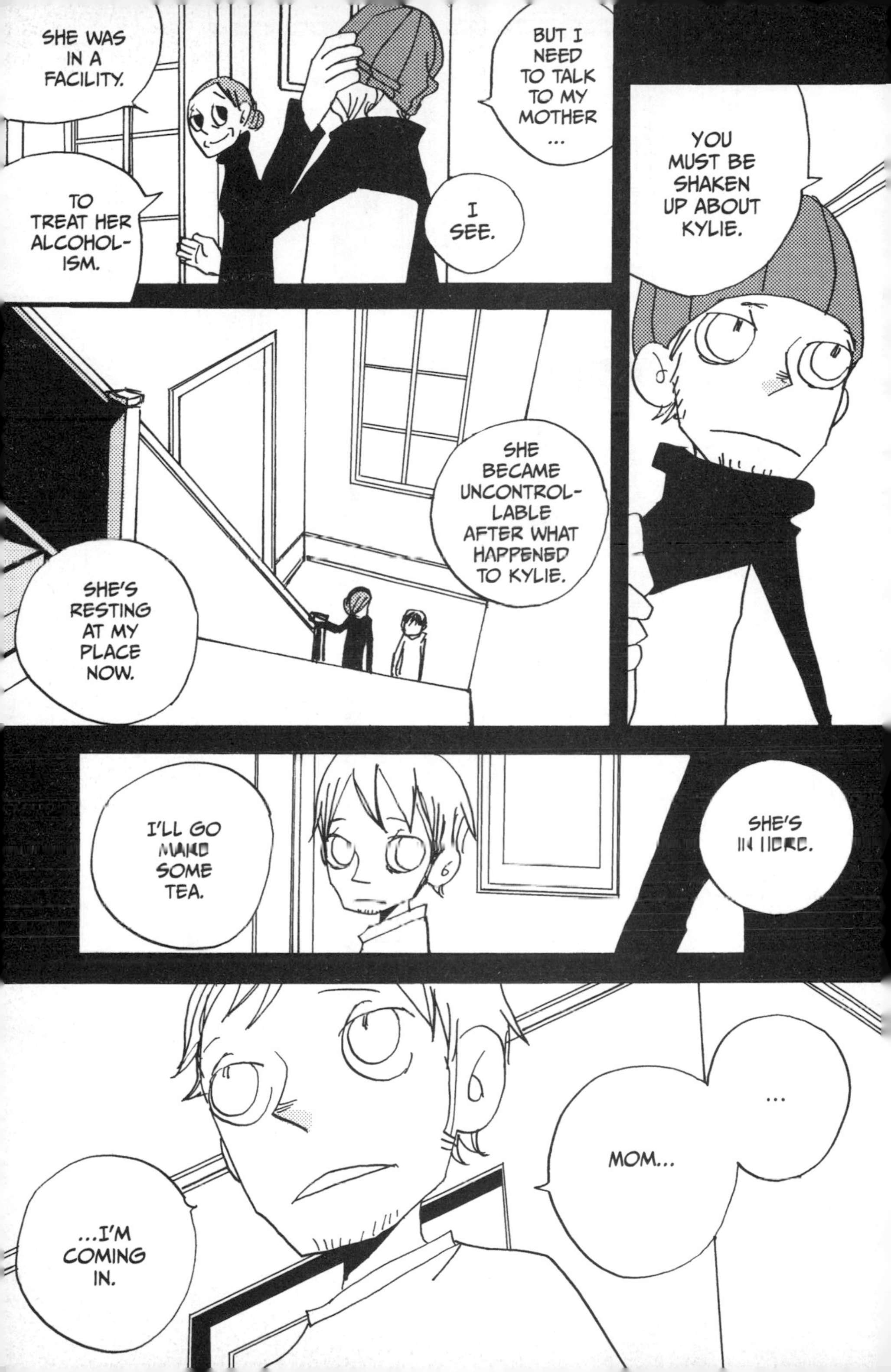
YOU MUST BE SHAKEN UP ABOUT KYLIE.
BUT I NEED TO TALK TO MY MOTHER ...
I SEE.
SHE WAS IN A FACILITY.
TO TREAT HER ALCOHOLISM.
SHE BECAME UNCONTROLLABLE AFTER WHAT HAPPENED TO KYLIE.
SHE'S RESTING AT MY PLACE NOW.
SHE'S IN HERE.
I'LL GO MAKE SOME TEA.
...
MOM...
...I'M COMING IN.

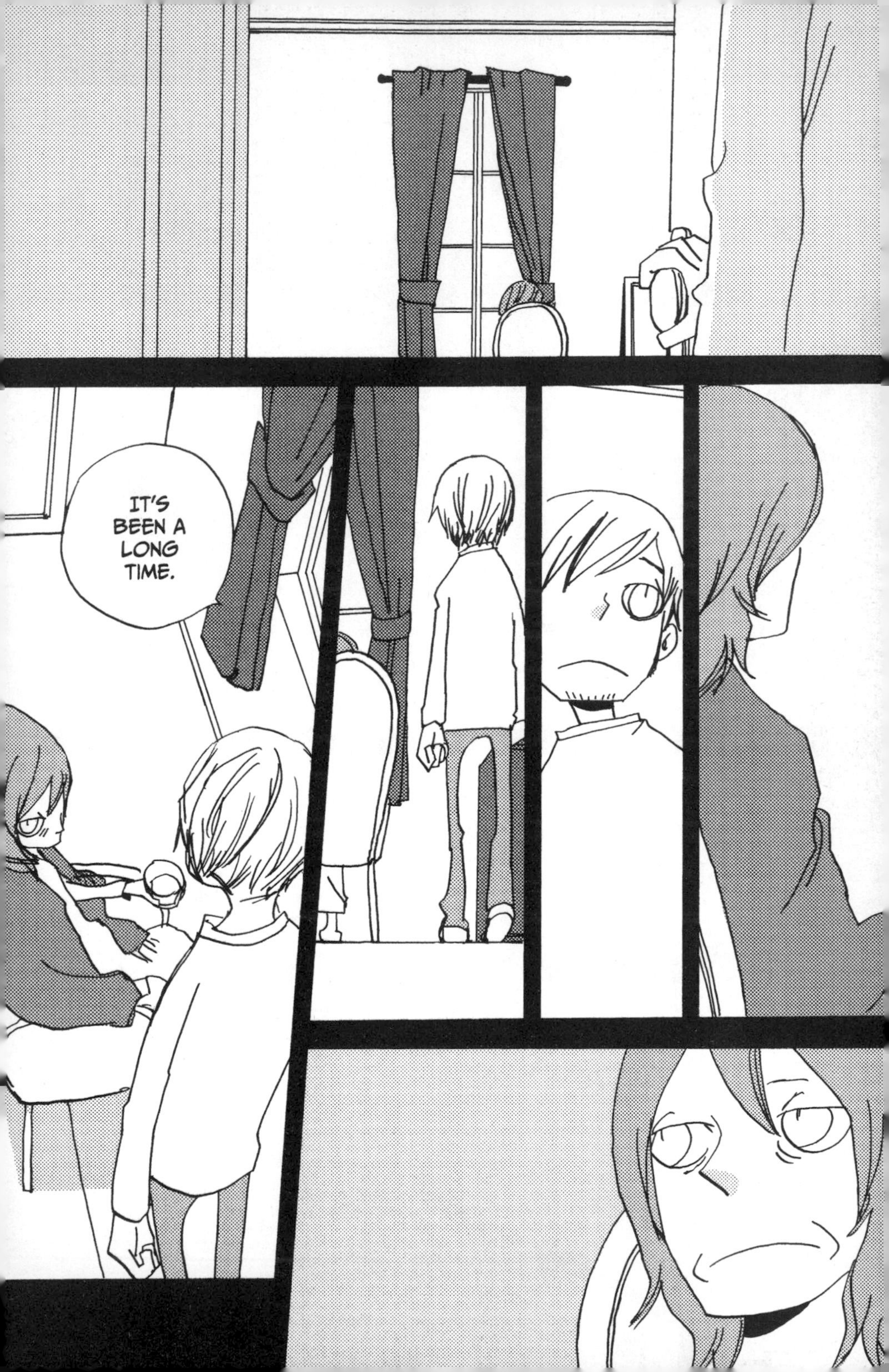
IT'S BEEN A LONG TIME.

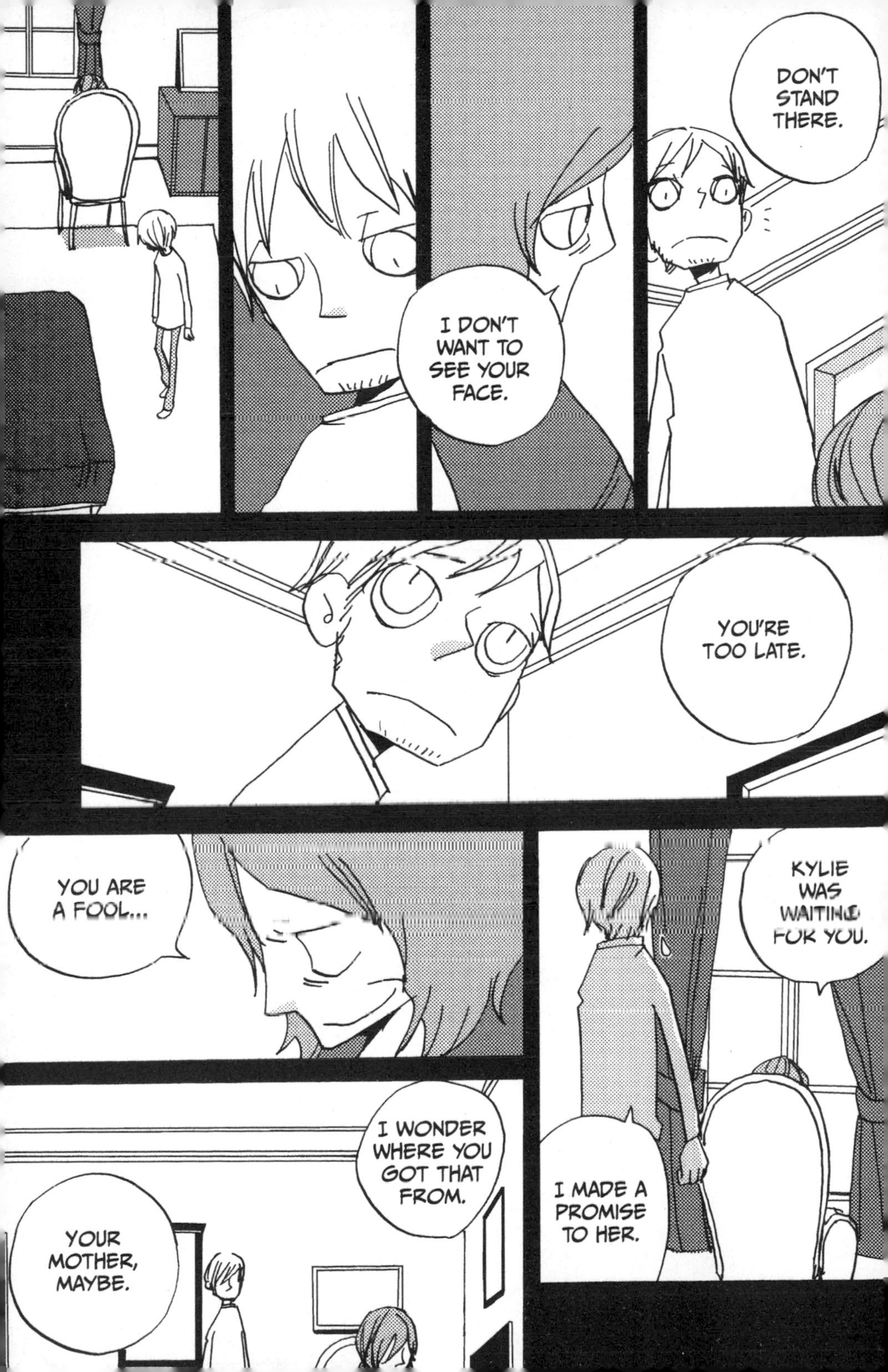
DON'T STAND THERE.
I DON'T WANT TO SEE YOUR FACE.
YOU'RE TOO LATE.
KYLIE WAS WAITING FOR YOU.
I MADE A PROMISE TO HER.
YOU ARE A FOOL...
I WONDER WHERE YOU GOT THAT FROM.
YOUR MOTHER, MAYBE.

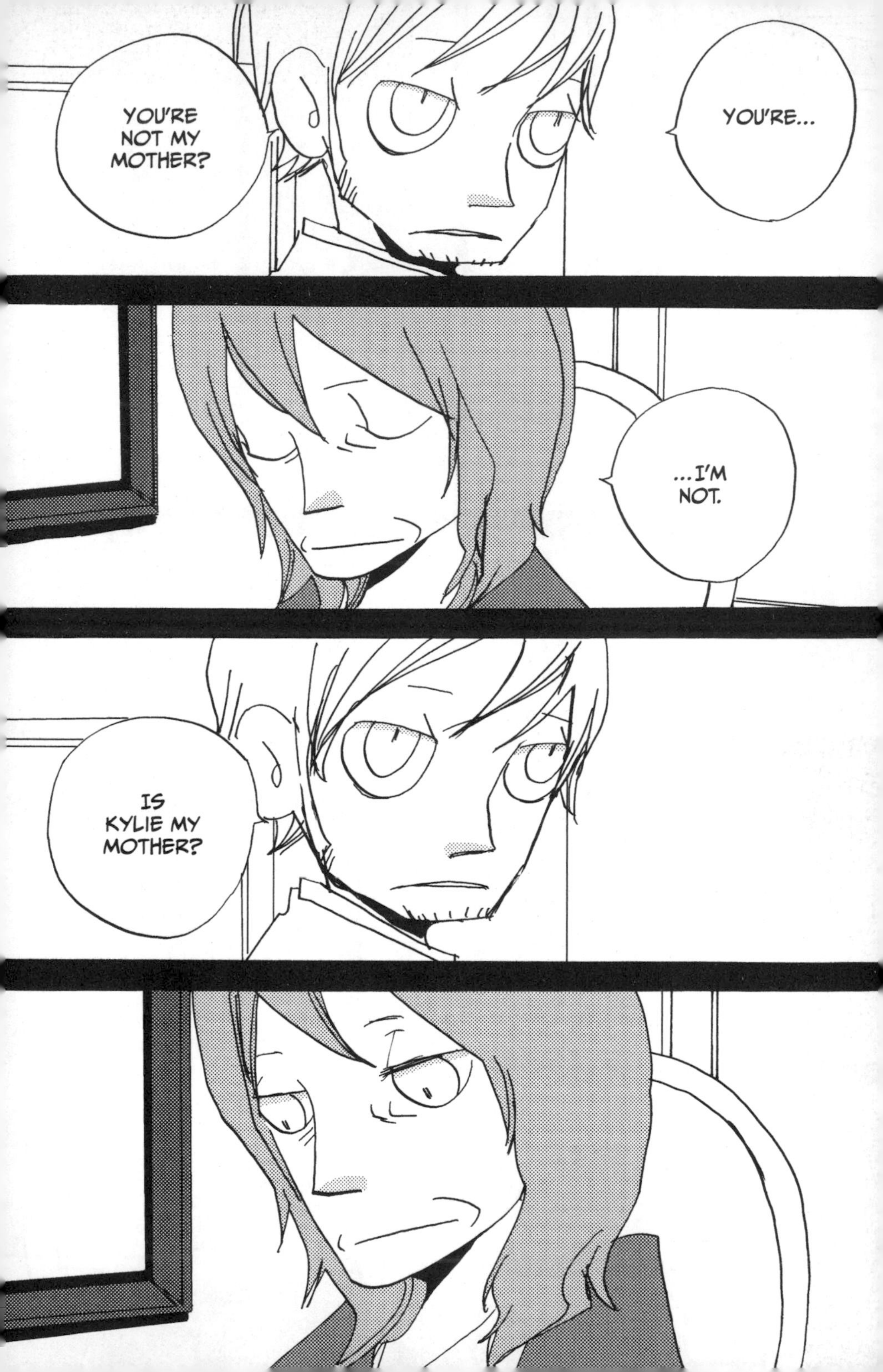
YOU'RE...
YOU'RE NOT MY MOTHER?
...I'M NOT.
IS KYLIE MY MOTHER?

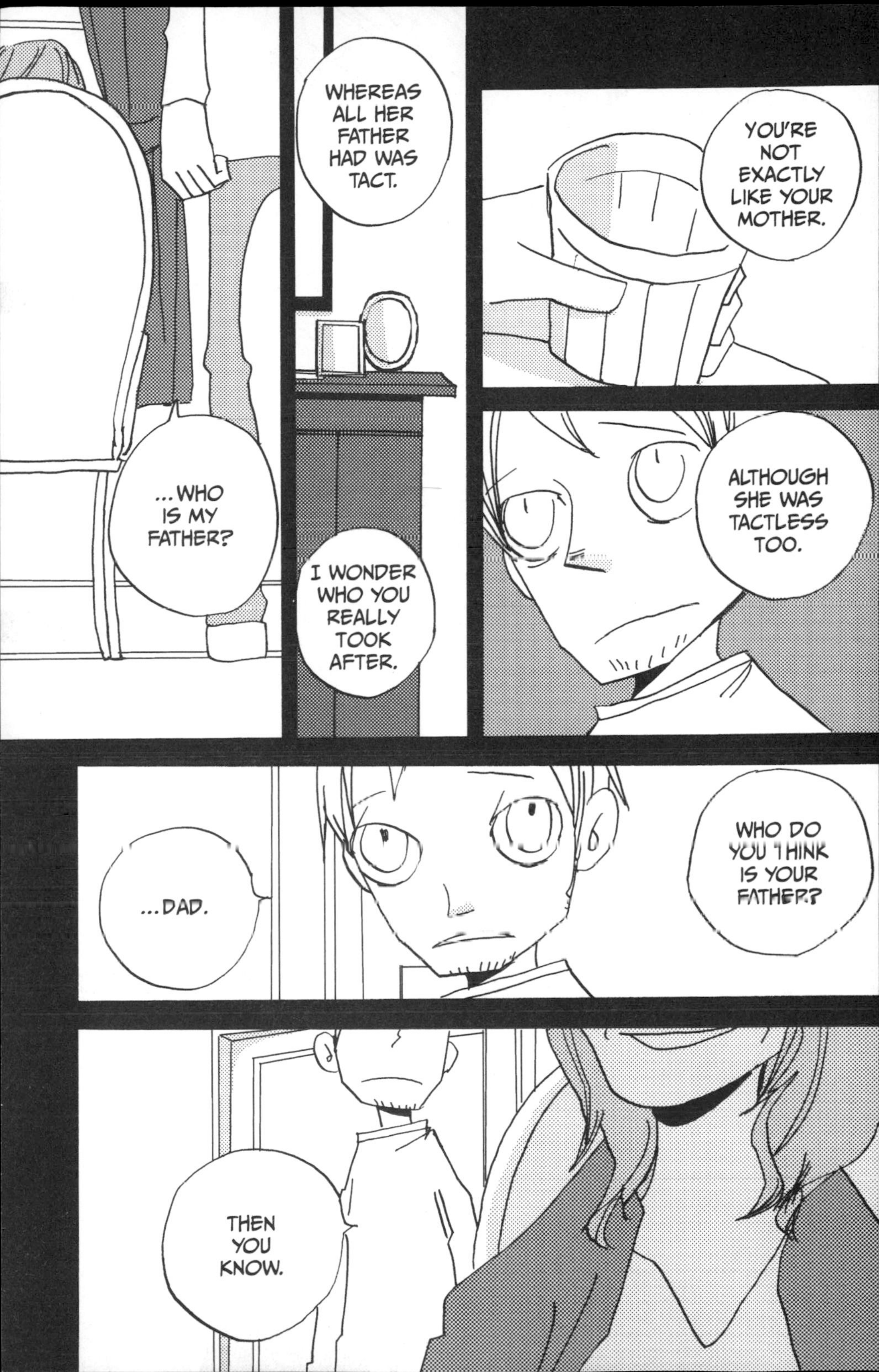
YOU'RE NOT EXACTLY LIKE YOUR MOTHER.
ALTHOUGH SHE WAS TACTLESS TOO.
WHEREAS ALL HER FATHER HAD WAS TACT.
I WONDER WHO YOU REALLY TOOK AFTER.
...WHO IS MY FATHER?
WHO DO YOU THINK IS YOUR FATHER?
...DAD.
THEN YOU KNOW.

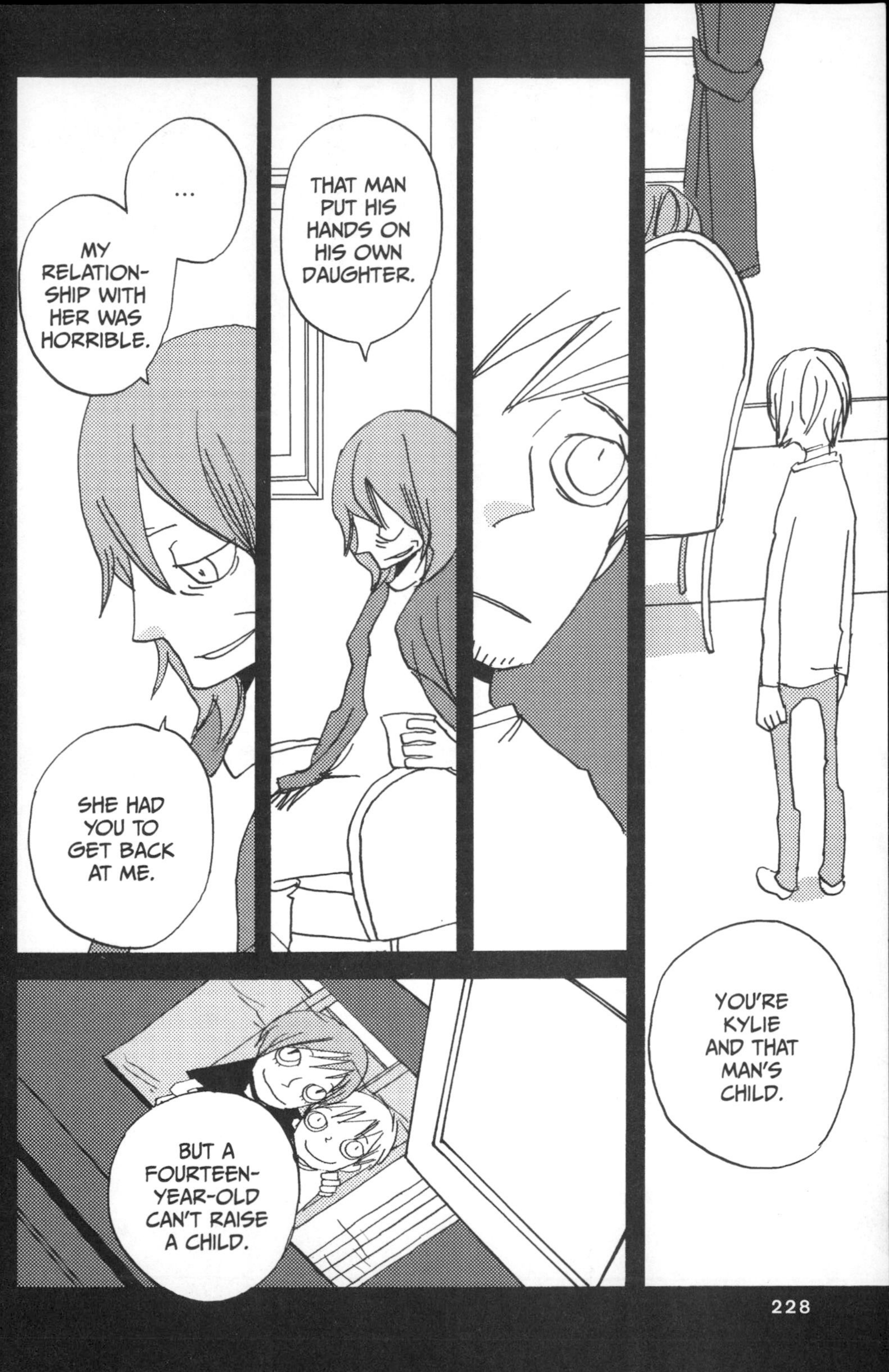
YOU'RE KYLIE AND THAT MAN'S CHILD.
THAT MAN PUT HIS HANDS ON HIS OWN DAUGHTER.
...
MY RELATIONSHIP WITH HER WAS HORRIBLE.
SHE HAD YOU TO GET BACK AT ME.
BUT A FOURTEEN-YEAR-OLD CAN'T RAISE A CHILD.

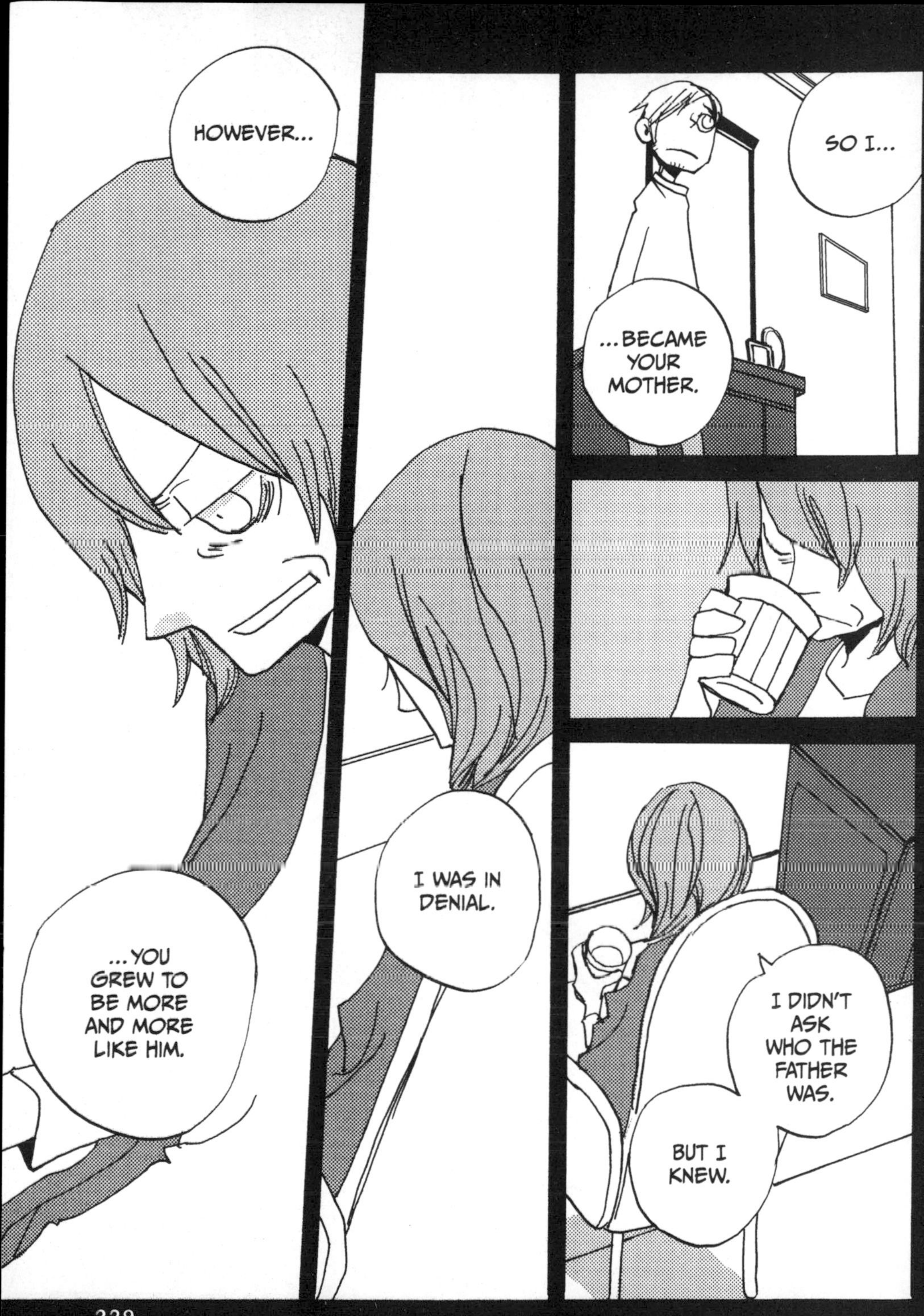
SO I...
...BECAME YOUR MOTHER.
I DIDN'T ASK WHO THE FATHER WAS.
BUT I KNEW.
I WAS IN DENIAL.
HOWEVER...
...YOU GREW TO BE MORE AND MORE LIKE HIM.

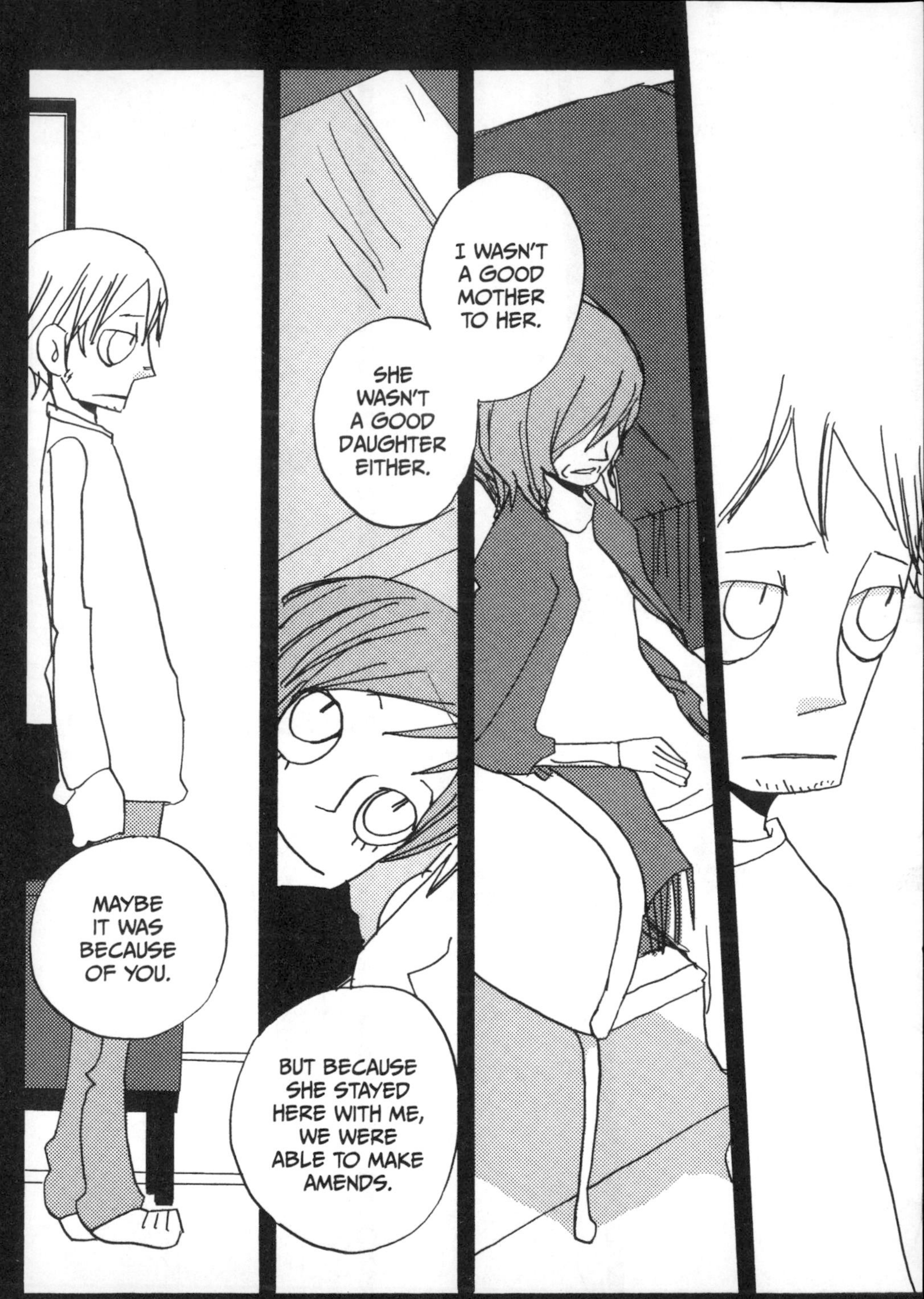
I WASN'T A GOOD MOTHER TO HER.
SHE WASN'T A GOOD DAUGHTER EITHER.
BUT BECAUSE SHE STAYED HERE WITH ME, WE WERE ABLE TO MAKE AMENDS.
MAYBE IT WAS BECAUSE OF YOU.

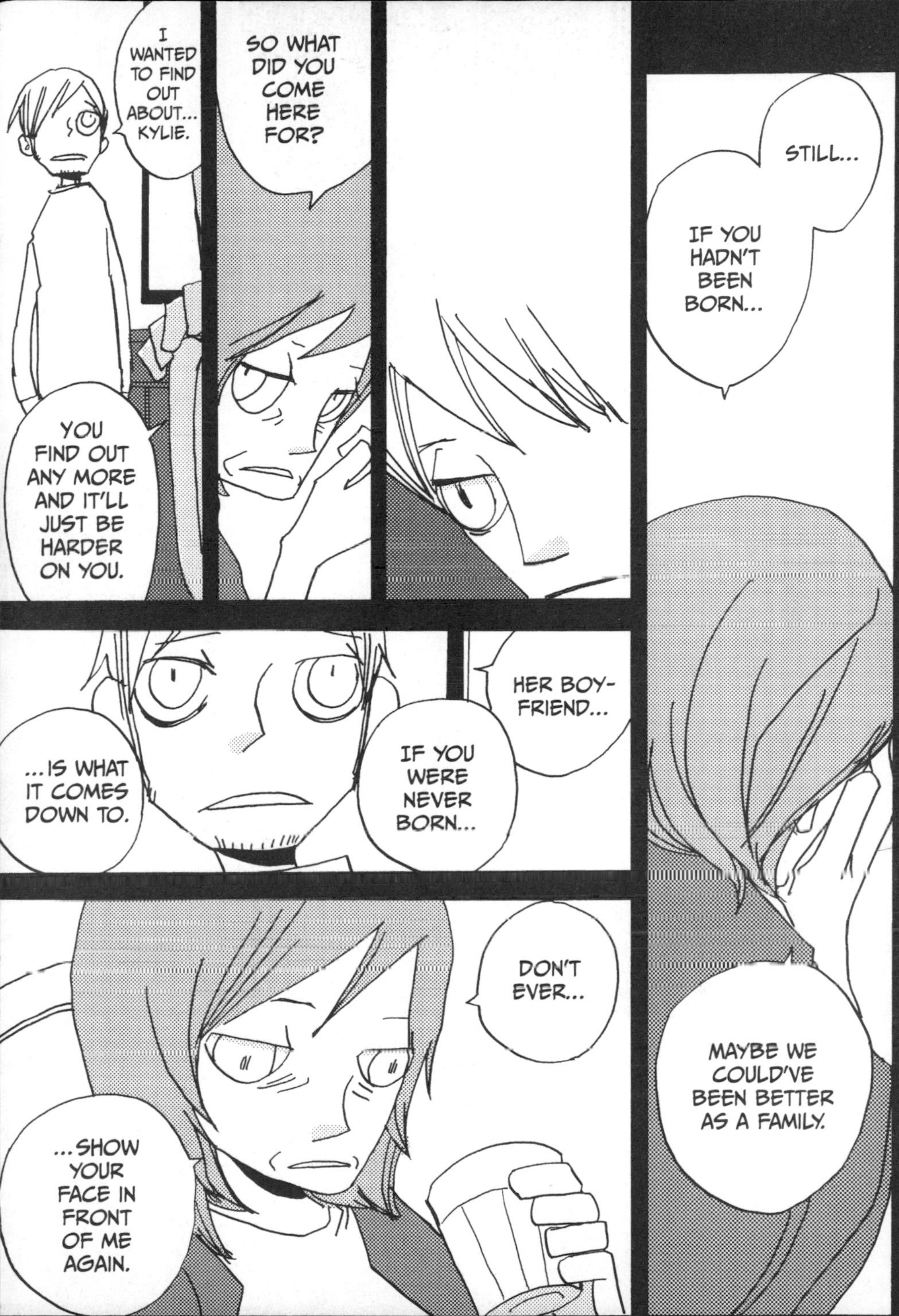
STILL...
IF YOU HADN'T BEEN BORN...
MAYBE WE COULD'VE BEEN BETTER AS A FAMILY.
SO WHAT DID YOU COME HERE FOR?
I WANTED TO FIND OUT ABOUT... KYLIE.
YOU FIND OUT ANY MORE AND IT'LL JUST BE HARDER ON YOU.
HER BOY-FRIEND...
IF YOU WERE NEVER BORN...
...IS WHAT IT COMES DOWN TO.
DON'T EVER...
...SHOW YOUR FACE IN FRONT OF ME AGAIN.

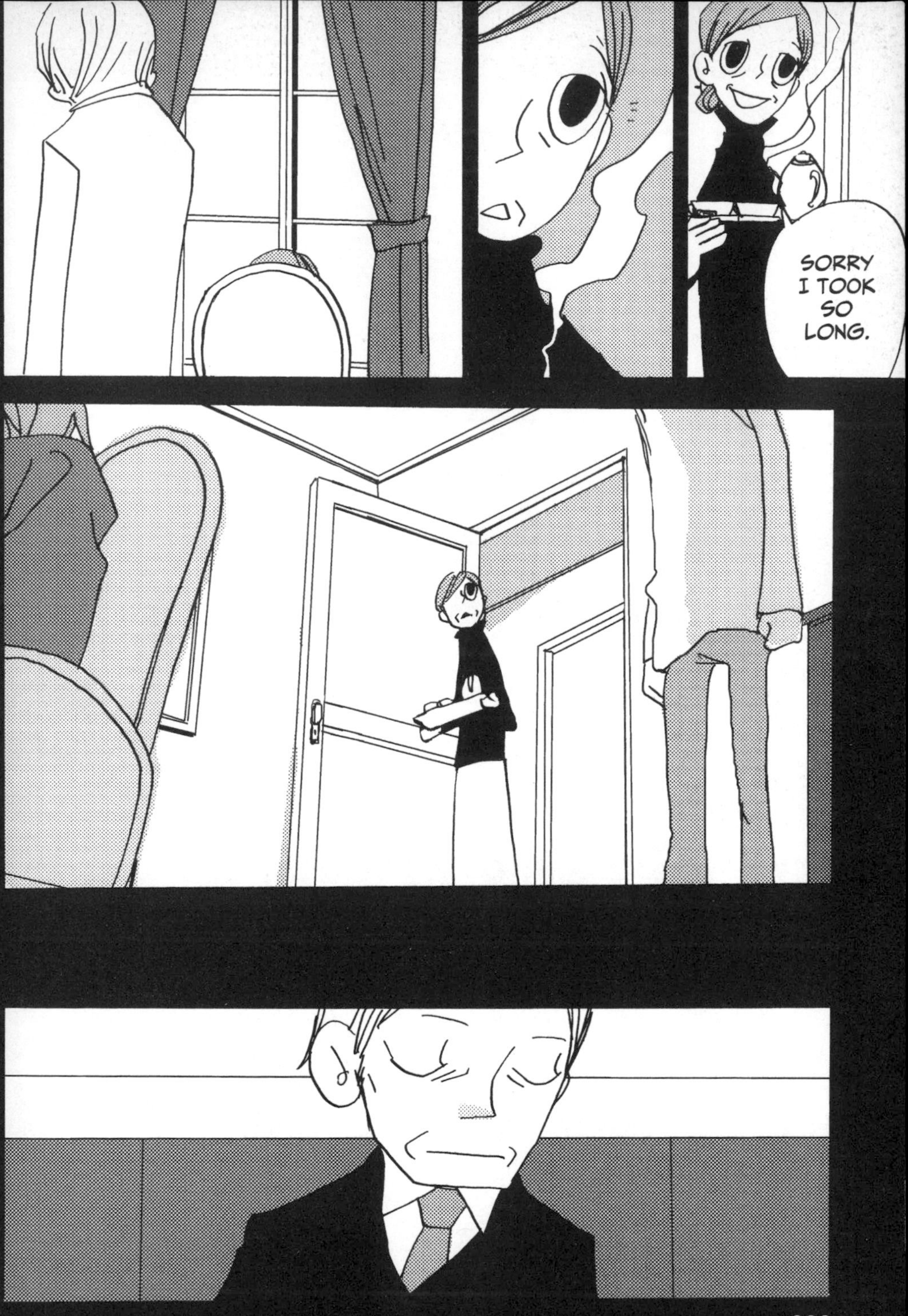
SORRY I TOOK SO LONG.

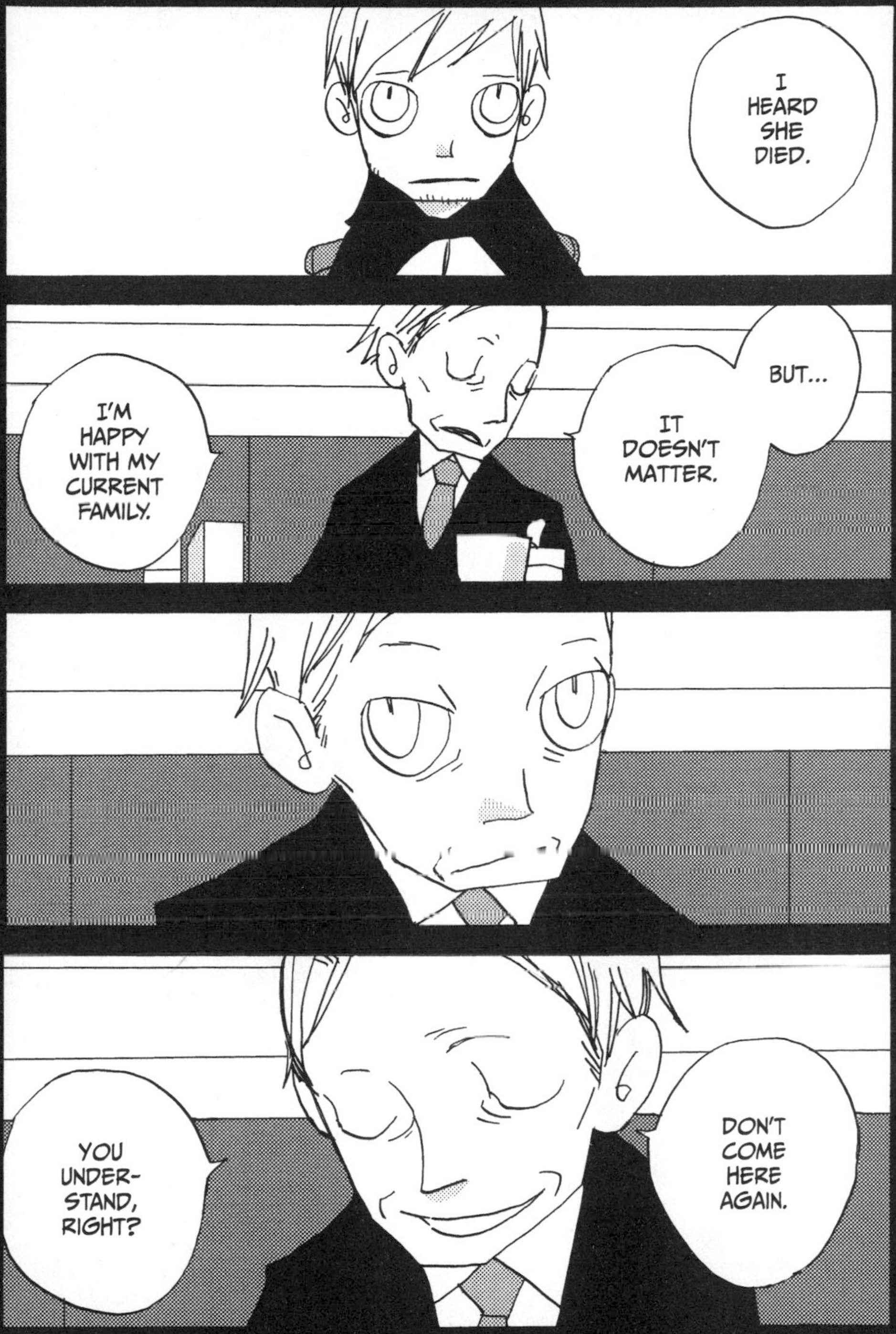
I HEARD SHE DIED.
BUT...
IT DOESN'T MATTER.
I'M HAPPY WITH MY CURRENT FAMILY.
DON'T COME HERE AGAIN.
YOU UNDER-STAND, RIGHT?

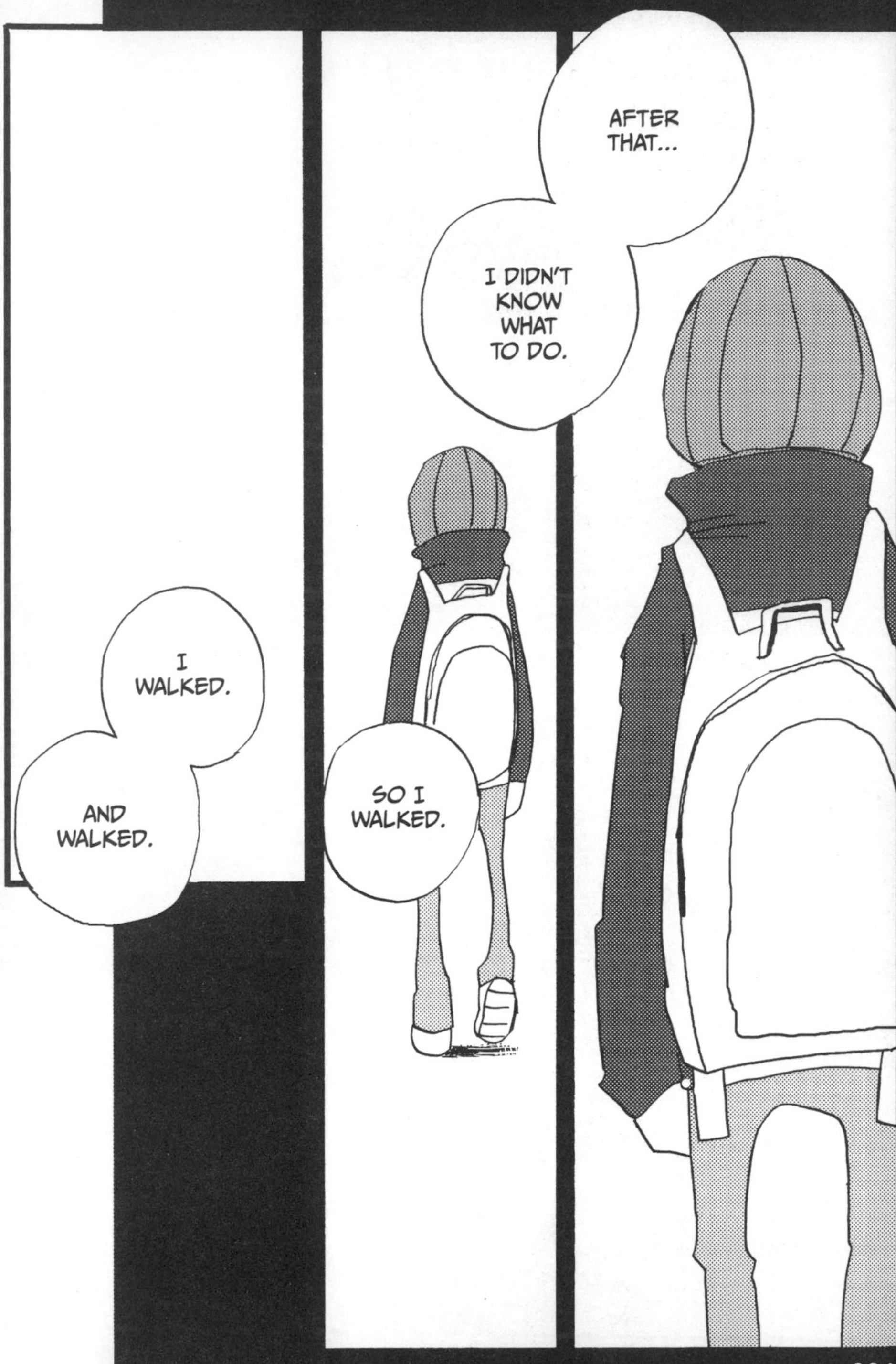
AFTER THAT...
I DIDN'T KNOW WHAT TO DO.
SO I WALKED.
I WALKED.
AND WALKED.

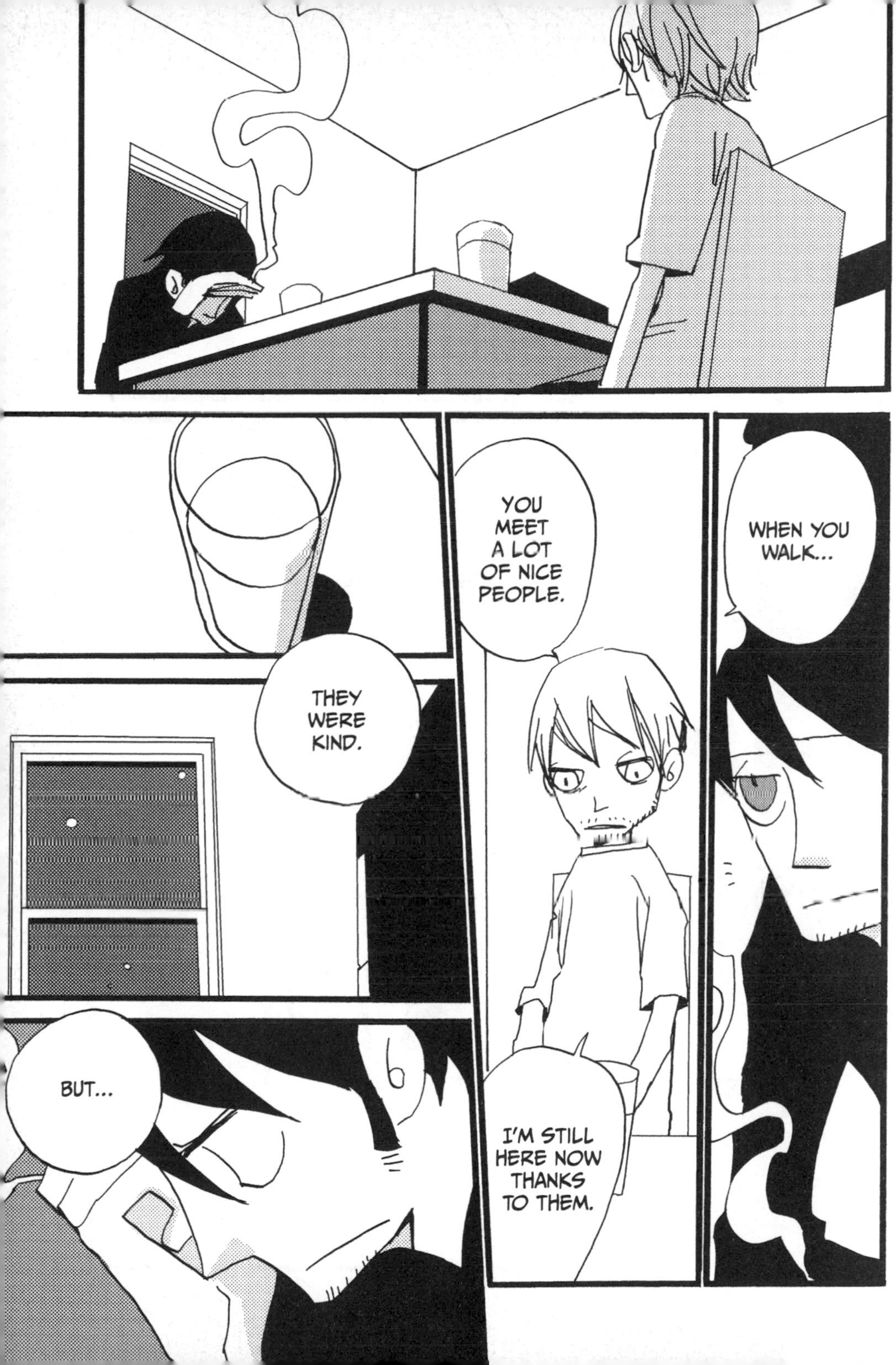
WHEN YOU WALK...
YOU MEET A LOT OF NICE PEOPLE.
I'M STILL HERE NOW THANKS TO THEM.
THEY WERE KIND.
BUT...

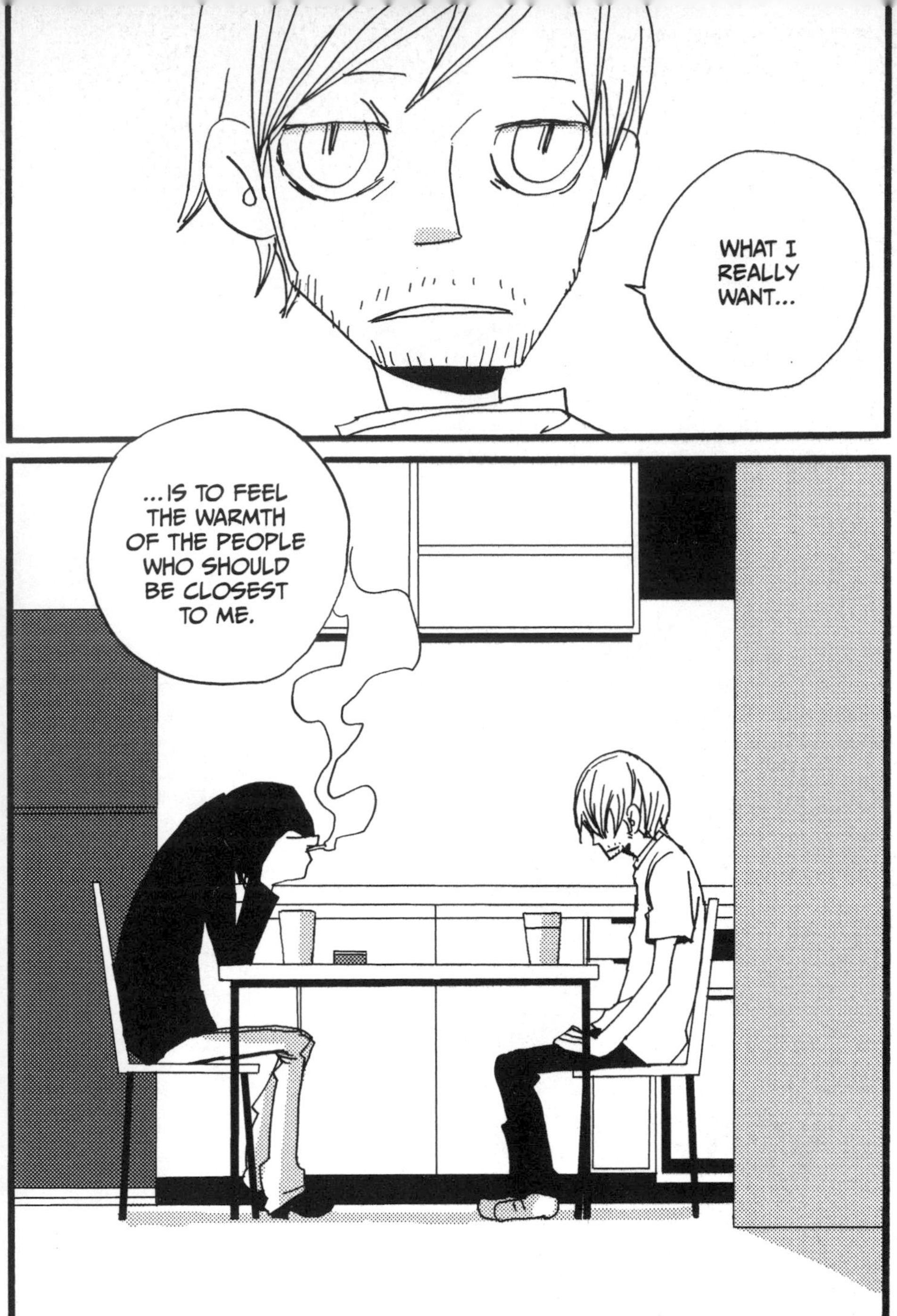
WHAT I REALLY WANT...
...IS TO FEEL THE WARMTH OF THE PEOPLE WHO SHOULD BE CLOSEST TO ME.

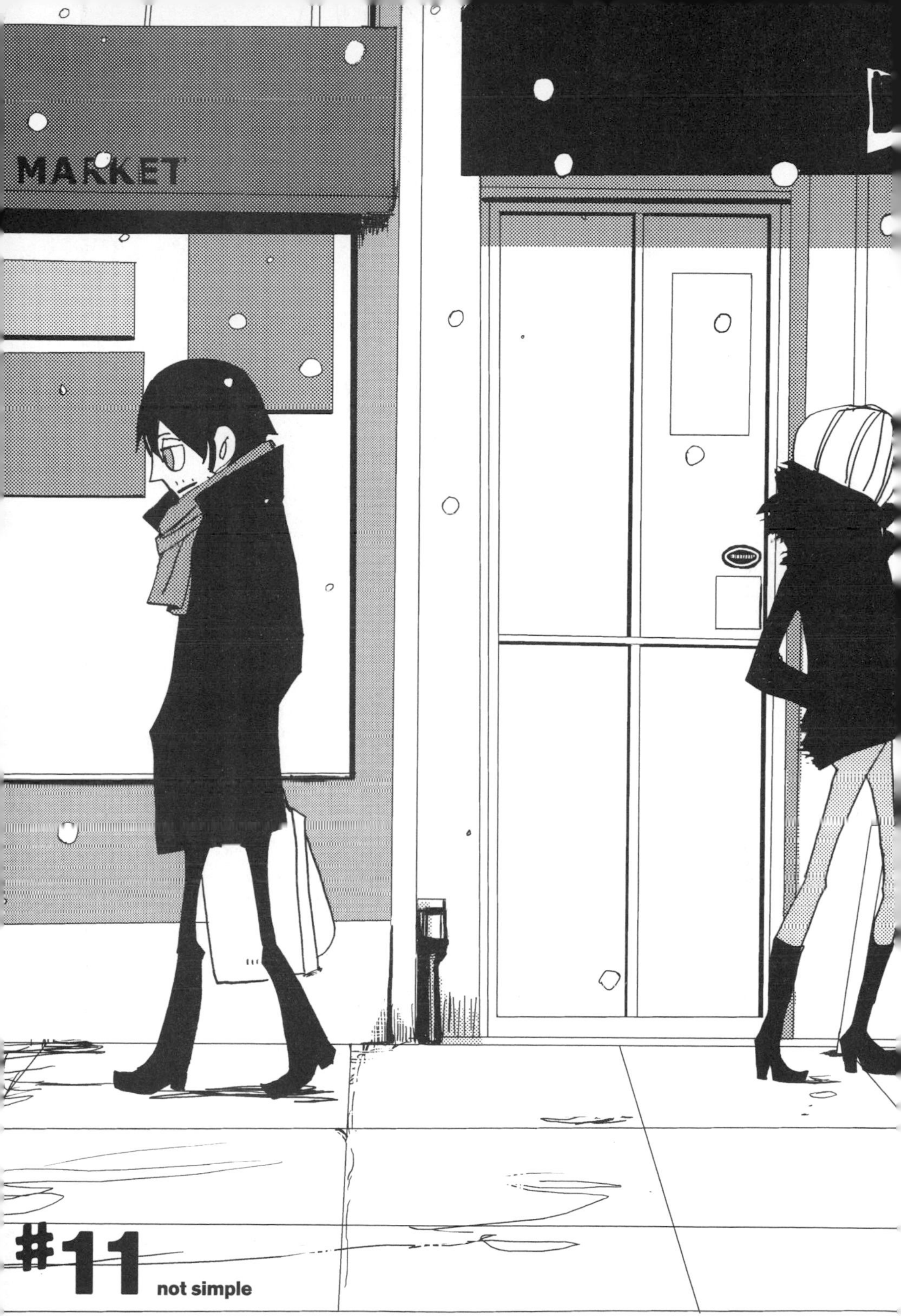
MARKET

#11 not simple

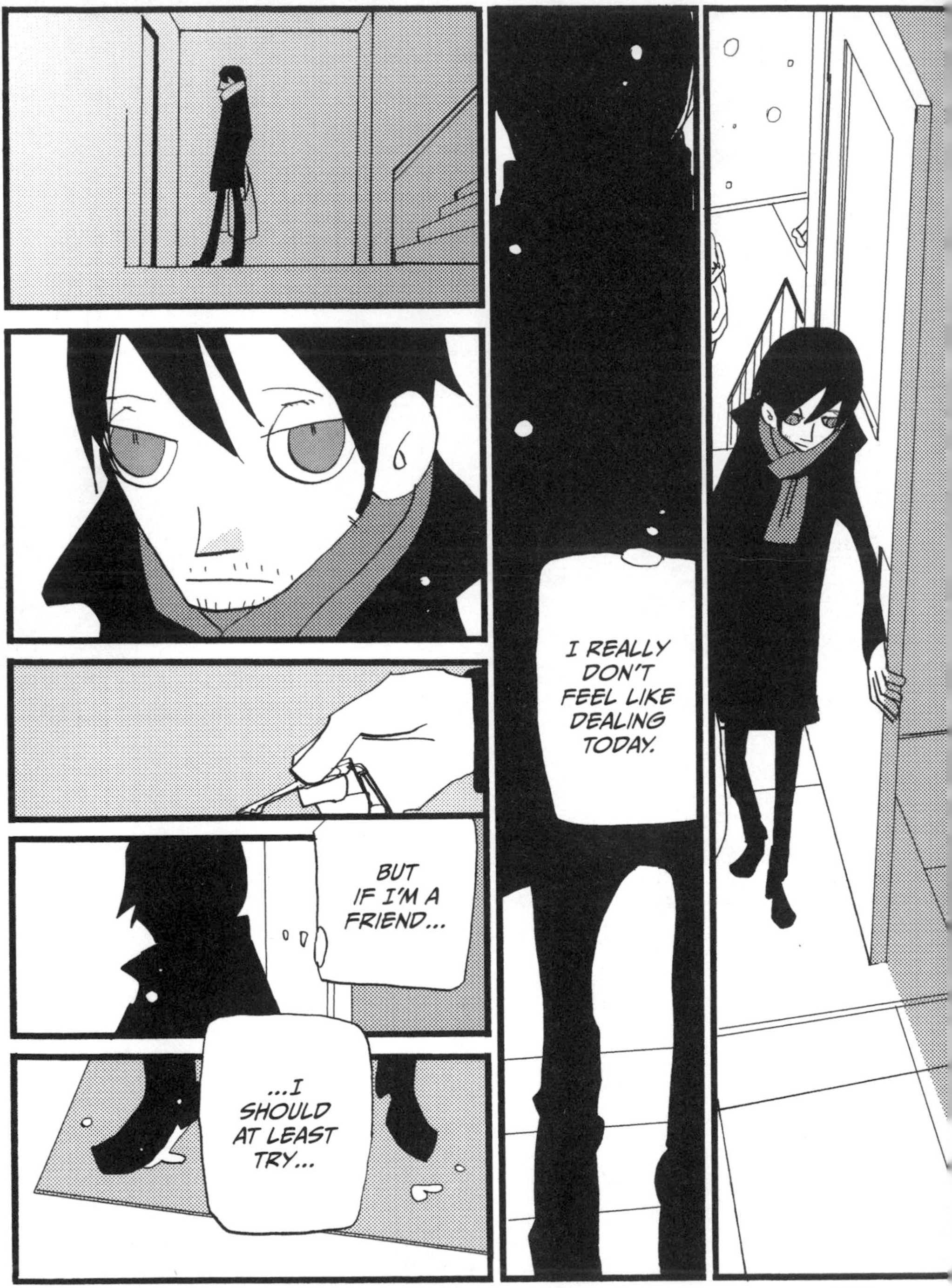
I REALLY DON'T FEEL LIKE DEALING TODAY.
BUT IF I'M A FRIEND...
...I SHOULD AT LEAST TRY...

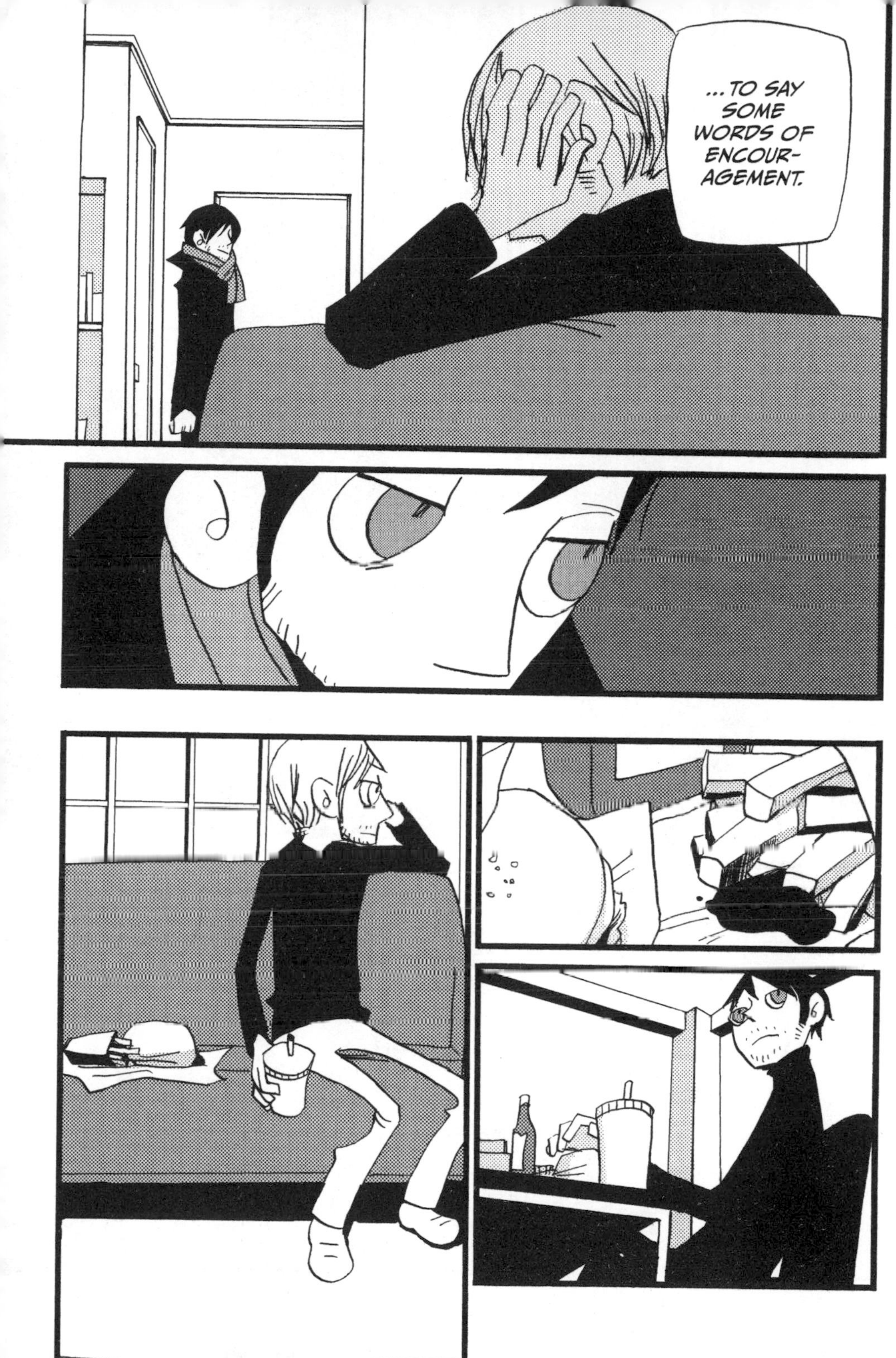
...TO SAY SOME WORDS OF ENCOUR-AGEMENT.

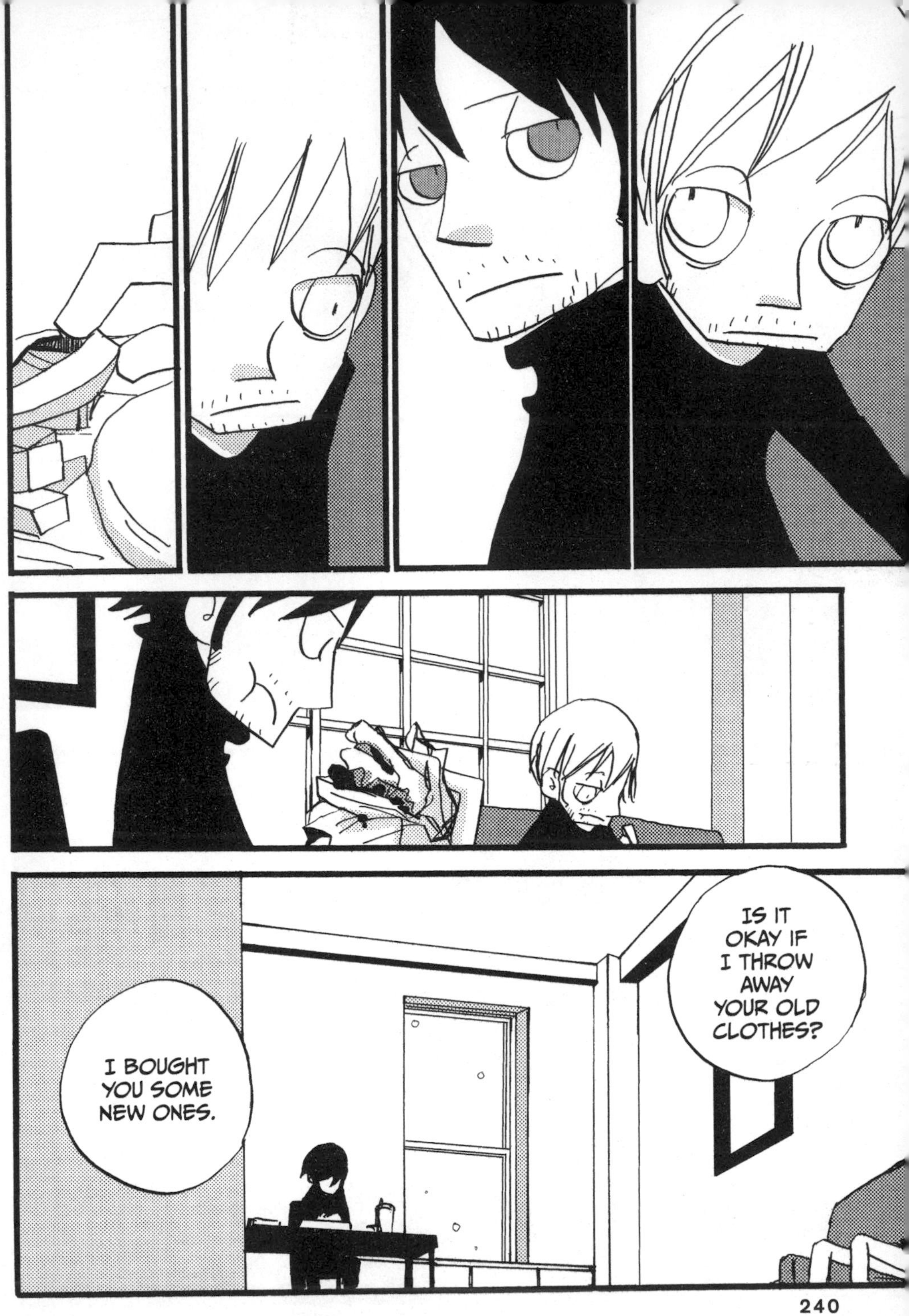
IS IT OKAY IF I THROW AWAY YOUR OLD CLOTHES?
I BOUGHT YOU SOME NEW ONES.

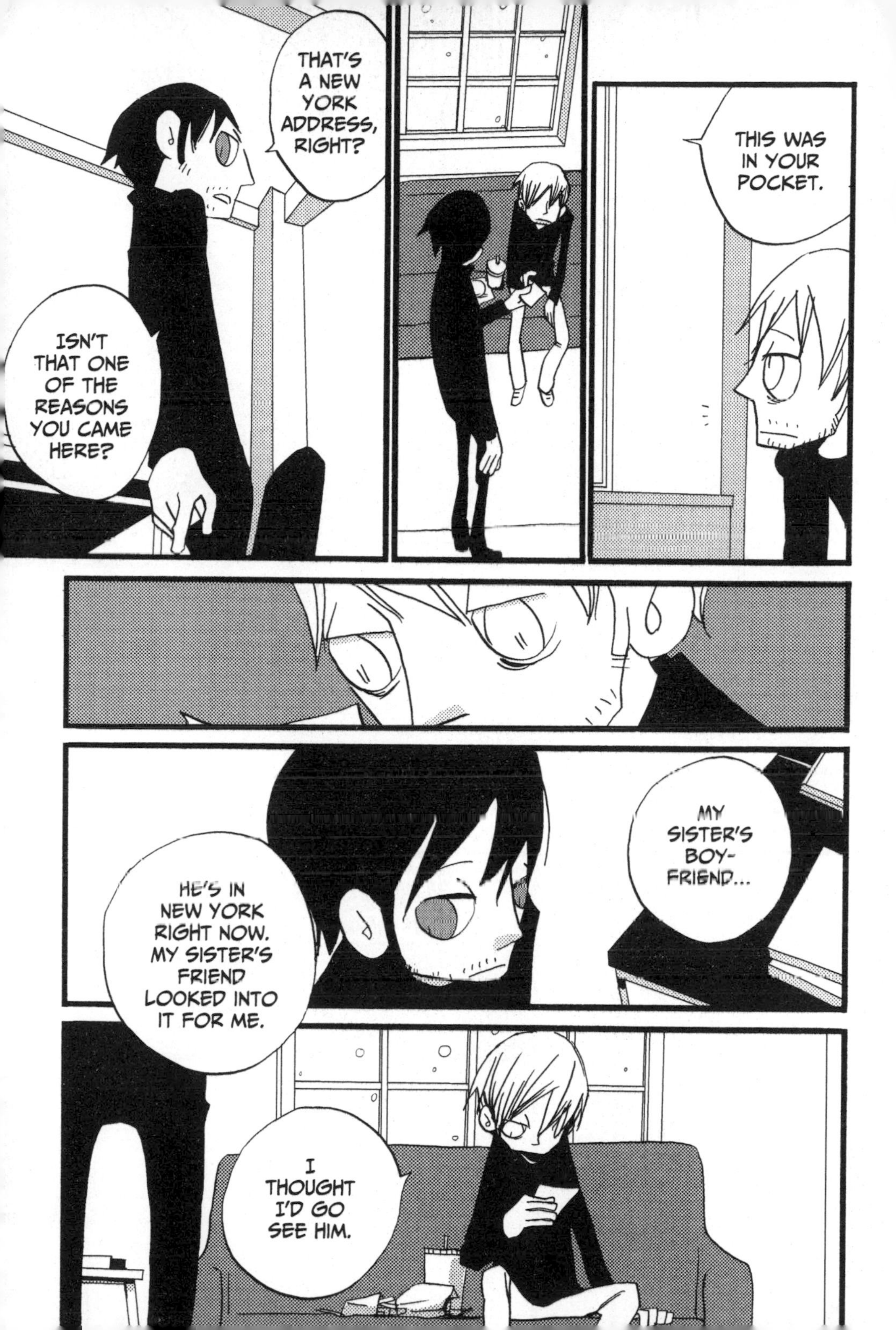
THIS WAS IN YOUR POCKET.
THAT'S A NEW YORK ADDRESS, RIGHT?
ISN'T THAT ONE OF THE REASONS YOU CAME HERE?
MY SISTER'S BOY-FRIEND...
HE'S IN NEW YORK RIGHT NOW. MY SISTER'S FRIEND LOOKED INTO IT FOR ME.
I THOUGHT I'D GO SEE HIM.

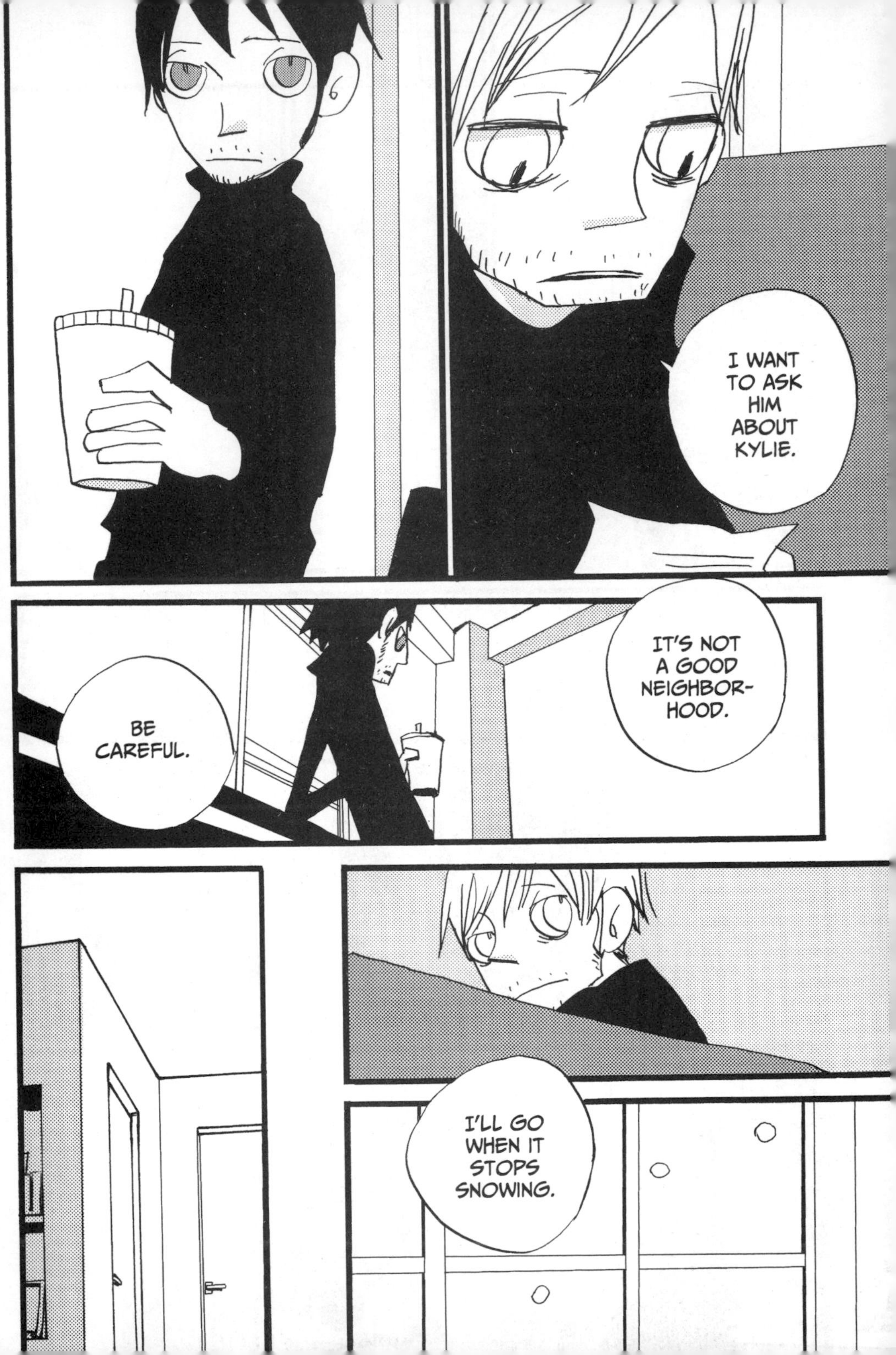
I WANT TO ASK HIM ABOUT KYLIE.
IT'S NOT A GOOD NEIGHBOR-HOOD.
BE CAREFUL.
I'LL GO WHEN IT STOPS SNOWING.

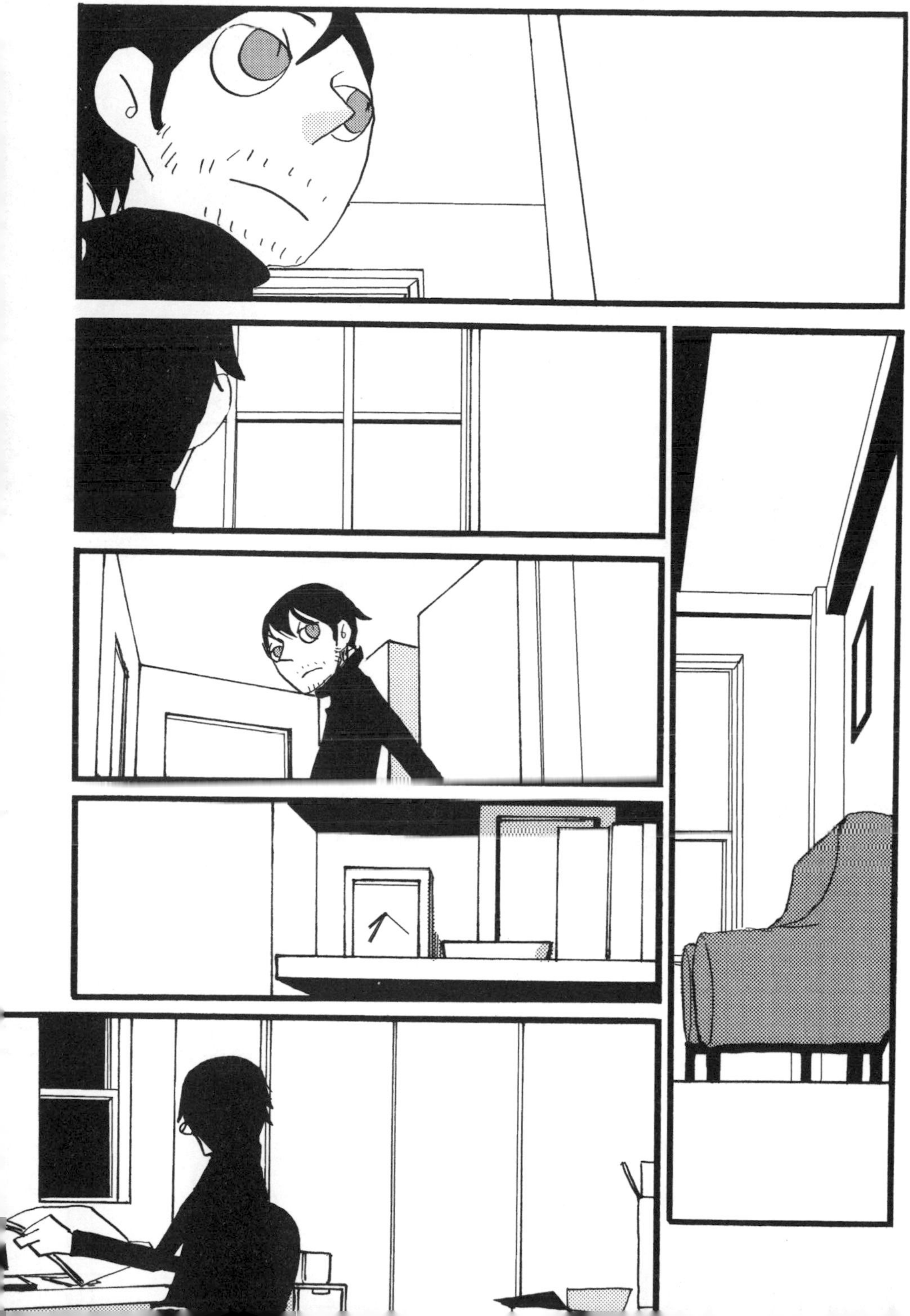

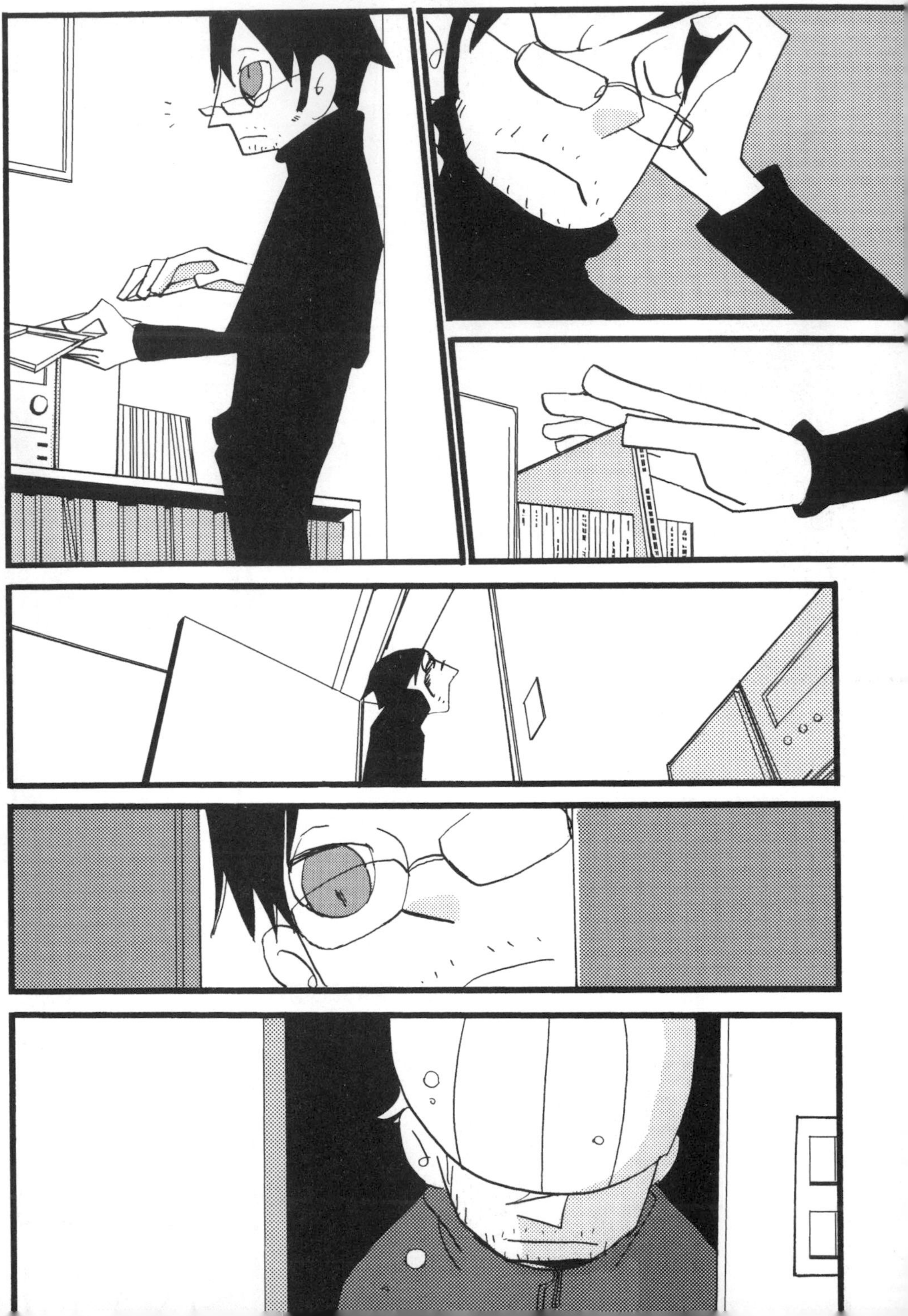

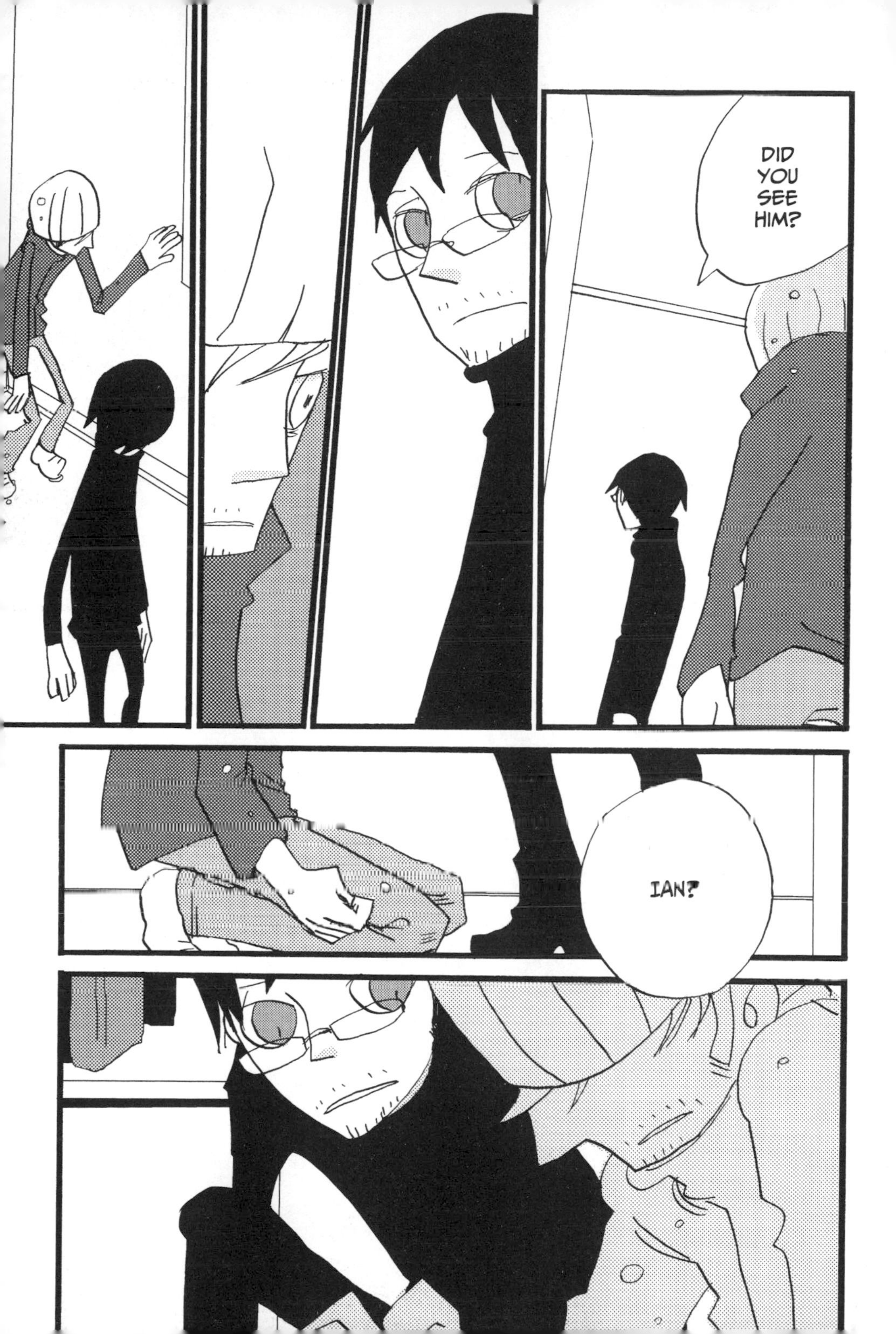
DID YOU SEE HIM?
IAN?

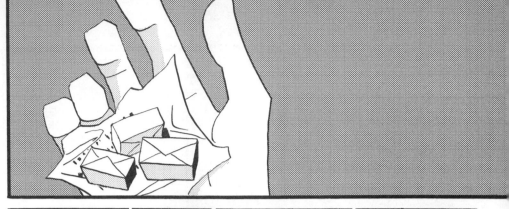

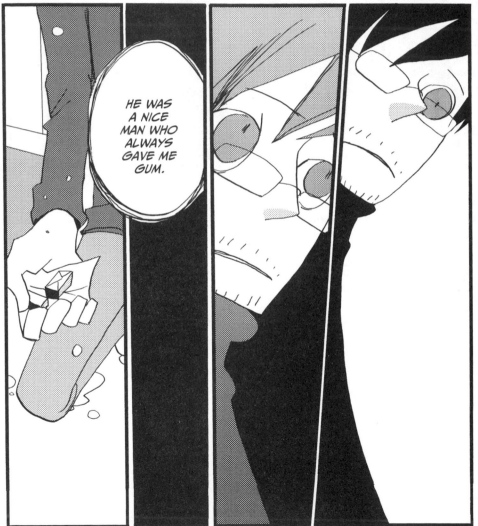

HE WAS A NICE MAN WHO ALWAYS GAVE ME GUM.

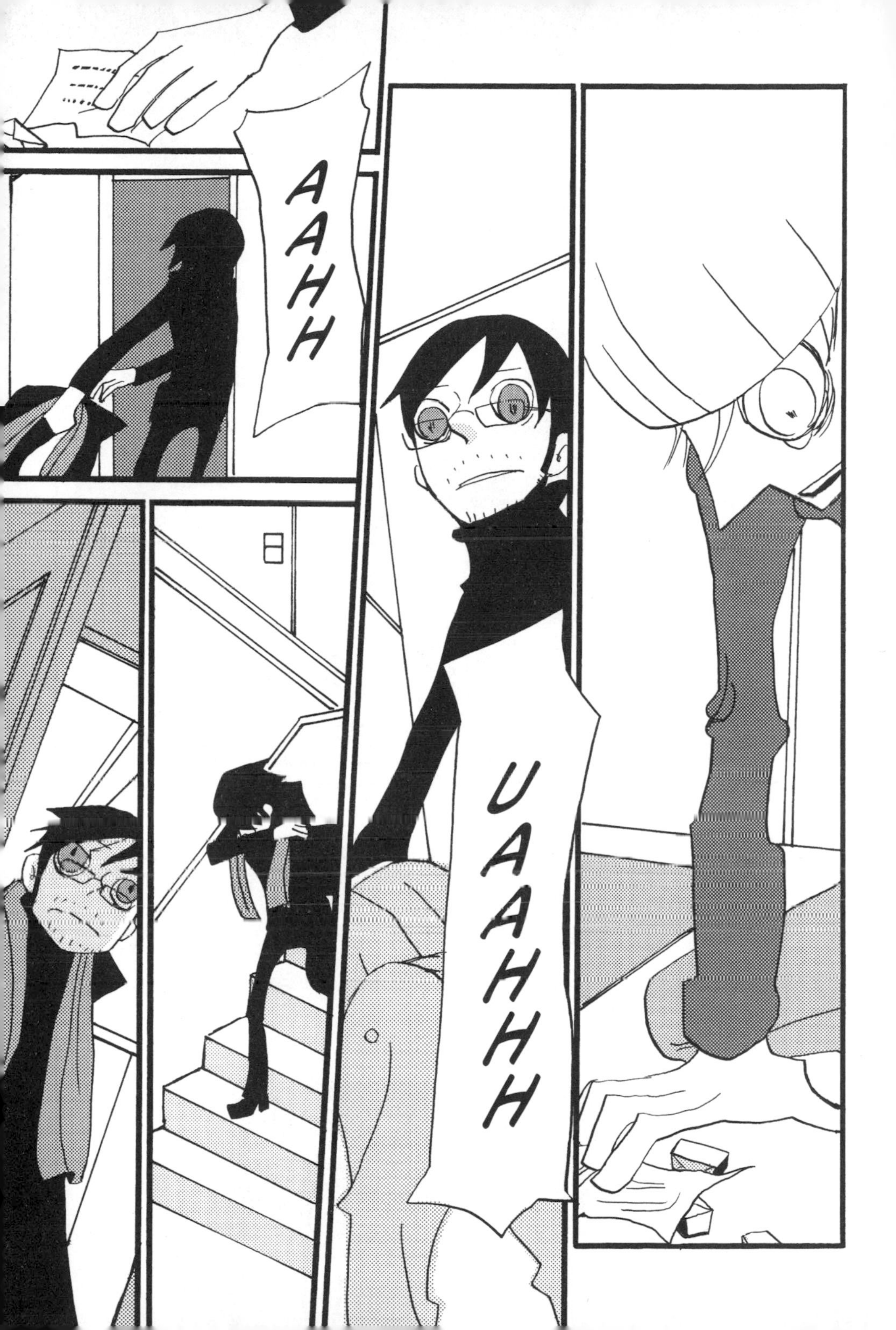
UAAHHH
AAHH

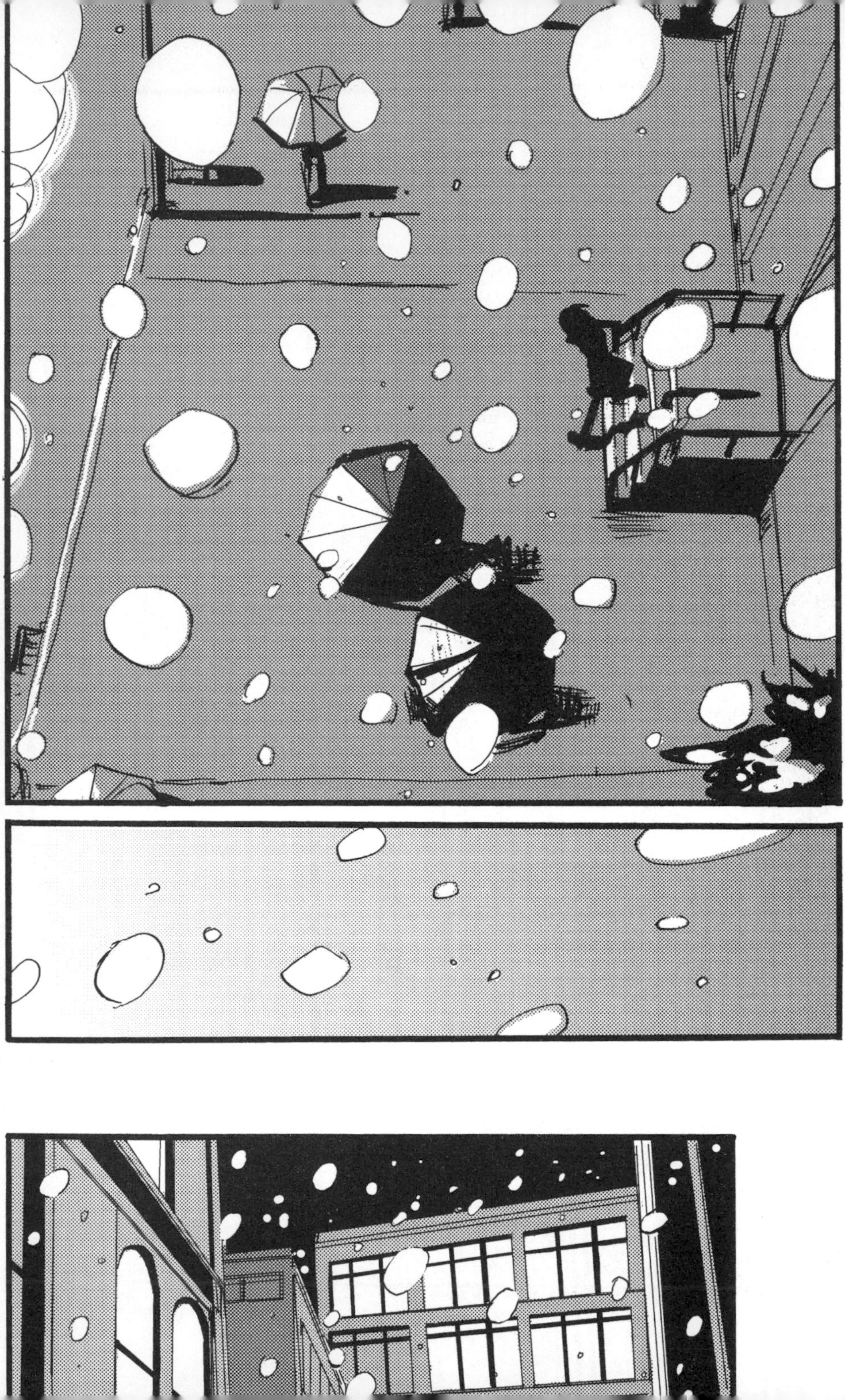

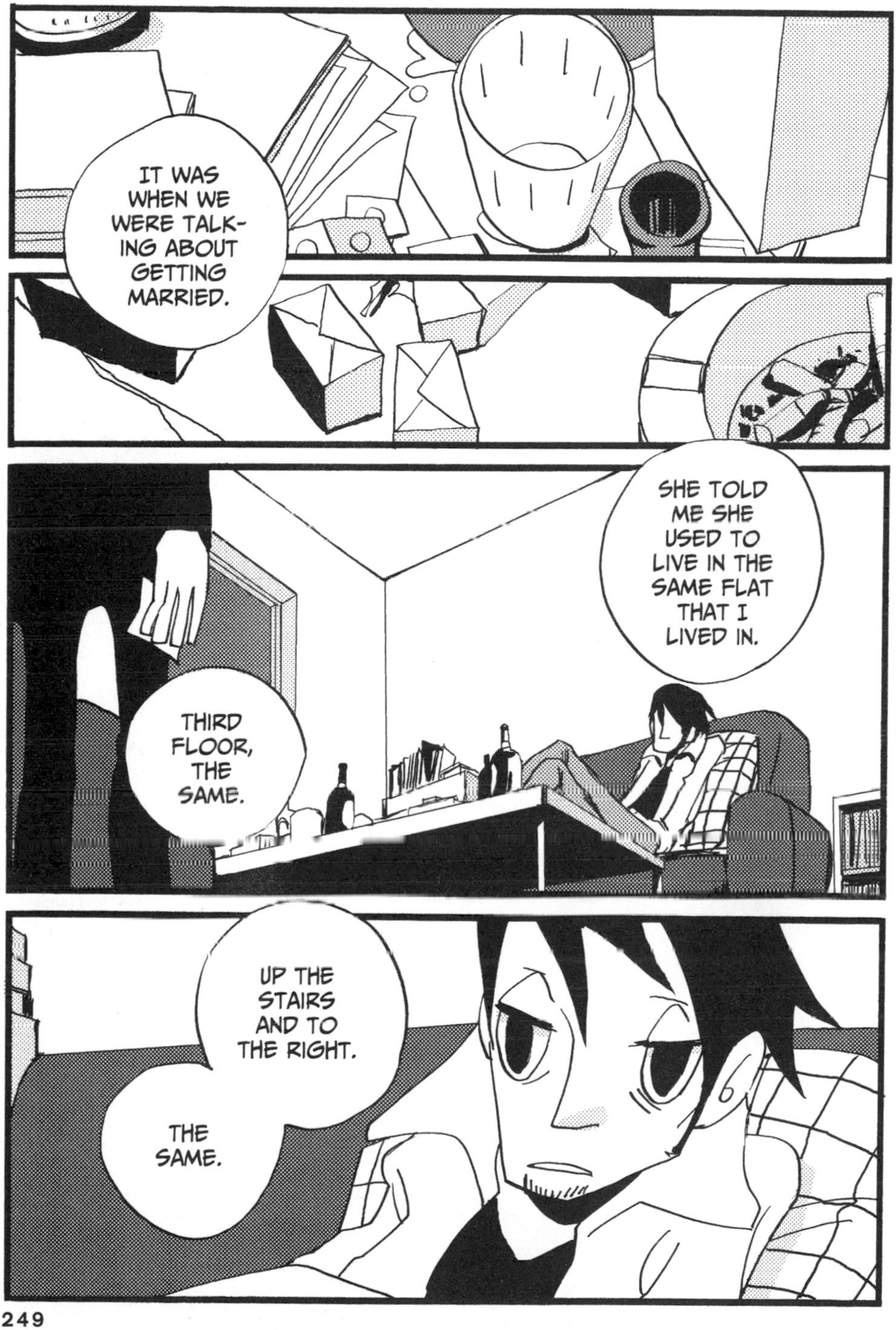
IT WAS WHEN WE WERE TALKING ABOUT GETTING MARRIED.
SHE TOLD ME SHE USED TO LIVE IN THE SAME FLAT THAT I LIVED IN.
THIRD FLOOR, THE SAME.
UP THE STAIRS AND TO THE RIGHT.
THE SAME.

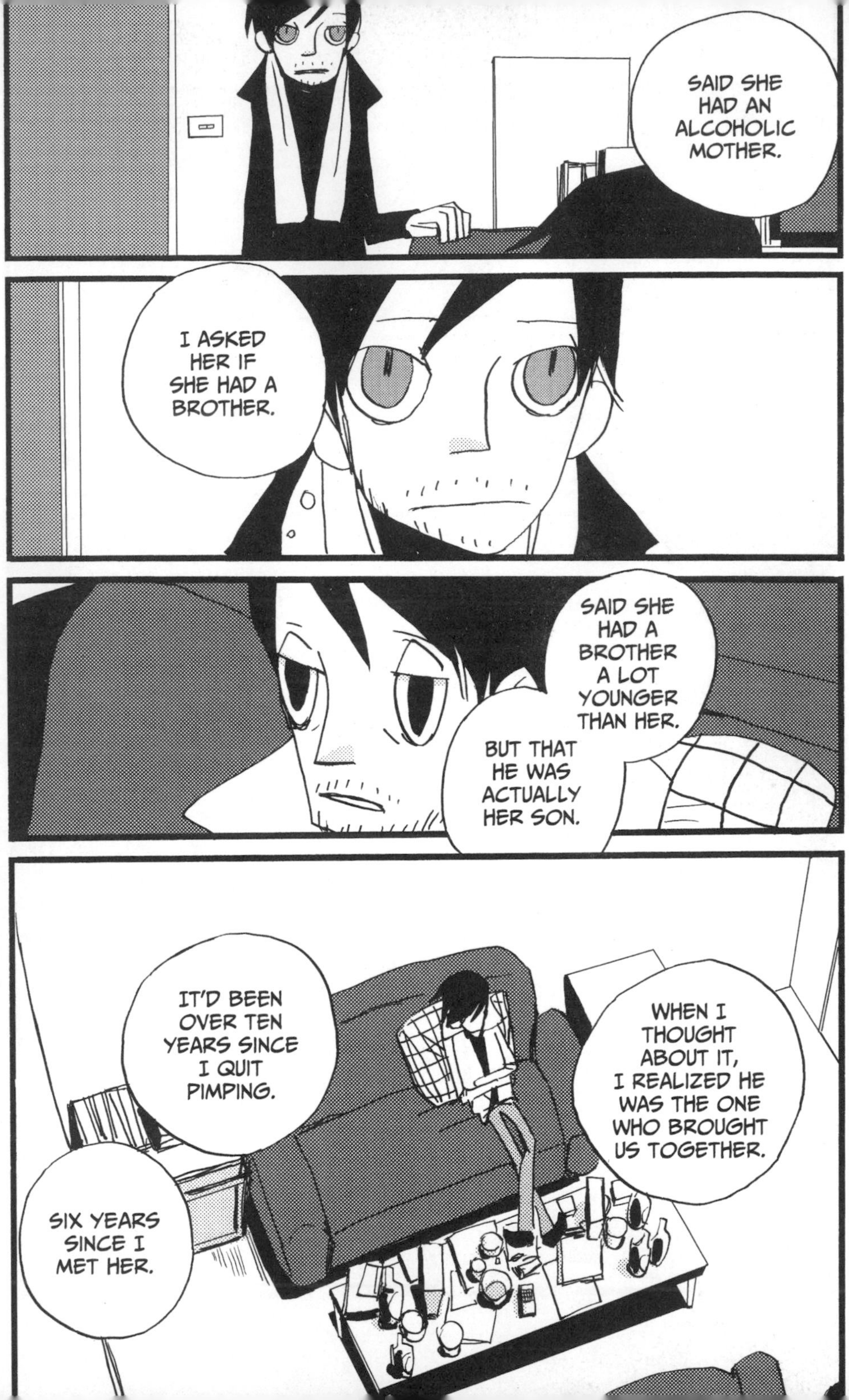
SAID SHE HAD AN ALCOHOLIC MOTHER.
I ASKED HER IF SHE HAD A BROTHER.
SAID SHE HAD A BROTHER A LOT YOUNGER THAN HER.
BUT THAT HE WAS ACTUALLY HER SON.
WHEN I THOUGHT ABOUT IT, I REALIZED HE WAS THE ONE WHO BROUGHT US TOGETHER.
IT'D BEEN OVER TEN YEARS SINCE I QUIT PIMPING.
SIX YEARS SINCE I MET HER.

I DIDN'T SAY ANYTHING FOR A WHILE.

THEN I TOLD HER.

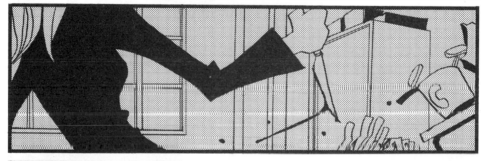

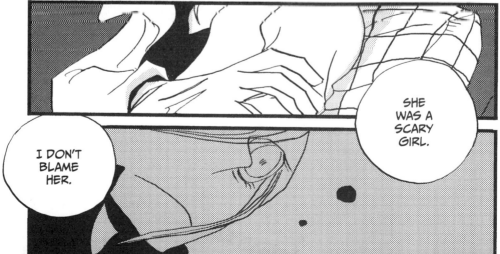

SHE WAS A SCARY GIRL.

I DON'T BLAME HER.

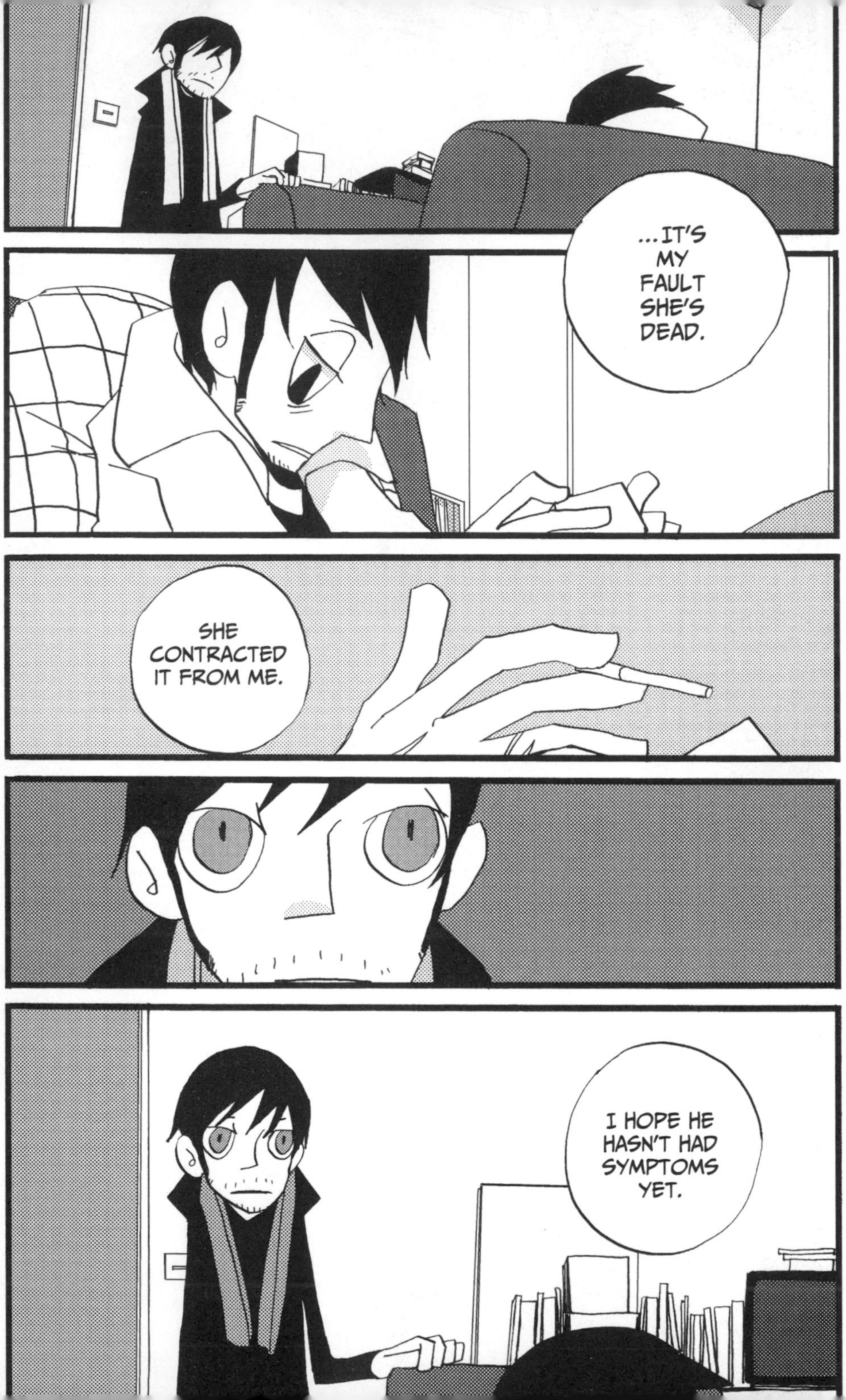
...IT'S MY FAULT SHE'S DEAD.
SHE CONTRACTED IT FROM ME.
I HOPE HE HASN'T HAD SYMPTOMS YET.

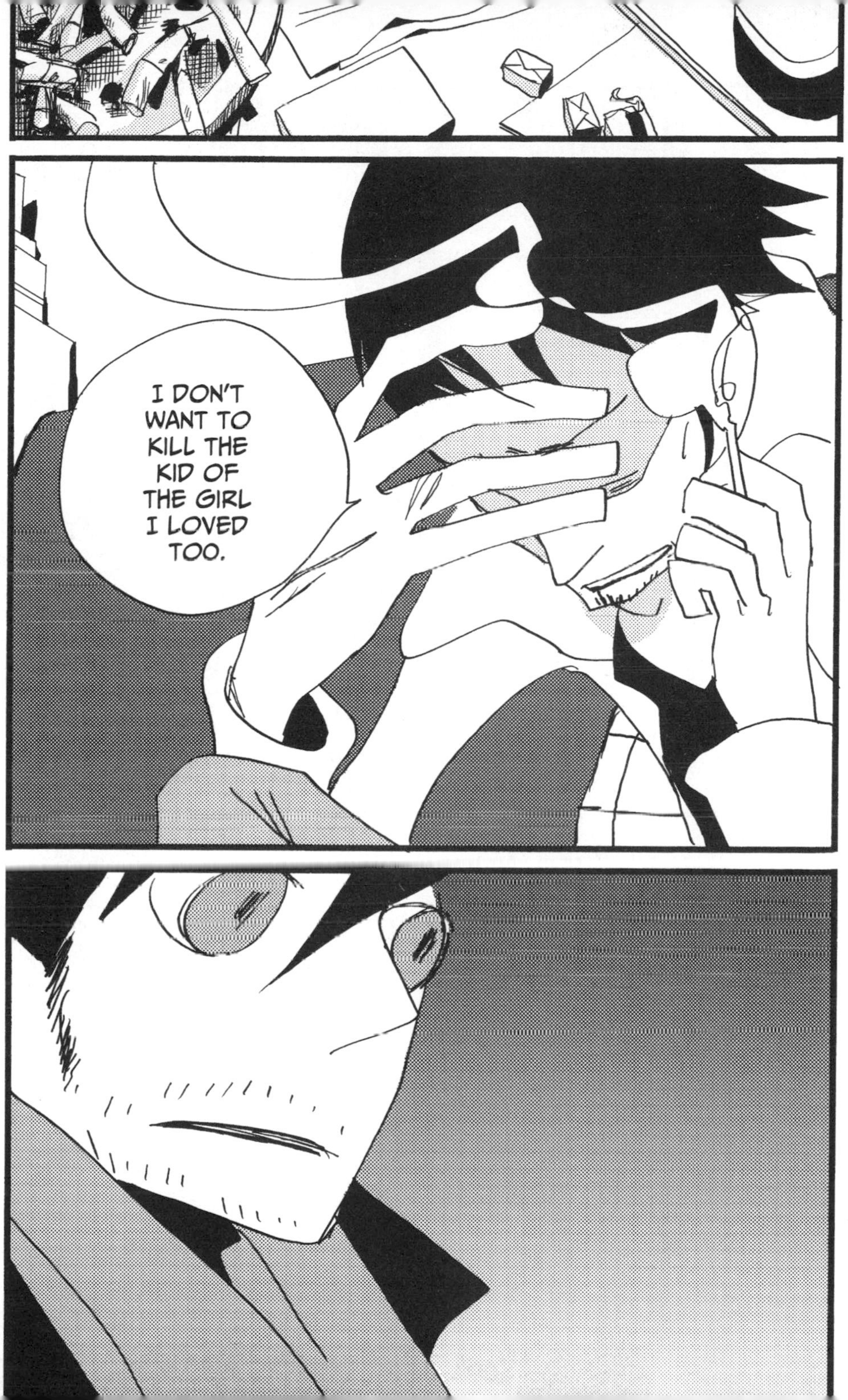
I DON'T WANT TO KILL THE KID OF THE GIRL I LOVED TOO.

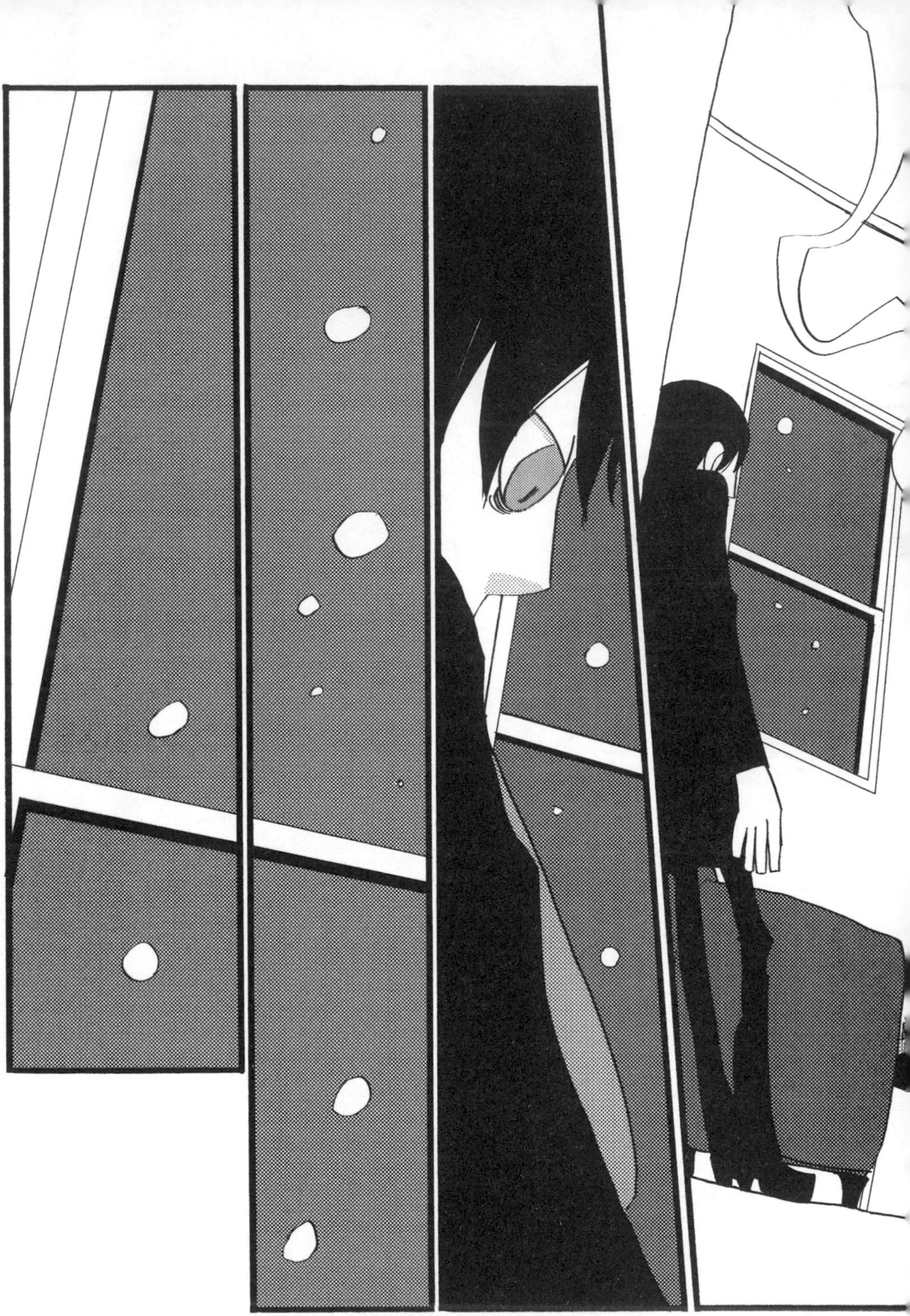

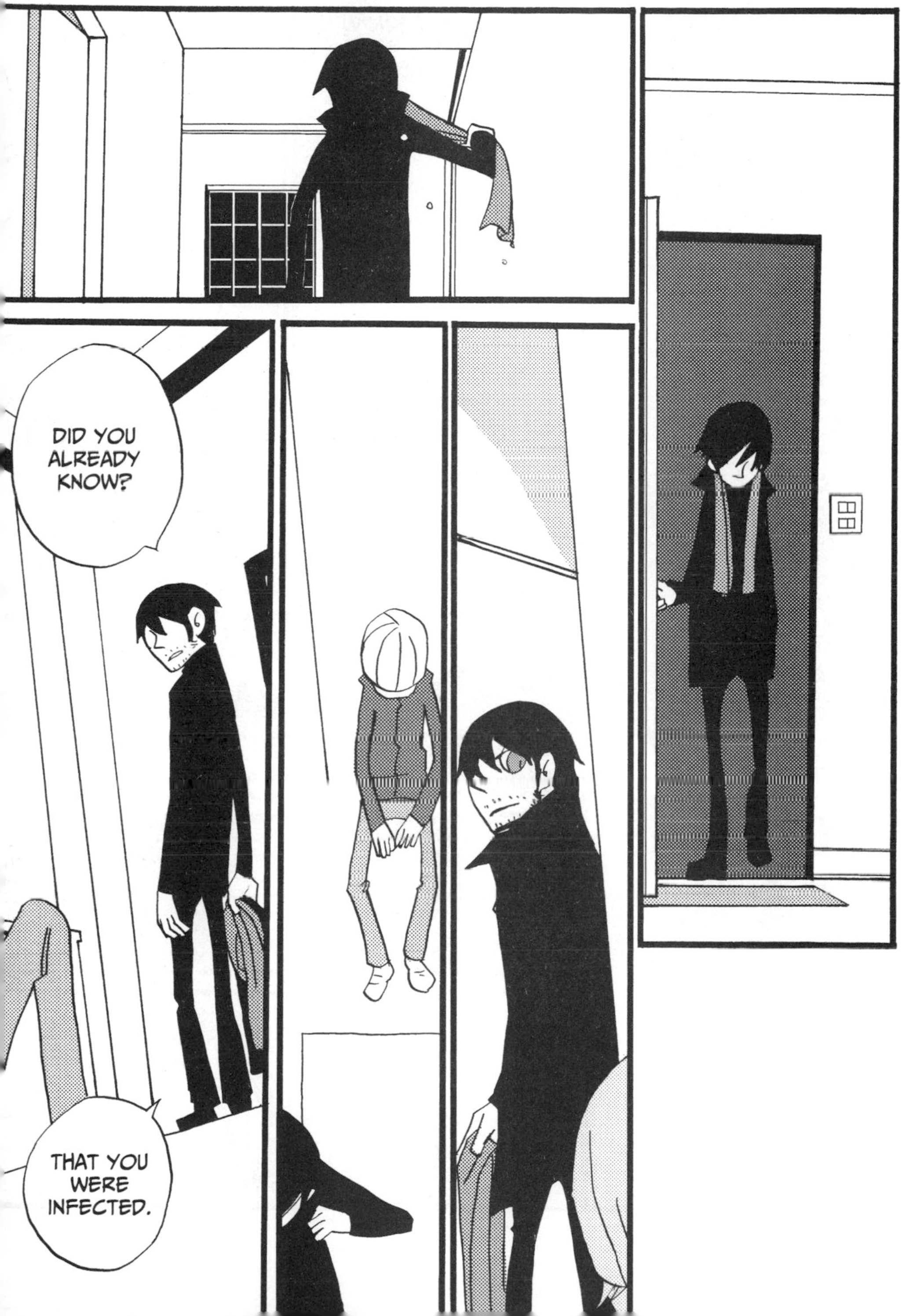
DID YOU ALREADY KNOW?
THAT YOU WERE INFECTED.

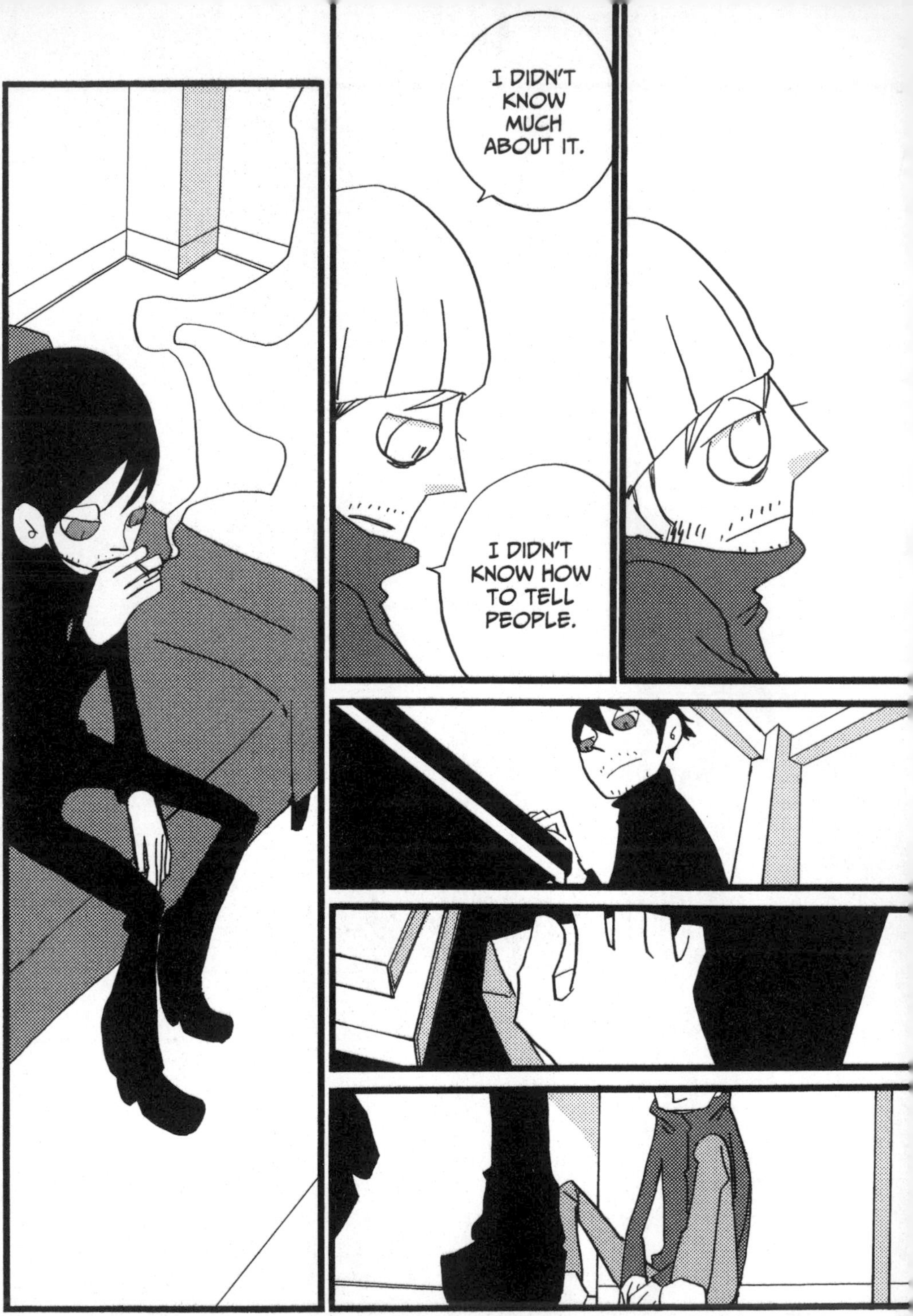
I DIDN'T KNOW MUCH ABOUT IT.
I DIDN'T KNOW HOW TO TELL PEOPLE.

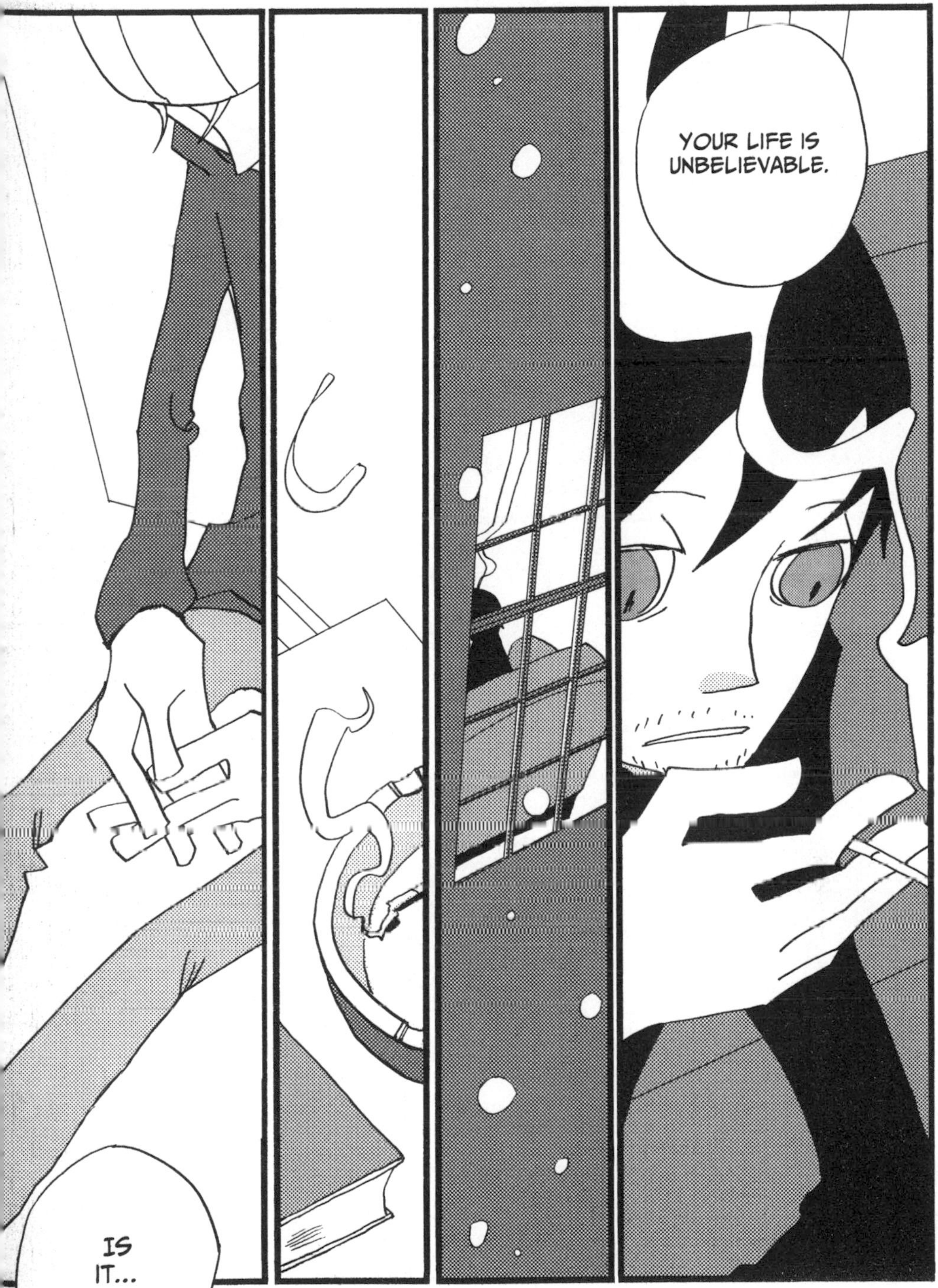
YOUR LIFE IS UNBELIEVABLE.
IS IT...

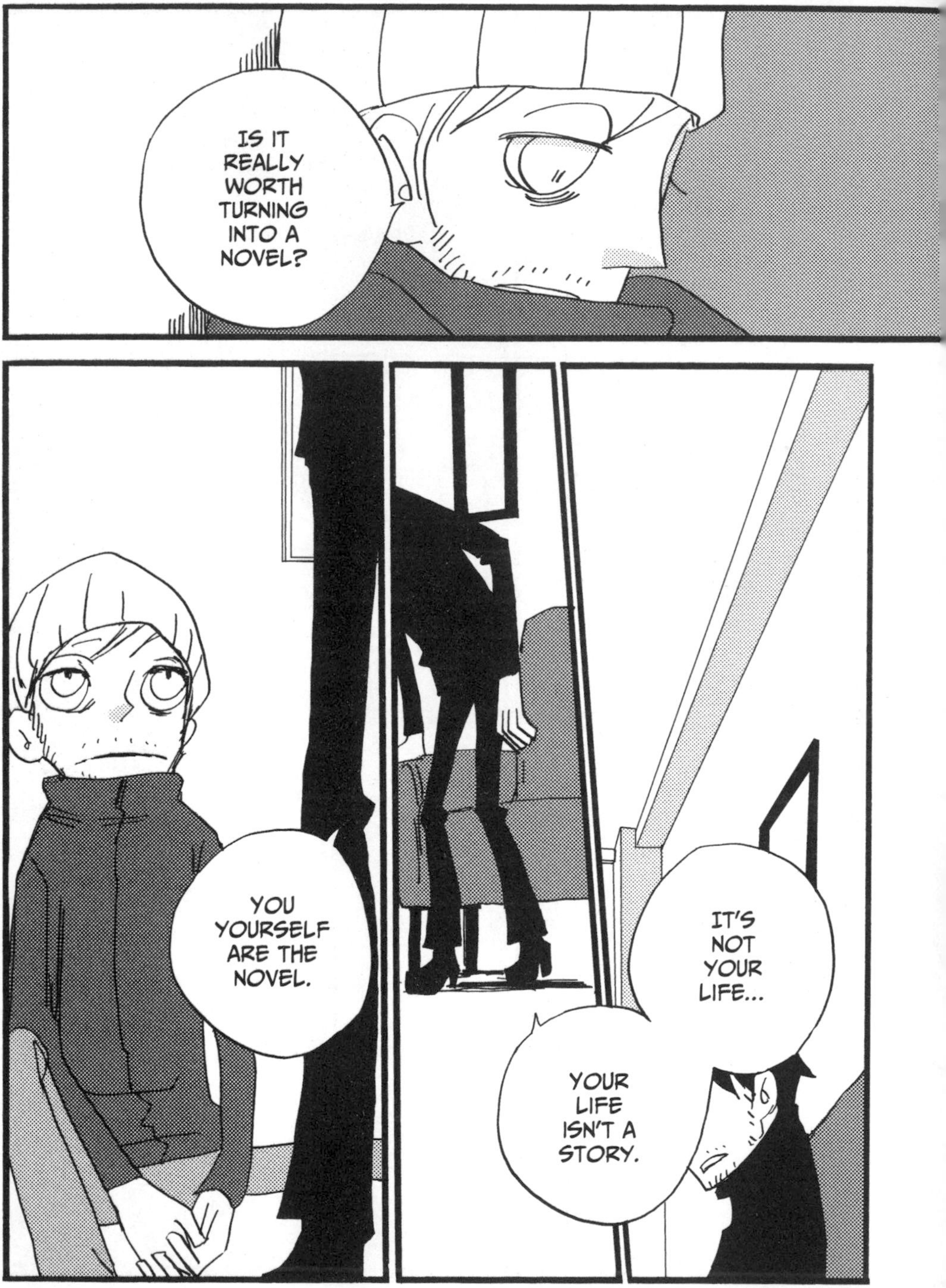
IS IT REALLY WORTH TURNING INTO A NOVEL?
IT'S NOT YOUR LIFE...
YOUR LIFE ISN'T A STORY.
YOU YOURSELF ARE THE NOVEL.

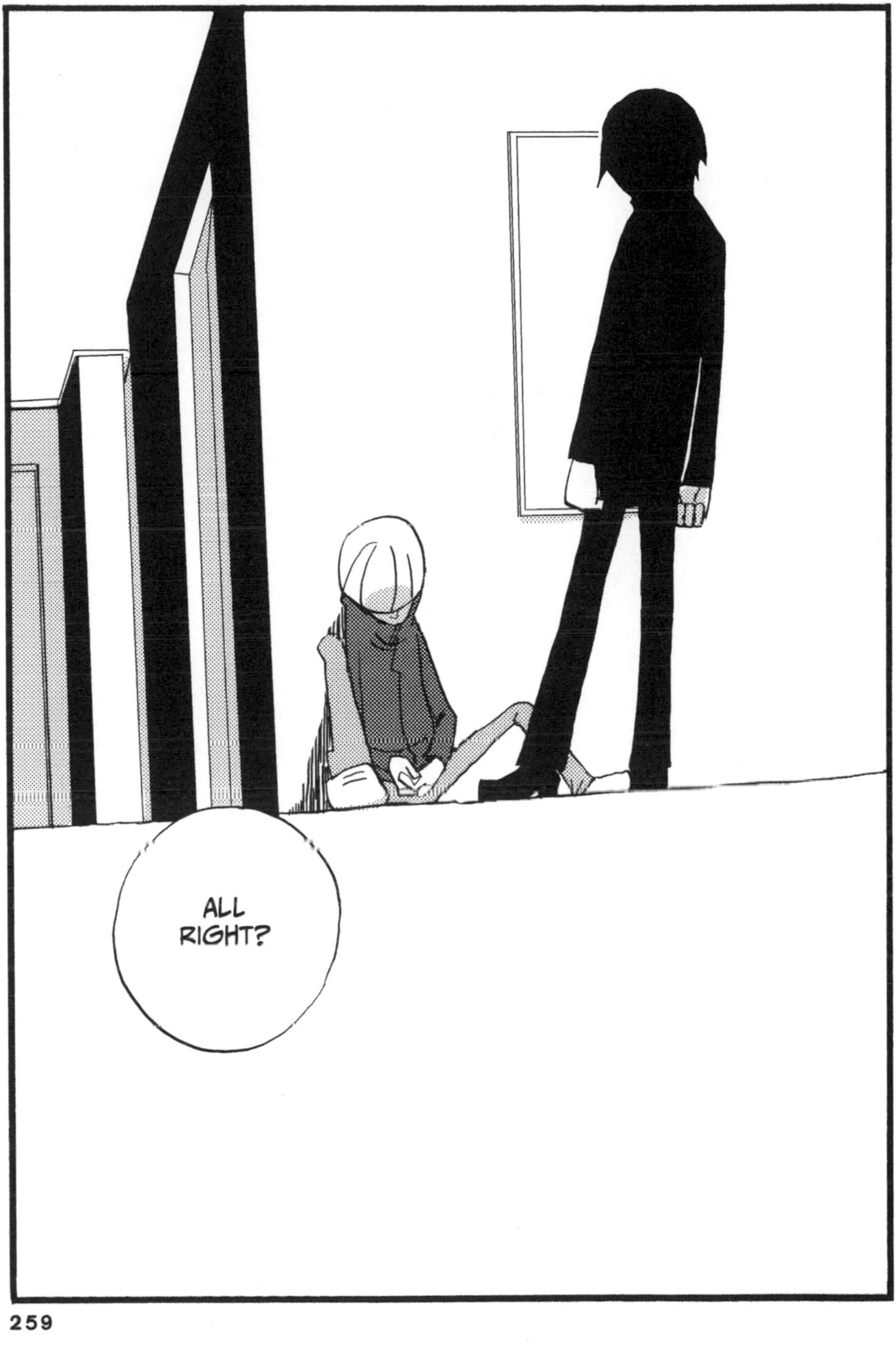
ALL RIGHT?

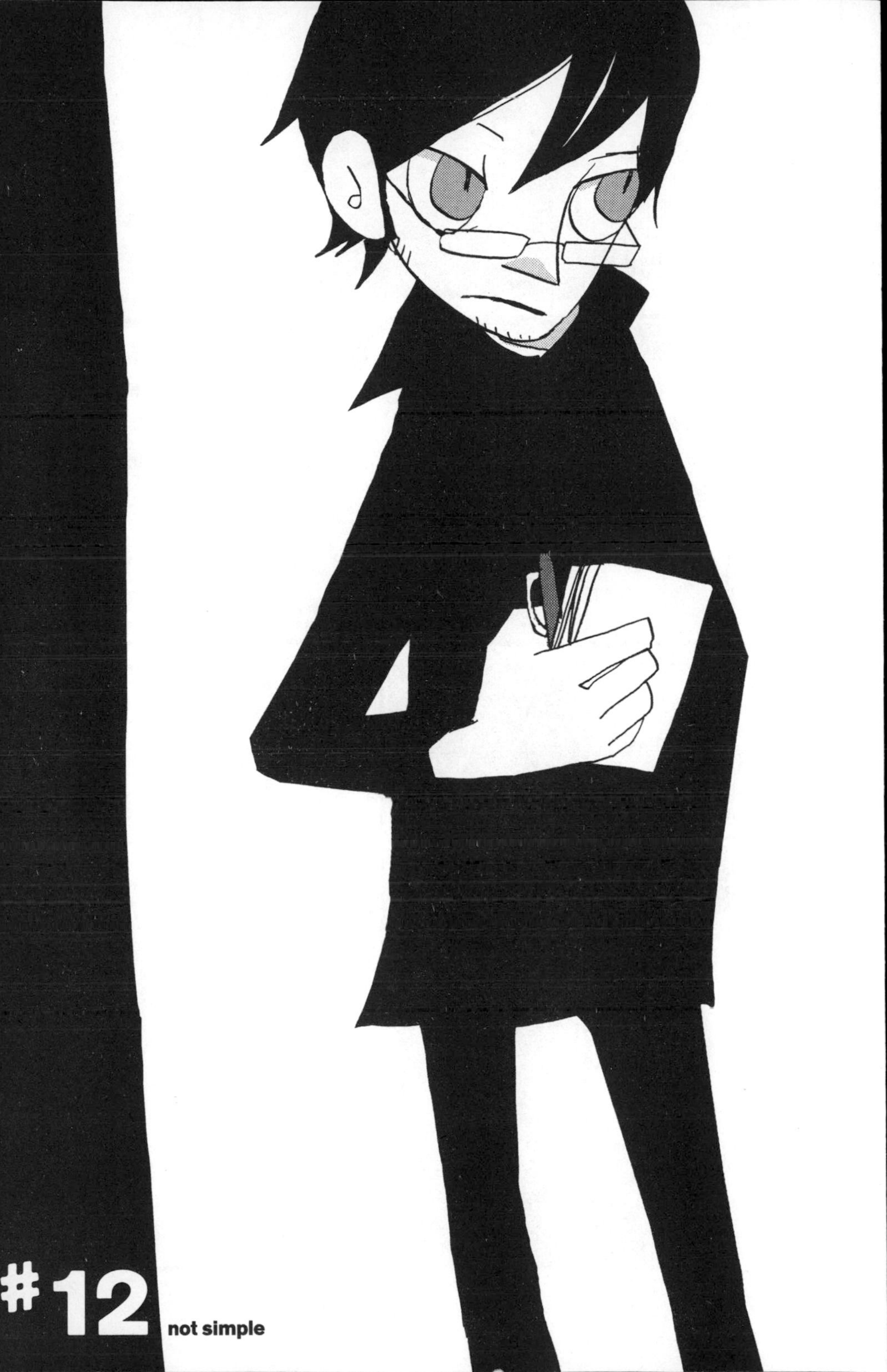

#12 not simple

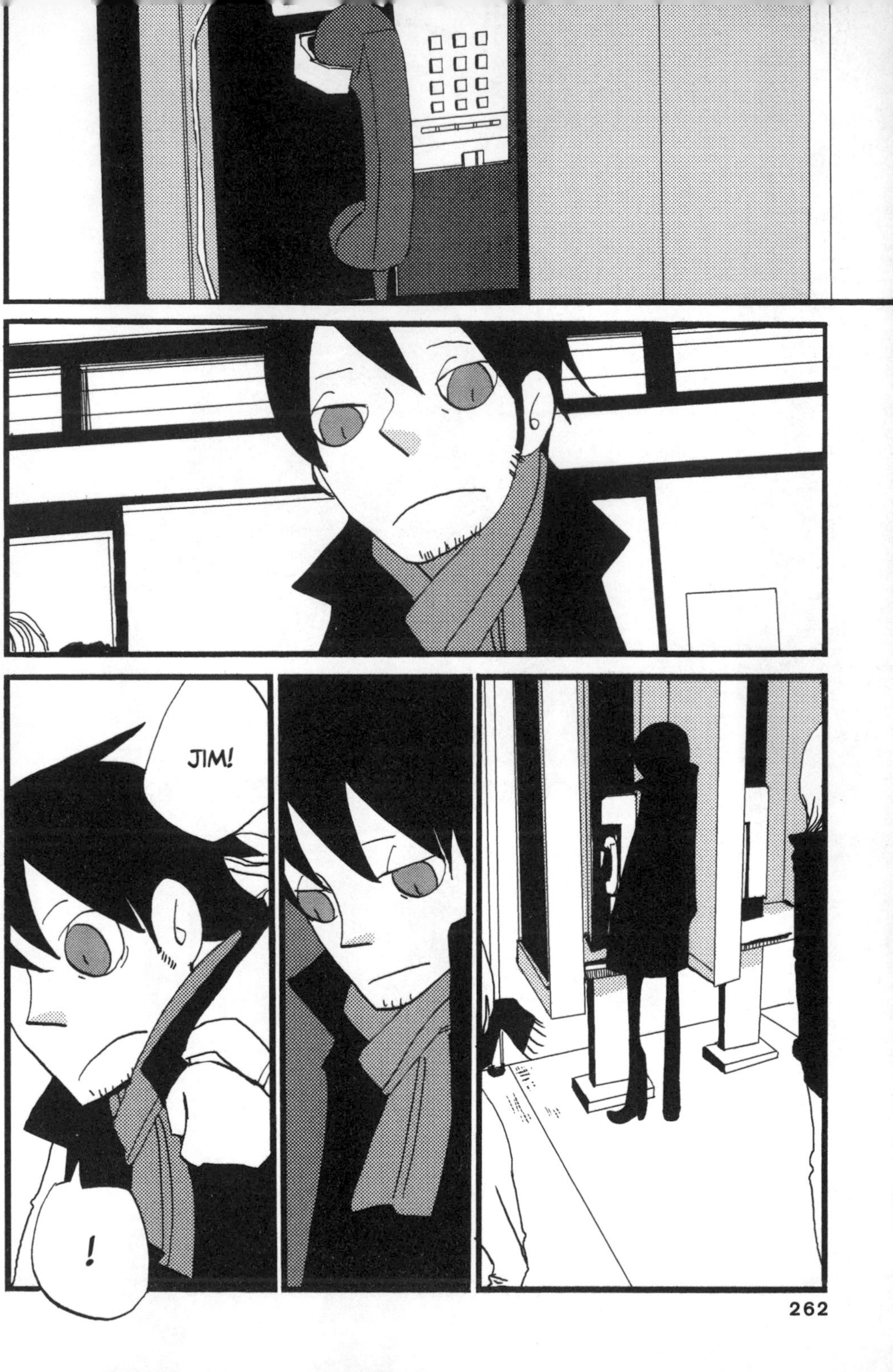
JIM!
!

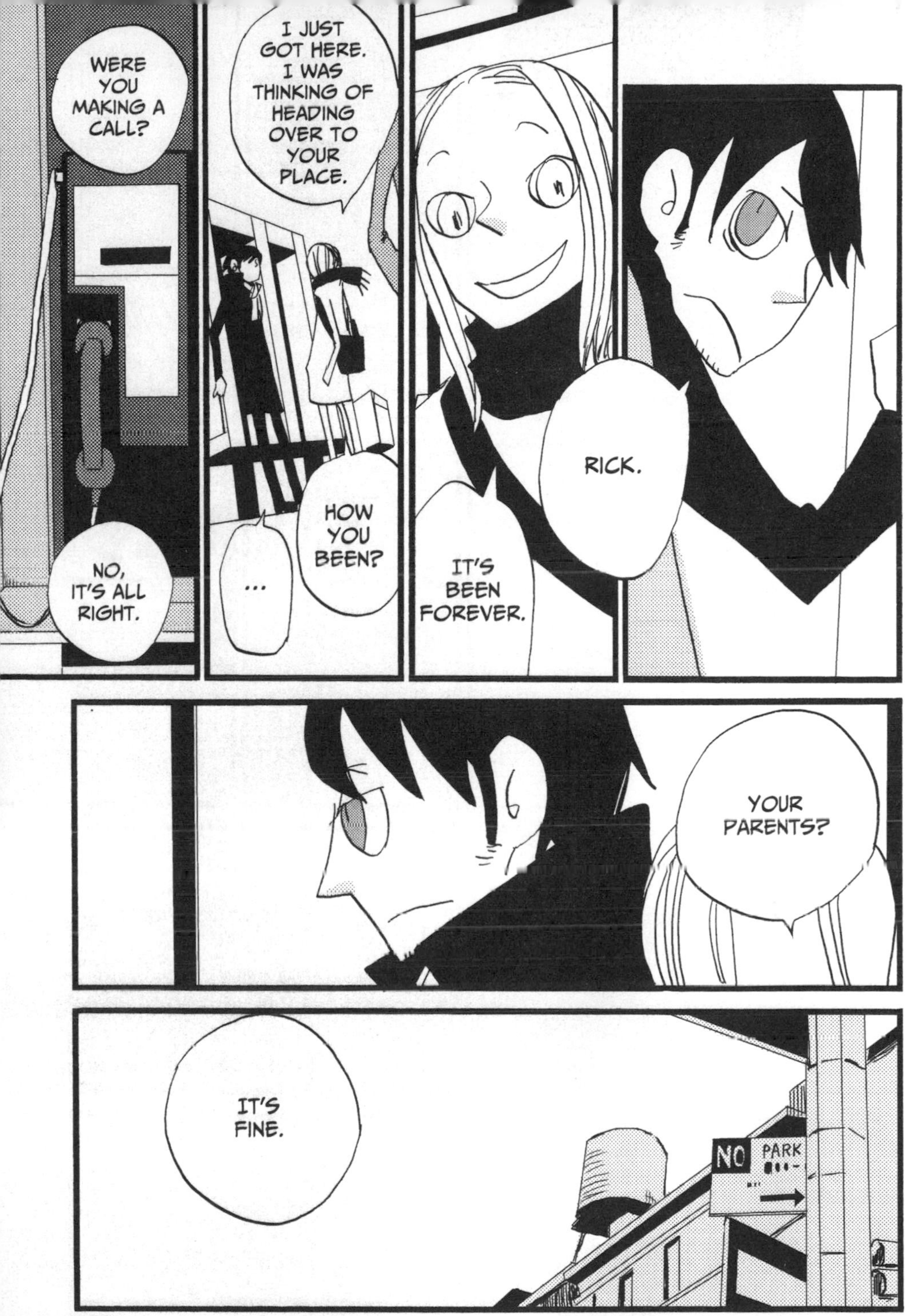
RICK.
IT'S BEEN FOREVER.
I JUST GOT HERE. I WAS THINKING OF HEADING OVER TO YOUR PLACE.
HOW YOU BEEN?
...
WERE YOU MAKING A CALL?
NO, IT'S ALL RIGHT.
YOUR PARENTS?
IT'S FINE.
NO
PARK

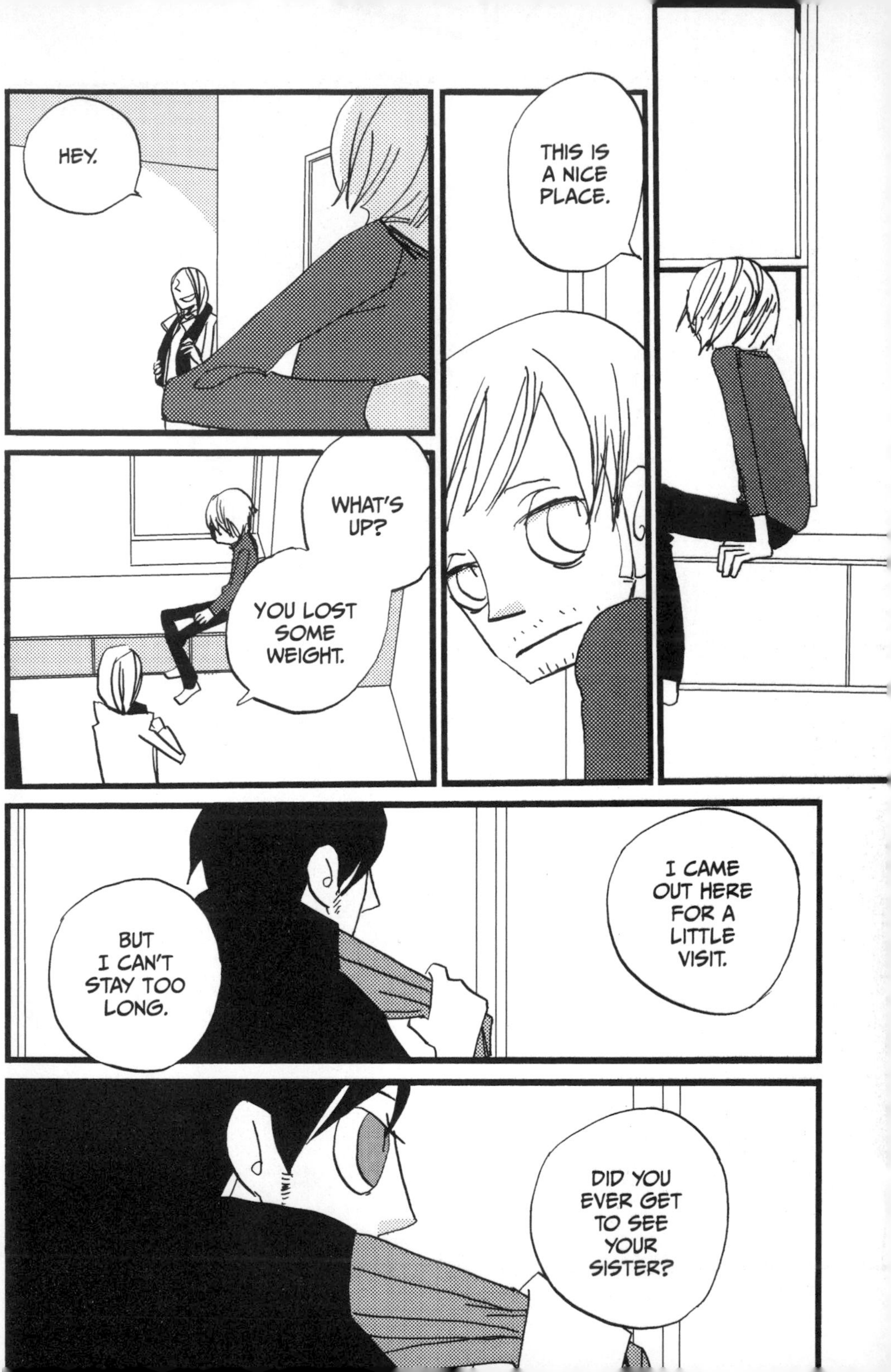
THIS IS A NICE PLACE.
HEY.
WHAT'S UP?
YOU LOST SOME WEIGHT.
I CAME OUT HERE FOR A LITTLE VISIT.
BUT I CAN'T STAY TOO LONG.
DID YOU EVER GET TO SEE YOUR SISTER?

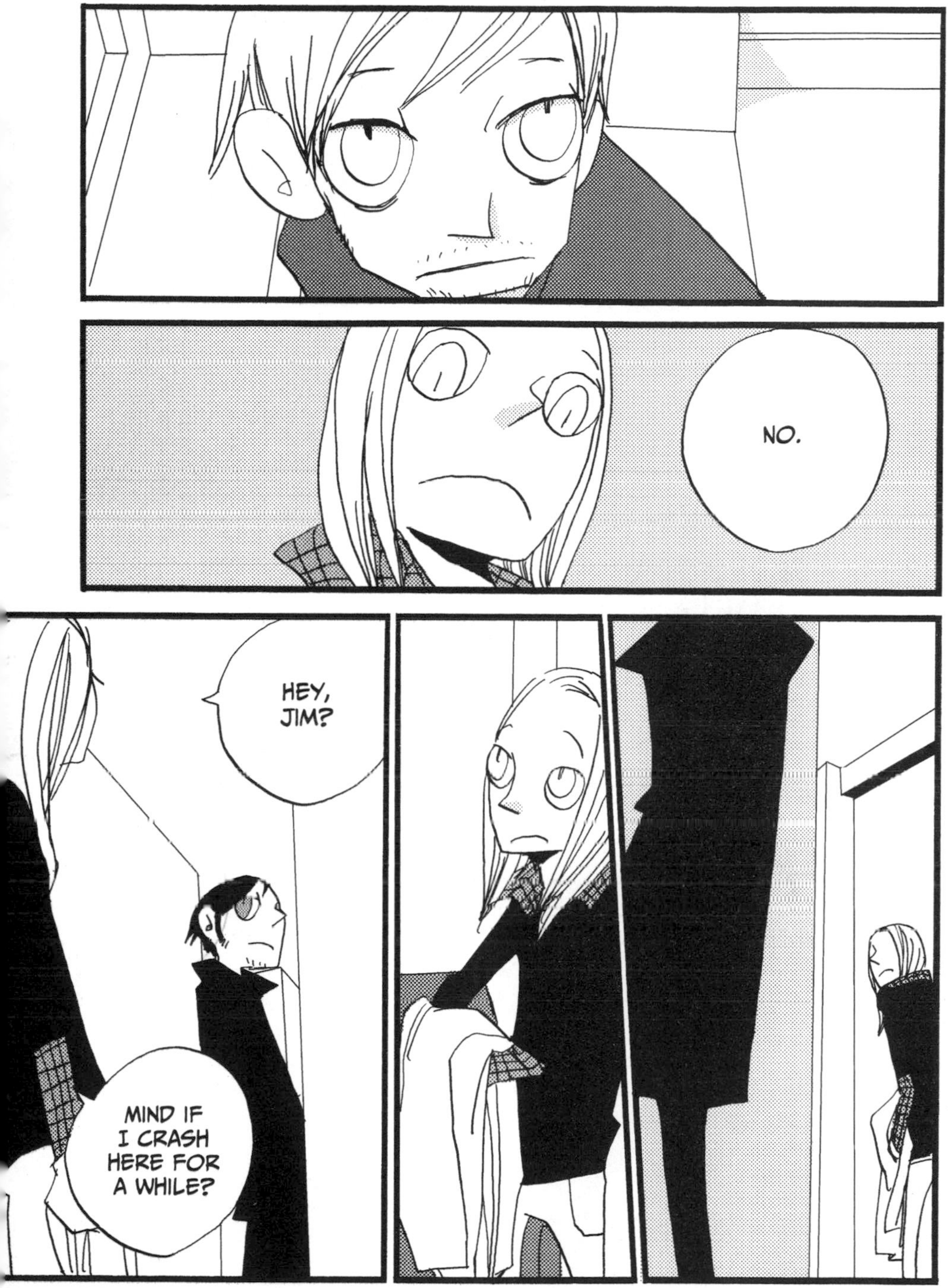
NO.
HEY, JIM?
MIND IF I CRASH HERE FOR A WHILE?

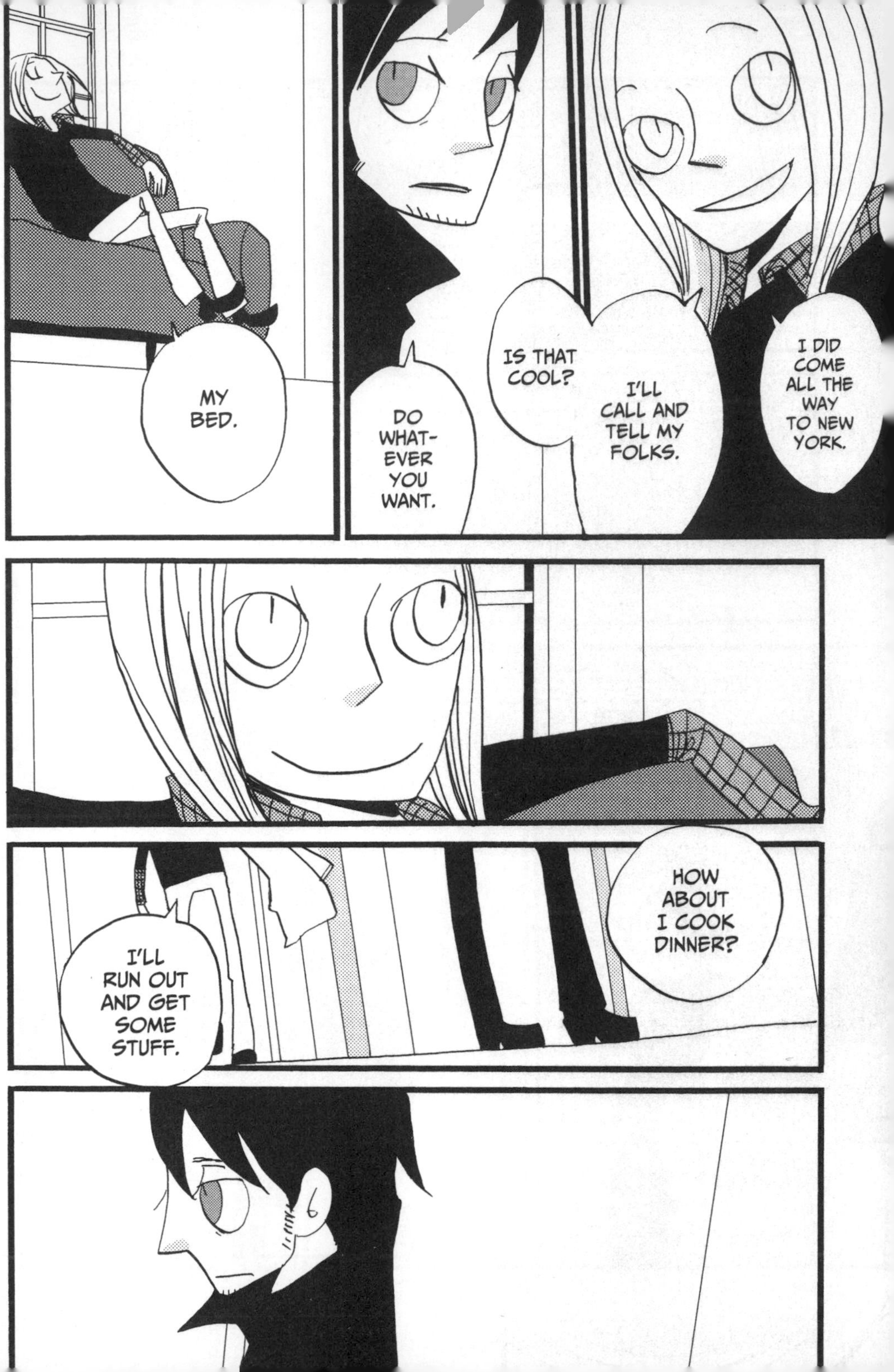
I DID COME ALL THE WAY TO NEW YORK.
I'LL CALL AND TELL MY FOLKS.
IS THAT COOL?
DO WHAT-EVER YOU WANT.
MY BED.
HOW ABOUT I COOK DINNER?
I'LL RUN OUT AND GET SOME STUFF.

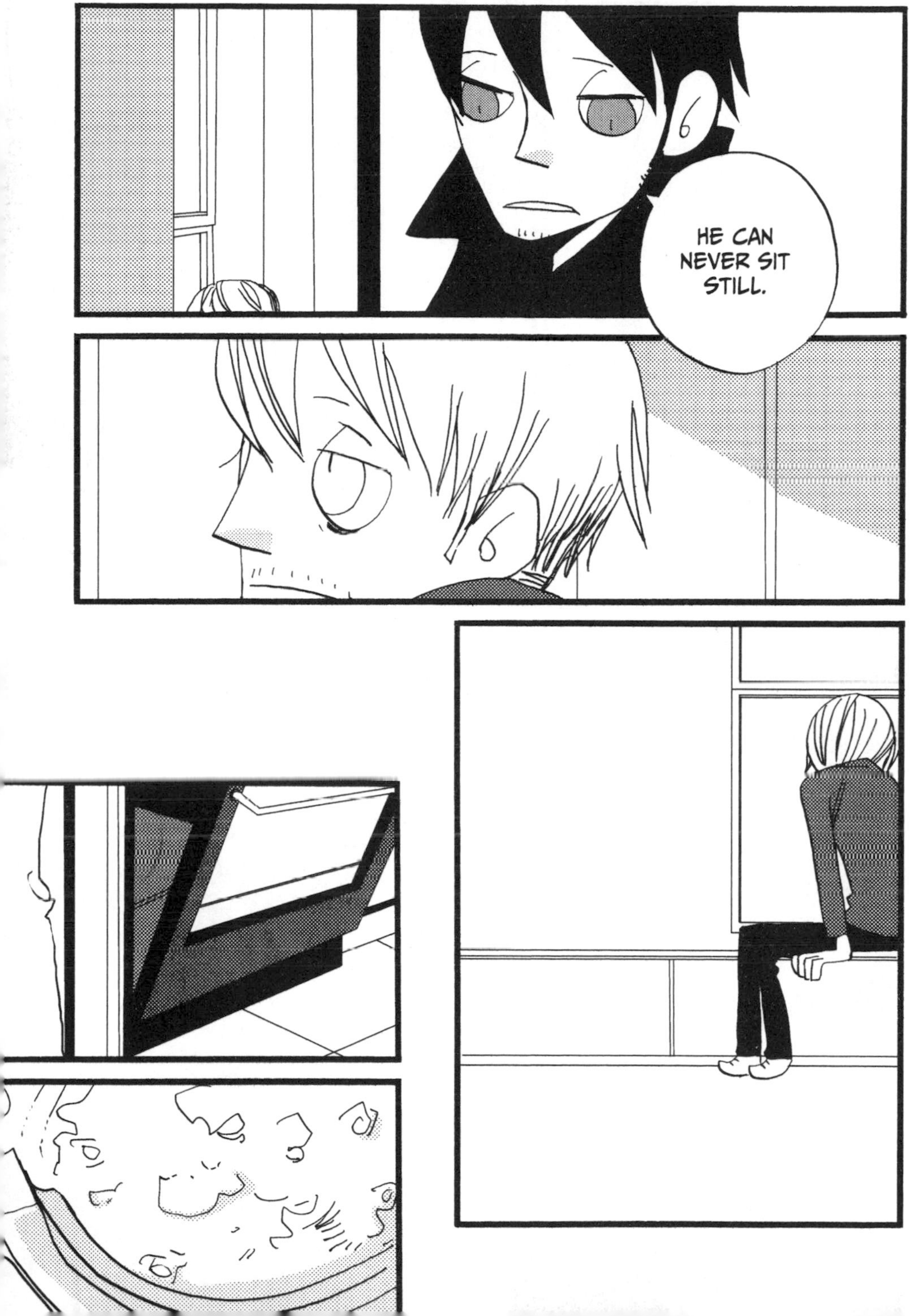
HE CAN NEVER SIT STILL.

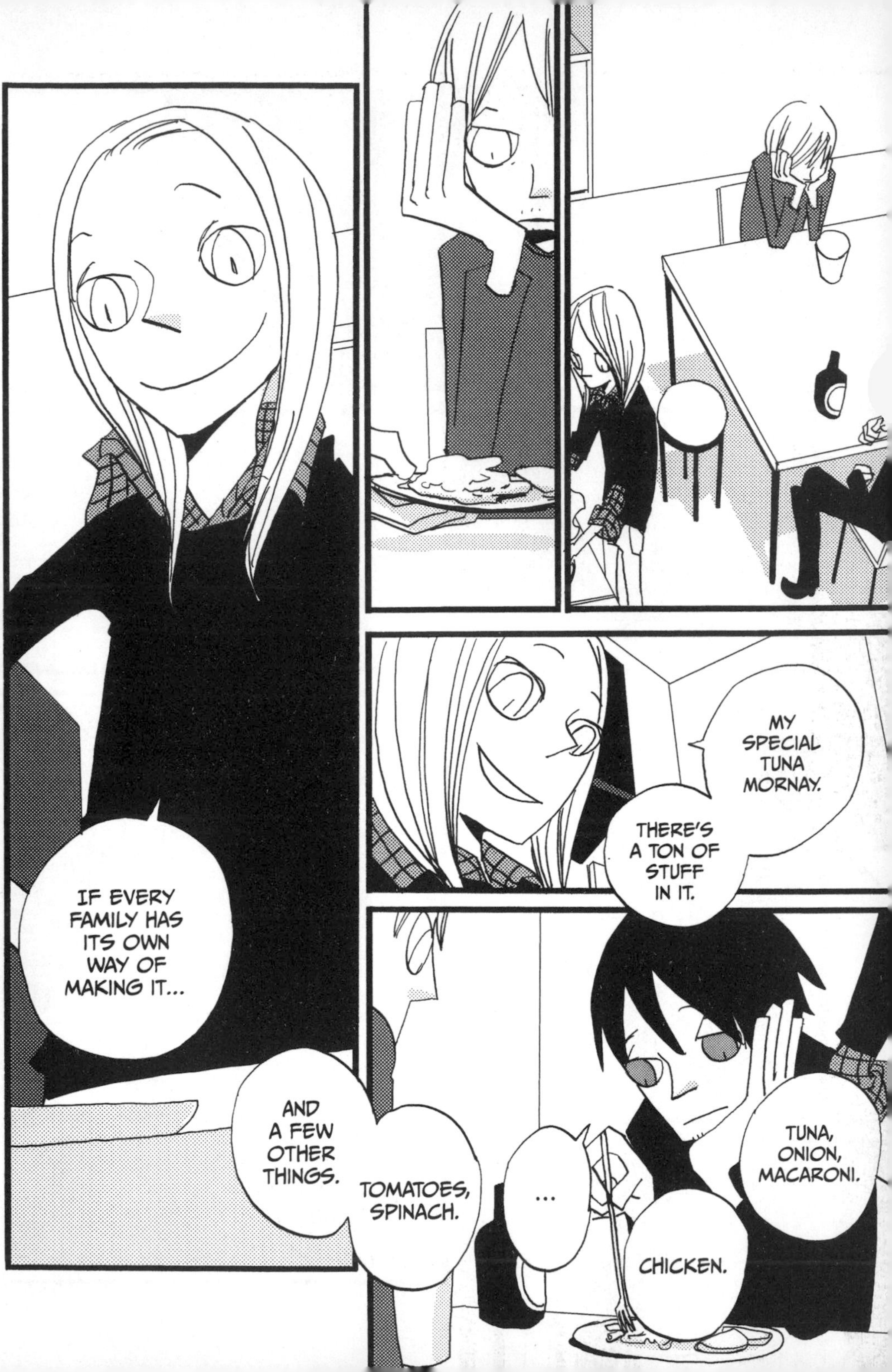
MY SPECIAL TUNA MORNAY.
THERE'S A TON OF STUFF IN IT.
TUNA, ONION, MACARONI.
CHICKEN.
...
TOMATOES, SPINACH.
AND A FEW OTHER THINGS.
IF EVERY FAMILY HAS ITS OWN WAY OF MAKING IT...

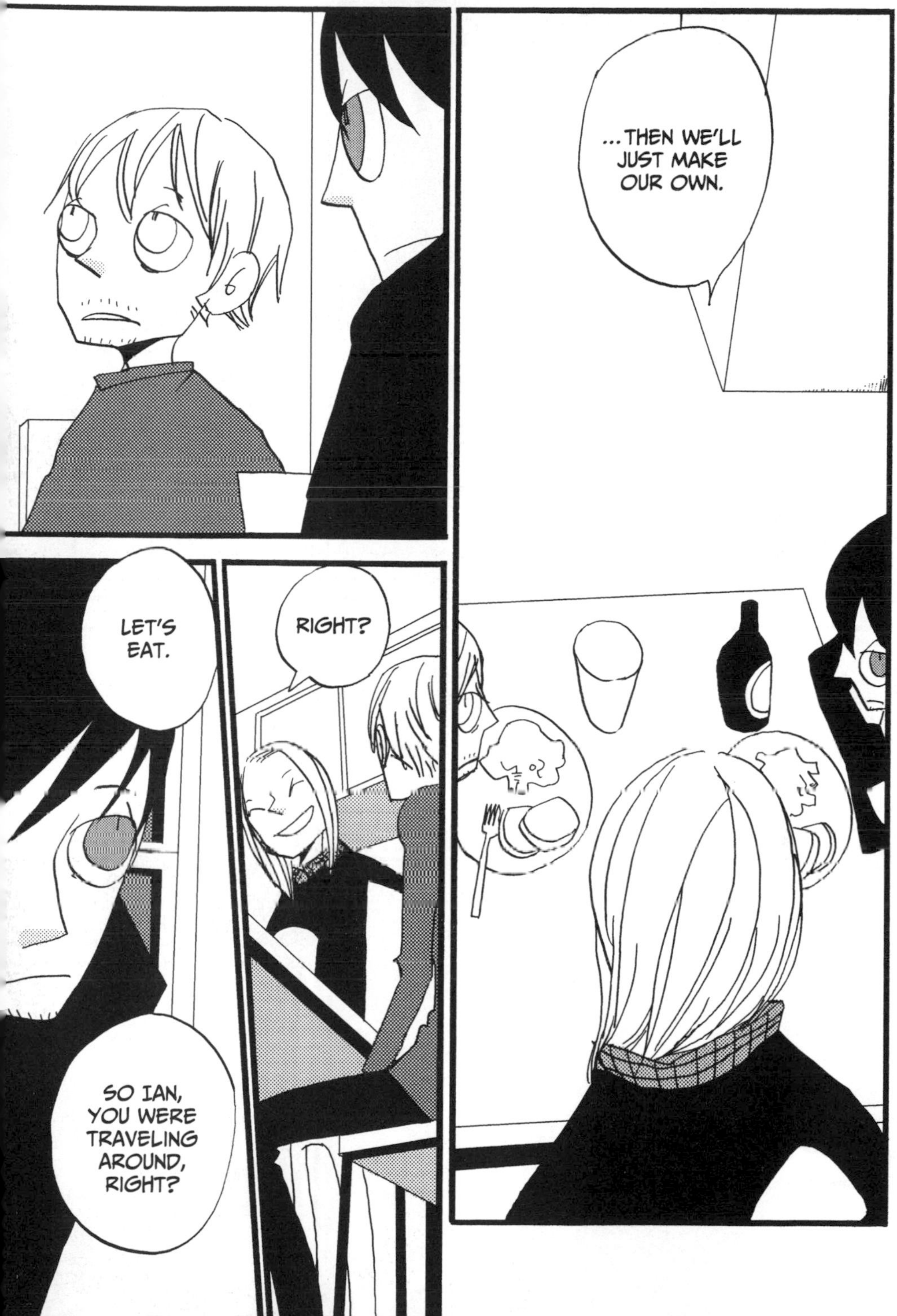
...THEN WE'LL JUST MAKE OUR OWN.
RIGHT?
LET'S EAT.
SO IAN, YOU WERE TRAVELING AROUND, RIGHT?

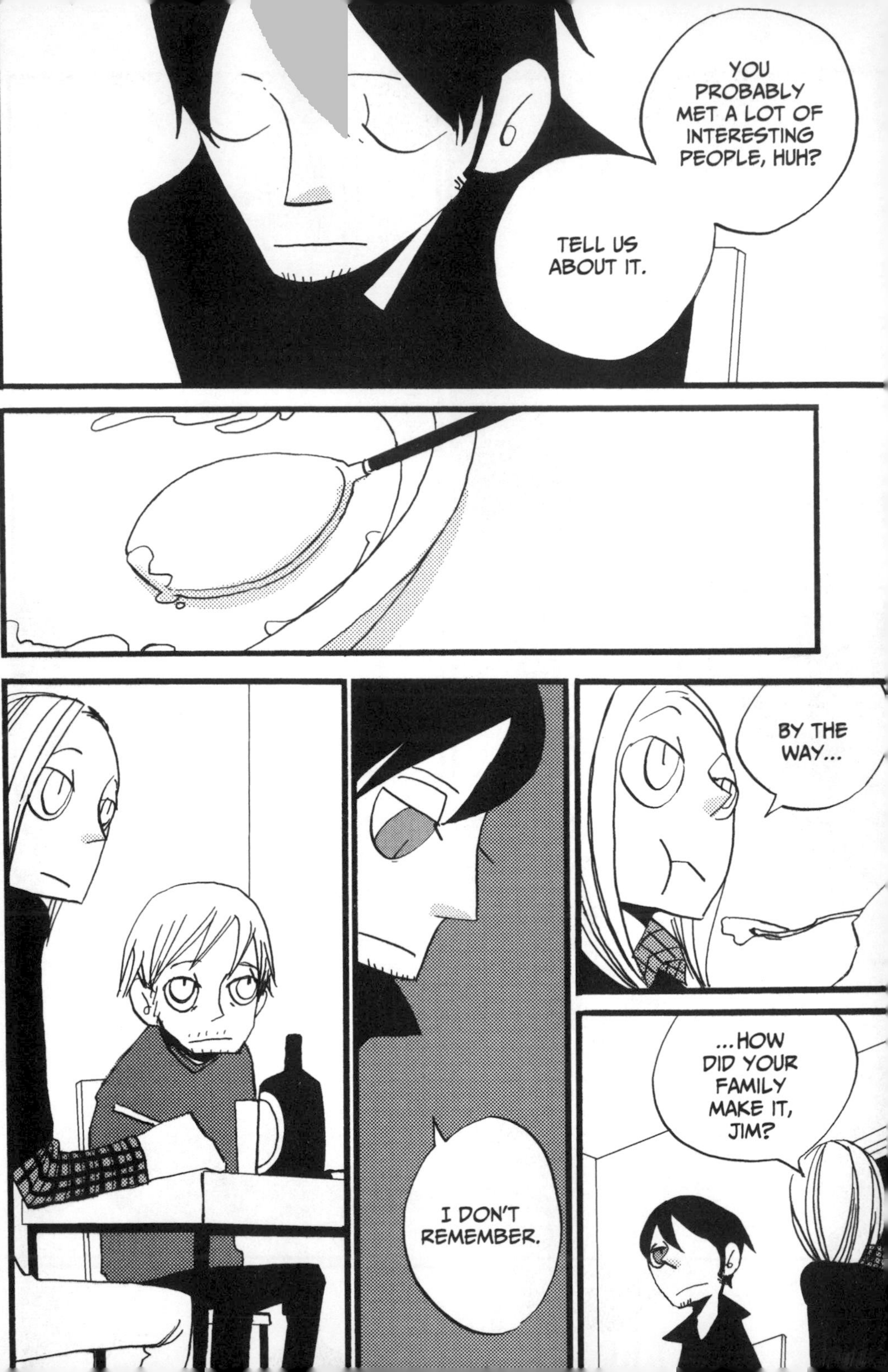
YOU PROBABLY MET A LOT OF INTERESTING PEOPLE, HUH?
TELL US ABOUT IT.
BY THE WAY...
...HOW DID YOUR FAMILY MAKE IT, JIM?
I DON'T REMEMBER.

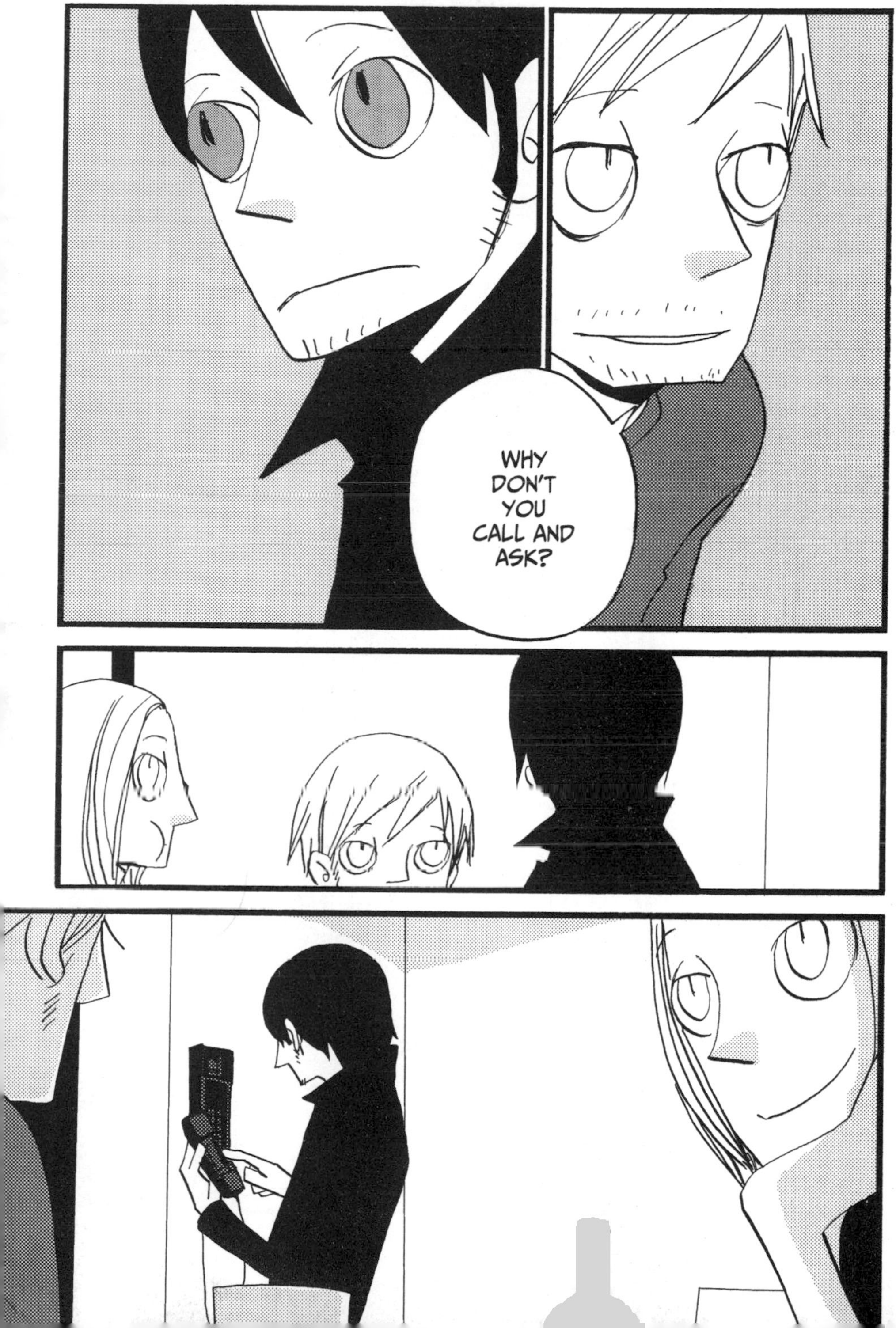
WHY DON'T YOU CALL AND ASK?

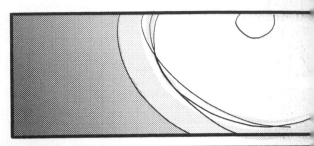

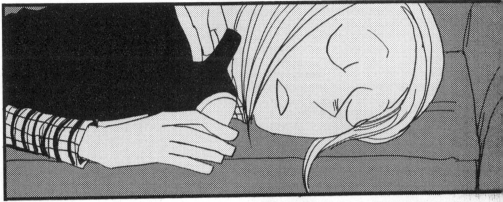

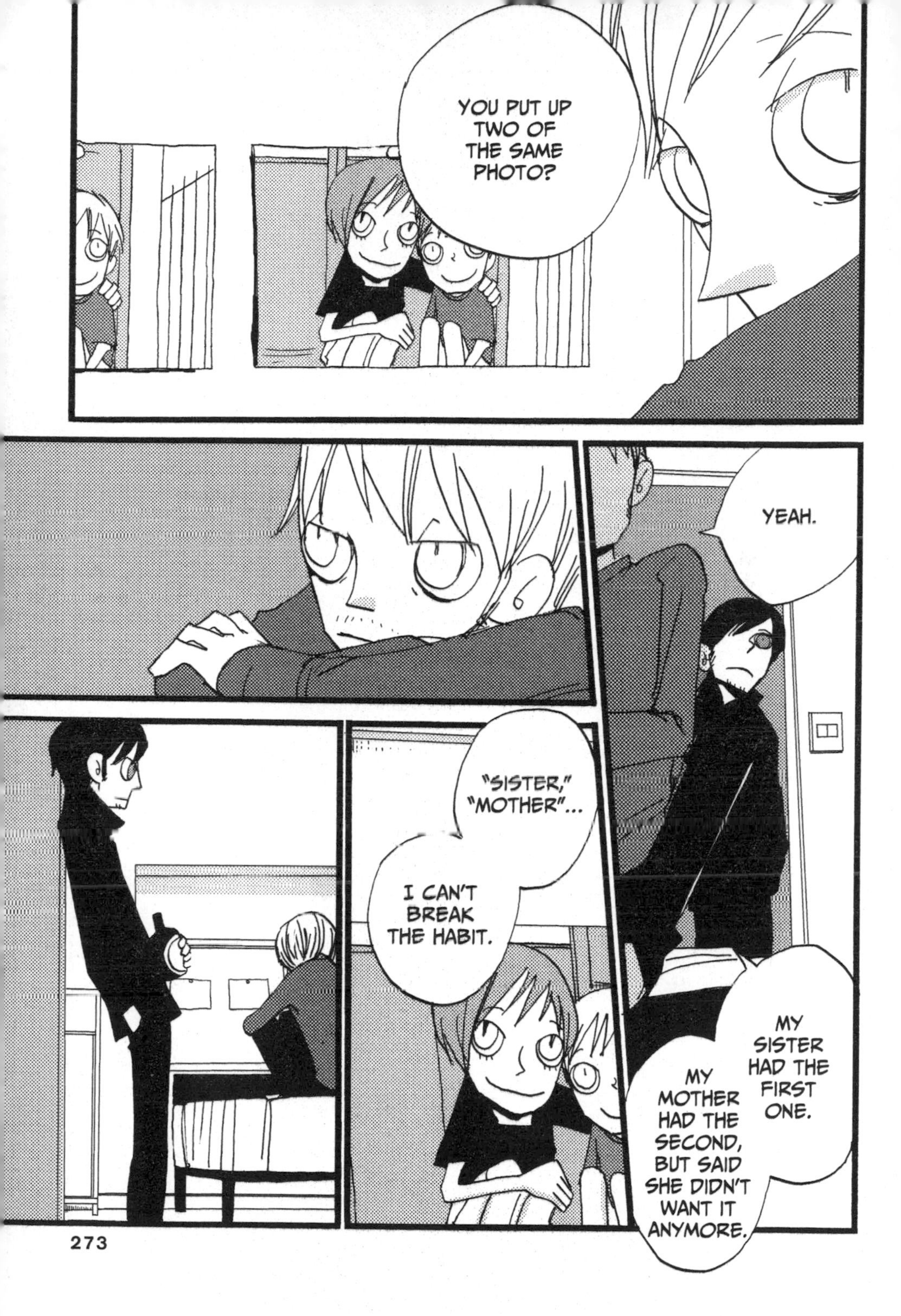
YOU PUT UP TWO OF THE SAME PHOTO?
YEAH.
MY SISTER HAD THE FIRST ONE.
MY MOTHER HAD THE SECOND, BUT SAID SHE DIDN'T WANT IT ANYMORE.
"SISTER," "MOTHER"...
I CAN'T BREAK THE HABIT.

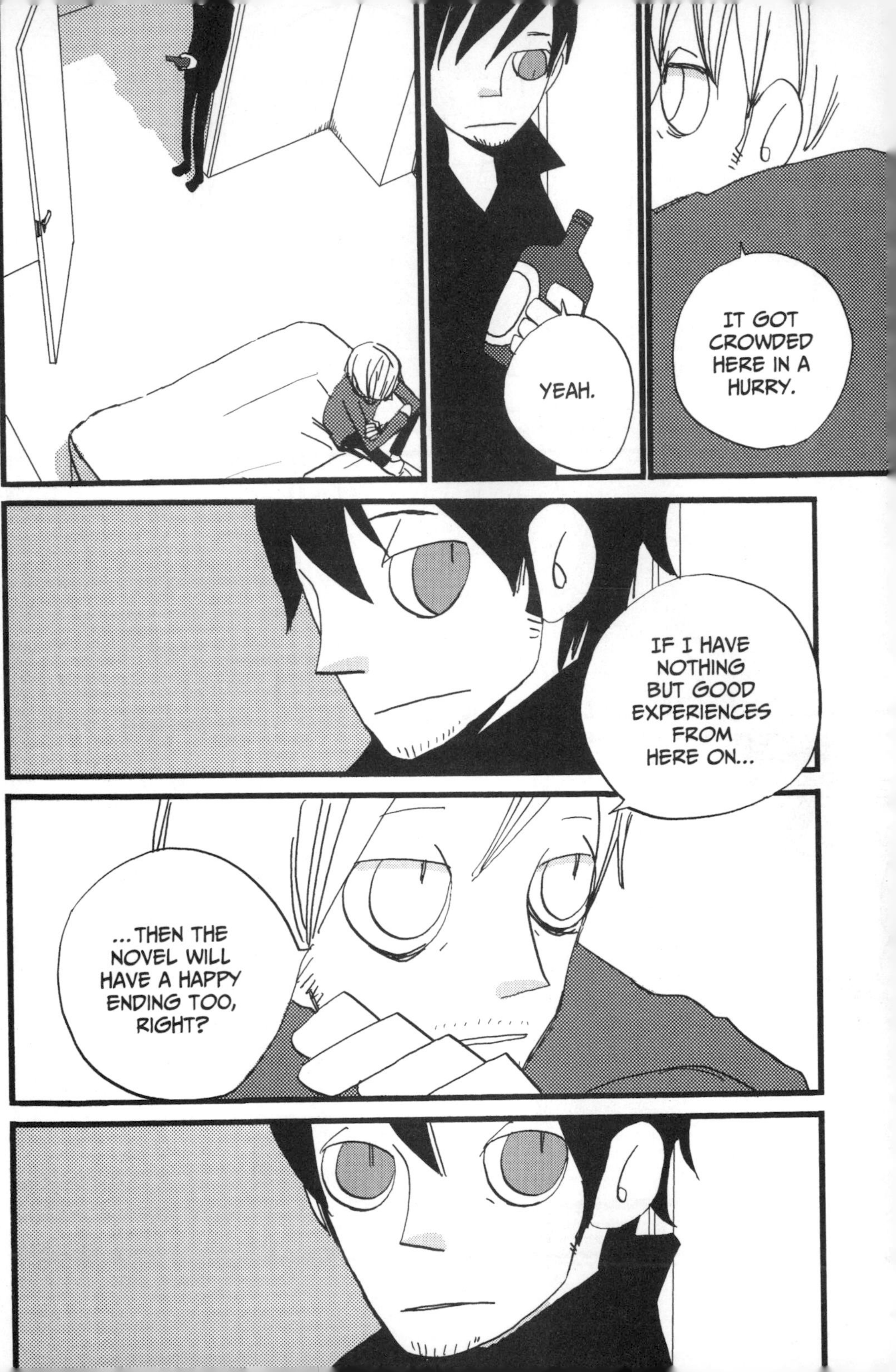
IT GOT CROWDED HERE IN A HURRY.
YEAH.
IF I HAVE NOTHING BUT GOOD EXPERIENCES FROM HERE ON...
...THEN THE NOVEL WILL HAVE A HAPPY ENDING TOO, RIGHT?

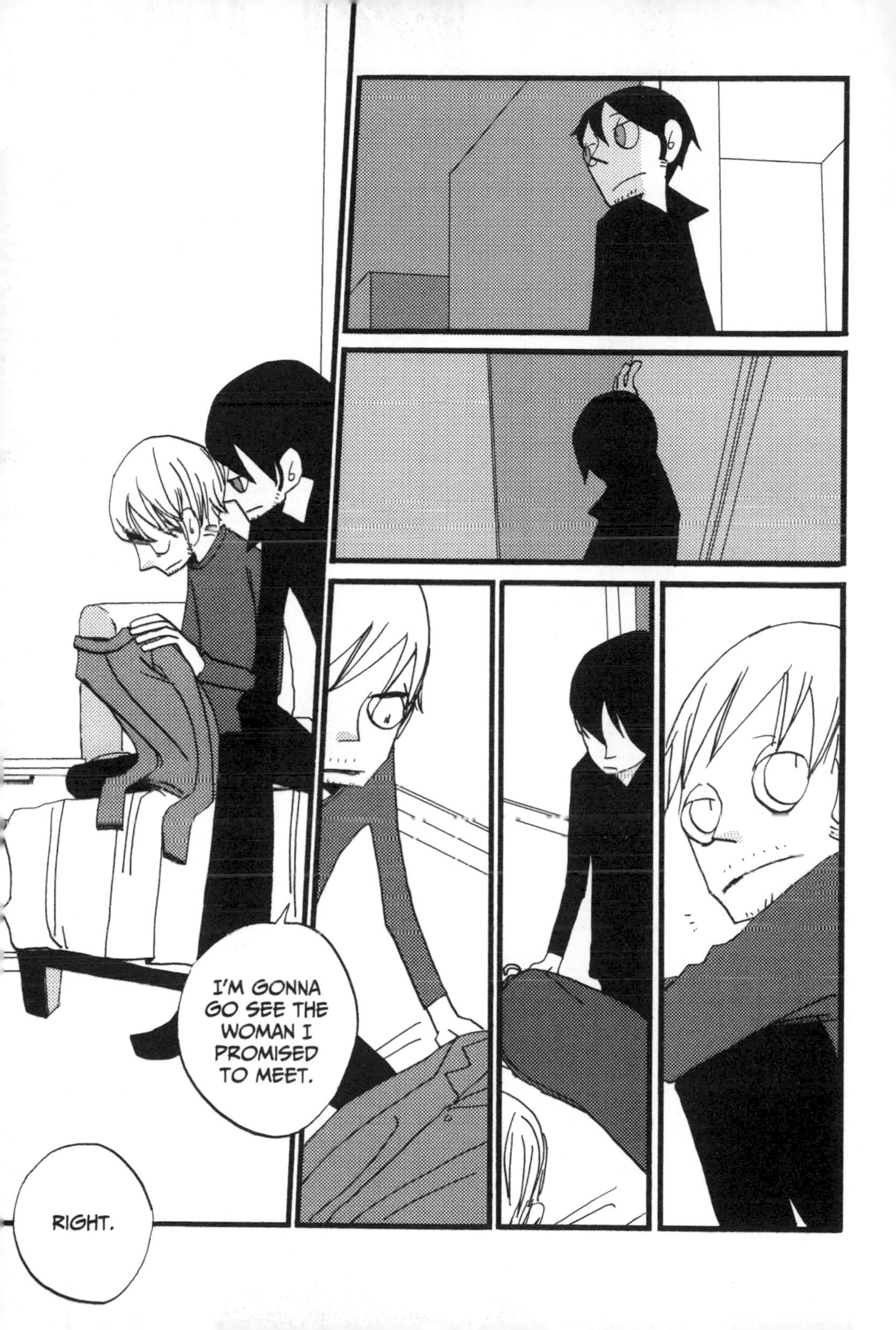
I'M GONNA GO SEE THE WOMAN I PROMISED TO MEET.
RIGHT.

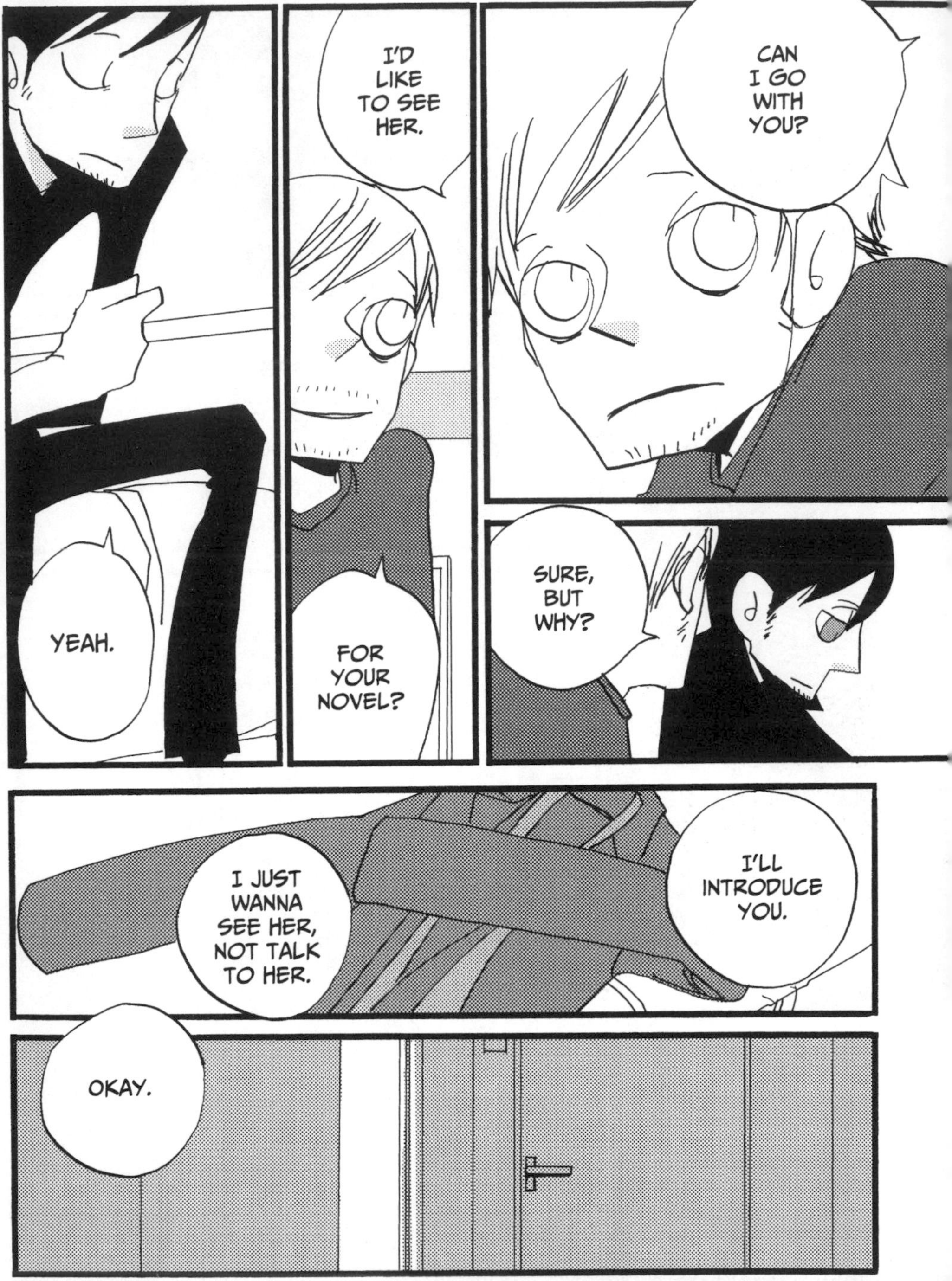
CAN I GO WITH YOU?
SURE, BUT WHY?
I'D LIKE TO SEE HER.
FOR YOUR NOVEL?
YEAH.
I'LL INTRODUCE YOU.
I JUST WANNA SEE HER, NOT TALK TO HER.
OKAY.

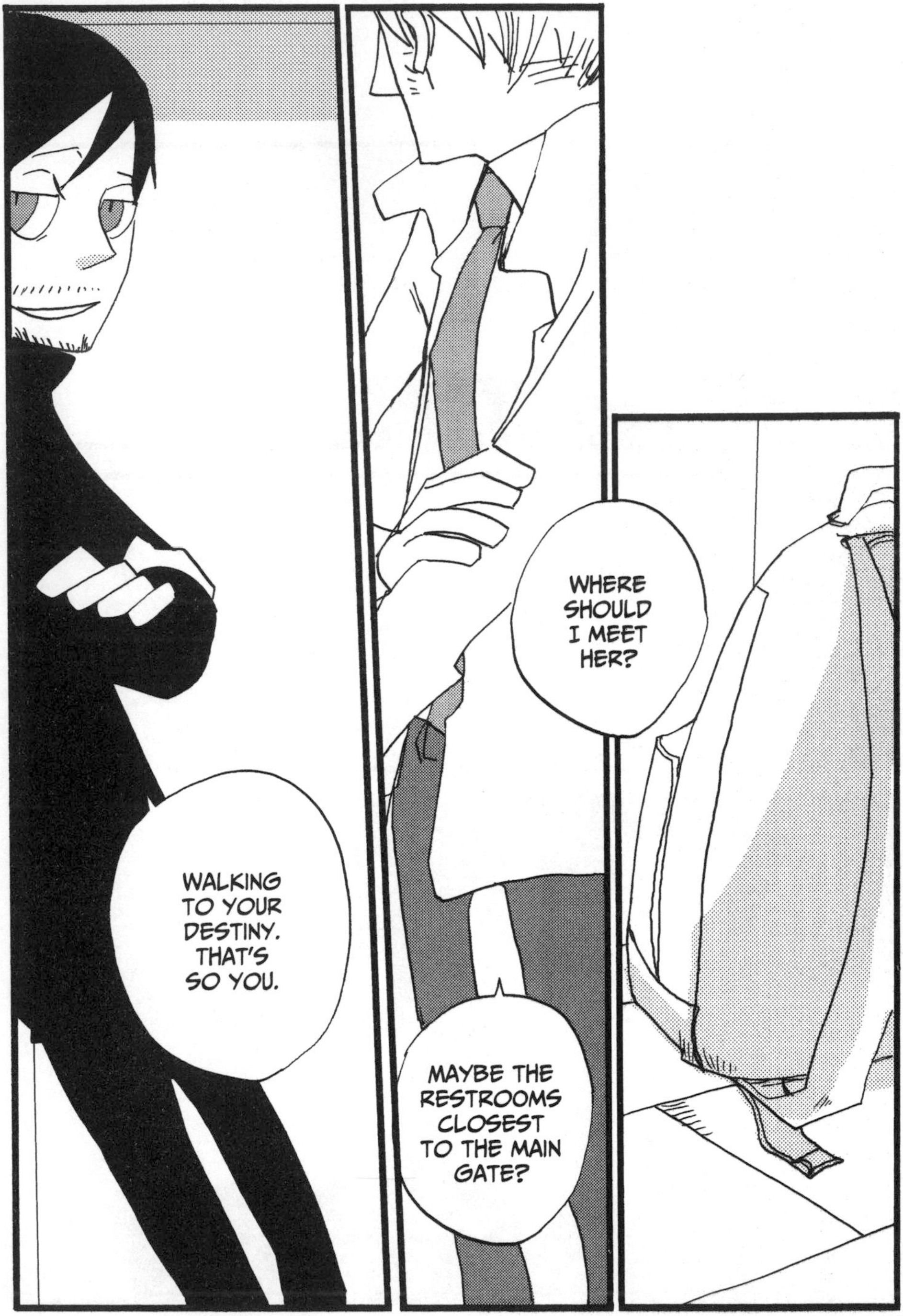
WHERE SHOULD I MEET HER?
MAYBE THE RESTROOMS CLOSEST TO THE MAIN GATE?
WALKING TO YOUR DESTINY. THAT'S SO YOU.

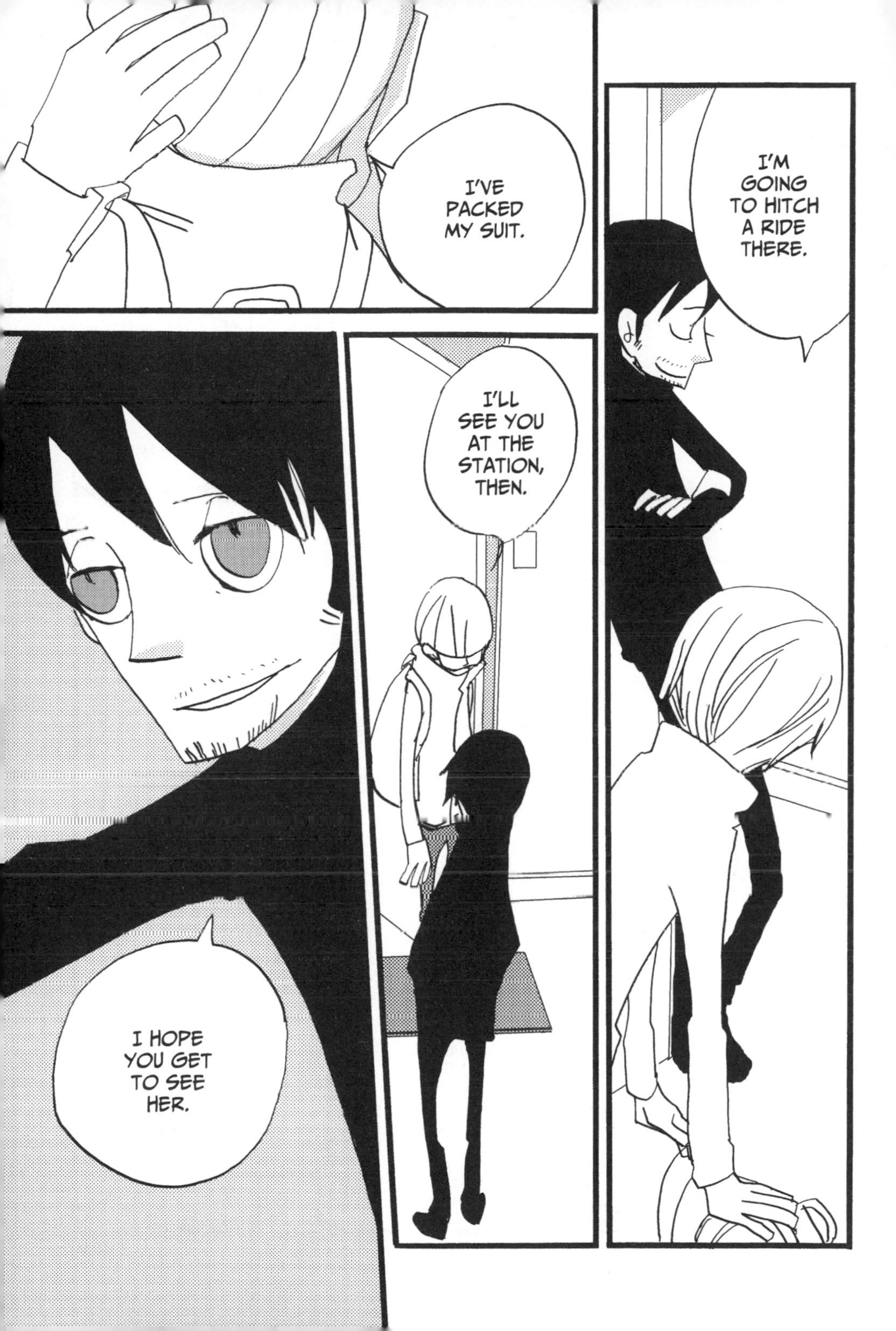
I'M GOING TO HITCH A RIDE THERE.
I'VE PACKED MY SUIT.
I'LL SEE YOU AT THE STATION, THEN.
I HOPE YOU GET TO SEE HER.

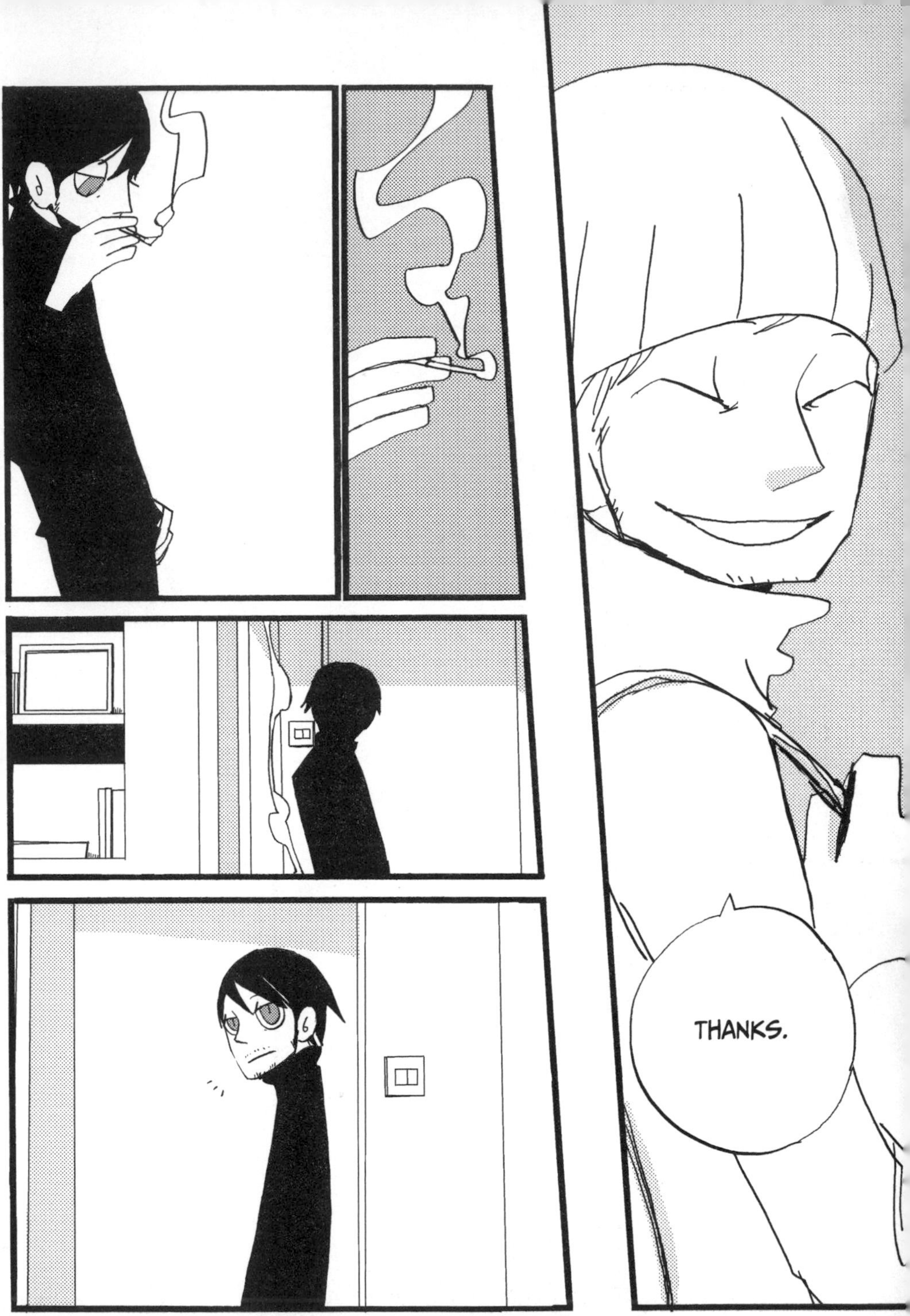
THANKS.

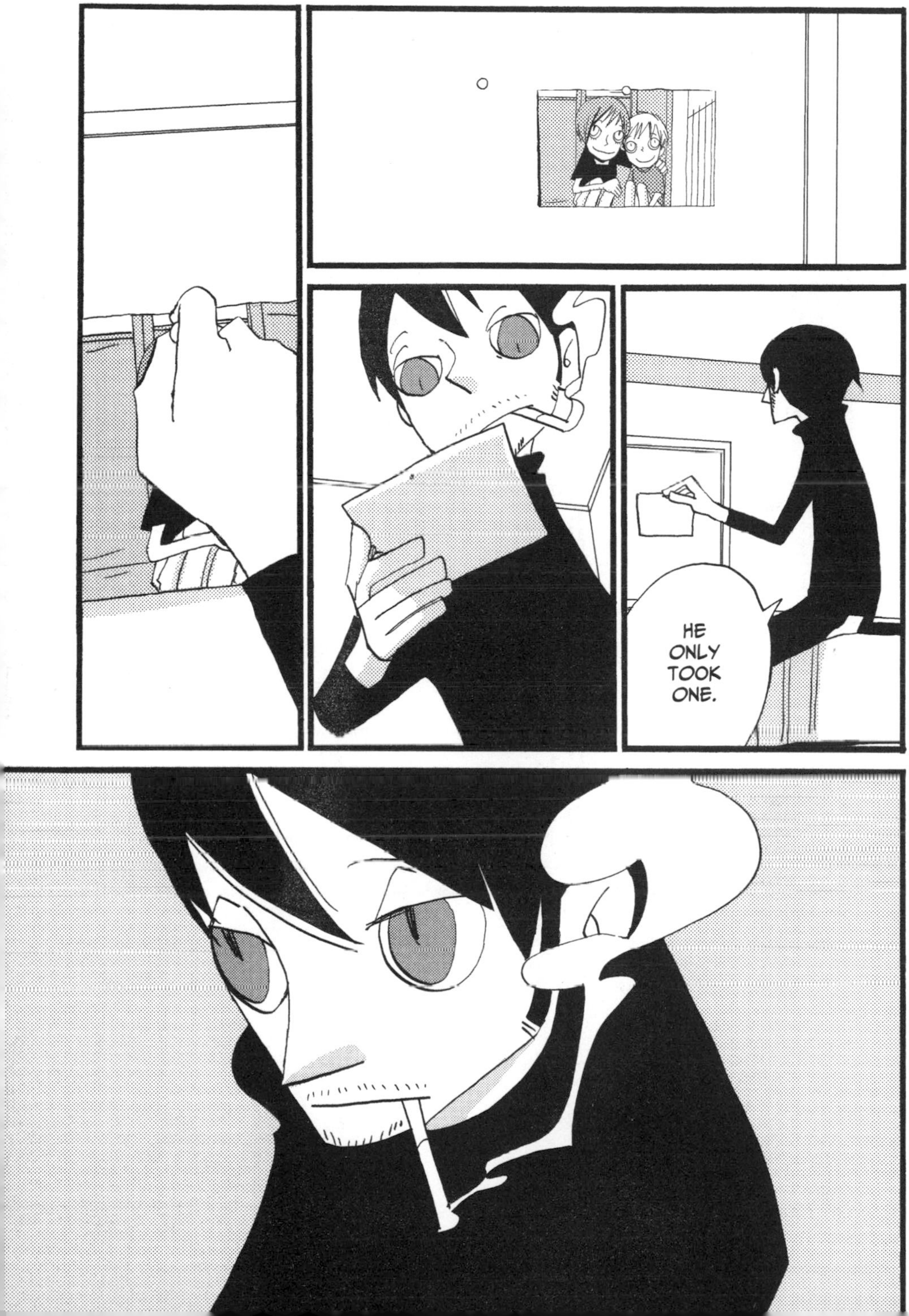
HE ONLY TOOK ONE.

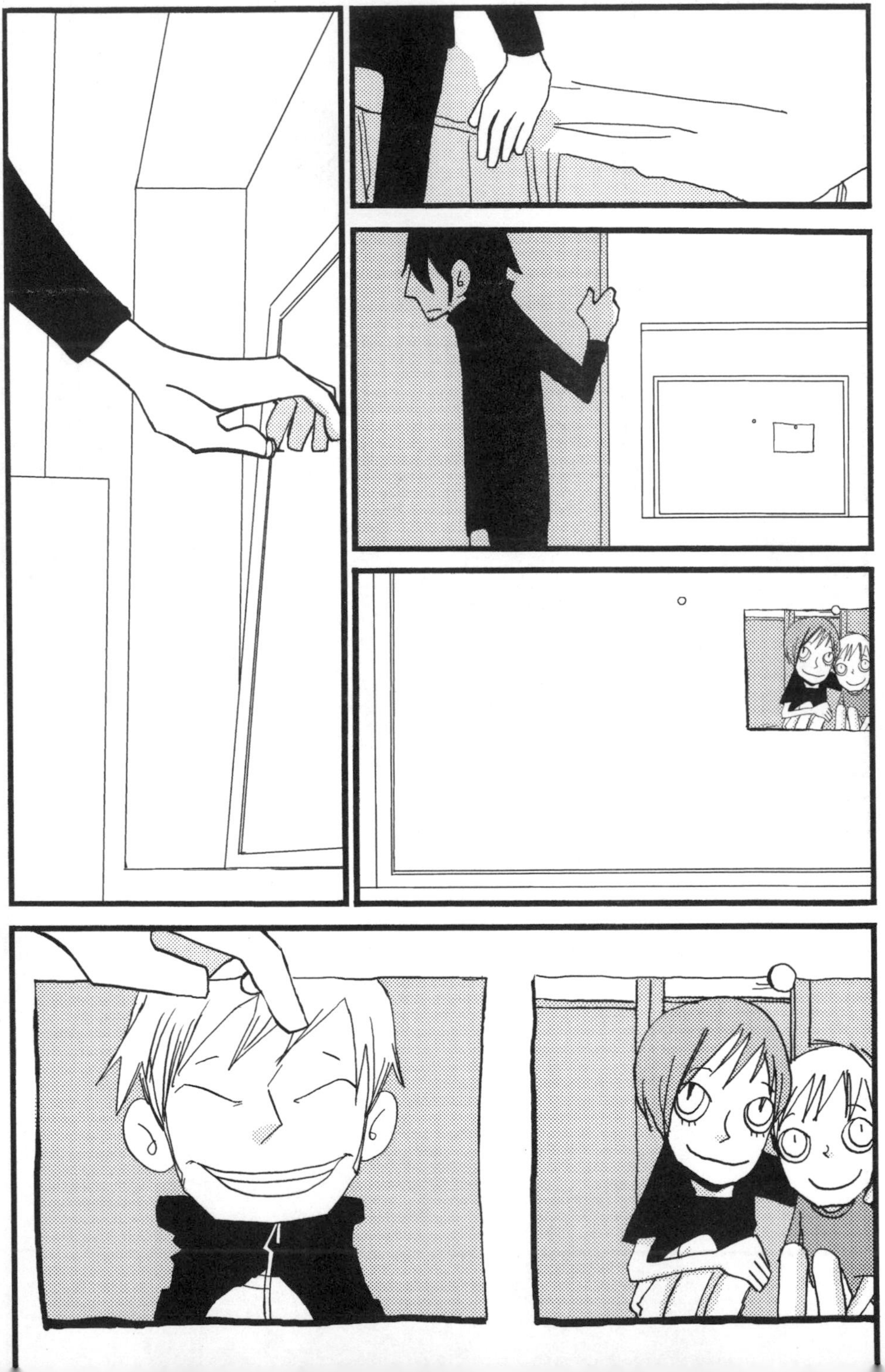

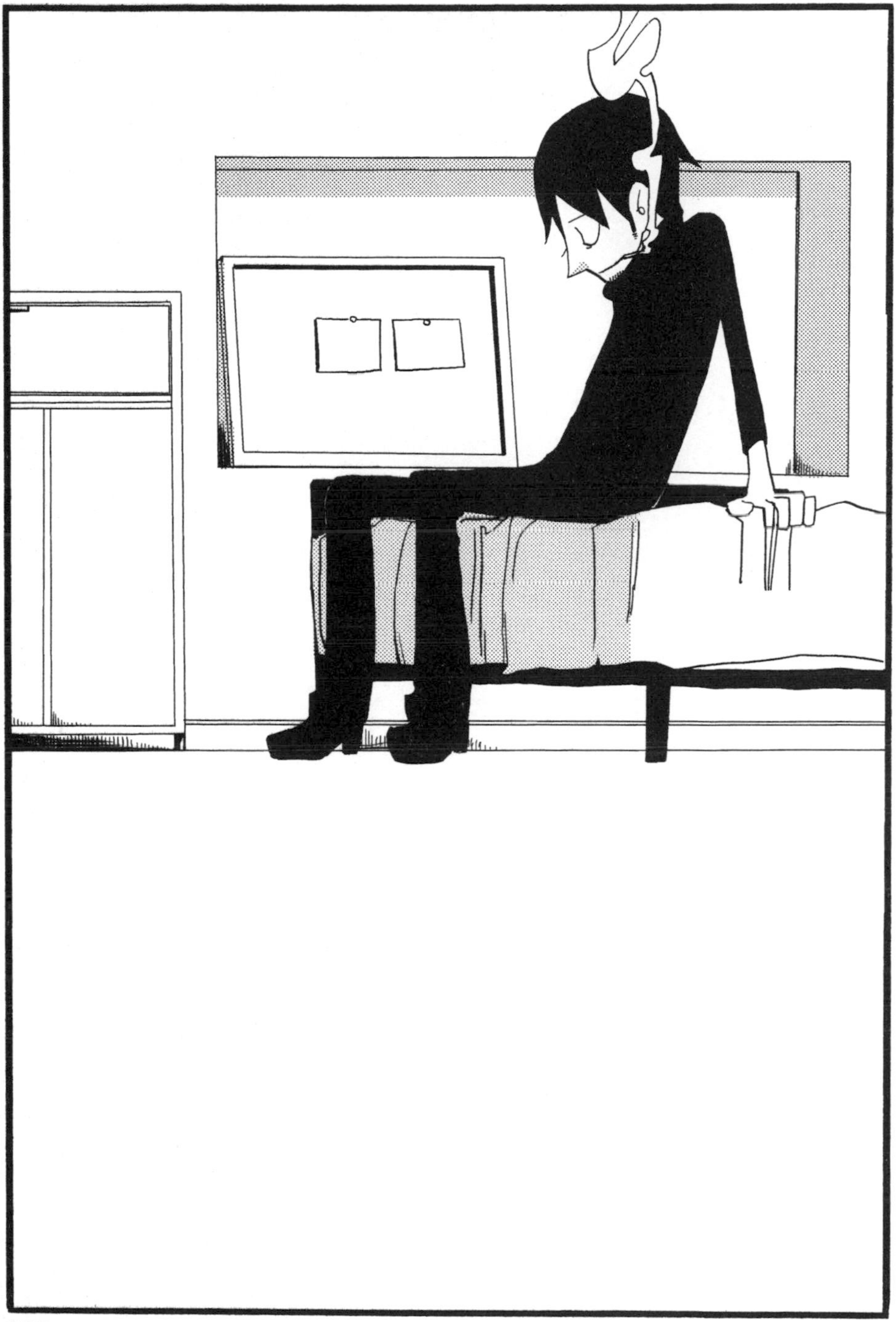

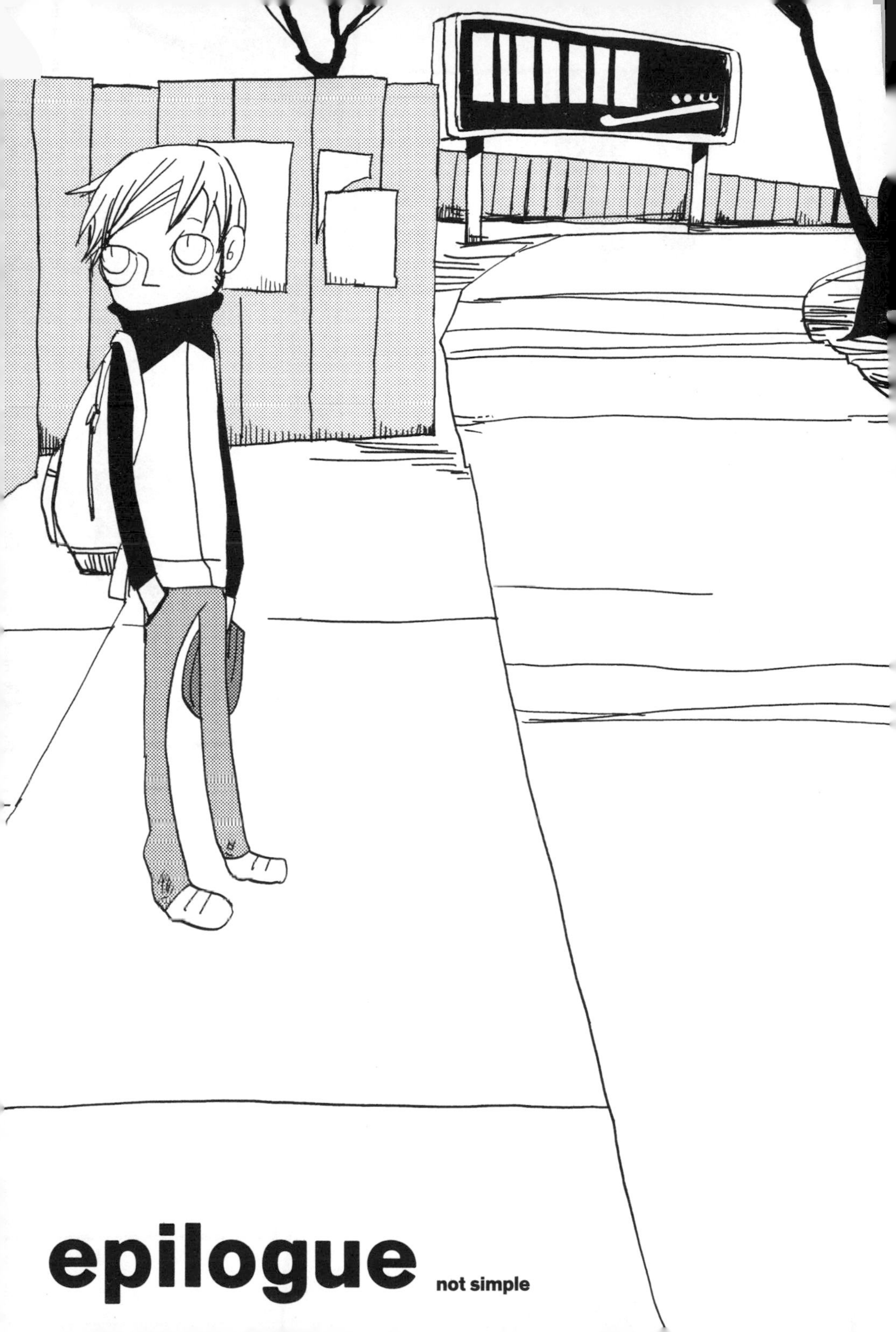

epilogue

not simple

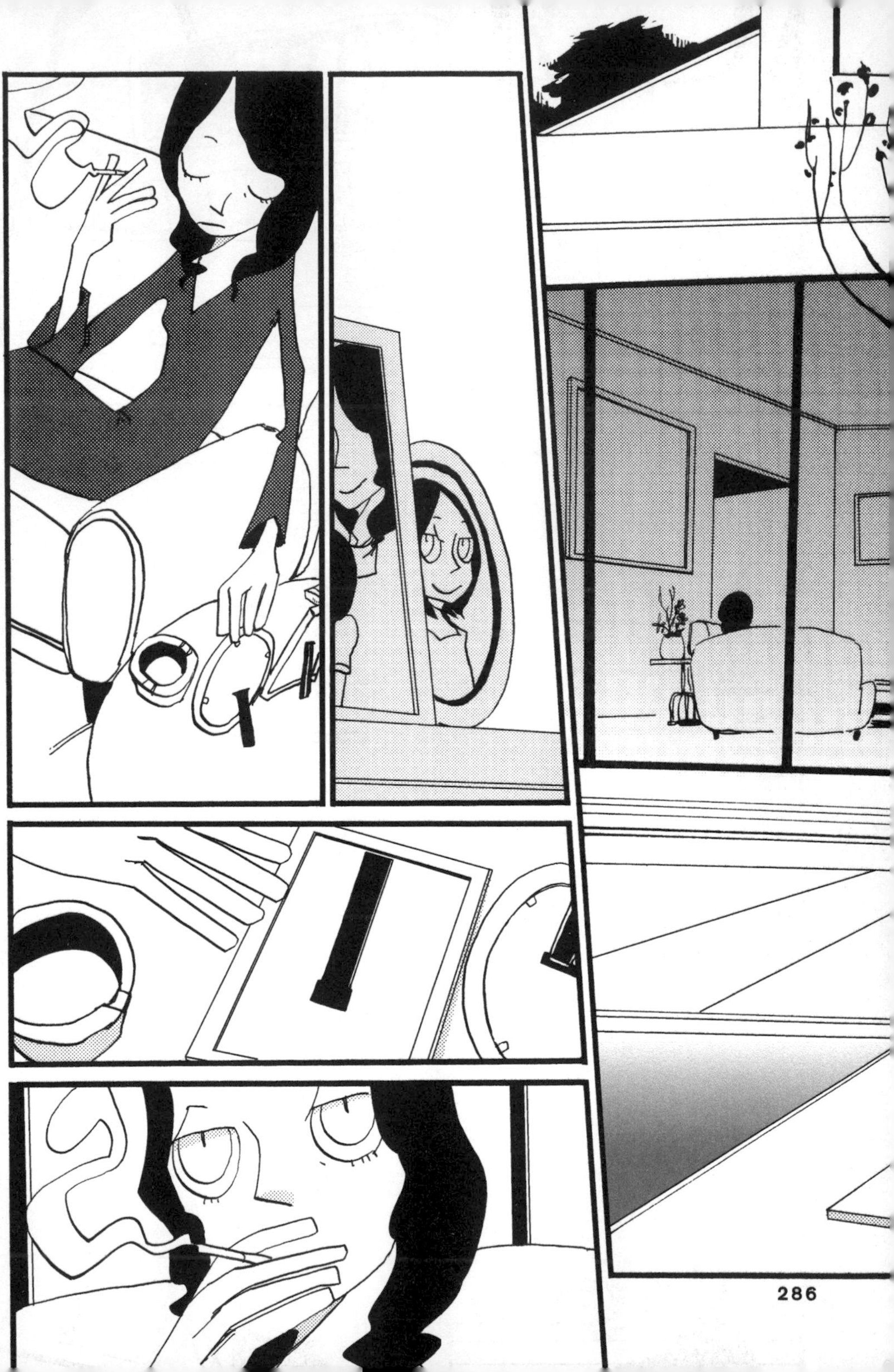

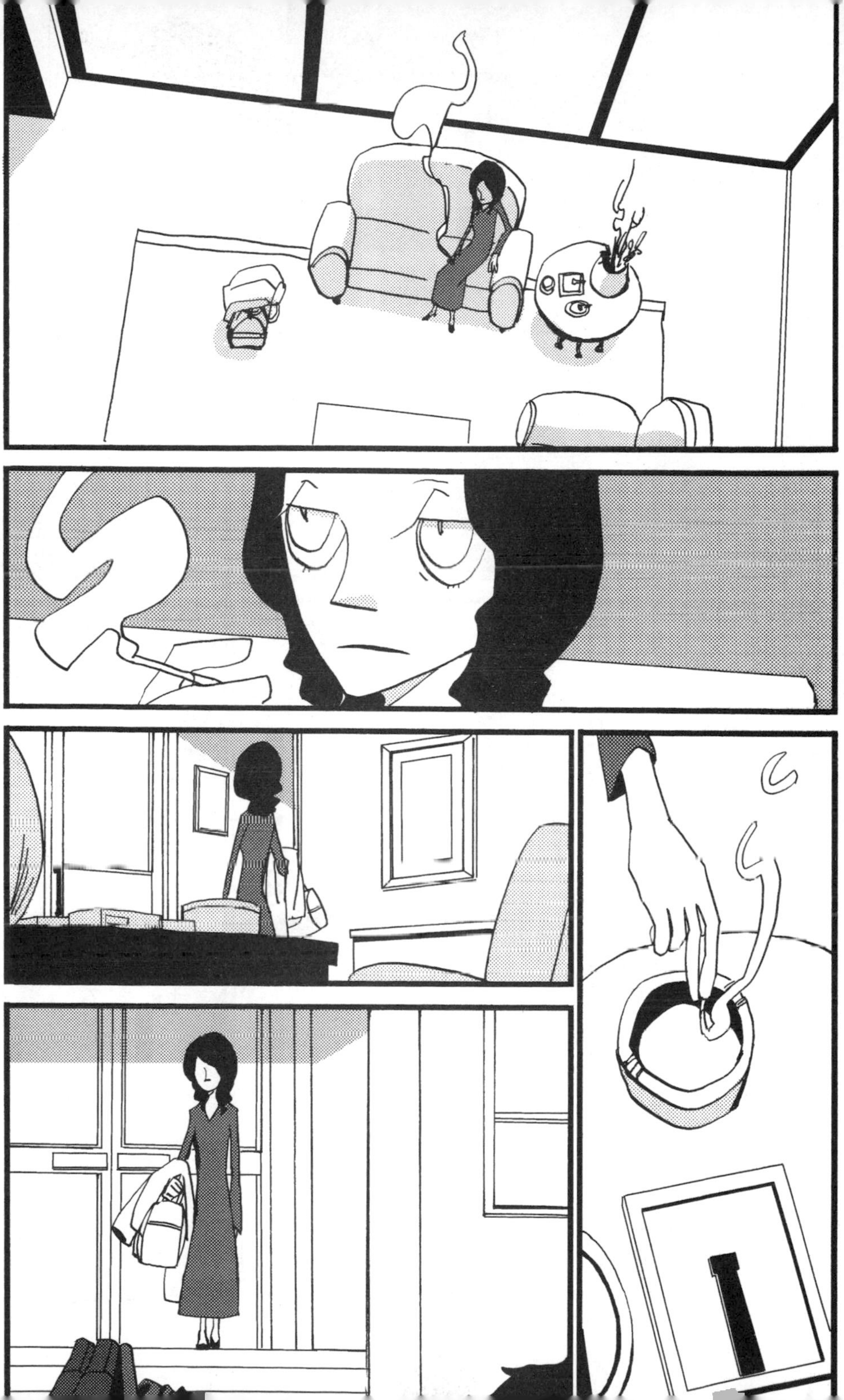

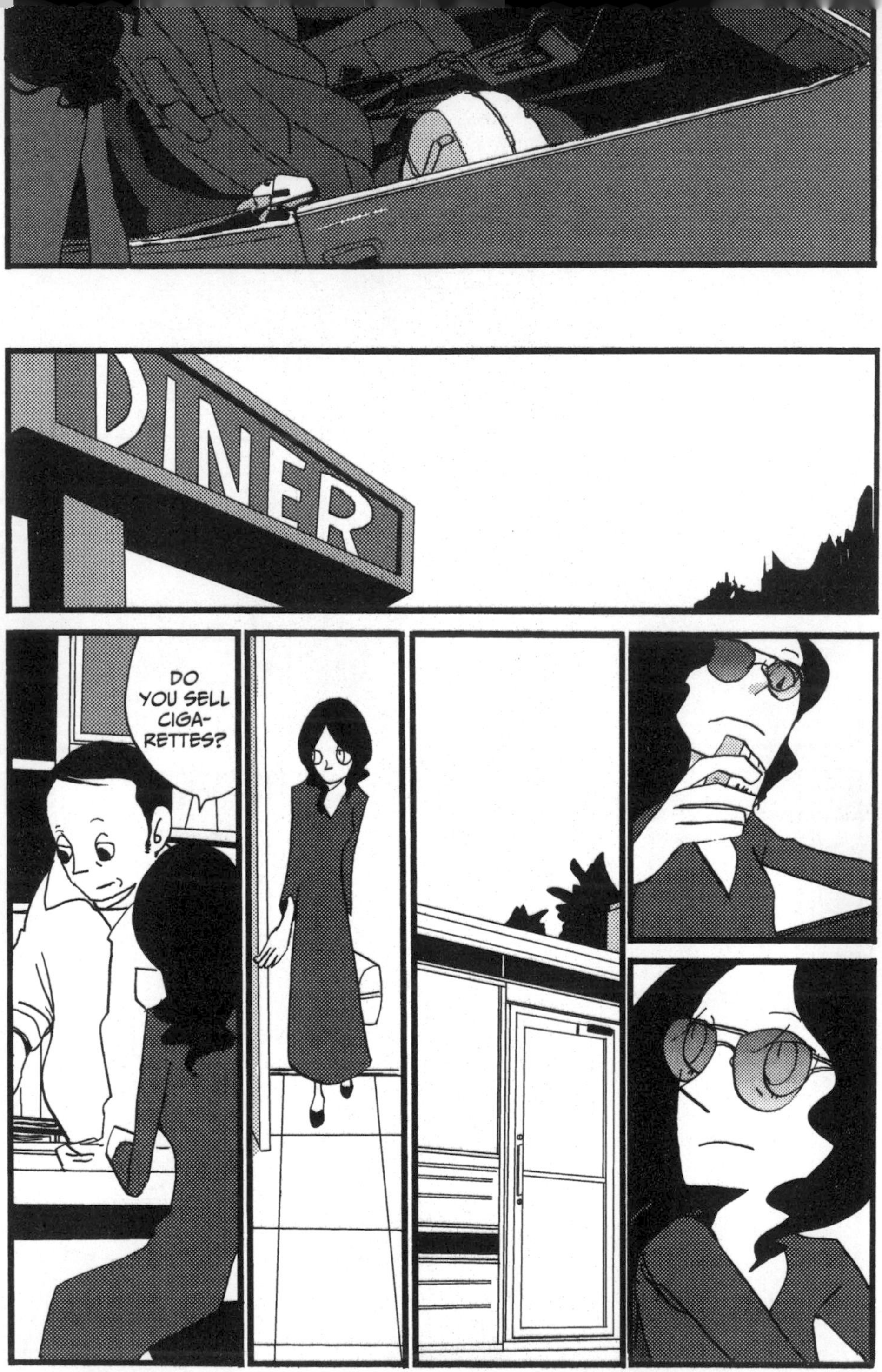
DINER
DO YOU SELL CIGA-RETTES?

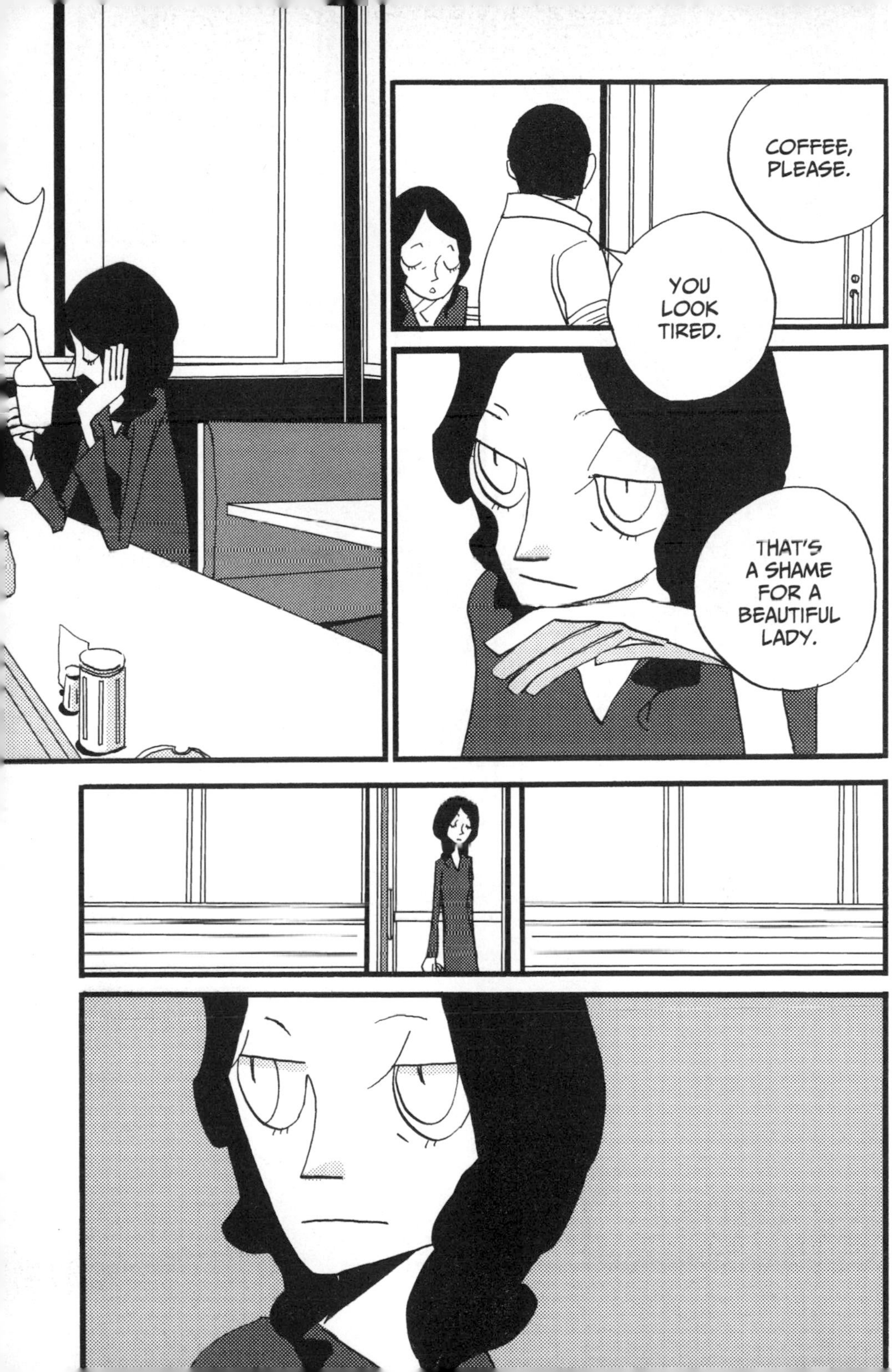
COFFEE, PLEASE.
YOU LOOK TIRED.
THAT'S A SHAME FOR A BEAUTIFUL LADY.

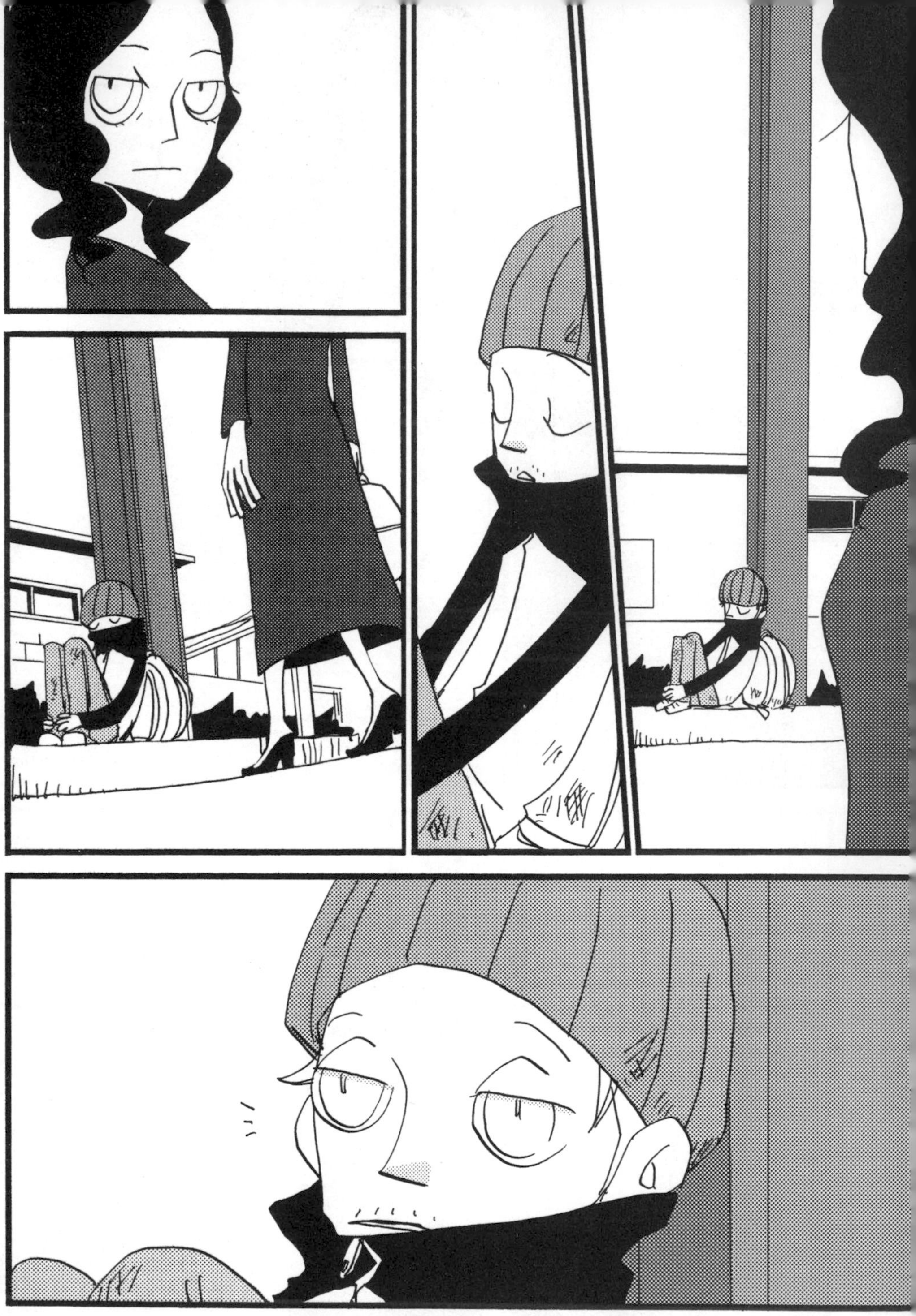

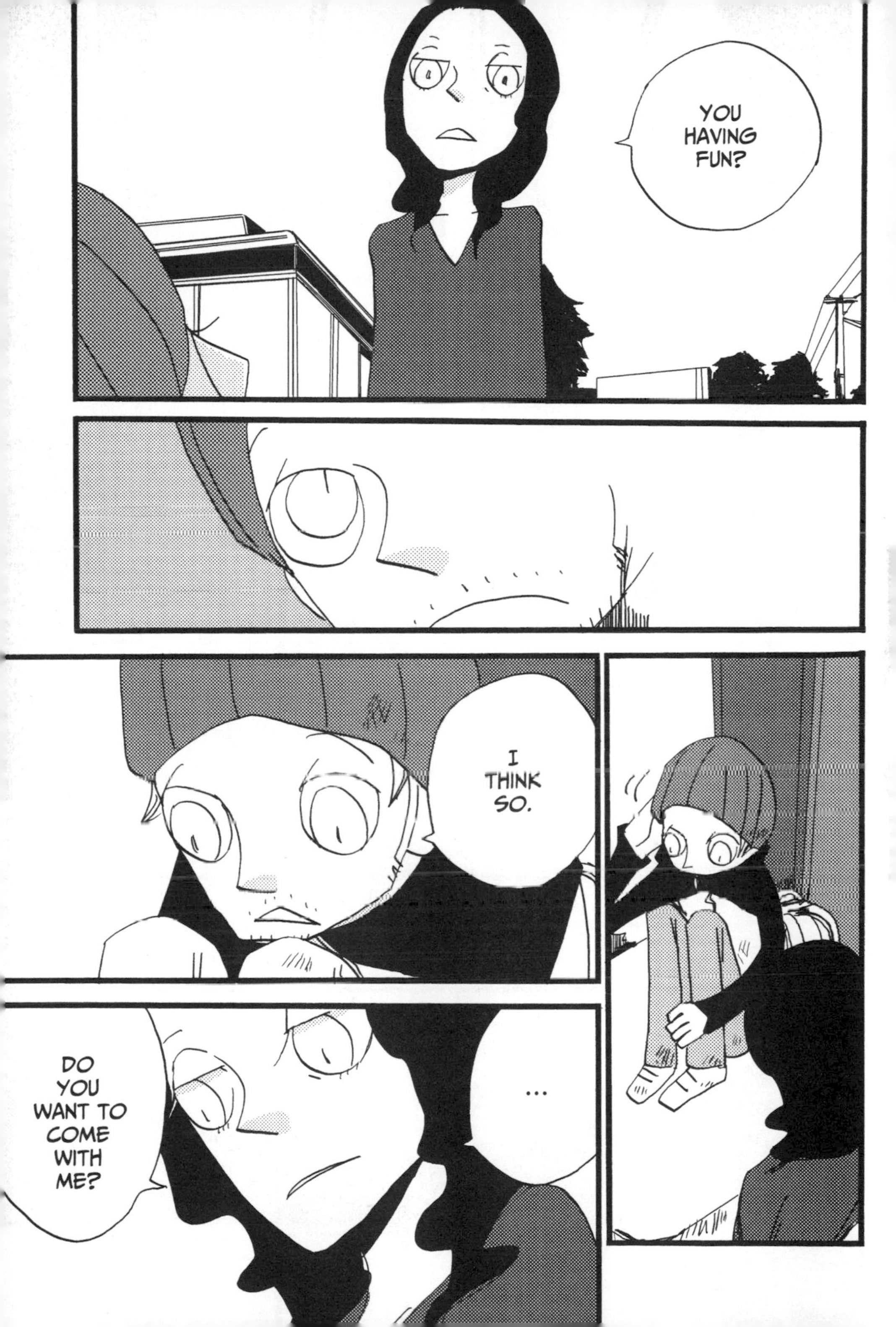
YOU HAVING FUN?
I THINK SO.
...
DO YOU WANT TO COME WITH ME?

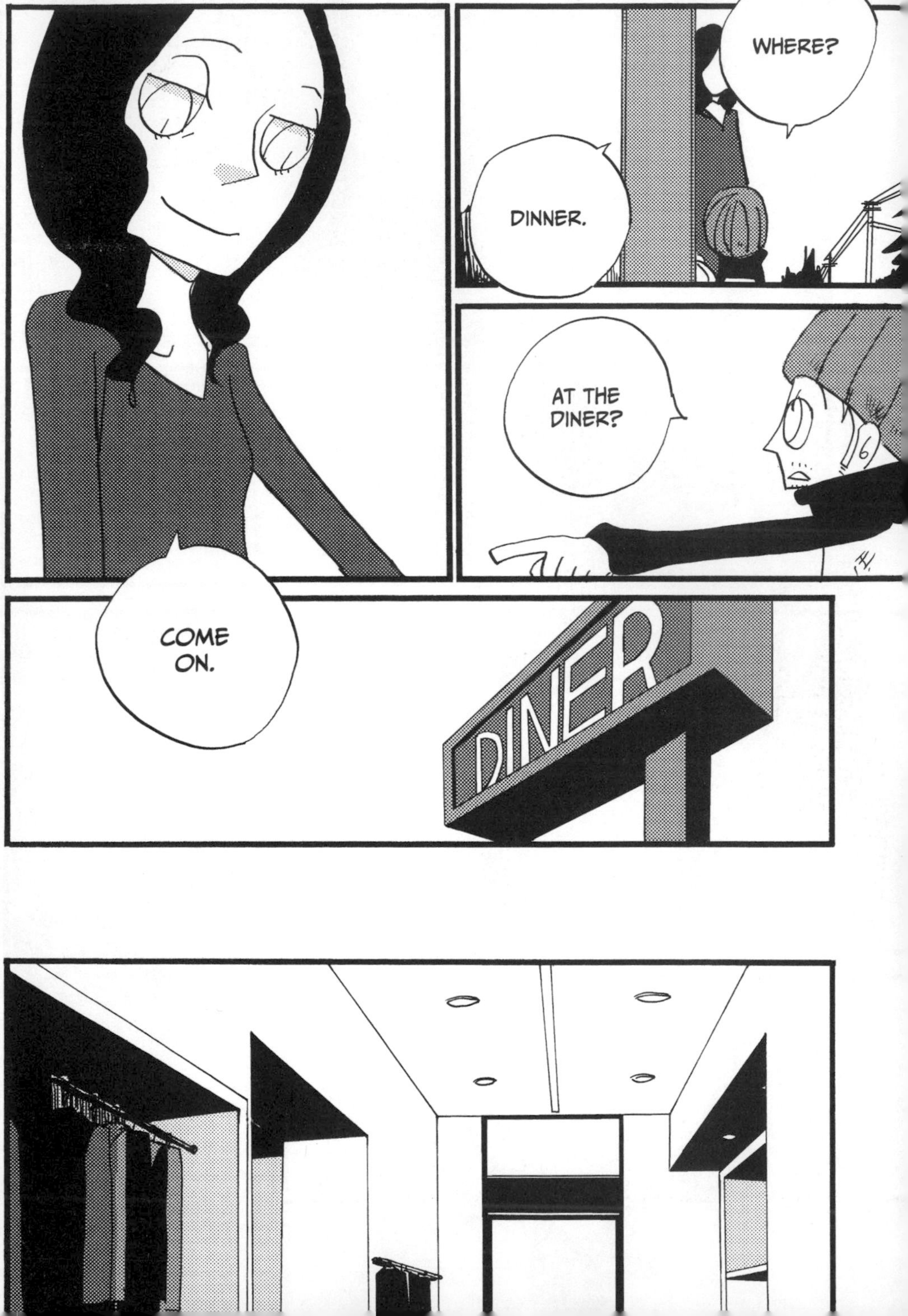
WHERE?
DINNER.
AT THE DINER?
COME ON.
DINER

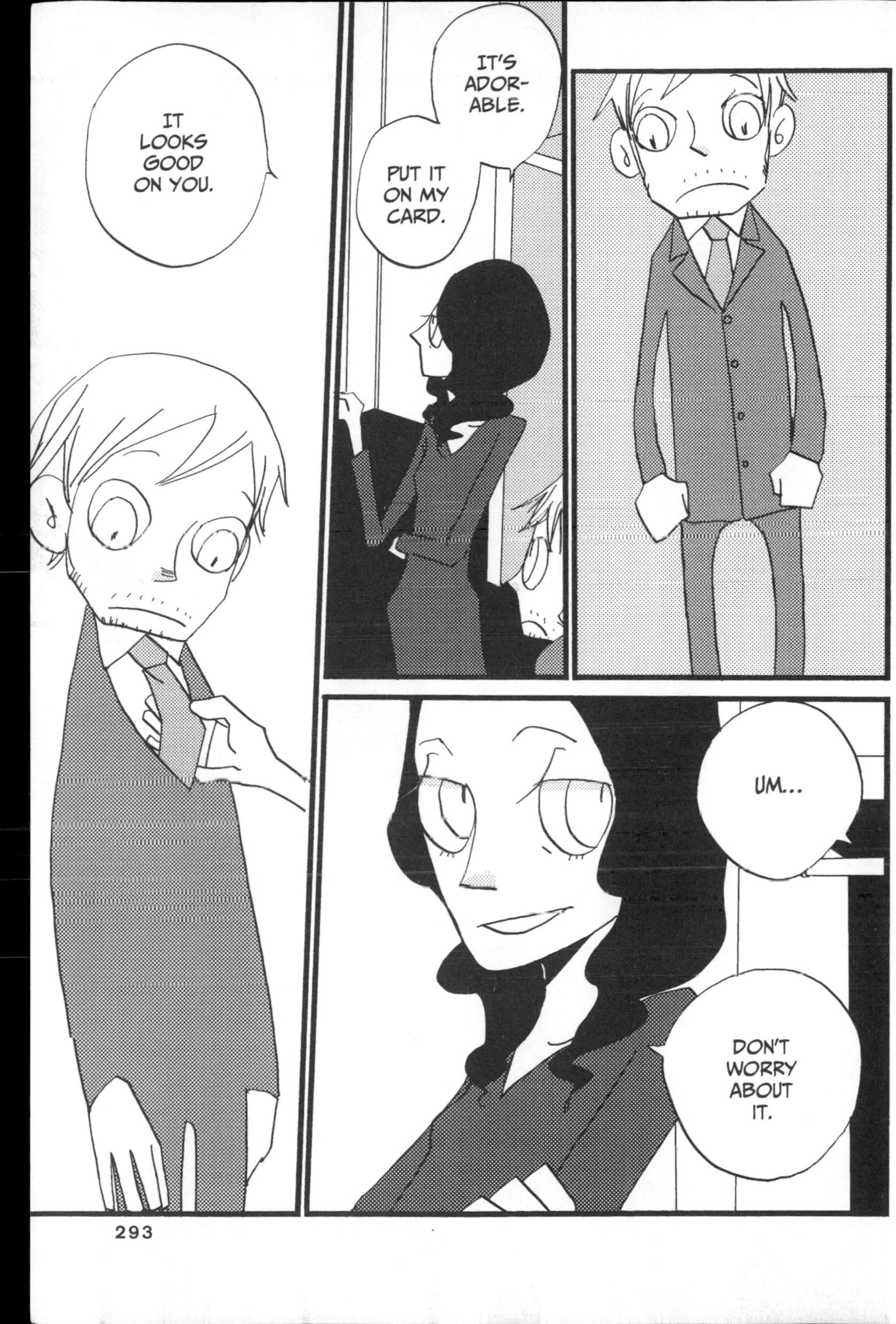
IT'S ADORABLE.
PUT IT ON MY CARD.
UM...
DON'T WORRY ABOUT IT.
IT LOOKS GOOD ON YOU.

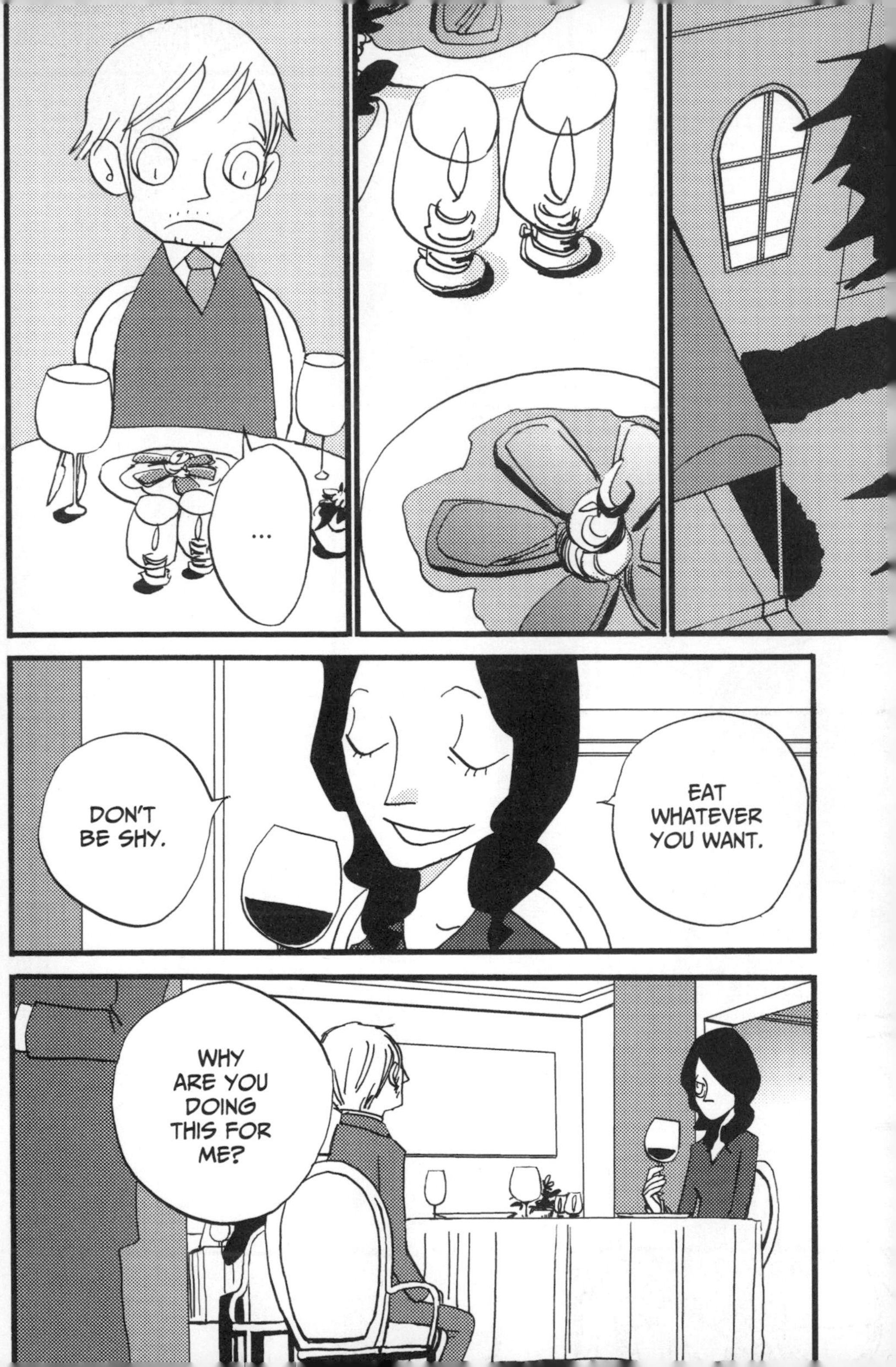
...
EAT WHATEVER YOU WANT.
DON'T BE SHY.
WHY ARE YOU DOING THIS FOR ME?

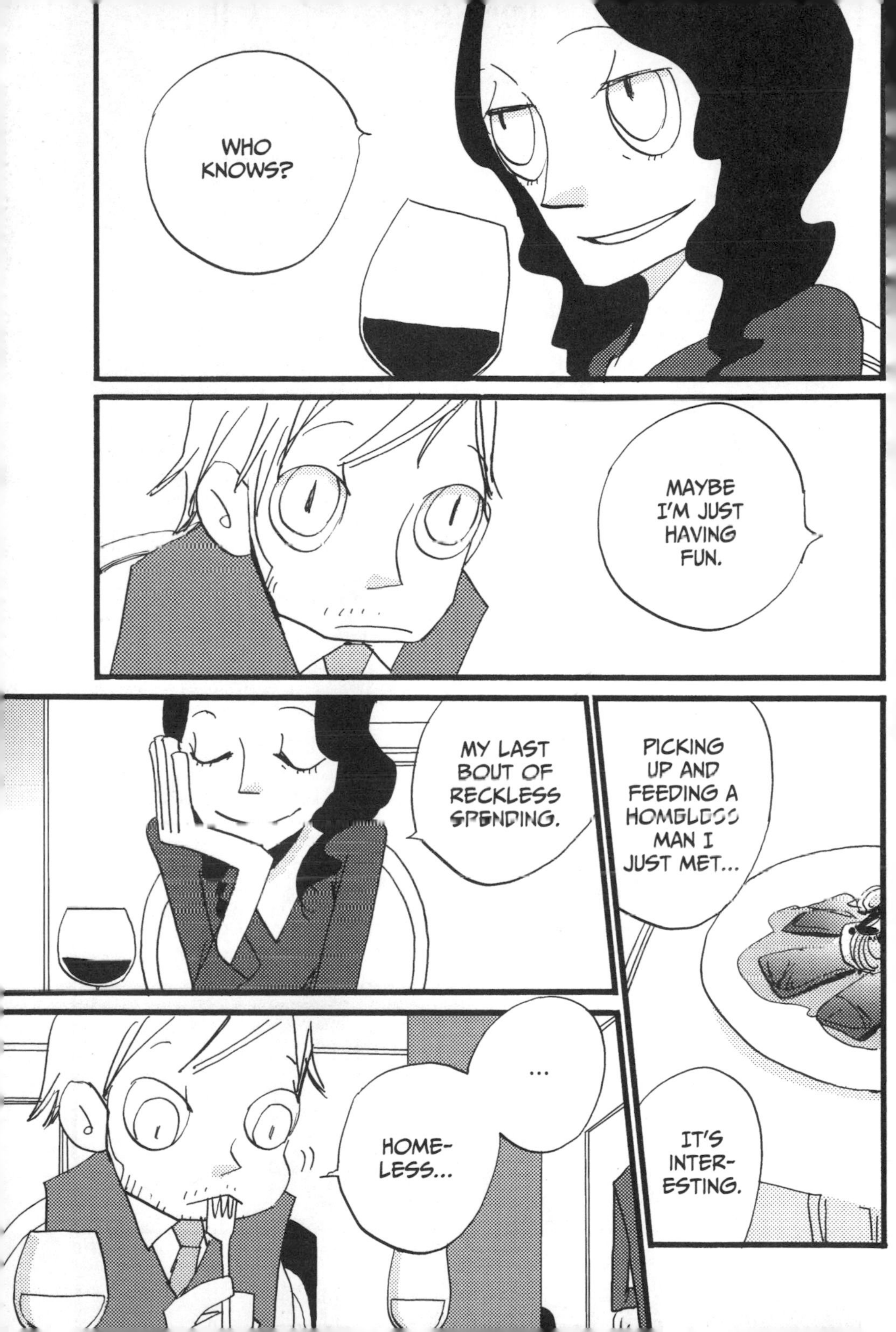
WHO KNOWS?
MAYBE I'M JUST HAVING FUN.
PICKING UP AND FEEDING A HOMELESS MAN I JUST MET...
IT'S INTER-ESTING.
MY LAST BOUT OF RECKLESS SPENDING.
...
HOME-LESS...

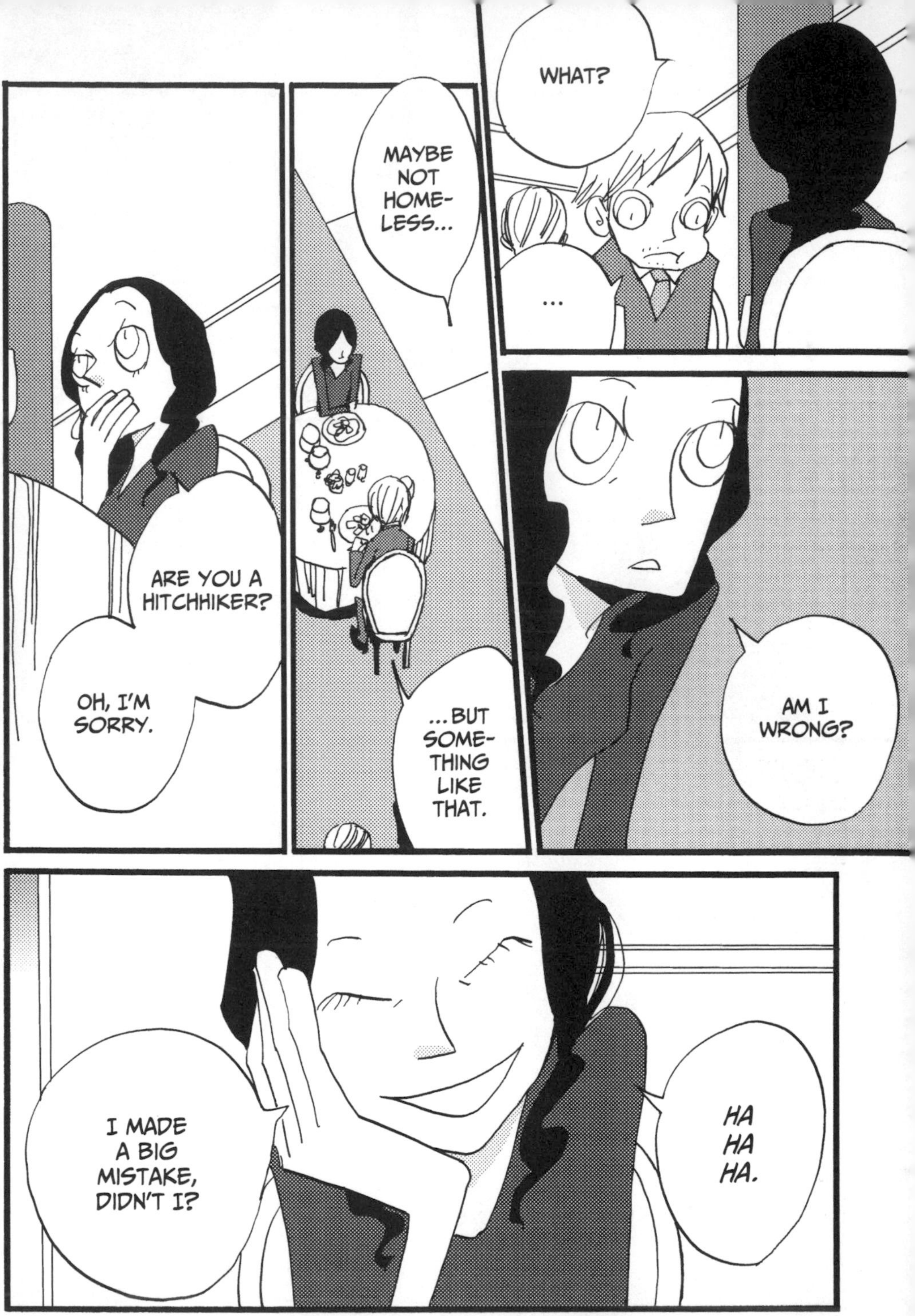
WHAT?
...
AM I WRONG?
MAYBE NOT HOMELESS...
...BUT SOMETHING LIKE THAT.
ARE YOU A HITCHHIKER?
OH, I'M SORRY.
HA HA HA.
I MADE A BIG MISTAKE, DIDN'T I?

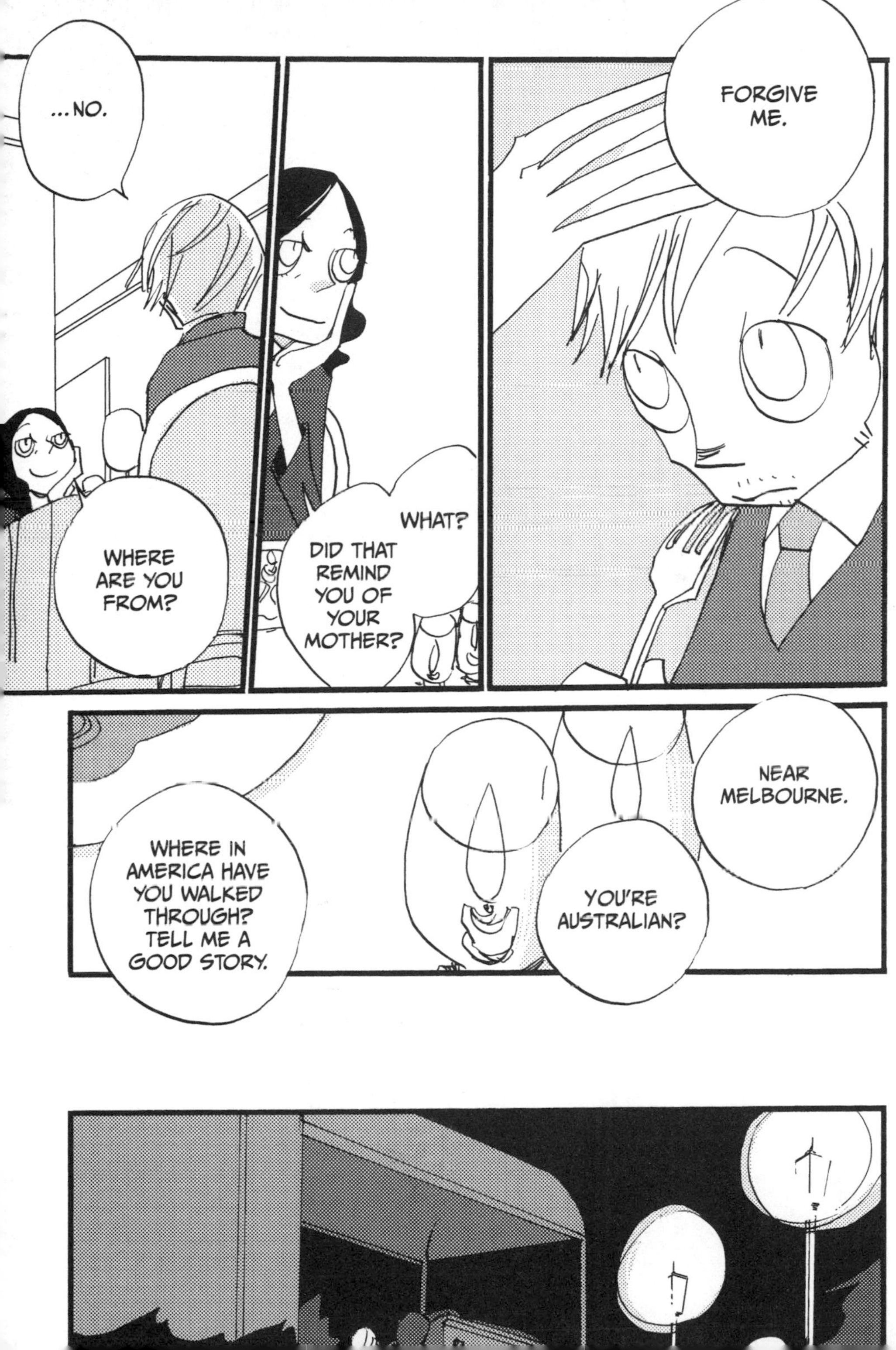
FORGIVE ME.
WHAT?
DID THAT REMIND YOU OF YOUR MOTHER?
...NO.
WHERE ARE YOU FROM?
NEAR MELBOURNE.
YOU'RE AUSTRALIAN?
WHERE IN AMERICA HAVE YOU WALKED THROUGH? TELL ME A GOOD STORY.

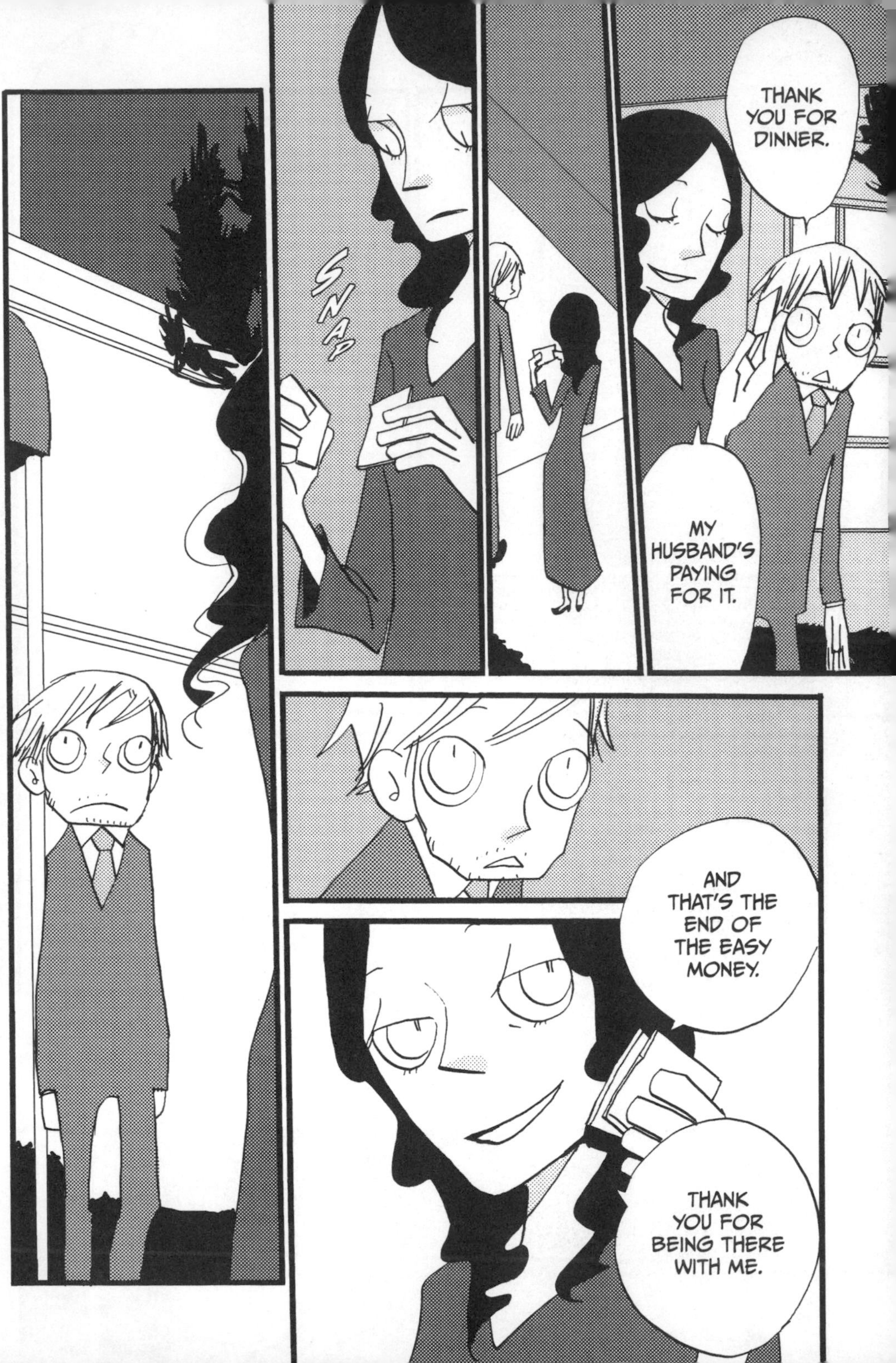
THANK YOU FOR DINNER.
MY HUSBAND'S PAYING FOR IT.
SNAP
AND THAT'S THE END OF THE EASY MONEY.
THANK YOU FOR BEING THERE WITH ME.

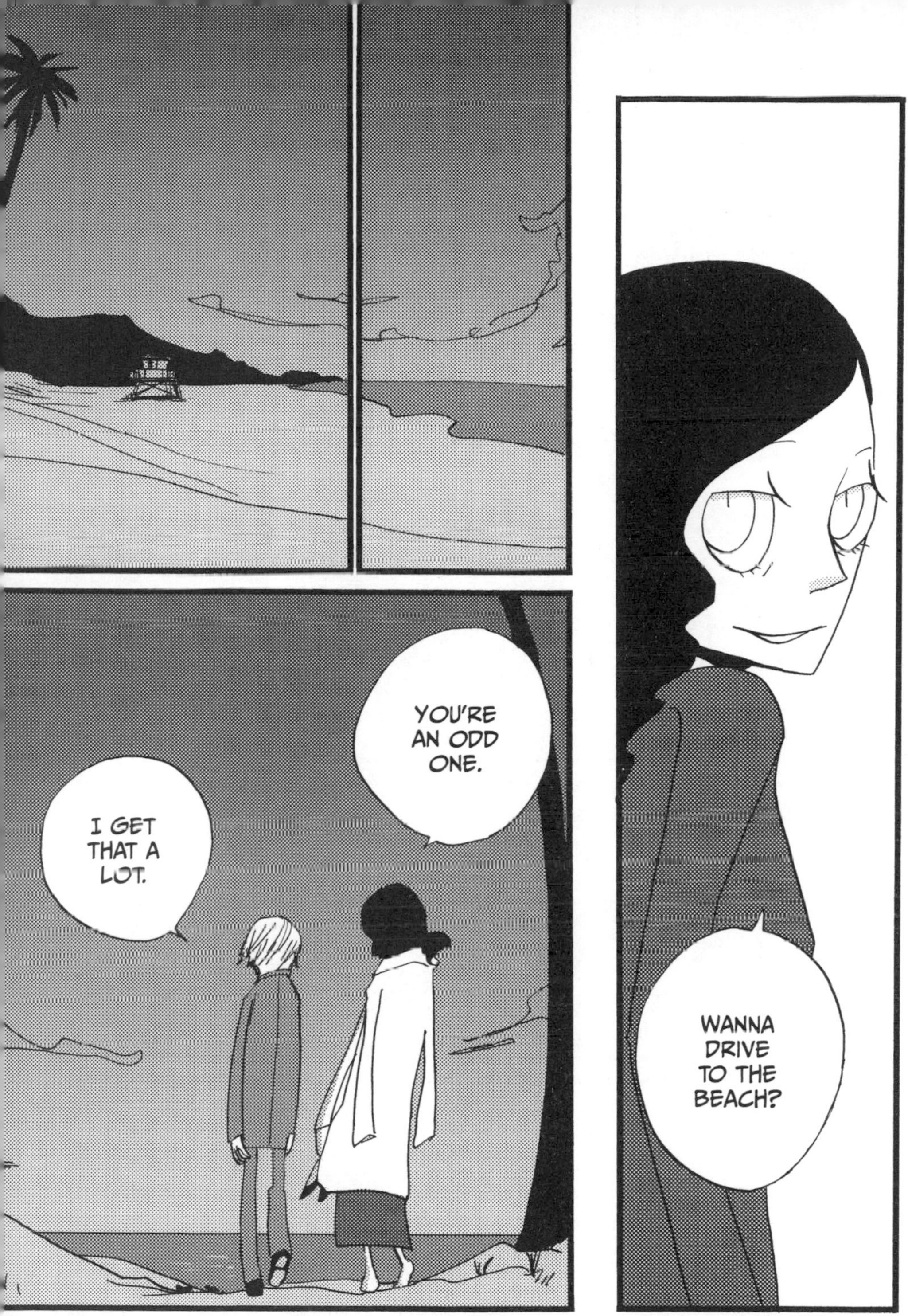
WANNA DRIVE TO THE BEACH?
YOU'RE AN ODD ONE.
I GET THAT A LOT.

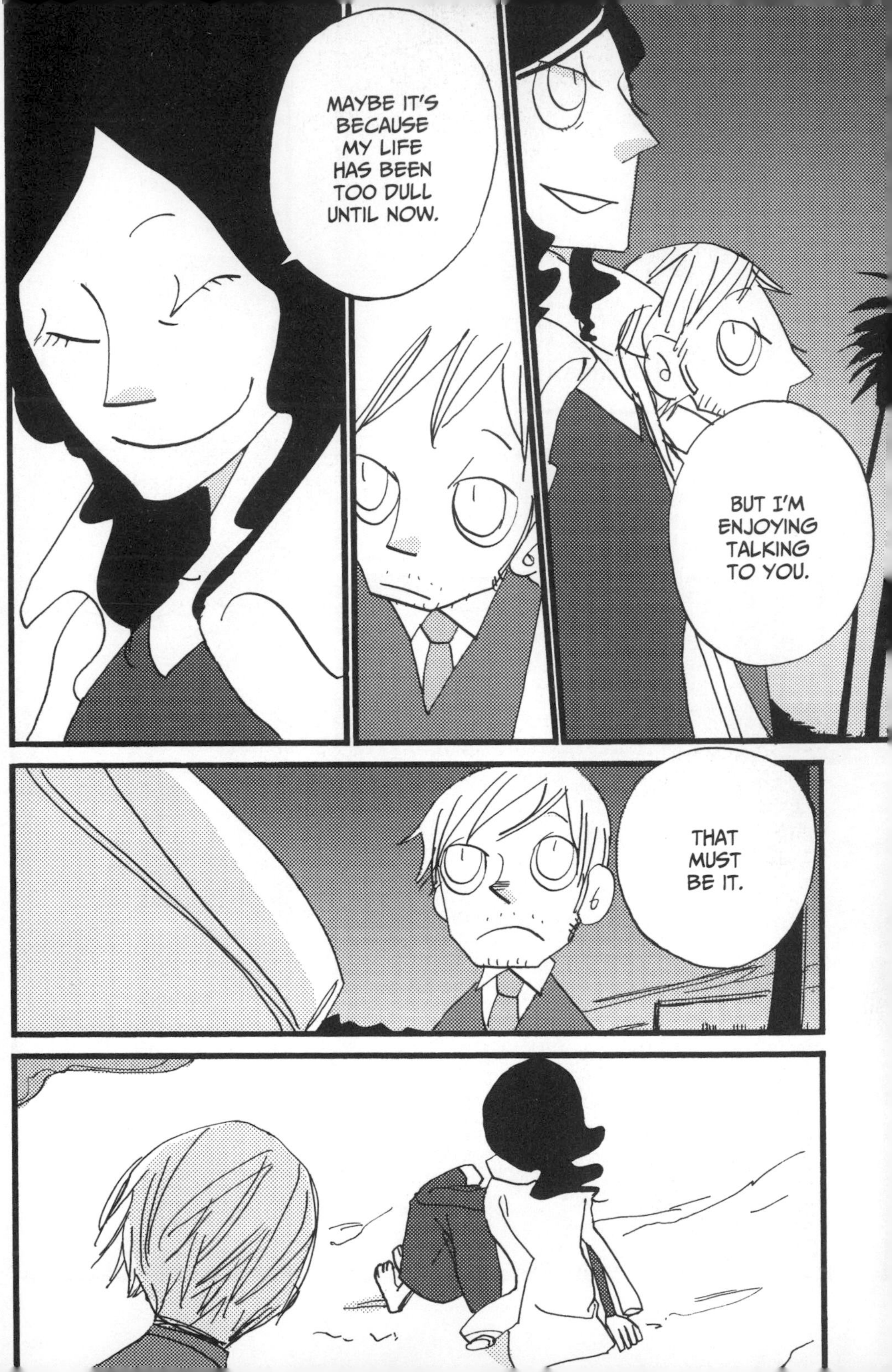
BUT I'M ENJOYING TALKING TO YOU.
MAYBE IT'S BECAUSE MY LIFE HAS BEEN TOO DULL UNTIL NOW.
THAT MUST BE IT.

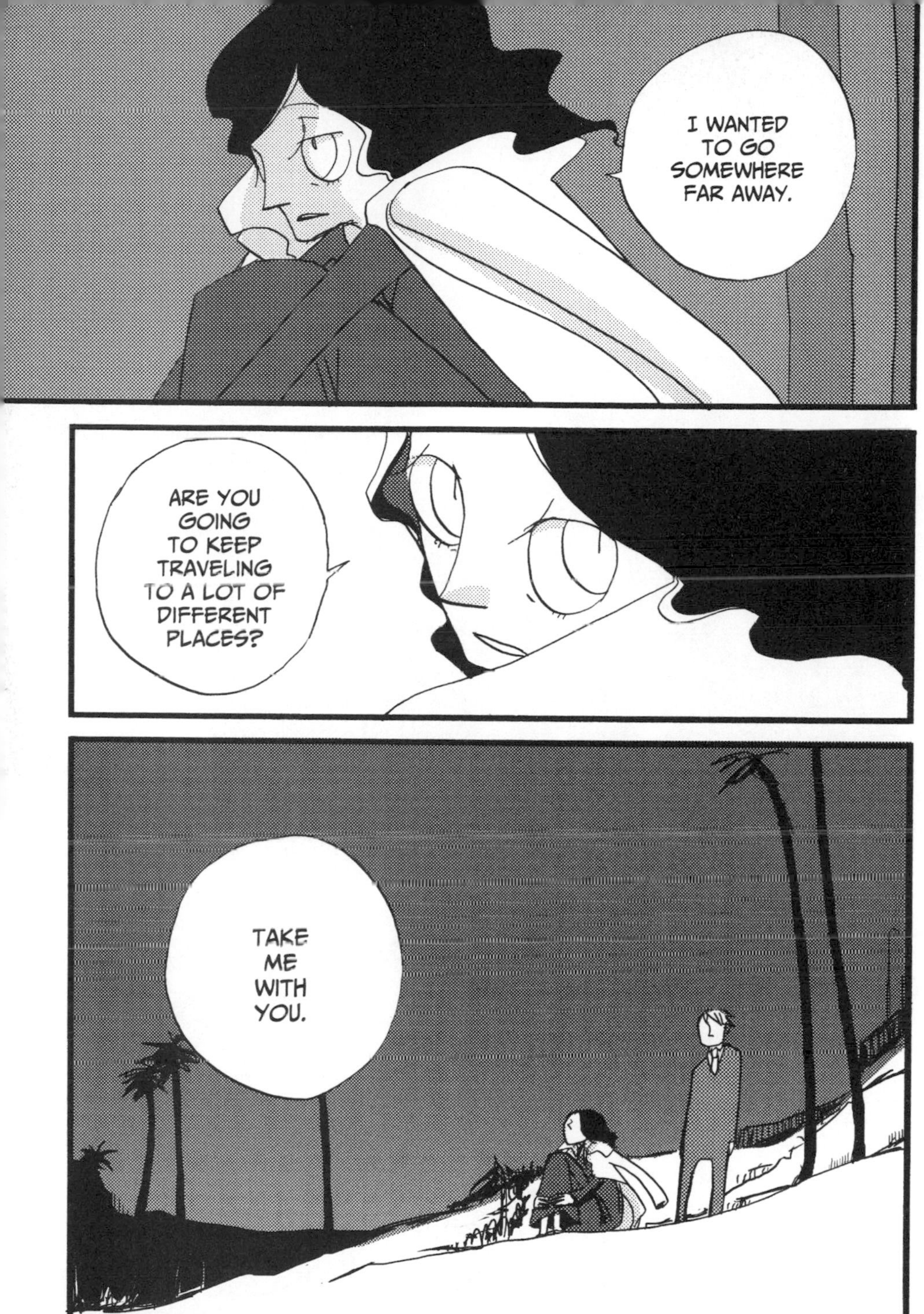
I WANTED TO GO SOMEWHERE FAR AWAY.
ARE YOU GOING TO KEEP TRAVELING TO A LOT OF DIFFERENT PLACES?
TAKE ME WITH YOU.

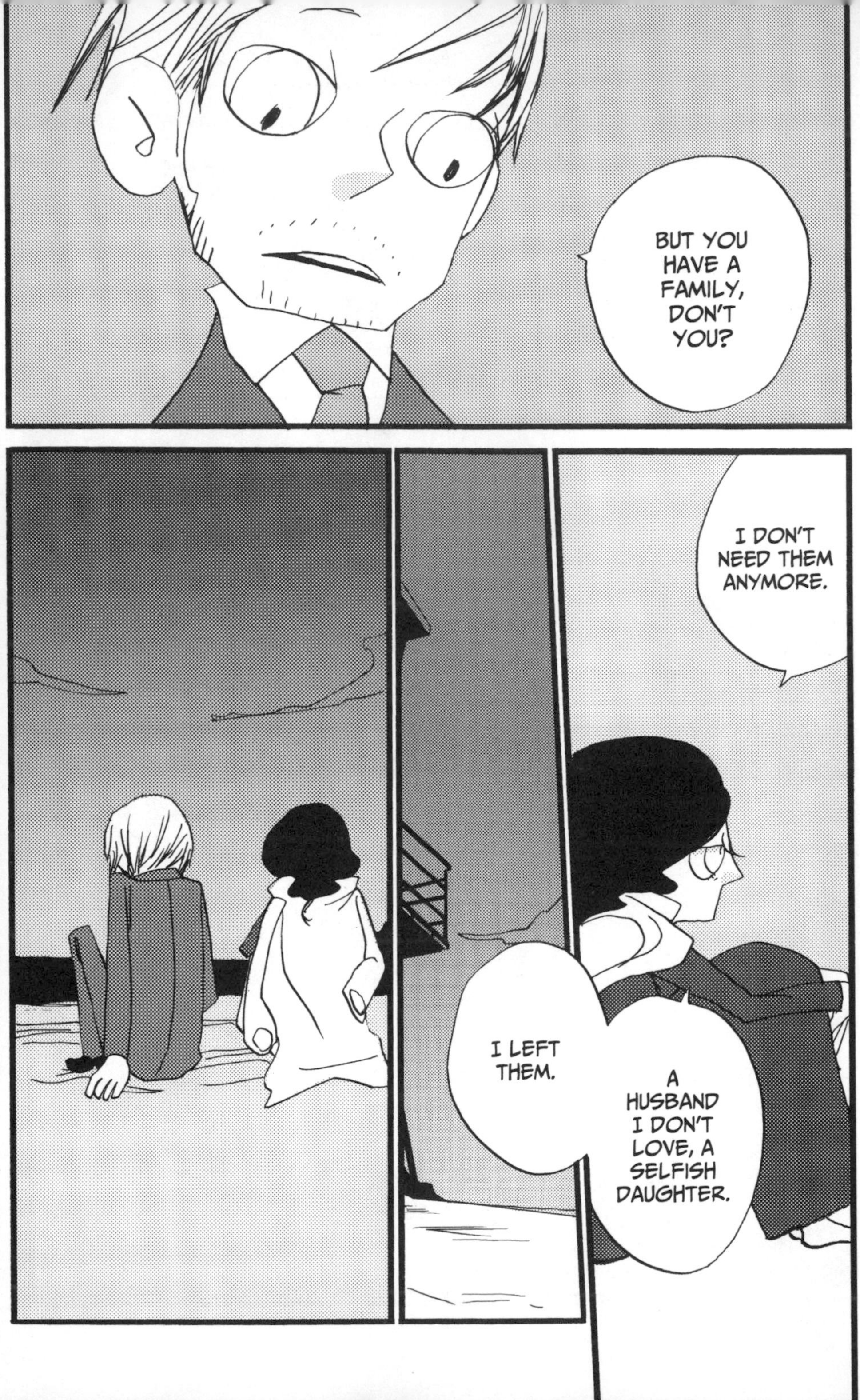
BUT YOU HAVE A FAMILY, DON'T YOU?
I DON'T NEED THEM ANYMORE.
I LEFT THEM.
A HUSBAND I DON'T LOVE, A SELFISH DAUGHTER.

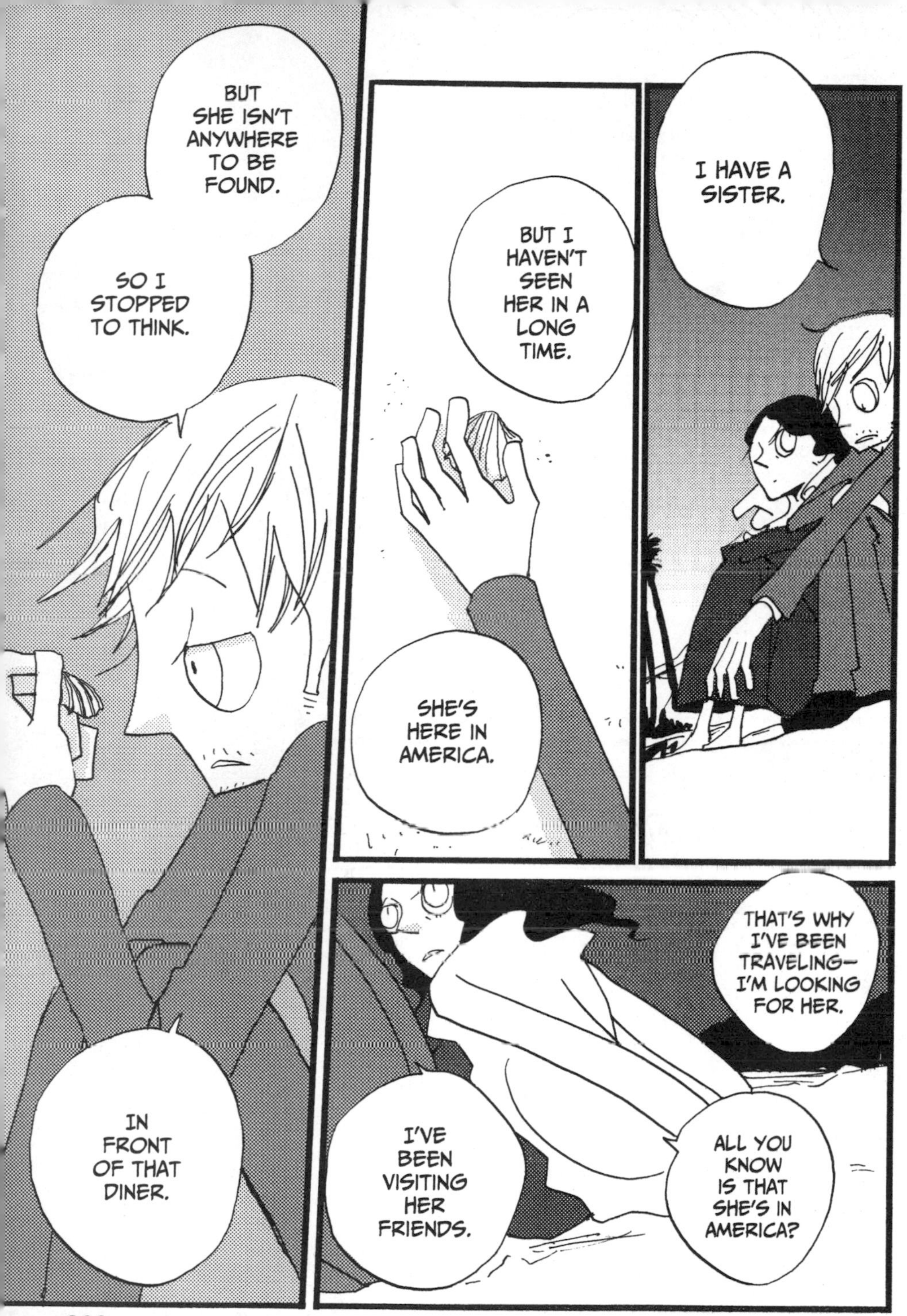
I HAVE A SISTER.
BUT I HAVEN'T SEEN HER IN A LONG TIME.
SHE'S HERE IN AMERICA.
THAT'S WHY I'VE BEEN TRAVELING— I'M LOOKING FOR HER.
ALL YOU KNOW IS THAT SHE'S IN AMERICA?
I'VE BEEN VISITING HER FRIENDS.
BUT SHE ISN'T ANYWHERE TO BE FOUND.
SO I STOPPED TO THINK.
IN FRONT OF THAT DINER.

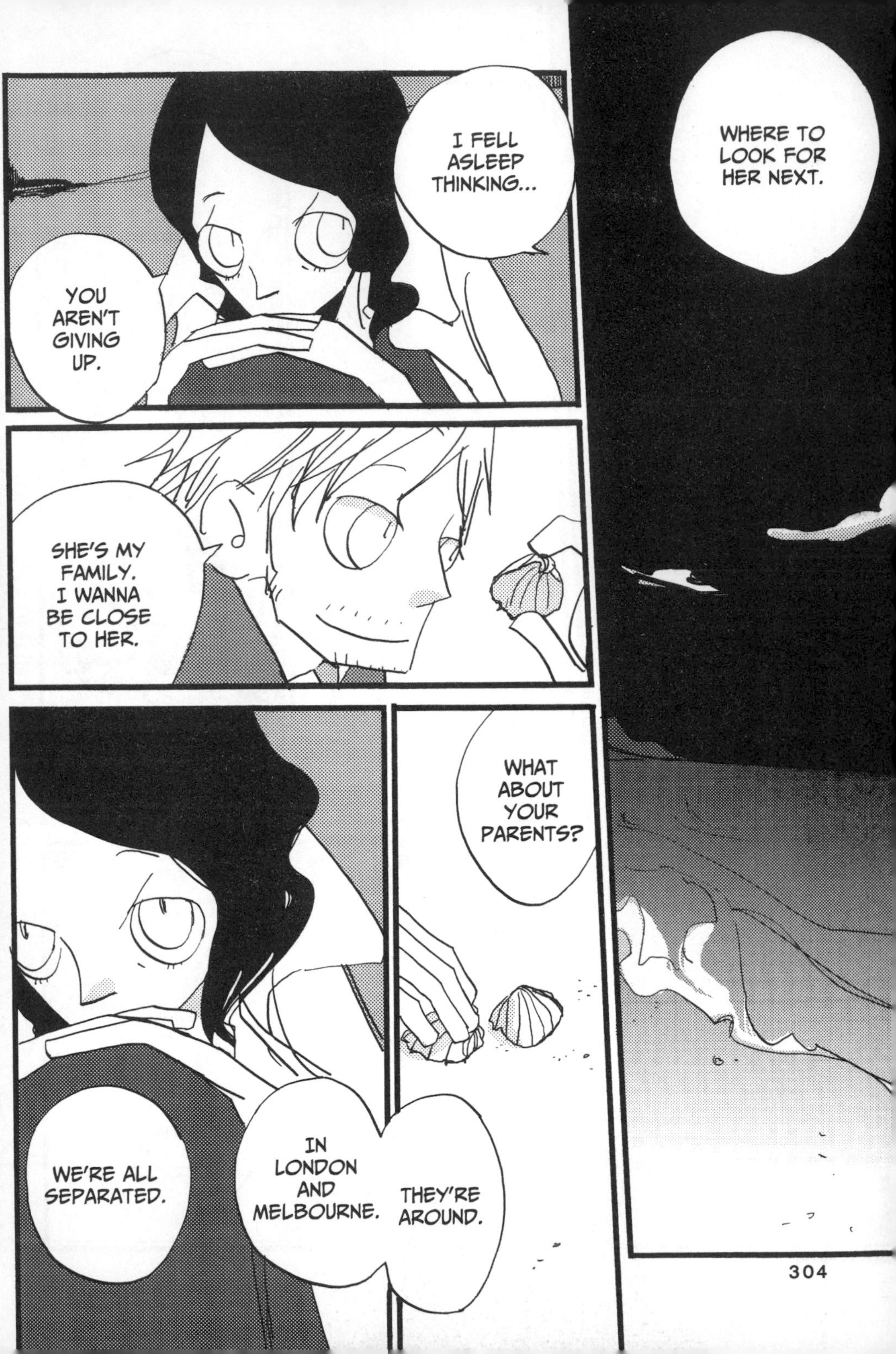
WHERE TO LOOK FOR HER NEXT.
I FELL ASLEEP THINKING...
YOU AREN'T GIVING UP.
SHE'S MY FAMILY. I WANNA BE CLOSE TO HER.
WHAT ABOUT YOUR PARENTS?
THEY'RE AROUND.
IN LONDON AND MELBOURNE.
WE'RE ALL SEPARATED.

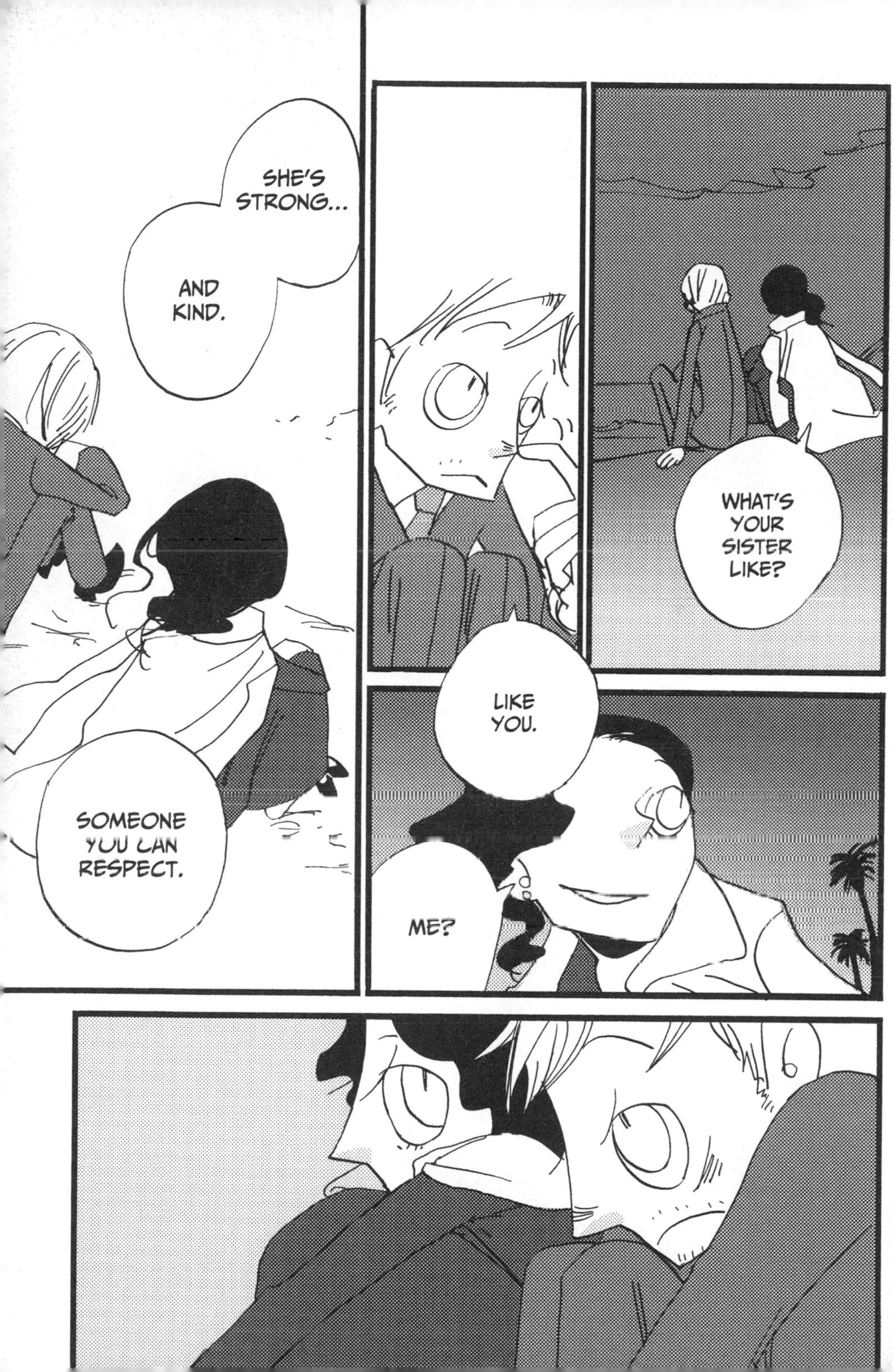
WHAT'S YOUR SISTER LIKE?
LIKE YOU.
ME?
SHE'S STRONG...
AND KIND.
SOMEONE YOU CAN RESPECT.

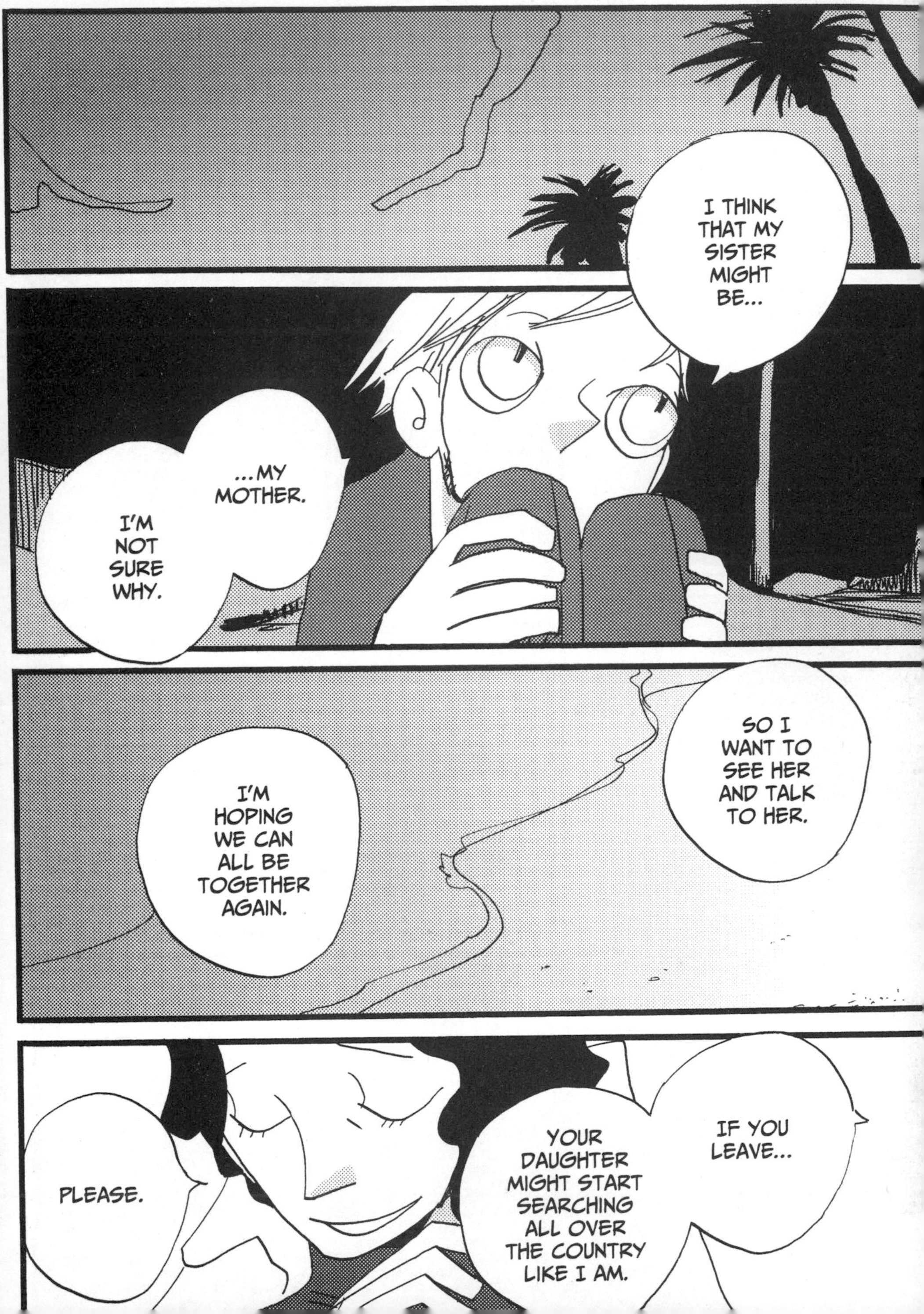
I THINK THAT MY SISTER MIGHT BE...
...MY MOTHER.
I'M NOT SURE WHY.
SO I WANT TO SEE HER AND TALK TO HER.
I'M HOPING WE CAN ALL BE TOGETHER AGAIN.
IF YOU LEAVE...
YOUR DAUGHTER MIGHT START SEARCHING ALL OVER THE COUNTRY LIKE I AM.
PLEASE.

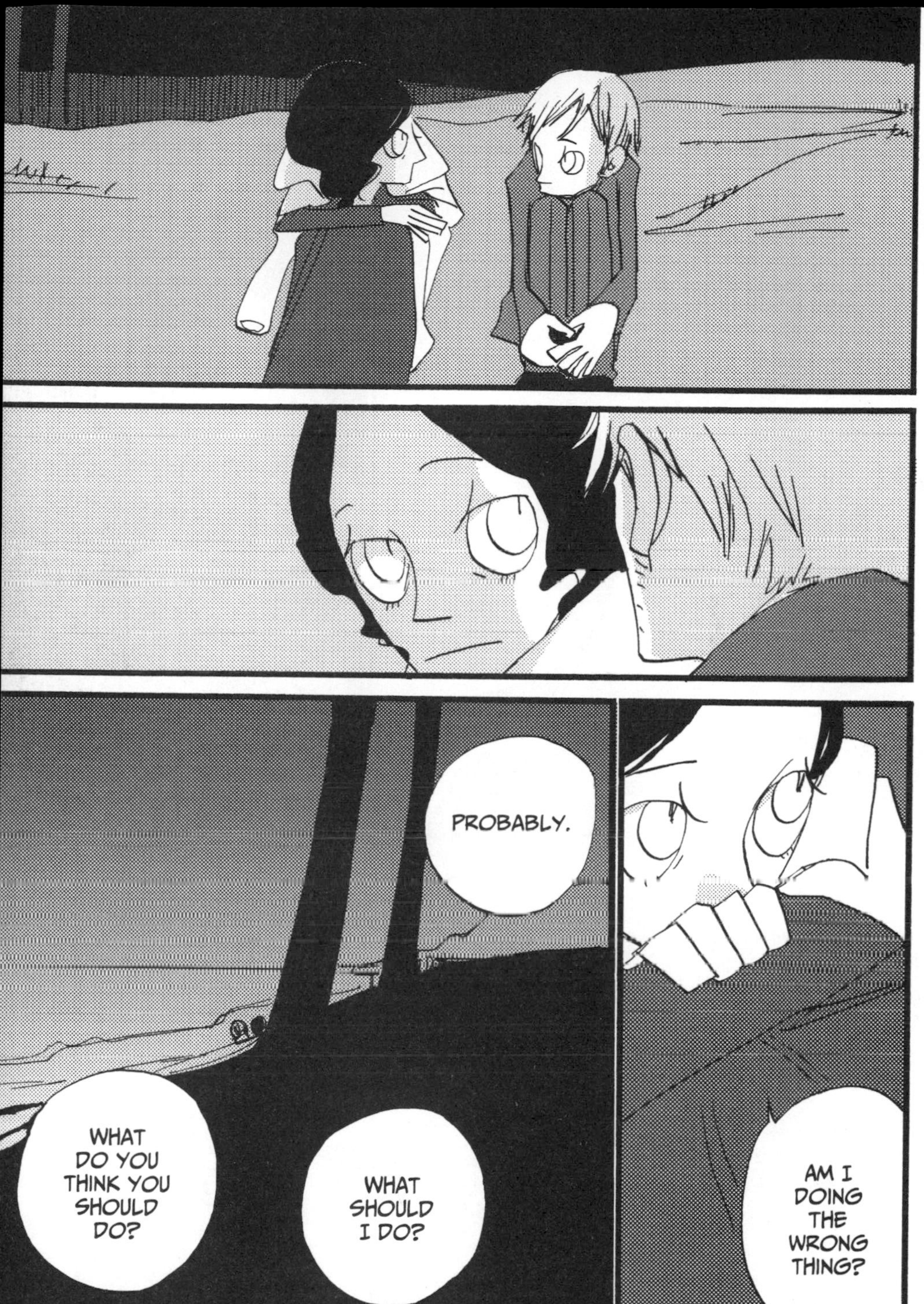
AM I DOING THE WRONG THING?
PROBABLY.
WHAT SHOULD I DO?
WHAT DO YOU THINK YOU SHOULD DO?

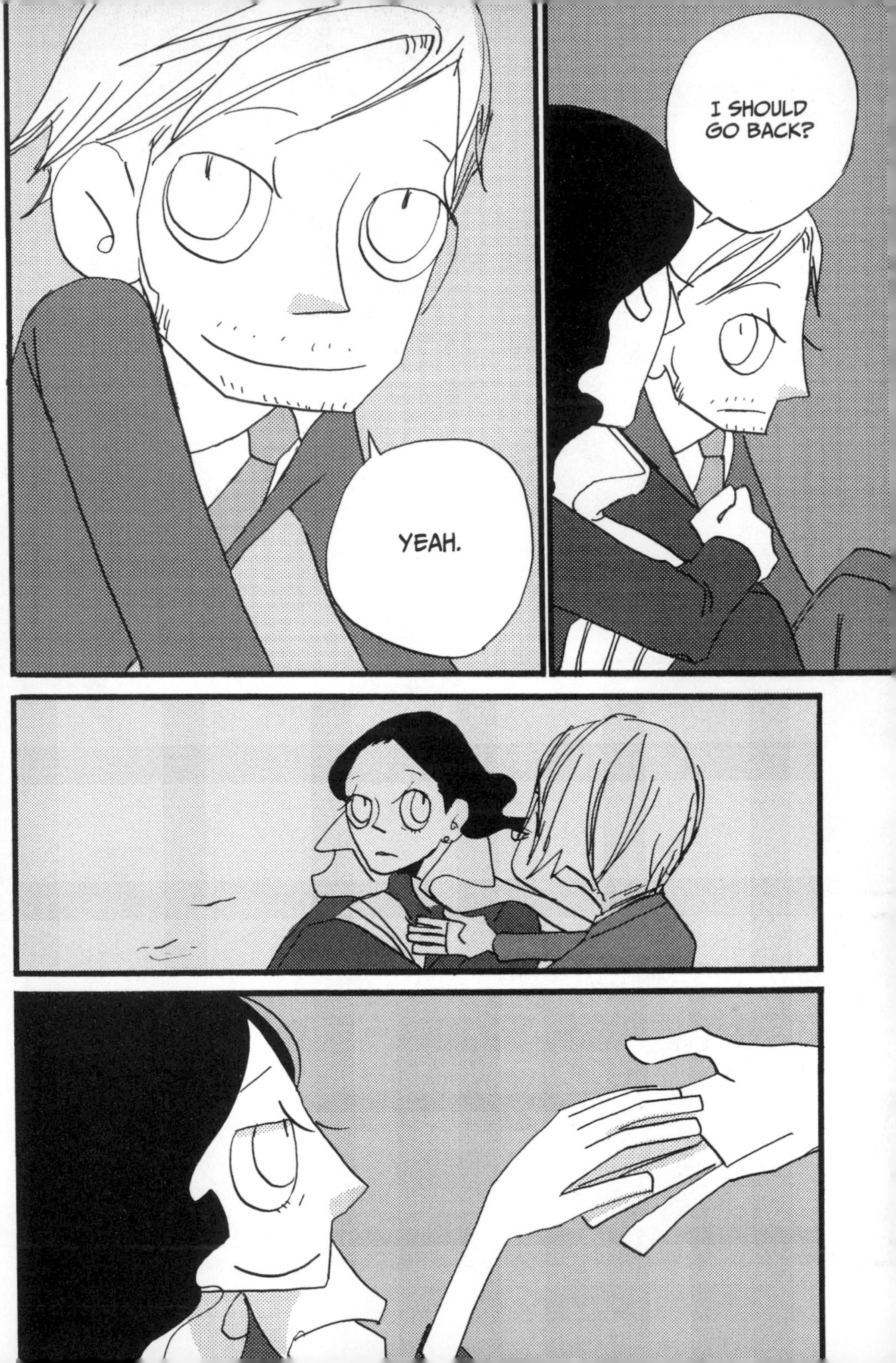
I SHOULD GO BACK?
YEAH.

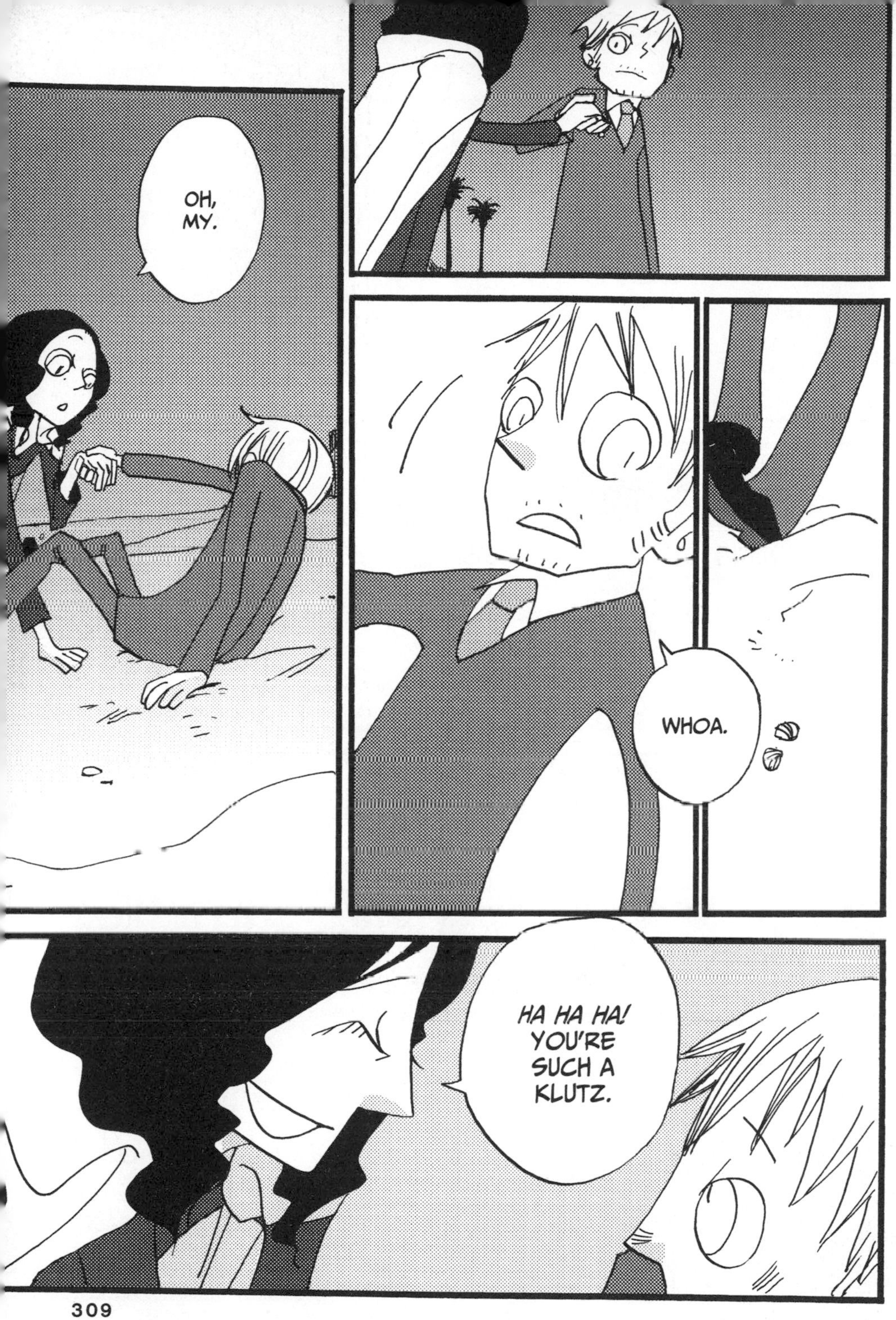
WHOA.
OH, MY.
HA HA HA! YOU'RE SUCH A KLUTZ.

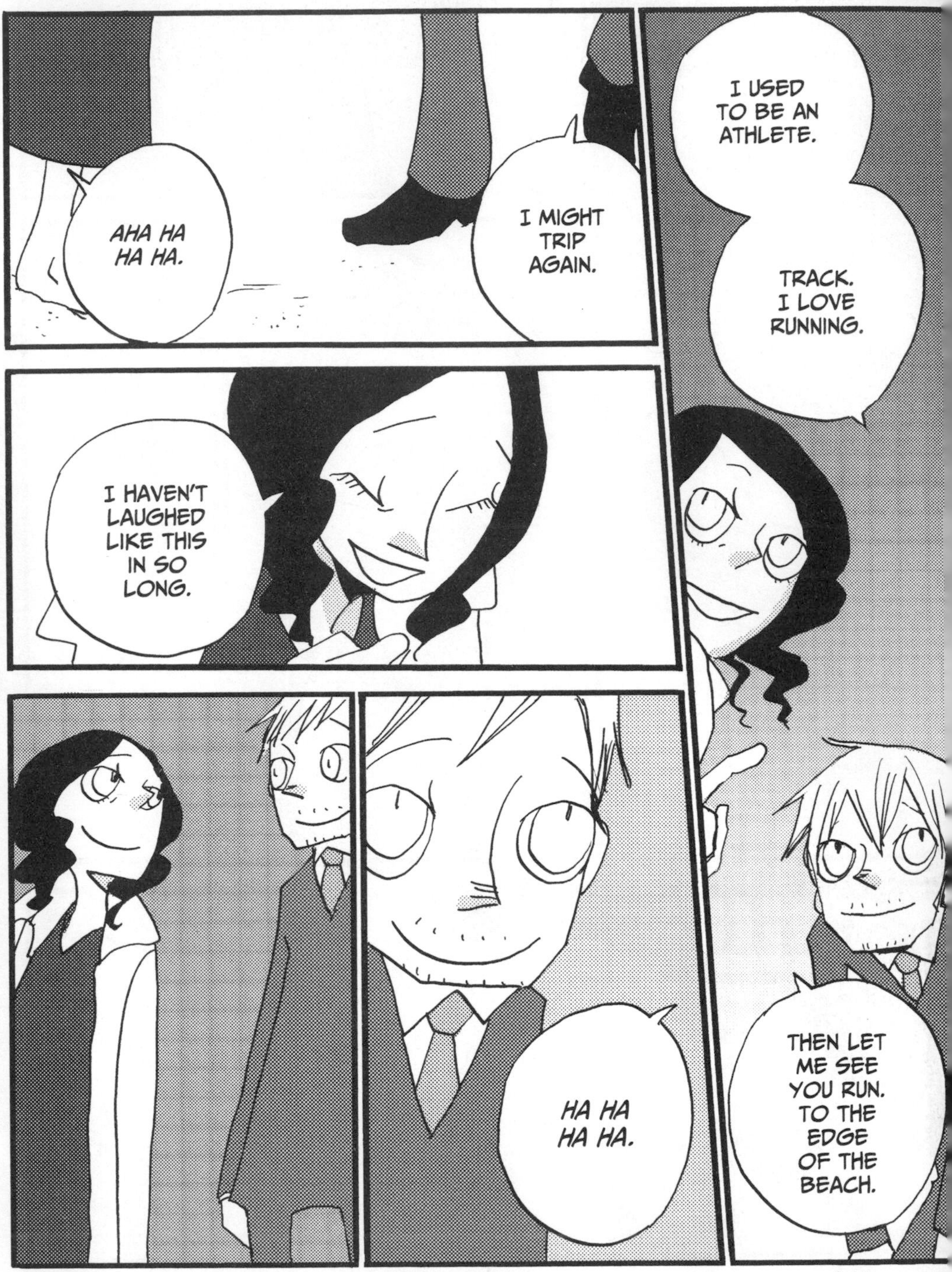
I USED TO BE AN ATHLETE.
TRACK. I LOVE RUNNING.
THEN LET ME SEE YOU RUN. TO THE EDGE OF THE BEACH.
I MIGHT TRIP AGAIN.
AHA HA HA HA.
I HAVEN'T LAUGHED LIKE THIS IN SO LONG.
HA HA HA HA.

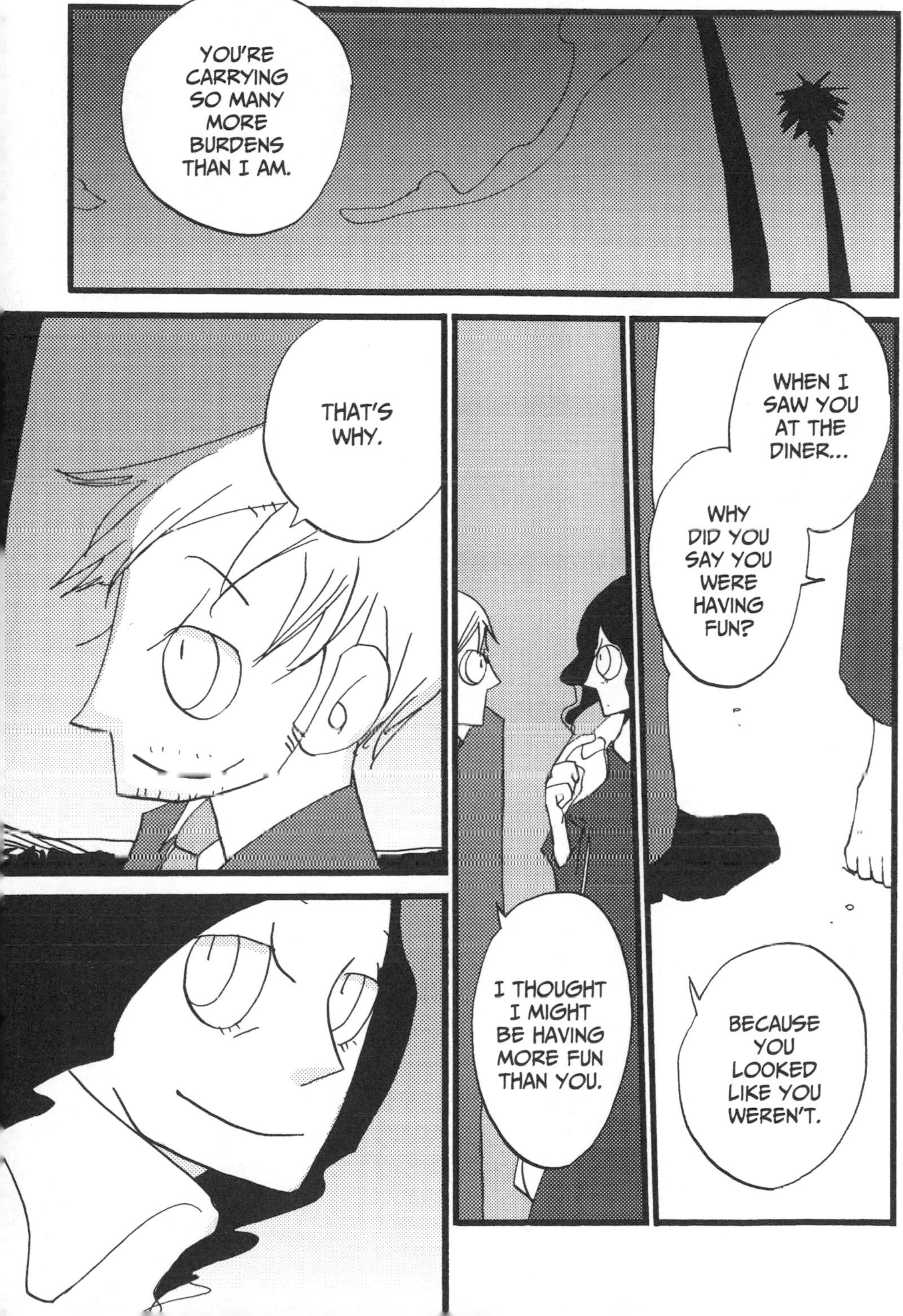
YOU'RE CARRYING SO MANY MORE BURDENS THAN I AM.
WHEN I SAW YOU AT THE DINER...
WHY DID YOU SAY YOU WERE HAVING FUN?
BECAUSE YOU LOOKED LIKE YOU WEREN'T.
I THOUGHT I MIGHT BE HAVING MORE FUN THAN YOU.
THAT'S WHY.

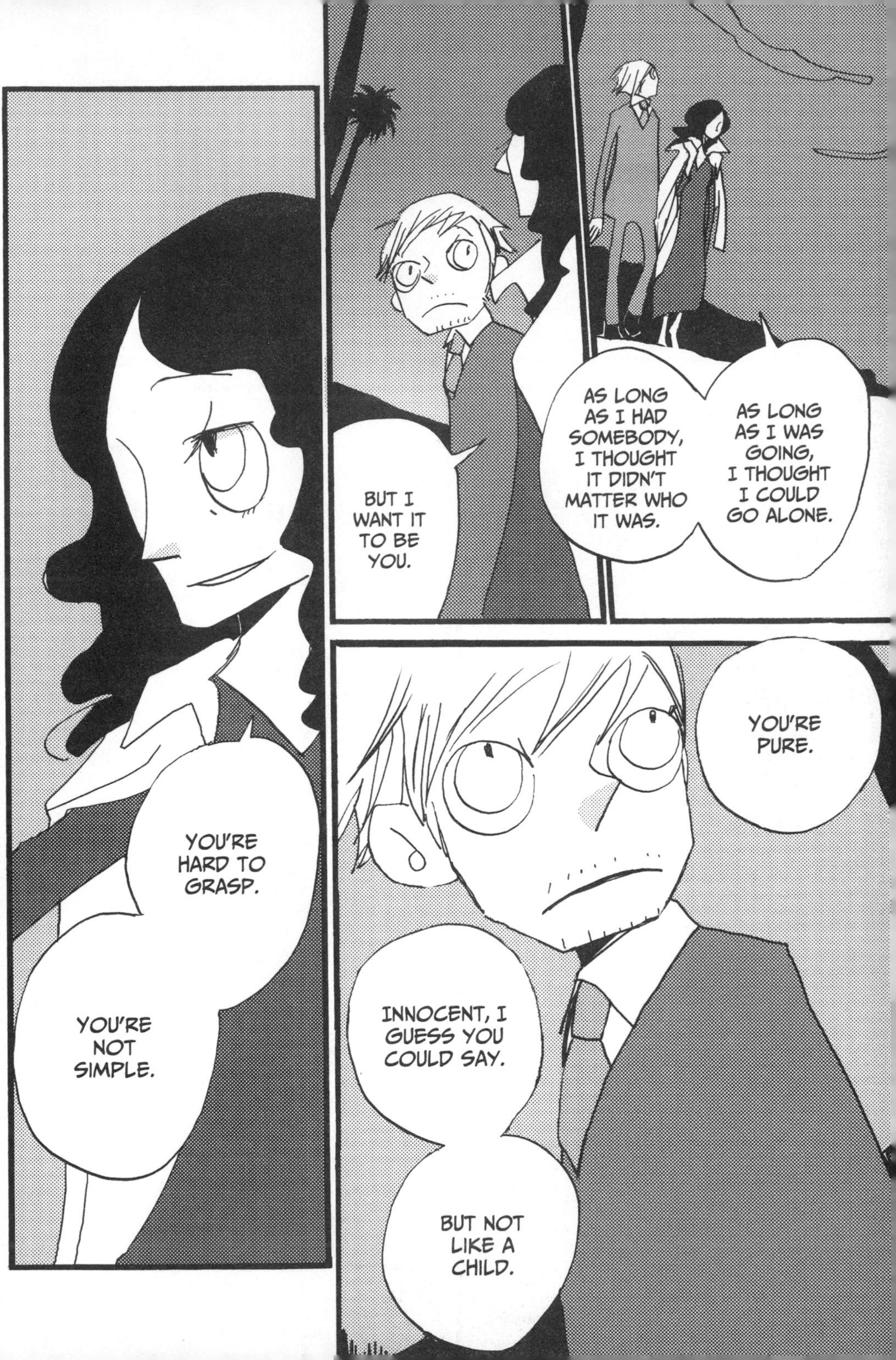
AS LONG AS I WAS GOING, I THOUGHT I COULD GO ALONE.
AS LONG AS I HAD SOMEBODY, I THOUGHT IT DIDN'T MATTER WHO IT WAS.
BUT I WANT IT TO BE YOU.
YOU'RE PURE.
INNOCENT, I GUESS YOU COULD SAY.
BUT NOT LIKE A CHILD.
YOU'RE HARD TO GRASP.
YOU'RE NOT SIMPLE.

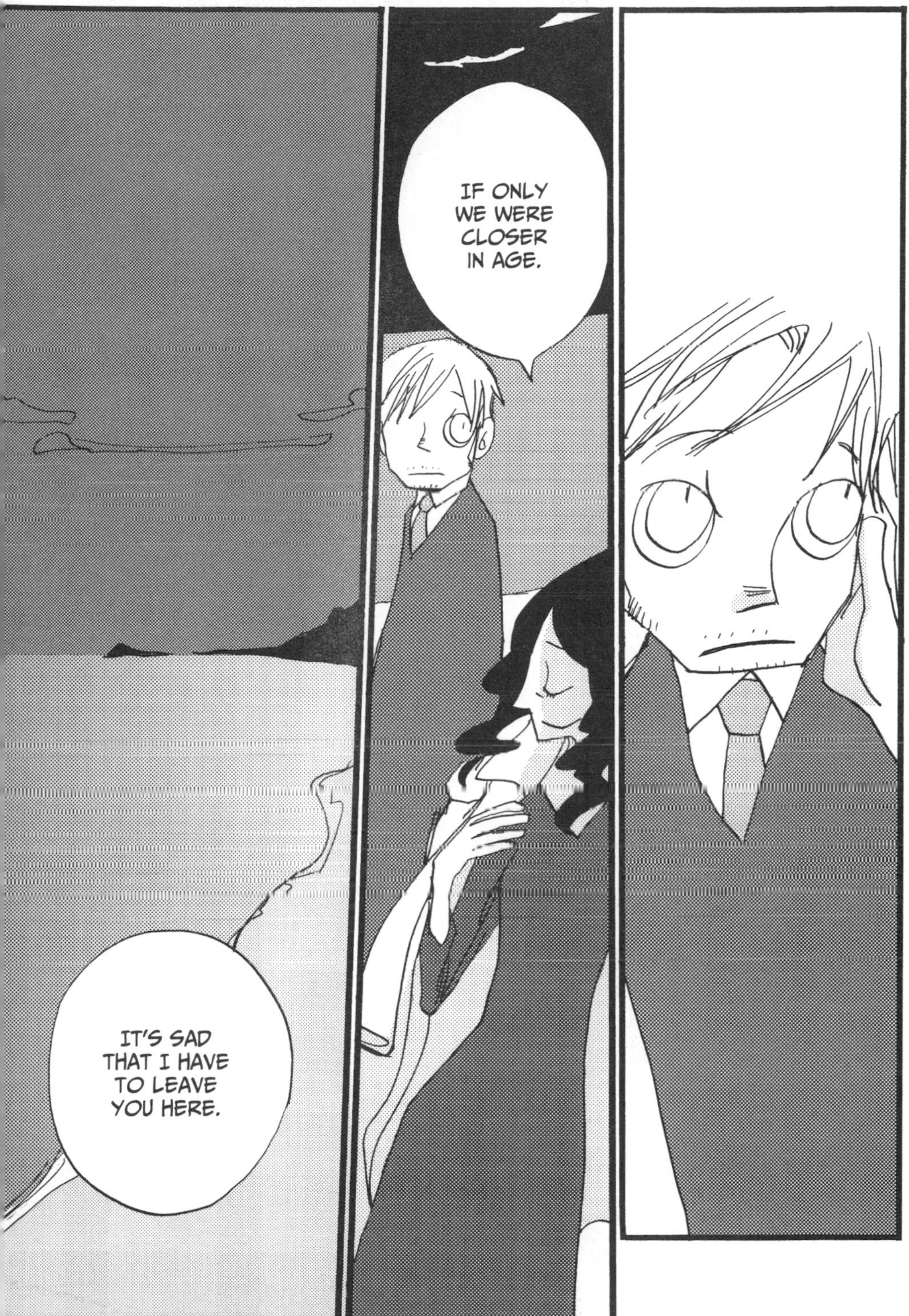
IF ONLY WE WERE CLOSER IN AGE.
IT'S SAD THAT I HAVE TO LEAVE YOU HERE.

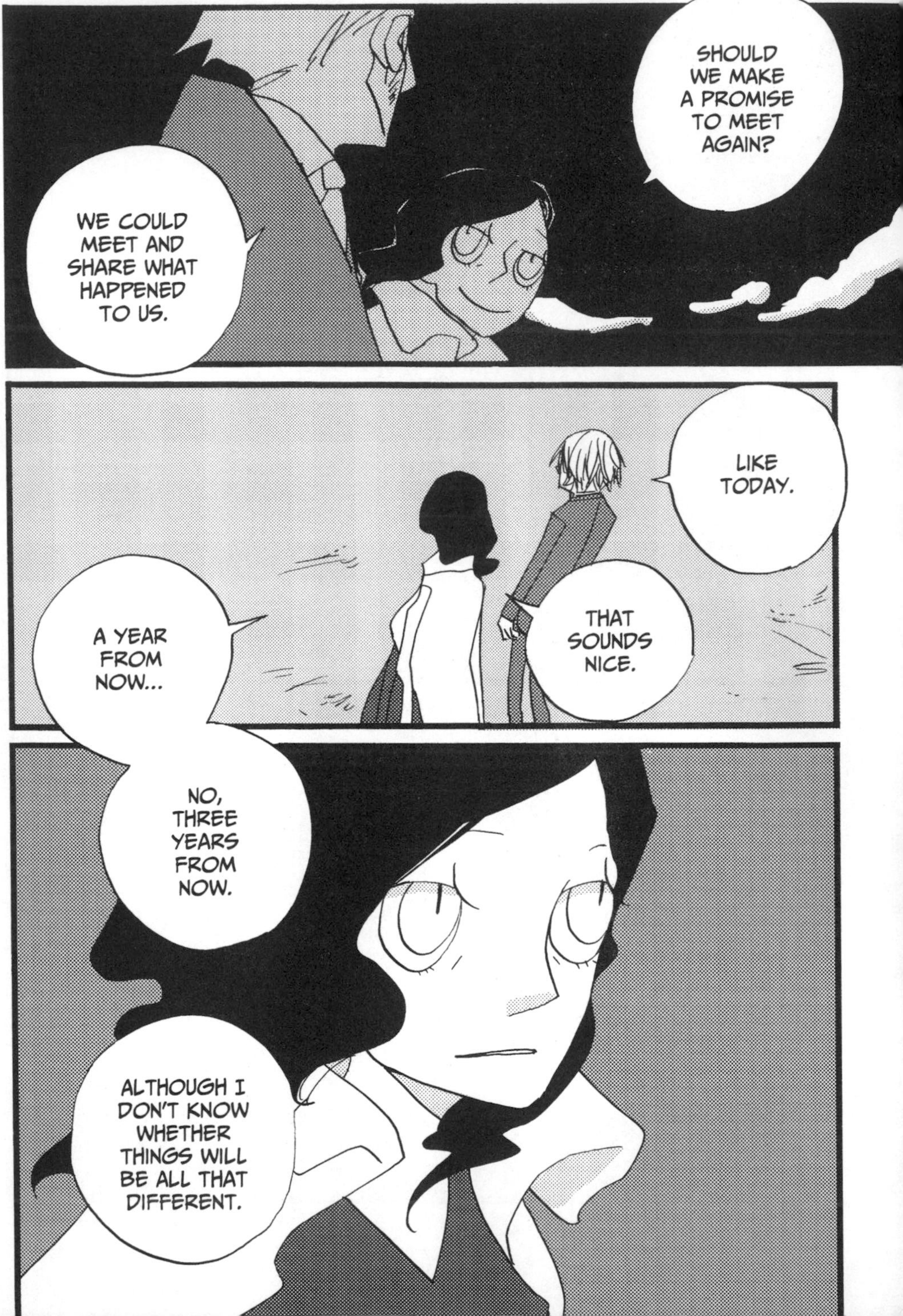
SHOULD WE MAKE A PROMISE TO MEET AGAIN?
WE COULD MEET AND SHARE WHAT HAPPENED TO US.
LIKE TODAY.
THAT SOUNDS NICE.
A YEAR FROM NOW...
NO, THREE YEARS FROM NOW.
ALTHOUGH I DON'T KNOW WHETHER THINGS WILL BE ALL THAT DIFFERENT.

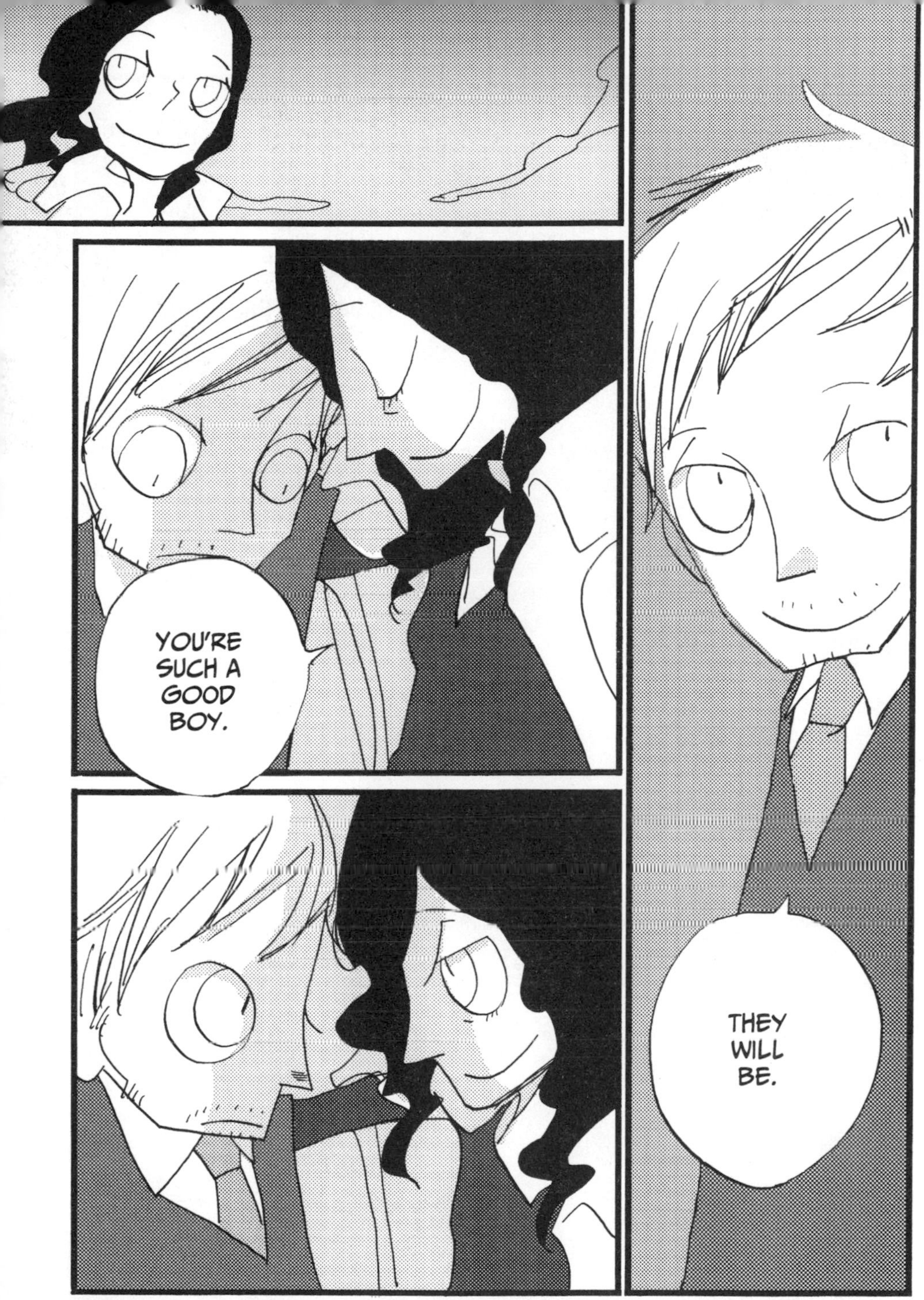
THEY WILL BE.
YOU'RE SUCH A GOOD BOY.

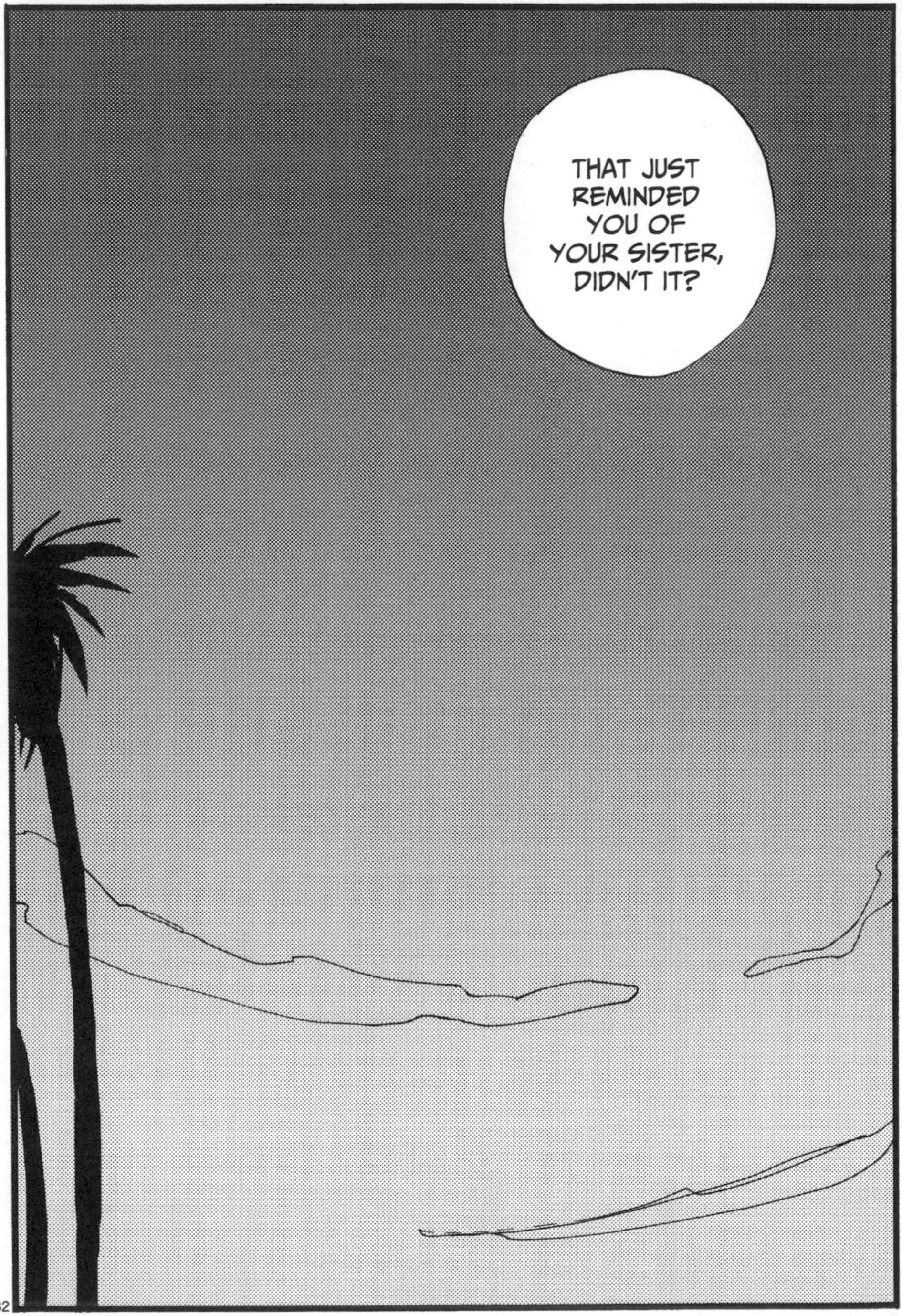
THAT JUST REMINDED YOU OF YOUR SISTER, DIDN'T IT?
32

end not simple

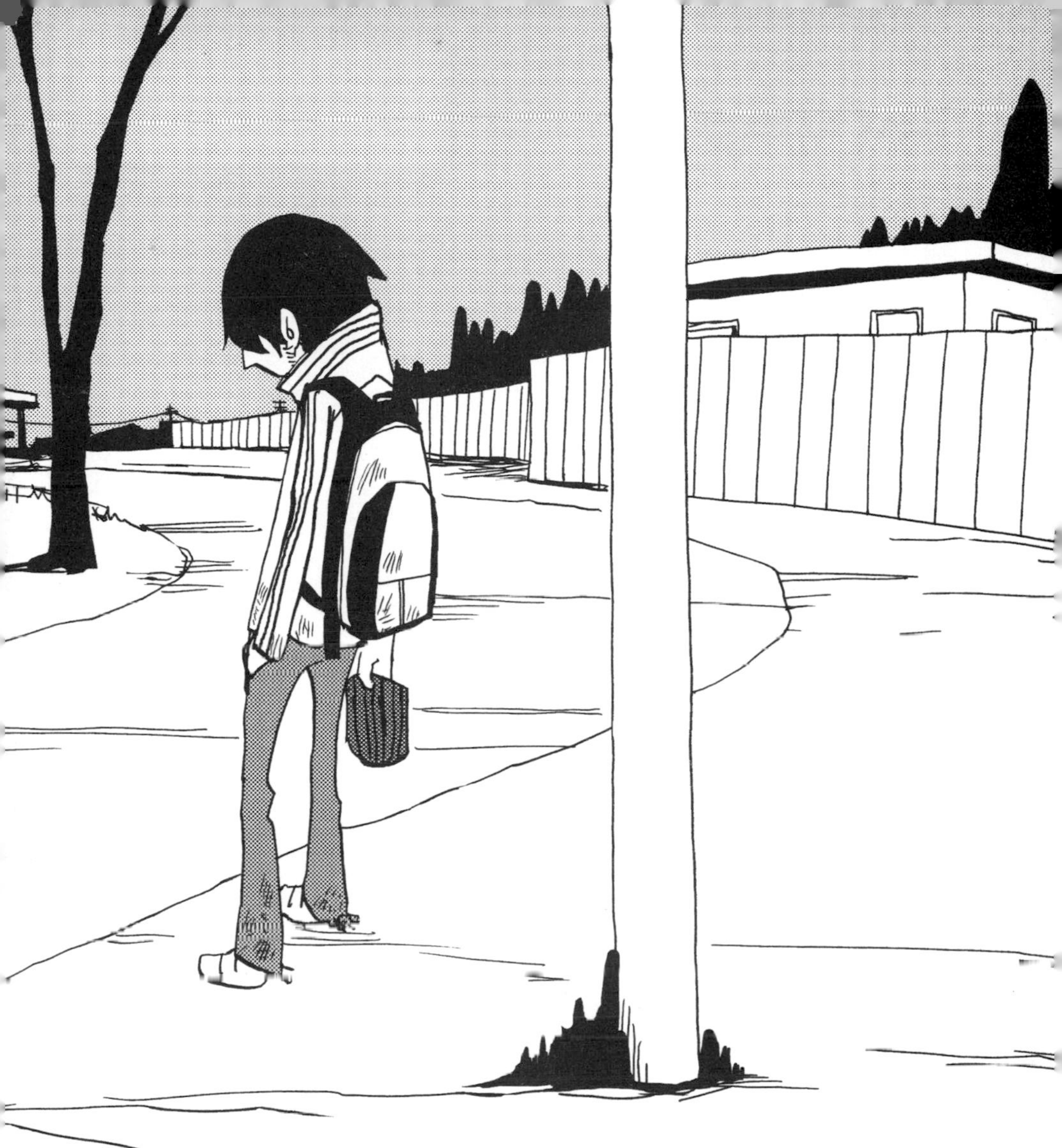

not simple

VIZ Signature Edition

story and art by **Natsume ONO**

title logo design by **chutte**

translation / **Joe Yamazaki**
english adaptation / **Anne Ishii**
touch-up art & lettering / **Gia Cam Luc**
design / **Fawn Lau**
editor / **Leyla Aker**

VP, production / **Alvin Lu**
VP, sales & product marketing / **Gonzalo Ferreyra**
VP, creative / **Linda Espinosa**
publisher / **Hyoe Narita**

Printed in the U.S.A.

Published by VIZ Media, LLC
P.O. Box 77010
San Francisco, CA 94107

10 9 8 7 6 5 4 3 2 1
First printing, January 2010

www.viz.com

PARENTAL ADVISORY
not simple is rated T+ for Older Teen and
is recommended for ages 16 and up.
ratings.viz.com

www.sigikki.com